THE YALE EDITION

OF

HORACE WALPOLE'S

CORRESPONDENCE

EDITED BY W. S. LEWIS

VOLUME THIRTEEN

HORACE WALPOLE'S
CORRESPONDENCE

WITH

THOMAS GRAY
RICHARD WEST
AND
THOMAS ASHTON

I

EDITED BY W. S. LEWIS

GEORGE L. LAM
AND
CHARLES H. BENNETT

NEW HAVEN
YALE UNIVERSITY PRESS
LONDON · GEOFFREY CUMBERLEGE · OXFORD UNIVERSITY PRESS
1948

LIST OF SUBSCRIBERS

H. M. KING GEORGE VI

AGNES SCOTT COLLEGE LIBRARY, Decatur, Georgia
ALAMEDA FREE LIBRARY, Alameda, California
ALBERTUS MAGNUS COLLEGE LIBRARY, New Haven, Connecticut
ALLEGHENY COLLEGE, THE REIS LIBRARY, Meadville, Pennsylvania
ALL SOULS COLLEGE LIBRARY, Oxford
JOSEPH W. ALSOP, JR, Esq., Avon, Connecticut
AMERICAN UNIVERSITY LIBRARY, Washington, D.C.
AMHERST COLLEGE, CONVERSE MEMORIAL LIBRARY, Amherst, Massa-
  chusetts
ATLANTA UNIVERSITY LIBRARY, Atlanta, Georgia
HUGH D. AUCHINCLOSS, Esq., McLean, Virginia
AVON OLD FARMS, Avon, Connecticut
F. W. BAIN, Esq., London
RICHARD B. BAKER, Esq., Providence, Rhode Island
BANGOR PUBLIC LIBRARY, Bangor, Maine
Sir T. D. BARLOW, K.B.E., London
BATH MUNICIPAL LIBRARY, Bath
C. F. BELL, Esq., Kensington
BERKELEY COLLEGE LIBRARY, YALE UNIVERSITY, New Haven, Con-
  necticut
THEODORE BESTERMAN, Esq., Paris
BIBLIOTECA NACIONAL DE PERÚ, Lima, Peru
Mrs NORMAN H. BILTZ, Reno, Nevada
BIRMINGHAM PUBLIC LIBRARY, Birmingham
CHARLES L. BLACK, Esq., Austin, Texas
Miss ANNA G. BLAIR, Edinburgh
BOSTON ATHENÆUM, Boston, Massachusetts
BOSTON COLLEGE LIBRARY, Chestnut Hill, Massachusetts
BOSTON PUBLIC LIBRARY, Boston, Massachusetts
BOSTON UNIVERSITY GRADUATE SCHOOL, Boston, Massachusetts

vii

BOWDOIN COLLEGE LIBRARY, Brunswick, Maine
JULIAN P. BOYD, Esq., Princeton, New Jersey
Miss EMMA JEANNETTE BRAZIER, New York, New York
BRISTOL PUBLIC LIBRARY, Bristol
WALLACE BROCKWAY, Esq., New York, New York
BROOKLYN COLLEGE LIBRARY, Brooklyn, New York
BROOKS SCHOOL, North Andover, Massachusetts
BROWN UNIVERSITY, JOHN HAY MEMORIAL LIBRARY, Providence, Rhode Island
BRYN MAWR COLLEGE LIBRARY, Bryn Mawr, Pennsylvania
JOHN N. BRYSON, Esq., Oxford
BUCKNELL UNIVERSITY LIBRARY, Lewisburg, Pennsylvania
CHARLES EATON BURCH, Esq., Washington, D.C.
BUTLER UNIVERSITY LIBRARY, Indianapolis, Indiana
CALHOUN COLLEGE LIBRARY, YALE UNIVERSITY, New Haven, Connecticut
CALIFORNIA STATE LIBRARY, Sacramento, California
CAMBRIDGE PUBLIC LIBRARY, Cambridge
CAMBRIDGE PUBLIC LIBRARY, Cambridge, New York
CARDIFF PUBLIC LIBRARY, Cardiff
The Right Honourable, the Countess of CARLISLE, London
CARNEGIE LIBRARY OF PITTSBURGH, Pittsburgh, Pennsylvania
LAURENCE R. CARTON, Esq., Towson, Maryland
CATHOLIC UNIVERSITY LIBRARY, Washington, D. C.
CHARLES L. COCKE MEMORIAL LIBRARY, Hollins College, Virginia
CHICAGO PUBLIC LIBRARY, Chicago, Illinois
CICERO PUBLIC LIBRARY, Cicero, Illinois
CLAREMONT COLLEGES LIBRARY, Claremont, California
ARTHUR H. CLARK COMPANY, Los Angeles, California
CLARK UNIVERSITY LIBRARY, Worcester, Massachusetts
CLEVELAND PUBLIC LIBRARY, Cleveland, Ohio
COE COLLEGE LIBRARY, Cedar Rapids, Iowa
COLBY COLLEGE LIBRARY, Waterville, Maine
COLGATE UNIVERSITY LIBRARY, Hamilton, New York
COLLEGE OF THE CITY OF NEW YORK, New York, New York
COLLEGE OF NEW ROCHELLE LIBRARY, New Rochelle, New York
COLLEGE OF ST TERESA LIBRARY, Winona, Minnesota
COLLEGE OF WOOSTER LIBRARY, Wooster, Ohio
COLORADO COLLEGE, COBURN LIBRARY, Colorado Springs, Colorado
COLUMBIA UNIVERSITY LIBRARY, New York, New York
G. MAURICE CONGDON, Esq., Providence, Rhode Island

CONNECTICUT COLLEGE, PALMER LIBRARY, New London, Connecticut
CONNECTICUT STATE LIBRARY, Hartford, Connecticut
REGINALD G. COOMBE, Esq., Greenwich, Connecticut
Mrs FRANK COOPER, Albany, New York
CORNELL UNIVERSITY LIBRARY, Ithaca, New York
THOMAS R. COWARD, Esq., New York, New York
HUGH B. COX, Esq., Washington, D. C.
CREIGHTON UNIVERSITY, Omaha, Nebraska
E. C. CULL, Esq., Dorking
DARTMOUTH COLLEGE, BAKER MEMORIAL LIBRARY, Hanover, New Hampshire
DAVENPORT COLLEGE LIBRARY, YALE UNIVERSITY, New Haven, Connecticut
RICHARD DAWSON, Esq., Dorking
DENVER PUBLIC LIBRARY, Denver, Colorado
DES MOINES PUBLIC LIBRARY, Des Moines, Iowa
DETROIT PUBLIC LIBRARY, Detroit, Michigan
Mrs ROBERT CLOUTMAN DEXTER, Belmont, Massachusetts
CHARLES D. DICKEY, Esq., Chestnut Hill, Philadelphia, Pennsylvania
DICKINSON COLLEGE LIBRARY, Carlisle, Pennsylvania
Mrs FRANK F. DODGE, New York, New York
E. H. DOUGLAS-OSBORN, Esq., Barnt Green, Worcestershire
DRAKE UNIVERSITY LIBRARY, Des Moines, Iowa
DREW UNIVERSITY LIBRARY, Madison, New Jersey
DUKE UNIVERSITY LIBRARY, Durham, North Carolina
DULUTH PUBLIC LIBRARY, Duluth, Minnesota
EDINBURGH PUBLIC LIBRARY, Edinburgh
EDINBURGH UNIVERSITY LIBRARY, Edinburgh
ALBERT H. ELY, Esq., Coldspring Harbor, Long Island, New York
EMORY UNIVERSITY LIBRARY, Emory University, Georgia
ENOCH PRATT FREE LIBRARY, Baltimore, Maryland
C. G. W. EVE, Esq., Oakham, Rutland
JOHN EVELYN, Esq., Portsmouth
FARMINGTON VILLAGE LIBRARY, Farmington, Connecticut
HENRY FIELD, Esq., Chicago, Illinois
MAURICE FIRUSKI, Esq., Salisbury, Connecticut
HARRY HARKNESS FLAGLER, Esq., Millbrook, New York
Mrs MARGARET MITCHELL FLINT, Westport, Connecticut
FLORIDA STATE COLLEGE FOR WOMEN LIBRARY, Tallahassee, Florida
GEORGE FOLDS, Esq., Rye, New York
FORBES LIBRARY, Northampton, Massachusetts

FORDHAM UNIVERSITY LIBRARY, New York, New York
FOWLER BROTHERS, Los Angeles, California
FRANKLIN AND MARSHALL COLLEGE LIBRARY, Lancaster, Pennsylvania
FREE LIBRARY OF PHILADELPHIA, Philadelphia, Pennsylvania
DONALD T. GAMMONS, Esq., Boston, Massachusetts
GEORGETOWN UNIVERSITY, RIGGS MEMORIAL LIBRARY, Washington, D. C.
GLASGOW ART GALLERIES, Glasgow
GLASGOW UNIVERSITY LIBRARY, Glasgow
HOWARD L. GOODHART, Esq., New York, New York
PHILIP L. GOODWIN, Esq., New York, New York
Mrs WILLIAM GREENOUGH, Newport, Rhode Island
LAUDER GREENWAY, Esq., Greenwich, Connecticut
Mrs OCTAVIA GREGORY, Parkstone, Dorset
WILLIAM V. GRIFFIN, Esq., New York, New York
FARNHAM P. GRIFFITHS, Esq., San Francisco, California
GRINNELL COLLEGE LIBRARY, Grinnell, Iowa
GROSVENOR LIBRARY, Buffalo, New York
GROTON SCHOOL LIBRARY, Groton, Massachusetts
GUILDHALL LIBRARY, London
SIDNEY LEWIS GULICK, JR, Esq., Oakland, California
HACKLEY PUBLIC LIBRARY, Muskegon, Michigan
Mrs CHANDLER HALE, Washington, D. C.
ALFRED E. HAMILL, Esq., Lake Forest, Illinois
ALLEN HAMILTON, Esq., M.D., Fort Wayne, Indiana
Mrs LEONARD COOMBES HAMMOND, San Francisco, California
HARVARD COLLEGE LIBRARY, Cambridge, Massachusetts
Miss BLANCHE HARVEY, Cleveland, Ohio
LEWIS HATCH, Esq., New York, New York
RICHARD L. HATCH, Esq., Sharon, Connecticut
Mrs HEPWORTH, London
EDWIN L. HILDRETH, Esq., Brattleboro, Vermont
FREDERICK W. HILLES, Esq., New Haven, Connecticut
HISTORICAL LIBRARY, MEDICAL SCHOOL, YALE UNIVERSITY, New Haven, Connecticut
HOBART COLLEGE LIBRARY, Geneva, New York
C. B. HOGAN, Esq., Woodbridge, Connecticut
E. C. HOHLER, Esq., Aylesbury
HOTCHKISS SCHOOL, Lakeville, Connecticut
HOUSE OF COMMONS LIBRARY, London
DAVID H. HOWIE, Esq., Cambridge, Massachusetts

LIVERPOOL PUBLIC LIBRARIES, Liverpool
LORAS COLLEGE LIBRARY, Dubuque, Iowa
LOS ANGELES PUBLIC LIBRARY, Los Angeles, California
LOUISIANA STATE UNIVERSITY LIBRARY, Baton Rouge, Louisiana
COMPTON MACKENZIE, Esq., Isle of Barra
REUBEN MCMILLAN FREE LIBRARY, Youngstown, Ohio
Mrs W. S. MCNEILL, Richmond, Virginia
MANCHESTER PUBLIC LIBRARIES, Manchester
ANTHONY F. MARRECO, Esq., London
MARYWOOD COLLEGE LIBRARY, Scranton, Pennsylvania
HAROLD R. MEDINA, Esq., MEDINA LIBRARY, Westhampton, New York
MIAMI UNIVERSITY LIBRARY, Oxford, Ohio
MILLS COLLEGE LIBRARY, Oakland, California
MINNEAPOLIS ATHENÆUM, Minneapolis, Minnesota
B. I. MISSELBROOK, Esq., Southampton
The Reverend HENRY MITCHELL, Wayne, Pennsylvania
LAURENCE P. MOOMAU, Esq., Westport, Connecticut
MOUNT HOLYOKE COLLEGE LIBRARY, South Hadley, Massachusetts
MOUNT UNION COLLEGE LIBRARY, Alliance, Ohio
MERRILL CALVIN MUNYAN, Esq., Washington, D. C.
EDWARD W. NASH, Esq., Washington, D. C.
The Right Honourable Lord NATHAN OF CHURT, London
THE NATIONAL CENTRAL LIBRARY, London
NATIONAL LIBRARY OF IRELAND, Dublin
A. E. NEERGAARD, Esq., M.D., New York, New York
NEWBERRY LIBRARY, Chicago, Illinois
NEW BRITAIN INSTITUTE LIBRARY, New Britain, Connecticut
NEW HAMPSHIRE STATE LIBRARY, Concord, New Hampshire
NEW HAVEN PUBLIC LIBRARY, New Haven, Connecticut
NEW JERSEY COLLEGE FOR WOMEN LIBRARY, New Brunswick, New
   Jersey
CHARLES NEWMAN, Esq., New York, New York
NEW YORK PUBLIC LIBRARY, New York, New York
NEW YORK STATE LIBRARY, Albany, New York
NEW YORK UNIVERSITY LIBRARY, New York, New York
NORFOLK PUBLIC LIBRARY, Norfolk, Connecticut
NORTH TEXAS STATE TEACHERS COLLEGE LIBRARY, Denton, Texas
NORTHERN ILLINOIS STATE TEACHERS COLLEGE, DeKalb, Illinois
NORTHWESTERN UNIVERSITY LIBRARY, Evanston, Illinois
OBERLIN COLLEGE LIBRARY, Oberlin, Ohio
OHIO STATE UNIVERSITY LIBRARY, Columbus, Ohio

OHIO WESLEYAN UNIVERSITY, CHARLES ELIHU SLOCUM LIBRARY, Delaware, Ohio

OKLAHOMA AGRICULTURAL AND MECHANICAL COLLEGE LIBRARY, Stillwater, Oklahoma

ASHLEY W. OLMSTED, Esq., Buffalo, New York

OXFORD AND CAMBRIDGE UNIVERSITY CLUB, London

R. HUNT PARKER, Esq., Roanoke Rapids, North Carolina

PASADENA PUBLIC LIBRARY, Pasadena, California

PEABODY INSTITUTE LIBRARY, Baltimore, Maryland

PEMBROKE COLLEGE LIBRARY, Cambridge

PENNSYLVANIA STATE COLLEGE LIBRARY, STATE COLLEGE, Pennsylvania

PENNSYLVANIA STATE LIBRARY AND MUSEUM, Harrisburg, Pennsylvania

PHILLIPS ACADEMY LIBRARY, Andover, Massachussetts

PHILLIPS EXETER ACADEMY, DAVIS LIBRARY, Exeter, New Hampshire

Miss MARION B. PHILLIPS, San Bernardino, California

PLAINFIELD PUBLIC LIBRARY, Plainfield, New Jersey

Miss PORTER'S SCHOOL, Farmington, Connecticut

PORTLAND PUBLIC LIBRARY, Portland, Maine

L. F. POWELL, Esq., Oxford

PRINCETON UNIVERSITY LIBRARY, Princeton, New Jersey

PROVIDENCE ATHENÆUM, Providence, Rhode Island

PUBLIC LIBRARY OF VICTORIA, Melbourne, Australia

PURDUE UNIVERSITY LIBRARY, Lafayette, Indiana

QUEENS COLLEGE LIBRARY, Flushing, New York

QUEENS UNIVERSITY OF BELFAST LIBRARY, Belfast

RANDOLPH–MACON WOMAN'S COLLEGE LIBRARY, Lynchburg, Virginia

READING UNIVERSITY LIBRARY, Reading

REDWOOD LIBRARY AND ATHENÆUM, Newport, Rhode Island

REFORM CLUB, London

RHODE ISLAND STATE COLLEGE LIBRARY, Kingston, Rhode Island

RICE INSTITUTE LIBRARY, Houston, Texas

The Right Honourable LORD ROTHSCHILD, Cambridge

THE ROYAL LIBRARY, Stockholm

THE ROYAL UNIVERSITY LIBRARY, Upsala

RUTGERS UNIVERSITY LIBRARY, New Brunswick, New Jersey

ST ANDREWS UNIVERSITY LIBRARY, St Andrews, Fife

ST BONAVENTURE COLLEGE, FRIEDSAM MEMORIAL LIBRARY, St Bonaventure, New York

ST JOSEPH'S COLLEGE LIBRARY, Emmitsburg, Maryland

ST LOUIS PUBLIC LIBRARY, St Louis, Missouri

St Louis University Library, St Louis, Missouri
St Mary's College Library, Notre Dame, Indiana
St Olaf College Library, Northfield, Minnesota
St Paul Public Library, St Paul, Minnesota
St Peter's College Library, Jersey City, New Jersey
Mrs James Sallade, Ann Arbor, Michigan
San Bernardino Valley Junior College Library, San Bernardino,
    California
San Francisco Public Library, San Francisco, California
Paul S. Schoedinger, Esq., Durham, New Hampshire
Seattle Public Library, Seattle, Washington
George Sherburn, Esq., Cambridge, Massachusetts
Richard Smart, Esq., London
Smith College Library, Northampton, Massachusetts
Mrs Theodore J. Smith, Geneva, New York
Willard Smith, Esq., Oakland, California
P. H. B. Otway Smithers, Esq., London
South African Public Library, Capetown
Southern Methodist University Library, Dallas, Texas
Southwestern College Library, Memphis, Tennessee
T. M. Spelman, Esq., Harrison, New York
Stanford University Libraries, Stanford, California
State University of Iowa Libraries, Iowa City, Iowa
James Strachey, Esq., London
Stratford Library Association, Stratford, Connecticut
Miss L. Stuart Sutherland, Lady Margaret Hall, Oxford
Swarthmore College Library, Swarthmore, Pennsylvania
Syracuse University Library, Syracuse, New York
Henry C. Taylor, Esq., Coldspring Harbor, Long Island, New York
Temple University, Sullivan Memorial Library, Philadelphia,
    Pennsylvania
Texas State College for Women Library, Denton, Texas
Thacher School Library, Ojai, California
Day Thorpe, Esq., Alexandria, Virginia
Toledo Public Library, Toledo, Ohio
Transylvania College Library, Lexington, Kentucky
Tulane University Library, New Orleans, Louisiana
A. P. Ulasto, Esq., Cambridge
Union College Library, Schenectady, New York
University Club Library, New York, New York
University College Library, Hull

University College Library, London
University College, Southampton
University of Alabama Library, University, Alabama
University of Arizona Library, Tucson, Arizona
University of Birmingham Library, Birmingham
University of British Columbia Library, Vancouver
University of Buffalo, Lockwood Memorial Library, Buffalo, New York
University of California at Los Angeles Library, West Los Angeles, California
University of California Library, Berkeley, California
University of Chicago Libraries, Chicago, Illinois
University of Cincinnati Library, Cincinnati, Ohio
University of Colorado Library, Boulder, Colorado
University of Connecticut Library, Storrs, Connecticut
University of Delaware Library, Newark, Delaware
University of Durham Library, Durham
University of Florida Library, Gainesville, Florida
University of Georgia Libraries, Athens, Georgia
University of Illinois Library, Urbana, Illinois
University of Kansas City, Kansas City, Missouri
University of Kansas Library, Lawrence, Kansas
University of Kentucky Library, Lexington, Kentucky
University of Liverpool Library, Liverpool
University of London Library, London
University of Manchester Library, Manchester
University of Maryland Library, College Park, Maryland
University of Melbourne, Melbourne
University of Michigan Library, Ann Arbor, Michigan
University of Minnesota Library, Minneapolis, Minnesota
University of Missouri Library, Columbia, Missouri
University of Nebraska Library, Lincoln, Nebraska
University of New Hampshire, Hamilton Smith Library, Durham, New Hampshire
University of New Mexico Library, Albuquerque, New Mexico
University of North Carolina Library, Chapel Hill, North Carolina
University of North Dakota Library, Grand Forks, North Dakota
University of Notre Dame Library, Notre Dame, Indiana
University of Oklahoma Library, Norman, Oklahoma

UNIVERSITY OF OMAHA LIBRARY, Omaha, Nebraska
UNIVERSITY OF OREGON LIBRARY, Eugene, Oregon
UNIVERSITY OF OSLO LIBRARY, Oslo
UNIVERSITY OF PENNSYLVANIA LIBRARY, Philadelphia, Pennsylvania
UNIVERSITY OF PITTSBURGH LIBRARY, Pittsburgh, Pennsylvania
UNIVERSITY OF RICHMOND LIBRARY, Richmond, Virginia
UNIVERSITY OF ROCHESTER LIBRARY, Rochester, New York
UNIVERSITY OF SHEFFIELD LIBRARY, Sheffield
UNIVERSITY OF SOUTHERN CALIFORNIA LIBRARY, Los Angeles, California
UNIVERSITY OF SYDNEY, Sydney
UNIVERSITY OF TENNESSEE LIBRARY, Knoxville, Tennessee
UNIVERSITY OF TEXAS LIBRARY, Austin, Texas
UNIVERSITY OF TORONTO LIBRARY, Toronto
UNIVERSITY OF UTAH LIBRARY, Salt Lake City, Utah
UNIVERSITY OF VERMONT, UNIVERSITY LIBRARIES, Burlington, Vermont
UNIVERSITY OF VIRGINIA LIBRARY, Charlottesville, Virginia
UNIVERSITY OF WASHINGTON LIBRARY, Seattle, Washington
UNIVERSITY OF WISCONSIN LIBRARY, Madison, Wisconsin
UNIVERSITY OF WYOMING LIBRARY, Laramie, Wyoming
VANDERBILT UNIVERSITY LIBRARY, Nashville, Tennessee
VASSAR COLLEGE LIBRARY, Poughkeepsie, New York
VERMONT STATE LIBRARY, Montpelier, Vermont
VIRGINIA STATE LIBRARY, Richmond, Virginia
GEORGE WAHR, Esq., Ann Arbor, Michigan
Mrs D. T. WALPOLE, London
Mrs CHRISTOPHER WARD, Greenville, Delaware
WASHINGTON UNIVERSITY LIBRARY, St Louis, Missouri
WATKINSON LIBRARY OF REFERENCE, Hartford, Connecticut
WAYNE UNIVERSITY LIBRARY, Detroit, Michigan
M. E. WEATHERALL, Esq., North Clifton, Guernsey
VANDERBILT WEBB, Esq., New York, New York
WELLESLEY COLLEGE LIBRARY, Wellesley, Massachusetts
WELLS COLLEGE LIBRARY, Aurora, New York
WESLEYAN UNIVERSITY LIBRARY, Middletown, Connecticut
WALDEMAR WESTERGAARD, Esq., Los Angeles, California
WESTERN COLLEGE LIBRARY, Oxford, Ohio
WESTERN KENTUCKY STATE TEACHERS COLLEGE LIBRARY, Bowling Green, Kentucky
WESTERN RESERVE UNIVERSITY, FLORA STONE MATHER LIBRARY, Cleveland, Ohio

TABLE OF CONTENTS

VOLUME I

LIST OF ILLUSTRATIONS

VOLUMES I AND II

*Grateful acknowledgment is made to Lord Waldegrave, the
British Museum, the National Portrait Gallery, Pembroke
College, Cambridge, and the Toledo Museum of Art, for
permission to reproduce illustrations listed here.*

INTRODUCTION

1.

THE biographers of Gray (and for a man who lived such an uneventful life he has had a great many) give much space to his early letters to Walpole and their two friends of the 'Quadruple Alliance' at Eton. This partiality is not hard to understand: the letters of Gray, Walpole, West, and Ashton bring back the friendships of one's own school days, or, rather, glorify them; what other schoolboys ever put into letters so much humour, criticism, sentiment, and affection? These precocious boys—of whom one was to write the most beloved poem of the century and another to give posterity the history of his time— admit us into their company. As we read their letters we are mindful of what the ministers of fate had in store for the writers, and the reading is wistful and pleasant and sad.

Gray, West, and Walpole had much in common: literary tastes, physical slightness, an aversion to games, and the circumstance, probably felt rather than discussed, that they came from unhappy homes. No boys can ever have enjoyed their school more; perhaps no boys of a literary cast ever enjoyed it as much. They did not suffer from the persecution which often afflicts such boys at school. Being 'literary' was not offensive to 'normal' Etonians of their time, since the normal Etonians, the bloods and future M.P.'s, also turned out verses; they were, indeed, 'the mob of gentlemen who wrote with ease.' The Quadruple Alliance also had the advantage of having Walpole, although the youngest of the four, as their leader. He assumed that rôle inevitably, not because he was the Prime Minister's son—however aware masters and tutors may have been of the relationship, not many of his contemporaries were sycophants—but because he was gay and gregarious and had a gift for friendship. Walpole had other intimates of a quite different character from Gray and West, Montagu and

Lyttelton. He was devoted to George Selwyn and John Dodd; Henry Conway was his closest friend. It is a mistake to picture Horace Walpole as an aesthete scorned by the rakish and manly.

Little is known about Eton at this time; even the School Lists for six of Walpole's eight years there are missing. What was studied and when, the routine of the day, the details of school life; knowledge of such matters is dim and uncertain. Perhaps the most revealing glimpse of Walpole's Eton appears in his letter to Montagu of 6 May 1736. It throws some light on Etonian pastimes; it throws more on Walpole and the Quadruple Alliance: 'An expedition against bargemen or a match at cricket may be very pretty things to recollect,' Walpole wrote, 'but thank my stars, I can remember things that are very near as pretty.' These included day-dreams in which his surroundings were transformed into classical and romantic places mentioned by Virgil and Mlle de Scudéry. Discussing Tibullus and Statius was more to the taste of the Quadruple Alliance than fighting with plough-boys or clubbing a ram to death.

The libraries which Walpole and Gray formed at Eton must have played an important part in the life of the Quadruple Alliance. Eton had a good bookshop, Pote's. One can picture the four friends exploring its shelves and carting back to their rooms the books which they wanted. We can pick some of them out in the catalogues Gray and Walpole made of their libraries. Gray's catalogue is now in the Pierpont Morgan Library and has been printed by Professor W. Powell Jones in *Thomas Gray, Scholar*, Cambridge, Mass., 1937, pp. 151–63. It seems likely that the first books listed in it came from Pote's. They are seventeenth-century editions of the classics, an extensive collection that proceeded far beyond the usual schoolboy authors. The catalogue of Walpole's library which was kept from 1763 on, was arranged alphabetically by authors. It does not indicate the books which Walpole bought while at school, but they can be identified when seen because he wrote his name in them and the date when he bought them. Apart from textbooks, those that have been recovered are all Latin or recent English authors: Virgil, Horace, Ovid, and Petronius; Congreve, Swift, Gay, Prior, Addison and Steele. Walpole made notes in many of these books, in the margins and on the fly-leaves and end-papers, a practice he continued throughout his life. The annotations frequently bear little relation to the book in which they were made. Thus, in his copy of Congreve, purchased in 1728 when he was ten or eleven, the youthful Horace laboriously copied out a portion of the 'nine times' table, from 9x3 to 9x9; on the back cover of Moll's *Maps of the Geography of the Ancients*, 1726, after showing the descendants of Demaratus, he added in French (without any nonsense about accents) a quatrain on Tasso; on the back cover of the first volume of a *History of England*, he wrote after testing his quill in a corner, 'sunning himself in all the bask of beauty.' 'I can't say I am sorry I was never quite a schoolboy,' he confessed to Montagu.

The Quadruple Alliance was broken by West's early death, the quarrel between Gray and Walpole, and their quarrels with Ashton. The first quarrel occurred while Gray and Walpole were on the Grand Tour. 'We had not got to Calais before Gray was dissatisfied,' Walpole wrote after Gray's death.[1] It would have been remarkable if they had not quarrelled: one of the travellers was a vivacious young man of fashion, the son of the most powerful man in England; the other was a scholar and a poet, the son of a milliner and a half-mad 'money scrivener,' who was travelling as his friend's guest. 'I am conscious that in the beginning of the differences between Gray and me, the fault was mine,' Walpole later wrote.[2] 'I was too young, too fond of my own diversions, nay, I do not doubt, too much intoxicated by indulgence, vanity, and the insolence of my situation, as a Prime Minister's son, not to have been inattentive and insensible to the feelings of one I thought below me; of one, I blush to say it, that I knew was obliged to me; of one whom presumption and folly perhaps made me deem not my superior *then* in parts, though I have since felt my infinite inferiority to him. I treated him insolently: he loved me, and I did not think he did. I reproached him with the difference between us, when he acted from conviction of knowing he

1. To Mason, 27 Nov. 1773.   2. To Mason, 2 March 1773.

was my superior. I often disregarded his wishes of seeing places, which I would not quit other amusements to visit, though I offered to send him to them without me. Forgive me, if I say that his temper was not conciliating; at the same time that I will confess to you that he acted a more friendly part, had I had the sense to take advantage of it—he freely told me of my faults. I declared I did not desire to hear them, nor would correct them. You will not wonder that with the dignity of his spirit, and the obstinate carelessness of mine, the breach must have grown wider, till we became incompatible.' The wonder is that these two were able to endure the discomforts and trials of their travels as long as they did. The annals of travel furnish many instances of devoted friends returning home by separate routes; Europe has always been strewn with the wrecks of friendships. The immediate cause of the Gray-Walpole quarrel at Reggio is not known, but it might have been anything. Nor are we able to afix the blame; as Mr Ketton-Cremer has said, only Mann and Chute could do that. The reader's sympathies tend to be with Gray, because Walpole was rich and fashionable, while Gray was poor, of humble parentage, and a poet; but, as in most quarrels, both sides were doubtless at fault.[3]

Of more importance than the quarrel is what the friends were able to do for each other after their reconciliation. Their second friendship lasted without interruption until Gray's death. It went unstressed by earlier editors; Mitford even denied its existence. In a passage which it would be difficult to match for inaccuracy he wrote: 'The warmth and affection of their early friendship was unfortunately never renewed, and their paths of life were for the future removed from each other.'[4] Actually, Walpole constituted himself the promoter and champion of Gray's poetical reputation, enduring with patience and kindness the poet's alarms and fluster. Gray helped Walpole with his antiquarian researches and corrected his works. 'Pray send me the proof-sheets to correct, for you know you are not capable of it,' Walpole quoted him as saying and acknowledged the truth of the charge.[5] 'Mr Gray

3. See also *Walpoliana* i. 95.
4. *The Correspondence of Horace Wal-* *pole and William Mason,* ed. John Mitford, 1851, i. p. ix.
5. To Mason, 15 May 1773.

was far from an agreeable confidant to self-love, yet I had always more satisfaction in communicating anything to him, though sure to be mortified, than in being flattered by people whose judgment I do not respect. We had besides known each other's ideas from almost infancy, and I was certain he would *understand* precisely whatever I said, whether it was well or ill-expressed.'[6] Gray's visits to Strawberry Hill are the measure of their mature friendship. There the two friends listened to the nightingales, admired the lilacs, pored over Walpole's latest treasures, and, reading aloud Lord Herbert of Cherbury's *Life,* 'could not get on for laughing and screaming.' When friends have quarrelled bitterly and are reconciled, they can hardly forget the break, but if they share tastes and interests they can construct another friendship. This, although they criticized each other to friends, is what Gray and Walpole managed to do. Five years before his death Gray read in a newspaper that Walpole was seriously ill. 'It would be a singular satisfaction to me if I might see three lines in your own hand, but it is impossible for me to judge whether this is a reasonable request. I flatter myself, if you can, you will indulge me in it. . . . Heaven preserve you, and restore you to health and ease.'[7] When Gray died his executors, Mason and Brown, apparently acting on Gray's instructions, gave Walpole 'a Goa-stone and a blood-stone seal.' Walpole preserved most of Gray's letters to him and thus helped to assure Gray a high place among English letter-writers. The companion portraits of Gray and Walpole by Eccardt that hung in the Blue Bedchamber at Strawberry Hill now hang, fittingly and properly, side by side in the National Portrait Gallery.

Walpole's quarrel with Ashton has received little attention, for no one cares about Ashton. He is put down as a time-server who attached himself to the Prime Minister's son at Eton with a view to securing future preferments. Doubtless this is over-simplifying, but when Ashton went into Orders preferments did flow from Sir Robert. Upon Walpole's return from Italy, Ashton lived with him, and though Walpole, under Middleton's teaching at Cam-

6. To Mason, 25 Sept. 1771. 7. Gray to Walpole 24 Sept. 1766.

bridge, had become something of an infidel, he went to hear his friend preach and praised him. In 1747 things began to go wrong. Walpole turned to Gray for advice. 'It is a misfortune to me to be at a distance from both of you at present,' Gray replied from Cambridge in November 1747, two years after his reconciliation with Walpole. 'I always believed well of his heart and temper, and would gladly do so still. If they are as they should be, I should have expected everything from such an explanation; for it is a tenet with me . . . that if ever two people who love one another come to breaking it is for want of a timely éclaircissement, a full and precise one, without witnesses or mediators, and without reserving any one disagreeable circumstance for the mind to brood upon in silence.' 'I believe,' Walpole wrote Mann, 25 July 1750, 'you have often heard me mention a Mr Ashton, a clergyman, who, in one word, has great preferments, and owes everything upon earth to me. I have long had reason to complain of his behaviour; in short, my father is dead, and I can make no bishops. He has at last quite thrown off the mask, and in the most direct manner, against my will, has written against my friend Dr Middleton. . . . I have forbid him my house.' And so, with the banging of the door behind him, Ashton leaves the Walpolian stage. He returns for only a moment in the brief 'Suite of Mr Ashton' which Walpole wrote in a Commonplace Book: 'In the winter of 1763 he had a stroke of apoplexy as he was preaching in the chapel at Eton College.'

Around the person of the fourth member of the Quadruple Alliance is the light of early morning. His three friends considered him to be the truest poet among them; each in his own way loved him. Gray and Walpole saw little of him after they left Eton, for West went to Oxford and died shortly after their return from their travels. But there is one incident which shows the Quadruple Alliance at its happiest, Walpole's visit to West at Christ Church, as reported by West in his letter of 1 June 1736. Walpole's letter of thanks to his host was 'in every sentence, word, and comma, so very gay, high-spirited, and allegro, that,' wrote West, 'I danced about the room all the while I read it like a madman,' while 'the great heads round the Theatre shouted for joy,' thus anticipating their animation when they beheld Zuleika Dobson nearly two centuries later.

West died in his twenty-sixth year, apparently of tuberculosis which seems to have been aggravated by the discovery that his mother was having an affair with his father's secretary. One story has it that she poisoned her husband. West's memory is kept green by the letters of the Quadruple Alliance and the sonnet which Gray addressed to him after his death.

2.

The material published here for the first time includes the complete text of Walpole's brief autobiography, 'Short Notes of My Life,' 'The Nicoll Affair,' and various passages from Walpole's unpublished manuscripts—his notes on Ashton, Lady Pomfret, Lady Mary Wortley Montagu, and his parody of a Roman guide-book.

We planned originally to include 'Short Notes' in the first volume of this edition. Mr Dayle Wallace had started to edit it, but a delay arising, it was necessary to postpone publication. This proved fortunate, because that summer (of 1937) the original manuscript turned up among the Walpole papers at Upton, Slough, where it had remained in the library of the first Richard Bentley since he acquired it from Miss Berry. It had not been seen since it was first published in 1843–4. The editor omitted certain passages and inaccurately transcribed others, errors faithfully copied by later editors who introduced further errors of their own. It is a satisfaction to be able to give the text Walpole wrote, for it is perhaps the most important Walpole manuscript in existence.

It cannot be said that Walpole appears at his best in the Nicoll affair, but his desire to perpetuate the family glory at Houghton by securing an heiress for his nephew should be judged by the practice of his time, when the *mariage de convenance* was an accepted custom, rather than by ours, when mercenary considerations never enter into marriage. Although the narrative is cast in the form of a letter to Mrs Harris, Lord Orford's grandmother, it has seemed best to include it here as an appendix.

The accounts of Ashton and the others are taken from two of the folio manuscript volumes which Walpole kept when a young man and which formed part of the Waldegrave Collection until their migration in 1942 to Farmington. We shall draw upon these volumes frequently in the future.

3.

It is now four years since Walpole's correspondence with the Berry sisters was published in this edition, a cæsural pause in the history of the undertaking which we hope will not recur. During the war nearly all of us were in the armed forces or in government service; one of our former undergraduate assistants, William W. Reiter, was lost in action over Wake Island. The present team, including part-time assistants, consists of twelve members. It is hoped that we shall now be able to press forward and finish the remaining forty or so volumes by 1965.

In the Preface to our first volume I expressed the hope that the readers of our edition would consider that they had a share in its fortunes and would contribute whatever additions or corrections they could supply. Although the proofs are remarkably accurate, in accord with the high printing standards of the Yale University Press, and have been read by half a dozen trained readers, yet regrettable typographical errors and editorial inconsistencies do occasionally creep in. Our reviewers have been loath to point these out in view of the magnitude of the whole work, but we are most grateful to those who have done so. A supplementary volume of additions and corrections will one day be printed.

No editors can ever have received more encouragement from their reviewers. Moments of despondency—during which we remind ourselves of our motto, 'Diligenter sed frustra'—have been frequently dispelled by the essays of historians and literary critics on both sides of the Atlantic.

The most frequent adverse criticism made of us has been that we have 'normalized' the text. Those who disapprove of this are about evenly divided between Britons and Americans, and are, I think, primarily concerned with literature; the historians have been lined up solidly on our side; the majority have apparently not cared one way or the other. When, at the beginning of our labours in 1933, I was faced with the question of whether or not to attempt an exact reproduction of the spelling, capitalization, and punctuation of the original letters, I was guided by the historians on my Advisory Committee at that time. The decision is stated in the Preface to the first volume of the Cole Correspondence at pp. xxxv–vi. In spite of the carefully expressed position of those who regret it, I am still convinced that it is sound.

On the point next most frequently raised, I think we have been wrong: the decision not to translate Greek and Latin quotations. One reviewer has said that the editors 'seem never to have decided whether they are annotating for scholars or schoolboys.' Although appearances may be against us, we agreed at the outset that we should annotate for scholars. As the Oxford Dictionary tells us that a scholar is a 'learned or erudite person, especially in the classical (i.e., Greek and Latin) languages and their literature,' we reasoned that since we were editing for scholars it was not necessary to translate the Greek and Latin passages. But this is where we went wrong, because today the word 'scholar' has taken on a much wider meaning. There are scholars of international reputation in something or other who cannot construe a page of the *Æneid* in an hour or read a line of the *Anabasis*. Briefly, the majority of our readers (including ourselves) are grateful for translations. Future correspondences will supply them.

Another reviewer has this to say on the Du Deffand Correspondence: 'One must deplore the lack, among references by contrast so full of genealogical facts, of a hoped-for documentation of the events which the blind worldling in her *tonneau* nevertheless felt forced to mention—a matter which the commentator would have done well to treat with the importance it deserved. Neither the *affaires de Genève* with their Versoix sequel, nor the

Voltairean project of the *évasion des clercs,* nor the Voltaire-Shakespeare dispute, nor the condemnation of Lally-Tollendal, not even the Hume-Rousseau struggle, nor American independence—not one of these major events in the republic of letters or of Western civilization receives the just part in the clarifications and the bibliographical material that the fate of some obscure person does.' This is true, but is it our business to 'document' these events? I think not. One of the editor's greatest difficulties is to know when to stop. The temptation is strong to go on and on with a fascinating problem, to annotate the annotation, to pile appendix upon appendix, but a line has to be drawn somewhere. I think it ought to be drawn when all information has been given which is needed to understand the text. If we can toss in a tidbit from Walpole's library, or a pertinent passage from a contemporary letter or manuscript, all well and good, but I do not think we should attempt a 'clarification' of the American War of Independence or other great issues. Such an enlargement of our design could delay its completion until the next century.

One further point is constantly before us: What should be annotated and what should be left alone because the reader will understand it? This is perhaps the most difficult question an editor has to answer. It is a matter upon which no law can be laid down, but upon it Dr Johnson has said the last word, as upon so many others: 'It is impossible for an expositor not to write too little for some, and too much for others. He can only judge what is necessary by his own experience; and how long soever he may deliberate, will at last explain many lines which the learned will think impossible to be mistaken, and omit many for which the ignorant will want his help. These are censures merely relative, and must be quietly endured.'

It should be borne in mind that, in the future, few will read this work all the way through. Those who want to read Walpole for fun without worrying too much if they do not understand everything he is talking about, can do so in one of the many selections of his letters. Those who use this work will be chiefly readers who will turn first to the *omnium gatherum* index—whose ordering is still far in the future—to be guided to the particular part of the correspondence which concerns them at the moment, whether it is Lally-Tollendal, or the Stamp Act, or hair-dressing. Any one wanting to know what Walpole and his friends had to say about the Hume-Rousseau quarrel will be sent by the index to a dozen correspondences in addition to Madame du Deffand's. We hope that the reader will then find what he is looking for.

Our task, as I see it, is to put at our readers' disposal as many letters to and from Walpole as can be found, and to save the reader the trouble of consulting the thousands of books needed to understand them. 'It is a little hard,' wrote John Wilson Croker in the *Quarterly Review,* of Vernon Smith's edition of Walpole's letters to Lady Ossory, that its readers 'should be obliged to provide themselves with the *Annual Register, Gentleman's Magazine,* and a succession of old Peerages, to discover the object and meaning of one of Walpole's jokes on Lady A or Lord B.' A later passage in this same review appears in the Preface to our first volume, but I repeat it here because our experience of the past fifteen years has reinforced our belief in it: 'What the reader most indispensably needs, and what registers and magazines cannot supply, is the explanation of small events, slight allusions, obscure anecdotes, traits of individual characters, the gossip of the circle, and all the little items and accidents of domestic, social, and political life, which constitute in a most peculiar degree the staple of Walpole's correspondence—the most frequent occasions and chief objects of either his wit or his sagacity, and without some knowledge of which his best letters would be little more than a collection of riddles.'

We must, then, when called upon to do so, 'study to know how many knots were in Hercules' club, of what colour Achilles' beard was, or whether Hector were not troubled with the toothache,' not to gain the name of speculative men, but to ease the labours of readers who do us the honour to consult us. If we are successful in this, it will be owing in no small part to the interest and help of the many friends who wish this undertaking well.

W. S. L.

MANUSCRIPTS AND BIBLIOGRAPHY

WALPOLE's correspondence with Gray now includes 139 letters, of which 126 are from Gray.

One hundred and eight of Gray's letters to Walpole were bequeathed by Mrs Damer, Walpole's executrix and legatee, to her Twickenham neighbour, Sir Wathen Waller, 1st Bt, in 1828. Their first appearance in the sale room was at Sotheby's, 5 December 1921, when they formed lot 198. The consignor was Sir Wathen A. Waller, 5th Bt, who bought them in at £410. Their second and final public appearance was at Christie's, 18 December 1947, as lot 16, where, following Sir Wathen's death, they were sold by Lady Waller. Messrs Maggs, acting on behalf of Mr Dudley Colman, paid £1250 for them. It is pleasant to record that, through the gift of Mr Colman, the letters have now come to rest in the library of Gray's adopted college, Pembroke, Cambridge. The manuscripts of sixteen of the remaining eighteen letters from Gray to Walpole are missing. Of the other two, that of 7 July ?1746 is in the Charles Roberts Autograph Collection at Haverford College, and that of 2 Sept. 1760 is now at Eton.

Of Walpole's thirteen surviving letters to Gray, the manuscripts of five (20 Feb. 1753, 25 Dec. 1755, 15 Feb. 1759, August 1760, and 25 March 1771), which formed part of Mrs Damer's bequest, are now WSL. Two others, ca 15 Oct. 1735 and 8 March 1768, from the Waller and the Lister Collections, are now in the Pierpont Morgan Library. Descriptions of the provenance of these manuscripts (and of Walpole's fragmentary letters of ca 3 Jan. 1763 and ca 26 Sept. 1766) and of the other letters listed below are given in the notes prefixed to each letter.

The regrettable one-sidedness of this correspondence is not likely to be balanced by a lumber-room discovery. Walpole wrote to William Mason 27 November 1773 that most of his early letters to Gray and West—'wretched boyish stuff'—had been destroyed by the recipients. Nor, apparently, did Gray keep many of Walpole's later letters, for Mason, who was Gray's executor, reported to Walpole, after going through the letters among Gray's effects,

'I do not find many of yours.' Those that he found were returned at
Walpole's request. Whether Miss Berry or Mrs Damer destroyed
more of them after Walpole's death we do not know, but it is perhaps significant that of the six letters from Walpole to Gray which
were printed by Miss Berry (Walpole's *Works*, Vol. V, pp. 353–
78), the manuscripts of only three (20 Feb. 1753, 15 Feb. 1759,
and 19 Nov. 1765) are known to have survived.

Both sides of the correspondence are contained in the *Correspondence of Thomas Gray,* ed. Paget Toynbee and Leonard
Whibley, Oxford, 1935, to which references are given in the List
of Letters which follows on p. xlix. The letters are also in *The Correspondence of Gray, Walpole, West and Ashton,* ed. Paget Toynbee, Oxford, 1915, and Walpole's side is in Mrs Toynbee's edition of Walpole's letters. Unlike our text, that of the Paget Toynbee and the Toynbee-Whibley edition preserves the spelling,
punctuation, capitalization, and abbreviations of the original
manuscripts. Other editions of Gray's letters are listed in C. S.
Northup's *Bibliography of Thomas Gray,* New Haven, 1917, pp.
167–72.

Walpole's correspondence with West now consists of thirty-
nine letters, of which twenty are from Walpole. The manuscripts
of all but one of Walpole's known letters to West have disappeared.
That one, 3 Jan. 1737, which formed part of Mrs Damer's bequest
to Sir Wathen Waller, is now WSL. Of West's letters to Walpole,
the manuscripts of the following have survived: 29 Oct. 1735,
1 June 1736, 31 Oct. 1736, 18 April 1737, 1 Dec. 1737, 7 Sept.
1738, 24 Sept. 1739, 15 Oct. 1739, 10 Nov. 1740, and 29 March
1741. These were also in Mrs Damer's bequest, were sold at Sotheby's 5 Dec. 1921 in lot 194, and were purchased from Maggs by
WSL in 1925. Another, 12 July 1737, has a manuscript source in a
transcript made by John Mitford in 1853, now British Museum
Add. MS 32,562. The source of the remainder of the Walpole-
West correspondence is Walpole's *Works,* Vol. IV, pp. 411–63,
where Miss Berry printed twenty-seven letters, the originals of
which are missing.

Walpole's correspondence with Ashton includes five letters, of which three are from Walpole. The MS of one of Walpole's letters, 14 May 1740, survives, and is now in the possession of Mr C. C. Auchincloss. Walpole's two other letters have a manuscript source in the Mitford transcript mentioned above. Of the two letters from Ashton, that of 7 August 1737 is now published for the first time from the original manuscript among the Berry Papers in the British Museum (Add. MS 37,728, f. 42). The manuscript of the other, 25 July 1741, is now WSL.

The correspondence with West and Ashton has been published in Paget Toynbee's *Correspondence of Gray, Walpole, West and Ashton,* to which references are given in the List of Letters.

Sources quoted in the biographical footnotes may be assumed to be supplemented by the *Dictionary of National Biography* and the *Complete Peerage* and *Complete Baronetage*. Our constant use of the Toynbee and Whibley notes in the *Correspondence of Thomas Gray* was acknowledged in our first proofs by the formula (T-W), but this was so ubiquitous as to be both unsightly and disconcerting, and we decided to strike it out. The work of these editors, especially in running down quotations and allusions, has greatly reduced our own labours.

All English books mentioned in the references, unless otherwise specified, are assumed to have been published in London.

Square brackets indicate editorial emendation; angular brackets, the restoration of the manuscript where it has been damaged.

In all the letters, the hyphenization and capitalization have been modernized here. The spelling has also been modernized (for lists of Walpole's obsolete spellings see COLE i. xliii and MONTAGU i. xxxiii), except that of proper names, which are spelled as in the manuscripts or printed sources. Gray's pointing has been revised; his omnipresent colons and other caprices of punctuation perhaps add distinction to his manuscripts, but are an annoyance in a printed text. Walpole's punctuation has as usual been retained. When we have used a printed source, however, we have occasionally revised the punctuation where we believed the transcription was incorrect.

W. S. L.
C. H. B.

ACKNOWLEDGMENTS

THE two men to whom our first acknowledgments are due are, alas, no longer alive. They were Sir Wathen Waller and Leonard Whibley.

Sir Wathen was the owner of virtually all of Gray's letters to Walpole. He granted us permission to have them photostated for use in this edition, but his generosity did not stop there. He was also a friend who was eager to help us in any way he could. When he led an expedition of discovery into the attics at Woodcote his joy at 'finding' was the equal of mine. The Walpole manuscripts, carefully preserved in wrappers upon which Sir Wathen wrote pertinent information in his clear hand, were always at our disposal. Most of them are now at Farmington, where Lady Waller assures me her husband hoped that they might one day be.

The Waller Collection of Gray's letters to Walpole is now at Pembroke College, Cambridge, whence so many of them were written. The retiring Master, Sir Montagu Butler, and the incoming Master, Mr S. C. Roberts, have both, on behalf of the College, granted permission to us to print these letters.

No one would have rejoiced more at the final disposition of Gray's letters to Walpole than Leonard Whibley, who was a Fellow of Pembroke for more than forty years. My friendship with him began in 1931 and continued with annual meetings until 1939; we wrote each other about once a fortnight until his death in 1942. A large proportion of our correspondence dealt with Gray and his friends. Whibley enjoyed copying long extracts from the records relating to Gray at Peterhouse and Pembroke and from books which he thought we might lack. Nothing was too much trouble for him to undertake; whatever he found he freely imparted to us for what use we might care to make of it. We have acknowledged his specific contributions in the notes, but they are only a small part of his total contribution to these volumes. The walks at Frensham and the hours spent in the library at the Dial House were devoted to Gray, about whom he knew more than any living man. The information acquired in this way cannot be placed, with credit, in a footnote.

Our particular thanks are due to Mr Carl Pforzheimer for permission to quote for the first time from Gray's 'Naturalist's Journal' from the manuscript in his possession, and to Sir John Murray for his permission to print extracts from Gray's notebook of his travels. The late F. L. Holland kindly permitted us to print for the first time the letters in his possession bearing upon the Nicoll affair. We are indebted to Mr Charles C. Auchincloss, Eton, and the Trustees of the Pierpont Morgan Library and Haverford College for permission to use letters in their possession.

Once more I have to acknowledge the help given us by members of the Advisory Committee: Messrs Chapman, Ketton-Cremer, Pottle, and Sir Owen Morshead have read the proofs and made many additions and corrections in them. Mr Allen T. Hazen's *Bibliography of Horace Walpole* has solved many bibliographical problems for us. That work and its predecessor, the *Bibliography of Strawberry Hill,* were undertaken to supplement the *Yale Edition of Horace Walpole's Correspondence.* Mr Hazen's two books set Walpolian studies upon a solid bibliographical foundation, after nearly two centuries of frequent, but not always successful, endeavours to place them there. Sir Owen Morshead and Messrs Chapman, Ketton-Cremer, Pottle, and Wilder have read and improved my Introduction, as has also Mr John Carter. A contribution of major importance has been made by Lord Waldegrave. In 1942 he turned over to me Walpole's three unpublished volumes of juvenilia. These have provided us with much of what is new in the appendix to the present correspondence.

We are much indebted to Professor William Powell Jones for reading the proofs, to Mrs Louis L. Martz for assisting Mr Bennett in the preparation of the volumes for the press, and to Professor Robert Halsband of Northwestern University for his comments on Walpole's anecdotes of Lady Mary Wortley Montagu.

Mr Lam began editing the letters to and from Gray in January 1938. His task was a particularly difficult one, for he had to try to solve the problems which had been too much for our predecessors. As recently as 1935 had appeared the Toynbee-Whibley edition of Gray's correspondence, a notable contribution to eighteenth-century studies. Mr Lam's five years' work on the correspondence has reduced still further the number of its unsolved enigmas. That some remain is perhaps not remarkable, since Walpole himself, when he re-read Gray's early letters after Gray's death, confessed that many passages in them had become meaningless to him. When in November 1942 Mr Lam went into the army, Mr Bennett took over, edited the appendices and 'Short Notes,' saw the volumes through the press, and compiled the index. These tasks occupied him about three years.

Most of the work on the edition is conducted in the Yale Library under the immediate supervision of Mr Warren Hunting Smith. He was absent on military service for three of the ten years which have elapsed since these two volumes were undertaken, but for the other seven years Messrs Lam or Bennett have had the daily benefit of his knowledge and experience. An ever increasing contribution has been made by Miss Julia McCarthy, my secretary at Farmington, whose knowledge of the contents of Strawberry Hill and Walpolian records and documents is invaluable. No editor was ever more fortunate in his associates than I have been.

For upwards of a quarter of a century I have turned for help to Mr A. J. Watson of the Manuscripts Department of the British Museum, and have never failed to receive it. He has given me the immediate benefit of his knowledge and memory, and the long-range benefit of his untiring interest. He has kept his mind and eyes open for unrecorded material that would be of importance to us. It is quite impossible for us to cite the full account of his assistance. I can only say that we of this edition think of him as one of ourselves.

Much valuable help in the editing was furnished by the following, on bursary appointments from Yale College: Vincent P. Adley, John Ervin, Nicholas L. Heer, George W. Kearns, Leigh M. Miller, E. P. B. Muggridge, Lee Wigren, and William R. Wray.

Our particular thanks should be expressed to the Yale University Library. For fifteen years, the Yale Librarians, Messrs Keogh, Knollenberg, and Babb, have done everything in their power to make our task easier; we have been the daily beneficiaries of one of the most devoted library staffs in the world. This undertaking would be impossible without their assistance.

Our additional thanks are due to the following: Mr Norman Ault, Oxford; Mr F. W. Bateson, Brill, Bucks; Prof. A. R. Bellinger, Yale University; Mr Charles S. Belsterling, New York City; Miss Edith R. Blanchard, Brown University Library; Mr Daniel S. Brinsmade, New Haven; the Marquess of Bristol; Mr Ralph S. Brown, Jr, Yale University; Mr G. H. Chettle, F.S.A.; Mr C. L. Chute, the Vyne, Hants; Mr A. J. Collins, British Museum; Mr A. E. Conybeare, Vice-Provost of Eton; Dr Thomas W. Copeland, Yale University; Dr Grover Cronin, Jr, Yale University; Dr Lewis P. Curtis, Yale University; Dr Philip B. Daghlian, University of Indiana; the late Earl of Derby; Prof. William H. Dunham, Jr, Yale University; the late Hugh Gatty, St John's College, Cambridge; His Eminence Giovanni, Cardinal Mercati, Vatican Library; Miss Ruth S. Granniss, Grolier Club Library; Mr H. J. Habakkuk, Pembroke College, Cambridge; Dr Albert Hartmann, Bavarian State Library, Munich; Prof. E. A. Havelock, Harvard University; Mr Robert H. Haynes, Harvard University Library; Sir Ambrose Heal, Beaconsfield, Bucks; Prof. George L. Hendrickson, Yale University; Miss Anna B. Hewitt, Haverford College Library; Mr F. L. Holland, West Horsley, Surrey; Dr Andrew G. Hoover, Oberlin College; Mr Arthur A. Houghton, Jr, Queenstown, Maryland; Prof. James Hutton, Cornell University; Mr William A. Jackson, Harvard University Library; Dr Gerrit P. Judd, Lancaster, Pa; Mr H. S. Kingsford, Society of Antiquaries of London; Prof. Otto Kinkeldey, Cornell University Library; Prof. John P. Kirby, Randolph-Macon College, Lynchburg, Va; the late Prof. Angelo Lipari, Yale University; Prof. E. L. McAdam, New York University; Prof. Maynard Mack, Yale University; Mr D. W. McClellan, Library of Congress; Sir Henry Marten, Provost of Eton; the Rev. William Mather, Swaffham, Norfolk; Mr Herman R. Mead, Henry E. Huntington Library; Sir Ellis Minns, Pembroke College, Cambridge; Dr Robert E. Moore, University of Minnesota;

Prof. George H. Nettleton, Yale University; Prof. Wallace Note-stein, Yale University; Mr James M. Osborn, Yale University; Miss Rose Phelps, University of Illinois Library School; the late Rev. Frank C. Porter, Yale University; Mr F. J. E. Raby, Ministry of Works, London; Miss Fannie Ratchford, University of Texas Library; Mr Paul North Rice, New York Public Library; Prof. R. Selden Rose, Yale University; Mr James Ross, Librarian of the Public Library of Bristol; Prof. Curt Sachs, New York University; Mr John Saltmarsh, King's College, Cambridge; Dott. Ferdinando Sartini, Director of the Florentine State Archives; Dr B. Schofield, British Museum; Prof. Edmund Silk, Yale University; Dean Hartley Simpson, Yale University; Mr W. Force Stead, Abingdon, Berks; Miss Dorothy Margaret Stuart, Alton, Hants; Dr Hale Sturges, Shaker Heights, Ohio; Messrs Lawrence E. Tanner and D. L. Powell, Keeper and Assistant Keeper of the Muniments in Westminster Abbey; Mr Thomas Thacher, New York City; Mr W. Threlfall, Borough Librarian, Bexleyheath, Kent; Dr Rosemond Tuve, Connecticut College; Miss Winifred Ver Nooy, University of Chicago Library; Dr William K. Wim-satt, Jr, Yale University; Dr C. E. Wright, British Museum; Mr Wayne S. Yenawine, University of Illinois Library.

The death of Robin Flower, Deputy Keeper of Rare Books in the British Museum, removes another member of the original Advisory Committee. Our unceasing demands upon him and his admirable staff were (and continue to be) carried out not only precisely and speedily, but with a sense of pleasure in sharing a large responsibility. He played an important part in preserving intact the Bentley-Walpole collection and other Walpole collec-tions. A warm friend whose gaiety and generosity contributed greatly to this undertaking.

W. S. L.

CUE-TITLES AND ABBREVIATIONS

Add. MS . . .	Additional Manuscript, British Museum.
Ædes Walpolianæ, *Works* ii . . .	Horace Walpole, *Ædes Walpolianæ: or, A* *Description of the Collection of Pictures at* *Houghton Hall in Norfolk, the Seat of . . . Sir* *Robert Walpole,* in *The Works of Horatio* *Walpole, Earl of Orford,* 1798, vol. ii.
Anecdotes, Works iii .	Horace Walpole, *Anecdotes of Painting in Eng-* *land,* in *The Works of Horatio Walpole, Earl* *of Orford,* 1798, vol. iii.
Army Lists . .	[Great Britain, War Office,] *A List of the Offi-* *cers of the Army and of the Corps of Royal* *Marines.*
BERRY . . .	*The Yale Edition of Horace Walpole's Cor-* *respondence: The Correspondence with Mary* *and Agnes Berry,* New Haven, 1944, 2 vols.
Bibl. Nat. Cat. .	Catalogue de la Bibliothèque nationale, Paris, 1897–.
BM Cat. . .	British Museum Catalogue.
BM Cat. of Engraved *British Portraits* .	F. O'Donaghue and H. M. Hake, *Catalogue of* *Engraved British Portraits . . . in the British* *Museum,* 1908–25.
BM, *Satiric Prints* .	British Museum, Department of Prints and Drawings, *Catalogue of Prints and Drawings* *. . . Political and Personal Satires,* prepared by F. G. Stephens, E. Hawkins, and M. D. George, 1870–1942, 7 vols.
'Book of Materials' .	Three manuscript volumes, the first two en- titled by Walpole 'Book of Materials,' the third entitled 'Miscellany'; begun in 1759, 1771, and 1786 respectively. The originals are in the Fol- ger Shakespeare Library; photostatic copies in the possession of W. S. Lewis.
Boswell, *Johnson* .	*Boswell's Life of Johnson,* ed. George Birkbeck Hill, revised by L. F. Powell, Oxford, 1934–, 6 vols.
Boswell Papers .	*Private Papers of James Boswell,* ed. Geoffrey Scott and Frederick A. Pottle, privately printed, 1928–34, 18 vols.

Burke, *Commoners* . John Burke, *A Genealogical and Heraldic History of the Commoners of Great Britain and Ireland,* 1833–8, 4 vols.

Burke, *Landed Gentry* . Sir John Bernard Burke, *A Genealogical and Heraldic History of the Landed Gentry of Great Britain.*

Burke, *Peerage* . . Sir John Bernard Burke and Ashworth P. Burke, *A Genealogical and Heraldic History of the Peerage and Baronetage.*

Burney, *Hist. of Music* . Charles Burney, *A General History of Music,* 1776–89, 4 vols.

Cobbett, *Parl. Hist.* . *The Parliamentary History of England,* ed. William Cobbett and John Wright, 1806–20, 36 vols.

COLE . . . . *The Yale Edition of Horace Walpole's Correspondence: The Correspondence with the Rev. William Cole,* New Haven, 1937, 2 vols.

Collins, *Peerage* . . Arthur Collins, *The Peerage of England,* 1768, 1779, 1812 (ed. Sir Samuel Egerton Brydges).

Country Seats . . *Horace Walpole's Journals of Visits to Country Seats, &c.,* ed. Paget Toynbee, published by the Walpole Society, Oxford, vol. xvi, 1928.

Cunningham . . *The Letters of Horace Walpole, Earl of Orford,* ed. Peter Cunningham, 1857–9, 9 vols.

Daily Adv. . . . *Daily Advertiser.* Film, 1731–95, in the Yale University Library, from the file in the Library of Congress.

Designs, 1753 . . *Designs by Mr R. Bentley for Six Poems by Mr T. Gray,* 1753.

'Des. of SH,' *Works* ii . Horace Walpole, 'A Description of the Villa of Mr Horace Walpole at Strawberry Hill near Twickenham,' in *The Works of Horatio Walpole, Earl of Orford,* 1798, vol. ii.

DNB . . . . *Dictionary of National Biography,* ed. Leslie Stephen and Sidney Lee.

DU DEFFAND . . . *The Yale Edition of Horace Walpole's Correspondence: The Correspondence with Mme du Deffand,* New Haven, 1939, 6 vols.

Eton Coll. Reg. . . R. A. Austen-Leigh, *Eton College Register 1698–1752,* Eton, 1927.

Foster, *Alumni Oxon.* . Joseph Foster, *Alumni Oxonienses: The Mem-*

	bers of the University of Oxford, 1500–1714, Oxford, 1891–2, 4 vols; *1715–1886,* London, 1887–8, 4 vols.
GEC	George Edward Cokayne, *The Complete Peerage,* revised by Vicary Gibbs *et al.,* 1910–; *The Complete Baronetage,* Exeter, 1900–9, 6 vols.
'Genesis of SH'	W. S. Lewis, 'The Genesis of Strawberry Hill,' *Metropolitan Museum Studies,* vol. v, pt i, June, 1934.
Genest	John Genest, *Some Account of the English Stage,* Bath, 1832, 10 vols.
GM	*The Gentleman's Magazine.*
Gray-HW-West-Ashton Corr.	*The Correspondence of Gray, Walpole, West and Ashton (1734–1771),* ed. Paget Toynbee, Oxford, 1915, 2 vols.
Gray's Commonplace Books	Gray's MS Commonplace Book in three volumes, covering approximately the years from 1737 to 1761. Contains notes of Gray's reading and copies of poems by himself, Walpole, and West. Left by Mason to Stonhewer, and by Stonhewer to Pembroke College, Cambridge.
Gray's Corr.	*Correspondence of Thomas Gray,* ed. Paget Toynbee and Leonard Whibley, Oxford, 1935, 3 vols.
Gray's MS Journal 1739–41	Gray's notebook of his travels in France and Italy, owned by Sir John Murray; photostatic copy owned by W. S. Lewis. Printed in part in Gosse, *The Works of Thomas Gray* (4 vols. 1884), i. 237–46.
Gray's Naturalist's Journal	Gray's copy, with MS notes, of *The Naturalist's Journal,* London, 1767, a diary or memorandum book in which Gray entered notes, chiefly on natural phenomena, from 1 Jan. 1767 to 16 May 1771. Now in the collection of Mr Carl H. Pforzheimer of New York City.
Grove's Dictionary of Music	*Grove's Dictionary of Music and Musicians,* ed. H. C. Colles, 1927–8.
Hazen, Bibliography of Walpole	A. T. Hazen, *A Bibliography of Horace Walpole,* New Haven, 1948.
Hazen, SH Bibliography	A. T. Hazen, *A Bibliography of the Strawberry Hill Press,* New Haven, 1942.

Hertford Corr. . .	Correspondence between Frances, Countess of Hartford, and Henrietta Louisa, Countess of Pomfret, between the years 1738 and 1741, 1805, 3 vols.
Hervey, Memoirs . .	John, Lord Hervey, Some Materials towards Memoirs of the Reign of King George II, ed. Romney Sedgwick, 1931, 3 vols.
Hist. MSS Comm. . .	Historical Manuscripts Commission.
Historic Doubts . .	Horace Walpole, Historic Doubts on the Life and Reign of King Richard the Third, 1768.
HW	Horace Walpole.
HW, Waldegrave MSS .	Three manuscript volumes by Walpole, formerly in the Waldegrave Collection, now in the possession of W. S. Lewis. The first volume contains Walpole's 'Commonplace Book' of miscellaneous anecdotes and verses, begun in 1740; the second volume contains copies of his juvenilia with notes; the third volume, copies of his political papers with notes.
Isenburg, Stammtafeln .	Wilhelm Karl Prinz von Isenburg, Stammtafeln zur Geschichte der europæischen Staaten, Berlin, 1936, 2 vols.
Johnson, Lives of the Poets . . .	Samuel Johnson, Lives of the English Poets, ed. George Birkbeck Hill, Oxford, 1905, 3 vols.
Journal of the Printing-Office . . .	Horace Walpole, Journal of the Printing-Office at Strawberry Hill, ed. Paget Toynbee, 1923.
Ketton-Cremer, Walpole	R. W. Ketton-Cremer, Horace Walpole. A Biography, 1940.
La Chenaye-Desbois .	François-Alexandre-Aubert de la Chenaye-Desbois and —— Badier, Dictionnaire de la noblesse, 3d edn, Paris, 1863–76, 19 vols.
Litta	Pompeo Litta, Famiglie celebri italiane, Milan, 1819–74.
London Past and Present	H. B. Wheatley and Peter Cunningham, London Past and Present, 1891, 3 vols.
Mason, Mem. Gray .	William Mason, The Poems of Mr Gray to which are prefixed Memoirs of his Life and Writings, 1775.
Mem. Geo. II . .	Horace Walpole, Memoirs of the Reign of King George the Second, ed. Henry R. V. Fox, Lord Holland, 1847, 3 vols.

Mem. Geo. III . .	Horace Walpole, *Memoirs of the Reign of King George the Third*, ed. G. F. Russell Barker, 1894, 4 vols.
Mitford, 1816 . .	*The Works of Thomas Gray*, ed. John Mitford, 1816, 2 vols.
Mitford, 1835–43 . .	*The Works of Thomas Gray*, ed. John Mitford, 1835–6, 4 vols; volume v, containing the correspondence of Gray and the Rev. Norton Nicholls, 1843.
MONTAGU . . .	*The Yale Edition of Horace Walpole's Correspondence: The Correspondence with George Montagu*, New Haven, 1941.
MS Cat. . . .	Horace Walpole, 'Catalogue of the Library of Mr Horace Walpole at Strawberry Hill, 1763,' unpublished MS in the possession of Lord Walpole, Wolterton Park, Norwich; photostatic copy in the possession of W. S. Lewis.
Musgrave, *Obituary* .	*Obituary Prior to 1800 . . . Compiled by Sir William Musgrave*, ed. Sir George J. Armytage, Harleian Society Publications, 1899–1901, 6 vols.
N&Q	*Notes and Queries*.
NBG	*Nouvelle biographie générale*, ed. Jean-Chrétien-Ferdinand Hoefer, Paris, 1852–66, 46 vols.
Nichols, *Lit. Anec.* .	John Nichols, *Literary Anecdotes of the Eighteenth Century*, 1812–15, 9 vols.
Nichols, *Lit. Illus.* . .	John Nichols, *Illustrations of the Literary History of the Eighteenth Century*, 1817–58, 8 vols.
Nicoll, *Drama 1700–50* .	Allardyce Nicoll, *A History of Early Eighteenth Century Drama, 1700–1750*, Cambridge, 1929.
OED	*New English Dictionary on Historical Principles*, ed. Sir James A. H. Murray *et al.*, Oxford, 1888–1933.
'Paris Journals' . .	Horace Walpole, *Paris Journals*, in *The Yale Edition of Horace Walpole's Correspondence: The Correspondence with Mme du Deffand*, New Haven, 1939, v. 255–417.
P. C. C. . . .	Prerogative Court of Canterbury.
Pope, *Works*, ed. Elwin and Courthope . .	*The Works of Alexander Pope*, ed. Whitwell Elwin and W. J. Courthope, 1871–89.
Ranfft	Michael Ranfft, *Merkwürdige Lebensgeschichte*

	aller Cardinäle der Röm. Cathol. Kirche, Regensburg, 1768–73, 4 vols.
Reminiscences . .	Paget Toynbee (ed.), *Reminiscences Written by Mr Horace Walpole in 1788*, Oxford, 1924.
Royal and Noble Authors, Works i . .	Horace Walpole, *A Catalogue of the Royal and Noble Authors*, in *The Works of Horatio Walpole, Earl of Orford*, 1798, vol. i.
SH	Strawberry Hill.
SH Accounts . .	*Strawberry Hill Accounts . . . Kept by Mr Horace Walpole from 1747 to 1795*, ed. Paget Toynbee, Oxford, 1927.
Sold London . . .	*A Catalogue of the Collection of Scarce Prints* [also MSS and books] *Removed from Strawberry Hill*, 13–23 June, 1842. The number following each entry is the lot number in the sale.
Sold SH . . .	*A Catalogue of the Classic Contents of Strawberry Hill Collected by Horace Walpole*, 25 April–21 May 1842. The roman and arabic numerals which follow each entry indicate the day and lot number in the sale.
Thieme and Becker .	Ulrich Thieme and Felix Becker, *Allgemeines Lexikon der bildenden Künstler von der Antike bis zur Gegenwart*, Leipzig, 1907–.
TLS	*The Times* (London) *Literary Supplement*.
Tovey, *Gray and His Friends* . . .	Duncan C. Tovey, *Gray and His Friends*, Cambridge, 1890.
Toynbee . . .	*The Letters of Horace Walpole*, ed. Mrs Paget Toynbee, Oxford, 1903–5, 16 vols.
Toynbee *Supp.* . .	*Supplement to the Letters of Horace Walpole*, ed. Paget Toynbee, Oxford, 1918–25, 3 vols.
Tracts of Geo. 3 . .	'A collection of tracts and pamphlets, historical and political, published during the reign of King George III,' 1760–90, 59 vols (2 vols numbered 47), collected by HW; sold SH iii. 110; now in the possession of W. S. Lewis.
T–W	Paget Toynbee and Leonard Whibley, editors of the *Correspondence of Thomas Gray*, Oxford, 1935.
Venn, *Alumni Cantab.* .	*Alumni Cantabrigienses*, Part I, to 1751, ed. John Venn and J. A. Venn, Cambridge, 1922–7, 4 vols.

Vict. Co. Hist.	.	*The Victoria History of the Counties of England.*
Waldegrave MSS .	.	*See* HW, Waldegrave MSS.
Walpole-Mason Corr.	.	*The Correspondence of Horace Walpole and the Rev. William Mason*, ed. John Mitford, 1851, 2 vols.
Walpoliana .	.	John Pinkerton, *Walpoliana* [1799], 2 vols.
Willis and Clark	.	Robert Willis and John W. Clark, *The Architectural History of the University of Cambridge*, Cambridge, 1886, 4 vols.
Winstanley, *Unreformed Cambridge*	.	D. A. Winstanley, *Unreformed Cambridge. A Study of Certain Aspects of the University in the Eighteenth Century*, Cambridge, 1935.
Works .	.	*The Works of Horatio Walpole, Earl of Orford*, 1798, 5 vols.
WSL (now WSL)	.	In the possession of W. S. Lewis.

LIST OF LETTERS BETWEEN WALPOLE AND GRAY

The dates of the letters from Gray are printed in italics. Missing letters are marked by an asterisk after the date. References in the second column are to *Correspondence of Thomas Gray*, ed. Paget Toynbee and Leonard Whibley, 1935.

Year	Date	YALE	T-W
1734	ca 12 April*		
	ca 16 April	i. 56	i. 1
	ca 20 Oct.*		
	31 Oct.	i. 57	i. 3
	*ca 7 Nov.**		
	ca 11 Nov.*		
	17 Nov.	i. 61	i. 5
	ca Nov.*		
	8 Dec.	i. 65	i. 9
	ca 20 Dec.*		
	23 Dec.	i. 67	i. 12
	ca 25 Dec.*		
	ca 29 Dec.	i. 68	i. 11
1735	*6 Jan.*	i. 70	i. 14
	ca 9 Jan.*		
	12 Jan.	i. 72	i. 16
	14 Jan.	i. 73	i. 17
	ca 17 Jan.*		
	19 Jan.	i. 75	i. 19
	21 Jan.	i. 76	i. 20
	27 Jan.	i. 77	i. 21
	4 Feb.	i. 79	i. 23
	Feb.*		
	25 Feb.	i. 81	i. 24
	5 March	i. 82	i. 26
	June*		
	3 July	i. 83	i. 27
	ca 15 Oct.	i. 85	i. 29
	ca 31 Dec.*		

Date	YALE	T-W	Year
3 Jan.	i. 95	i. 35	1736
11 March	i. 98	i. 38	
June*			
11 June	i. 101	i. 44	
15 July	i. 103	i. 45	
Aug.*			
Aug.*			
Aug.	i. 105	i. 46	
*19 Sept.**			
Sept.*			
26 Sept.	i. 111	i. 49	
6 Oct.	i. 113	i. 51	
13 Oct.	i. 114	i. 54	
27 Oct.	i. 115	i. 55	
29 Dec.	i. 119	i. 58	
Jan.*			1737
16 Jan.	i. 125	i. 60	
ca 14 July*			
ca 16 July	i. 136	i. 64	
ca 22 Aug.	i. 140	i. 67	
ca 12 Nov.	i. 141	i. 68	
29 Dec.	i. 145	i. 71	
10 Jan.	i. 146	i. 73	1738
ca 12 Jan.*			
15 Jan.	i. 148	i. 74	
Feb.*			
23 Feb.	i. 151	i. 79	
7 March	i. 152	i. 81	

	YALE	T-W		YALE	T-W	
1738 March*			20 Feb.	ii. 46	i. 342	**1751**
20 March	i. 154	i. 82	3 March	ii. 47	i. 343	
ca 26 March*			April*			
28 March	i. 155	i. 83	16 April	ii. 49	i. 345	
19 Sept.	i. 161	i. 92	Sept.*			
			29 Sept.	ii. 51	i. 350	
1745 7 Nov.*			8 Oct.	ii. 52	i. 346	
ca 8 Nov.*			Nov.*			
			26 Nov.	ii. 56	i. 355	
1746 3 Feb.	ii. 1	i. 228	31 Dec.	ii. 57	i. 356	
March*						
28 March	ii. 4	i. 230	28 May	ii. 58	i. 362	**1752**
April–June*			ca July*			
7 July	ii. 5	i. 231	8 July	ii. 59	i. 362	
20 Oct.	ii. 6	i. 249	July–Aug.*			
15 Dec.	ii. 9	i. 257	ca Aug.	ii. 60	i. 363	
			17 Dec.	ii. 61	i. 366	
ca Jan.*						
1747 Jan.	ii. 11	i. 262	ca Jan.*			**1753**
Feb.*			ca 11 Feb.*			
8 Feb.	ii. 13	i. 264	13 Feb.	ii. 63	i. 372	
ca 19 Feb.	ii. 18	i. 268	ca 15 Feb.*			
ca 22 Feb.	ii. 21	i. 271	ca 17 Feb.*			
1 March	ii. 22	i. 272	20 Feb.	ii. 64	i. 373	
ca May*			27 Feb.	ii. 66	i. 375	
12 May	ii. 25	i. 281				
ca 15 June	ii. 26	i. 282	Jan.*			**1754**
Aug.*			15 Feb.	ii. 67	i. 390	
19 or 26 Aug.	ii. 30	i. 286	3 March	ii. 69	i. 391	
9 Sept.	ii. 31	i. 287	17 March	ii. 80	i. 400	
Nov.*			April*			
? 10 Nov.	ii. 32	i. 288	11 April	ii. 81	i. 401	
			ca 21 May*			
1748 Jan.*			23 May	ii. 82	i. 402	
ca Jan.	ii. 34	i. 294				
			July*			**1755**
1749 12 Nov.	ii. 42	i. 325	22 July	ii. 83	i. 426	
			8 Aug.	ii. 84	i. 429	
1750 12 June	ii. 43	i. 326	10 Aug.	ii. 84	i. 429	
			ca 12 Aug.*			
1751 ? 10 Feb.	ii. 44	i. 341	14 Aug.	ii. 85	i. 430	

Year	Date	YALE	T-W
1755	ca 15 Aug.*		
	14 Oct.	ii. 86	i. 441
	25 Dec.	ii. 86	i. 448
1756	30 July	ii. 89	ii. 467
	ca 2 Aug.*		
	4 Aug.	ii. 91	ii. 473
	Aug.*		
	29 Aug.	ii. 92	ii. 478
	8 Sept.	ii. 93	ii. 479
	ca 10 Sept.*		
	12 Sept.	ii. 94	ii. 480
	19 Sept.	ii. 95	ii. 481
	21 Sept.	ii. 96	ii. 481
1757	11 March	ii. 97	ii. 496
	11 July	ii. 97	ii. 507
	10 Aug.	ii. 99	ii. 512
	13 Oct.	ii. 100	ii. 533
	21 Oct.	ii. 101	ii. 535
1758	17 Jan.	ii. 101	ii. 556
	July (two letters)*		
	22 July	ii. 102	ii. 575
1759	14 Feb.	ii. 103	ii. 614
	15 Feb.	ii. 103	ii. 614
1760	ca April	ii. 105	ii. 664
	Aug. (fragment)	ii. 106	ii. 694
	2 Sept.	ii. 107	ii. 696
	ca 28 Oct.	ii. 116	ii. 708
1761	ca 2 Jan.	ii. 118	ii. 717
	ca May	ii. 118	ii. 737
	10 Sept.	ii. 119	ii. 750
	ca 12 Sept.*		
1762	11 Feb.	ii. 119	ii. 774
	Feb.*		
	28 Feb.	ii. 121	ii. 774

Date	YALE	T-W	Year
ca 3 Jan.	ii. 123		1763
ca 5 Jan.	ii. 124	ii. 767	
ca Sept.*			
12 Sept.	ii. 125	ii. 815	
ca 15 Sept.*			
19 Sept.	ii. 129	ii. 818	
27 Jan.	ii. 130	ii. 829	1764
Jan.*			
31 Jan.	ii. 132	ii. 830	
ca Feb. (two letters)*			
?18 March	ii. 132	ii. 834	
April*			
25 April	ii. 134	ii. 835	
July*			
10 July	ii. 135	ii. 835	
17 Aug.	ii. 136	ii. 841	
30 Dec.	ii. 136	ii. 855	
14 April	ii. 138	ii. 868	1765
20 Oct.*			
ca 12 Nov.	ii. 140	ii. 900	
19 Nov.	ii. 142	ii. 902	
13 Dec.	ii. 146	ii. 906	
25 Jan.	ii. 148	iii. 911	1766
24 Sept.	ii. 158	iii. 937	
ca 26 Sept. (fragment)	ii. 159	iii. 938	
24 Dec.	ii. 159	iii. 984	1767
14 Feb.	ii. 161	iii. 1006	1768
18 Feb.	ii. 166	iii. 1013	
25 Feb.	ii. 171	iii. 1017	
26 Feb.	ii. 175	iii. 1021	
6 March	ii. 178	iii. 1024	
8 March	ii. 181	iii. 1025	
ca April	ii. 184	iii. 1056	1769
26 May	ii. 185	iii. 1060	

1770	YALE	T-W
ca Aug.*		
12 Sept.	ii. 185	iii. 1145
Sept.*		
17 Sept.	ii. 186	iii. 1148

1771	YALE	T-W
17 March	ii. 187	iii. 1175
ca 23 March*		
25 March	ii. 188	iii. 1175

LIST OF LETTERS BETWEEN WALPOLE AND WEST

REFERENCES in the second and third columns are to *The Correspondence of Gray, Walpole, West and Ashton*, ed. Paget Toynbee, 1915, and to Mrs Toynbee's edition of Walpole's letters.

1735	YALE	P. TOYNBEE	MRS TOYNBEE
Oct.*			
29 Oct.	i. 90	i. 46	
9 Nov.	i. 93	i. 49	i. 8
1736 ca 23 May*			
1 June	i. 99	i. 76	
17 Aug.	i. 107	i. 97	i. 20
ca 20 Aug.	i. 109	i. 99	
Oct.*			
31 Oct.	i. 116	i. 109	
ca Dec.*			
1737 3 Jan.	i. 120	i. 118	
12 Jan.	i. 123	i. 122	
Feb.*			
27 Feb.	i. 127	i. 125	
April*			
18 April	i. 128	i. 132	
12 July	i. 133	i. 146	
ca Aug.*			
1 Dec.	i. 144	i. 162	
1738 7 Sept.	i. 157	i. 190	
1739 ca 4 April, O.S.*			

1739	YALE	P. TOYNBEE	MRS TOYNBEE
21 April, N.S.	i. 162	i. 207	i. 25
ca April*			
ca 15 May, N.S.	i. 167	i. 214	i. 29
18 June, N.S.	i. 170	i. 224	i. 31
21 June, O.S.	i. 172	i. 225	
20 July, N.S.	i. 177	i. 232	i. 32
28 Sept., N.S.	i. 180	i. 244	i. 36
24 Sept., O.S.	i. 184	i. 243	
15 Oct., O.S.	i. 185	i. 250	
11 Nov., N.S.	i. 188	i. 254	i. 40
14 Dec., N.S.	i. 192	i. 266	i. 43
13 Dec., O.S.	i. 195	i. 264	
1740 23 Jan., O.S.	i. 197	i. 271	
24 Jan., N.S.	i. 199	i. 273	i. 46
27 Feb., N.S.	i. 200	i. 276	i. 48
22 March, N.S.	i. 203	i. 279	i. 53
16 April, N.S.	i. 206	i. 283	i. 55
April*			
7 May, N.S.	i. 211	i. 290	i. 61
June*			
14 June, N.S.	i. 222	i. 313	i. 71
31 July, N.S.	i. 225	i. 324	i. 80
ca Aug.*			

		P. YALE	TOYNBEE	MRS TOYNBEE
1740	2 Oct., N.S.	i. 229	i. 339	i. 86
	10 Nov., O.S.	i. 234	i. 346	
	4 Dec., N.S.	i. 236	i. 349	i. 91
1741	ca Jan.*			
	ca Feb.*			

		P. YALE	TOYNBEE	MRS TOYNBEE	
29 March, O.S.					1741
		i. 239	ii. 1		
10 May, N.S.		i. 241	ii. 9	i. 97	
22 June, O.S.		i. 243	ii. 11		
April*					1742
4 May		i. 247	ii. 34	i. 218	

LIST OF LETTERS BETWEEN
WALPOLE AND ASHTON

		P. YALE	TOYNBEE	MRS TOYNBEE
1735	ca Oct.*			
1736	ca March*			
1737	Aug. (two letters)*			
	7 Aug.	i. 138		
1739	ca 4 April, O.S.*			
	? July*			
	July	i. 176	i. 236	i. 35

	P. YALE	TOYNBEE	MRS TOYNBEE	
March*				1740
ca 27 April, O.S.*				
14 May, N.S.	i. 214	i. 293	i. 64	
28 May, N.S.	i. 219	i. 307	i. 68	
July*				
ca 27 May, N.S.*				1741
June–July*				
July*				
25 July, O.S.	i. 246	ii. 15		

LIST OF LETTERS TO AND FROM
WALPOLE IN APPENDIX 1

		YALE
1751	20 June	
	from Horace Walpole, Sr	ii. 214
	21 June	
	to Horace Walpole, Sr	ii. 215
	21 June	
	from Horace Walpole, Sr	ii. 216
	22 June	

	YALE	
to Horace Walpole, Sr	ii. 205	1751
24 June		
to Francis Capper	ii. 206	
28 June		
to Margaret Nicoll	ii. 210	
7 Aug.		
to Mrs Harris	ii. 193	

SHORT NOTES

WALPOLE'S SHORT NOTES

THE manuscript of Walpole's 'Short Notes' consists of five sheets (one of which serves as a cover), folded into ten leaves which measure approximately 12¼ x 7¾ inches. Walpole originally folded each leaf again and wrote his notes down the right-hand side, leaving the left side blank for insertions; but after thus completing fifteen columns (which he erroneously numbered 1–11, 13–16), he added two more on the verso of leaf 9, then added another in the blank portion of leaf 8 recto, and concluded the notes at the top of leaf 7 recto.

'Short Notes' were first printed in 1843–4, when they were included in the fourth volume of the concluding series of Walpole's letters to Mann, published by Richard Bentley. The text prepared by the anonymous editor was reprinted by Cunningham and Mrs Toynbee in their collected editions of Walpole's letters. In 1937 the original manuscript was rediscovered among the Walpole papers which Bentley had acquired from Mary Berry, and passed into Mr Lewis's possession. The manuscript is here printed in full for the first time. The new material, which is indicated in the text by asterisks, amounts to about one-tenth of the whole.

When were the notes compiled? The early years of Walpole's life are rather sparsely reported, but in 1757–8 the record becomes more copious, suggesting that this was the period of compilation. An examination of the MS, with attention to the evidence provided by handwriting, changes of quill, variations in colour of ink, and the different watermarks in the five sheets, supports this conjecture. By May of 1759 at the latest, Walpole was almost certainly entering each event very soon after it occurred. But his interest in his autobiography declined, and in the latter part of the MS we again find groups of separated events, such as those for 1777–8, apparently entered at one sitting. The record ends in 1779, with an entry referring to Walpole's commentary on Mason's poems.

We do not know why Walpole dropped the notes eighteen years before his death. Records of a similar nature, his account-book and his printing-house journal, he continued for another decade and more. Perhaps he mislaid the MS, and thought it hardly worth the trouble of looking for it in order to enter the doings of his increasingly uneventful life, which, moreover, was being fully documented in the ever-growing correspondence that he already knew would survive him.

C. H. B.

Short Notes
of the life of
Horatio Walpole
youngest Son of
Sr Robert Walpole Earl of Orford
and of
Catherine Shorter, his first Wife.

I was born in Arlington street near
St James's London Sept 24. 1717. O.S. My
Godfathers were Charles Fitzroy Duke of
Grafton, & my uncle Horatio Walpole;
my Godmother, my aunt Dorothy Lady
Viscountess Townshend.
In 1725 I went to Bexley in Kent with
my cousins the four younger Sons of
Lord Townshend & with a Tutor, Edward
Weston, one of the Sons of Stephen Bishop
of Exeter, & continued there some months.
The next summer year, I had the same education
at Twickenham, Middlesex; & the
intervening winters I went every day
to study under Mr Weston at Ld Townshend's
April 26. 1727. I went to Eton school,
where Mr Henry Bland, (since Prebendary
of Durham) eldest son of Dr Henry Bland,
Master of the school, & since Provost of Eton
& Dean of Durham, was my Tutor.
I left Eton school Sept. 23. 1734: and
March 11th 1735 went to King's college
Cambridge. My public Tutor was Mr John
Smith; my private Mr Anstey, afterwards
Mr John Whaley was my Tutor. I went to
lectures in civil law to Dr Dickens of
Trinity hall. to mathematical lectures to
blind Professor Saunderson, for a short time:
afterwards Mr Trevigar read lectures to me
in mathematics & philosophy. I heard Dr
Battie's anatomical lectures. I had learned
French at Eton; I learned Italian at Cambridge
of Signor Piazza: at home I learned to dance
& fence; & to draw of Bernard Lens, master
to the Duke & Princesses.

I was inoculated for the small pox in 1724.

See my Notes & next page.

THE FIRST PAGE OF WALPOLE'S 'SHORT NOTES'

HORACE WALPOLE'S SHORT NOTES

Short Notes of the life of Horatio Walpole, youngest son of Sir Robert Walpole, Earl of Orford, and of Catherine Shorter, his first wife.

I WAS born in Arlington Street[1] near St James's London Sept. 24, 1717, O.S. My godfathers were Charles Fitzroy Duke of Grafton,[2] and my uncle Horatio Walpole;[3] my godmother, my aunt, Dorothy Lady Viscountess Townshend.[4]

I was inoculated for the smallpox in 1724.[5]

In 1725 I went to Bexley in Kent with my cousins the four younger sons[6] of Lord Townshend and with a tutor, Edward Weston,[7] one of

1. Extending southward from Piccadilly, between St James's Street and the Green Park. Sir Robert Walpole's first house in Arlington Street, which he occupied from 1716 until 1732, and which stood on the site of what was later No. 17, was demolished before 1743 (*post* i. 12 and n. 76). See also *post* i. 56 n. 1; H. B. Wheatley, *Round about Piccadilly*, 1870, pp. 170, 172. An entry in Lord Townshend's account-book, under date of 4 Oct. 1717, may tell us when HW was baptized: 'Paid the christening of Mr Walpole's child, £10-15-0' (*Genealogical Magazine* 1899, ii. 365). See n. 4 below.

2. Charles Fitzroy (1683–1757), 2d D. of Grafton (1690); Lord Chamberlain 1724–57, in which capacity he was influenced by Sir Robert Walpole to suppress Gay's *Polly* (1729), Sir Robert having been popularly identified with the highwayman Macheath in *The Beggar's Opera* (John, Lord Hervey, *Some Materials towards Memoirs of the Reign of King George II*, ed. Romney Sedgwick, 1931, i. 98).

3. Horatio Walpole ('old' Horace) (1678–1757), cr. (1756) Bn Walpole of Wolterton. See *post* i. 23–4.

4. Dorothy Walpole (1686–1726), Sir Robert's younger sister, m. (1713), as his second wife, Charles Townshend (1674–1738), 2d Vct Townshend of Raynham, Norfolk (GEC; Collins, *Peerage*, 1812, v. 652).

5. 'Mr Horatio Walpole, third son to the

Right Honourable Robert Walpole, Esq., had the smallpox inoculated on him a few days ago' (*London Journal* 10 Oct. 1724, p. 3). HW was probably inoculated by Claudius Amyand (d. 1740), the King's surgeon, who performed most of the twenty recorded inoculations in London that year (James Jurin [see *post* i. 15 n. 95], *An Account of the Success of Inoculating the Smallpox in Great Britain for the Year 1724*, [1725,] p. 13). Communications on the subject of inoculation had begun to appear in the Royal Society's *Philosophical Transactions* by 1714, and a few years later Lady Mary Wortley Montagu and her husband succeeded in introducing the practice into England. See *Philosophical Transactions . . . Abridged*, vi. 1809, p. 88; Lady Mary Wortley Montagu, *Letters and Works*, edn 1887, i. 184–5; Leslie Stephen in DNB *sub* Montagu.

6. George (1715–69), Augustus (1716–46), Horatio (ca 1717–1764), and Edward (ca 1719–1765) (DNB *sub* Charles Townshend; *East Anglian* 1903–4, n.s. vol. x. 348). The house where HW stayed has not been identified. In 1730 the Hon. Thomas Townshend (1701–80), half-brother of HW's cousins, married George Selwyn's sister Albinia (ca 1715–1739), whose father, Col. John Selwyn of Matson (see *post* i. 14 n. 94), at some unspecified period leased Danson Hill in Bexley parish. HW's first two

the sons of Stephen,[8] Bishop of Exeter, and continued there some months. The next summer, I had the same education at Twickenham,[9] Middlesex; and the intervening winters I went every day to study under Mr Weston at Lord Townshend's.[10]

April 26, 1727, I went to Eton school,[11] where Mr Henry Bland,[12] (since prebendary of Durham) eldest son of Dr Henry Bland,[13] master

letters, addressed to his mother and probably written during this or an earlier Bexley stay, mention visits to Mrs Selwyn. Both Thomas Townshend and his brother Roger are buried in the church at nearby Chislehurst, of which Thomas owned the manor, which had been conveyed to him by his father-in-law (*Archæologia Cantiana* xiii. 397, 400, xviii. 378n, 381; Edward Hasted, *History of Kent*, 2d edn, 1797–1801, ii. 9, 172, 183; Daniel Lysons, *Environs of London*, 1791–6, iv. 345. In preparing this note the editors received the kind assistance of Mr W. Threlfall, Borough Librarian of Bexley).

7. Edward Weston (1703–70), second son of Bp Weston; Eton and King's. W. P. Courtney in DNB lists his various public employments, including his secretaryship to Lord Townshend at Hanover during the King's residence there in 1729. A letter from Stephen Poyntz to Weston shows that HW was in Weston's charge as early as 25 July 1724 (Hist. MSS Comm. X, App. pt i. 239). Although it would be reasonable to suppose that Weston, a studious man who later wrote *The Country Gentleman's Advice to his Son on Coming of Age* and other improving pieces, had considerable influence upon HW at this time, he is unmentioned by HW in any other MS or letter which has been seen. This is the more curious since Weston received benefits from Bute and George Grenville, recommended the issue of a general warrant against Wilkes in 1763, and was attacked by Junius.

8. Stephen Weston (1665–1742), D.D., was consecrated Bishop of Exeter in 1724 through the influence of Sir Robert Walpole, whose master he had been at Eton. Weston's unsuccessful attempt at farming by Virgilian rules is mentioned by HW in his 'Epistle to Thomas Ashton' (*Works* i. 6).

9. On 19 Sept. 1726 Sir Robert wrote to Edward Weston from Chelsea asking him

to stay at 'Twittenham' till the end of October, instead of moving to town, 'as it will be very inconvenient as long as my family continues at Chelsea for my boy [Horace] to go and come every day' (Hist. MSS Comm. X, App. pt i. 240). If, as is likely, HW was again with his cousins, he and the young Townshends may have stayed with their half-brother, the Hon. William Townshend (ca 1702–1738: see *post* i. 7), who was living at Twickenham about this time (R. S. Cobbett, *Memorials of Twickenham*, 1872, pp. 51, 66, 67).

10. Lord Townshend's London house at this time has not been identified; his official letters 1724–9 are headed merely 'Whitehall' (William Coxe, *Memoirs of Sir Robert Walpole*, 1798, ii. 295, 328, 638). In 1720–1 he had a house in Paradise Row, Chelsea, but seems to have left it before 1725 (W. H. Godfrey, *Parish of Chelsea*, pt i, n. d., 26: *Survey of London* ii).

11. Only two lists of pupils have survived for the period of HW's residence: for 1728 and for 1732. In the latter the names are not divided into forms; in the 1728 list HW's name appears among the oppidans (the boys who, unlike the collegers on the foundation, lived in a boarding-house outside the college) in the third form of the lower school. Two 'Mr Townshends' are listed immediately above HW's name, presumably his cousins George and Augustus (*Eton Coll. Reg.* pp. vii, 340; R. A. Austen-Leigh, *Eton College Lists 1678–1790*, Eton, 1907, pp. xxi, 27, 30).

12. Henry Bland (ca 1703–1768), D.D. (1747), rector of Bishopwearmouth 1735–68 and of Washington, co. Durham, 1737–68. He became a prebendary of Durham in 1737 (*Eton Coll. Reg.* 32).

13. Henry Bland (d. 1746), D.D., headmaster of Eton 1720–28; a friend of Sir Robert Walpole (COLE i. 52 n. 8; *Works* ii. 238).

of the school, and since Dean of Durham and provost of Eton,[14] was my tutor.[15]

I was entered at Lincoln's Inn May 27th 1731, my father intending me for the law, but I never went thither, not caring for the profession.[16]

I left Eton School Sept. 23, 1734:[16a] and March 11th 1735 went to King's College[17] Cambridge. My public tutor was Mr John Smith:[18] my private Mr Anstey.[19] Afterwards Mr John Whaley[20] was my tutor. I

14. HW first wrote 'Provost of Eton and Dean of Durham,' but reversed the order. Dr Bland became Dean of Durham in 1728, and Provost of Eton in 1733 (*Etoniana* 22 Sept. 1920, p. 414; *Eton Coll. Reg.* p. xxi).

15. Probably Bland was an ordinary tutor attached to the school, such as was assigned to every boy; but it is possible that he had accompanied HW to Eton as a private tutor. See *Eton Coll. Reg.* p. xxiv, and *Etoniana* 23 April 1919, pp. 364-5. See also HW to Conway 29 June 1744.

16. See *Records . . . of Lincoln's Inn, Admissions*, 1896, i. 403. HW's attitude towards the law is shown in his 'Book of Materials' dated 1759, in which he collected a number of quotations and references under the heading 'Nonsense of the law' (p. 16). See also *post* Appendix 1.

16a. Mr A. E. Conybeare, Vice-Provost of Eton, informs us that seventeen was the usual leaving age of the oppidans of that period; but the fact that HW left on the day before his seventeenth birthday is apparently of no significance.

17. Where HW's father had preceded him. Mr John Saltmarsh, Librarian of King's College, writes (1937), 'There is no record of Horace Walpole's admission to this College, since only admissions of members of the Foundation were formally recorded, and as a Fellow-Commoner he was a non-member of the Foundation. However . . . in the Michaelmas Term 1735 the Mundum Book [an account book of the College] records the receipt of 10/- from Mr Walpole "pro detrimentis," and the same figure reappears in each term until the Baptist Term [beginning June 24] in 1738, with the exception of the Michaelmas Term 1736. In addition, a charge of 5/2 "pro coals" appears in the Christmas Term in 1735, 1736, and 1737. . . . To what extent these charges indicate residence I am uncertain. . . . Nor am I quite certain of

the meaning of the word "detriments" at this time. [Though orginally signifying a bill for extras,] in modern times it has become the charge paid by members of the College for keeping their names on the books, that is to say, for retaining their membership of the College.'

18. John Smith (1705-75) had become a fellow of King's in 1726, and was later bursar of the college (*Eton Coll. Reg.* 313-14). Cole, in one of his candid appraisals, characterized Smith as 'a steady, rational, and judicious man,' 'shy and reserved,' 'always cool and temperate; no great talker, but a most shrewd and sensible thinker' (Nichols, *Lit. Illus.* viii. 583). Harwood describes him as 'eminent for his knowledge of civil law, and esteemed an excellent algebraist' (Thomas Harwood, *Alumni Etonenses*, Birmingham, 1797, p. 310).

19. James Anstey (1714-42), fellow of King's 1735-42, Sir Robert Walpole's chaplain; born at W. Lockinge, Berks, son of James Anstey, 'gentleman'; ordained deacon (Lincoln) 1738, and priest (Norwich) 1741. He died at Chelsea, where he had been confined for insanity, said to have been brought on by a lawsuit (Venn, *Alumni Cantab.*; *Eton Coll. Reg.* 5; Thomas Harwood, *op. cit.* p. 322).

20. John Whaley (1710-45), fellow of King's 1731-45; ordained deacon 1745. HW reprinted some eulogistic verses by Whaley, entitled 'A Journey to Houghton,' at the end of *Ædes Walpolianæ* (1747). In his own copy of the *Ædes* (now in the Dyce Collection, Victoria and Albert Museum) HW wrote, 'John Whaley born in the city of Norwich about the year 1709, educated on the Foundation at Eton School, and from thence elected to King's College, Cambridge, and afterwards chosen Fellow there. He published a volume of poems and translations [*A Collection of Poems*] in 1732, octavo, and a second volume [*A Col-*

went to lectures in civil law to Dr Dickins[21] of Trinity Hall, to mathematical lectures to blind Professor Saunderson,[22] for a short time:[23] afterwards Mr Trevigar[24] read lectures to me in mathematics and philosophy. I heard Dr Battie's[25] anatomical lectures. I had learned French[26] at Eton; I learned Italian at Cambridge of Signor Piazza.[27] At

lection of Original Poems and Translations] in 1745, about which time he took orders and died in December of the same year. In both volumes are several pieces by the Rev. Sneyd Davies, rector of Kingsland, Herefordshire.' The 1745 volume is dedicated to HW; his copy of it is now in the Dyce Collection. For Cole's low opinion of Whaley, who was dissipated and frequently in trouble, see COLE ii. 299 n. 7; see also Nichols, Lit. Illus. i. 502. Though no letters from HW to Whaley appear to have survived, HW preserved eight of Whaley's to him, dated between 10 Aug. 1735 and 4 Dec. 1744.

21. Francis Dickins (d. 1755), LL.D., of Ripplington, East Meon, Hants; fellow of Trinity Hall 1704–55; Regius Professor of Civil Law 1714–55 (Venn, Alumni Cantab.).

22. Nicholas Sanderson (or Saunderson) (1683–1739), LL.D., Lucasian Professor of Mathematics 1711–39. He became blind in infancy after an attack of smallpox (Venn, Alumni Cantab.).

23. About two weeks, after which Dr Sanderson warned HW, to his mortification, that he would never learn mathematics. See BERRY ii. 208, and HW to Mann 13 Dec. 1759.

24. Luke Trevigar (1705–72), fellow of Clare 1728–38; ordained deacon (Ely) 1729, priest 1730; rector of Hurstmonceux, Sussex, 1743–72 (Venn, Alumni Cantab.). HW had hired Trevigar as a private instructor in mathematics, and he came to HW every day for a year, but to no avail (HW to Mann 13 Dec. 1759).

25. William Battie (1703–76), M.D. (1737), fellow of King's 1725–39; fellow of the Royal College of Physicians 1738, president 1764; founded the Battie scholarship at Eton. He specialized in mental cases, and was physician to St Luke's in London, besides being proprietor of a private asylum (Eton Coll. Reg. 23; Nichols, Lit. Anec. iv. 611). He attended Lord Orford, HW's nephew, during Orford's attacks of insanity in 1773–4 (COLE i. 298; HW to Lady Ossory

30 Dec. 1773, to Mann 19 Jan. 1774). According to HW, Battie died worth £100,000 (HW to Lady Ossory 16 Aug. 1776).

26. HW's French grammar, by John Palairet, with HW's signature and the date, 1730, is now WSL. His instructor may have been M. François Julien, a French teacher employed at Eton ca 1728–34 (Etoniana 11 Nov. 1939, p. 401; see also ibid. 1 May 1925, p. 604).

27. Girolamo Bartolomeo Piazza (d. ca 1745), born at Alessandria, was a teacher of Italian and French at Cambridge, and assistant to Samuel Harris and Shallet Turner, successively Regius Professors of Modern History. Cole, who had also studied Italian under Piazza, wrote of him, 'He had been a Dominican friar, and I remember his once showing me his letters of priest's orders: but, on his coming to England, to show himself a true convert, he forgot his vows, and took a wife, a French Huguenot woman, by whom he had a son and two daughters. . . . He was always very poor and necessitous, and had been often publicly relieved by the University, and oftener by the private Colleges and his scholars, who were the more generous to him as he always behaved himself decently and soberly, and was constantly clean and neat. . . . Though Mr Piazza was looked upon as an honest man, yet he was never esteemed as one of abilities, even in the two modern languages he taught' (Nichols, Lit. Anec. ix. 338). Piazza, who had been a delegate judge of the Inquisition in Osimo, was the author of A Short and True Account of the Inquisition and its Proceeding, as it is Practised in Italy, printed in English and French, London 1722 (HW's copy is MS Cat. E.9.35), which Cole stigmatized as being 'stuffed with idle stories . . ., and legendary tales of saints wrote in such a manner as was thought most proper to persuade that he was a true convert to the Church of England' (Winstanley, Unreformed Cambridge, p. 368; see also ibid. pp. 155–6, BM Cat. sub Piazza, and Gray's Corr. i. 52 n. 4).

home I learned to dance and fence; and to draw of Bernard Lens,[28] master to the Duke and Princesses.[29]

In 1736 I wrote a copy of Latin verses published in the *Gratulatio Acad[emiæ] Cantab[rigiensis]*[30] on the marriage of Frederic Prince of Wales.[31]

My mother died Aug. 20, 1737.[32]

Soon after, my father gave me the place of Inspector of the Imports and Exports in the Custom House, *worth[32a] £500 a year,*[33] which I resigned[34] on his appointing me Usher of the Exchequer in the room of Colonel William Townshend Jan. 29, 1738;[35] *a place worth above

28. Bernard Lens (1682–1740), miniature-painter and water-colourist. See COLE ii. 222–3 and nn. 6–7. Cole recalled having seen Lens with HW ca 1732 in Sir Robert's house at Chelsea, but remarked that HW profited little from the instruction (ibid.). A drawing by Lens of HW as a boy has been preserved at Chewton Priory.

29. I.e., the Duke of Cumberland and the Princesses Mary and Louisa, with whom HW played as a child (COLE ii. 222 n. 6; HW to Mann 29 May 1786).

30. *Gratulatio Academiæ Cantabrigiensis Auspicatissimas Frederici Walliæ Principis et Augustæ Principissæ Saxo-Gothæ Nuptias Celebrantis*, Cambridge, 1736. See Hazen, *Bibliography of Walpole* 105–7. HW's verses, printed on leaf O₁ verso, are headed 'Ad Principissam' and signed 'Horatius Walpole Coll. Regal. Socio-Commensalis' (HW's *Fugitive Verses*, ed. W. S. Lewis, 1931, pp. 99–100). Among the contributions are some verses in Italian, 'Al Re,' by G. B. Piazza (*ante* i. 6 n. 27), printed on leaf I₂.

31. Frederick Louis (1707–51), Prince of Wales, married Augusta (1719–72), daughter of Frederick, Duke of Saxe-Gotha, 27 April 1736.

32. Catherine Shorter, Lady Walpole, died of dropsy at Sir Robert's house in Chelsea, and was buried in Houghton Church. See *post* i. 140 n. 1. 'If my loss consisted solely in being deprived of one that loved me so much, it would feel lighter to me than it now does, as I doted on her' (HW to Lyttelton 18 Sept. 1737).

32a. Passages enclosed in asterisks are now printed for the first time.

33. HW's appointment was entered in the Customs Book xiv, pp. 254–5, as fol-

lows: 'Dec. 7 [1737.] Treasury letters patent appointing Horatio Walpole, Inspector General of Exports and Imports, and to make and keep a particular, distinct and true account of the importations and exportations of all commodities into and out of this kingdom, and to and from what places the same are exported and imported, and also upon what shipping such exports and imports are made, and to examine into the decay (if any) of the trades of this kingdom into foreign parts, and into the increase of freight of foreign shipping using this His Majesty's kingdom of Great Britain: and out of the said account once in every year and as often as he shall be thereunto required by the Treasury or Board of Trade or Customs Commissioners to make and present a fair and exact scheme of the Balance of Trade as it then stands between Great Britain and other parts of the world: all in succession to Anthony Balam, Esq., deceased: with yearly salaries of £500 to himself and £280 for clerks and substitutes' (W. A. Shaw, *Calendar of Treasury Books and Papers 1735–1738*, 1900, pp. 350–1).

34. The Customs House records show that HW surrendered the office on 13 Feb. 1737/8 (Shaw, *idem* 533, 625).

35. Entries referring to HW's appointment to this place, the full designation of which was 'Usher of the Receipt of the Exchequer and Keeper of the Council Chamber of the Star Chamber within the Palace of Westminster,' are dated 31 Jan. and 4 Feb. 1737/8 in the King's Warrant Book xxxii, pp. 490, 495–6 (Shaw, *idem* 624). The Hon. William Townshend (see *ante* i. 4 n. 9) had died 28 Jan. 1738 (GM 1738, viii. 52). This office, which HW held for the

£1500 a year.*³⁶ And as soon as I came of age I took possession of two other little patent places in the Exchequer, called Controller of the Pipe,³⁷ and Clerk of the Estreats,³⁸ *worth united about £300 a year.*³⁹ They had been held for me by Mr Fane.⁴⁰

My father's second wife Mrs Maria Skerret died June 1738.⁴¹

I had continued at Cambridge, though with long intervals, till towards the end of 1738, and did not leave it in form till 1739,⁴² in which year March 10th⁴³ I set out on my travels with my friend Mr Thomas Gray, and went to Paris. From thence, after a stay of about two months,⁴⁴ we went with my cousin Henry Conway⁴⁵ to Rheims in

rest of his life, was the chief source of his income. The duties pertaining to it, which were performed by deputy and included such tasks as shutting the gates of the exchequer and providing paper and pens for the exchequer and treasury, are described by HW in his 'Account of my Conduct Relative to the Places I Hold under Government,' written in 1782 (*Works* ii. 367–8). See also Appendix 7.

36. I.e. ca 1759, when HW was writing these notes. In 1738, according to HW, it was 'reckoned worth £900 a year' ('Account of my Conduct,' *Works* ii. 364), though the *Historical Register* for 1738 ('Chronological Diary' p. 7), in announcing HW's appointment, described it as 'a place of £1200 *per annum.*' By 1782 HW's income from the office averaged £1800 (*Works* ii. 367).

37. HW's appointment to this place is entered in the King's Warrant Book xxxiii, p. 183, and is dated by Shaw [? Dec. 14] 1738 (Shaw, op. cit. p. 634). The office was that of Controller of the Great Roll, and HW was required to swear 'that he would well and faithfully control the said Great Roll and all foreign accounts which shall be enrolled therein except such for which nothing is to be answered' (ibid.). See Hazen, *SH Bibliography* 170–2.

38. I.e., clerk or keeper of the foreign extracts in the Court of Exchequer. HW's patent was dated 1 Nov. 1738 (Shaw, *idem* 633).

39. The income was the same in 1782 ('Account of my Conduct,' *Works* ii. 364). HW held these places also for the rest of his life.

40. Henry Fane (d. 1777), of Wormsley, later (1742–57) one of the chief clerks of the Treasury; younger brother of Thomas, 8th Earl of Westmorland; M.P. for Lyme

Regis 1757–77 (Shaw, ibid. pp. 633–4; Burke, *Landed Gentry* 1939, p. 742; Collins, *Peerage*, 1812, iii. 302–3; *Court and City Register* 1757, p. 107). See also HW to Mann 28 Aug. 1742.

41. Maria Skerrett (ca 1702–1738), who had been Sir Robert's mistress and whom he had married earlier that year. She was a close friend of Lady Mary Wortley Montagu; they are the 'Phryne' and 'Sappho' of Pope's *Moral Essays* iii. 119–22. When Sir Robert announced his marriage, Thomas Robinson wrote to Lord Carlisle, 16 March 1737/8, 'All the well wishers to Sir R. W. have been to wish him and his Lady joy on his change of condition. I did it to both with great sincerity. Everybody gives her a very good character, both as to her understanding and good nature' (Hist. MSS Comm. XV, App. pt vi. 194). She died in Downing Street of a puerperal fever (GM 1738, viii. 324), and was buried at Houghton. See also *post* i. 151 n. 1.

42. Mr Saltmarsh informs us that HW took his name off the college books at the beginning of the Michaelmas term in 1738. His payments last appear in the accounts for the Long Vacation term in that year.

43. Doubtful in MS: perhaps '20th.' Neither date is correct. According to Gray, writing to his mother 1 April 1739, N.S., they left Dover 29 March N.S. (18 March O.S.) (*Gray's Corr.* i. 99). See also HW to West 21 April 1739, N.S., n. 1. For a full account of the tour, see Leonard Whibley, 'The Foreign Tour of Gray and Walpole,' *Blackwood's* June 1930, ccxxvii. 813–27.

44. They left Paris 1 June N.S. See HW to West 21 April 1739, N.S., n. 44.

45. Henry Seymour Conway (1719–95), statesman, Field Marshal, and HW's most

Champagne, stayed there three months,[46] and passing by Geneva,[47] where we left Mr Conway,[48] Mr Gray and I went by Lyons to Turin[49] over the Alps, and from thence to Genoa,[50] Parma, Placentia, Modena, Bologna[51] and Florence.[52] There we stayed three months, chiefly for the sake of Mr Horace Mann,[53] the English Minister. Clement XII dying while we were in Italy, we went to Rome in the end of March 1740[54] to see the election of the new Pope;[55] but the Conclave continuing, and the heats coming on, we (after an excursion to Naples[56]) returned in June to Florence,[57] where we continued in the house of Mr Mann till May of the following year 1741, when we went to the fair of Reggio.[58] There Mr Gray left me,[59] going to Venice with Mr Francis Whithed

intimate life-long friend. He had been lodging with Gray and HW in Paris (*Gray's Corr.* i. 109).

46. They lodged at M. Hibert's, Rue Saint-Denis (ibid. i. 112).

47. The latter part of HW to West 28 Sept. 1739, N.S., is dated 2 Oct. N.S. from Geneva.

48. He was back in Paris by 6 March 1740, N.S., and in London by June (HW to Conway 6 March and 5 July 1740, N.S.).

49. This is not a very clear statement of their itinerary. The three travellers made a five-and-a-half-day trip (27 Sept.–2 Oct.) from Lyon to Geneva, where Gray and HW stayed about a week. They were back in Lyon by 13 Oct., and on 31 Oct. set out for Turin, which they reached on 7 Nov. In Lyon they lodged at the Hôtel de Bourgogne; in Turin, at the Auberge Royale (Gray's MS Journal 1739–41; HW to West 28 Sept. 1739, N.S.; *Gray's Corr.* i. 121, 123, 125).

50. They left Turin 18 Nov., and on the 20th reached Genoa, where they stayed for a week, lodging at the Santa Marta (*Gray's Corr.* i. 129; Gray's MS Journal 1739–41). See also HW to West 14 Dec. 1739, N.S., n. 1.

51. The proper order here is Placentia (i.e. Piacenza, which according to Gray 'made so frippery an appearance' that they stopped only long enough to dine), Parma, etc. They left Genoa 28 Nov. and on 3 Dec. reached Bologna, where they stopped for twelve days, at the Pellegrino (*Gray's Corr.* i. 132; Gray's MS Journal 1739–41).

52. Gray and HW left Bologna on 15 Dec. for Florence, which they reached on the afternoon of the next day (*Gray's Corr.*

i. 134–5). For notes on their lodgings in Florence, see HW to West 4 Dec. 1740, N.S., n. 4.

53. Ca 1706–1786: later Sir Horace Mann, Bt; HW's correspondent. He represented England at the Court of Tuscany from 1738 until his death. Officially he was chargé d'affaires 1738–40, resident 1740–65, envoy extraordinary 1765–82, and envoy extraordinary and plenipotentiary 1782–6 (D. B. Horn, *British Diplomatic Representatives 1689–1789*, 1932, p. 81).

54. HW and Gray reached Rome 26 March (HW to West 22 March 1740, N.S.).

55. Clement XII died 6 Feb. 1740. See HW to West 22 March 1740, N.S., n. 1. For an account of the Conclave, which ended 17 August with the election of Lambertini (Benedict XIV), see HW to West 7 May 1740, N.S., to Ashton 28 May, and to West 31 July.

56. They left Rome for Naples 12 June, and stayed there about nine days ('Gray's Notes of Travel,' Tovey, *Gray and His Friends* 223; *Gray's Corr.* i. 169).

57. HW and Gray arrived in Florence ca 8 July (*Gray's Corr.* i. 165; HW to Conway 5 July 1740, N.S.).

58. See HW to West 10 May 1741, N.S., and n. 1.

59. See Whibley's account of the quarrel which resulted in this separation, the causes of which will probably never be satisfactorily explained, in *Gray's Corr.* iii. 1200–2; see also Mann to HW 23 May 1741, N.S. Gray and HW were not reconciled until Nov. 1745, when they were brought together through the mediation of 'a lady who wished well to both parties' (Mason, *Mem. Gray* 41). According to HW's

and Mr John Chute[60] for the festival of the Ascension.[61] I fell ill at Reggio of a kind of quinsy, and was given over for fifteen hours, escaping with great difficulty.[62]

I went to Venice with Henry Clinton Earl of Lincoln[63] and Mr Joseph Spence, Professor of Poetry,[64] and after a month's stay there,[65]

note in his copy of the *Mem. Gray* (now in the Harvard Library) the lady was a Mrs Kerr, but she has not been further identified.

60. 'The Chutheds': HW's correspondent John Chute (1701–76), and Chute's friend Francis Whithed (1719–51). See Gray to HW 8 Feb. 1747, n. 31.

61. Which in 1741 fell on 11 May. It was the day on which was celebrated the traditional espousal of Venice and the Adriatic. See *Gray's Corr.* i. 182.

62. Joseph Spence (see *post* n. 64) wrote to his mother from Bologna 29 May 1741: 'We are got on as far as Bolonia in our way to Venice; and have been, as I told you in my last, a opera-hunting at Reggio. After we had been there a day or two, we heard that Mr Walpole (who we thought was gone) was still there, but that he was ill abed. We went, you may be sure, immediately to see him; and found him very ill, with a quinsy; and swelled to such a degree as I never saw any one in my life. We went from him to the opera; whence I got to bed, at two; and between three and four, was surprised with a message that Mr Walpole was extremely worse, and desired to speak with me immediately. I dressed as soon as I heard it; stepped into his coach, which waited at the door: and found him scarce able to speak. I soon found there, upon talking with his servants, that he had been all this while without any physician; and had doctored himself. So I sent immediately for the best physician the place could afford; and dispatched an express to Florence, to our Minister there, with orders to bring a physician from thence who is a very good one and my particular friend, Dr Cocchi; and who (which was a very material thing in these parts) understands and talks English, like an Englishman. In about twenty hours time, Mr Walpole began to grow better; and we left him with his Florentine doctor in a fair way of recovering soon. I was with him perpetually till the doctor came; and if he had been worse, had got leave of Lord Lincoln to stay behind for some days to take care of him: but I thank God all went well, before my Lord went away; and so we took our leaves of him with pleasure, and hope to see him next week at Venice, wh[i]ther he is bound as well as we, and then for England. You see what luck one has sometimes in going out of one's way: if Lord Lincoln had [not] wandered to Reggio, Mr Walpole (who is one of the best natured, and most sensible, young gentlemen that England affords) would in all probability have been now under the cold earth' (Add. MS Egerton 2234, ff. 263–4). For a note on Dr Cocchi see *post* 2 Oct. 1740, N.S., n. 9.

63. Henry Fiennes-Clinton (after 1768 Pelham-Clinton) (1720–94), 9th E. of Lincoln, who became 2d D. of Newcastle in 1768. In 1743 HW described him as 'a very dark thin young nobleman, who did not look so much of the Hercules as he said he was himself' (Waldegrave MSS 2. 99). HW also satirized good-naturedly his vanity and amorous propensities in a mock letter from 'Thamas Kouli Kan' (included in HW to Mann 13 Feb. 1743 and Waldegrave MSS 2. 68–70) and in 'Patapan' (see *post* i. 14).

64. Lord Lincoln's tutor, Joseph Spence (1699–1768), friend of Pope, professor of poetry at Oxford 1728–38, and author of *Polymetis*. HW and Gray had first met Spence and Lord Lincoln at Turin in Nov. 1739 (see HW to West 11 Nov. 1739, N.S., and to Spence 21 Feb. 1741, N.S.), and they met again in Florence, where Spence mentioned dining with HW 'almost every day' (Spence to his mother 7 Nov. 1740, Egerton MS 2234). But HW's memory is at fault if he means to imply that he travelled with Spence and Lord Lincoln from Reggio to Venice: see Spence's letter to his mother *ante* n. 62, and *Hertford Corr.* iii. 206, 209, 221.

65. HW left Venice in company with Spence and Lord Lincoln on 12 July, and they were in Genoa by the 19th. See HW to Mann 19 July 1741, N.S., and Mann to HW 23 July.

returned with them by sea from Genoa, landing at Antibes, and by
the way of Toulon, Marseilles, Aix,[66] and through Languedoc to Montpellier,[67] Toulouse and Orléans, arrived at Paris,[68] where I left the Earl
and Mr Spence, and landed at Dover Sept. 12, 1741, O.S.,[69] having been
chosen Member of Parliament for Kellington[70] in Cornwall at the preceding General Election,[71] which parliament put a period to my
father's administration, which had continued above twenty years.[72]

Feb. 9th 1742. My father resigned, and was created Earl of Orford.[73]
He left the house in Downing Street[74] belonging to the Exchequer, and

66. HW wrote to Mann 7 August from Aix (missing: see Mann to HW 21 and 27 August 1741, N.S.).

67. They had reached Montpellier by 11 August, and left it on the 15th (Mann to HW 2 Sept. 1741, N.S.; Spence to his mother 14 Aug. 1741, N.S.).

68. Ca 30 August (Spence to his mother 21 Aug. and 1 Sept. 1741, N.S.). HW stopped at the Hôtel de Luxembourg, Rue des Petits Augustins; Lord Chesterfield was there at the same time (HW's marginal notes in Maty's *Chesterfield*, p. 28: corrected copy issued with vol. xi, 1867–8, of *Miscellanies* of the Philobiblon Society).

69. He reached London 14 Sept. O.S. (*Daily Adv.* 16 Sept. 1741). HW had expected to leave Paris 27 Sept. N.S. (HW to Mann Sept. 1741), but his plans were for some reason altered. He arrived at Calais on his homeward journey 20 Sept. N.S. (9 Sept. O.S.) (HW to Mann 11 Sept. 1741, O.S.).

70. An alternative spelling of Callington (C. S. Gilbert, *An Historical Survey of the County of Cornwall*, 1817–20, ii. 467).

71. HW had been returned one of the two members for Callington 14 May 1741; he sat in Parliament for that borough until 1754 (Return of Members of Parliament, pt ii, 1878, pp. 86, 98). In a 'State of Cornish Boroughs' prepared for Lord Edgcumbe in 1760 it is said of Callington: 'Lady Orford has this borough without any opposition. There have been several attempts to elect a Member here against her Ladyship's family interest, but without success' (L. B. Namier, *The Structure of Politics at the Accession of George III*, 1929, ii. 372–3, 375: see also i. 178). Margaret Rolle (1709–81), later Cts of Orford, HW's sister-in-law, owned the manor of Callington, which on the death of her son, Lord Orford, in 1791,

passed to his maternal cousin Lord Clinton (Gilbert, op. cit. ii. 468; GEC *sub* Orford). In both the 1741 and the 1747 election HW was not unopposed. In 1741 he and Thomas Copleston, the other successful candidate, received 44 votes each, while the defeated candidates, Messrs Mitford and Bennet, received 23 and 21 votes respectively; the figures in the 1747 election were HW 71, Copleston 57, Calmady 31, Potter 15 (GM 1741, xi. 229; 1747, xvii. 305).

72. Sir Robert had been First Lord of the Treasury 1715–17, and was reappointed to the post in April 1721. By the end of 1741 his administration was tottering. After several adverse votes in the House of Commons, on 28 Jan. 1742 he suffered a serious defeat in the debate over a Chippenham election and decided to resign (*Journals of the House of Commons* xxiv. 65–6; HW to Mann 16 Dec. 1741).

73. The patent for his peerage was dated 6 Feb. 1742; he resigned the premiership 11 Feb. (*Journals of the House of Lords* xxvi. 55; *Daily Adv.* 12 Feb. 1742). Why Sir Robert selected the title of Orford is unknown. His bitter enemy Samuel (later Lord) Sandys was infuriated by the choice, since the title had formerly been held by Lady Sandys' granduncle, Edward Russell, E. of Orford. See HW to Mann 9 Feb. 1742, O.S.

74. Where Sir Robert had lived since 22 Sept. 1735: see Gray to HW 16 Apr. 1734, n. 1. 'That house belonged to the crown: King George I gave it to Baron Bothmar, the Hanoverian minister, for life. On his death [1732] King George II offered it to Sir Robert Walpole; but he would only accept it for his office of First Lord of the Treasury, to which post he got it annexed forever' (*Ædes Walpolianæ, Works* ii. 266). The house as remodelled for Sir Robert became and has remained the official resi-

retired to one in Arlington Street,[75] opposite to that in which I was born, and which stood where the additional building to Mr Pelham's house now stands.[76]

   March 23d 1742. I spoke in the House of Commons, for the first time, against the motion for a secret committee on my father.[77] This speech was published in the magazines, but was entirely false, and had not one paragraph of my real speech in it.[78]

dence (No. 10) of the prime minister, though it has not always been used as such. See the London County Council's *Survey of London* xiv, 1931, pp. 122, 126. In a MS copy of *Ædes Walpolianæ* (sold London 1124) now in the Metropolitan Museum of Art, New York, HW inserted a set of drawings which show a plan of the house and elevations of the walls of seven of the rooms, with notes giving dimensions, locations of pictures, etc., in HW's hand (*Survey of London* xiv. 117: reproduced in plates 147–54). Lord Orford did not leave the house in Downing Street until ca 21 July 1742, when he and HW removed to Lord Orford's house in Chelsea for a short time before departing for a three-months visit to Houghton (HW to Mann ca 21 July and 29 July 1742).

75. Shortly before 1 Nov. Lord Orford and HW returned from Norfolk and took up their residence in the Arlington Street house (later No. 5) which Lord Orford had long owned, and which he had had 'laid together' with a smaller adjoining house for HW (HW to Mann 1 Nov. 1742, 6 Jan. 1743; H. B. Wheatley, *Round About Piccadilly*, 1870, p. 171).

76. 'At the house now inhabited by Earl Gower, and built by Mr Pelham, is a fine room and ceiling designed by Kent, as the rest of the house was. Where the great room stands was formerly a house inhabited by Sir R. Walpole during his administration and where his youngest son Horace was born: on the rest of the ground of Mr Pelham's house stood the house of Mr Pultney, afterwards Earl of Bath, the great opponent of Sir Rob. Walpole' (HW's 'Anecdotes of the Streets of London,' in 'Book of Materials' 1759, p. 45). Henry Pelham (d. 1754), the statesman, moved into his Arlington Street house early in May 1743 (HW to Mann 12 May 1743).

77. The motion 'for appointing a committee to inquire into the conduct of Robert Earl of Orford during the last ten years,' which had been made by Lord Limerick and seconded by Sir John St Aubyn, was passed by a vote of 252 to 245. The committee was duly appointed and, after some preliminary trouble with obstinate witnesses, published two reports; but the evidence they were able to collect against Lord Orford was not conclusive, and both the investigation and its results were quickly forgotten (William Coxe, *Memoirs of Sir Robert Walpole*, 1798, i. 708–31; I. S. Leadam in DNB).

78. For the 'real speech' see HW to Mann 24 March 1742, O.S., where HW in a note again describes the printed speech as 'fictitious.' Until 1771 the publication of parliamentary debates was liable to prosecution, as constituting a breach of privilege, with the result that the reports which appeared in magazines had to be disguised, and were notoriously unauthentic (see Hill and Powell in Boswell's *Johnson* i. 501–12; W. E. H. Lecky, *A History of England in the Eighteenth Century*, New York, 1892–3, iii. 476–83; bibliography by H. H. Bellot et al. in *Bulletin of the Institute of Historical Research* x. 171–7). The fabricated speech attributed to HW, probably written by Thomas Gordon (d. 1750), the translator of Tacitus, was printed in *London Magazine* xi. 657–60 and xii. 1–2 (Appendix to 1742, Jan. 1743), the same version appearing also in *Scots Magazine* Jan. 1743, v. 13–15, and in Richard Chandler's *History and Proceedings of the House of Commons* xiii (1743), pp. 191–6. It was eventually included, still in HW's name, in the report of the debate in Cobbett, *Parl. Hist.* xii. 536–41. Johnson, though he also 'reported' this debate for GM, wrote no speech for HW (Boswell's *Johnson* i. 511; 'Debates in the Senate of Lilliput,' GM 1743, xiii. 345–60; Cobbett, *Parl. Hist.* ix, p. [ii]; GM 1856, cci.

WALPOLE'S HOUSE IN ARLINGTON STREET

July 14th I wrote 'The Lesson for the Day,' in a letter to Mr Mann;[79] and Mr Coke,[80] son of Lord Lovel, coming in while I was writing it, took a copy, and dispersed it till it got into print,[81] but with many additions,[82] and was the origin of a great number of things of that sort.[83]

In the summer of 1742 I wrote 'A Sermon on Painting,'[84] for the amusement of my father in his retirement. It was preached before him by his chaplain;[85] again before my eldest brother at Stanno[86] near Houghton; and was afterwards published in the *Ædes Walpolianæ*.[87]

June 18, 1743, was printed in a weekly paper called *Old England or the Constitutional Journal,* my parody on some scenes of *Macbeth,* called 'The Dear Witches.'[88] It was a ridicule of the new ministry.[89]

667. In writing this note the editors have received assistance from an unpublished Yale dissertation by Medford Evans, 'Johnson's Debates in Parliament,' 1933).

79. See HW to Mann 14 July 1742 for the original text of the 'Lesson,' which is a scriptural parody satirizing the office-seekers who obtained preferment after Sir Robert Walpole's downfall. HW wrote also a slightly expanded version, of which two copies in his hand are known: one formerly in the Waller Collection (see Toynbee *Supp.* ii. 78–80), the other in HW, Waldegrave MSS 2.56–8. See Hazen, *Bibliography of Walpole* 19–21.

80. Edward Coke (1719–53), styled Vct Coke 1744–53; son of Thomas Coke (1697–1759), who was cr. Bn Lovel 1728 and E. of Leicester 1744. Edward Coke was M.P. for Norfolk 1741–7, for Harwich 1747–53; m. (1747) Lady Mary Campbell, from whom he was separated in 1750.

81. It was published 5 Aug. 1742 (*Daily Adv.*) under the title *The Lessons for the Day. Being the First and Second Chapters of the Book of Preferment.* The source of this edition was not, as HW seems to imply, the version sent to Mann, but the expanded version mentioned in n. 79 above. (See HW's note on HW to Mann 14 July 1742.)

82. HW wrote only the 'second chapter,' and even that was greatly expanded from his original. The author of the additions was unknown to him (HW, Waldegrave MSS 2.55); it may have been Sir Charles Hanbury Williams, in whose collected *Works* (1822), ed. Edward Jeffery, the pamphlet is included (iii. 28–39).

83. In Waldegrave MSS 2.55 HW speaks of 'swarms of papers in the same way, that came out on all subjects for a long time afterwards'; see also HW to Mann 28 Aug. 1742, in which he transcribes one imitation. Others are as follows: *The Evening Lessons for the Day, being the Third and Fourth Chapters of the Book of Preferment,* 1742; *The Lessons for the Day, being the Fifth and Sixth Chapters,* etc., n.d.; *A Lesson for the Day . . . by Michael Ben Haddi,* 1744. See Hazen, *Bibliography of Walpole* 21–2.

84. *Works* ii. 279–87; a copy in HW's hand is in HW, Waldegrave MSS 2. 58–68. The text is from Psalms cxv. 5–6: 'They have mouths but they speak not,' etc. HW described the sermon as 'a sort of essay on [Lord Orford's] collection of pictures' (Waldegrave MSS 2. 57). In it he attempted to combine a commentary on the paintings with a eulogy of his father.

85. Perhaps the Rev. Thomas Deresley, presented to the vicarage of Houghton Church by Sir Robert in 1731 (Francis Blomefield and Charles Parkin, *An Essay towards a Topographical History of Norfolk,* 1805–10, vii. 111).

86. Robert Walpole (ca 1701–1751), who succeeded his father as 2d E. of Orford in 1745, had a small house at Stanhoe, near King's Lynn, which was occupied by his mistress, Hannah Norsa (HW to Mann 10 June 1743; MONTAGU i. 109 n. 28).

87. See *post* i. 17. The sermon is printed on pp. 87–99 of the first edn of *Ædes*.

88. HW preserved the first leaf, the one that contains 'The Dear Witches' (inscribed 'This belongs to George's Coffeehouse, Temple Bar'), at the back of Waldegrave MSS 2. In the printed text the proper

The same summer I wrote 'Patapan, or the little White Dog,'[90] a tale imitated from Fontaine. It was never printed.

Oct. 22d 1743 was published No. 38 of the *Old England Journal*, written by me to ridicule Lord Bath.[91] It was reprinted with three other particular numbers.[92]

In the summer of 1744 I wrote a parody[93] of a scene in Corneille's *Cinna;* the interlocutors, Mr Pelham, Mr Arundel and Mr Selwyn.[94]

names and such words as Court, Treasury, etc., are identified by initial and terminal letters only. HW's MS copy, in the same volume of MSS, pp. 76–92, gives the names in full, besides many explanatory notes which were not printed. The title, as HW explains in his introductory letter to the printer, is taken from *Spectator* No. 45. See Hazen, *Bibliography of Walpole* 153–4.

89. Some of those named are Lord Wilmington, Samuel Sandys, Sir John Rushout, Lord Bath, and Lord Carteret.

90. 'Wrote at Houghton 1743'; in Waldegrave MSS 2. 94–112. This skit, which has never been printed, is in verse interspersed with prose, and is copiously annotated. It is a close imitation of La Fontaine's *Le Petit Chien*, with Arthur Onslow, Lord Lincoln, Signora Grifoni, *et al.*, substituted for the original characters. The fantastic amorous adventures were not meant to parallel any actual scandal, as HW points out (MSS 2. 95); but his father's political enemies are incidentally satirized with telling effect. Patapan, the dog in the case, was a white Roman spaniel given to HW at Florence by Mme Grifoni. He is mentioned frequently in the Mann correspondence, and when he died in 1745 there were expressions of grief on both sides (HW to Mann 25 April 1743, 29 April 1745, O.S.; Mann to HW 29 June 1745, N.S.; Waldegrave MSS 2. 101, 102).

91. William Pulteney (1684–1764), cr. E. of Bath 1742; originally Sir Robert Walpole's political ally, but after 1725 his enemy. Though Pulteney declined an offer of the prime ministership after Sir Robert's downfall, he held the chief power in the government until July 1742, when his acceptance of a peerage ended his active political career. He had attacked Sir Robert in the *Craftsman*, and now was himself the butt of satire, from the pen of HW, Hanbury Williams, and others. In the paper

here mentioned (of which HW's annotated MS copy is in Waldegrave MSS 2. 112–18), HW represents Bath as 'William Poney' and the King as Sir Richard Steele in a theatrical allegory referring to the change of government.

92. HW's letter is printed on pp. 10–17 of *Four Letters published in Old England: or, The Constitutional Journal* (viz. of *Oct. the 8th, 22d, 29th, and Nov. the 5th*), 1743. The three other papers are not by HW.

93. Unpublished: in Waldegrave MSS 2. 124–34. The scene HW imitates is II. i. Pelham is represented as threatening to resign as prime minister, but is persuaded by Selwyn and Arundel to abandon his resolution.

94. Pelham is the Augustus of the original, Selwyn is Cinna, and Arundel is Maximus. HW's note on Selwyn (see also *ante* i. 3 n. 6) is as follows: 'John Selwyn formerly served in the Army under the Duke of Marlborough; but being a sensible shrewd man, chose to quit that life for more certain lucrative employments. He was much in the confidence of Sir R. Walpole and Lord Townshend, and by their favour raised much money in the stocks, and was made Groom of the Bedchamber to the King, and then Treasurer to the Queen. He never meddled in Parliament, nor hurt himself by choosing his attachments there too rashly. He died in 1751' (Waldegrave MSS 2. 123). Of Richard Arundel (d. 1758: see MONTAGU i. 33, n. 1) HW writes: 'Mr Arundel, a younger son of Lord Arundel's, was a bosom friend of Mr Pelham's, and married one of the Duke of Rutland's sisters [Frances, d. 1769], as Mr Pelham married the other [Catherine, d. 1780]. He was reckoned an honest man, very silent, and shrewd, and had humour; but very indolent. He was Paymaster of the Board of Works, then Master

My father died March 28, 1745.[95] He left me the house in Arlington Street in which he died, £5000 in money[96] and £1000 a year from the collector's place in the Custom House, and the surplus to be divided between my brother Edward and me, *which brings me about £300 a year more;[97] so that my income is in all about £3300 a year[98] clear.*

April 12, 1746, was published in a magazine, called *The Museum,*

of the Mint, and at this time one of the Lords of the Treasury' (Waldegrave MSS 2. 123).

95. Lord Orford died 18 March, O.S. (if HW was trying to adjust to N.S. he missed it by a day), at one o'clock in the morning (*Daily Adv.*, 18 March). He was buried at Houghton 25 March (GEC). In a note in *Mem. Geo. II* (i.225) and elsewhere, HW says flatly that his father 'was killed by Jurin's medicine for the stone,' a powerful caustic which lacerated the bladder.

John Ranby, the King's surgeon, who attended Lord Orford and performed an autopsy, published (10 April 1745: *Daily Adv.*) a pamphlet entitled *A Narrative of the Last Illness of the Right Honourable the Earl of Orford*, to which HW certainly contributed a portion (see p. 15), and perhaps had a hand in writing the whole. The implicit censure of Dr James Jurin, a physician of formidable eminence, provoked a pamphlet war which was notable for having inspired Fielding's virtually unknown *Charge to the Jury . . . on the Trial of A.B.C.D. and E.F., all M.D.* (published 3 July 1745: *Daily Adv.*), an amusing satire upon the pedantry, dogmatism, and incompetence of the medical profession, to which is appended a Swiftian 'Project for the advancement of physic in this island, by abolishing the College [of Physicians].' See a note on the *Charge* and the entire controversy in the *Times Literary Supplement* 4 March 1926, p. 168.

96. 'I give and bequeath unto my son Horatio Walpole the sum of five thousand pounds to be . . . paid to him within one year after my decease with the . . . interest for the same in the mean time after the rate of four pounds by the hundred for a year; and I also give and bequeath unto my said son Horatio Walpole . . . all that my house in Arlington Street . . . for the residue of my term and interest therein to

come and unexpired; but upon this condition nevertheless that he and they do permit and suffer my daughter Lady Maria Walpole and Isabella Leneve now living with me to dwell and inhabit in the said house until my said daughter shall happen to marry, my said daughter and the said Isabella Leneve paying to my said son the yearly rent or sum of one hundred pounds' (Lord Orford's will, P.C.C. 91 Seymour). By 1782 HW had received only £1000 of the cash bequest, with no interest ('Account of My Conduct,' *Works* ii. 365). HW's lease of the Arlington Street house expired in 1781 (ibid.). HW's half-sister, Lady Maria Walpole (ca 1725–1801), Sir Robert's legitimized daughter by Maria Skerrett, married Charles Churchill in 1746. For a note on Isabella Leneve, her companion, see MONTAGU i. 62.

97. By 1782 it had risen to £400: 'King George I had graciously bestowed on my father the patent place of collector of the customs for his own life, and for the lives of his two elder sons Robert and Edward; but my father reserved in himself a right of disposing of the income of that place as he should please during the existence of the grant. Accordingly . . . he bequeathed, by an instrument under his hand, £1000 a year to me out of the patent for the remainder of the term, and devised the remainder, about £800 a year, to be divided between my brother Edward and me' (*Works* ii. 364–5). When Sir Edward Walpole died in 1784 HW was deprived of this £1400 (HW to Lady Ossory 18 Jan. 1792).

98. Presumably his income ca 1759 (when this portion of the notes was written), though how HW made the (probably inaccurate) calculation which produced this figure is not clear. See *ante* i. 7–8 and *post* i. 25; see also HW to Newcastle 12 Nov. 1758.

my 'Scheme for a tax on message cards and notes';[99] and soon after, an advertisement of a pretended new book;[100] which I had written at Florence in 1741.[101]

In July of the same year I wrote 'The Beauties,'[102] which was handed about, till it got into print very incorrectly.

In August I took a house within the precincts of the Castle at Windsor.[103]

Nov. 4th and 5th Mrs Pritchard[104] spoke my 'Epilogue to *Tamerlane*'[105] on the suppression of the rebellion, at the theatre in Covent Garden. It was printed by Dodsley the next day.[106]

About the same time I paraphrased some lines of the first book of Lucan;[107] but they have not been printed.

99. The 'Scheme,' which satirizes the fashionable practice of sending written messages on the most trivial occasions, was printed on pp. 46–53 of *The Museum* for 1746. It is also in *Works* i. 132–9, with notes, and in Waldegrave MSS 2. 134–44, with additional notes.

100. 'The History of Good-Breeding,' published in the 5th number of *The Museum*, 24 May 1746, pp. 169–72; it is also in *Works* i. 141–5 and Waldegrave MSS 2. 146–50. The 'Advertisement' consists of the title-page and the table of contents, with such chapter-headings as: 'Inquiry whether Adam called Eve "Madam" or "My dear" before company: the latter opinion condemned by the Council of Nice'; 'What persons are qualified to give balls,' etc.

101. I.e., the 'Advertisement'; according to a note in the MS, the 'Scheme' was written in London.

102. *Works* i. 19–24. 'Some copies of this poem having got about, it was printed without the author's knowledge, and with several errors. It was reprinted more correctly in the second volume of a miscellany of poems in three volumes published by Dodsley 1748' (HW, Waldegrave MSS 2. 153: the poem, with some unpublished annotation, is on pp. 154–60). For a full account of this elegant trifle, which was written in less than three hours for the amusement of Lady Caroline Fox and in compliment to the ladies of their acquaintance, see HW's *Fugitive Verses*, ed. W. S. Lewis, 1931, pp. 23–33. The unauthorized first edn was announced 23 Sept. 1746 (*Daily Adv.*); its inaccuracies, though

plentiful, are not serious. Dodsley printed it, still without HW's name, in his *Collection of Poems*, 1748, ii. 321–7. HW first publicly acknowledged the authorship in *Fugitive Pieces* (see *post* i. 29). See Hazen, *Bibliography of Walpole* 22–4.

103. HW's 'little tub of forty pounds a year' (HW to Conway 3 Oct. 1746), which he rented from a Mr Jordan. He had moved in by 21 August 1746, but gave it up the following summer when he leased Strawberry Hill (MONTAGU i. 44; HW to Mann 21 Aug. 1746, and to Conway 3 Oct. 1746, 8 June 1747).

104. Hannah Pritchard, née Vaughan (1711–68), at this time at Covent Garden, followed Garrick to Drury Lane in 1747. She spoke the 'Epilogue' in the character of the Comic Muse.

105. *Works* i. 25–7. 'Tamerlane [by Nicholas Rowe] is always acted with an Occasional Prologue in honour of King William [III], on the 4th and 5th of November, being the anniversaries of his birth and landing. This Epilogue was spoken on those two days in honour of William Duke of Cumberland, who had defeated the Young Pretender in Scotland in the foregoing April' (HW's note in Waldegrave MSS 2. 159; text on pp. 160–2). The annual performances of *Tamerlane* were given regularly at Drury Lane until 1815, and occasionally also at Covent Garden.

106. Nov. 5, according to *Daily Adv.* Dodsley included it also in his *Collection*, 1748, ii. 327–30.

107. These still unpublished lines, dated 'Windsor October 1746,' were transcribed

In 1747 I printed my account of the collection *of pictures* at Houghton, under the title of *Ædes Walpolianæ*.[108] It had been drawn up in the year 1743.[109] I printed but 200 copies,[110] to give away. It was very incorrectly printed; another edition, more accurate and enlarged,[111] was published March 10th 1752.

In May 1747 I took a small house[112] near Twickenham for seven years. I afterwards bought it by Act of Parliament[113] (it belonging to minors[114]) and have made great additions and improvements to it. In one of the deeds I found it was called Strawberry Hill.[115]

in Waldegrave MSS 2. 164–6, under the title 'Imitation of Lucan, Lib. 1, v. 32[-66]. Addressed to Mr Pitt.' HW's original MS is also now WSL.

108. *Ædes Walpolianæ: or, a Description of the Collection of Pictures at Houghton Hall in Norfolk, the Seat of the Right Honourable Sir Robert Walpole, Earl of Orford.* Though the title-page bears the date 1747, the printing was not completed or the distribution made until the summer of 1748: see HW to Mann ca Aug. 1748. The printer was probably John Hughs (ca 1703–1771), who certainly printed the second and third editions (Nichols, *Lit. Anec.* v. 35; Hazen, *Bibliography of Walpole* 26–32). For some notes on the collection of pictures, which HW's nephew the 3d E. of Orford sold in 1779 to Catherine of Russia for £40,555, see COLE ii. 168–70.

109. The Dedication to his father is dated from Houghton 24 Aug. 1743.

110. A mistake: only 100 copies of this edition were printed (HW to Mann ca Aug. 1748). In his own copy of the edition (Victoria and Albert Museum) HW gives a list of 83 persons who received copies. No copy has been seen by the editors which has not been corrected extensively by HW.

111. The chief additions were a long note on Sir Thomas Chaloner on p. 47 (of the 1752 edn), an anecdote added on p. 51, a note on the Sibylline oracles, p. 63, an account of Lord Danby inserted in the text on p. 72, and a long passage on the controversy over the immaculate conception, pp. 77–9. The enlarged edition was reprinted in *Works* ii. 237–87, omitting Whaley's verses (*ante* i. 5 n. 20).

112. The house and its surroundings are described in HW to Conway 8 June 1747. For a note on Mrs Chenevix, from whom

HW took the lease, see *post* i. 103. A memorandum of HW's original agreement, now WSL, reads in part as follows: 'Memorandum that it is agreed between the Honourable Horace Walpole, Esq. of the one part and Elizabeth Chenevix of the parish of Saint Martin in the Fields in the county of Middlesex of the other part, dated this 27th day of June in the year of Our Lord 1747: First, the said Elizabeth Chenevix does consent and agree to let her house, out-houses, furniture and lands thereunto belonging situate in the parish of Twickenham in the county of Middlesex at and under the yearly rent of sixty pounds to be paid half-yearly; and the said Horace Walpole, Esq. does hereby bind himself to accept the same as tenant to the said house and lands . . . for one whole year and no longer, to commence from the twentieth day of May last past.'

113. Private Act 22 Geo. II, c. 44: 'An Act for sale of divers lands and tenements in Twickenham in the County of Middlesex, devised by the will of Paul Mansfield, deceased, pursuant to an agreement for that purpose, and for the benefit of his grandchildren.' It is printed in *SH Accounts* 183–9. A copy annotated by Kirgate is now WSL.

114. Two of the three heirs for whom the property was held in trust were minors, Paul and Martha Mortimer. The date of conveyance was 1 June 1749; the sum to be paid by HW was £1356 10s. (*SH Accounts* 183–4, 186).

115. 'It was built [1698] by the Earl of Bradford's coachman, and was called by the common people, "Chopped-Straw-Hall," they supposing, that by feeding his lord's horses with chopped straw, he had saved money enough to build his house; but the

In this year (1747) and the next and in 1749 I wrote thirteen[116] numbers in a weekly paper called *Old England or the Broadbottom Journal:* but being sent to the printer[117] without a name they were published horridly[118] deformed and spoiled.[119]

I was rechosen in the new Parliament for Kellington[120] in Cornwall. About the same time was published *A Letter to the Tories,* written, as I then believed, by Mr George Lyttelton,[121] who with his family had

piece of ground on which it stands is called in all the old leases, "Strawberry-Hill-Shot," from whence it takes its name' ('Des. of SH,' *Works* ii. 399 n.; see also Cobbett, op. cit. 295). Gray seems to have called the house 'Strawberry Hill' before HW did: see Gray to HW 19 (or 26) Aug. 1747. In October 1747 HW jokingly called it 'Kyk in de Pot' in a letter to Montagu; and not until the spring of 1748 did he begin to refer to it in his letters as Strawberry Hill (MONTAGU i. 52, 56; HW to Mann 7 June 1748).

116. A mistake for fifteen: 14 Feb., 7 March, 16 May, 13 June, 20 June, 4 July, 1 Aug., 22 Aug., 10 Oct., 24 Oct., 5 Dec. 1747; 23 Jan., 23 April, 25 June 1748; 11 Feb. 1749. HW transcribed them, from his original copies, in Waldegrave MSS 3. 1–52, 58–63 (also WSL are HW's drafts of 16 May, 13 June, 4 July, 24 Oct., and 5 Dec. 1747; see letter in *Times Literary Supplement* 24 Jan. 1935, p. 48). These papers, in which HW first achieved the strength and clarity characteristic of his mature political style, treat such subjects as the dissolution of Parliament (18 June 1747), the rivalry between the Prince of Wales and the Duke of Newcastle, and the current war, that of the Austrian Succession. Taken as a whole the papers constitute a vigorous attack on Pelham, Pitt, and the other members of the coalition government.

117. John Purser (d. 1771), at this time in Red Lion Court, Fleet Street. He printed the *Daily Journal* in 1728, and *Fog's Weekly Journal* after 1731 (H. R. Plomer, *Dictionary of Printers and Booksellers . . . 1726 to 1775,* Oxford, 1932, p. 205; *London Magazine* Oct. 1771, xl. 524).

118. Previously printed 'horribly.'

119. HW's more temperate note preceding his transcripts in Waldegrave MSS 3 is as follows: 'These papers are here transcribed from the original copies, which

were often altered, and sometimes very absurdly, by the editor, to whose want of judgment they were left.' The editor at this time, who used the pseudonym 'Argus Centoculi,' is said to have been John Banks (1709–51) (Theophilus Cibber, *Lives of the Poets,* 1753, v. 313–14). Though a few of the papers, e.g. 10 Oct., 5 Dec., and 23 Jan., followed HW's MS quite closely, most of them, as HW says, were extensively revised. The changes were usually in the direction of moderation and greater disguise, owing, doubtless, to the printer's having been prosecuted three times for libel (Plomer, loc. cit.). The effect of the first paper, for example, is considerably diminished by the addition of an awkward compliment to the very ministers whom HW was satirizing. But the editorial emendation was illogical, as HW points out in a note on 20 June: 'In this paper was a strong instance of the absurdity of the editors; instead of *Pelhasgæ* [as HW had written it in the motto, referring to Henry Pelham], they printed *Pelhamgæ* at length, and disguised the name of the Duke of Buckingham [which HW had written out, since he had been dead a century] under the foolish appellation of *Bucco.*'

120. See *ante* i. 11 n. 71. The new Parliament was summoned to meet on 13 Aug. 1747.

121. George Lyttelton (1709–73), created Baron Lyttelton 1756. HW's copy of the *Letter to the Tories,* 1747, bound with his own *Letters to the Whigs* (see *post* i. 19), was sold London 1033 and is now WSL. HW's later uncertainty that the *Letter* was by Lyttelton is shown in a MS note on p. 2 of his copy of the *Second and Third Letter to the Whigs:* 'After these two Letters came out, there was a denial of [Lyttelton's] being the author printed in a daily paper, but not signed by himself, and it was said that the *Letter to the Tories* was wrote by

come over to Mr Pelham. As Mr Lyttelton had been a great enemy of, and writer against,[122] my father, and as Mr Pelham had used my father and his friends extremely ill, and neglected the Whigs to court the Tories,[123] I published an answer to that piece, and called it *A Letter to the Whigs*.[124] It was a careless performance and written in five days. At the end of the year I wrote two more letters to the Whigs:[125] but did not publish them till April the next year, when they went through three editions[126] immediately. I had intended to suppress them, but some attacks being made by the Grenvilles[127] on Lord Ch[ief] Justice Willes[128] (an intimate friend of my father) particularly by obtaining an Act of

Dr Thirlby; but neither of these facts was ever authenticated.' The attribution to Edward Walpole's friend Styan Thirlby (ca 1686–1753: see MONTAGU i. 14 n. 4) has not been elsewhere noted. The unsigned denial of Lyttelton's authorship appeared in the *General Advertiser* for 5 April 1748, reprinted from Fielding's *Jacobite's Journal* for 2 April. It was probably written by Fielding himself (see W. L. Cross, *History of Henry Fielding*, 1918, ii. 80, 92), though possibly drafted by Lyttelton, as HW seems to have thought. HW replied in *Old England* for 23 April 1748.

Whether Lyttelton wrote the *Letter to the Tories* remains uncertain. At the time it was generally believed to be his, and not only by his enemies, as some complimentary verses in GM for Nov. 1748 (xviii. 520) show. But Fielding's denial, HW's doubt, and Ayscough's failure to include it in Lyttelton's collected works (1774), weigh heavily against the attribution.

122. Particularly in his *Letters from a Persian* (1735). In Feb. 1741 he had supported Sandys's motion for Sir Robert's dismissal.

123. For Pelham's defection, see *Mem. Geo. II* i. 167, 229–36.

124. HW's anonymous *Letter to the Whigs*, which was a defence of the freedom of the press embodied in an attack on the Ministry, was published 23 July 1747 (*Daily Adv.*). See Hazen, *Bibliography of Walpole* 32–4.

125. *A Second and Third Letter to the Whigs*, published 26 March 1748 (*Daily Adv.*). In the second letter HW again defended the freedom of the press, and in the third he eulogized his father's administration in contrast to that of the Pelhams. In

both letters he quoted from Lyttelton's *Letters from a Persian,* and by collating the third and fifth editions and comparing certain emendations with passages in the *Letter to the Tories* he attempted to reinforce his contention that Lyttelton wrote the latter. (HW's annotated copies of the two editions of the *Persian Letters* were sold London 1033 and are now WSL.)

126. 'The third edition of Three Letters to the Whigs' (actually it was the second edition of the *Second and Third Letter*) was announced in *Daily Adv.* 27 May 1748. See Hazen, *Bibliography of Walpole* 34–6.

127. All four brothers (a fifth had died in May 1747) had by this time achieved political prominence: Richard (1711–79), styled Vct Cobham 1749–52, E. Temple 1752, M.P. for Buckingham 1734–41, 1747–52, and for Bucks 1741–47; George (1712–70), M.P. for Buckingham 1741–70; James (1715–83), M.P. for Bridport 1747–54; and Henry (1717–84), governor of Barbados 1746–56.

128. Sir John Willes (1685–1761), Chief Justice of the Court of Common Pleas 1737–61. In his letter to Mann of 11 March 1748, HW describes the 'attack' as 'a sort of private affair between the Chief Justice Willes and the Grenvilles'; and in a MS note in his own copy (*ante* i. 18 n. 121) of the *Second and Third Letter,* appended to his 'Advertisement' mentioning the intended suppression of the letters, he says, 'The Assizes transferred by Act of Parliament and by the interest of the Grenvilles from Aylesbury to Buckingham where the two elder were chosen, was a derogation from the rights of the Judges who have a right to fix the Assizes, and was levelled at Lord Ch. Justice Willes, in whose circuit those

Parl[iament] to transfer the assizes from Ailesbury to Buckingham,[129] I printed them and other pieces.[130]

On the same occasion I had a remarkable quarrel with the Speaker of the House of Commons, Mr Onslow.[131] The bill was returned from the Lords with amendments.[132] The friends of the Chief Justice resolved to oppose it again. Mr Potter[133] desired me to second him.[134] He rose, but entering on the merits of the bill, Mr T. Townshend[134a] and my uncle Horace Walpole (to prevent me) insisted that nothing could be spoken to but the amendments. The Speaker supporting this, I said I had intended to second Mr Potter, but should submit to his *oracular* decision, though I would not to the complaisant peevishness of anybody else. The Speaker was in a great rage and complained to the House. I said I begged his pardon, but had not thought that submitting to him was the way to offend him.[135] During the course of the same

towns lay, and one of whose sons [Edward Willes (d. 1787), M.P. for Aylesbury 1747–54] was elected at Aylesbury.'

129. Where they had been held regularly since 1720, except in 1747, the year in which Justice Willes's son was elected for Aylesbury. The proposed Act, therefore, merely enforced the traditional practice; but Willes's supporters, arguing that the Grenvilles were motivated only by family interest, waged a bitter fight against the bill when it was brought in by Richard Grenville on 19 Feb. 1748. It was finally passed by the Commons on 15 March, and on 13 May received the royal assent and became law (21 Geo. II, c. 12). The Act remained in force until 1849 (Cobbett, *Parl. Hist.* xiv. 202–46; *Journals of the House of Commons* xxv. 530, 570, 659; *Victoria History of the County of Buckingham,* ed. William Page, 1905–28, iv. 548).

130. Presumably the pamphlets described *post* nn. 138 and 141.

131. Arthur Onslow (1691–1768), M.P. for Guildford 1720–7, Surrey 1727–61; Speaker of the House of Commons 1728–61.

132. After passing the Commons on 15 March the bill was sent to the Lords for consideration, whence it was returned 5 April, and on 6 April the amendments (six trifling verbal changes) were moved in the Commons by George Grenville and accepted (*Journals of the House of Commons* xxv. 570, 617, 620). No other record of the altercation HW describes has been found.

133. Thomas Potter (1718–59), M.P. for St Germans 1747–54, for Aylesbury 1754–7, and for Okehampton 1757–9; an associate of Wilkes and collaborator with him in the 'Essay on Woman.'

134. The MS of HW's undelivered seconding speech is now WSL. HW's preliminary note is as follows: 'When the Buckingham Assizes Bill was sent back from the Lords, a motion was intended to be made for postponing the passing of it for three months, Mr Potter to move and I to second with the following speech.' At the end of the speech HW has written: 'This speech [was] not spoke, Mr Potter who was to have made the motion having been several times called to order by Mr T. Townshend and Mr H. Walpole Sen. who insisted on his speaking only to the amendments. Mr H. W. Junior then said, "Sir, I did indeed intend to have seconded this motion, but am so little master of order, that for fear of squabbling with you about what is so much your province, I shall submit to your oracular decisions, not to the complaisant peevishness of anybody else." Here the Speaker bounced, and said he never was so treated before, etc. Mr H. W. then said, "Sir, I ask your pardon, but I should not have thought that submitting to you, was the way to offend you." '

134a. See *ante* i. 3 n. 6.

135. HW had great respect for the Speaker's character and abilities, and at the time of Onslow's retirement (1761) eulo-

bill, Sir William Stanhope[136] had likewise been interrupted in a very bitter speech against the Grenvilles. I formed part of the speech I had intended to make,[137] into one for Sir William, and published it in his name.[138] It made great noise. Campbell answered it[139] for a bookseller.[140] I published another, called 'The Speech of Richard White-Liver,'[141] in answer to Campbell's. All these things were only excusable by the lengths to which party had been carried against my father—or rather were not excusable even then.

In 1748 were published in Dodsley's *Collection*[142] of miscellaneous

gized him highly in his memoirs; but it was perhaps the recollection of this quarrel which caused HW to insert the reservation that Onslow 'was so minutely attached to forms that it often made him troublesome in affairs of higher moment' (*Mem. Geo. III* i. 39).

136. Sir William Stanhope (1702–72), K.B. 1725; M.P. for Lostwithiel 1727, for Bucks 1727–41, 1747–68; Lord Chesterfield's younger brother (DNB *sub* P. D. Stanhope; Return of Members of Parliament pt ii, 1878, pp. 51, 61, 72, 85, 98, 109, 123, 137).

137. Not the second speech, which was to have been delivered during the debate of 5–6 April (*ante* n. 132), but evidently a speech HW had intended to make some time between 19 Feb. (*ante* n. 129) and 3 March, when the 'Stanhope' speech was published (see next note).

138. *The Original Speech of Sir W——m St——pe, on the First Reading of the Bill for Appointing the Assizes at Buckingham, Feb. 19, 1748,* was published 3 March 1748 (*Daily Adv.*). It was reprinted in GM for March 1748 (xviii. 99–101), *London Magazine* for May 1748 (xvii. 202–5), and *The Foundling Hospital for Wit,* No. VI, 1749, pp. 14–21; and it appears in Stanhope's name in Cobbett, *Parl. Hist.* xiv. 204–9. See Hazen, *Bibliography of Walpole* 36–9.

139. Presumably Dr John Campbell (1708–75), though other evidence for his authorship of it is lacking. The pamphlet was published 7 March 1748 (*Daily Adv.*) under the title *A Speech without Doors, in Answer to a Supposed Speech within; on the Merits of the Great Cause of Aylesbury versus Buckingham.* (The original pamphlet has not been seen by the editors, but it was reprinted in *The Foundling Hospital for Wit,* No. VI, 1749, pp. 21–9.) The vagar-

ies of parliamentary reporting at that time (see *ante* i. 12 n. 78) are well illustrated by the history of this pamphlet, which was compiled by a hack and probably bore little resemblance to anything that was actually said in the House of Commons. First it was listed in the 'Register of Books' in GM for March 1748 (xviii. 144), and in the same issue it was reprinted (pp. 101–4) immediately following HW's speech for Stanhope, as though they were both actual speeches delivered in the debate; then in *London Magazine* for May 1748 (xvii. 205–9) Campbell's tract was again reprinted as a genuine speech, this time attributed to Pitt ('Julius Florus': see *London Magazine* 1743, xii p. [ii]). It was reprinted as Pitt's in Cobbett, *Parl. Hist.* xiv. 210–15, and is included—though with due warning—in the list of Pitt's speeches in Basil Williams's authoritative *Life of Pitt,* 1913, ii. 341 (see also ibid. i. 202; ii. 335).

140. The pamphlet was 'printed for A. Moore, near St Paul's' (*Daily Adv.*). Nothing further is known of this bookseller, except that the same name and address appear in an imprint as early as 1722 (H. R. Plomer, *Dictionary of Printers and Booksellers . . . 1726 to 1775,* Oxford, 1932, pp. 174–5).

141. *The Speech of Richard White-Liver, Esq., in behalf of Himself and his Brethren. Spoken to the most August Mob at Rag-Fair.* Like the two preceding 'speeches' it was announced in GM for March 1748 (xviii. 144), and was also reprinted in the *Foundling Hospital,* 1749, pp. 30–4. Only one copy of the original pamphlet, in the University of Illinois Library, has been traced.

142. Robert Dodsley's *A Collection of Poems by Several Hands* was published 14

poems, three of mine: 'An Epistle to Mr Ashton from Florence,'[143] written in 1740; 'The Beauties'; and the 'Epilogue to *Tamerlane*.'

I next wrote two papers of *The Remembrancer*, and two more of the same in the year 1749.[144] In the latter year too I wrote a copy of verses 'On the Fireworks for the Peace'; they were not printed.[145]

About the same time I wrote a pamphlet called 'Delenda est Oxonia.'[146] It was to assert the liberties of that university, which the ministry had a plan of attacking by vesting in the Crown the nomina-

Jan. 1748 (*Daily Adv.*). See Gray to HW ca Jan. 1748, n. 1. HW's contributions are in Vol. ii: the 'Epistle' on pp. 305-20, 'The Beauties' on pp. 321-7, and the 'Epilogue' on pp. 327-30.

143. This was the first printing of the 'Epistle,' which is the most ambitious of HW's early poems. See Gray to HW ?10 Nov. 1747, n. 8.

144. HW's MS copies of these papers are in Waldegrave MSS 3. 53-8, 63-7. Only three were printed: No. 32, 16 July 1748; No. 38, 27 Aug. 1748; and No. 97, 14 Oct. 1749. The fourth was never completed. HW notes on *The Remembrancer*: 'This paper was published for the Prince's party, by one Ralph [James Ralph, ca 1705-1762, satirized in the *Dunciad*]. . . . [It] was dropped on the death [1751] of the Prince.' HW's last contribution (No. 97) caused the printer (?Owen: see *post* n. 146) to be prosecuted, as HW notes on his copy of the MS: 'This paper, for which the printer was taken up, was occasioned by the Duke's [i.e. the Duke of Cumberland] very tyrannic behaviour to the Army.' The unpublished paper, as HW says in another MS note, 'was intended as a supplement to the Duke's history, particularly of his behaviour in his Rangership of Windsor Great Park, where he disobliged the whole country: particularly by shutting up the road from Windsor to Sunning Hill Wells, and arbitrarily depriving all the neighbouring gentlemen of the privilege of sporting thereabouts.'

In 1753 Ralph started another journal, *The Protester*. HW contributed to No. 23, 3 Nov. 1753, and noted on his copy in Waldegrave MSS 3. 79-82: 'This was a weekly paper written by Ralph, and supported at the expense of the Duke of Bedford and Alderman Beckford. There was

but one number printed after this, Ralph being bought off by the Court. . . .'

145. These verses (47 lines), which are in Waldegrave MSS 2. 178, are to the effect that the Treaty of Aix-la-Chapelle brought an ill-conducted war to an inglorious conclusion. The construction of the elaborate fireworks had been started by July 1748, and the disappointing display finally took place on 27 April 1749 (GM 1748, xviii. 331; 1749, xix. 186-7). Handel's 'Royal Fireworks' music was composed for this occasion. See HW to Conway 6 Oct. 1748, to Mann 3 May 1749. HW's original MS, from which the lines were transcribed in Waldegrave MSS, is also now WSL.

146. Printed by Paget Toynbee in the *English Historical Review* for 1927, xlii. 95-108, from HW's copy in Waldegrave MSS 3. 68-79. HW's note is as follows: 'This pamphlet was wrote in 1749, upon a resolution then taken by the Ministry, but afterwards dropped, to vest the nomination of the Chancellorship of Oxford in the King, in order to its being conferred on the Duke [of Cumberland], whenever Lord Arran should die. This pamphlet was seized at Owen's the printer before publication, by the Secretary of State's messengers, who were sent thither after some of the *Remembrancers*. It was designedly coloured very strongly, in order to pass the better for an Oxford performance: though the intention was very Whig; to preserve the liberties of the University, and to show that the scheme of the Ministry was parallel to the behaviour of K. James II, which had given rise to the Revolution.' 'Owen' is presumably William Owen (d. 1793), at Homer's Head near Temple Bar, publisher of *The Remembrancer*; but he does not seem to have been a printer (H. R. Plomer, *Dictionary of Printers and Booksellers . . . 1726 to 1775*, Oxford, 1932, pp. 187-8).

tion of the Chancellor. This piece (which I think one of my best) was seized at the printer's and suppressed.

One night in the beginning of November 1749 I was returning from Holland House[147] by moonlight about ten at night. I was attacked[148] by two highwaymen in Hyde Park, and the pistol of one of them going off accidentally razed the skin under my eye, left some marks of shot on my face and stunned me. The ball went through the top of the chariot, and, if I had sat an inch nearer to the left side, must have gone through my head.

Jan. 11th 1751. I moved the address to the King on his speech at the opening of the session.[149]

March 20th[150] 1751 died my eldest brother, Robert Earl of Orford.

About this time I began to write my memoirs.[151] At first I intended only to write the history of one year.[152]

About the same time happened a great family quarrel.[153] My friend Mr Chute had engaged Miss Nicholl, a most rich heiress, to run away from her guardians, who had used her very ill; and he proposed to marry her to my nephew Lord Orford, who refused her, though she

147. The Kensington residence of Henry Fox (1705–74), cr. Bn Holland 1763. See HW to Mann 5 May 1747, and Lord Ilchester's *The Home of the Hollands 1605–1820* and *Chronicles of Holland House 1820–1900* (both 1937).

148. The robbery occurred on 8 Nov., the robbers being James Maclaine—a noted highwayman who was executed in 1750—and William Plunkett. HW inserted an advertisement in the newspapers for the recovery of his watch and seals, and received in reply a remarkable document compounded of threats and apologies, demanding twice the sum offered as a reward, and naming a meeting-place. HW declined this assignation, but eventually recovered his property for the twenty guineas originally offered ('A.B. and C.D.' to HW [10 Nov. 1749]; *Daily Adv.* 10 Nov. 1749, 4 Oct. 1750; *St James's Evening Post* 9–11 Nov. 1749; HW in *The World* 19 Dec. 1754; Toynbee *Supp.* iii. 132–5). See also HW to Mann 18 Oct. 1750; Toynbee in *TLS* 5 Feb. 1920; Ketton-Cremer, *Walpole* 145–7.

149. HW is mistaken as to the date of the motion, which was made 17 Jan. 1751. His speech (in Waldegrave MSS 2. 180–4) was conciliatory in tone and, though eloquent

on the subject of the peace with Spain, did not go much beyond conventional adulation. In the debate which followed, Pelham, Pitt, and HW's uncle Horace sided with HW in support of the motion, which was carried by 203 to 74 (Cobbett, *Parl. Hist.* xiv. 788–828; *Mem. Geo. II* i. 8–9).

150. HW, writing these notes later, apparently attempted to adjust the date to New Style, but subtracted instead of adding eleven days. Lord Orford died 31 March 1751, O.S. (HW to Mann 1 April 1751. O.S.). He was buried 7 April at Houghton.

151. The earliest reference to HW's historical memoirs appears in Gray to HW 8 Oct. 1751 (*post* ii. 53).

152. This is borne out by HW's 'Postscript' to the 1751 memoirs (*Mem. Geo. II* i. xxix–xxxvii), in which there is no suggestion that he intended to carry on the work. Actually the memoirs, and the more informal journals which succeeded them in 1772, were continued to August 1791 (the last portion, from 1783, now WSL, has not yet been published). An earlier essay in memoir-writing is described *post* ii. 9 n. 5.

153. HW's 'Narrative' and other letters and documents in this affair are printed *post* ii. 193 ff., Appendix 1.

had above £150,000. *We consulted my uncle Horace Walpole, who placed her with his lawyer Mr Capper and then tried to get her for his third son, and excluded Mr Chute from seeing her. This treacherous behaviour I resented warmly, and broke entirely with my uncle and his whole family, and* wrote a particular account of the whole transaction.

In this year too I imitated a fable of Fontaine, called 'The Funeral of the Lioness.'[154]

In 1753[155] I was appointed by Sir Hans Sloane's will one of his trustees.

Feb. 8th 1753 was published a paper I had written in a periodical work called *The World*,[156] published by E. Moore. I wrote eight more numbers,[157] besides two that were not printed then,[158] and one, containing a character of Mr Fox, which I had written some years before.[159]

This year I published[160] a fine edition of six poems of Mr T. Gray, with prints from designs of Mr R. Bentley.[161]

154. Written before 8 Oct. 1751 (see *post* ii. 53 and n. 3); first printed in *Works* iv. 377–80. The original MS, now in the Merritt Collection at Harvard, was transcribed by HW in Waldegrave MSS 2. 186–8. The fable imitated is *Les Obsèques de la lionne*, with some echoes of *Les Animaux malades de la peste*.

155. Previously printed '1752'; Sir Hans (b. 1660), the founder of the British Museum, died 11 Jan. 1753. By his will dated 20 July 1749 he bequeathed to the nation, for the sum of £20,000, his vast collection of books, MSS, and natural history specimens, which in 1754, pursuant to an Act of Parliament (26 Geo. II, c. 22), was transferred, along with the Cottonian and Harleian collections, to Montagu House. See HW to Mann 14 Feb. 1753.

156. 'A weekly paper with this title came out January 4th 1753 (to be continued every Thursday) by Edward Moore [1712–57], author of several plays and poems: the assumed name was Adam Fitz-Adam' (HW, Waldegrave MSS 2. 189). HW's first contribution, No. 6, was on the absurdity of attempting to imitate nature on the stage and in gardens, confectionery, etc. Printed in *Works* i. 146–50 (Waldegrave MSS 2. 190–4).

157. There were only seven more: No. 8, 22 Feb. 1753; No. 10, 8 March 1753; No. 14, 5 April 1753; No. 28, 12 July 1753; No. 103,

19 Dec. 1754; No. 160, 22 Jan. 1756; and No. 195, 23 Sept. 1756. HW's set of these numbers, extensively annotated by him for his *Fugitive Pieces*, is now WSL. They appear in *Works* i. 151–89 (Waldegrave MSS 2. 194–218, 226–42). In general HW dealt satirically with such non-political matters as the New Style calendar, letter-writing, the superiority of elderly mistresses, and British politeness. See also *post* i. 28 n. 186.

158. These papers, proposing a 'scheme for encouragement of learning by destroying books', were first printed in HW's *Fugitive Pieces*, 1758, pp. 169–89 (see also p. vi). They are in *Works* i. 195–204. The MSS are now WSL, together with the MS of an uncompleted third paper on the same subject and a fourth MS on humility. See also Hazen, *Bibliography of Walpole* 157–8.

159. This eulogistic *World Extraordinary* (*Works* i. 190–4) was published, apparently at Fox's own request, 4 Jan. 1757 (*Daily Adv.*; HW to Fox 20 Dec. and ? Dec. 1756). HW's copy of the major portion of it, in the form of a 'Letter to the Right Honourable Lady Caroline Fox,' is in Waldegrave MSS 2. 172–4, dated 'Strawberry Hill 1748.'

160. At Dodsley's book-shop 29 March 1753 (*Daily Adv.*).

161. Richard Bentley (1708–82). His original drawings for Gray's poems were sold London 1044, and are now WSL. For a

In November I wrote a burlesque poem, called 'The Judgment of Solomon.'[162]

In December died Erasmus Shorter Esq.[163] the last and youngest of my mother's brothers.[164] He dying without a will, his fortune of £30,000 came in equal shares between my brother Sir Edward,[165] me, and my cousins, Francis Earl of Hertford,[166] Colonel Henry Seymour Conway and Miss Anne Seymour Conway.[166a]

In 1754 I was chosen for Castle Rising[167] in Norfolk in the new parliament.

In July of that year I wrote 'The Entail,'[168] a fable in verse.

About the same time I erected a cenotaph for my mother[169] in West-

discussion of the *Designs by Mr R. Bentley for Six Poems by Mr T. Gray*, see Hazen, *Bibliography of Walpole* 113–20 and *post* 29 Sept. 1751, 8 Oct. 1751, 8 July 1752, 17 Dec. 1752, 13 and 20 Feb. 1753.

162. Waldegrave MSS 2. 218–22: an obscene parody of 1 Kings iii. 16–28, unpublished. There is also a MS, with designs by Bentley, which was in the possession of Sir Wathen Waller, Bt, and is now WSL.

163. 'Last Friday [23 Nov.] died at his lodgings in Chancery Lane, Capt. Shorter, brother to the first Lady of Sir Robert Walpole, Earl of Orford. He died a bachelor, and very rich. Two servants of the deceased were taken up the next day, by order of the heirs, on suspicion of embezzling some of his effects' (*Daily Adv.* 26 Nov. 1753). HW seems to have interceded in favour of one of the servants: see HW to Bentley 19 Dec. 1753. See also MONTAGU i. 156–7 and HW to Mann 6 Dec. 1753.

164. The others were John Shorter and Arthur Shorter (d. ?1753). John, whose obituary has not been found, was Commissioner for Managing the Duties on Stamped Vellum, Parchment, Paper, etc., 1734–7 (J. B. Whitmore and A. W. Hughes Clarke, *London Visitation Pedigrees, 1664,* 1940, p. 124; *London Gazette* 18–21 May 1734, 20–24 April 1736, and 29 March–2 April 1737).

165. Sir Edward Walpole (1706–84), K.B. 1753 (investiture 27 Aug., installation 27 Dec.) (W. A. Shaw, *Knights of England,* 1906, i. 169).

166. Francis Seymour Conway (1718–94), cr. (1750) E. and (1793) M. of Hertford.

166a. See *post* 29 Dec. 1737, n. 13, and 10 Nov. 1740, O.S., n. 4.

167. At this time the Earl of Orford held the nomination of one of the two members for Castle Rising, a Norfolk borough. HW and the Hon. Thomas Howard were elected 20 April 1754 without opposition (L. B. Namier, *The Structure of Politics at the Accession of George III,* 1929, i. 178; GM 1754, xxiv. 200; Return of Members of Parliament ii. 114).

168. *Works* i. 28–9; Waldegrave MSS 2. 222–4. 'This piece was occasioned by the author being asked (after he had finished the little castle at Strawberry Hill and adorned it with the portraits and arms of his ancestors) if he did not design to entail it on his family?' (HW, *Works* i. 28). It was probably inspired by some verses entitled 'The Caterpillar and Butterfly' in GM 1750, xx. 36–7. See HW's *Fugitive Verses,* ed. W. S. Lewis, 1931, pp. 44–6. A MS of the verses in HW's hand with drawings by Bentley was in the possession of Sir Wathen Waller, Bt, and is now WSL. It is reproduced in W. S. Lewis, *Bentley's Designs for Walpole's Fugitive Pieces,* 1936.

169. See *post* i. 140. An entry in the Westminster Abbey Chapter Book, dated 30 May 1747, reads as follows: 'Ordered, that leave be given to put up a monument to the memory of —— Lady Walpole, the first wife of the late Right Honourable Robert Earl of Orford deceased, in one half the arch adjoining to the monument lately put up for General Monk, in K. Henry VII's Chapel—upon the payment of twenty guineas.' An entry in the Treasurers' Accounts shows that the £21 was paid in that year (information kindly supplied by Messrs L. E. Tanner and D. L. Powell of the Muniment Room).

minster Abbey; having some years before prepared a statue of her by Valory at Rome.[170] The pedestal was carved by Rysbrack.[171]

In March 1755 I was very ill used by my nephew Lord Orford upon a contested election[172] in the House of Commons, on which I wrote him a long letter[173] with an account of my own conduct in politics.

*In April 1756 my uncle Horace Walpole having drawn in my nephew Lord Orford to alter the settlement of his estate, I entered into a new dispute with my uncle on behalf of my nephews Lord Malpas and Mr Cholmondeley[174] and my sister Lady[175] Mary Churchill,

170. The monument, which is conspicuously placed in the south aisle of Henry VII's Chapel, is shown in a print by J. Bluck in Rudolph Ackermann's *Westminster Abbey*, 1812, facing ii. 158, and in two photographic views in H. J. Feasey's *Westminster Abbey*, 1899, plates 69-70. 'The tomb consists of the figure of a matron (copied by Valory at Rome from the Pudicitia or Livia Mattei) standing on a kind of square Roman altar, with a border of rich foliage on the sides, by Rysbrack' (HW, Waldegrave MSS 2. 225). HW commissioned the statue when he was in Italy in 1741. The correct name of the sculptor, with whom HW had no direct dealings, was Filippo Valle, or Della Valle (1693-1770), a Florentine who by 1725 was in Rome, where he became a member of the Accademia di San Luca. The statue he copied for the monument was an antique 'Pudicitia,' perhaps representing the Empress Livia, in the Villa Mattei in Rome; in 1774 Pope Clement XIV acquired it for the Vatican, where it is now No. 23 in the Braccio Nuovo. HW paid Valle 600 Roman crowns—about £150 (*Enciclopedia Italiana*; Frédéric de Clarac, *Musée de sculpture antique et moderne*, 1826-53, vol. iv of plates, 762B, fig. 1895, vol. iv of text, p. 346: see also ibid. 343; Walther Amelung, *Die Sculpturen des Vaticanischen Museums*, Berlin, 1903-8, i. 33-7: photograph, pl. 4 in vol. i of plates; Mann to HW 5 March 1743, N.S.). The full story of HW's troubles with the statue—the long delays in execution and in shipment, and his disappointment with it when it finally arrived—is told in his correspondence with Mann 1 July 1741, N.S.—14 Aug. 1743, O.S.

171. John Michael Rysbrack (1693-1770): see *Anecdotes, Works* iii. 477-80;

Katherine Esdaile's study in *The Architect* for 3 March and 7 April 1922, pp. 164-8, 249-52; Rysbrack to HW 26 June 1754.

172. 'Tuesday, March 25. Simon Lutterell, Esq., took his seat in the House of Commons for the borough of St Mitchell's, Cornwall; Mr Hussey, the other member declared duly elected, was on the western circuit. This was the great contested election in the Commons, when Mr F[o]x and the D. of B[edfor]d joined interest in opposition to the Hon. Mr L[e]gge and the D. of N[ewcast]le, the former of whom carried the question in favour of Robert Clive and John Stephenson, Esqrs, on two divisions in the Committee; but in the report lost it, by the Tories joining the old minister. They rather chose to trust the men they knew, they said, than the men they did not know' (GM 1755, xxv. 183). The Committee's report on the election at Mitchell (also called Midsholl and St Michael's: disfranchised in 1832) is printed in *Journals of the House of Commons* xxvii. 253-63; see also HW to Bentley 27 March 1755, *Mem. Geo. II* ii. 10-14, and A. Mervyn Davies, *Clive of Plassey*, 1939, pp. 137-8. The part played by HW and Lord Orford in the affair is unknown, except that HW evidently supported the Bedford-Fox faction and Lord Orford the Newcastle faction: see HW to Fox 21 Nov. 1762.

173. Apparently not preserved.

174. These were George Cholmondeley (1724-64), styled Vct Malpas, and Robert Cholmondeley (1727-1804), both sons of HW's brother-in-law George Cholmondeley (1703-70), 3d E. of Cholmondeley 1733.

175. Though a natural child, she had been granted precedence as an Earl's daughter in 1742. See BERRY i. 42 n. 4.

LADY WALPOLE'S MONUMENT IN WESTMINSTER ABBEY

who were all injured by that disposition; and I wrote an account of that whole affair.*¹⁷⁶

In Feb. 1757 I vacated my seat for Castle Rising in order to be chosen for Lynn:¹⁷⁷ and about the same time used my utmost endeavours, but in vain, to save the unfortunate Admiral Byng.¹⁷⁸

May 12th of that year I wrote in less than an hour and half the 'Letter from Xo Ho.'¹⁷⁹ It was published on the 17th and immediately passed through five editions.¹⁸⁰

June 10th was published a catalogue of the collection of pictures of Charles I,¹⁸¹ to which I had written a little introduction. I afterwards wrote short prefaces or advertisements in the same manner to the

176. This account, 'Case of the Entail of the Estate of Sir Robert Walpole Earl of Orford,' is now WSL. With it are copies in HW's hand of the letters which passed between Lord Malpas and Horace Walpole, Sr (10 and 11 April 1756), and HW's correspondence on the subject with his uncle and Lord Orford.

177. At this election for King's Lynn, 24 Feb. 1757, HW was chosen to succeed his cousin 'Pigwiggin,' Horatio Walpole (1723–1809), M.P. for Lynn 1747–57, who had just succeeded his father, HW's uncle Horace, as Lord Walpole of Wolterton (Return of Members of Parliament, pt ii, 1878, p. 114; *Mem. Geo. II* ii. 327; Lord Orford to HW Feb. 1757). HW had the refusal of Lynn in 1747, but left it to his cousin (HW to Mann 5 June 1747). That the choice of HW, though inevitable as Lord Orford's nominee, was far from popular at Lynn appears from a letter of Edmund Pyle (1702–76), D.D., Chaplain-in-Ordinary to George II: 'The intended representative for Lynn is a most delicate Italian fop. And, *inter nos*, will not go to that place to be chosen [he didn't]. Whether the Earl, his nephew, has pressed him enough on this subject I can't say. But I can say that (if I know anything of the spirit of the better and worser sort of people there) it is a slight they will not forget, how little so ever they may talk of it just at the time when it is put upon them' (*Memoirs of a Royal Chaplain, 1729–1763,* ed. Albert Hartshorne, 1905, p. 287).

178. John Byng (1704–57), 4th son of George, 1st Vct Torrington; rear-admiral 1745. Sent to prevent the French from taking Minorca, he was defeated (20 May 1756) and recalled, after which he was sentenced to death by court-martial for neglect of duty, and executed 14 March 1757. For HW's detailed account of the affair see *Mem. Geo. II* ii. 284–300, 306–72; see also HW to Mann 3 March and 17 March 1757.

179. *A Letter from Xo Ho, a Chinese Philosopher at London, to his Friend Lien Chi, at Peking* (*Works* i. 205–9). In it HW satirizes the 'incomprehensible' English, mentioning among other things the execution of Byng, the changes in the Ministry, and the national insensibility to climate. The disguise of a Chinese philosopher was borrowed by Goldsmith for his *Citizen of the World* (1762). HW's annotated copy of the 1st edn of the *Letter* is now WSL. (See W. S. Lewis in *Times Literary Supplement* for 30 Aug. 1928, xxvii. 617; Hazen, *Bibliography of Walpole* 39–42).

180. The first announcement in *Daily Adv.* was on 19 May; the second edition was published 20 May, the third 24 May, the fourth 31 May (*London Evening Post*), and the fifth 27 June.

181. *Catalogue and Description of King Charles the First's Capital Collection of Pictures, Limnings, Statues, Bronzes, Medals, and other Curiosities, now first published from an original manuscript in the Ashmolean Museum at Oxford. The whole transcribed and prepared for the press, and a great part of it printed, by the late ingenious Mr Vertue, and now finished from his papers.* HW's 'Advertisement' is in *Works* i. 234–7. This MS catalogue and those mentioned below, published by William Bathoe, had been purchased by Bathoe at the sale of Vertue's library, etc., 16–19 and 21–2 March 1757 (*Daily Adver-*

catalogues of the collections of James II[182] and the Duke of Buckingham.[183]

June 25th I erected a printing-press[184] at my house at Strawberry Hill.

Aug. 8th published two odes by Mr Gray,[185] the first production of my press.

In September I erected a tomb in St Anne's churchyard, Soho, for Theodore King of Corsica.[186]

In October 1757 was finished at my press an edition of Hentznerus translated by Mr Bentley, to which I wrote an advertisement.[187] I dedicated it to the Society of Antiquaries, of which I am a member[188] as well as of the Royal Society.[189]

tiser; Works i. 238). See also post 1 Sept. 1759 (i. 33).

182. A Catalogue of the Collection of Pictures, etc., belonging to King James the Second; to which is added, a Catalogue of the Pictures and Drawings in the Closet of the late Queen Caroline, etc., 1758. HW's 'Advertisement' is in Works i. 238–9.

183. A Catalogue of the Curious Collection of Pictures of George Villiers, Duke of Buckingham, 1758. See Works i. 240–1.

184. See HW to Chute 12 July 1757, and to Mann 4 Aug. 1757; see also Hazen, SH Bibliography, and SH Accounts 94–9.

185. The first printing of 'The Progress of Poesy' and 'The Bard.' Two thousand copies were printed at SH, and published by Dodsley. See post ii. 97–8 and Hazen, SH Bibliography 23–31.

186. Theodore (1690–1756), Baron de Neuhoff. See post ii. 170, and DU DEFFAND i. 182–3. HW had espoused his cause, as that of a king who held his title by virtue of being 'the choice of his subjects,' in The World for 22 Feb. 1753, when Neuhoff was under imprisonment for debt in the King's Bench. HW recommended that a subscription be opened at Dodsley's shop, and 'about £50 was collected for him by the means of this paper, notwithstanding the ugly circumstances of his history. He pretended to be much disappointed at not receiving more, as his whole debt, he said, was £1500. He sent in a few days to Dodsley to desire the subscription might be opened again, and being denied, he sent a lawyer to Dodsley to threaten to prosecute him for the paper, as it had done him great hurt, he

said, and had prevented several contributions. . . . Such was the gratitude of the only King whom the author ever thought of attempting to serve!' (HW, Waldegrave MSS 2. 195: see also Works i. 156–8 and Toynbee Supp. ii. 92–3, 96–8). For the monument HW wrote an epitaph (Works i. 158, HW to Mann 29 Sept. 1757), of which he printed two dozen copies at SH (Hazen, SH Bibliography 164–5). The monument, which is at the west door of St Anne's, survived the destruction of the church in 1940.

187. Works i. 220–2. 'Began to print Hentznerus's account of England, with a translation by Richard Bentley; the advertisement by H. Walpole' (Journal of the Printing-Office 3, under 8 Aug.). Paul Hentzner (1558–1623), a German jurisconsult, published his Itinerarium Germaniæ, Galliæ, Angliæ, Italiæ at Nuremberg in 1612. HW printed a small octavo, with the Latin and English on opposite pages, entitled A Journey into England, by Paul Hentzner, in the Year MDXCVIII, Strawberry Hill, 1757. The whole edition, numbering 220 copies, was finished 17 Oct. (Hazen, SH Bibliography 31–3).

188. HW was elected a Fellow of the Society of Antiquaries 19 April 1753, his sponsors being Lord Fitzwilliam, Charles Lyttelton, Henry Baker, George Vertue, and Joseph Ames (A List of the Members of the Society of Antiquaries of London, 1798, p. 12; information kindly supplied by Mr H. S. Kingsford). See post i. 47 and nn. 325–32; and Hazen, SH Bibliography 172–5.

189. HW was elected a Fellow of the

In April 1758 was finished the first impression of my *Catalogue of Royal and Noble Authors*,[190] which I had written the preceding year in less than five months.[191]

About the same time Mrs Porter[192] published Lord Hyde's play to which I had written the advertisement.[193]

In the summer of 1758 I printed some of my own fugitive pieces, and dedicated them to my cousin General Conway.[194]

About autumn I erected at Linton in Kent a tomb for my friend Galfridus Mann;[195] the design was Mr Bentley's.

The beginning of October I published Lord Whitworth's *Account of Russia*,[196] to which I wrote the advertisement.[197]

Nov. 22d was published a pamphlet written by Mr R. Bentley, called *Reflections on the Different Ideas of the French and English with regard to Cruelty*.[198] It was designed to promote a bill (that I

Royal Society 19 Feb. 1747 (*The Record of the Royal Society of London*, 1912, p. 343).

190. *Works* i. 245–577. The printing of the first volume was begun on 17 Oct. 1757. See Hazen, *SH Bibliography* 33–7.

191. There are references to the writing of the *Catalogue* in Spence to HW 27 Oct. 1757 and HW to Mann 20 Nov. 1757.

192. See *post* i. 96 n. 10.

193. *Works* i. 228–9. The play was *The Mistakes, or the Happy Resentment*, a comedy by Henry Hyde (1710–53), styled Vct Cornbury until 1751, when he became Lord Hyde of Hindon. He had presented it 'many years ago' to Mrs. Porter 'to dispose of for her benefit' (*Works* i. 228). HW subscribed for twenty-one copies (*The Mistakes*, p. xv). See Hazen, *Bibliography of Walpole* 125–8.

194. The printing of *Fugitive Pieces in Verse and Prose* was completed 13 July (200 copies). See Hazen, *SH Bibliography* 39–42.

195. Galfridus Mann (ca 1706–1756), Sir Horace Mann's twin brother, of Boughton Malherbe in Kent, the manor of which (with various others) he had purchased from Lord Chesterfield in 1750. By his wife Sarah (ca 1716–1804), daughter of John Gregory of London, he was the father of Sir Horace Mann (1744–1814), 2d Bt (Edward Hasted, *History of Kent*, Canterbury, 1797–1801, v. 405–6; GM 1804, ii. 889). The tomb at Linton (which was the Mann family's chief estate, at that time in the

possession of Sir Horace's older brother Edward Louisa Mann) had been erected by 24 Oct. 1758: for a description see HW to Mann of that date. Bentley's original designs for the tomb are now WSL.

196. *An Account of Russia as it was in the Year 1710*, by Charles Whitworth (1675–1725), Bn Whitworth, envoy and ambassador to Russia 1704–12 (D. B. Horn, *British Diplomatic Representatives 1689–1789*, 1932, pp. 110–11.) The printing was completed 29 Sept. 1758; 600 of the 700 copies were sold for the benefit of the poor of Twickenham, at 3s. a copy (Hazen, *SH Bibliography* 42).

197. *Works* i. 223–7. HW explains that 'Lord Whitworth's MS was communicated to me by Richard Owen Cambridge, Esq., having been purchased by him in a very curious set of books, collected by Monsieur Zolman [probably Frederick Zoleman, d. 1748: GM xviii. 380], secretary to the late Stephen Poyntz, Esq.'

198. *Reflections on the Different Ideas of the French and English in regard to Cruelty; with Some Hints for Improving our Humanity in a Particular Branch*. By a Man . . . 1759. HW's Dedication is addressed 'To the Most Humane Person alive, [Whoever that is].' This pamphlet is attributed to HW by Halkett and Laing on the strength of a statement by Isaac Reed in his copy of the pamphlet (now WSL) which was quoted in GM 1807, lxxvii pt ii. 1132. Reed had seen what he called 'the original

meditated) of perpetual insolvency. I wrote the dedication. It was *not* printed at Strawberry Hill.

Dec. 5th was published the second edition of my *Catalogue of Authors*. Two thousand were printed, but *not* at Strawberry Hill.[199] I was much abused for it in the *Critical Review*,[200] and more gently in the *Monthly Review*.[201] By the former for disliking the Stuarts;[202] by the latter for liking my father: opinions I am not likely to change. In the *Gentleman's Magazine* of February following was another railing criticism, but so foolish that some parts of my book were printed in italics to turn them into puns, and it was called unintelligible for such reasons as my not having specified Francis I, by his title of King of France![203]

1759.[204]

Feb. 2d I published Mr Spence's parallel[205] of Magliabecchi[206] and Mr Hill,[207] a tailor of Buckingham; calculated to raise a little sum of money for the latter poor man. Six hundred copies were sold in a fortnight, and it was reprinted in London.[208]

copy' in HW's handwriting in the possession of HW's deputy, Charles Bedford, and was convinced of HW's authorship from internal evidence as well. See Hazen, *Bibliography of Walpole* 128–30.

199. On 30 April 1758 HW had sold the copyright for two years to Robert Dodsley and Josiah Graham, for £200, which he presented to the impecunious Bentley. See Hazen, *SH Bibliography* 36, and *Journal of the Printing-Office* 7, 31.

200. For Dec. 1758 (vi. 483–90). The reviewer, while praising the work as 'agreeable and entertaining, animated with pertinent and humorous reflections' (p. 486), castigates the author for 'the most flagrant prejudices of education and party' (p. 483). He adds (p. 485), 'We have known party introduced into balls, assemblies, horse-races, puppet shows, fashions, colours, and complexions; we have seen it even foisted into dictionaries, and now it has descended to catalogues.'

201. For Dec. 1758 (xix. 557–69); the reviewer was Owen Ruffhead (B. C. Nangle, *The Monthly Review*, Oxford, 1934, pp. 39, 73). His attack on Lord Orford, mentioned below, is on pp. 566–7.

202. '[The author] has, as far as in him

lies, authenticated all the cruel calumny which has been invented and levelled at the characters of Mary Queen of Scots, and her unfortunate posterity' (p. 483), and so on, through a page and a half in defence of Mary, James I, and Charles I.

203. The GM review appeared in the January, not the February issue (xxix. 19–23). HW's account of the Earl of Surrey is printed in the review, with certain words italicized and discussed tartly in footnotes. Note 14, to which HW here alludes, is typical: 'The addition of two words would have acquainted every reader who was meant by Francis the First' (p. 21).

204. At about this time HW started entering events in the MS as they occurred. See prefatory note.

205. *A Parallel, in the manner of Plutarch, between a most celebrated man of Florence, and one scarce ever heard of in England*, by Joseph Spence. See COLE i. 40 n. 14 and Hazen, *SH Bibliography* 44–6.

206. Antonio Magliabechi (1633–1714), Florentine scholar and librarian to Cosimo III de' Medici.

207. Robert Hill (1699–1777), a learned tailor whom Spence had befriended.

208. An announcement in *Daily Adv.* for

Feb. 10.[209] Some anonymous author (I could not discover who it was, it was said to be Dr Hill[210]) published a pamphlet, called *Observations on the account given of the Catalogue of R. and N. Authors of England etc. in article 6th of the* Critical Review *No. 35, for December 1758, where the unwarrantable liberties taken with that work and the honourable author of it are examined and exposed.* This defence of me was full of gross flattery, and displeased me so much, that I was going to advertise my disapprobation of it and ignorance of the author, but was dissuaded by my friends.

March 17. I began to distribute some copies of my fugitive pieces collected and printed together at Strawberry Hill; and dedicated to General Conway.

In this month I happened to hear that James Earl Waldegrave, Knight of the Garter,[211] liked my niece Maria,[212] second daughter of my brother Sir Edward. I immediately contrived that he should have meetings with her, and in two days less than a month drew him to make his declaration and proposal of marriage.

May 5th[213] was published a pamphlet called *Remarks on Mr Walpole's Catalogue of Royal and Noble Authors etc. in which many of his censures and arguments are examined and disproved; his false principles are confuted, and true ones established; several material facts are set in a true light, and the characters and conduct of several crowned heads and others are vindicated. Part the first.* And it advertised that in a few days would be published, 'Walpolian principles exposed and confuted.'[214] It was written by one Carter,[215] who had been

12 Feb. probably refers to the second printing.

209. The pamphlet was first announced in *Daily Adv.* for 12 Feb.

210. John Hill (ca 1716–1775), M.D. A bibliography of his writings, comprising 76 titles (including this pamphlet), was compiled by G. F. Russell Barker for DNB. See also *post* ii. 105.

211. James Waldegrave (1715–63), styled Vct Chewton 1729–41; succeeded his father as 2d E. Waldegrave 1741; K.G. 1757. See *post* ii. 88 n. 15.

212. Maria Walpole (1736–1807), second illegitimate daughter of Sir Edward Walpole. For her marriage to Lord Waldegrave on 15 May 1759, see MONTAGU i. 231–5. Her second marriage, to the D. of Gloucester (6 Sept. 1766), is discussed *post* i. 48 n. 335.

213. No newspaper advertisement of the pamphlet has been found, but it was announced in GM for May (xxix. 230).

214. The advertisement, printed on the verso of the title-page, reads in full as follows: 'In a few days will be published Walpolian Principles Exposed and Confuted (price sixpence). N.B. The Introduction may be had separate by those who buy this.' But according to a note by Richard Bull in his copy (now WSL) of the *Remarks*, 'The Walpolian Principles never were printed; the Introduction was printed and sold separate, but as so very few got abroad, they [i.e. the *Remarks* and the 'Introduction'] are very rarely met with together.'

215. I.e., William Cartwright (ca 1730–1799). For a note on him, and an alternative identification of the author as George Osborn, see Appendix 8.

bred a surgeon and who had married the daughter of Deacon of Manchester who was hanged in the last rebellion.[216] This Carter had lost an estate of £800 a year which had been intended for him, rather than renounce his principles, and was turned a non-juring preacher, and had lately been sent away from an apothecary's where he lodged, for his treasonable conversation, and for sending fifteen or sixteen letters every post-night, which the people of the house suspected were written for purposes not more innocent. Whatever his designs were, he had too little prudence to do much harm, and too little sense. His book was a rhapsody of Jacobitism, made still more foolish by the style and manner, and of the lowest scurrility. I wish I may never have wiser enemies, or tyranny abler advocates! It is observable, that this Carter distributed hand-bills and left them at doors, promising this answer and begging assistance towards it.

In May too was published in the *Critical Review*[217] a letter to the authors of it from some anonymous person, denying the fact, mentioned in the life of the D. of Wharton in the same *Catalogue*,[218] of Serjeant Wynne[219] borrowing and using Bishop Atterbury's speech—

216. Cartwright's wife was Sarah Sophia (ca 1731–1801), daughter of Thomas Deacon (1697–1753), non-juring bishop (consecrated by Archibald Campbell in 1733) of the Manchester congregation which he had himself founded. It was Deacon's son, Mrs Cartwright's brother, who was 'hanged in the last rebellion': Thomas Theodorus Deacon (b. ca 1723), a lieutenant in the Jacobite regiment raised at Manchester. He was taken prisoner at Carlisle and executed on Kennington Common 30 July 1746 (Henry Broxap, *Biography of Thomas Deacon*, Manchester, 1911, pp. 97, 109–10, 155–7; B. G. Seton and J. G. Arnot, *The Prisoners of the '45*, Edinburgh, 1928–9, ii. 150–1).

217. Vol. vii. 453–7. The letter was by William Wynne (see n. 219).

218. The passage referred to is in ii. 133 of the 1759 *Royal and Noble Authors*. HW tells an anecdote of how Philip, Duke of Wharton, tricked the prosecution at Bishop Atterbury's trial for treason in 1723, and adds this footnote: 'Serjeant Wynne served the Bishop in much the same manner: being his counsel, he desired to see the Bishop's speech [Atterbury's defence before

the House of Lords 11 May 1723]; and then spoke the substance of it himself.'

219. William Wynne (1692–1765), barrister of the Middle Temple, serjeant-at-law (1736); m. (1728) Grace Brydges (d. 1779) (DNB *sub* Edward Wynne; R. A. Roberts, *A Calendar of the Inner Temple Records*, iv, 1933, p. 325). Wynne himself was the author of the letter in the *Critical Review*, which was reprinted in 1765 in E. Wynne's *A Miscellany, containing Several Law Tracts*, pp. 209–19, and again in 1790 in John Nichols's edition of Atterbury's *Miscellaneous Works*, 1789–98, iv. 440–7 (see also p. 462). Wynne denies having even seen Atterbury's speech before its delivery, and his denial is supported by an examination of the published versions of the speeches which appeared in 1723: *The Defence of Francis, Late Lord Bishop of Rochester, at the Bar of the House of Lords, on Thursday the 9th, and Saturday the 11th of May 1723. . . . By William Wynne Esq., one of his Lordship's Counsel;* and *The Speech of Francis, Late Lord Bishop of Rochester, at the Bar of the House of Lords*, etc. (a more authentic version of Atterbury's speech was printed in *Miscellaneous Works* iv. 383–439, further

yet it was absolutely true. Mr Morrice,[220] the Bishop's grandson, often told it to Mr Selwyn;[221] Mr Fox remembered the fact, when he was at Oxford;[222] and Mr Baptist Leveson Gower[223] says, he perfectly remembers it, and that his (then) party affected to cry him up for it, that he got £3000 the first year on the credit of it; but they were forced to drop him, as he had no parts to support his reputation. In truth, when I wrote the passage in question, I did not know Mr Wynne was still living, am sorry to have shocked a man who had given me no provocation, and therefore to avoid adding one mortification to another, which I did not mean, I have chosen to make no reply.[224]

In August, I wrote a copy of verses, called 'The Parish Register of Twickenham';[225] it is a list of all the remarkable persons who have lived there.

Sept. 1. I began to look over Mr Vertue's MSS,[226] which I bought last year for £100, in order to compose the lives of English painters.

corrected v. 365–94). Wynne's chief speech was delivered two days before Atterbury's own defence; his second speech, a relatively brief résumé, immediately preceded Atterbury's. Neither bears any closer resemblance to Atterbury's than, as Wynne himself puts it, 'necessarily arises from a reference to the same facts, papers, and letters' (ibid. iv. 443–4). Wynne's Toryism and his being an opponent of Sir Robert, who as prime minister had directed the prosecution of Atterbury, account for HW's attack.

220. Francis Morice (1721–78), only son of William Morice, High Bailiff of Westminster 1719–31, by his first wife, Mary Atterbury (d. 1729); rector and vicar of various parishes in County Clare, Ireland; m. (1764) Mary Spaight (G. F. Russell Barker and A. H. Stenning, *The Record of Old Westminsters,* 1928, ii. 665; Robert Folkestone Williams, *Memoirs and Correspondence of Francis Atterbury, D.D.,* 1869, ii. 336n, 399).

221. HW first had the story from Cæsar Ward, the bookseller (HW to Hailes 8 Nov. 1767).

222. Henry Fox matriculated at Christ Church, Oxford, in 1721, aged 15 (Foster, *Alumni Oxon.*).

223. Baptist Leveson-Gower (ca 1704–1782), son of John, Lord Gower; matriculated at St. John's, Cambridge, 1720; M.P. for Newcastle-under-Lyme 1727–61; Com-

missioner of Trade 1745–9 (Venn, *Alumni Cantab.*).

224. HW removed the offending note from the 1770 printing of *Royal and Noble Authors,* and it is not in the 1798 *Works;* but it appears in all the separate editions of *Royal and Noble Authors,* including the 1806 edition by Thomas Park, who however contradicts it (iv. 124).

225. *Works* iv. 382–3. Two MSS of the poem in HW's hand are now WSL.

226. On 22 August 1758 HW had purchased some forty volumes of the MSS of George Vertue (1684–1756), engraver and antiquary, from Vertue's widow. These MSS, which were used as the basis for HW's *Anecdotes of Painting* (see *post* i. 34), were sold London 1110 to Horatio Rodd for £26; they were later sold to Thomas Thorpe, from whom the greater part were purchased by Dawson Turner in 1848. At Turner's sale in 1859 they were bought by the British Museum, which had already acquired some of the other MSS (HW to Grosvenor Bedford 29 Aug. 1758; HW to Zouch 12 Jan. 1759; Walpole Society, vol. xviii, 1930, p. xv). From the originals in the BM, the Walpole Society has published five volumes drawn from the notebooks, *viz.* xviii (1930), xx (1932), xxii (1934), xxiv (1936), and xxvi (1938). At the time the last volume was published, one more was planned.

21. I gave my Lady Townshend[227] an epitaph and design for a tomb for her youngest son[228] killed at Ticonderoga; neither were used.

Oct. 28. I finished the eighth book of my memoirs.[229]

29. I began the account[230] of a new discovery of painting upon wax; it was invented at Paris by the Comte de Caylus,[231] and was improved here by Mr Müntz.[232]

Nov. 12. I dismissed Mr Müntz *for very impertinent behaviour;*[233] and upon his leaving me, laid aside[234] the intention of publishing the account of the new encaustic.

1760.

Jan. 1. I began the lives of English artists from Vertue's MSS: that is, *Anecdotes of Painting*[235] etc.

227. Etheldreda Harrison (ca 1703–1788), m. (1723) Charles Townshend, 3d Vct Townshend.

228. The Hon. Roger Townshend (ca 1731–1759), Lt-Col. of Foot, was killed at Ticonderoga 25 July 1759 (the news of his death reached England ca 8 Sept.). Lady Townshend later erected a monument to him in Westminster Abbey. She preserved, though she did not use, the epitaph and design (the latter by Bentley) which HW sent to her in a letter of 21 Sept. 1759 (now WSL) (Collins, *Peerage*, 1812, ii. 477; *Daily Adv.* 10 Sept. 1759; HW to Lord Strafford and to Conway 13 Sept. 1759).

229. The eighth book of the memoirs, for the year 1758, was begun 17 Aug. 1759, and was completed, according to a note in the MS, on 27 Oct.

230. See HW to Mann 9 Sept. 1758, where he says that he is already writing the account. HW's MS has not been found.

231. Anne-Claude-Philippe de Thubières de Grimoard de Pestel de Lévis (1692–1765), Comte Caylus, archæologist, engraver, and man of letters. He published his *Mémoire sur la peinture à l'encaustique et sur la peinture à la cire* in 1755 (Bibl. Nat. Cat.; Samuel Rocheblave, *Essai sur le Comte de Caylus*, 1889, p. 1). See also DU DEFFAND v. 271 and n. 103.

232. Johann Heinrich Müntz (1727–98), a Swiss painter in HW's employ since 1755 (HW to Bentley 10 June and 5 July 1755).

233. The circumstances of Müntz's offending are not known, but a letter from him to HW of this same date is in the high style of outraged sensibility. There seems to have been an intrigue with a female servant of HW's whom, according to Edwards, Müntz married; but HW states that it was 'extreme impertinence' and not love that caused Müntz's downfall (Edward Edwards, *Anecdotes of Painters*, 1808, p. 16; HW to Montagu 17 Nov. 1759, MONTAGU i. 259).

234. HW had begun printing the account on 7 Nov., but apparently only the title-page and dedication (to Lady Hervey) were completed. In the following year Müntz published his own account (written in an ungrammatical style which shows it to have been entirely independent of HW's MS), under the title *Encaustic: or, Count Caylus's Method of Painting in the Manner of the Ancients*. Müntz projected also a more elaborate 'Treatise on Practical Painting, Colours, and Colouring,' advertised 3 Jan. 1760 as to be published 'next month,' but it never appeared. The Society of Artists in 1762 exhibited some of his drawings and paintings, among them a landscape in encaustic (*Journal of the Printing-Office* 9, 36; Hazen, *SH Bibliography* 143; HW's *Anecdotes of Painting*, vol. v, ed. F. W. Hilles and P. B. Daghlian, 1937, p. 104; *Daily Adv.* 3 Jan. 1760; Algernon Graves, *Society of Artists of Great Britain 1760–1791*, 1907, p. 180).

235. See *ante* i. 33. The first two volumes were published in 1762 under the title *Anecdotes of Painting in England, with*

About the same time, there being thoughts of erecting a monument for Sir Charles Hanbury Williams in Westminster Abbey, I wrote an epitaph[236] for it.

March 13, wrote the *Dialogue between Two Great Ladies.* It was published April 23d,[237] being deferred till after the trials of Lord G. Sackville[238] and Lord Ferrers.[239]

April. In this month wrote a poem on the destruction of the French navy,[240] as an exercise for Lord Beauchamp[241] at Christ Church Oxford.

Aug. 14, finished the first volume of my *Anecdotes of Painting in England.*

Sept. 5th, began the second volume.

Oct. 23d, finished the second volume.

some account of the principal artists, and incidental notes on other arts, collected by the late Mr George Vertue, and now digested and published from his original MSS, by Mr Horace Walpole. See Hazen, *SH Bibliography* 55–62.

236. The epitaph is included in HW to Fox 6 Feb. 1760 and in 'Book of Materials' 1759, p. 57. Williams was buried 10 Nov. 1759 in the north aisle of Westminster Abbey, but no monument was ever erected (Westminster Abbey Registers, ed. J. L. Chester, 1876, p. 395). See also *post* ii. 10 n. 10.

237. *A Dialogue between Two Great Ladies* was first announced in *Daily Adv.* for 24 April. Of this rare 19-page pamphlet only two copies have been traced by Mr Hazen, one at King's College and the other in the New York Public Library. It is a dialogue between 'M.T.,' i.e. Maria Theresa, and 'E.,' standing for 'Empress,' i.e. Catherine the Great.

238. Lord George Sackville (1716–85) (after 1770 Sackville-Germain), created Vct Sackville in 1782. Having been arraigned for disobeying orders while serving as commander-in-chief of the British forces in the Allied army against the French, he was tried by court-martial at the Horse Guards 3 Feb.–5 April 1760, was found guilty and deprived of his rank. See *Mem. Geo. II* iii. 266–74. In HW's *Dialogue* there is a possible allusion to Sackville in Maria Theresa's remark, 'If generals are victorious, is it not enough to reward them? Is victory to be a perpetual exemption from blame?' (p. 14.) Shortly after-

wards she says, 'Did not they [the English] lately put an admiral to death, for supposing he had beaten the French when he had not?' (pp. 15–16.) HW would not have wished that his pamphlet should be suspected of drawing a parallel between Sackville's pending case and that of the ill-fated Byng, and it seems to have been for that reason that he postponed its publication.

239. Laurence Shirley (1720–60), 4th E. Ferrers, was tried in Westminster Hall 16–18 April and found guilty of the murder of his steward. He was executed at Tyburn 5 May. See HW's account of the trial, which he attended, in HW to Montagu 19 April 1760 (MONTAGU i. 279–81) and to Mann 20 April 1760; and of the execution, which he did not witness, in HW to Mann 7 May 1760.

240. The verses have not been found, but from Beauchamp's letters to HW it is clear the poem was an ambitious one, with King Arthur, Merlin, and Queen Elizabeth all participating. Beauchamp to HW ?28 April 1760 is given over to a long criticism which was presumably made by Beauchamp's tutors. The incident which the verses commemorated seems to have been Admiral Hawke's defeat of the French invasion fleet under Marshal de Conflans, 20–21 Nov. 1759.

241. Lord Hertford's son Francis Seymour-Conway (after 1807 Ingram-Seymour-Conway) (1743–1822), styled Vct Beauchamp 1750–93; 2d M. of Hertford 1794. He matriculated at Christ Church, Oxford, 2 Feb. 1760.

1761.

Jan. 4th, began the third volume.

In March, I was appointed trustee for Mrs Day[242] by Richard Lord Edgcumbe, in his will.

May 30th, wrote a mock sermon to dissuade Lady Mary Coke[243] from going to the King's Birthday,[244] as she had lately been ill.

June 11th, wrote an epigram on the Duchess of Grafton[245] going abroad.

June 29, resumed the third volume of my *Anecdotes of Painting* which I had laid aside after the first day.

July 16, wrote 'The Garland,' a poem on the King, and sent it to Lady Bute,[246] but not in my own hand,[247] nor with my name, nor did I ever own it.

242. Ann Franks (d. 1790), alias Nancy Day, said to have been born near Plymouth of poor parents; mistress of Richard, Lord Edgcumbe, by whom she had two daughters. He died 10 May of this year (will dated 19 Feb. 1761). Shortly afterwards she married Sir Peter Fenouilhet (d. 1774), Exon of the Yeomen of the Guard, but was soon separated from him and went to live with her daughters in Calais. In 1760 she sat to Sir Joshua Reynolds (portrait formerly in the possession of Lord Northbrook: in Northbrook sales 11 June 1937, No. 15, and 25 Feb. 1938, No. 120) (W. A. Shaw, *Knights of England*, 1906, ii. 290; Algernon Graves and W. V. Cronin, *History of the Works of Sir Joshua Reynolds*, 1899–1901, i. 236; E. K. Waterhouse, *Reynolds*, 1941, pp. 47–8; *Town and Country Magazine* 1770, ii. 569–70; *Times* 19 Sept. 1790, p. 2). See also HW to Mme du Deffand ca 8 June 1773, DU DEFFAND iii. 366.

243. Lady Mary Campbell (1727–1811), m. (1747) Edward, Vct Coke; HW's correspondent. The 'sermon' is printed in Lady Mary's *Letters and Journals*, Edinburgh, 1889–96, vol. iii, pp. xii–xiv, under the title, 'A Sermon on abstaining from Birthdays on certain occasions; preached before the Right Honourable the Lady Mary Coke, on Sunday, May 31st, 1761, by H.W., D.D., Chaplain to her Ladyship, and Minister of St Mary, Strawberry Hill.' The text, which HW expounds learnedly, is 'Blessed is the woman that abstaineth from

Birthdays, because of the angels.—*Epistle of St Luke to the Camelinthians*, chap. 3, v. 7.'

244. 4 June 1761, on which day 'the ball was opened at St James's . . . by the Duke of York and the Princess Augusta. The concourse of nobility and gentry was so great that several ladies fainted through the excessive heat' (*London Chronicle* 4–6 June 1761, ix. 542).

245. HW's correspondent, Anne Liddell (ca 1738–1804), m. (1756) Augustus Henry Fitzroy, 3d D. of Grafton 1757, from whom she was divorced in 1769; married secondly (1769) John Fitzpatrick, 2d E. of Upper Ossory. HW included the epigram in a letter to Lady Ailesbury 13 June 1761 (also in 'Book of Materials' 1759, p. 106).

246. Mary Wortley-Montagu (1718–94), daughter of Lady Mary Wortley Montagu, m. (1736) John Stuart, 3d E. of Bute. HW's flattering verses, written in the first year of the young George III's reign, were sent to Lady Bute as one through whom they were sure to reach the King. They should be read in the light of HW to Bute Dec. 1760, 'The mere love of the arts, and the joy of seeing on the throne a prince of taste, are my only inducements for offering my slender services.' See HW's *Fugitive Verses*, ed. W. S. Lewis, 1931, pp. 134–7.

247. HW sent the verses to his deputy, Grosvenor Bedford, to be copied and returned to him (HW to Bedford ?19 July 1761). Bedford's copy is now (1947) in the possession of Sir John Murray. It was

Aug. 22d, finished the third volume of my *Anecdotes of Painting*.

Dec. 20, wrote a few lines to Lady Mary Coke on her having St Antony's fire in her cheek.[248]

—— 23, wrote a portrait of Lord Granville in verse,[249] to serve as an epitaph for him.

1762.

March 24th I was chosen a member of the Society of Arts and Sciences.[250]

June 12th I was attacked in a new weekly paper, Numb. 2, called *The North Briton*,[251] and accused of having *flattered* the Scotch, in my

printed in the *Quarterly Review*, March 1852, xc. 311–13, where it was the excuse for a ferocious attack on HW.

248. He sent them to Montagu 23 Dec. 1761. (MONTAGU i. 413). The original MS is reproduced in Lady Mary's *Letters and Journals*, vol. iii, facing p. xxiv.

249. *Works* i. 31. See *post* ii. 123, and Hazen, *SH Bibliography* 175–9, where the possibility of this entry's having been pre-dated a year is discussed. An examination of the MS does not resolve the ambiguity. The entry is at the bottom of a page and therefore could have been inserted later, under the wrong year; but this and the preceding entry appear to have been written at the same time. Granville did not die until 2 Jan. 1763, but had been declining for a year or more (Basil Williams, *Carteret and Newcastle*, Cambridge, 1943, pp. 214–15).

250. I.e., the Society for the Encouragement of Arts, Manufactures, and Commerce (since 1908 known as the Royal Society of Arts), founded in 1754 (H. T. Wood, *A History of the Royal Society of Arts*, 1913, pp. 11, 17–18). HW seems to have taken little part in their activities, and by 1781 had dropped his connection with them (HW to Lord Hailes 10 Feb. 1781).

251. No. 2 of Wilkes's *North Briton*, written as usual in the character of a Scotchman, is on Bute's appointment as prime minister. It contains recommendations for the pension list, including 'the patriots at the Cocoa Tree,' a coffeehouse which at that time was recognized as the ministerial club. The passage referring to HW is as follows:

'I am happy to find that the English are

not so sparing and penurious to us, both of money and praise, as they used to be. We are certainly growing into fashion. The most rude of our bards are admired; and I know some choice wits here, who have thrown aside Shakespeare, and taken up Fingal, charmed with the variety of character and richness of imagery. Mr Horace Walpole, in that deep book called *Royal and Noble Authors*, says we are *the most accomplished nation in Europe; the nation to which, if any one country is endowed with a superior partition of sense* (and he ought to have added of humour and taste, in both which we excel) *I should be inclined to give the preference in that particular*. How faithful is this masterly pen of Mr Walpole! How unlike the odious, sharp, and strong incision-pen of Swift! who has only called us *a poor, fierce, northern* people, and asserted *that the pensions and employments possessed by the natives of Scotland in England amounted to more than the whole body of their nobility ever spent at home; and all the money they raised upon the public was hardly sufficient to defray their civil and military lists*. This was at the latter end of Queen Anne's reign. How very different is the case now! I beg to recommend Mr Walpole too, for so very particular a compliment (which I hope flowed from his *heart*, still more than from his *head*) and entreat his lordship to put him on the list, immediately after my countrymen, and the Cocoa.'

The quotation from *Royal and Noble Authors* is in the prefatory paragraph to the section on Scots authors (1759 edn, ii. 201; *Works* i. 492). The quotation from

Catalogue of Royal and Noble Authors. I made no answer to it. I could not have been charged with anything of which I am less guilty than flattery. The passage was written and published five years before this period, and in the reign of the late King, when partiality to Scotland was no merit at Court; and so little was it calculated to make a friend of Lord Bute, that having had occasion to write two or three letters to him, I constantly disclaimed any desire or intention of having a place.[252] I have copies of these letters, and of others to the Duke of Newcastle,[253] and Mr Pitt,[254] equally and as fully disinterested. Before this accusation was made, Lord Bute had had two levees;[255] I was at neither, nor ever was at the levee of any minister, but my father, and once at the Duke of Newcastle's,[256] while my father was in power.—I believe the author of *The North Briton* will ask for and have a place before I shall.

Aug. 2d, began the *Catalogue of Engravers.*
Oct. 10th, finished it.[257]

I had been told that Bishop Warburton[258] resented something in the chapter of architecture in the second volume[259] of my *Anecdotes of Painting,* and that he intended to abuse me in the new edition of Mr Pope's works which he proposed to have printed at Birmingham.[260]

Swift, which is slightly paraphrased, is in 'The Public Spirit of the Whigs' (the page references in Temple Scott's edition of Swift, 1897–1922, are v. 336, 338). 'Attack' will seem a strong word for so mild a notice, but HW's fear of criticism on the possession of his places was acute.

252. Five letters from HW to Bute written before this time have been preserved: 20 Oct. 1760, Dec. 1760, 10 May 1761, 27 May 1761, and 15 Feb. 1762. HW is probably referring to the ones included among 'Letters to and from Ministers' in *Works* ii: Dec. 1760, pp. 376–7, and 15 Feb. 1762, pp. 378–9.

253. HW to Newcastle 12 Nov. 1758 and ?Oct. 1761.

254. HW to William Pitt 19 Nov. 1759.

255. Bute had been appointed prime minister on 26 May. Only one levee before 12 June, at the Cockpit on 9 June, was noticed in the newspapers; but Bute also gave 'a grand entertainment' on the King's birthday (4 June), to which HW may be referring (*Daily Adv.* 27 May 1762; *London Chronicle* 5–8 and 8–10 June: xi. 542, 549).

256. In 1782 HW repeated this, as having occurred 'forty years ago' when Newcastle was Secretary of State ('Account of My Conduct Relative to the Places I Hold under Government,' *Works* ii. 369).

257. The printing of the *Catalogue of Engravers* (*Works* iv. 1–118), which was published in 1764 as a supplement to the *Anecdotes of Painting,* was started the day before HW completed the writing of it; the printing was finished 9 May 1763 (Hazen, *SH Bibliography* 55).

258. William Warburton (1698–1779), Bp of Gloucester. It was Garrick who told HW of the Bishop's resentment: see *post* n. 265.

259. A mistake for the first volume, of which it is Chapter V, pp. 105–16: 'State of Architecture to the end of the Reign of Henry VIII' (*Works* iii. 92–102). The first two volumes of the *Anecdotes of Painting* had been published 15 Feb. 1762 (Hazen, *SH Bibliography* 55; *Daily Adv.*).

260. Warburton's edition of Pope was first published in 1751 (HW's copy was sold SH iii. 165, MS Cat. K.3.17). Baskerville did not accede to Warburton's request that he print an edition at Birmingham (letter

As I had not once thought of him in that work, it was not easy to guess at what he was offended. On looking over the chapter, I concluded he had writ some nonsense about the Phenicians,[261] but having read very few of his works,[262] it was impossible for me to know where to find it. As I would not disoblige even a coxcomb unprovoked, and know how silly a literary controversy is in which the world only laughs at both sides, I desired Dr Charles Lyttelton,[263] Bishop of Carlisle, to ask him if what I had said of the Phenicians was the rock of offence, and to assure him I had read few of his things, and had had no intention of laughing at him. I name Bishop Lyttelton, because if it had not come from one of his own order, all-arrogant and absurd as Warburton is, one should scarce believe it possible that he could have pushed vanity and folly to such a height as appeared in his answer. He replied, 'The Phenicians! no, no'; he alluded to 'my note in the edition of Pope,[264] in which I have spoken of Gothic architecture; I have exhausted the subject.' I will only remark on this excess of impertinent self-conceit, that if he can *exhaust* subjects in so few lines, it was very unnecessary for him to write so many thousands. After this, I would as soon have a controversy with a peacock, or with an only daughter that her parents think handsome. The fowl, the miss, and the bishop, are alike incorrigible. The first struts naturally, the second is spoiled; reason itself has been of no use to the last.[265]

from Shenstone to Percy 16 May 1762, *Letters of William Shenstone*, ed. Marjorie Williams, Oxford, 1939, p. 625; Ralph Straus and R. K. Dent, *John Baskerville*, 1907, p. 38).

261. HW had introduced the Phœnicians as follows: 'Let but France and England once dispute which first used a hatchet, and they shall never be accorded till the chancery of learning accommodates the matter by pronouncing that each received that invaluable utensil from the Phœnicians. Common sense, that would interpose by observing how probable it is that the necessaries of life were equally discovered in every region, cannot be heard; a hammer could only be invented by the Phœnicians, the first polished people of whom we are totally ignorant' (*Works* iii. 93).

262. Besides the edition of Pope mentioned *ante* n. 260, HW possessed copies of Warburton's *Doctrine of Grace*, 1763 edn (sold SH iii. 74, MS Cat. I.9.43–4: now WSL), the first volume of his *Divine Lega-*

tion *of Moses*, 1738 (sold SH iii. 40, MS Cat. H.3.17), and seven or more of his shorter works (five of these are now WSL). HW had undoubtedly at least looked through all of these books. In his 'Book of Materials' 1759, p. 17, he quotes a phrase ('a sombrous rankness of expression') from the *Doctrine of Grace* illustrating Warburton's 'nonsense.'

263. See *post* i. 92 n. 14.

264. Warburton's note on *Moral Essays*, Epistle IV, l. 29 ('Load some vain church with old theatric state').

265. Warburton wrote to Garrick as follows: 'I have my fribbles as well as you. In the "Anecdotes of Painting," just published, the author, by the most unprovoked malice, has a fling at your friend obliquely, and puts him in company where you would not expect to find him (it is vol. i, p. 106, 107), with Tom Hearne and Browne Willis. It is about Gothic edifices, for which I shall be *about his pots,* as Bentley said to Lord Halifax of Rowe. But I say it better; I mean the

1763.

Beginning of September wrote the dedication and preface to Lord Herbert's life.[266]

*Oct. 10th, began the memoirs of 1759.

Oct. 28th, finished that year.

Oct. 29, began the year 1760.

Nov. 9th, finished that year.*

1764.

May 29, began an answer to a pamphlet against Mr Conway, called *An Address to the Public on the Late Dismission of a General Officer.*[267] My answer was finished June 12th, but not published till Aug. 2d, under the title of *A Counter Address to the Public,* etc.[268]

galley-pots and washes of his toilet. I know he has a fribble-tutor [Gray] at his elbow, as sicklied over with affectation as himself' (17 Feb. 1762). And again on 22 April: 'It was most kindly done of you to represent my complaint to Mr Walpole. If an abuse had been intended, it was altogether *unprovoked.* His denying any such intention on his honour, gives me full satisfaction: though neither I nor my friends know what the passage aims at, if it had not that intention. It is p. 106–7. And to confess to you, *inter nos,* when the new antiquarian Bishop of Carlisle mentioned this affair to me, impertinently enough, for I never had that familiarity of acquaintance with him to expect he should busy himself in my concerns, I gave him to understand, that Mr Walpole must give me farther satisfaction than what he had brought, which was that gentleman's declaring on his honour he had not me in his thoughts. And my reason was this: I knew Mr W. to be a wag, and such are never better pleased than when they have an opportunity of laughing at an antiquarian' etc., etc. (*Private Correspondence of David Garrick,* 1831–2, i. 138–9, 141).

The passage in the *Anecdotes* to which Warburton took exception begins as follows: 'Indeed Tom Hearne, Brown Willis, and such illustrators did . . . now and then stumble upon an arch, a tower, nay a whole church, so dark, so ugly, so uncouth, that they were sure it could not

have been built since any idea of grace had been tranported into the island' (*Works* iii. 93). A comparison between this and Warburton's note on Gothic architecture confirms HW's assertion that no malice towards the bishop was intended.

266. See *post* ii. 125. The book was dedicated to Herbert's descendant Henry Arthur Herbert (ca 1703–1772), cr. (1748) E. of Powis, from whom HW obtained the MS.

267. By William Guthrie (1708–70), a hack-writer for the government (see *Mem. Geo. III* ii. 4). It was published 24 May (*Daily Adv.*).

268. *Works* ii. 549–76: *A Counter Address to the Public, on the Late Dismission of a General Officer,* of which the 2d edition was announced in *Daily Adv.* for 9 Aug., the 4th, 31 Aug. It was written in reply not only to Guthrie's *Address* but also to a letter printed in the *Gazetteer* for 9 May (*Works* ii. 550). On 17 Feb. Conway had opposed general warrants and supported Wilkes by voting with the minority on the question of adjourning the debate. This so angered George III that he insisted on Conway's dismissal from both the Bedchamber and his regiment (see George III to Grenville 18 Feb. 1764, Grenville to Lord Hertford 18 April 1764, *Grenville Papers,* ed. W. J. Smith, 1852–3, ii. 261–7, 296–9; *Mem. Geo. III* i. 287–302, 319–31; MONTAGU ii. 120; *Journals of the House of Commons* xxix. 846; Cobbett, *Parl. Hist.* xv. 1404). One of HW's copies of the pamphlet is

June. I began *The Castle of Otranto,* a Gothic story, and finished it Aug. 6th.[269]

Oct. 15, wrote the 'Fable of the Magpie and her Brood'[270] for Miss Hotham,[271] then near eleven years old, great-niece of Henrietta Hobart Countess Dowager of Suffolk.[272] It was taken from *Les nouvelles ré[c]réations de Bonaventure des Périers,*[273] valet-de-chambre to the Queen of Navarre.[274]

Dec. 24. *The Castle of Otranto* was published;[275] 500 copies.

1765.

April 11th. The second edition of *The Castle of Otranto.* 500 copies.
Sept. 9th, set out for Paris.[276]
End of this year wrote the letter from K. of Prussia to Rousseau.[277]

1766.

April 22d, arrived in London from Paris.

now WSL. See Hazen, *Bibliography of Walpole* 50–2.

269. See Hazen, *Bibliography of Walpole* 52–67; see also *post* ii. 137, and HW to Cole 9 March 1765, COLE i. 88.

270. *Works* i. 34–6. On 17 Oct. HW printed 200 copies at SH (Hazen, *SH Bibliography* 191–5).

271. Henrietta Gertrude (1753–1816), dau. of Sir Charles Hotham, 8th Bt.

272. Henrietta Hobart (ca 1681–1767), m. (1706) Charles Howard, 9th E. of Suffolk: HW's neighbour at Marble Hill (see *post* i. 160 n. 4), Twickenham, and the chief source of his 'Reminiscences' written in 1788. Miss Hotham lived with her at Marble Hill (*Works* i. 34n).

273. Bonaventure des Périers (d. ca 1544), French satirist. His *Nouvelles récréations et joyeux devis* was first published at Lyon in 1558 (NBG). HW's copy, Lyon, 1561, was sold SH iii. 105.

274. Marguerite d'Angoulême (1492–1549), author of the *Heptameron;* sister of Francis I; m. (1527) Henri d'Albret, King of Navarre.

275. See *post* ii. 137 n. 1.

276. See HW's first 'Paris Journal,' DU DEFFAND v. 258–314.

277. 'Le Roi de Prusse à Monsieur Rousseau,' written 23 Dec. 1765 (*Works* iv. 250; DU DEFFAND v. 289), which had been circulating in Paris since 28 Dec. (L. J. Courtois, 'Chronologie critique de la vie et des œuvres de Jean-Jacques Rousseau,' *Annales de la Société Jean-Jacques Rousseau,* vol. xv, Geneva, 1923, p. 181). For the text of the letter see COLE i. 110–11. It was first printed, with a translation, in *St James's Chronicle* 1–3 April 1766. In the issue for 8–10 April was printed an aggrieved response from Rousseau, dated from Wootton 7 April, on which the editors commented, referring to HW's letter: '. . . We believe the World will not look upon [it] in that heinous light in which it is considered by Mons. Rousseau. The imposture was a very innocent one, and we do not imagine that many readers were deceived by it. It was indeed nothing more than a harmless piece of raillery, not calculated to injure the philosopher in this country. It was handed about town for several weeks before it made its way into the *St James's Chronicle,* and we are told that it was a *jeu d'esprit* of an English gentleman, now at Paris, well known in the *Catalogue of Noble Authors.*' See Hazen, *Bibliography of Walpole* 160–2.

June 28, 29. Wrote *An Account of the Giants lately Discovered.*[278] It was published Aug. 25th following.

Aug. 18, began 'Memoirs of the Reign of George III.'[279]

1767.

Feb. 1, began the detection of the *Testament politique*[280] of my father, at Strawberry Hill; and finished it the next time I went thither, Feb. 17th. Did not print it,[281] as no translation was made into English of that fictitious work.

March. Wrote to the Mayor of Lynn[282] that I did not intend to come into Parliament again.

A bad translation of *The Castle of Otranto* into French,[283] was published at Paris this month.

May 28. My letter to the Mayor of Lynn was first published in the *St James's Chronicle.*[284]

Aug. 20, I went to Paris.[285] Wrote there an account of my whole concern in the affair of Rousseau,[286] not with intention to publish it yet.

In Sept. were published in the *Public Advertiser* two letters[287] I had written on political abuse in newspapers. They were signed, *Toby,* and *A Constant Correspondent.*

Oct. 12, returned from Paris.

278. *Works* ii. 93–102. See Hazen, *Bibliography of Walpole* 67–9.

279. First published in 1845. See Hazen, *Bibliography of Walpole* 93–5.

280. *Testament politique du Chevalier Walpoole, Comte d'Orford, et ministre d'Angleterre,* Amsterdam, 1767. This two-volume 'brochure,' which had been sent to HW by Mme du Deffand the middle of January (DU DEFFAND i. 212), was probably (as HW believed) by the author of a three-volume *Histoire du ministère du chevalier Robert Walpool, devenu ministre d'Angleterre et comte d'Oxford* [sic], Amsterdam, 1764, which has been attributed to Jean-Baptiste Dupuy-Demportes (d. 1770) (NBG; Bibl. Nat. Cat.; note by Antoine-Alexandre Barbier in *Correspondance littéraire, philosophique et critique par Grimm, Diderot . . . etc.,* ed. Maurice Tourneux, 1877–82, vii. 232).

281. It was printed posthumously in *Works* ii. 323–38 under the title 'Detection of a Late Forgery called *Testament Politique du Chevalier Robert Walpoole.*'

282. HW to William Langley 13 March 1767.

283. *Le Château d'Otrante, histoire gothique . . . traduite sur la seconde édition anglaise* by Marc-Antoine Eidous. See DU DEFFAND i. 256.

284. It was also printed in GM June 1767, xxxvii. 293, and elsewhere.

285. See 'Paris Journals,' DU DEFFAND v. 315–24.

286. 'A Narrative of what passed relative to the quarrel of Mr David Hume and Jean-Jacques Rousseau, as far as Mr Horace Walpole was concerned in it,' *Works* iv. 249–56: appendix of letters 257–69. It is dated 13 Sept. 1767. See *post* ii. 170 n. 28.

287. 28 Aug. and 2 Sept. The second is written in the character of a hack-writer who has indulged in political abuse, but has resolved to mend his ways after reading the satirical letter by 'Toby.' HW's MSS of the letters are now WSL.

1768.

Feb. 1, published my *Historic Doubts on Richard III*.[288] I had begun it in the winter of 1767; continued it in the summer, and finished it after my return from Paris. Twelve hundred copies[288a] were printed and sold so very fast, that a new edition was undertaken the next day of 1000 more, and published the next week.[289]

March 15. I finished a tragedy called *The Mysterious Mother*,[290] which I had begun Dec. 25, 1766: but I had laid it aside for several months while I went to Paris, and while I was writing my *Historic Doubts on Richard III*. The two last acts were not now as much finished as I intended.

June 20, received a letter from Voltaire[291] desiring my *Historic Doubts*. I sent them, and *The Castle of Otranto*, that he might see the preface, of which I told him.[292] He did not like it, but returned a very civil answer,[293] defending his opinion. I replied[294] with more civility, but dropping the subject, not caring to enter into a controversy; especially on a matter of opinion; on which, whether we were right or wrong, all France would be on his side, and all England on mine.

Nov. 18, at the desire of her son George William Hervey Earl of Bristol,[295] I wrote the elegy for the monument of Mary Lepelle Lady Hervey,[296] to be erected in the church at Ickworth in Suffolk.

288. *Historic Doubts on the Life and Reign of King Richard the Third* (in *Works* ii. 105–84). It was published by James Dodsley, to whom HW sold the copyright for £100 (Toynbee *Supp.* ii. 138). See Hazen, *Bibliography of Walpole* 69–74, and *post* ii. 161.

288a. In HW to Lord Hailes 2 Feb. 1768 he says there were 1250 copies.

289. On 12 Feb. (*Daily Adv.* 8, 12 Feb. 1768).

290. *Works* i. 37–129. HW printed fifty copies at SH 14 June–6 August 1768 (Hazen, *SH Bibliography* 79).

291. Dated from Ferney 6 June 1768 (printed in HW's *Works* v. 629–30).

292. In HW to Voltaire 21 June 1768. HW had attacked Voltaire, because of his criticism of Shakespeare, in the preface to the second edition of *The Castle of Otranto* (*Works* ii. 9–11).

293. 15 July 1768 (HW's *Works* v. 632–6).

294. 27 July 1768.

295. See *post* i. 183 n. 17.

296. The elegy, a poem of 36 lines, is included in HW to Sir Edward Walpole ca 28 April 1769. See also Lord Bristol to HW 18 Dec. 1768, which seems to suggest that HW had revised an earlier version. The inscription preceding it on the tombstone, which is a flat stone in the pavement of the chancel of Ickworth Church, is as follows: 'Here lyeth the body of the Right Honble Mary, Lady Hervey, relict of John, Lord Hervey, and daughter of Brigadier Lepell, one of the Maids of Honour to Caroline, Princess of Wales; born 26 Sept. [1700], died 2 Sept. 1768' (*Ickworth Parish Registers*, Wells, 1894, pp. 69, 76). The elegy as inscribed (ibid. pp. 76–7) shows only trifling variations from HW's copy; and, as Lord Bristol requested, it is signed 'Hon. Horace Walpole Esq. fecit.' A MS copy in HW's hand is now WSL.

I should have mentioned that on the dissolution of the Parliament[297] this year, I refused to serve again, agreeably to a letter I had written to the Mayor of Lynn, and which was published in the newspapers.

1769.

April 24, Mrs Clive[298] spoke an 'Epilogue'[299] I had written for her on her quitting the stage. It alluded to Robertson's *History of Charles V,* then lately published.[300]

May. Mr David Hume had introduced to me[301] one Diverdun,[302] a Swiss in the Secretary's office. This man wrote *Mémoires littéraires de la Grande Bretagne;* and Mr Hume desired I would give him a copy of Lord Herbert's *Life,* that he might insert an extract in his journal.[303] I did. In April this Diverdun went to travel with a young English gentleman,[304] and a few days afterwards a Swiss clergyman[305] delivered to me from him his *Mémoires* for the year 1768; he had published but one before, for 1767. In this new journal I found a criticism[306] on my *Historic Doubts,* with notes by Mr Hume, to which the critic declared he gave the preference.[307] Mr Hume had shown me the notes last year

297. Parliament was dissolved 11 March 1768 (Return of Members of Parliament ii. 123).

298. Catherine Raftor ('Kitty Clive') (1711–85), the actress, m. (1732) George Clive, from whom she was soon separated. She had come to Twickenham, where she first lived in a cottage near Marble Hill, ca 1748; since about 1754 she had lived with her brother, James Raftor, at Little Strawberry Hill (Cliveden), a small house on the SH property where the Berrys later lived (*Works* iv. 392n.; R. S. Cobbett, *Memorials of Twickenham,* 1872, p. 245; HW to Bentley 3 Nov. 1754, 4 Aug. 1755; MONTAGU i. 70; Mrs Clive to HW n.d.).

299. *Works* iv. 399–400. Mrs Clive appeared that night (at Drury Lane) as 'Flora' in Mrs Centlivre's *The Wonder* and as 'Mrs Riot' in Garrick's *Lethe* (Genest v. 226).

300. *The History of the Reign of the Emperor Charles V,* by William Robertson (1721–93), was published in March 1769 (GM xxxix. 156). HW's 'Epilogue' begins:

'With glory satiate, from the bustling stage,
Still in his prime—and much about my
    age—
Imperial Charles (if Robertson says true)
Retiring, bade the jarring world adieu.'

301. In Hume to HW 11 Nov. 1768.

302. Jacques-Georges Deyverdun (1734?–1789), a Swiss employed as clerk in the Secretary of State's office, first (1766–8) in the northern department under Conway and later (1768–9) in the southern department. He was an intimate friend of Edward Gibbon, who was his collaborator in the *Mémoires* here mentioned (V. P. Helming, 'Edward Gibbon and Georges Deyverdun,' *PMLA* 1932, xlvii. 1028–49; *Royal Kalendar* 1767, p. 113; 1768, p. 118; 1769, p. 117).

303. I.e., in the projected third volume of the *Mémoires,* which never appeared (Helming, op. cit., p. 1028).

304. Sir Richard Worsley (1751–1805), 7th Bt (*Memoirs of the Life of Edward Gibbon,* ed. G. B. Hill, 1900, pp. 176–7).

305. Not identified.

306. Pp. 1–25, with Hume's notes appended pp. 26–35.

307. 'Les arguments de Mr Walpole nous avaient ébloui sans nous convaincre. Les réflexions suivantes nous ont ramené au sentiment général. Elles sont de M. Hume qui nous les a communiqué avec la permission d'en enricher nos *Mémoires*' (pp. 25–6). Though HW assumed that the review was by Deyverdun, it was by Gibbon, and was included by Lord Sheffield in Gibbon's *Miscellaneous Works,* 1796–1815, iii. 156–7. A

in MS,[308] but this conduct appeared so paltry, added to Mr Hume's total silence, that I immediately wrote an answer,[309] not only to these notes but to other things[310] that had been written against my *Doubts*. However, as I treated Mr Hume with the severity he deserved, I resolved not to print this answer, only to show it to him in MS and to leave it behind as an appendix to and confirmation of my *Historic Doubts*.

About the same time Voltaire published in the *Mercure* the letter he had written to me,[311] but I made no answer, because he had treated me more dirtily than Mr Hume had. Though Voltaire with whom I had never had the least acquaintance or correspondence, had voluntarily written to me first and asked for my book, he wrote a letter to the Duchesse de Choiseul,[312] in which, without saying a syllable of his having written to me first, he told her I had officiously sent him my works and declared war with him, in defence *de ce bouffon de Shakespeare*,[313] whom in his reply to me, he pretended so much to admire. The Duchess sent me Voltaire's letter,[314] which gave me such contempt for his disingenuity that I dropped all correspondence with him.

In July and August finished two more books of my memoirs for the years 1765, 1766.[315]

MS draft (not in Gibbon's autograph) of the article is among the Gibbon papers in the BM (Add. MS 34,882, ff. 11–26).

308. See *post* ii. 176 and 182.

309. Published posthumously in *Works* ii. 185–220, under the title 'Supplement to the *Historic Doubts on the Life and Reign of King Richard III*, with remarks on some answers that have been made to that work.' It is dated 10 May 1769, with a postscript dated 6 August 1769. Each of Hume's sixteen notes is taken up and answered.

310. I.e., the review by Willam Guthrie in the *Critical Review* for Feb. 1768, xxv. 116–26 (see *post* ii. 180 and MONTAGU ii. 254); F. W. Guydickens's *Answer to Mr Horace Walpole's Late Work*, etc. (see *post* ii. 172); and a series of six letters signed 'Impartialis' in the *London Chronicle* 12 March–31 May 1768 (see COLE i. 139 n. 18, 144).

311. I.e., the letter of 15 July 1768 (see *ante* i. 43). It was printed in the *Mercure de France* for May 1769, pp. 134–43.

312. 15 July 1768: Voltaire enclosed for her approval his letter to HW. The letter to the Duchesse is in his *Œuvres*, ed. Mo-

land, xlvi. 84–5: reprinted in DU DEFFAND vi. 144.

313. 'Il m'a envoyé ses ouvrages dans lesquels il justifie le tyran Richard trois, dont ni vous ni moi ne nous soucions guère. Mais il donne la préférence à son grossier bouffon Shakespeare sur Racine et sur Corneille; et c'est de quoi je me soucie beaucoup. Je ne sais par quelle voie M. Walpole m'a envoyé sa déclaration de guerre . . .' (ibid.).

314. HW complained about it to Mme du Deffand both at the time and in 1773, and again to Lort as late as 1781 (DU DEFFAND ii. 120, iii. 316; HW to Lort 2 Nov. 1781). Yet Voltaire had not asked HW for the *Castle of Otranto*, the preface to which was the cause of his annoyance, but only for the *Historic Doubts*. See a study of the quarrel by M. B. French and E. Allison Peers, 'Walpole's Relations with Voltaire,' in *Modern Philology* 1920–1, xviii. 189–200.

315. HW has noted in the MS that he finished the year 1765 on 3 July 1769, and the year 1766 on 7 August.

*August 16, set out for Paris.[316]

October 11, arrived in London from Paris.

—— 18, began another book of the memoirs.

Dec. 1, finished the memoirs to the end of 1st parliament of George III.*

1770.

*June 9th, began the last volume of my *Anecdotes on Painting*. Aug. 2d, finished it.*[317]

In this summer wrote an answer to Dr Milles's remarks[318] on my *Richard III*.

1771.

*July 7. Set out for Paris.[319]

Sept. 6, arrived in London from Paris.*

End of Sept. wrote the advertisement to the letters of King Edward VI.[320]

This year wrote the memoirs of 1768, 1769, 1770.[321]

1772.

*Jan. 7, began the memoirs of 1771.

April 20,* finished my memoirs, which conclude with the year 1771; intending for the future only to carry on a journal.[322]

316. See HW's 'Paris Journals,' DU DEF-FAND v. 324–33.

317. The printing of the fourth volume of the *Anecdotes* was started shortly after 20 Nov. 1770 and completed 13 April 1771, but it was not published until Oct. 1780 (Hazen, *SH Bibliography* 63; see also HW to Lady Ossory 23 Sept. 1780).

318. 'Observations on the Wardrobe Account for the Year 1483,' by Jeremiah Milles (1714–84), D.D., Dean of Exeter and President of the Society of Antiquaries; delivered before the Society 8 March 1770, and printed in *Archæologia* (HW's set of which is now WSL) i (1770), pp. 361–83. HW's 'Reply to the Observations of the Rev. Dr Milles,' *Works* ii. 221*–244*, is dated 28 Aug. 1770. It was included by

HW in the unfinished quarto edition of his works, from which an offprint of about six copies was made (Hazen, *SH Bibliography* 91, 95, and *Bibliography of Walpole* 73, 75).

319. See 'Paris Journals,' DU DEFFAND v. 333–42.

320. *Copies of Seven Original Letters from King Edward VI to Barnaby Fitz-Patrick*, printed at SH 1–13 June 1772 (Hazen, *SH Bibliography* 99–101). See COLE i. 219–22.

321. According to HW's notes on the MS the year 1768 was begun 27 April 1771, completed 1 July; 1769 begun 5 Oct., completed 17 Nov.; 1770 begun 17 Nov., completed 7 Jan. 1772.

322. See *ante* i. 23 n. 152.

This year, the last and some time before, wrote some *Hieroglyphic Tales;*[323] there are only five.[324]

I had long left off going to the Antiquarian Society. This summer I heard[325] that they intended printing some more foolish notes[326] against my *Richard III,* and though I had taken no notice of their first publication,[327] I thought they might at last provoke me to expose them. I determined to be at liberty by breaking with them first; and Foote[328] having brought them on the stage[329] for sitting in council, as they had done, on Whittington and his cat,[330] I was not sorry to find them so ridiculous, or to mark their being so, and upon that nonsense and the laughter that accompanied it, I struck my name out of their book. This was at the end of July.[331] *See my letters to Mr Norris,[332] secretary to the society.*

In July wrote the life of Sir Thomas Wyat,[333] for No. II of my edition of *Miscellaneous Antiquities.*[334]

323. *Works* iv. 321–52. In 1785 HW printed at SH six copies, besides a set of proofs which has survived (Hazen, *SH Bibliography* 132–4). The MSS of the first four *Tales* are now WSL, together with an unpublished one. HW has noted on the first that it was written 21 Aug. 1766, on the third, July 1771, and on the fourth, 23 Dec. 1771.

324. There are six in the printed collection.

325. From Cole, 9 July 1772 (COLE i. 268, 270).

326. By Robert Masters (1713–98): 'Some Remarks on Mr Walpole's *Historic Doubts on the Life and Reign of King Richard III,*' included in *Archæologia* ii (1773), pp. 198–215 (also separately published in 1772). The original paper was read before the Society of Antiquaries 7 and 14 Jan. 1771 (ibid. 198). See *post* i. 49.

327. Dr Milles's 'Observations.'

328. Samuel Foote (1720–77).

329. In *The Nabob,* first performed at the Haymarket 29 June 1772 (Mary M. Belden, *Dramatic Work of Samuel Foote,* 1929, p. 195. It was not published until 1778; HW's copy is now WSL).

330. Act III, sc. 1, takes place at a meeting of the Antiquarian Society, to which Sir Matthew Mite, the nabob, has been elected. In his inaugural address, which is on Dick Whittington, Sir Matthew says: 'The commerce this worthy merchant carried on, was chiefly confined to our coasts; for this pur-

pose, he constructed a vessel, which, from its agility and lightness, he aptly christened a cat. . . . From thence it appears, that it was not the whiskered, four-footed, mouse-killing cat, that was the source of the magistrate's wealth, but the coasting, sailing, coal-carrying cat.' The paper on Whittington was read before the Society ca December 1771 by Samuel Pegge (Richard Gough to Michael Tyson, 27 Dec. 1771, in *Lit. Anec.* viii. 574–5). It was not printed in *Archæologia,* and no record of the debate on it seems to have survived; but that Sir Matthew Mite's explanation may have been advanced seriously is suggested by the letter cited above, in which Gough (who was a member of the Council of the Society) remarks, 'I firmly believe, if not a rebus for some ship which made his fortune, [Whittington's cat] was the companion of his arm chair, like Montaigne's.' See also Samuel Lysons's *The Model Merchant of the Middle Ages* (1860), pp. 38–41, for a discussion and dismissal of the boat theory; and James Tait in DNB *sub* Whittington, where the legend is disentangled from the documented facts.

331. Before July 28 (COLE i. 270).

332. William Norris (1719–91), F.S.A. 1754, secretary to the Society 1759–86. HW's letters have not been found.

333. Sir Thomas Wyatt (ca 1503–1542), the poet.

334. A series begun by HW 'in imitation

Sept. 16. The Duke of Gloucester notified to the King his marriage[335] with my niece Lady Waldegrave.

The last day of September I was seized with a most severe fit of the gout in all my limbs, which, with several relapses, lasted five months and a half. Wrote some lines to Lady Anne Fitzpatrick with a present of shells.[336]

1773.

My nephew Lord Orford[337] went mad, by quack medicines that he had taken for the scurvy, which by carelessness and catching cold flew up into his head.

[March 1 and 2] wrote[338] 'Nature will Prevail, a Moral Entertainment in one Act,'[339] which I sent (anonymously) to Mr Colman,[340] manager of Covent Garden. He was much pleased with it, but thinking it too short for a farce, pressed to have it enlarged, which I would not take the trouble to do for so slight and extemporary a performance.

*June. The physicians having no hopes of Lord Orford's recovery,

of Peck's *Desiderata Curiosa*, and . . . solely calculated for amusement' (preface to the advertisement). No. 1, consisting of extracts from the third book of Sir William Segar's *Honour Military and Civill* (1602), was printed 22–28 June 1772; No. 2, on Wyatt, was printed 21 Sept.–10 Dec. 1772. Each printing was of 525 copies, and the two numbers were published simultaneously by John Bell 1 Jan. 1773; but the sales were disappointing and HW dropped the project (Hazen, *SH Bibliography* 103–5; *Daily Adv.* 1 Jan. 1773). No. 2 consists chiefly of Wyatt's 'Defence after the Indictment and Evidence' (pp. 21–54) which Gray had transcribed (see *post* ii. 116 n. 62); HW's 'Life of Sir Thomas Wyat the Elder' is on pp. 4–20.

335. The marriage between Lady Waldegrave and William Henry (1743–1805), D. of Gloucester, the King's brother, had taken place secretly 6 Sept. 1766. It was the rumour of this match, and the Duke of Cumberland's marriage in 1771, which were largely responsible for the Royal Marriage Act of March 1772. See *Mem. Geo. III* iii. 267–71 and *The Last Journals of Horace Walpole*, ed. A. Francis Steuart, 1910, i. 27–71, 93–102.

336. 'To Lady ——, when about five years old, with a present of shells. 1772' (*Works*

iv. 387). Lady Anne Fitzpatrick (ca 1769–1841), elder daughter of Lord and Lady Ossory, never married, and later lived with her sister Lady Gertrude at Farming Woods, Northants, which they inherited from their father. She was probably illegitimate (her mother did not marry Lord Ossory until 1769), which would account for a certain confusion as to the date of her birth (see GEC *sub* Upper Ossory). But HW's calling her 'about five' in 1772 is almost certainly wrong. In a note to 'The Three Vernons,' 1774 (see *post* i. 49), he again describes her as 'about five.'

337. George Walpole (1730–91), 3d E. of Orford. For a detailed account of his derangement see HW to Mann 17 Feb. 1773; see also COLE i. 298–9.

338. HW did not insert the date.

339. *Works* ii. 289–304. See *post* i. 50. The MS is now WSL. HW's original title, which he crossed through in the MS, was 'The Contrast, a Comedy in Two Acts.' HW has noted after *Finis*, 'Begun March 1st, finished next day, 1773,' and, in a later hand, 'Acted in 1779,' which is one year late.

340. George Colman (1732–94), the dramatist, and manager of Covent Garden 1767–74. See HW to Colman March 1773 (two letters) and 2 March 1778.

and his affairs being in the utmost confusion, at the desire of his mother[341] and nearest relations I undertook the management of them, intending to try if by my great care and economy I could put them into some order and save money to pay his debts and the mortgages on his estate.*

1774.

*Jan. 28. My nephew Lord Orford being suddenly returned to his senses,[342] I gave up the charge of his affairs, and was thanked by him and my relations for my care of them.

May.* Wrote an introduction to, and a parody of Lord Chesterfield's three first letters.[343]

At the beginning of this year, *or end of the last, I forget which, I* wrote my answer[344] to Mr Masters's remarks in the *Archæologia*.

In July wrote the verses on 'The Three Vernons.'[345]

1775.

In Feb. wrote the 'Epilogue to *Braganza*,'[346] and three letters to the author, Mr Jephson, on tragedy.[347]

*Aug. 16, set out for Paris.[348]

341. Margaret, Lady Orford (see *post* i. 227 n. 19). HW's troubles with Lord Orford's affairs are the chief topic of most of his letters during this period, particularly those to Mann in Florence, where Lady Orford was living, and to Lady Ossory. See especially his account of Houghton's desolation in the letter of 1 Sept. 1773 to Lady Ossory.

342. See HW to Lady Ossory 29 Jan. and to Mann 2 Feb. 1774.

343. *Works* iv. 355–60. The letters are headed 'The New Whole Duty of Woman, in a series of letters from a mother to a daughter.' Lord Chesterfield's *Letters to his Son* had just been published (see HW to Mason 7 April 1774). The MS is now in the Pierpont Morgan Library.

344. *Works* ii. 245*–251*. See *ante* i. 47 n. 326.

345. *Works* iv. 388–9; printed in GM for Nov. 1787, lvii. 1002–3, from a 'genuine transcript,' 'an incorrect copy . . . having been printed in the newspapers' (in *St James's Chronicle* 17 Nov. 1787). The Misses Vernon were Lord Ossory's half-sisters, the

Dowager Lady Ossory's daughters by her second husband, Richard Vernon (1726–1800): Henrietta (1760–1838), m. (1776) George Greville, Earl Brooke of Warwick Castle; Caroline Maria (1762–1833), m. (1797) Robert Percy Smith; and Elizabeth (d. 1830), who never married, and after 1804 lived mainly with her niece, Caroline Fox, at Little Holland House (Collins, *Peerage* 1812, viii. 309; GEC *sub* Brooke and Lyveden; Lord Ilchester, *The Home of the Hollands 1605–1820*, 1937, pp. 106–7, 110, 151–2; idem, *Chronicles of Holland House 1820–1900*, 1937, pp. 110, 210).

346. *Works* iv. 400–1 (actually written before 29 Jan., when Mason wrote to HW about it). *Braganza*, by Robert Jephson (1736–1803), was first performed at Drury Lane 17 Feb. (Genest v. 448–9), the leading rôle being played by Mrs Yates, who spoke HW's epilogue.

347. *Works* ii. 305–14. The first letter is dated 24 Feb. 1775.

348. See 'Paris Journals,' DU DEFFAND v. 342–53.

Oct. 17, returned from Paris.

General Cholmondeley[349] left me one of the executors of his will.*

1777.

In April my nephew Lord Orford went mad again,[350] and was under my care, but as he had employed a lawyer[351] of whom I had a bad opinion in his affairs, I refused to take care of them.

1778.

Lord Orford recovering in March,[352] I gave up the care of him.

In June was acted 'Nature will Prevail,' *see above,* at the little theatre in the Haymarket, with success.[353] At the end of July wrote my answer to the editor of Chatterton's works.[354]

    *Aug. 15, wrote a poetic card to Lady Blandford.[355]

    [In the winter wrote 'The Junto,' a poem.][356]

349. Hon. James Cholmondeley (1708–75), general, brother of HW's late brother-in-law Lord Cholmondeley. HW declined the executorship (HW to Lady Ossory 21 Oct. 1775). For the terms of the will see MONTAGU ii. 312; see also DU DEFFAND iv. 225 n. 3.

350. See HW to Sir Edward Walpole 21–25 April, and HW to Mann 28 April and 14 May 1777.

351. Probably either Coney or Lucas, Lord Orford's attorneys in 1781 (HW to Mann 26 Feb. 1781), both of whom HW despised. Lucas is mentioned frequently in the Mann correspondence 1781–4 as Lord Orford's chief agent in the settlement of his mother's estate.

352. See HW to Mann 27 March and 9 April 1778.

353. The first performance was on 10 June, and it was acted six more times (Genest vi. 31–2). Colman, to whom the play was first submitted, had succeeded Foote as manager of the Haymarket in 1777.

354. 'A Letter to the Editor of the Miscellanies of Thomas Chatterton,' Works iv. 206–20. The editor, who signed himself 'J.B.,' was John Broughton (d. 1801), a Bristol attorney whose address, according to later Bristol directories, was Small Street in 1787, College Green 1793–4, and Castle Green 1797 (F. A. Hyett and Wil-

liam Bazeley, The Bibliographer's Manual of Gloucestershire Literature, Gloucester, 1895–6, iii. 321; Felix Farley's Bristol Journal 27 June 1801; GM 1801, lxxi pt ii. 675. The references to the Bristol directories and Journal were kindly supplied by Mr James Ross of the Bristol Public Library). For HW's dealings with Chatterton, see his correspondence with Chatterton and Michael Lort: see also E. H. W. Meyerstein, A Life of Thomas Chatterton, 1930, pp. 253–84; E. R. Wasserman, 'The Walpole-Chatterton Controversy,' Modern Language Notes 1939, liv. 460–2; and Ketton-Cremer, Walpole 290–302.

355. Works iv. 391–2. Lady Blandford was Maria Catherina (ca 1697–1779), dau. of Peter S. C. de Jong, burgomaster of Utrecht; m. (1729) William Godolphin, Marquess of Blandford (d. 1731); m. secondly (1734) Sir William Wyndham, Bt. (The date of her birth is doubtful. GEC Comp. Baronet., following GM and Annual Register, describes her as 96 at the time of her death; HW to Lady Ossory 23 Nov. 1775 said she was 78, but in 1778 [Works iv. 392n] described her as 84.)

356. Bracketed in MS, probably because HW saw that he had entered it under the wrong year. The MS of this unpublished poem of 81 lines, dated 1777, is now WSL. It opens with a stanza celebrating George

Began the life of Mr Thomas Baker.[357] Finished it at Christmas.*

1779.

In the preceding autumn had written a defence of myself ag[ainst] the unjust aspersions[358] in the preface to the *Miscellanies* of T. Chatterton. Printed 200 copies at Strawberry Hill this January, and gave them.[359] It was much enlarged from what I had written in July.

I had been seized with the gout in eight places at the end [of] October. The fit lasted fourteen weeks,[360] and left me very lame, till June.

At the end of May wrote a commentary and notes[361] to Mr Mason's later poems.

II's reign when 'Fortune's fav'rite Chatham held the helm' and contrasts those glorious days with 1777 when England has

'Another George—but check the soaring song:
Remember, Muse, *a King can do no wrong.*
Yet ah! some Kings, in sober law's despite,
Choose none but Ministers that ne'er do right.'

The remainder of the poem is devoted to these Ministers.

357. 'The Life of the Reverend Mr Thomas Baker, of St John's College in Cambridge' (*Works* ii. 339–62). See *post* ii. 133 and HW to Cole 26 Oct. 1778 (COLE ii. 129–30).

358. Printed in COLE ii. 102 n. 1.

359. I.e., it was not published for sale. See Hazen, *SH Bibliography* 116–18. HW's copy is now WSL.

360. See HW to Cole 4 Nov. 1778 (COLE ii. 132–3). He was unable to write any letters with his own hand until 24 Dec. (to Lady Ossory).

361. Edited by Paget Toynbee under the title *Satirical Poems published anonymously by William Mason, with Notes by Horace Walpole*, Oxford, 1926. HW's MS of the commentary and notes, which were written in interleaved copies of the original editions of the six poems, is now in the Harvard University Library.

CORRESPONDENCE

HORACE WALPOLE'S CORRESPONDENCE

Introductory Note by Walpole

Printed from MS in Waller Collection.[1] The date of this note is uncertain, but the hand is HW's in the middle 'eighties. The letters were returned by Mason to HW in the spring of 1773. See HW to Mason 9 May 1772, Mason to HW 20 March 1773.

THESE first letters from Mr Gray to Mr Walpole were written when they were both lads just removed from school to the University, where they and Mr Ashton had assumed feigned names,[1a] and assigned others[2] to their particular acquaintance, that they might correspond with the greater freedom. This puerility, excusable at their ages of eighteen and seventeen, would have been ridiculous at a riper age, and they soon laid it aside. Consequently when Mr W. entrusted these letters to Mr Mason[3] that he might select such as were proper for publication, all those childish distinctions were struck out,[4] and Mr Mason made a very judicious selection for the press.[5] Mr W. notwithstanding was so partial to those early blossoms of his friend's wit, genius and humour, that he could not determine to destroy them—yet as they are too trifling for the public eye, he begs his executor[6] to burn them after reading, or at least after having transcribed such as would be no reflection on the taste and good sense, of the writer.

H. W.

To Gray, ca Friday 12 April 1734

Missing: mentioned in the following letter.

1. Now at Pembroke College. See *ante*, p. xxxiii.

1a. Gray was called 'Orosmades' or 'Orozmades'; HW, 'Celadon'; West, 'Favonius,' 'Zephyrus,' 'Zephyrille'; and Ashton, 'Almanzor.' The use of nicknames was apparently customary at Eton. In a MS version of 'Nugæ Etonenses 1765–1766' in the Eton College Library there is an alphabetical list of Eton boys and their nicknames. See *Etoniana* 15 July 1907, pp. 155–7.

2. See *post* 29 Oct. 1735.

3. William Mason (1725–97), poet and dramatist; Fellow of Pembroke College, Cambridge, 1747; rector of Aston, Yorks,

1754–97; HW's and Gray's correspondent and Gray's literary executor.

4. They were cut out with scissors (see *post* 16 April 1734 and *passim*).

5. Of the thirty-eight surviving letters of Gray to HW written between 1734 and 1738, Mason printed parts of six.

6. HW's executor at this time was his cousin, the Hon. Henry Seymour Conway (1719–95), field marshal, 1793 (*Eton Coll. Reg.*; DNB). After Conway died, HW appointed Mary Berry (1763–1852) his literary executrix. She printed nineteen of Gray's letters to HW, written 1746–68.

From GRAY, ca Tuesday 16 April 1734

Printed from MS in Waller Collection.

Dated by the postmark, the address (see note below), and the reference to 'Passion Week' (see below). The letter was written in answer to HW's missing letter to Gray ca 12 April 1734. Gray was in the country, possibly with his uncle, William Antrobus, at Everdon, Northants, or with his aunt, Mrs Jonathan Rogers, at Cantshill, in Britwell, near Burnham, Bucks (see *post* Aug. 1736, and 9 Sept. 1747).

The date shown in eighteenth-century postmarks on letters sent to or through London is invariably that of arrival in London; the use of date stamps was confined to the General Post Office and no provincial date stamps appeared until 1798 (John G. Hendy, *History of the Early Postmarks of the British Isles*, 1905, p. 5; C. F. Dendy Marshall, *British Post Office*, 1926, p. 209). This fact, together with the fact that until 1741 mail 'for all parts of England' left London on Tuesdays, Thursdays, and Saturdays, and arrived on Mondays, Wednesdays, and Fridays (John Chamberlayne, *Magnæ Britanniæ Notitia*, 1735, pt i. 260–3; GM 1741, xi. 330), is taken into consideration in the conjectural dating of some of Gray's and Walpole's early letters.

Address: To the Honourable Mr Horatio ⟨Wal⟩pole at the house of th⟨e Right⟩
 Honourable Sir Robert W⟨alpole⟩ in St James's Square,[1] London.
Postmark: [?] 17 AP.

[ca April 16, 1734.]

⟨   ⟩[2]

I BELIEVE by your not making me happy in a longer letter than that[3] I have just received, you had a design to prevent my tiring you with a tedious one; but in revenge for your neglect I'm resolved to send you one five times as long. Sir, do you think, that I'll be fobbed off[4] with eleven lines and a half after waiting this week in continual expectation and proposing to myself all the pleasure that you, if you would, might give me? Gadsbud![5] I am provoked into a fermentation! When I see you next, I'll firk you, I'll rattle you with a *certiorari*.[6] Let me tell you I am at present as full of wrath and choler as—as—you are of wit and good-nature; though I begin to doubt your title to the last of them,

1. From 1732 to 1735 Sir Robert Walpole lived in Lord Ashburnham's house (known since 1771 as London House) on the east side of St James's Square. After the completion of alterations he removed to Downing Street 22 Sept. 1735. See *Daily Adv.* 25 Oct., 27 Nov. 1732; *London Daily Post* 23 Sept. 1735; A. I. Dasent, *History of St James's Square*, 1895, pp. 155, 220.

2. Piece cut away. Probably 'My dearest Celadon': see *post* 14 Jan. 1735.

3. Missing.

4. Mistress Quickly in 2 *Henry IV* II. i. Gray repeats this passage *post* 25 Feb. 1735 and refers to Mistress Quickly.

5. Sir Paul Plyant in Congreve's *Double Dealer* II. iv: 'Gadsbud! I am provoked into a fermentation, as my Lady Froth says.'

6. Sir Paul Plyant (ibid. II. iv): 'Pray, your Ladyship, give me leave to be angry. I'll rattle him up, I warrant you, I'll firk him with a *certiorari*.'

since you have balked me in this manner. What an excuse do you make with your Passion Week and fiddle-faddle,[7] as if you could ever be at a loss what to say! Why, I, that am in the country, could give you a full and true account of half a dozen intrigues; nay, I have an amour carried on almost under my window between a boar and a sow, people of very good fashion, that come to an assignation, and squeak like ten masquerades; I have a great mind to make you hear the whole progress of the affair, together with the humours of Miss Pigsnies, the lady's confidante, but you will think perhaps I invent it, and so I shall let it alone. But I wonder you are not ashamed of yourself: in town, and not able to furnish out an epistle as long as a cow's tail! (excuse the rusticity of my simile). In short, I have tried and condemned you in my mind; all that you can allege to save yourself won't do, for I find by your excuses you are brought to your *dernière chemise;*[8] and as you stand guilty, I adjudge you to be drawn to the place of execution, your chamber, where, taking pen in hand, you shall write a letter as long as this to him who is nothing when not

Your sincere friend and most devoted humble servant,

T. GRAY

<   >[9]

To GRAY, ca Sunday 20 October 1734

Missing. Probably written in St James's Square between 9 Oct., the date on which Gray began residence at Peterhouse, and 31 Oct., the date of Gray's answer.

From GRAY, Thursday 31 October 1734

Printed from MS in Waller Collection.
Misdated 1735 by Mason. The day and month are supplied by the postmark; the year is clearly the year Gray entered Cambridge.
Address: To the Honourable Horace Walpole Esq. at the house of the Right Honourable Sir Robert Walpole in St James's Square, London.
Postmark: CAMBRIDGE 1 NO.

7. Lady Plyant (ibid. II. v): 'Fiddle faddle, don't tell me of this and that.'
8. The supposed French translation of Cibber's *Love's Last Shift* was *La Dernière chemise de l'amour.*
9. Piece cut out, carrying with it part of the address on the other side.

[Cambridge, Oct. 31, 1734.]

⟨   ⟩

FOR God's sake send me your *quære's* and I'll do my best to get information upon those points you don't understand. I warrant, you imagine that people in one college know the customs of others, but you mistake, they are quite little societies by themselves; the dresses, language, customs, etc., are different in different colleges; what passes for wit in one would not be understood if it were carried to another: thus the men of Peterhouse, Pembroke, and Clare Hall of course must be Tories; those of Trinity, rakes; of King's, scholars; of Sidney, Whigs; of St John's, worthy men; and so on. Now, what to say about this *terra incognita* I don't know: first then, it is a great old town, shaped like a spider, with a nasty lump[1] in the middle of it and half a dozen scambling long legs. It has fourteen parishes, twelve colleges, and four halls;[2] these halls only entertain students who after a term of years are elected into the colleges.[3] There are five ranks in the university, subordinate to the vice-chancellor, who is chose annually; there are: ⟨masters, fellows, fellow-commoners, pensione⟩rs,[4] and sizars. The masters of colleges are twelve gray-haired gentlefolks who are all mad with pride; the fellows[5] are sleepy, drunken, dull, illiterate things; the fellow-commoners[6] are imitators of the fellows, or else beaux, or else

1. Market Hill.

2. As late as 1800 (see *Cambridge University Calendar, for . . . 1800*) Clare, Pembroke, and St. Catharine's were referred to as 'Halls'; the name Trinity Hall still survives.

3. Gray is mistaken; there was no difference between halls and colleges.

4. The missing words have been supplied in pencil by HW.

5. 'It is a just remark that the fellows, not a few in some colleges, are very far from considering the end for which their fellowships were originally founded' (*Free Thoughts upon University Education; occasioned by the Present Debates at Cambridge*, 1751, pp. 42–3).

6. 'A fellow-commoner . . . is one who sits at the same table and enjoys the conversation of the fellows. It differs from what is called a gentleman-commoner at Oxford, not only in the name but also in the greater privileges and licences indulged

to the members of this order, who do not only enjoy the conversation of the fellows but likewise a full liberty of following their own imaginations in everything. For as tutors and governors of colleges have usually pretty sagacious noses after preferment, they think it impolitic to cross the inclinations of young gentlemen who are heirs to great estates, and from whom they expect benefices and dignities hereafter, as rewards for their want of care of them while they are under their protection. From hence it comes to pass that pupils of this rank are excused from all public exercises, and allowed to absent themselves at pleasure from the private lectures in their tutors' rooms as often as they have made a party for hunting, or an engagement at the tennis-court, or are not well recovered from their evening's debauch' (Francis Coventry, *History of Pompey the Little: or, the Life and Adventures of a Lap-dog*, 1751, pp. 232–3; see also pp. 233–53).

nothing; the pensioners[7] grave, formal sots who would be thought old, or else drink ale and sing songs against the excise.[8] The sizars[9] are graziers' eldest sons who come to get good learning that they may all be archbishops of Canterbury. These two last orders are qualified to take scholarships, one of which your humble servant has had given him.[10] First they led me into the Hall and there I swore allegiance to the King,[11] then I went to a room where I took fifty thousand Latin oaths,[12] such as to wear a square cap,[13] to make six verses upon the Epistle or Gospel every Sunday morning, to chant very loud in Chapel, to wear a clean surplice, etc., etc. Now as to eating, the fellow-commoners dine at the fellows' table, their commons is worth 6s. 4d. a week, the pensioners pay but 2s. 4d.; if anybody don't like their commons they send down into the kitchen to know what's for sizing,[14] the cook sends up a catalogue of what there is, and they choose what they please; they are obliged to pay for commons whether they eat it or no; there is always plenty enough; the sizars feast upon the leavings of the rest. As to dress, the fellow-commoners usually wear a prunella gown[15] with sleeves, a

7. 'The majority of the undergraduates were admitted as pensioners. . . . Many of them were destined to be clergymen' (Winstanley, *Unreformed Cambridge* 200–1; see also Christopher Wordsworth, *Social Life at the English Universities in the Eighteenth Century*, Cambridge, 1874, pp. 98–9).

8. The proposed excise on wine and tobacco, in addition to customs already imposed, provoked violent parliamentary and popular opposition, and was dropped by Sir Robert Walpole in April 1733.

9. They were the children of poor clergymen, small farmers, artisans, and petty tradesmen, and performed various menial tasks in the colleges. See Winstanley, *Unreformed Cambridge* 201–3; Wordsworth, loc. cit.

10. On 17 Oct. 1734 Gray was admitted to a Cosin Scholarship, worth £10 a year and 5s. on Founder's Day for a 'dainty meal' (T. A. Walker, *Admissions to Peterhouse*, Cambridge, 1912, p. 267; idem, 'Thomas Gray in Peterhouse,' *Athenæum*, 1906, i. 76, 107–8; 'Correspondence of John Cosin, D.D.,' *Surtees Society*, 1872, lv. 222). See also *post* i. 80 n. 9.

11. By the Act of 1 George I c. 13 sect. 12 (1714) members of the University, scholars on the foundation, and exhibitioners were

required to take and subscribe the oaths of allegiance, abjuration (to abjure the authority of the Pope), and supremacy (to acknowledge the House of Hanover and renounce the Old Pretender).

12. The provisions of the Cosin Scholarship.

13. Undergraduates of King's, Trinity College, and those on the foundation, such as the Cosin Scholars, wore a square cap (*pileus quadratus*), while pensioners and sizars wore a round cap (*pileus rotundus*). See 'Habitus Academici in Universitate Cantabrigiensi' in David Loggan's *Cantabrigia Illustrata*, ed. J. W. Clark, Cambridge, 1905, plate vii; E. C. Clark, 'College Caps and Doctors' Hats,' *Archæological Journal*, 1904, lxi. 36–47; Wordsworth, op. cit. 508–12.

14. In 1736–7 Gray's sizings or 'extras' amounted to £6 3s. 11d. and his commons to £4 13s. 4d. for the forty weeks he was in residence (T. A. Walker, 'Thomas Gray in Peterhouse,' *Athenæum*, 1906, i. 76).

15. Originally silk, afterwards worsted. A regulation passed by the Senate 26 June 1750 provided that bachelors' gowns should be made of 'prunello or princes stuff' (Charles H. Cooper, *Annals of Cambridge*, 1842–52, iv. 278).

hat and no band,[16] but their proper habit has its sleeves trimmed with gold lace; this they only wear at public ceremonies; neither do the noblemen use their pr[oper] habit commonly but wear only a black paduasoy[17] gown. The men of King's[18] are a sort of university by themselves and differ in customs from all the rest; everybody hates 'em, and when Almanzor[19] comes to me our peoples stare at him like a lord mayor's show, and wonder to see a human creature among them. If I tell you I never stir out perhaps you won't believe me, especially when you know there's a club of wits kept at the Mitre,[20] all such as come from Eton, where Almanzor would introduce me if I so pleased. Yet you will not think it strange that I don't go abroad when I tell you that I am got into a room, such ⟨a⟩ hugeous one that little i is quite lost in it, so ⟨that⟩ when I get up in the morning I begin to travel ⟨tow⟩ards the middle of it with might and main, and with much ado about noon bate at a great table which stands half-way [in] it. So then by that time (after having pursued my journey full speed) that I arrive at the door it is so dark and late, and I am so tired, that I am obliged to turn back again. So about midnight I get to the bedside; then, thinks you, I suppose he goes to sleep. Hold you a bit: in this country it is so far from that, that we go to bed to wake and rise to sleep, in short, those that go along the street do nothing but walk in their sleep, they run against every post they meet. But I beg pardon for talking so much of myself since that's not what you care for—(to be continued).

16. An 'ordinary broad-brimmed low-crowned billy-cock hat of the period subsequent to the Restoration' (Wordsworth, op. cit. 509; Loggan, loc. cit.).

17. A kind of say or serge (OED). The orders and regulations passed by the Senate 26 June 1750 provided that 'every person *in statu pupillari* shall wear clothes of a grave colour in the judgment of the officers of the University, without lace, fringe or embroidery, without cuffs or capes of a different colour from their coats' (Cooper, loc. cit.).

18. The scholars of King's were all Etonians, who, after three years' residence, were elected to a life fellowship. They proceeded to the degrees of B.A. and M.A. without the customary examinations, and they wore a gown with long sleeves. In the eighteenth century the scholars of King's were all fellow-commoners. See King's College Statutes II, III, VI, XXVI (*Documents*

Relating to the University and Colleges of Cambridge, 1852, ii. 484–92, 498, 543–5; Winstanley, *Unreformed Cambridge* 189–91). In 1735 there were fifty fellows and twenty scholars at King's (John Chamberlayne, *Magnæ Britanniæ Notitia*, 1735, pt ii. 245).

19. Thomas Ashton's pseudonym. 'Almanzor' was the hero of *The Conquest of Granada*, whose character Dryden shaped on Homer's Achilles and Tasso's Rinaldo (see *Gray-HW-West-Ashton Corr.* i. pp. xix–xx).

20. The Mitre Tavern was in Trumpington Street, near the SE corner of King's College quadrangle; the site is now occupied by the east wing of the Hall built by William Wilkins in 1824–8 (Willis and Clark i. 552–3, 564–6; Winstanley, *Unreformed Cambridge* 207).

From GRAY, ca Thursday 7 November 1734

Missing. Written before 17 Nov. at Cambridge, probably in the week of 3–9 Nov. It contained allusions to a 'guzzling affair' at a Cambridge tavern (*post* 17 Nov. 1734).

To GRAY, ca Monday 11 November 1734

Missing. Probably written in St James's Square before 17 Nov., the date of Gray's answer. It contained HW's promise to visit Gray and mention of the affair at the tavern (*post* 17 Nov. 1734).

From GRAY, Sunday 17 November 1734

Printed from MS in Waller Collection.
The date of the year is established by the reference to Stephens (see n. 18).

To mie Nuss att London

With care   Present
Carridge pade   These

[Cambridge,] 23d Sunday after Trin[ity].

Honner'd Nurse,

THIS comes to let you know that I am in good health, but that I should not have been so if it had not been for your kind promise of coming to tend me yourself and see the effect of your own prescription. And I should desire of you, so please you, as how that you would be so good as to be so kind as to do me the favour of bringing down with you a quantity of it, prepared as your grandmother's aunt, poor Mrs Hawthorn (God[1] rest her soul, for she was as well a natured a good gentlewoman as ever broke bread[2] or trod upon shoe-leather,[3] though I say it that should not say it, for you know she was related to me, and marry, not a jot the worse, I trow!) used to make it. Now I

1. Changed by HW to 'fudge' and then smudged.
2. Mistress Quickly, of Anne Page: 'An honest maid as ever broke bread' (*Merry Wives of Windsor* I. iv).
3. Second Commoner: 'As proper men as ever trod upon neat's leather have gone upon my handiwork' (*Julius Cæsar* I. i).

would not put you to this trouble if I could provide myself of the ingredients here, but truly, when I went to the poticaries for a drachm of spirit of ridicule, the saucy jackanapes of a prentice-boy fleered at me, I warrant ye, as who should say, you don't know your errand. So by my troth, away ambles me I (like a fool as I came) home again, and when I came to look of your receipt, to be sure, there was spirit of RIDICULE in great letters, as plain as the nose in one's face. And so, back hurries I, in a making-water-while,[4] as one may say; and when I came there, says I, you stripling, up-start, worsted-stocking, white-livered, lath-backed,[5] impudent princox,[6] says I, abuse me that am your betters every day in the week, says I, you ill-begotten, pocky, rascally, damned son of a bitch, says I—for you know, when he put me in such a perilous passion how could one help telling him his own—why, 'twould have provoked any Christian[7] in the world, though 'twere a dog, to speak. And so if you'll be so kind, I'll take care you shall be satisfied for your trouble. So, this is all at present from

Your ever-dutiful and most obedient and
most affectionate loving god-daughter,
PRU. OROSMADES[8]

A Discourse

Πάντα κόνις, καὶ πάντα πιὸς, καὶ πάντα τόβακκο.[9]

If I should undertake to prove to you that everything is tobacco it might be looked upon as an absurdity, after the reverend and learned Dean Swift has made it so manifest that everything is a pudding.[10] But I

4. Widow Blackacre, to Manly: 'O no, stay but a making water while (as one may say) and I'll be with you again' (Wycherley, *Plain Dealer* III. i).

5. Widow Blackacre, to Freeman (ibid. II. i): 'Thou pitiful, paltry, lath-backed fellow.'

6. Capulet, to Tybalt: 'You are a princox' (*Romeo and Juliet* I. v).

7. Changed by HW to 'man,' an emendation (violating Gray's masquerade) which attests HW's temporary piety. See also n. 1 above.

8. Or Orozmades (*post* 6 Jan. 1735), Gray's pseudonym. Ormazd is the omniscient lord of Zoroastrianism. 'Orosmades' occurs in

Lee's *Rival Queens* II. i (see *Gray's Corr.* i. 6, n. 9) and in Giovanni Paolo Marana's *Letters writ by a Turkish Spy*, 1687–93 (see 5th edn 1702, viii. 77), the style of which was imitated by Gray in *post* 6 Jan. 1735.

9. 'All is dust, and all is pie, and all is tobacco,' an adaptation of the first line of the epigram attributed to Glycon in the *Greek Anthology* x. 124: Πάντα γέλως, καὶ πάντα κόνις, καὶ πάντα τὸ μηθέν ('all is laughter, and all is dust, and all is nothing'). The epigram is No. 31 in Thomas Johnson's *Novus Græcorum epigrammatum et poemation delectus . . . In usum Scholæ Etonensis*, 3d edn, 1706, p. 11.

10. 'The universe itself is but a pudding

conceive it will not be so difficult to show that tobacco is everything (at least here), for there is not a soul in our college (a body I should say) who does not smoke or chew. There is nothing but whiffing, from fellow to sizar; nay, even the very chimneys, that they mayn't be thought particular, must needs smoke like the rest, whilst unfashionable I labour through clouds of it with as much pains as Milton's poor Devil took when he travelled through Chaos.[11] But as to the guzzling affair,[12] you mistook in thinking it was the old fellows that were with me, no— 'twas a thousand times worse—they were all young ones. Do but imagine me pent up in a room hired for the purpose, and none of the largest, from seven o'clock at night till four in the morning, 'midst hogsheads of liquor and quantities of tobacco, surrounded by thirty of these creatures, infinitely below the meanest people you could ever form an idea of, toasting bawdy healths and deafened with their unmeaning roar. Jesus![13] But I must tell you of a fat mortal,[14] who stuck close to me and was as drunk as ⟨   ⟩[15] (which story I'm afraid by the by was t⟨oo⟩ well-fancied to be real)—well, he was so maudlin and so loving, and told me long stories, interrupted by the sourest interjections, with moral discourses upon God knows what, that I was almost drunk too. Oh, I must just beg lea⟨ve to men⟩tion[16] one more[17] who, they tell me, has no fault but that he's a little too *foppish* and talks like a London rake. This fine gentleman is quite master of the *Spectator* and retails it for ever; among the rest he gave his humble opinion of the present state of the play-house, that Stevens[18] had a very

---

of elements. Empires, kingdoms, states, and republics are but puddings of people differently made up. The celestial and terrestrial orbs are deciphered to us by a pair of globes or mathematical puddings' (Henry Carey, *A Learned Dissertation on Dumpling; its Dignity, Antiquity, and Excellence. With a Word upon Pudding*, 1727, p. 21). The attribution of this pamphlet to Swift probably resulted from the fact that *Namby Pamby*, also by Carey but at that time supposed to be by Swift, was printed with it as an appendix.

11. *Paradise Lost* ii. 927–67.

12. In some Cambridge tavern, probably in the week of 3–9 Nov., since the comparison of Stephens and Quin (see below) may have been suggested by a letter in *The Grub-street Journal* of 31 Oct. Gray either wrote to HW that week, or HW heard else-

where about the guzzling affair, which apparently was thought to be not without effect upon Gray's health.

13. Scored through in the MS.

14. Not identified.

15. Undecipherable. T-W suggest 'Mrs Edwards who died of drams,' mentioned in HW to Mann 2 Dec. 1748 (see *Gray's Corr.* i. 7).

16. Piece cut out; the emendation in pencil is by HW.

17. Not identified.

18. Samuel Stephens (ca 1695–ca 1765), a button-maker of Paternoster Row (see *post* 3 Jan. 1736). He made his début as Othello at Covent Garden 19 Oct. 1734, and according to Thomas Davies (*Dramatic Miscellanies*, 1785, i. 147–9) 'his figure was not unsuitable to the part,' though he was 'bulky' and 'near his fortieth year.' *The Grub-*

graceful motion, spoke well, etc., but that he must needs give his voice for Mr Quin;[19] Mrs Thurmond[20] too was in great favour with him. As for the operas, he could not understand them but had heard Margaretta[21] and Nicolini[22] highly commended by those that were judges.[23] By God, says another, those operas are the ruin of the nation,[24] no honest people can go to 'em, and those that do, are ashamed of themselves, else why should they go in masks and disguises thither? Nobody in the company found out his blunder,[25] so nobody laughed but I, which was taken for applause. You'll think it a strange compliment when I tell you how often I thought of you all the while, but will forgive me when you recollect that 'twas a great piece of philosophy in me to be able in the midst of noise and disturbance to call to mind the most agreeable thing in nature. When you could give me so much pleasure absent, what must you do when with me, though perhaps it's policy in you to stay away so long, that you may increase my desire of seeing you? In your next send me word how soon you design to come to the relief

Of your ⟨   ⟩

street Journal 31 Oct 1734 reported: 'Mr Stevens has a melodious voice, enters into the passions, and varies his manner accordingly, and has surprised the town by treading the stage so gracefully the first time he came upon it.' See Genest iii. 456–7, 459; Autobiography and Correspondence of Mary Granville, Mrs Delany, ed. Lady Llanover, 1861–2, i. 513.

19. James Quin (1693–1766) returned to Drury Lane after sixteen years' absence and acted Othello on 10 Sept. 1734, with Mrs Thurmond as Desdemona (Genest iii. 436). For a comparison of Quin with Stephens and Colley Cibber see GM 1734, iv. 593.

20. —— Lewis (fl. 1715–37), of Epsom, Surrey, m. (before 1715) John Thurmond, actor and dancer. She acted at Drury Lane 1718–32, 1734–7, and at Goodman's Fields 1732–4. See DNB; William R. Chetwood, General History of the Stage, 1749, p. 226; Davies, op. cit. iii. 375–6.

21. Francesca Margherita de l'Epine (d. 1746), m. (1718) John Christopher Pepusch, composer. She came to England in 1692, and was the first Italian (the Earl of Hali-

fax's 'tawny Tuscan') to sing there in public (10 Jan. 1693). From 1704–18 she sang at Drury Lane, and retired in 1718 with £10,000 (Burney, Hist. of Music iv. 195–6; Sir John Hawkins, General History of the Science and Practice of Music, 1776, v. 153–5; Grove's Dictionary of Music; see also the Earl of Halifax's 'On Orpheus and Signora Francisca Margarita').

22. Nicolino Grimaldi (b. ca 1673), called Nicolini, originally a soprano, later a contralto. He made his English début 14 Dec. 1708, and was still singing in 1730 when Burney saw him in Broschi's Idaspes at Venice (Burney, op. cit. iv. 207, 257, 539).

23. Addison in The Spectator Nos 13, 405, and Steele in The Tatler No. 115.

24. For attacks on the Italian opera, see Harmony in an Uproar in John Arbuthnot, Miscellaneous Works, Glasgow, 1751, ii. 33–4, 42; Hogarth's satiric engravings listed in BM, Satiric Prints iii. 9–10, 95–6, 117–18.

25. The 'blunder,' as Mr R. W. Ketton-Cremer points out, was doubtless the young man's confusing operas with masquerades.

To Gray, ca November 1734

Missing. Probably written in St James's Square. This 'diverting letter in the poetical strain' (mentioned *post* 8 Dec. 1734) is alluded to by HW in his 'Memoir of Gray' (HW, Waldegrave MSS 1. 65–6: printed in *Gray's Corr.* iii. 1286–8): 'One of his first pieces of poetry was an answer in English verse to an epistle from H.W.'

From Gray, Sunday 8 December 1734

Printed from MS in Waller Collection.
Dated by the postmark and the address (see *ante* 16 April 1734, n. 1).
Address: To the Honourable Horatio Walpole Esq. at the house of the Right
    Honourable Sir Robert Walpole in St James's Square, London.
Postmark: CAMBRIDGE 9 DE.

[Cambridge, Dec. 8, 1734.]

<   >

I (though I say it) had too much modesty to venture answering your dear, diverting letter in the poetical strain myself, but when I was last at the DEVIL,[1] meeting by chance with the deceased Mr Dennis[2] there, he offered his service, and, being tipped with a tester,[3] wrought what follows—

> From purling streams and the Elysian scene,[4]
> From groves, that smile with never-fading green
> I reascend; in Atropos' despite
> Restored to Celadon[5] and upper light:
> Ye gods, that sway the regions under ground,
> Reveal to mortal view your realms profound;
> At his command admit the eye of day;
> When Celadon commands, what god can disobey?
> Nor seeks he your Tartarean fires to know,
> The house of torture, and th' abyss of woe;
> But happy fields[6] and mansions free from pain,

1. The Devil Tavern in Fleet Street (see *Dunciad* i. 325).
2. John Dennis (1657–6 Jan. 1734), dramatist and critic. He was abused by Pope (first in *An Essay on Criticism* iii. 25–8) and satirized by Swift (in his imitation of Horace, *Epist.* I. v). The name has been scored through by HW and then written in again above the line; Gray's writing, nevertheless, is legible.
3. Colloquial for sixpence.
4. Cf. *Rape of the Lock* iv. 45.
5. HW's pseudonym. Celadon, an amorous shepherd, was the hero of Honoré d'Urfé's voluminous pastoral romance, *L'Astrée.*
6. *Paradise Lost* i. 249.

Gay meads, and springing flowers best please the gentle swain.
   That little, naked, melancholy thing,
My soul,[7] when first she tried her flight to wing,
Began with speed new regions to explore,
And blundered through a narrow postern door:
   First most devoutly having said its prayers,
It tumbled down a thousand pair of ⟨stairs⟩;[8]
Through entries long, through cellars vast and deep,
Where ghostly rats their habitations keep,
Where spiders spread their webs, and owlish goblins sleep.
After so many chances had befell,
It came into a mead of asphodel:
Betwixt the confines of the light and dark
It lies, of 'Lyzium the St James's Park:
Here spirit-beaux flutter along the Mall,
And shadows in disguise skate o'er the iced canal:
Here groves embowered, and more sequestered shades,
Frequented by the ghosts of ancient maids,
Are seen to rise: the melancholy scene
With gloomy haunts, and twilight walks between
Conceals the wayward band: here spend their time
Greensickness girls, that died in youthful prime,
Virgins forlorn, all drest in willow-green-i,
With Queen Elizabeth and Nicolini.
   More to reveal, or many words to use,
Would tire alike your patience and my muse.
Believe, that never was so faithful found
Queen Proserpine to Pluto under ground,
Or Cleopatra to her Marc Antony
As Orozmades to his Celadony.
   PS.
Lucrece for half a crown will show you fun,
But Mrs Oldfield[9] is become a nun.
Nobles and cits, Prince Pluto and his spouse
Flock to the ghost of Covent Garden house:[10]

---

7. Probably an imitation of the dying Hadrian's verses to his soul: 'Animula vagula blandula' (Ælianus Spartianus, *Life of the Emperor Hadrian*, tr. by William Maude, New York, 1900, p. 23; Matthew Prior, *Poems on Several Occasions*, ed. A. R. Waller, Cambridge, 1905, p. 101; see also Pope's 'Dying Christian to his Soul').

8. Piece cut out; the word is restored in pencil by HW.

9. Anne Oldfield (1683–1730), actress at Drury Lane; mistress of Arthur Mainwaring and of Charles Churchill (see *post* 28 Sept. 1739).

10. Opera at Covent Garden was on the decline because of the rivalry of the 'Opera

Plays, which were hissed above, below revive;
When dead applauded, that were damned alive.
The people, as in life, still keep their passions,
But differ something from the world in fashions.
Queen Artemisia[11] breakfasts on bohea,[12]
And Alexander[13] wears a ramillie.[14]

To GRAY, ca Friday 20 December 1734

Missing. Probably written in St James's Square, and carried to Gray by one of Sir Robert Walpole's footmen. See following letter.

From GRAY, Monday 23 December 1734

Printed from MS in Waller Collection.

The year date is conjectural, but the Peterhouse records show Gray to have been charged full commons for December 1734; whereas *post* 3 Jan. 1736 shows that Gray spent the Christmas season of 1735–6 in London. Gray's '24' is corrected to '23' because his attendance at St Mary's 'yesterday' must have occurred on the Sunday which in 1734 fell on 22 Dec.

Dec. 24 [23, 1734], Peterhouse.

<   >

AFTER having been very piously at St Mary's Church[1] yesterday, as I was coming home somebody told me that you was come, and that your servant had been to inquire for me; whereupon, throwing off all the prudery and reserve of a Cambridge student, in a great ecstasy, I run in a vast hurry to set the bells aringing, and kindle a thousand bonfires—when, amidst these convulsions of joy, I was stopped by one of our College, who informed me that a fine gentleman in a laced hat and scarlet stockings wanted me. So, you may conclude, as soon as I set eyes on him, I was ready to eat him for having your livery on; but he soon checked me by acquainting me 'twas not you that was come, but—your service. Now undoubtedly after being so terribly balked, one could not

of the Nobility' at the King's Theatre in the Haymarket (see *The Prompter* No. 13, 24 Dec. 1734).

11. Artemisa, the heroine of Rowe's *Ambitious Stepmother*, last acted at Drury Lane 26 Jan. 1722 (Nicoll, *Drama 1700–1750*, pp. 98, 350).

12. Considered, in the eighteenth century, the finest tea (OED; GM 1734, iv. 575).

13. Character in Lee's *Rival Queens*.

14. 'A wig having a long plait behind tied with a bow at top and bottom' (OED).

1. St Mary the Great, where the university sermons were preached on Sundays. On weekdays Gray would have attended chapel at Peterhouse.

have lived but by the help of hartshorn, Hungary-water,[2] and your journal, which gives one a greater flow of spirits, than ei⟨ther of them.⟩[3] ⟨ . . . , ⟩[4] nothing gave me half so much pleasure as to find that after the toil of the day was over, you could be so good as to throw away a moment in thinking of me, and had spirits enough left to make all the hideosities you underwent agreeable by describing them.—By all that's frightful, I was in agonies for you, when I saw you planted at the upper end of a table so elegantly set out; like the king of monsters in the fairy tales. Never was any one's curiosity half so much raised by a blot, as mine is by that in your diary. 'Tis so judicious a scratch, so genteel a blur, that I shall never be easy till I know what it conceals, no more than I shall be till I receive the things that are to come by word of mouth, which (if 'twere possible) would make me wish to see you more than ever. Sure[5] West is ⟨as⟩ much improved ⟨as he sa⟩y⟨s⟩[6] Plato[7] is, since you could have the ⟨con⟩science to persuade him to come to Cambridge.

To GRAY, ca Wednesday 25 December 1734

Missing. Probably written in St James's Square, and received by Gray the following day at midnight (post ca 29 Dec. 1734).

From GRAY, ca Sunday 29 December 1734

Printed from MS in Waller Collection.

Date conjectural. The reference to the 'hard frost' on the '26th instant' may be whimsical; no frost is reported in the newspapers. 'Next March' implies that the letter was written before February.

Address: ⟨To the Honourable Horatio⟩ Wal⟨pole Esq. at the house of t⟩he Right ⟨Honourable Sir Robert Wa⟩lpole in ⟨St James's Square, Lond⟩on.

2. 'Made of rosemary flowers infused in rectified spirit of wine, and thus distilled' (OED). It was used against apoplexy. In 1730 it was sold (at 1s. 3d. a half pint) at the Hungary Water Warehouse, Ludgate Hill (Fog's Weekly Journal 9 May 1730). See also Gergely Czuczor and János Fogarasi, Magyar Nyelv Szótára, Budapest, 1862–74, iv. 68 sub 'magyarviz.'

3. Piece cut out; emendation in pencil by HW.

4. Perhaps 'Dearest Celadon.'

5. This sentence has been heavily scored through by HW.

6. Gray apparently wrote 'you say,' and then altered it to 'he says.'

7. Not identified. He was an Etonian, at this time probably in London, and subsequently, in 1735, at Cambridge (post 9 Nov. 1735).

Prescript: You don't send me word when you think you shall come to Sarag.[1]

From St Peter's Charnel-house [ca Dec. 29, 1734].

Dear *Dimidium animæ meæ*,[2]

AS you take a great deal of pleasure in concluding that I am dead, and resolve not to let me live any longer; methinks you ought to be good to my ashes, and give 'em leave to rest in peace, but instead of that, whereas I ought to be divested of all human passions and forget the pleasures of your world, you must needs be diverting me, so that I made every nail in my coffin start with laughing. It happened that on the 26th instant at twelve of the clock at midnight, being a hard frost, I had wrapped myself up in my shroud very snug and warm, when in comes your letter, which (as I told you before) made me stretch my skeleton-jaws in such a horse-laugh that all the dead popped up their heads and stared. But to see the frowzy countenances of the creatures, especially one old Lady Carcase that made most hideous grimaces, and would needs tell me that I was a very uncivil person to disturb a woman of her quality, that did me the honour to lie so near me, and truly she had not been in such a surprise this threescore and ten year come next March; besides, her commode was discomposed, and in her hurry she had lost her wedding-ring, which she was buried in; nay, she said, she believed she should fall in fits, and certainly that would be her death. But I gave her a Rowland for her Oliver,[3] egad: I told her Ladyship the more she stirred, the more she'd stink, and that, to my knowledge, though she put a good face upon the matter, she was not sound. So she laid her down very quietly, and crept under her winding-sheet for fear of spirits. Now your arrival only can deliver me from such a state of separation; for, as your soul is large enough to serve for both of us, it will be ill-natured of you if you don't re-animate my corpse. At least I hope for a place in your heart, as formerly; though, by your last letter

---

1. Crossed out by HW, who wrote 'Cambr.' below. Gray, immersed in oriental lore (see *post* 6 Jan. 1735), is perhaps playing upon the name of the ancient city of Saraka in southern Arabia (Ptolemy, *Geogr.* VI. vii. 41), whence the Saracens took their name, and so might be comparing Cambridge to a dead city in the desert. See *Paulys Real-Encyclopädie der classischen*

Altertumswissenschaft, Stuttgart, 1894–, 2d ser. i pt ii. 2387–8.

2. Horace, *Carm.* I. iii. 8.

3. 'If I do not give every foreigner a Rowland for every Oliver, I shall be very much mistaken' (*True Briton* No. 63, 6 Jan. 1724). See also *1 Henry VI* I. ii. 30; Southerne, *Oroonoko* II. i.

but one, it seems you have either forgot yourself, or entertain a less favourable opinion of me than that with which you once honoured

Your friend, the defunct ⟨   ⟩

As my letter ends so prettily in that p . . .⁴

From GRAY, Monday 6 January 1735

Printed from MS in Waller Collection.
Dated by the probable reference to Epiphany, and the two fragments of the ad-
dress (see *ante* 16 April 1734, n. 1).
  Address: ⟨To the Honourable Horace Walpo⟩le ⟨Esq. at his house in St
Jam⟩es⟨'s Square, London.⟩

[Cambridge, Jan. 6, 1735.]

To the faithful Miradolin,¹
third son of the Vizier-azem,²
continuance of health and long life.³

WHEN the dew of the morning⁴ is upon me, thy image is before
mine eyes; nor when the night overshadoweth me dost thou de-
part from me. Shall I ne'er behold thine eyes until our eternal meeting
in the immortal chioses of paradise?⁵ And sure at that hour, thy soul

4. The rest of this leaf has been torn away, carrying with it the greater part of the address.

---

1. The late Professor Edward Bensly first traced most of the oriental names and images of this letter to the *Letters writ by a Turkish Spy, who lived Five and Forty Years, undiscovered, at Paris*, 1687–93, an adaptation and continuation of Giovanni Paolo Marana's *L'Espion du Grand Seigneur*, Paris, 1684 (also published in Italian the same year), by William Bradshaw and Robert Midgley (*Gray's Corr.* i. 14–16; Bolton Corney, 'Authorship of the Turkish Spy,' GM 1841, n.s. xv pt i. 265–70. For the influence of the *Turkish Spy* see Martha Pike Conant, *The Oriental Tale in England in the Eighteenth Century*, New York, 1908, xvii. 157–63). The 22d edn of the *Turkish Spy* was published in 1734. HW's copy was sold SH iii. 79. For HW's 'Thamas Kouli Kan, Schah Nadir, to Henry Clinton

Earl of Lincoln' (HW, Waldegrave MSS 2.68–70), written in 1743 in the style of the *Turkish Spy*, see HW to Mann 13 Feb. 1743, O.S.
  Several letters in the *Turkish Spy* are addressed 'To Mirmadolin, Santone of the Vale of Sidon' (*Turkish Spy*, edn 1702, vol. VI, bk ii, letter 6; p. 67, and *passim*). 'Santone' in Turkish means a holy man, or hermit. Many of Gray's images are not borrowings but adaptations and analogies.
  2. More than a score of letters are addressed 'To the invincible Vizir Azem' (*Turkish Spy* I. i. 7; p. 11, and *passim*), the 'principal minister of the empire, favoured of God' (ibid. I. iii. 20; p. 209). HW was Sir Robert's third son.
  3. ' 'Tis a common aphorism that health, long life, and honour descend from above' (ibid. IV. iii. 6; p. 184).
  4. 'The wholesome and fragrant dew of the morning' (ibid. IV. i. 18; p. 64).
  5. 'A little chiose or bower'; 'the delec-

will have little need of ablution in the sight of Israphiel,[6] the Angel of Examination. Surely, it is pure as the snow on Mount Ararat and beautiful as the cheeks of the houries. The feast of Ramadan[7] is now passed away, and thou thinkest not of leaving Candahar:[8] what shall I say unto thee, thou unkind one? Thou hast lost me in oblivion, and I am become as one whom thou never didst remember. Before, we were as two palm-trees[9] in the Vale of Medina;[10] I flourished in thy friendship, and bore my head aloft, but now I wander in solitariness, as a traveller in the sandy deserts of Barca,[11] and pine in vain to taste of the living fountain of thy conversation. I have beheld thee in my slumbers, I have attempted to seize on thee, I sought for thee, and behold, thou wert not there! Thou wert departed as the smoke, or as the shadows, when the sun entereth his bedchamber. Were I to behold thy countenance, though afar off, my heart should bound as the antelope; yea, my soul should be as light as the roe-buck on the hills of Erzerom. I swear by Abubekir,[12] thou art sweet in my thoughts as the pineapple of Damascus to the taste, and more refreshing than the fragrant breezes of Idumea. The chain of destiny has linked me unto thee, and the mark which Gabriel stamped on my forehead at my nativity was born for Miradolin. Let not the Demon Negidher[13] separate us, nor the evil Tagot interpose between us. Be thou unto me as Mohammed to Ajesha,[14] as the bowers of Admoim[15] to those whom the sun hath over-

table chioses of paradise'; 'the chioses of Eden on the banks of immortal streams' (ibid. IV. i. 9; p. 28, VI. iii. 13; p. 175, and V. iii. 8; p. 151). OED does not record this spelling under 'kiosk.'

6. The name occurs in a list of the archangels, 'Gabriel, the friend of the prophet, . . . Michael, Israphiel, and the Messenger of Death,' and in an account of Gabriel's and Israphiel's visit to the tomb of the prophet (ibid. V. iii. 8; p. 151, and ibid. VIII. ii. 9; pp. 77–8). Israfil, the third archangel, preceded Gabriel as the companion of Mohammed. According to one Moslem tradition, which Gray apparently follows, Israfil is the four-winged archangel who reads the tablets of destiny and is ready to receive the souls of men (Encyclopædia of Islam, Leyden, 1913–38).

7. Christmas. During the thirty days of Ramadan, the ninth month of the Mohammedan calendar, the faithful fast throughout the day, and feast at night (Koran ii. 179–83).

8. London. 'The description thou hast made of Candahar . . . that impregnable city' (Turkish Spy III. ii. 21; p. 167).

9. 'The righteous shall flourish like the palm tree' (Psalms xcii. 12).

10. 'O Medina Telnabi! How sweet is thy name among the Mussulmans!' (Turkish Spy VIII. ii. 9; p. 78).

11. 'The parching deserts of Arabia' (ibid. V. i. 1; p. 4).

12. Abū Bekr 'Abd Allāh (d. 634), the first caliph, one of Mohammed's fathers-in-law. Gray's spelling rests on the letter addressed to 'Abubechir Hali, merchant in Aleppo' (ibid. III. ii. 13; p. 144).

13. Negidher, the spirit of envy, and Tagot appear in the Turkish Spy VI. ii. 17; p. 112.

14. 'Ā'isha Bint Abī Bekr (ca 614–78), dau. of Abū Bekr 'Abd Allāh, was one of Mohammed's favourite wives.

15. 'Let thy heart be like the valley of Admoim, fragrant as a grove of spices'

taken, or as the costly sherbets of Stamboul[16] to the thirsty. The grace
of providence and the smiles of heaven be upon thee. My white angels
guard thee from the efforts of the rebellious genii.

Adieu,

OROZMADES

The last day of the Ramadan,
6th of the 1st moon.[17]

To GRAY, ca Thursday 9 January 1735

Missing. Mentioned *post* 12 Jan. 1735. Probably written in St James's Square in
reply to *ante* 6 Jan. 1735, which, unless sent by messenger, would not have reached
HW before Wednesday morning, as the post left Cambridge Tuesday night. HW's
reply probably reached Gray by Friday.

From GRAY, Sunday 12 January 1735

Printed from MS in Waller Collection.
Address: To the Honourable Horace Walpole Esq. at his house in St. James's
Square, London. *Postmark:* SAFFRON WALDEN[1] 13 IA.

[Cambridge,] Jan. 12 [1735].

> How severe is forgetful old age
> To confine a poor devil so?
> That I almost despair
> To see even the air;
> Much more my dear Damon—hey ho![2]

THOU dear envious imp, to set me a-longing with accounts of
plays and operas and masquerades, after hearing of which I can no
more think of logic and stuff than you could of divinity at a ball, or of
caudle and caraway-comfits after having been stuffed at a christening.

(ibid. V. i. 10; pp. 39–40). See also ibid. VII.
ii. 21; p. 93.
  16. 'The wholesome sherbets of Asia'
(ibid. II. iii. 36; p. 280).
  17. I.e. Jan. 6, Epiphany, the last day of
the Christmas holidays, not the 30th of
Ramadan which, in 1735, fell on 23 Feb.
(see Sir Wolseley Haig, *Comparative Tables
of Muhammadan and Christian Dates*,
1932). Gray imitates such formulæ as 'Paris,

15th of the 11th moon, of the year 1637'
(*Turkish Spy* I. i. 8; p. 17, and *passim*).

  1. Letters from Cambridge to London
were sometimes postmarked at the nearby
post towns of Saffron Walden or Royston.
  2. The first stanza of 'Song of Hey ho,' in
the *Fourth Part of Miscellany Poems . . .
by the Most Eminent Hands*, 5th edn, 1727,
p. 116. In line 2, read 'lover' for 'devil.'

Heaven knows! we have nobody in our college that has seen London, but one, and he, I believe, comes out of Vinegar Yard, and looks like toasted Cheshire cheese strewed with brown sugar. I beg you, give me the minutest circumstances of your diversions and your indiversions; though if it is as great a trouble to you to write as it is a pleasure to me to get 'em by heart, I fear I shan't hear from you once in a twelvemonth, and dear now, be very punctual and very long. If I had the least particle of pleasure you should know it, and so you should if I had anything troublesome, though in Cambridge there is nothing so troublesome as that one has nothing to trouble one. Everything is so tediously regular, so samish, that I expire for want of a little variety. I am just as I was, and so is everything about me. I hope you'll forgive my formality, in being just the same friend of yours, and just the same servant,

OROZMADES

From GRAY, Tuesday 14 January 1735

Printed from MS in Waller Collection.
Dated by the postmark, the address, and the reference to the *Epistle to Dr Arbuthnot*.
Address: To the Honourable Mr Horace Walpole at the house of the Right Honourable Sir Robert Walpole in St James's Square, London.
Postmark: CAMBRIDGE 15 IA.

[Cambridge, Jan. 14, 1735.]

Tityre, dum patulæ recubo sub tegmine fagi.[1]

THOUGH you'll think perhaps it's a little too cold weather for giving oneself languishing airs under a tree, however supposing it's by the fireside, it will be full as well; so as I was going to say—but, I believe, I was going to say nothing, so I must begin over again—

My dearest Celadon,[2]

Yesterday morning (being the morning I set apart for lying abed till one o'clock), I was waked about ten with hollowing and the noise of a bagpipe at the door; so I got up, and opened the door, and saw all the court full of strange appearances. At first I concluded 'twas you with a whole masquerade at your heels, but upon more mature deliberation

1. 'Tityre, tu patulæ recubans sub tegmine fagi' (Virgil, *Ecl.* i. 1). 2. Scored through in MS, but the phrase is legible.

imagined it might be Amadis de Gaul come to set me free from this enchanted castle, with his train of conquered monsters and oddities.[3] The first, whom I took for the knight in person, had his face painted after the manner of the ancient Britons;[4] he played melodiously on the aforenamed instrument, and had a plough[5] upon his back. What it meant, I did not apprehend at first; he said nothing at all, but made many very significant grimaces. Before him, and on each side, a number of folks, covered over with tags and points, formed themselves into a country-dance. There followed something which I apprehended was the beauteous Oriana,[6] in a white dimity petticoat and bodice; her head and face were veiled. She was supported by her two gentlemen-ushers, and seemed to be very obstreperous, for she struggled and kicked, and snorted and fizzled. I concluded she was falling in fits, and was running with my Hungary-water bottle, when she was so violent that she got loose from her attendants and run away upon all fours into the middle of the court, and her hood falling off discovered a large pair of ears. In short, Oriana was metamorphosed into a very genteel jackass. Upon this the whole crowd set up a great shout of 'God speed the plough.' After all I was informed by a negro gentlewoman with a very long beard,[7] who had a great deal to do in the ceremony, that it was Plough Monday,[8] and that all this was the custom of the country; they march in this manner through all the colleges in town. The term is now begun again,[9] and I have made such a wonderful progress in philosophy, that I begin to be quite persuaded that black is white, and that fire will not burn, and that I ought not either to give credit to my eyes or feeling. They tell me too that I am nothing in the world, and that I only fancy I exist. Do but come to me quickly, and one lesson of thine, my dear philosopher, will restore me to the use of my senses, and make me think myself something, as long as I am,

Your friend and servant,

T. GRAY

3. Amadis delivers his brother, Don Galaor, from the castle on Dolorous Isle, ruled by the giant Madarque. Amadis is followed by Madarque, whom he has just conquered, and his dwarf Ardian (*Amadis de Gaule* iii. 2).

4. That is, blue.

5. Called the 'fool plough,' dragged by a procession of peasants on Plough Monday.

6. The heroine of *Amadis de Gaule*.

7. One of the men was dressed as a much-bedizened old woman and called 'Bessy' in Plough Monday processions (Robert Chambers, *Book of Days*, Edinburgh, 1863, i. 94–6).

8. The first Monday after Twelfth Night, i.e. 13 Jan. in 1735.

9. Lent Term began 13 Jan. (John Chamberlayne, *Magnæ Britanniæ Notitia*, 1735, i. 285).

PS. The enclosed is the oath of matriculation.¹⁰ I am charmed with Pope's letter¹¹—never did anybody long for anything, as I do for your masquerade;¹² pray d'ye design to go as a judge, or a devil, or undisguised, ⟨or as an angel in propria persona⟩.¹³ I wonder how you can dislike *The Distressed Mother*.¹⁴ ⟨   ⟩¹⁵

To GRAY, ca Friday 17 January 1735

Missing. Probably written in St James's Square. Mentioned *post* 19 Jan. 1735.

From GRAY, Sunday 19 January 1735

Printed from MS in Waller Collection.
Misdated by Gray. Dated by the postmark, the address, and the reference to the 'long Christmas' which Gray spent at Cambridge the previous year.
Address: To the Honourable Mr Horace Walpole at his house in St James's Square, London. *Postmark:* CAMBRIDGE 20 IA.

[Cambridge,] Sunday, Jan. 21 [19, 1735].

⟨   ⟩

YOU have performed your promise as fully as I could have wished it. There seems to have been no occasion for ushering it in with an apology, since I have long learned to be more than contented with whatever comes from a hand so dear. The things that are to be delivered by word of mouth¹ give me so much impatience that I would desire you to send down your mouth by the coach, if I were not appre-

10. Missing. On the day of matriculation (the second day of the term) each student was given a printed copy of the Latin matriculation oath by the vice-chancellor at the Senate House, where the oath was administered. For the text of the oath see Adam Wall, *Account of the Different Ceremonies Observed in the Senate House of the University of Cambridge*, Cambridge, 1798, p. 39; see also Gilbert Ainslie, *Historical Account of the Oaths and Subscriptions Required in the University of Cambridge on Matriculation*, Cambridge, 1833, p. 59.
11. The *Epistle to Dr Arbuthnot*, which was published 2 Jan. 1735 (*London Evening Post* 31 Dec. 1734–2 Jan. 1735).
12. That is, for HW's account of it: probably the first of three balls held at the

King's Theatre in the Haymarket this year (see *post* 19 Jan. 1735). 'At the King's Theatre in the Haymarket on Thursday next, being the 16th day of January, will be a ball. Tickets will be delivered to the subscribers on Wednesday next at White's Chocolate House in St James's Street' (*London Evening Post* 7–9 Jan. 1735). See also *Daily Adv.* 11 Jan., 14 Jan. 1735.
13. Heavily scored through by HW.
14. By Ambrose Philips (ca 1675–1749). HW probably attended the performance at Covent Garden on either 9 or 10 Jan. 1735 (*Daily Adv.* 9 Jan., 10 Jan. 1735).
15. A line cut out in MS.

1. HW left for King's College, Cambridge, 11 March 1735 (*ante* i. 5).

hensive what a loss it would be to the next masquerade, and what a dearth of pretty things it might occasion in town; however, I hope you'll not fail to send your thoughts by the post—without a mask. You are extremely good in making me a feast every other day; I have kept myself alive all this long Christmas by the help of your letters and a few mince pies, which an old gentlewoman[2] in this town sends me, and in whose favour I have made no small progress, I can assure you. You must know, I make my addresses to her by calling her 'Grandmother,' insomuch that she sends her niece every day to know how I do. N.B. The other ⟨day she⟩[3] was dying, as every one thought but herself, and when the physician told her how dangerous her case was, she fell into a violent passion with him: marry come up! she die! no indeed wouldn't she! die, quotha! she'd as soon be hanged! In short she was so resolutely bent upon not dying that she really did live, and is now as well as

Your sincerest friend,

OROZMADES

PS. Punch[4] is more smart than ordinary.

From Gray, Tuesday 21 January 1735

Printed from MS in Waller Collection.
Address: To the Honourable Mr Horace Walpole at the house of the Right Honourable Sir Robert Walpole in St James's Square, London.
Postmark: CAMBRIDGE 22 IA.

Tuesday, Jan. 21 [1735], P.C.[1]

I, OROZMADES, master of the noble science of defence,[2] hearing of the great reputation of thee, Timothy Celadon, do challenge and invite thee to contend with me at long-love, great-affection, or what-

2. Not identified.

3. Piece cut out; the words are restored in pencil by HW.

4. Although this may refer to an Eton contemporary, the allusion is probably to an incident at the ball or masquerade in the Haymarket on Thursday 16 Jan. (*ante* 14 Jan. 1735, n. 12). Gray may have read in the *Daily Advertiser,* 18 Jan. 1735, that Punch 'dispersed bills amongst the company of a puppet show of seven acts to be opened on Thursday next near Westminster.' The bill, which satirized Sir Robert

Walpole and his brother Horace, is quoted by Lord Egmont in Hist. MSS Comm., *Diary of the First Earl of Egmont,* 1920–3, ii. 145–6; see also *Fog's Weekly Journal* 25 Jan. 1735.

———

1. That is, Peterhouse (St Peter's College).

2. This challenge is imitated from *Spectator* No. 436. A genuine handbill in similar terms dated 3 July 1709, is quoted by W. B. Boulton in *Amusements of Old London,* 1901, i. 18.

ever other weapon you shall make choice of, in King's College Quadrangle, a week hence precisely.

Vivat Rex.

And that you may not fail me, I believe I shall see you at London beforehand; Almanzor persuades me, and I have a month's mind[3] to it myself, though I think it a foolish undertaking enough. Would you advise me to come, or not?[4] for I stand wavering. But pray, don't importune,[5] don't press, dear Sir Celadon. O Jesus![6] I believe, if you should importune, I shall—be very coming—if I do venture, I must borrow your disguise,[7] for nobody but you must know that I am in town. Well! be it as it will, you have got my soul with you already; I should think 'twould be better for you to bring it hither to the rest of me, than make my body take a journey to it; besides it would be cheaper to me, for that can come down in the coach with you, but my limbs must pay for their passage up. I hate living by halves, for now I lead such a kind of I don't know how—as it were—in short, what the devil d'ye mean by keeping me from myself so long? I expect to be paid with interest, and in a short time to be a whole thing, whereas, at this present writing, I am but a

Demi-Oroz.

From Gray, Monday 27 January 1735

Printed from MS in Waller Collection.
Address: To ⟨t⟩he Honourable Horace Walpole Esq. at the house of the ⟨R⟩ight
Honourable Sir Robert Walpole ⟨i⟩n St James's Square, London.

Jan. 27 [1735],[1] Rome[2] ⟨   ⟩.

My ⟨   ⟩[3]

DON'T believe that I would refuse to do anything for your sake, since at this present I am starving for you, and losing my dinner, that I may have the better opportunity of writing. You could not have

---

3. Foible, of Mrs Marwood: 'She has a month's mind; but I know Mr Mirabell can't abide her' (Congreve, *Way of the World* III. vi). HW planned to leave for King's 19 Feb. (*post* 25 Feb. 1735).
4. Gray remained at Cambridge (see next letter). He was charged full commons until about the end of July.
5. Lady Wishfort, of Sir Rowland: 'O then he'll importune, if he's a brisk man' (Congreve, *Way of the World* III. v).

6. HW first wrote 'Crimini' over this, but later restored 'Jesus' above the line.
7. An allusion to the masquerades of the previous letters.

1. Year added by Mason at heading of the letter.
2. Perhaps suggested by the pomp and circumstance attending the Senate House examinations (see below).
3. Probably 'My dear Celadon'; cut out.

given me a fairer occasion for showing my obedience to your commands than you have done in bidding me stay where I am, for though before I was quite set upon coming to town, you give me so many reasons against it that I am perfectly easy, and shall expect your coming with great resignation, that is, if you don't make it too long first. I read yesterday in the news[4] that Sir R.W.'s youngest son, a young gentleman of great hopes, was coming to Trinity College, Cambridge; pray, let me know whether you are acquainted with him, and what hopes we may entertain of him; there are few here but what give a good character of him, especially a long, ungainly mortal[5] of King's College and a little, waddling freshman[6] of Peterhouse, who pretend to be intimate with him. I can't see how it should be, but, however, everybody begins to envy the⟨m already; they are p⟩eople of very bad repute; one of 'em is neither a Whig nor a Tory, and the other passes for a conjurer. There is nothing to be seen in the streets at present but new-made bachelors, who walk to and fro to show their new gowns; their examination is now over,[7] during which time they are obliged to set in the Theatre[8] for three days, from eight in the morning till five at night, without any fire; the first two days they are liable to all the impertinent questions which any master of arts is pleased to ask them;[9] they must answer everything in philosophy which is proposed to them, and all this in Latin. The third day the first moderator[10] takes 'em out, half a dozen at a time, into a gallery atop of the Theatre, in sight of everybody but out of hearing; he examines them again as long as he will, and in what sciences he pleases. The junior moderator does the same thing in the afternoon, and then both the proctors, if they have a mind, but they seldom do. The next day the vice-chancellor and two proctors tell them whether they shall have their degrees or not, and put on their bachelor's gown and cap.[11] Then they go all into the schools,[12] and one fel-

4. Not located.
5. Ashton.
6. Gray himself.
7. The Senate House examinations began the first Monday in Lent Term, that is, 13 Jan. of this year (Adam Wall, *Account of the Different Ceremonies observed in the Senate House of the University of Cambridge*, Cambridge, 1798, p. 43).
8. Another name for the Senate House (Edmund Carter, *History of the University of Cambridge*, 1753, p. 13).
9. Richard Cumberland (B.A. Cantab. 1750) states in his *Memoirs*, 1807, i. 105: 'It was hardly my lot during that examination to enjoy any respite. I seemed an object singled out as every man's mark, and was kept perpetually at the table under the process of question and answer.'
10. For this, and the other Cambridge officers, see *Historical Register of . . . Cambridge*, ed. J. R. Tanner, Cambridge, 1917, p. 438.
11. Called 'huddling' (Christopher Wordsworth, *Scholæ Academicæ*, Cambridge, 1877, pp. 59–61).
12. The sophs' schools (ibid. 22–31, 60–1).

low[13] belonging to each of the colleges gets into the rostrum and asks each of his bachelors some strange question. This was one, which was asked t'other day: *Mi fili, Domine, Domine N., quid est matrimonium?* The answer was, *Est conjunctio nunc copulativa, nunc disjunctiva.* So then everybody must laugh, and the ceremony is ended. I tell you this because it will be mine own case some time or other, so I hope you will excuse me for tiring you with the account. And now, my dearest Hamlet, heaven send me safe from Wittemberg, or thee ⟨   ⟩

PS. My letter last time was too late for the post, so I hope you'll forgive it.

From Gray, Tuesday 4 February 1735

Printed from MS in Waller Collection.
Dated by the postmark and the address.
Address: ⟨To⟩ the H⟨onourable Horace Wal⟩pole Esq. a⟨t his house in St⟩ James's Squa⟨re, London⟩. *Postmark:* 5 FE.

[Cambridge, Feb. 4, 1735.]

⟨   ⟩

I HAVE so little to write and so much to say that, when you really do come, you may expect for the first fortnight to do nothing but hearken to my questions, and to spend the next month in answering them: nay, I assure you, I limit the time only that you may rest a while to take breath, otherwise I could listen to you for the whole two years[1] with an infinite deal of pleasure. I am forming the image to myself of your journey hither. I suppose you will come down Essex way, and if you do, first you must cross Epping Forest, and there you must be robbed.[2] Then you go a long way, and at last you come to Gogmagog

---

13. Called the 'father' (*Cambridge University Calendar 1802*, p. xlvii).

1. HW apparently intended to stay only two years, since 'noblemen or *tanquam nobiles*' could proceed to the degree of M.A. after being 'members of the university of two years' standing or more' (*post* 3 July 1735, n. 5). Actually he stayed 'though with long intervals, till towards the end of 1738, and did not leave it in form till 1739' (*ante* i. 8).
2. Since December 1734 a great number

of robberies had been committed by a gang of deer-stealers 'lurking about Epping Forest,' who, under the leadership of Dick Turpin, of Epping, turned highwaymen and housebreakers. They were known as the 'Essex Gang.' Seven of them were arrested by the end of February and were subsequently condemned to death, while the rest were thought to have been dispersed by the beginning of March. Dick Turpin escaped, and was not executed until 7 April 1739 (*London Evening Post* 21 Dec. 1734—11 March 1735, *passim*; see also

Hills,[3] and then you must be overturned. I hope you have not hurt yourself. But you must come at last to Foulmoor Fields,[4] and then you must fall squash into a bog; pray, don't be frighted for in about an hour and half you may chance to get out. Now perhaps if it is not dark you m⟨ay see the⟩[5] top of King's Chapel, though if it should be night it is very likely you won't be able to see at all. However, at last you get into Cambridge, all bemudded and tired, with three wheels and a half to the coach, four horses lame, and two blind. The first thing that appears is a row of almshouses;[6] and presently on the right hand you'll see a thing like two Presbyterian meeting-houses,[7] with the back side of a little church[8] between them, and here you must find out by sympathy that this is Peterhouse, and that I am but a little way off. I shall soon feel how near you are; then you should say—no, no, I should say—but I believe I shall be too much overjoyed to say anything. Well, be that as it will, I still hope you will be almost as much so: dear Sir, you are welcome to Cambridge. What d'ye think? Pilk Hale[9] about three months ago had a great inclination to visit Malepert,[10] but thought it would not be well-bred not to let him know it beforehand, and being at a loss who he should send, I persuaded him to go himself and let him know Mr Hale would wait upon him in the afternoon. And so he did. Mal. promised to return it very soon, and ever since the other has stayed at home with all his fine things set out to the best advantage, and is quite sure he'll come and expects him every hour ⟨   ⟩.

GM 1735, v. 106, 162; New Newgate Calendar, ed. Andrew Knapp and William Baldwin, 1809–10, i. 546–59; Complete Newgate Calendar, ed. G. T. Crook, 1926, iii. 88–92).

3. Four miles SE of Cambridge. 'The badness of the way in that place' was remedied by the completion of a new four-mile road from Cambridge to Gogmagog Hills (Daniel Defoe, A Tour through . . . Great Britain, 2d edn, 'with very great additions . . . which bring it down to the beginning of the year 1738,' 1738, i. 101).

4. A mere, now drained, nine miles south of Cambridge, on the Cambridge-Barkway road. The Essex road did not pass through Fowlmere.

5. Words supplied in pencil by HW.

6. Possibly the Perse Almshouses (since removed to Newnham Street) on the southern corner of the old Botanic Gardens and Free School Lane. See the map of Cambridge in Daniel and Samuel Lysons, Magna Britannia ii, 1808, pt i. 100; Thomas D. Atkinson and John W. Clark, Cambridge Described and Illustrated, 1897, p. 202.

7. Facing south on Trumpington Street. The first building, a range of chambers, was pulled down ca 1738 to make room for the 'New Building,' where Gray lived after his return from Italy. The second was the library. See Willis and Clark i. 34–6.

8. Peterhouse Chapel.

9. Probably William Hale (1716–93), admitted pensioner at Peterhouse 12 July 1734, who, as a descendant of Bernard Hale, Master of Peterhouse 1660–3, nominated Gray to a Hale Scholarship, worth £13 6s. 8d. a year, which Gray held from 27 June 1735 throughout his undergraduate years at Peterhouse (T. A. Walker, Admissions to Peterhouse, Cambridge, 1912, p. 268; idem, 'Thomas Gray in Peterhouse,' Athenæum, 1906, i. 76; Eton Coll. Reg.).

10. Probably another Etonian.

To Gray, February 1735

Missing. Probably written in St James's Square. A letter concerning HW's departure for Cambridge Thursday 27 Feb. 1735 (postponed from Wednesday 19 Feb.) is implied in *post* 25 Feb. 1735, *post* 5 March 1735. The letter referred to as 'your last letter . . . directed to me at King's College' (*post* 5 March 1735) is probably the same one.

From Gray, Tuesday 25 February 1735

Printed from MS in Waller Collection.
Address: To the Honourable Mr Horace Walpole at his house ⟨in⟩ St James's Square, Londo⟨n.⟩ *Postmark:* CAMBRIDGE 26 FE.

Feb. 25 [1735], Pet. Col.

May it please your We-ship,

IN consideration of the time your petitioner has passed in your Honour's service, as also on account of the great services your petitioner's relations have had the honour to perform for your Honour's ancestors; since it is well-known that your petitioner's grandmother's aunt's cousin-german had the honour to pull out your Honour's great-uncle's wife's brother's hollow tooth; as also, to go further backwards, your petitioner's relation was physician to King Cadwallader,[1] one of your Highness's forefathers, and cured him of a fish's bone, which had stuck in his throat fifteen years and three days, and would neither come up nor down; also the Emperor Maximus,[2] a very near relation of your Serene Haughtiness's, entertained your petitioner's progenitor in his army as a jester, who is said to have had so much wit that he could devour ten peck-loaves at a meal, and toss off as many hogsheads of strong beer without taking breath: I could enumerate more than all this, but hope this will be sufficient to prevail upon your generosity to make me your first minister and confidant.

1. Cadwaladr (d. 682), 'last King of the Britons' (*Annales Cambriæ*, ed. John Williams, 1860, p. 8). Gray probably refers to the pedigree presented ca 1723 by HW's cousin John Philipps (later 6th Bt) to HW's brother Robert. This chart (now WSL) traces the descent of HW's maternal grandmother, Elizabeth, dau. of Sir Erasmus Philipps, 3d Bt, of Picton Castle, from Rhys ap Gruffydd (d. 1197), Prince of South Wales, Cadwaladr's lineal descendant. See Montagu i. 69, n. 14.

2. Magnus Maximus (d. 388), a Spaniard, general of the Roman troops in Britain, ca 369; usurper of the imperial throne 383–8 (*Paulys Real-Encyclopädie der classischen Altertumswissenschaft*, Stuttgart, 1894–); Sir John Philipps's alleged ancestor (Montagu i. 69; Burke, *Peerage*, 1928, *sub* St David's).

And your petitioner shall *ever pray*.

Thou hast been for this month like an auctioneer's mallet, just a-coming! just a-coming! And pray, what has next Thursday in it more than last Wednesday to make me expect you with any tolerable certainty? When these two eyes behold thee I question whether I shall believe them. Three long months is a long while for a poor lone woman[3] to bear; and I have borne, and borne, and been fubbed off, and fubbed off, from this day to that day by you, thou honey-suckle villain (as Mrs Quickly says). Oh! thou art an infinitive thing upon my score of impatience.[4] Remember you are a day in my debt for every hour you have made me wait, and I shall come upon you for the payment, and perhaps with interest—I begin to bear my crest aloft when I hear of your pride. I dare not tell T. Ashton[5] anything about it, for he hopes to see you behave with great affability to everybody, and you'll have many lectures upon that subject. I begin to pity the poor man that is to be with you.[6] He is extremely modest, and as humble as you could wish; you may snub him with a look; I fancy he will intrude very little. Make haste and pack up your things; the coach is at the door; drive away to ⟨   ⟩[7]

From Gray, Wednesday 5 March 1735

Printed from MS in Waller Collection.
Dated by Mason: 1735.
Address: To the Honourable ⟨Mr Horace⟩ Walpole at ⟨his house in⟩ St James's ⟨Square, London⟩.

March 5 [1735], Cambridge.

⟨   ⟩

IF you please to remember that about a fortnight ago you sent me to Almanzor's room, there to wait for you, and there it seems I might have stayed till this time, and been never the nearer. After all this, I see nothing should hinder but that about the 29th of next February there may be some small probability of your being just a-going to think of

3. Altered by HW to 'creature.'
4. Mrs Quickly, of Falstaff: 'He's an infinitive thing upon my score. . . . A hundred mark is a long one for a poor lone woman to bear; and I have borne, and borne, and borne; and have been fubbed off, and fubbed off, and fubbed off, from this day to that day, . . . Ah, thou honey-suckle villain!' (2 *Henry IV* II. i). See also *ante* 16 April 1734.
5. Scored through, but easily decipherable.
6. Probably Gray alludes either to HW's servant at Cambridge or to his tutor.
7. Piece cut out.

setting out on the 29th of February, Anno Domini 1737, at which time your humble servant will most punctually meet you. But in the mean time I would advise with you how Almanzor and I shall pass the time: whether you think it best for us to double ourselves up nicely in the corner of some old draw,[1] that, at your arrival, we may come out spick and span new in all our pleats (but perhaps by that time we may grow out of fashion, or moth-eaten), or to compose ourselves with a good dose of laudanum for a year or two, and so dream of you; ⟨but then you may⟩[2] find it too hard a matter to wake us, or perhaps you will let us lie and snore on till Doomsday. Prithee don't mind finances[3] and my Lord Chancellor,[4] but make haste hither. Oh! I forgot how obligingly in your last letter[5] to me you let us both know that you did not care a farthing whether you saw us this twelvemonth, for I imagine you meant it to both, because it was directed to me at King's College. I own I quite believe you, but did not think you would mortify me so much as to tell me so; however I have learned to be pleased with anything that comes from you, and still try to persuade myself that you would think Cambridge more disagreeable without than you will with

Yours most faithfully,

⟨Orozmades⟩

To Gray, June 1735

Missing. Probably written in St James's Square. HW informed Gray of his projected visit to Houghton (post 3 July 1735).

From Gray, Thursday 3 July 1735

Printed from MS in Waller Collection.
Dated by the postmark and the address.
Address: To the Honourable Horace Walpole Esq. in St James's Square, London. *Postmark:* CAMBRIDGE 4 IY.

1. I.e., drawer.
2. Piece cut out; the words are restored in pencil by HW.
3. HW had no independent income until the end of 1737 (*post* 29 Dec. 1737; Montagu i. 9).
4. Not explained. Lord Talbot, then Lord Chancellor, was at odds with Sir Robert Walpole over the bishopric of Glouces-

ter. See Hervey, *Memoirs* ii. 399–405; Hist. MSS Comm., *Diary of the First Earl of Egmont*, 1920–3, ii. 137–8, 151. Sir Owen Morshead has suggested that Gray may allude to the Chancellor of Cambridge (the Duke of Somerset) who was notorious for his pride.
5. Probably the second letter above, missing.

[Cambridge,] July 3d [1735].

My dearest Horace,

D*ONEC gratus eram tibi.*[1]
I was happier than Dr Heighington[2] or his wife Lydia;[3] however I find being from you agrees as ill with me as if I never had felt your absence before. I have composed a hymn about it mighty moving, and thrum it perpetually, for I've changed my harp into a harpsichord and am as melodious as the day is long. I am sorry I can give you no further information about Mr Cornwallis;[4] there was a congregation held yesterday, but nothing further done about his degree[5] for the present. I received a long letter, mighty pretty, in Latin, from West yesterday,[6] partly about buttered turnips, partly about an eclipse, that I understood no more than the man in the moon; he desired his love to you in English. I wish a great deal of happiness to you, a good journey to Houghton,[7] and a more entertaining companion than

Yours most sincerely,

T. GRAY

1. Horace, *Carm.* III. ix. 1.
2. Musgrave Heighington (1679–ca 1774), organist and composer (see DNB; Robert Surtees, *History and Antiquities of . . . Durham*, 1816–40, i. 99; Charles J. Palmer, *Perlustration of Great Yarmouth*, 1872–5, i. 383). While organist at Yarmouth, he gave concerts at Spalding, assisted by his wife and son (Nichols, *Lit. Anec.* vi. 11–12), and at Houghton.
3. Anne Conway, presumably a relative of HW's cousin Henry Seymour Conway, m. (before 1733, probably in Dublin where their son, Conway, was born) Musgrave Heighington (Surtees, op. cit. i. 99). 'Lydia' is one of the speakers in the ode which Gray quotes and which is included in Heighington's *Six Select Odes of Anacreon in Greek and Three of Horace in Latin, set to Music* (?1745), dedicated to Robert, 2d E. of Orford. These odes were 'chiefly composed for the private entertainment, and some of them by the particular command of your Lordship's noble father, under whose patronage, had fate permitted, they were designed to appear in public.' Gray no

doubt heard of the adaptation of the ode from HW. Among the subscribers to the *Six Select Odes* are HW and several Walpoles and Conways. HW's copy of the 'Odes of Horace, set to music by Dr M. Heighington' was sold London 1057.
4. Hon. Frederick Cornwallis (1713–83), at Eton 1725–8; admitted pensioner at Christ's College, Cambridge, 9 Feb. 1732; fellow 1738 (see *post* 20 March 1738); Canon of Windsor 1746; Bp of Lichfield 1750–68; Dean of St Paul's 1766–8; Abp of Canterbury 1768–83 (*Eton Coll. Reg.*; Venn, *Alumni Cantab.*).
5. Presumably his M.A., for which, as a nobleman's son, he could apply after being a member of the university for two years or more.
6. Missing.
7. Houghton Hall, Sir Robert Walpole's Norfolk seat, described in HW's *Ædes Walpolianæ*, 1747, and in Daniel Defoe, *Tour through . . . Great Britain*, 2d edn, 1738, i. 81–3. Sir Robert left London for Houghton 11 July (*London Daily Post* 11 July 1735).

To Gray, ca Wednesday 15 October 1735

Printed from MS in the Pierpont Morgan Library, formerly in the possession of Sir Thomas Villiers Lister. For the history of the Lister Collection see Berry i. p. xxxiii.

Endorsed by HW: To Mr Gray.

Dated by the apparent duration of HW's journey to Cambridge. HW left London 9 Oct., reached Newmarket the next day, and spent three days there (see below). Evidently written on HW's arrival at Cambridge. HW's notes are written in the margin.

From Cambridge [ca Oct. 15], 1735.
In the style of Addison's Travels.[1]

Dear Sir,

I BELIEVE you saw in the newspapers that I was going to make the tour of Italy,[2] I shall therefore give you some account of the places I have seen which are not to be found in Mr Addison, whose method I shall follow. On 9th of October 1735 we set out from Lodone[3] (the Lugdunum of the ancients) the capital city of Lombardy in a chariot and four. About 11 o'clock, we arrived at a place the Italians call Tempialbulo.[4] Virgil seems to have prophesied of this town, when he says,

Amisit verum vetus Albula nomen.[5]

By Time the founder's great design was crossed,
And Albula its genuine title lost.

Here are no remains of Roman antiquity, but a statue of Marc Aurelius,[6] which the Lombards call Guglielmo Terzo one of their kings, and some learned men,[7] St George and the Dragon. It is an equestrian

1. *Remarks on Several Parts of Italy*, first published in 1705. HW's copy, 3d edn, 1726 (now WSL) was sold SH iii. 156. The press-mark is K.5.21, and it was evidently bought by HW at Eton when he bought Addison's other works, as appears from his signature and the date 1729 which he inscribed on a fly-leaf of the first volume of Addison's *Miscellaneous Works*, 1726 (press-marks K.5.18–20).

2. 'Horatio Walpole, Esq., third son to Sir Robert Walpole, is going to make the tour of Italy, with a governor and two servants' (*London Evening Post* 4–7 Oct. 1735).

3. 'London' (HW). 'Lombardy' in the next line is possibly an allusion to Lombard Street. The places mentioned in this letter are on the London-Newmarket road.

4. 'White Chapel' (HW).

5. Virgil, *Æneid* viii. 332.

6. 'Statue of King William at a stone-cutter's' (HW). A pedestal for an equestrian statue of William III had been erected in St James's Square in 1732, but no statue was completed for it until 1808 (*London Past and Present* ii. 302; see also A. I. Dasent, *The History of St James's Square*, 1895, pp. 51–2, 59). HW's note suggests that the cutting of an earlier statue was at least commenced.

7. 'See Addis[on's] *Trav[els]*, p. 26' (HW). 'In Pavia . . . is likewise a statue in brass of Marcus Antoninus on horseback, which the people of the place call Charles the Fifth, and some learned men Constantine the Great.'

statue, and almost equal to that of Charlemagne, at the Great Cross[8] at Lodone. The church[9] is an old Gothic building, and reckoned the most ancient in Italy. Here was some time ago an altar-piece of the Lord's Supper, in which the painter[10] having quarrelled with the abbot[11] of this church, represented him like Judas, with this epigram:

Falleris, hac qui te pingi sub imagine credis,
  Non similis Judas est tibi—pœnituit.[12]

Think not, vain man, thou here art represented,
Thou art not like to Judas—he repented.

From thence we made the best of our way to a town, which in English we should call Stony-Stratford,[13] and corresponds with the description which Virgil has given of it—

—vivo præter vehor ostia saxo
Straffordi, Megarosque sinus, Tapsumque iacentem.[14]

Those that follow are little dirty towns, that seem to have been built only to be knocked on the head,[15] like

Antitheum, Glaucumque, Medontaque, Thersilochumque.[16]

The next town of note is Arc,[17] so called from its being built in the

8. 'Statue of King Charles [I] at Charing Cross' (HW), by Hubert Le Sueur (d. 1670). 'On horseback, bigger than the life, done in brass, standing on a high pedestal of white marble, curiously adorned with warlike trophies, all encircled with iron bars or rails: which said statue was made by that famous statuary Laseur' (Robert Seymour, *Survey of the Cities of London and Westminster*, 1733–5, ii. 656).

9. St Mary Matfelon or St Mary's, Whitechapel, built before 1329 (Wilberforce Jenkinson, *London Churches before the Great Fire*, 1917, pp. 271–2), enlarged in 1591, and rebuilt in 1673–5 (*London Past and Present* ii. 503).

10. James Fellowes (fl. 1710–30).

11. 'Dr White Kennet [1660–1728] Bishop of Peterborough' (HW). HW's version of this story is inaccurate. Fellowes had no quarrel with Kennett, but was commissioned to paint him as Judas, in an altarpiece, by Richard Welton (ca 1672–1726), D.D., rector of St Mary Matfelon and a non-juror. See William Newton, *Life of Dr White Kennett*, 1730, p. 140.

12. These lines, together with a third

one, 'Sed Judæ similem si vis, te reddere,' were sent to Dean Kennett 'upon its [the altar-piece] being taken down.' From a 'News Letter. 1714, May 6. London' in the Portland papers (Hist. MSS Comm., *Report on the Manuscripts of . . . the Duke of Portland* v. 435).

13. Perhaps referring to the stone pillars of the bridge over the Lea, at the entrance (*ostium*) of Stratford, Essex. There is, of course, a town of Stony Stratford in Bucks.

14. Virgil, *Æneid* iii. 688–9 (adapted), where Æneas speaks of voyaging past the mouth of the Sicilian river, Pantagias, past the Megarian bay and low-lying Thapsus.

15. 'Expression of Addison on this line' (HW). Not found in Addison.

16. Virgil, *Æneid* vi. 483 (adapted). The allusion to Antitheus is HW's own addition. The historical Antitheus was archon at Athens in the 160th Olympiad. Why HW added him is not clear. Glaucus died by the hand of Teucer, Medon was slain by Æneas, and Thersilochus by Achilles (*Iliad* xii. 387, xv. 332, xxi. 209).

17. 'Bow' (HW): i.e., Stratford-le-Bow.

shape of a bow; *ab Eoo curvatur in Arcum.*[18] From Arc we travelled through a very pleasant country to Epino,[19] whose forest is celebrated by Virgil in these lines.

> Sylva Epini[20] late dumis, atque ilice nigra
> Horrida, quam densi complerant undique sentes;
> Rara per occultos ducebat semita calles.[21]

> Epinum's woods[22] with shrubs and gloomy oak
> Horrid, and all with brambles thick o'ergrown,
> Through which few narrow paths obscurely led.
> Mr Trap.[23]

We were here shown at a distance the thickets rendered so famous by the robberies of Gregorio.[24] Here I was met by a very distant and troublesome relation:[25] my namesake hints at such an one in those lines of his—

> Accurrit quidam notus mihi nomine tantum,
> Arreptaque manu, quid agis, Cosinissime[26] rerum.[27]
> Horace.

> There stepped up one to me I hardly knew,
> Embraced me, and cried, Cousin, how d'ye do.[28]
> Mr Creech.[29]

18. Virgil, *Æneid* iii. 533.

19. 'Epping Forest' (HW).

20. Substituted for 'fuit.'

21. Virgil, *Æneid* ix. 381–3.

22. Substituted for 'A grove there was' (Joseph Trapp, *Works of Virgil*, 1731, iii. 188). HW's edition of Trapp's Virgil was sold SH iii. 141 (press-marks K.7.1–3).

23. Joseph Trapp (1679–1747), D.D., poet and divine; Professor of Poetry at Oxford 1708–18. His translation of the *Æneid* was first published 1718–20.

24. 'Gregory a noted highwayman. See Addison's *Travels*, p. 1' (HW). 'We were here [Cassis] shown at a distance the deserts, which have been rendered so famous by the penance of Mary Magdalene' (Addison, *Remarks* 13, the first page of the text). Samuel Gregory, a blacksmith, long sought as one of the leaders of the 'Essex Gang' (*ante* 4 Feb. 1735, n. 2), was arrested with his brother at an alehouse in Rake, Hants, 8 April, and taken to Winchester jail (*London Daily Post* 21 April 1735; *London Evening Post* 10–13 May 1735). He was later committed to Newgate, and was sentenced to death 24 May 1735 at the Old Bailey sessions for his part in robbing Joseph Lawrence, a farmer near Edgware, Middlesex, on 4 Feb. 1735. He was executed at Tyburn 3 June 1735 (*London Evening Post* 3–5 June 1735; see also ibid. 4–6 Feb., 24–27 May 1735).

25. Not identified.

26. Substituted by HW for 'dulcissime.'

27. Horace, *Serm.* I. ix. 3–4 (adapted).

28. The first four lines of 'Satire IX [Bk I], The Description of an impertinent Fop that plagued Horace in his Walk' (Thomas Creech, *Odes, Satires, and Epistles of Horace*, 5th edn, 1720, p. 217) read:

'As I was walking through the streets of Rome,
And musing on I know not what nor whom,
A fop came up, by name scarce known to me,
He seized my hand, and cried, *Dear Sir, how d'ye!*'

29. Thomas Creech (1659–1700), Fellow

We lay that night at Oggerell,[30] which is famous for nothing but being Horace's *oppidulo, quod versu dicere non est.*[31]

In our way to Parvulun[32] we saw a great castle[33] belonging to the Counts of Suffolcia; 'tis a vast pile of building, but quite in the old taste. Parvulun is a small village, but formerly remarkable for several miracles[34] said to be performed there by a Welsh saint,[35] who, like Jupiter, was suckled by a goat, whence they think it *porrum et cæpe*[36] *nefas violare.* Juvenal.[37] The wonders of Parvulun are in great repute all over Lombardy. We had very bad ways from hence to Pont Ossoria,[38] where are the ruins of a bridge that gives name to the town. The account they give of it is as follows: St Bona[39] being desirous to pass over the river, met with a man who offered to carry her over; he took her up in his arms and under pretence of doing her service, was going to ravish her; but she praying to the Virgin Mary for help the wretch fell into the stream and was drowned, and immediately this bridge rose out of the water for her to go over. She was so touched with this signal deliverance, that she would not leave the place but continued there till her

of All Souls, whose suicide Hearne attributes to lack of preferment (Thomas Hearne, *Remarks and Collections*, Oxford, i, 1885, p. 305). His translation of Horace was published in 1684.

30. 'Hockerel' (HW). Hockerill, Herts.

31. Horace, *Serm.* I. v. 87, 'the little town which it is not possible to name in verse' (once thought to be Equus Triticus or Equotriticus, which could not be used in a dactylic hexameter line) where Horace spent the night on his trip from Rome to Brundisium.

32. 'Littlebury' (HW).

33. 'Audley Inn, the seat of the Earl of Suffolk' (HW). Henry Howard (1706–45), 10th E. of Suffolk, was the last Suffolk to possess Audley End. The house was built, 1603–16, by Thomas Howard, 1st E. of Suffolk, at a cost of £190,000. When HW revisited Audley End in May 1762, he found it a 'monument . . . of its former grandeur' (Montagu ii. 30; see also Richard, Lord Braybrooke, *The History of Audley End*, 1836).

34. 'Winstanley's wonders, or tricks in mechanics' (HW). Henry Winstanley (1644–1703), engineer and engraver, was appointed, 18 March 1679, Clerk of the Works for Audley End and Newmarket,

then Crown properties (*Calendar of Treasury Books 1676–79*, pt ii. 1286). He 'had a house near Audley Inn at Littlebury, where were several mechanic tricks to surprise the populace' (HW's *Catalogue of Engravers, Works* iv. 95–6). See also Thomas Bird, 'Henry Winstanley's House at Littlebury,' N&Q 1892, ser. VIII. ii. 466–7. HW had a print of 'Henry Winstanley's house at Littlebury, in Essex, an etching by the artist, oblong, large half sheet, extra rare,' sold London 1270.

35. St David (d. ca 589), patron saint of Wales.

36. Onion. HW's pun is on the Welch custom of wearing leeks (*porrum*) on St David's Day (1 March).

37. Juvenal, *Sat.* xv. 9.

38. 'Bone Bridge' (HW). Bourn Bridge, seven miles north of Littlebury.

39. St Bona (ca 1156–1208) took the veil of the Canon Regulars at Pisa at the age of ten, and, when thirteen, undertook a pilgrimage to the Holy Land, where she was captured by the Saracens. The Bollandists relate two miracles of her walking across rivers in Spain with her train of pilgrims following her, when the bridges were swept away by swift currents. See *Acta Sanctorum* under 29 May, xx. 143–8.

89

death in exercises of devotion, and was buried in a little chapel at the foot of the bridge, with her story[40] at length and this epitaph,

Hac sita sunt fossa Bonæ Venerabilis ossa.[41]

From Pont Ossoria we travelled by land to Nuovo Foro[42] (the Novum Forum of Iockius) where are held the greatest races in all Italy: We were shown in[43] the treasury of the Benedictines' convent[44] an ancient gold cup[45] which cost an hundred guineas (a great sum in those days) and given as the friar told us that attended us, by a certain German prince, he did not very well know who, but he believed his name was one King George.[46] The inhabitants are wonderfully fond of horses, and to this day tell you most surprising stories of one Looby,[47] a Boltognian. I saw a book dedicated to the head of that family, entitled *A Discourse on the Magnanimity of Bucephalus, and of the Duke of Boltogne's horse Looby.*

I stayed here three days, and in my way to Pavia,[48] stopped at the pal-

40. HW is exercising his fancy.
41. 'Epitaph of Venerable Bede' (HW).
42. 'Newmarket' (HW).
43. HW first wrote 'at.'
44. HW possibly refers to the Coffee Room (subsequently occupied by the Jockey Club, founded ca 1750), or to the royal palace, at either of which places he might have seen the King's Plate (see next note). See J. P. Hore, *History of Newmarket, and the Annals of the Turf*, 1886, i. 20, 144–8; Frank Siltzer, *Newmarket*, 1923, p. 108.
45. The King's Plate of a hundred guineas was run for on Newmarket Heath on the first Thursday of October. This race was founded by Charles II in 1665, and was first run on 11 Oct. 1666 (Hore, op. cit. ii. 246–50). It appears from a Treasury warrant 29 Sept. 1709 to John Charlton, Master of the Jewel Office (quoted by Siltzer, op. cit. 66), that the Plate was a gold cup with a cover, weighing 24 ounces. In 1734, fifteen King's Plates of a hundred guineas each were offered at the races held at Newmarket, Winchester, Salisbury, etc. (John Cheny, *Historical List of all Horse-Matches*, 1734, p. 4).
46. 'See p. 78' (HW). 'The cupola [of the Rotunda at Ravenna] . . . the inhabitants say . . . was cracked by thunder that destroyed a son of one of their Gothic princes,

who had taken shelter under it. . . . I asked an abbot that was in the church, what was the name of this Gothic prince, who, after a little recollection, answered me that he could not tell precisely, but that he thought it was one Julius Cæsar' (Addison, *Remarks* 78).
47. 'See p. 30. Duke of Bolton' (HW). 'When I was at Milan I saw a book newly published that was dedicated to the present head of the Borromean family, and entitled, *A Discourse on the Humility of Jesus Christ, and of St Charles Borromée*' (Addison, *Remarks* 30). Charles Paulet (1685–1754), 3d D. of Bolton, owned Looby, who won the fourth royal plate of a hundred guineas 18 June 1734 at Salisbury (Cheny, op. cit. 8). The 'great match' between Looby, 'carrying eight stone six pound,' and Conqueror, a gelding, 'carrying eight stone one pound,' owned by Thomas Panton, Master of the King's Running Horses at Newmarket, was run at Newmarket 6 Oct., on the four-mile course, for a purse of '500 guineas a side, play or pay.' The betting was estimated between £10,000 and £30,000, and 'the odds at the ditch before starting were six to five and five to four on Conqueror,' who won the race. See *London Evening Post* 25–27 Sept., 2–4, 7–9 Oct. 1735; *Gray's Corr.* i. 32.
48. 'Cambridge' (HW).

ace of Delfini,[49] which is built on the top of a large barren mountain, and at a distance looks like the Ark resting on Mount Ararat. This mountain is called Gog, and opposite to one called Magog. They are very dangerous precipices and occasioned the famous verse,

Incidit in Gogum qui vult vitare Magogon.[50]

I need not repeat the history of Gog and Magog,[51] it being known to every child, and to be found at large in most books of travels.

Pavia and its university are described by Mr Addison,[52] so I shall only mention a circumstance which I wonder escaped that learned gentleman. It is the name of the town, which is derived from the badness of the streets; *Pavia a non pavendo*, as *Lucus a non lucendo*.[53]

Till next post, adieu!

Yours ever,

HORATIUS ITALICUS

To ASHTON, ca October 1735

Missing. Mentioned Ashton to West Oct. 1735 (*Gray-HW-West-Ashton Corr.* i. 44).

To WEST, October 1735

Missing. Probably written at King's College, Cambridge; answered *post* 29 Oct. 1735.

From WEST, Wednesday 29 October 1735

Printed from MS now WSL.

With the letters from West is the following note by HW, on a slip of paper:

49. 'Lord Godolphin's house on Gogmogog Hills' (HW). Francis Godolphin (1678–1766), 2d E. of Godolphin, 'has here a fine house on the very summit of the hill, to which his Lordship frequently resorts, especially in the racing season' (Daniel Defoe, *Tour through . . . Great Britain*, 2d edn, 1738, i. 90).

50. '*Incidit in Scyllam qui vult vitare Charibdin*' (HW). An adaptation of *Alexandreis* v. 301 by Philippe Gaultier de Châtillon (12th c.): 'Incidis in Scyllam cu-

piens vitare Charybdim' (see *Patrologia Latina*, ed. J. P. Migne, vol. ccix, Paris, 1855, p. 514).

51. Ezekiel xxxviii–xxxix.

52. 'In Pavia is an university of seven colleges, one of them called the college of Borromée, very large, and neatly built' (Addison, *Remarks* 26).

53. A proverb, based on Quintilian's example of false etymology, 'Lucus, quia umbra opacus, parum luceat' (*Inst. Orator.* I. vi. 34; see also *The Spectator* No. 59).

'From Richard West, only son of Lord Chancellor West of Ireland,[1] by Elizabeth, daughter to Dr Burnet Bishop of Salisbury.'
Address: To Horatio Walpole Esq. at King's College, Cambridge.
Postmark: OXFORD 30 OC.[2]

Ch[rist] Ch[urch],[3] Oct. 29, 1735.

My dearest Celadon,

CRIMINE quo merui juvenum placidissime[4]—
After a long tedious melancholy silence comes a letter, or rather the shadow of a letter, so short—I thought it a dream indeed.

Tu querar, ah Celadon, (nisi differat aura querelas)
vel scripsisse parum, vel siluisse nimis.[5]

Suffer then my poor little desponding letter to make its appearance before all like a ghost wrapped up in a white sheet, and to make its apology thus—

You say I have an aversion to Statius, and Statius surely is an honourable man,[6] and even his enemies must confess he has some perfections; but could you think I meant to wound you through his sides, or could I dream of your dear Pegasus, when I abused Domitian's horse?[7]

Moreover, you treat me as a dreamer of dreams, and you call me by the heathenish name of Watteau,[8] and you say I write down my *falsa insomnia,* and all that. If that be the case, I am absolved already, for

1. Richard West (d. 1726), barrister-at-law (Inner Temple) 1714; M.P. Grampound 1720–1, Bodmin 1721–6; Lord Chancellor of Ireland, 1725; Lord Justice of Ireland, 1726. See also *post* ca 12 Nov. 1737, n. 11.

2. The date stamp indicates that the letter passed through London, there being no direct post between Oxford and Cambridge.

3. West matriculated at Christ Church, Oxford, 22 May 1735 (Foster, *Alumni Oxon.*).

4. Statius, *Sylvæ* V. iv ('Ad Somnum') 1, adapted. Statius complains: 'O youthful Sleep, gentlest of the gods, by what crime or error have I deserved that I alone should lack thy bounty?'

5. Which may be paraphrased: 'Let me complain, Celadon (unless the wind should disperse my complaints), either you write too little or keep silent too much.' These

lines may be original; they have not been traced.

6. *Julius Cæsar* III. ii. 105.

7. Suetonius mentions Domitian's white horse in *De Vita Cæsarum* viii. Domitianus 2.

8. Like West, Jean-Antoine Watteau (1684–1721) had a feeble constitution, and, fearing premature death, was melancholy and retiring. See the contemporary biographical portrait by his friend, Jean de Julienne, in Pierre Champion, *Notes critiques sur les vies anciennes d'Antoine Watteau,* Paris, 1921, p. 51; see also Pierre-Jean Mariette, *Abecedario,* ed. Ph. de Chennevières and A. de Montaiglon, vi. 105, 119 (*Archives de l'art français,* xii, 1859–60). Watteau was a favourite with HW at this time: copies in water-colour, signed and dated by HW 1736 and 1738, of two pictures by Watteau are now WSL.

dreams you know always go by contraries; so that Statius has no longer any occasion to complain of sleep.⁹

But to waive this plea, surely you are not so far of Quarles' opinion as to think crimes committed actual sins;¹⁰ if so, many a virgin has dreamed away her virginity. And now, to end like an orator with a curious peroration,

> O pardon, pardon a distempered mind;
> Mercy's the sweetest attribute of heaven.
> Forget, forgive—humanity may err—
> I've injured Statius, I have wronged his muse,
> And I have suffered—O my Celadon!
> Shall one rash dream, th'infirmity of sleep,
> Throw down the merit of my waking hours?
> Damned visionary curse! so fares the wretch,
> Whose sleep-beguiled hand stabbed his poor sire,
> And waking finds despair—forget, forgive—
> My dreams are guilty, but my heart is free.¹¹

By this time I think I must have mollified you, and so I conclude, sleeping or waking, my dear Celadon,

Your very faithful humble servant,

R. WEST

PS. I must ask a few questions. Are you to travel soon?¹² Is Orosmades defunct? Does Almanzor exist? Is the divine Plato alive? What sort of a thing is Tydeus?¹³

I saw Ch. Lyttleton¹⁴ about a week ago. I wish I could hear from you by the minutes.

9. See n. 4 above.

10. *Sic* in MS. West must have intended something like 'crimes dreamed but not committed,' etc. Cf. 'On Dreams,' in Francis Quarles's *Divine Fancies* iv. 50:

'Who dreams a sin, and not his dreams forbid it
An entertainment, sins as if he did it;
Which if thy slumb'ring soul could not prevent,
Th'art safe, if thou hast dream'd thou didst repent.'

11. Dryden and Lee, *Œdipus* III. i: 'My hands are guilty, but my heart is free.'

12. Rumours of HW's 'tour of Italy' ap-

peared in the newspapers early this month (*ante* ca 15 Oct 1735, n. 2).

13. Not identified (see *post* 9 Nov. 1735).

14. Charles Lyttelton (1714–68), 3d son of Sir Thomas Lyttelton, 4th Bt, of Hagley Park, Worcs; HW's correspondent; Eton 1725–8; matriculated at Oxford, from University College, 10 Oct. 1732; barrister-at-law (Middle Temple), 1738; D.C.L., 1745; Dean of Exeter 1748–62; Bp of Carlisle 1762–8 (*Eton Coll. Reg.;* Foster, *Alumni Oxon.*). HW probably saw him at Hagley Park the previous Sept. (HW to Lyttelton 18 Aug. 1735).

Sic raro scribis ut tota non quater hora—[15]

Oh why must envious space our friendship part?
Letters are feeble transcripts of the heart.
Forth from my mind so swift ideas flow,
The dull line loiters, and the words move slow.[16]

Still by the pen's delay my fancy's crost,
And ere I write, a thousand thoughts are lost.
Then oh! since writing is but vain at best,
Read all you can—and you may dream the rest.[17]

Meantime how heavily my days now roll!
The morning lecture! and the evening bowl!
The cobweb-school! The tutor's flimsy tale!
The feast of folly! and the flow of ale![18]

Who would not laugh if such strange things[19] there be?[20]
For me I hate the odious scene,—and dream of thee.

To West, Sunday 9 November 1735

Reprinted from *Works* iv. 411–12.

King's College, Nov. 9, 1735.

Dear West,

YOU expect a long letter from me, and have said in verse all that I
intended to have said in far inferior prose. I intended filling three
or four sides with exclamations against an university life, but you have
showed me how strongly they may be expressed in three or four lines. I
can't build without straw; nor have I the ingenuity of the spider to spin
fine lines out of dirt: a master of a college would make but a miserable
figure as a hero of a poem, and Cambridge sophs are too low to introduce into a letter that aims not at punning:

Haud equidem invideo vati, quem pulpita pascunt.[1]

---

15. Horace, *Serm.* II. iii. 1, adapted: 'Sic
raro scribis, ut toto non quater anno Mem-
branam poscas.'
  16. Cf. Pope, *Essay on Criticism*, line 371.
  17. Cf. Pope, *Eloisa to Abelard*, line 124.
  18. Cf. Pope, *Satires and Epistles of
Horace Imitated*, Sat. II. i. 128.
  19. Corrected from 'scenes.'

20. Cf. Pope, *Epistle to Dr Arbuthnot*,
line 213.

1. Juvenal, *Sat.* vii. 93 conflated in part
with Virgil, *Ecl.* i. 11. It may be freely
translated, 'Yet I cannot begrudge a poet
who earns his living from the playhouse.'

But why mayn't we hold a classical correspondence? I can never forget the many agreeable hours we have passed in reading Horace and Virgil; and I think they are topics will never grow stale. Let us extend the Roman Empire, and cultivate two barbarous towns o'errun with rusticity and mathematics. The creatures are so used to a circle, that they plod on in the same eternal round, with their whole view confined to a *punctum, cujus nulla est pars:*

Their time a moment, and a point their space.[2]

Orabunt causas melius, cœlique meatus
Describent radio, et surgentia sidera dicent:
Tu coluisse novem musas, Romane, memento;
Hæ tibi erunt artes.—[3]

We have not the least poetry stirring here; for I can't call verses on the 5th of November[4] and 30th of January[5] by that name, more than four lines on a chapter in the New Testament is an epigram. Tydeus rose and set at Eton: he is only known here to be a scholar of King's. Orosmades and Almanzor are just the same; that is, I am almost the only person they are acquainted with, and consequently the only person acquainted with their excellencies. Plato improves every day: so does my friendship with him. These three divide my whole time—though I believe you will guess there is no quadruple alliance:[6] that was a happiness which I only enjoyed when you was at Eton. A short account of the Eton people at Oxford would much oblige, my dear West,

Your faithful friend,

Hor. Walpole

To Gray, ca 31 Dec. 1735

Missing. Mentioned *post* 3 Jan. 1736.

2. Cf. Pope, *Essay on Man* i. 72.
3. Virgil, *Æneid* vi. 849–52, adapted.
4. 'Guy Fawkes Day,' when the ceremonies in connection with the election of the vice-chancellor took place at Cambridge (see *post* 27 Oct. 1736).
5. Anniversary of Charles I's martyrdom.

For an account of the ceremonies at Cambridge on that day see Adam Wall, *Account of the Different Ceremonies Observed in the Senate House of the University of Cambridge*, 1798, pp. 51–2.
6. Of Gray, HW, West, and Ashton.

From Gray, Saturday 3 January 1736

Printed from MS in Waller Collection.
Dated by the references to *Artaserse* and *Zara*.

Jan. 3 [1736], London.[1]

<   >[2]

A THOUSAND thanks for the thousand happy New Years you sent
me,[3] and which, I suppose, a thousand good-natured people have
made you a present of, in the overflowings of their zeal:

—May each revolving year
With blessings crowned, like this, returning smile
On ‹Celadon›,[4] the happiest of his kind—

I need not wish anything further, since (as I wish what you do) to be
sure you know my wishes already. Wise folks say, the wise man's happiness is in himself; pray, are you the wise man? They tell you too that
mortal happiness is not of long continuance; heaven send, yours may
last till you wish for a little misery; nay! and longer still. I can't tell
whether our situations are much changed since this time twelvemonth;
certain I am however, that there is a great alteration: I don't succeed to
your diversions in town, I believe, and yet am absent from Cambridge[5]
without regret, nay with pleasure, though not infinitely happier here.
I have very little to tell you as to the place called London: *Adriano*[6] expired a few days ago, and his ancient predecessor *Artaxerxes*[7] succeeds

1. No doubt Gray spent Christmas with
his parents at their house at the corner of
Cornhill and St Michael's Alley. Gray was
born there, and his mother and her elder
sister, Mary Antrobus (1683–1749), con-
ducted a millinery business there from ca
1705 till Gray's father died, in 1741, when
Gray's mother and aunt removed to Stoke
Poges. The house was destroyed in the
great fire at Cornhill 25 March 1748. See
Gray's Corr. i. 51, 304–5, 324, iii. 1196–7;
Mason, *Mem. Gray* 120; Bernard Drew,
The London Assurance, n.d., pp. 125–6;
London Magazine 1748, xvii. 139–40.

2. Probably 'Dear Celadon'; the words
on the other side of the MS were restored
by HW.

3. HW to Gray ca 31 Dec. 1735, missing.

4. Piece cut out, except for the bottom
strokes of the letters.

5. Gray was not charged for commons at
Peterhouse from 26 Dec. 1735 to 23 Jan.
1736.

6. *Adriano in Siria*, opera in three acts,
words by Pietro Metastasio (1698–1782) and
music by Francesco Maria Veracini (1685–
1750). First acted in London 25 Nov. 1735 at
the Haymarket, it was taken off the bill
after the tenth night (30 Dec.), and revived
7 Feb. 1736 (Nicoll, *Drama 1700–50*, p. 388;
Hugo Riemann, *Musiklexikon*, Berlin,
1929; Burney, *Hist. of Music* iv. 391).

7. Hasse's *Artaserse* was arranged as a
pasticcio to include songs and airs by Ric-
cardo Broschi (1700–56) and others. It
opened 29 Oct. 1734 at the Haymarket, and

him for the present, which I think to visit tonight. The ⟨town (in sub-missio⟩n[8] to your judgment) don't much admire Delane;[9] Mrs Porter[10] acts in the *Albion Queens*,[11] but I shall stay for another play before I see her; neither have I much inclination for old Cibber[12] in *Sir Courtly Nice*,[13] nor for young Mrs Cibber[14] in Voltaire's *Zara*,[15] in which she performs the principal part for the first time of her appearance in that way. I went to *King Arthur*[16] last night, which is exceeding fine; they have a new man to ⟨supply⟩[17] Delane's place, one Johnson,[18] with the

was given 28 times during the season of 1734–5; it was revived 3 Jan. 1736 (Nicoll, op. cit. 390; Riemann, op. cit.; Burney, op. cit. iv. 381–2; Robert Eitner, *Quellen-Lexikon*, Leipzig, 1900–4; Oscar G. Sonneck, 'Die drei Fassungen des Hasse'schen "Artaserse," ' *Sammelbände der Internationalen Musikgesellschaft*, Leipzig, xiv, 1912–13, p. 227).

8. Piece cut out; the missing words have been restored in pencil by HW.

9. Dennis Delane (ca 1707–50). He acted Lord Hardy in Steele's *Funeral, or Grief à la mode*, 31 Dec. 1735, 1 Jan. 1736 at Covent Garden (*Daily Adv.* 1 Jan. 1736). 'Delane's person and voice were well adapted to the parts he generally acted . . . but his attachment to the bottle prevented his rising to any degree of excellence. . . . His address and manner were easy and polite' (Thomas Davies, *Memoirs of the Life of David Garrick*, 1808, i. 27; see also DNB; George D. Burtchaell and Thomas U. Sadleir, *Alumni Dublinenses*, Dublin, 1935; Nicoll, *Drama 1700–50*, p. 356).

10. Mary Porter (d. 1765), at Lincoln's Inn Fields 1699–1705; Haymarket 1705–8, 1710–11; Drury Lane 1708–10, 1711–43. Occasionally she acted at Covent Garden (see Thomas Davies, *Dramatic Miscellanies*, 1785, iii. 495–500; HW to Lady Ossory 3 Nov. 1782). See also *post* 23 Feb. 1738.

11. Tragedy in five acts by John Banks (fl. 1677–1704), published, 1684, as *The Island Queens: or the Death of Mary Queen of Scotland*, but not performed until 6 March 1704, when it was given under its new title at Drury Lane (see Genest i. 423, ii. 299). Mrs Porter acted Queen Elizabeth in *The Albion Queens* at Covent Garden 7 Jan. 1736 (*Daily Adv.* 7 Jan.).

12. Colley Cibber (1671–1757) began acting in 1690; at Drury Lane as actor, drama-

tist, and manager 1696–1733; poet laureate, 1730. He acted Sir Courtly Nice at Drury Lane 29 Dec. 1735, 2 Jan. 1736 (Genest iii. 378–82, 474; *Daily Adv.* 29 Dec. 1735, 2 Jan. 1736).

13. Comedy by John Crowne (ca 1640–1712), first printed and acted 1685. See Arthur F. White, *John Crowne*, Cleveland, 1922, pp. 24–6, 51, 139; Genest i. 438, vi. 195.

14. Susannah Maria Arne (1714–66), actress and singer, m. (1734), as his second wife, Theophilus Cibber, from whom she was separated in 1742. See DNB; *Account of the Life of . . . Susannah Maria Cibber*, 1887, p. 10; Genest v. 100–2.

15. *Zaïre* (1732). It was translated as *The Tragedy of Zara*, 1736, by Aaron Hill (1685–1750), and was performed at Drury Lane from 12 Jan. to 27 Jan. 1736, with Mrs Cibber acting Zara and her husband Nerestan (Nicoll, *Drama 1700–50*, p. 336; Genest iii. 474–5; C. Parfaict, *Dictionnaire des théâtres de Paris*, 1756, vi. 311–12).

16. By Dryden, with music by Henry Purcell (1659–95), revived at Goodman's Fields 19 Dec. 1735 as *Merlin, or the British Enchanter: and King Arthur, the British Worthy* ('a dramatic opera' in five acts), and acted thirty-six times successively (Genest iii. 482; Edward J. Dent, *Foundations of English Opera*, Cambridge, 1928, p. 206; BM Cat.).

17. The upper part of the word is cut out.

18. —— Johnson (d. 1746), 'commonly called *tall Johnson*, being near seven feet high, the son-in-law of Aaron Hill, and by him instructed' (Thomas Davies, *Dramatic Miscellanies*, 1785, i. 143); not to be confused with Benjamin Johnson (?1665–1742) of Drury Lane. See Genest iii. 481–2, 552, iv. 187, 195. In 1739 he married Urania Hill

finest person and face in the world to all appearance; but as awkward as a button-maker;[19] in short, if he knew how to manage his beauties to advantage, I should not wonder if all the women run mad for him. The enchanted part of the play is not machinery, but actual magic. The second scene is a British temple,[20] enough to make one go back a thousand years and really be in ancient Britain. The songs are all church-music,[21] and in every one of the choruses Mrs Chambers[22] sung the chief part, accompanied with

Roarings, squallings and squeakations dire.[23]

Mrs Giffard[24] is by way of Emmeline, and should be blind, but, heaven knows! I would not wish to see better than she does, and seems to do; for when Philidel[25] restores her to sight, her eyes are not at all better than before; she is led in at first by a creature that was more like a devil, by half, than Grimbald[26] himself. She took herself for *Madame la Confidente*, but everybody else took her to be in the circumstances of damnation: when Emmeline comes to her sight, she beholds this Mrs Matilda first, and cries out

Are women all like thee? such glorious creatures![27]

(Dorothy Brewster, *Aaron Hill*, New York, 1913, p. 246).

19. I.e., Samuel Stephens (*ante* 17 Nov. 1734, n. 18).

20. 'The scene represents a place of heathen worship; the three Saxon gods, Woden, Thor, and Freya, placed on pedestals. An altar.' Dryden in his dedication says that he informed himself 'out of Beda, Bochartus, and other authors, concerning the rites and customs of the heathen Saxons' (*King Arthur*, ed. Edward Taylor, 1843, pp. 14, 19).

21. Characteristics of the church style, modal phrases and cadences, homophonic and polyphonic choral technique, can be discovered in the score of *King Arthur*, particularly in the soprano solo, 'The lot is cast.' See Fritz de Quervain, *Der Chorstil Henry Purcells*, Bern, 1935; J. A. Westrup, *Purcell*, 1937, pp. 34, 41, 239–57.

22. —— Chambers (fl. 1733–52), probably the Miss Chambers who acted Grideline in Addison's *Rosamond* (music by Lampe) at Lincoln's Inn Fields 7 March 1733 (Burney, *Hist. of Music* iv. 656). She is remembered for her Polly in the *Beggar's Opera* at Covent Garden 18 Sept. 1752

(Genest iv. 368; *BM Cat. of Engraved British Portraits* iii. 99).

23. 'Gorgons, and Hydras, and Chimeras dire' (*Paradise Lost* ii. 628).

24. Anna Marcella Lydal (ca 1707–77), dau. of a Dublin actor, m. (before 1730 at Dublin), as his second wife, Henry Giffard (d. 1772), actor, and manager of Goodman's Fields 1731–42. She acted at Goodman's Fields 1731–6, 1740–2; Lincoln's Inn Fields 1736–7, 1742–3; Drury Lane 1737–40, 1743–7; Covent Garden 1747–8 (Genest iii. 356 and *passim*, iv. 20 and *passim*, under the several theatres for the years given above; see also Daniel Lysons, *Environs of London*, 1792–6, ii. 53–4; William R. Chetwood, *General History of the Stage*, 1749, pp. 166–7).

25. An airy spirit, acted by a Mrs Hamilton (Genest iii. 482; see also ibid. 512).

26. An earthy spirit, 'the grossest, earthiest, ugliest fiend in hell' (*King Arthur* IV. i), acted by William Lyon (d. ca 1748). See David E. Baker, *Biographia Dramatica*, 1812, i pt ii. 466; Genest iii. 482.

27. 'Are women such as thou? Such glorious creatures?' (*King Arthur* III. ii).

which set the people into such a laugh as lasted the whole act. The frost scene is excessive fine; the first scene of it is only a cascade that seems frozen, with the Genius of Winter asleep and wrapped in furs, who upon the approach of Cupid, after much quivering and shaking, sings the finest song[28] in the play. Just after, the scene opens, and shows a view of arched rocks covered with ice and snow to the end of the stage; between the arches are upon pedestals of snow eight images of old men and women that seem frozen into statues, with icicles hanging about them and almost hid in frost, and from the end come singers, viz. Mrs Chambers, etc., and dancers all rubbing their hands and chattering with cold,[29] with fur gowns and worsted gloves in abundance. There are several more beautiful scenes; but, rather than describe 'em, I ought to beg pardon for interrupting your happiness so long, and conclude myself

Your poor servant ever,

⟨OROZMADES⟩[30]

To ASHTON, ca March 1736

Missing. Probably written in Downing Street; mentioned in Gray to HW 11 March 1736.

From GRAY, Thursday 11 March 1736

Printed from MS in Waller Collection.
The date of the year is determined by the reference to Gray's return to Cambridge shortly after 'Monday' 1 March 1736. The Peterhouse records show that he was absent from Cambridge from ca 12 Feb. to ca 5 March.
Address: To the Honourable Mr Horace Walpole, near Whitehall,[1] Westminster. *Postmark:* SAFFRON WALDEN 12 MR.

28. Bass solo, 'Great love I know thee now' (*King Arthur*, ed. Edward Taylor, pp. 26, 72–3).

29. Four-part chorus—a frequently cited example of tone painting—to the verses (ibid. 26, 75–8),

'See, see, we assemble,
Thy revels to hold;
Though quiv'ring with cold,
We chatter and tremble.'

30. Piece cut out, but part of a 'd' is visible.

———

1. I.e., his father's house in Downing Street, property of the Crown, since 1735 the official residence of the First Lord of the Treasury. Sir Robert Walpole occupied it from 22 Sept. 1735 (*ante* 16 April 1734, n. 1) to ca 24 July 1742 (HW to Mann 30 June 1742, O.S.).

St. Peters House *was founded by Hugh de Beelsham Bishop of Ely in 1284 near to St. Peters Church from whence it seeme to have received its Name It's first endowment was for a Master and 14 Fellons. but eight more Fellowships and forty two Scholars have been added to that Foundation. the College Chapple was built by Contribution. but Matthew Wren Bp: of Ely and Master of this College bore ye Chief expence of it.*

GRAY'S CHAMBERS IN PETERHOUSE, 1734–9

March 11 [1736], Cambridge.

My dearest Horace,

I WAS obliged by an unexpected accident[2] to defer my journey some-what longer than Monday, though it gave not at all the more time for pleasure; if it had, I should have been at the masquerade[3] with you. Ashton terrifies me with telling me that according to his last advices[4] we are to remain in a state of separation from you the Lord knows how much longer;[5] we are inconsolable at the news, and weep our half pint apiece every day about it; if you don't make more haste, instead of us you may chance to find a couple of fountains by your fireside. If that should be our fate, I beg I may have the honour of washing your hands and filling your tea-kettle every morning, < >[6]

To WEST, ca Sunday 23 May 1736

Missing. Written at Cambridge, and referred to by West as 'your late panegyric' (*post* 1 June 1736) on Oxford; it also evidently contained a copy of the same verses which were enclosed in HW to Lyttelton 22 May 1736. HW wrote to Montagu 20 May and to Lyttelton 22 May about his 'jaunt to Oxford.' It is evident from Ashton to West June 1736 (*Gray-HW-West-Ashton Corr.* i. 82) that West included extracts from Walpole's letter in a missing letter to Ashton.

From WEST, Tuesday 1 June 1736

Printed from MS now WSL.
Address: To Horace Walpole Esq. at King's College, Cambridge.
Postmark: OXFORD 2 IV.

Christ Church, June 1, [17]36.

My dear Walpole,

O XFORD is so confounded and pleased with your late panegyric[1] that she knows not what to do with herself; the royal statue in the dome at Queen's College[2] has been thrice seen publicly to dance a cou-

2. Probably Gray was detained in London by business connected with the affairs of his aunt, Sarah Gray (1678–1736), who died in London, and was buried 16 Feb. at Wanstead, Essex (Charles Hall Crouch, 'Ancestry of Thomas Gray the Poet,' *Genealogists' Magazine*, 1927, iii. 74, 77). By her will, dated 31 Dec. 1735, proved 16 Feb. 1736, she left all her property to her 'nephew, Thomas Gray' (*Gray's Corr.* iii. 1307).

3. A ball, 'being the last this year,' was held 'at the King's Theatre in the Haymarket on Thursday . . . the 4th of March' (*Daily Adv.* 26 Feb., 2 March 1736).
4. HW to Ashton ca March 1736, missing.
5. HW wrote to Montagu 2 May 1736 from Cambridge.
6. Piece cut out.

———

1. HW to West ca 23 May 1736, missing.
2. The recently erected marble statue of

rant, and last night all the great heads round the Theatre[3] shouted for
joy, to the great astonishment of all that were present, and besides all
this in Magdalen Chapel a frolic boy and a pious youth[4] were heard repeating English verses round the Lyttleton monument.[5] Indeed your
last letter was in every sentence, word, and comma, so very gay, high-
spirited, and *allegro,* that I danced about the room all the while. I read
it like a madman, or like one bit by Lyne's *Tarantula,*[6] till at last I fell
into a breathing sweat, and fell asleep; and you are like, as you deserve,
to be troubled with the dream, which is a translation of '*O fons Blan-
dusiæ,*'[7] etc., in the third book of Horace's *Odes*[8]—I own I ought to be
deterred from tacking verses to the end of my letters since I have read
yours, where the prose and poetry are both so exquisite that for the future I shall never venture to send you either, except when I am in a
dream as at present, though I must confess I never dream on two-
headed Parnassus.[9] I desire my service to Dod,[10] and Mr Whaley;[11] and
am, dear Sir,

Yours,

R. W.

Queen Caroline, benefactor of the college, by Sir Henry Cheere (1703–81), finished in May 1735 but not set up until Feb. 1736 in the open cupola over the main gate of Queen's College in High Street. See John R. Magrath, *The Queen's College,* Oxford, 1921, ii. 93–4; *Gray-HW-West-Ashton Corr.* i. 76 n. 2; *London Evening Post* 4–7 Jan. 1735.

3. The heads of the 'sages of antiquity' on the stone pillars of the grilled fence behind the Sheldonian Theatre, facing Broad Street.

4. Thomas (1622–35) and John (1618–35), eldest sons of Sir Thomas Lyttelton, 1st Bt, of Franckley, Worcs (Charles Lyttelton's great-grandfather), were drowned 9 May 1635 in the Cherwell, near Magdalen College, after an unsuccessful attempt by John to save his younger brother. See HW to Lyttelton 22 May 1736 for HW's verses beginning:
'The frolic boy, unfortunately gay,
   Too near the current urg'd his little
      play. . . .'

5. By Nicholas Stone (1586–1647), on the east wall of the antechapel in Magdalen College chapel. See Stone's note-book in

Walpole Society vii. 74, which gives a photograph. See also *Anecdotes, Works* iii. 168, and Collins, *Peerage,* 1812, viii. 341.

6. Richard Lyne (1715–67), Eton 1730–4; scholar (1734), Fellow (1737–46) of King's; Fellow of Eton 1752–67; D.D., 1764; Royal Chaplain 1744–67. His *Tarantula,* with other poems by him, was included in *Musæ Etonenses,* 1755. See *Eton Coll. Reg.;* R. A. Austen-Leigh, 'Authors' List for *Musæ Etonenses,* 1755,' *Etoniana,* 20 June 1917, pp. 334–6.

7. Lambinus's reading; modern texts read 'Bandusiæ.'

8. No. xiii.

9. 'Parnassusque biceps' (Ovid, *Met.* ii. 221).

10. John Dodd (1717–82), of Swallowfield, Berks; M.P. Reading 1740–1, 1755–82. He entered King's as a fellow-commoner in 1735, and became one of HW's closest friends there; they were born on the same day, and were the subject of verses by Sneyd Davies (*Eton Coll. Reg.;* Cole ii. 299, n. 7).

11. John Whaley (see *ante* i. 5 n. 20), tutor to both HW and Dodd.

To the Fountain Blandusia

Blandusian Nymph, to grace thy spring,
Flow'rets and hallow'd wine I bring:
Tomorrow dooms the sportive kid
　　Beneath thy grot to bleed.
See! his ripe front the horn displays,
Prophetic pledge of amorous[12] frays:
His blood, alas! runs youth in vain,
　　His blood thy streams shall stain.
Thy shade still mocks the Dog-Star's heat,
Still underneath thy cool retreat
To rest the flocks and herds repair,
　　And breathe thy gentler air.
Thy waters too shall live in verse,
While I the sacred grot rehearse,
—Whence thou more tuneful than my song
　　Run'st murmuring along.

You know Dryden and Congreve and Cowley have in all their translations from Horace's *Odes* paraphrased him extremely. Backed by Milton's authority,[13] I am entirely for a close translation of him, with little variation. No paraphrase I ever read of him has hit the *curiosa felicitas*[14] of expression which is the principal beauty in Horace—the phrase 'Runs youth' is imitated from Milton's 'Ran nectar' in his Fourth Book.[15] Adieu, and remember me to Gray, and where is Ashton?

To GRAY, June 1736

Missing. Probably written at King's. In it HW asked Gray to do an errand for him at Mrs Chenevix's toyshop (see *post* 11 June 1736).

From GRAY, Friday 11 June 1736

Printed from MS in Waller Collection.
The date of the year is determined by the reference to *Atalanta*.
Address: To the Honourable Mr Horace Walpole at King's College, Cambridge.
Postmark: 12 IV.

12. Corrected from 'future.'
13. Of his translation of 'The Fifth Ode of Horace. Lib. I,' Milton wrote, 'Rendered almost word for word without rhyme according to the Latin measure, as near as the language will permit.'
14. Petronius, *Satyricon* 118.
15. *Paradise Lost* iv. 240.

June 11 [1736], London.[1]

Dear Sir,

IT was hardly worth while to trouble you with a letter till I had seen somewhat in town; not that I have seen anything now but what you have heard of before, that is, *Atalanta*.[2] There are only four men[3] and two women[4] in it. The first is a common scene of a wood, and does not change at all till the end of the last act, when there appears the Temple of Hymen with illuminations; there is a row of blue fires burning in order along the ascent to the temple; a fountain of fire spouts up out of the ground to the ceiling, and two more cross each other obliquely from the sides of the stage; on the top is a wheel that whirls always about, and throws out a shower of gold-colour, silver, and blue fiery rain. Conti[5] I like excessively in everything but his mouth[6] which is thus, 🐷 ; but this is hardly minded, when Strada[7] stands by him. Operas and plays, and all things else at present, are beat off the stage, and are forced to yield to Spring Garden,[8] where last night were above fifteen hundred people. I won't say more of it till I have seen it myself, but as the beauty of the place, when lighted up, and a little music are

1. Gray left Cambridge 6 June ('Chronological Table,' *Gray's Corr.*).

2. Opera in three acts by Handel, first performed at Covent Garden 12 May 1736 in honour of the marriage (27 April 1736) of Frederick, Prince of Wales, and Augusta, Princess of Saxe-Gotha. Gray must have heard it Wednesday 9 June. See *London Evening Post* 11–13 May 1736; Nicoll, *Drama 1700–50*, p. 390; *Daily Adv.* 12 May 1736.

3. Conti (see below) as Meleagro; John Beard (ca 1717–91), tenor, as Aminta; Gustavus Waltz (fl. 1732–9), bass, Handel's cook, as Nicandro; Thomas Reinhold (ca 1690–1751), bass, as Mercurio (Burney, *Hist. of Music* iv. 396; *Georg Friedrich Händels Werke*, 1882, vol. lxxxvii; Grove's *Dictionary of Music*).

4. Strada (see below) as Atalanta, and Maria Anna Caterina Negri (b. 1701), contralto, as Irene (Burney, loc. cit.; F. J. Fétis, *Biographie universelle des musiciens*, Paris, 1873–5).

5. Gioacchino Conti (1714–61), called Gizziello, male soprano who made his London début in a revival of Handel's *Ario-*

dante at Covent Garden 5 May 1736. 'Conti was at this time a young singer, more of promising than mature abilities, and so modest and diffident that when he first heard Farinelli, at a private rehearsal, he burst into tears, and fainted away with despondency' (Burney, *Hist. of Music* iv. 394–5; Grove's *Dictionary of Music*).

6. 'Poor Conti! . . . I remember here (but he was not ripe then) he had a very promising squeak with him, and that his mouth, when open, made an exact square' (Gray to Chute and Mann July 1742, *Gray's Corr.* i. 214).

7. Anna Strada del Pò (fl. 1729–38), soprano, who came to England in July 1729 and joined Handel's company. 'She had so little of a Venus in her appearance that she was usually called the *pig*' (Burney, *Hist. of Music*, iv. 342). She left England 17 June 1738, at the end of an operatic season which drove both Handel and his rival, Heidegger, to bankruptcy (ibid. iv. 426–7).

8. Or Vauxhall Gardens, which had been opened under the management of Jonathan Tyers (d. 1767) in June 1732 (DNB).

the only diversions of it, I don't suppose it will be an⟨y⟩ long time in vogue.⁹ I beg your excuse that I have not yet ⟨execu⟩ted my commission¹⁰ at Chenevix,¹¹ but some time the next week I will take care to do my duty. I have also a commission for your man¹² (with your leave), that is, to call at Crow's¹³ for me, and bid him send me *Atalanta*¹⁴ with all the speed he possibly can, which I must owe him for till I come down again, which won't (I believe) be a vast while.¹⁵ Pray, bid Ashton write, and I hope you'll write yourself. Adieu!

> Yours ever,
>
> OROZMADES

From GRAY, Thursday 15 July 1736

Printed from MS in Waller Collection.
Dated by the reference to the explosion at Westminster Hall, 14 July 1736.

9. The gardens continued to be fashionable until the nineteenth century, and were not closed officially until 25 July 1859 (*London Past and Present* iii. 429).

10. Probably contained in HW to Gray June 1736, missing.

11. 'A toywoman at Charing Cross, famous for her high prices and fine language' (note by HW, now missing, in HW, Waldegrave MSS 1: quoted in *Gray's Corr.* i. 227, n. 16), whose shop was on the 'corner of Warwick Street, near Pall Mall' (*Daily Adv.* 17 March 1739). This was presumably the same toywoman named Chenevix who in May 1747 (*ante* i. 17) turned over to HW her lease of the house which became SH; and it has been thought that her maiden name was Mary Roussel, who d. 1755 (R. A. Austen-Leigh in N&Q 1934, clxvi. 46, and in *Proceedings of the Huguenot Society*, 1945, xvii. 312–13). But the memorandum of HW's original agreement (printed in part *ante* i. 17 n. 112) is made out in the name of Elizabeth Chenevix. Her husband was almost certainly Paul Daniel Chenevix, a goldsmith, brother of Richard, Bp of Waterford (N&Q loc. cit. and clxvii. 15); and it may be that Mary Roussel was his sec-

ond wife, and HW's Mrs Chenevix his first. At all events there is evidence that Mrs Chenevix's maiden name was not Roussel but Deard. In the *Tunbridge Wells Guide* for 1780, in some anecdotes (pp. 2–3) referring to the period 1725–34, she is said to have been the daughter of the 'well-known and original Mr [John] Deard, or Bubble Boy,' whose 'elegant toy-shop' was in Fleet Street, facing St Dunstan's (information from Sir Ambrose Heal; and see Musgrave's *Obituary*). For further evidence that Mrs Chenevix was a Deard, see MONTAGU i. 83 n. 23.

12. Not identified.

13. Cambridge bookseller and binder whose name appears in the accounts of the library of Pembroke College between 1735 and 1741. Among the subscribers to *Atalanta* is listed a 'Mr Crow Senʳ of Cambridge. 7 Books.'

14. The score was published by John Walsh, music printer in Catherine Street, Strand, ca 5 June (*Fog's Weekly Journal* 5 June 1736; *London Evening Post* 8–10 June 1736).

15. Gray returned to Cambridge 23 Oct. ('Chronological Table,' *Gray's Corr.*).

[London, July 15, 1736.]

Dear Sir,

I SYMPATHIZE with you in the sufferings which you foresee are coming upon you;[1] we are both at present, I imagine, in no very agreeable situation. For my own part I am under the misfortune of having nothing to do, but it is a misfortune which, thank my stars, I can pretty well bear. You are in a confusion of wine and bawdy and hunting and tobacco,[2] and, heaven be praised, you too can pretty well bear it; while our evils are no more, I believe we shan't much repine. I imagine however you'll rather choose to converse with the living dead that adorn the walls of your apartments, than with the dead living that deck the middles of them, and prefer a picture of still-life to the realities of a noisy one; and, as I guess, will learn to imitate them, and for an hour or two at noon will stick yourself up as formal as if you had been fixed in your frame for these hundred years with an upright pink in one hand and a great seal-ring in the other.[3] I know nothing but that the judges were all blown up yesterday in Westminster Hall[4] by some unlucky boy that had affixed a parcel of squibs and crackers to several Acts of Parliament, whose ruins were scattered about the Hall with a great noise and displosion; it set the Lord Chancellor[5] a-laughing, and frighted everybody else out of their senses, and Lord Hardwick[6] ordered the Grand Jury to represent it as a libel.[7] Yes! I know besides, that I shall be always yours,

<   >

1. Unexplained.

2. HW spent two weeks at Houghton and returned to King's ca 26 July (see HW to Lyttelton 27 July 1736; HW to Sir Robert Walpole 27 July 1736). Sir Robert set out for Houghton 3 July for a fortnight's stay (*Daily Adv.* 1 July, 5 July 1736).

3. In the manner of Holbein.

4. 'Yesterday between one and two . . . a large parcel in a brown paper was laid near the Chancery Court, and kicked down on the landing place on the steps going to the two courts of King's Bench and Chancery, to which was put a lighted match which burnt till it came to the paper, wherein were enclosed several chambers or parcels of gunpowder which blew up, making several large reports that put the courts of justice and all Westminster Hall into great confusion; enclosed in the brown pa-

per were five acts of parliament, great part of which were burnt; and the explosion dispersed a great quantity of printed bills' (*London Evening Post* 13–15 July 1736).

5. Charles Talbot (1685–1737), cr. (1733) Bn Talbot of Hensol; Lord Chancellor 1733–7.

6. Philip Yorke (1690–1764), cr. (1733) Bn Hardwicke and (1754) E. of Hardwicke; Chief Justice of the King's Bench 1733–7; Lord Chancellor 1737–56.

7. The printed bills, dated 'Wednesday, July 14th 1736,' announced the public burning of five Acts of Parliament. See text of bill in Philip C. Yorke, *Life and Correspondence of Philip Yorke Earl of Hardwicke,* Cambridge, 1913, i. 138. 'One of these printed bills being carried into the court of King's Bench, it was referred to the grand jury then sitting, who found it a vile

TO GRAY, August 1736

Missing. Mentioned *post* Aug. 1736. The letter, probably addressed to Gray in London, was carelessly folded and 'had been opened without breaking the seal.'

From GRAY, August 1736

Missing. Probably written in London shortly before Gray's departure for Burnham early in August. Mentioned *post* Aug. 1736.

From GRAY, August 1736

Printed from MS in Waller Collection.
Dated by the postmark and the reference to Burnham (*post* 17 Aug. 1736). The impression of the date stamp is imperfect, and only the month is decipherable.
Address: To the Honourable Mr Horace Walpole at King's College, Cambridge.
Postmark: [?] AV.

[Burnham, August 1736.]

<   >

I WAS hindered in my last,[1] and so could not give you all the trouble I would have done; the description of a road,[2] which your coach-wheels have so often honoured,[3] it would be needless to give you; suffice it, that I arrived at Birnam Wood[4] without the loss of any of my fine jewels,[5] and that no little cacaturient[6] gentlewoman made me any reverences by the way. I live with my uncle,[7] a great hunter in imagination; his dogs take up every chair in the house,[8] so I'm forced to stand at

and scandalous libel, published and dispersed by persons unknown' (*London Evening Post* 13–15 July 1736). The author, Robert Nixon (d. ?1746), a nonjuring clergyman, was admitted to bail 28 Sept.; was tried before Lord Hardwicke 7 Dec. 'for a high misdemeanour, in being the author, printer, and publisher, of a most scandalous and insolent libel dispersed in Westminster Hall on the 14th of July last' (ibid. 7–9 Dec. 1736); and was fined £5 and sentenced to five years' imprisonment 10 Feb. 1737 (ibid. 8–10 Feb. 1737). See also Yorke, op. cit. i. 137–40; Hervey, *Memoirs* ii. 567–8; George Harris, *Life of Lord Chancellor Hardwicke*, 1847, i. 325–7; GM 1737, vii. 121 and 1746, xvi. 383.

1. Missing.
2. The Windsor road.
3. On the way to Eton.
4. Burnham, Bucks.
5. The Windsor road passes across Hounslow Heath.
6. Not in OED. Apparently derived from the Latin '*cacaturio*' (Martial, XI. lxxvii).
7. Jonathan Rogers (1677–1742), attorney, who m. (1710) Anne Antrobus, Gray's aunt (George Lipscomb, *History and Antiquities of . . . Buckingham*, 1847, iii. 217).
8. 'Cant's Hall, a small house . . . not far from the common' (MS note by Cole in his copy of Mason's *Memoirs*, first printed by Mitford in *Works of Gray*, 1835–6, i. p.

this present writing, and though the gout forbids him galloping after
'em in the field, yet he continues still to regale his ears and nose with
their comfortable noise and stink; he holds me mighty cheap, I perceive, for walking, when I should ride, and reading, when I should
hunt. My comfort amidst all this is, that I have at the distance of half a
mile through a green lane[9] a forest[10] (the vulgar call it a common) all
my own; at least as good as so, for I spy no human thing in it but myself;
it is a little chaos of mountains and precipices; mountains, it is true,
that don't ascend much above the clouds, nor are the declivities quite
so amazing as Dover Cliff; but just such hills as people, who love their
necks as well as I do, may venture to climb, and crags that give the eye
as much pleasure as if they were more dangerous. Both vale and hill is
covered over with most venerable beeches, and other very reverend
vegetables, that, like most ancient people, are always dreaming out
their old stories to the winds:

> And, as they bow their hoary tops, relate
> In murm'ring sounds the dark decrees of Fate;
> While visions, as poetic eyes avow,
> Cling to each leaf, and swarm on ev'ry bough.[11]

At the foot of one of these squats me I, *il penseroso*, and there grow to
the trunk for a whole morning,

> —the tim'rous hare and sportive squirrel
> Gambol around me—[12]

like Adam in Paradise, but commonly without an Eve; and besides, I
think he did not use to read Virgil as I usually do there. In this situation I often converse with my Horace aloud too, that is, talk to you, for
I don't remember that I ever heard you answer me; I beg pardon for

cv, quoted in *Gray's Corr.* i. 47) at Cantshill in Britwell, near Burnham, the lease of
which was left to Mrs Rogers by the will
(26 Nov. 1728) of her brother, Robert Antrobus, vicar of Burnham. See Thomas A.
Walker, *Admissions to Peterhouse,* Cambridge, 1912, p. 200.

9. Now called Green Lane, along which
stand several villas (*Vict. Co. Hist., Bucks,*
iii. 167).

10. Burnham Beeches.

11. The lines, presumably Gray's own,
were perhaps inspired by some Latin verses
of West's. See *Gray's Corr.* i. 47, n. 7. Mr
Ketton-Cremer calls our attention to an ap-

parent echo, in the first couplet, of two
lines from Matthew Green's *The Spleen:*

'Here nymphs from hollow oaks relate
The dark decrees and will of fate.'

But it is unlikely that Gray had seen
Green's poem before its publication in
1737. The echo is probably accidental unless there should be a common source.

12. An echo of *Paradise Lost* iv. 343–5:

'Sporting the lion ramp'd, and in his paw
Dandled the kid; bears, tigers, ounces,
    pards
Gambol'd before them. . . .'

taking all the conversation to myself, but it is your own fault indeed. We have old Mr Southern[13] at a gentleman's house a little way off, who often comes to see us. He is now seventy-seven year old,[14] and has almost wholly lost his memory, but is as agreeable as an old man can be;[15] at least I persuade myself so when I look upon him, and think of Isabella[16] and Oroonoko.[17] I shall be in town in about three weeks, I believe; if you direct your letters to London, they will take care to send 'em safe; but I must desire you would fold 'em with a little more art, for your last had been opened without breaking the seal. Adieu,

Dear [?]d,[18] yours ever,

T. GRAY

PS. Regreet Almanzor[19] from me,
Wish Pol. Cutchee[20] joy from me,
Give Cole[21] an humble service from me.

To WEST, Tuesday 17 August 1736

Reprinted from Works iv. 415–16.

King's College, August 17, 1736.

Dear West,

GRAY is at Burnham, and, what is surprising, has not been at Eton. Could you live so near it without seeing it? That dear scene of our quadruple alliance would furnish me with the most agreeable recollec-

13. Thomas Southerne (ca 1659–1746), dramatist.

14. No record of his birth survives, but he was admitted as a pensioner at Trinity College, Dublin, 30 March 1676, 'aged 17' (George D. Burtchaell and Thomas U. Sadleir, *Alumni Dublinenses*, Dublin, 1935).

15. 'He lived nine years longer, and died at the great age of eighty-six [26 May 1746: see J. W. Dodds, *Thomas Southerne*, New Haven, 1933, p. 10]. Mr Gray always thought highly of his pathetic powers, at the same time that he blamed his ill taste for mixing them so injudiciously with farce, in order to produce that monstrous species of composition called tragi-comedy' (Mason, *Mem. Gray* 25).

16. The heroine of Southerne's *Fatal Marriage, or the Innocent Adultery*, 1694.

17. The hero of Southerne's *Oroonoko*, 1696.

18. Deleted word, of which only the last letter is decipherable.

19. Ashton.

20. Mary, daughter of John Cutchy (or Cuchee), barber of Trinity College, Cambridge; married ca 1736 Thomas Watson Ward (ca 1718–50), Esq. of Great Wilbraham. Cole calls her a celebrated beauty (Venn, *Alumni Cantab. sub* Ward; W. M. Palmer, *William Cole of Milton*, Cambridge, 1935, pp. 83, 143). Her marriage must be the occasion for this reference.

21. William Cole (1714–82), divine, antiquary; HW's correspondent. He was at Eton 1726–32; admitted sizar at Clare College, Cambridge, 24 Jan. 1733; migrated to King's in 1735, and admitted scholar. See COLE i. p. xxv; Venn, *Alumni Cantab.*

tions. 'Tis the head of our genealogical table, that is since sprouted out into the two branches of Oxford and Cambridge. You seem to be the eldest son, by having got a whole inheritance to yourself; while the manor of Granta[1] is to be divided between your three younger brothers, Thomas of Lancashire,[2] Thomas of London,[3] and Horace. We don't wish you dead to enjoy your seat, but your seat dead to enjoy you. I hope you are a mere elder brother, and live upon what your father left you, and in the way you were brought up in, poetry: but we are supposed to betake ourselves to some trade, as logic, philosophy, or mathematics. If I should prove a mere younger brother, and not turn to any profession, would you receive me, and supply me out of your stock, where you have such plenty? I have been so used to the delicate food of Parnassus, that I can never condescend to apply to the grosser studies of Alma Mater. Sober cloth of syllogism colour suits me ill; or, what's worse, I hate clothes that one must prove to be of no colour at all. If the Muses *cœlique vias et sidera monstrent,* and *qua vi maria alta tumescant* why *accipiant:*[4] but 'tis thrashing, to study philosophy in the abstruse authors. I am not against cultivating these studies, as they are certainly useful; but then they quite neglect all polite literature, all knowledge of this world. Indeed such people have not much occasion for this latter; for they shut themselves up from it, and study till they know less than any one. Great mathematicians have been of great use: but the generality of them are quite unconversible; they frequent the stars, *sub pedibusque vident nubes,*[5] but they can't see through them. I tell you what I see: that by living amongst them, I write of nothing else; my letters are all parallelograms, two sides equal to two sides; and every paragraph an axiom, that tells you nothing but what every mortal almost knows. By the way, your letters come under this description; for they contain nothing but what almost every mortal knows too, that knows you—that is, they are extremely agreeable, which they know you are capable of making them:—no one is better acquainted with it than

Your sincere friend,

Hor. Walpole

1. I.e., the Cam.
2. Ashton was baptized at Bolton-le-Sands, Lancs (*Eton Coll. Reg.*).
3. Gray was born in London.
4. See Virgil, *Georg.* ii. 475–80.
5. Virgil, *Ecl.* v. 57.

From WEST, ca Friday 20 August 1736

Reprinted from *Works* iv. 416–18.

[Oxford, ca] Aug. [20], 1736.

My dearest Walpole,

YESTERDAY I received your lively—agreeable—gilt[1]—epistolary—parallelogram, and today I am preparing to send you in return as exact a one as my little *compass* can afford you. And so far, Sir, I am sure we and our letters bear some resemblance to parallel lines, that, like them, one of our chief properties is seldom or never to meet. Indeed, lately my good fortune made some inclination from your university to mine; but whether I can reciprocate or no I leave you to judge from hence—

I sent Asheton word that I should more than probably make an expedition to Cambridge this August;[2] but Prinsep,[3] who was to have been my fellow-traveller, and would have gone with me to Cambridge, though not to King's, is unhappily disappointed,[4] and therefore my measures are broke, and I am very much in the spleen—else by this time I had flown to you with all the wings of impatience,

Ocyor cervis, et agente nimbos
Ocyor *Euro*.[5]

But now, alas! as Horace said on purpose for me to apply it,

Sextilem totum mendax desideror—[6]

This melancholy reflection would certainly infect all the rest of my letter if I were not revived by the sal volatile of your most entertaining letter. I am afraid the younger brother will make much the better gentleman, and so far verify the proverb,[7] and indeed all my brothers are so very forward that like the first and heaviest element, I shall have nothing but mere dirt for my share—and really such is the case of most

---

1. I.e., gilt-edged.
2. See West to Ashton July 1736 (*Gray-HW-West-Ashton Corr.* i. 91).
3. John Prinsep (1716–69), son of Reginald Prinsep, of Tamworth, Staffs; Eton 1731–5; Balliol College, Oxford, 1735–8; editor of *Musæ Etonenses*, edn 1755 (*Eton Coll. Reg.*; Foster, *Alumni Oxon.*; *Gray-HW-West-Ashton Corr.* i. 80).
4. In his succession to a fellowship at King's. Two vacancies occurred, and Prinsep was fourth on the list. See ibid. i. 80–5 and Tovey, *Gray and His Friends*, pp. 72–3.
5. Horace, *Carm.* II. xvi. 23–4: i.e., Favonius (West) would fly 'swifter than Eurus,' the east wind.
6. Horace, *Epist.* I. vii. 2.
7. The younger brother is the ancienter (or better) gentleman (V. S. Lean, *Collectanea*, Bristol, 1902–4, ii. pt ii. 737).

of your landed elder brothers, while the younger run away with the more fine and delicate elements. As for my patrimony of poetry, my dearest Horace, *ut semper eris derisor!*[8] what little I have I borrowed from my friends, and, like the poor ambitious jay in the trite fable, I live merely on the charity of my abounding acquaintance. Many a feather in my stock was stolen from your treasures; but at present I find all my poetical plumes moulting apace, and in a small time I shall be nothing further than, what nobody can be more, or more sincerely,

Your humble servant and obliged friend,

R. WEST

Gray at Burnham, and not see Eton? I am Asheton's ever, and intend him an answer soon.[9] I beg pardon for what's over leaf, but as I am moulting my poetry, it is very natural to send it you, from whom and my other friends it originally came. I translated, and now I have ventured to imitate the divine lyric poet.[10]

Ode. To Mary Magdalene

Saint of this learned awful grove,
While slow along thy walks I rove,
The pleasing scene, which all that see
    Admire, is lost to me.

The thought which still my breast invades,
Nigh yonder springs, nigh yonder shades,
Still, as I pass, the memory brings
    Of sweeter shades and springs.

Lost and enwrapt in thought profound,
Absent I tread Etonian ground;
Then starting from the dear mistake,
    As disenchanted, wake.

What though from sorrow free, at best
I'm thus but negatively blest:
Yet still, I find, true joy I miss;
    True joy's a social bliss.

8. Horace, *Serm.* II. vi. 53–4.
9. Ashton wrote to West 12 Aug. (*Gray-HW-West-Ashton Corr.* i. 96).

10. I.e. Horace: see *ante* 1 June 1736.

Oh! how I long again with those,
Whom first my boyish heart had chose,
Together through the friendly shade
    To stray, as once I strayed.

Their presence would the scene endear,
Like paradise would all appear,
More sweet around the flowers would blow,
    More soft the waters flow.

Adieu!

From GRAY, Sunday 19 September 1736

Missing. Probably written at Burnham and addressed to HW at Cambridge (see *post* 26 Sept. 1736).

To GRAY, September 1736

Missing. 'A little billet' (see *post* 26 Sept. 1736), probably written at Chelsea (see Whaley to HW 19 Sept. 1736).

From GRAY, Sunday 26 September 1736

Printed from MS in Waller Collection.
Dated by the postmark; for the date of the year see *ante* Aug. 1736.
Address: To the Honourable Horatio Walpole Esq. of King's College, Cambridge. *Postmark:* 27 SE.

[Burnham, Sept. 26, 1736.]

⟨   ⟩

IT rains, 'tis Sunday, this is the country; three circumstances so dull in conjunction with the dulness of my nature are like to give birth to an admirable production; I hope you will receive it, as you would a Michaelmas goose from a tenant, since I send it, not that I believe you have a taste for an awkward fat creature, but because I have no better way of showing my goodwill. Your name, I assure you, has been propagated in these countries by a convert of yours, one Cambridge;[1] he has brought over his whole family to you; they were before pretty good Whigs, but now they are absolute Walpolians. We have hardly any-

---

1. Crossed out in the MS. Mason substitutes two asterisks for the name (Mason, *Mem. Gray* 26), as also in Gray to Mason 23 July 1759 (ibid. 275); hence HW's allusion to Cambridge as 'the proprietor of the asterisk' (HW to Mason 10 July 1775). Richard Owen Cambridge (1717–1802), son of Nathaniel Cambridge, of Whitminster,

body in the parish but knows exactly the dimensions of the hall and saloon[2] at Houghton, and begins to believe that the lantern[3] is not quite so great a consumer of the fat of the land as disaffected persons have said; for your reputation we keep to ourselves that of your not hunting,[4] nor drinking hogen,[5] e'er a one of which would be sufficient here to lay your honour in the dust. I received a little billet[6] from my dear Horace, as if he had not heard from me; whereas I wrote last Sunday; we have not so good an opportunity here, as I could wish, not lying conveniently for the post; but to⟨morrow se'nnight⟩[7] I hope to be in town, and not long after at Cambridge.[8]

Yours most faithfully,

T. G.

PS. My love to Ashton.

Glos; at Eton in 1732, a form below HW and Gray; entered St John's College, Oxford, 1735 (*Eton Coll. Reg.*). He spent his vacations with his uncle, Thomas Owen, a retired attorney, at Britwell Place, Bucks, near Burnham, and had apparently just returned from a visit to Houghton. 'During one of the Oxford vacations, he accepted from his schoolfellow, Mr Horace Walpole, an invitation to King's College, Cambridge, where, after spending some time, they agreed to make the tour of Norfolk together, and conclude it by visiting Houghton' (*Works of Richard Owen Cambridge*, ed. George Owen Cambridge, 1803, p. vi). In 1751 Cambridge settled at Twickenham (R. S. Cobbett, *Memorials of Twickenham*, 1872, pp. 236–8).

2. The hall, 'a cube of forty,' and the salon, thirty feet wide, forty long, and forty high (*Ædes Walpolianæ, Works* ii. 249, 263).

3. The Houghton lantern, a 'favourite object of Tory satire at the time' (Mason, *Mem. Gray* 26), 'for eighteen candles, of copper gilt' (*Ædes Walpolianæ, Works* ii. 263) hung in the hall. In the *Craftsman* No. 107, 20 July 1728, is a letter with a ballad entitled 'The Norfolk Lanthorn.' This 'famous lantern that produced so much patriot wit,' as HW called it, was bought by Chesterfield in 1750 and was replaced by a French lustre (HW to Mann 25 July 1750; *Ædes Walpolianæ*, loc. cit.).

4. Sir Robert Walpole 'had usually two annual meetings at Houghton; the one in the spring, to which were invited only the most select friends and the leading members of the cabinet, continued about three weeks. The second was in autumn, towards the commencement of the shooting season. It continued six weeks or two months, and was called the congress. . . . He kept a public table to which all the gentlemen in the county found a ready admission' (William Coxe, *Memoirs of the Life and Administration of Sir Robert Walpole*, 1800, iii. 351). See also the satirical essay, *The Norfolk Congress; or A full and true Account of the Hunting, Feasting, and Merrymaking of Robin and his Companions . . .* in the appendix to the third volume of *The Craftsman*, 1731, pp. 317–22.

5. Strong beer, a large bottle of which was buried under the foundation stone of Houghton (GM 1735, v. 216). The praises of the 'Hogen of Houghton' were sung in a ballad, *Prosperity to Houghton*, ?1728 (BM Cat.), by Philip Floyd. HW's copy of this ballad, with his MS notes, is now WSL, and is reproduced in *A Selection of Letters of Horace Walpole*, ed. W. S. Lewis, New York, 1926, i. 127.

6. Missing.

7. The salutation on the other side is cut out; the words were restored in pencil by HW. Gray left Burnham before Friday 1 Oct., since he went to the theatre in London that night (*post* 6 Oct. 1736).

8. Gray left London ca 22 Oct. (Gray to Birkett 8 Oct. 1736, *Gray's Corr.* i. 52).

From GRAY, Wednesday 6 October 1736

Printed from MS in Waller Collection.
Dated by the allusions to performances at Covent Garden.
Address: To the Honourable Mr Horace Walpole at Chelsea.[1]
Postmark: Pe[nny] P[os]t Paid.[2]

[London, Oct. 6, 1736.]

< >

THE best news from Cornhill-shire[3] is that I have a little fever, which denies me the pleasure of seeing either you, or Alexander,[4] or Downing Street today, but when that leaves me at my own disposal I shall be at yours. Covent Garden has given me a sort of surfeit of Mr Rich[5] and his cleverness, for I was at *The Way of the World* when the machine broke t'other night;[6] the house was in amaze for above a minute, and I dare say a great many in the galleries thought it very dexterously performed, and that they screamed as naturally as heart could wish, till they found it was no jest, by their calling for surgeons,[7] of whom several luckily happened to be in the pit. I stayed to see the poor creatures[8] brought out of the house, and pity poor Mrs Buchanan[9] not

1. See *post* 31 Oct. 1736, nn. 16, 18.
2. The limits of the Penny Post extended ten miles from the General Post Office, Lombard Street, London. The triangular stamp in its earliest form introduced in 1681, and still in use in 1777, contained no date. See John G. Hendy, *History of the Early Postmarks of the British Isles*, 1905, pp. 52–7.
3. See *ante* 3 Jan. 1736, n. 1.
4. Delane acted Alexander in Lee's *Rival Queens* at Covent Garden 6 Oct. (*Daily Adv.* 6 Oct. 1736; Genest iv. 308).
5. John Rich (ca 1682–1761), pantomimist; manager of Lincoln's Inn Fields 1714–32, Covent Garden 1732–61. He is generally credited with introducing the pantomime on the English stage (but see Nicoll, *Drama 1700–50*, p. 252) in 1716. Rich's pantomimes 'were full of wit, and coherent, and carried on a story' (HW to Lady Ossory 3 Nov. 1782).
6. Friday 1 Oct., during the performance of Rich's pantomime, *The Necromancer* (1723), on the same bill with Congreve's *Way of the World.* 'Last night in the entertainment . . . at the Theatre Royal in Covent Garden, when the machine wherein

were Harlequin, the miller's wife, the miller, and his man, was got up to the full extent of its flying, one of the wires which held the hind part of the car broke first, and then the other broke, and the machine and all the people in it fell down upon the stage, by which unhappy accident' the four actors received serious injuries (*London Evening Post* 30 Sept.–2 Oct. 1736).
7. Apparently William Bromfield (1712–92), 'an eminent surgeon,' who was assisted by 'Mr Sherwood [?James Sherwood (d. 1757) (*London Magazine* 1757, xxvi. 203)], Mr Metcalf [?Theophilus Metcalfe (d. 1757) (GM 1757, xxvii. 93)], and Mr Kirwood.' See *London Evening Post* 2–5 Oct. 1736.
8. Only John Todd, who acted the miller's man, and died 3 Oct. 1736, has been identified (ibid.).
9. Mrs Elizabeth Buchanan (d. ?1736) (Genest iii. 389, 479, 481). Davies, who saw her as Cressida 20 Dec. 1733 at Covent Garden, wrote some fifty years later: 'Mrs Buchanan, a very fine woman and a pleasing actress, who died soon after in childbed' (Thomas Davies, *Dramatic Miscellanies,* 1785, iii. 171–2).

a little, whom I saw put into a chair in such a fright that as she is big with child, I question whether it may not kill her.

I am

Yours ever,

T. G.

From GRAY, Wednesday 13 October 1736

Printed from MS in Waller Collection.

Dated by the postmark, which on London letters was usually the same as the date of writing (see *post* 19 Sept. 1738), and the reference to *Othello* at Drury Lane.

Address: To the Honourable Mr Horace Walpole, of King's College, Cambridge.

Postmark: 13 OC.

[London, Oct. 13, 1736.]

<   >

I BROUGHT my neck safe to town, and, I promise you, when I break it, it shall not be after the dogs, nor from so mean an elevation as the saddle;[1] no, let me fall from Dover Cliff, or Leucate's promontory,[2] and if I cannot die like a hero, let it be at least like a despairing lover.[3] Mem.: I won't swing in a cambric handkerchief,[4] nor swallow verdigris. But, however, I that have preserved my neck in the country have not been able to do as much by my throat in London; which I made so sore, coming from *Othello* on Wednesday last,[5] that I should not be easily persuaded even at this present to swallow a bumper, though it were crowned with my dear Horace's health; it has not as yet turned to an absolute squinancy,[6] or a fever; but if you have a mind, I can very easily improve it into either of 'em. You have imitated your

1. An allusion to the equestrian tastes of Gray's uncle, Jonathan Rogers.

2. A white cliff on Cape Ducato, at the SW extremity of Santa Maura (ancient Leucas), an Ionian island. The temple of Apollo Leucatas stood on the cliff, and at the annual expiatory rites in honour of Apollo, a condemned criminal was obliged to plunge from the Leucadian rock into the sea for the sake of averting evil (Strabo, *Geogr.* X. ii. 9). Virgil (*Æneid* iii. 274–5) speaks of its dangers to mariners.

3. Sappho, rejected by Phaon, was the first to fling herself from the Leucadian rock, according to Menander (quoted by Strabo, loc. cit.). See *The Spectator* Nos. 223, 227, 233.

4. Perhaps an allusion to the suicide (22 May 1736) of Count Karl Heinrich Hoym (1694–1736), convicted of treason, and imprisoned in 1734 at the fortress of Koenigstein (*Allgemeine Deutsche Biographie*, Leipzig, 1875–1912). Gray might have read about it in GM 1736, vi. 292, where Hoym is said to have 'hanged himself on the 21st of April at night, with a handkerchief fastened to a hook in the wall.'

5. I.e., Tuesday, 5 Oct., at Drury Lane (*Daily Adv.* 5 Oct. 1736).

6. Quinsy.

namesake[7] very happily, I believe, for I have not the Latin to look at; I wish poor Mr Iccius[8] in Ireland had taken the poet's good advice. Pray add my admiration of the first stanzas to good Mr Ashton's, and give him my service for his, and believe me,

Yours ever,

T. GRAY

From GRAY, Wednesday 27 October 1736

Printed from MS in Waller Collection.
The date of the year is determined by the reference to Cole.
Address: To the Honourable Horatio Walpole Esq. at the Treasury, London.
Postmark: CAMBRIDGE 29 OC.

[Cambridge,] Oct. 27 [1736].

HERE am I, a little happy to think I shan't take degrees,[1] and really, now I know there is no occasion, I don't know but I may read a little philosophy;[2] it is sufficient to make a thing agreeable not to have much need of it: such is my humour, but let that pass. West supped with me the night[3] before I came out of town; we both fancied, at first, we had a great many things to say to one another, but when it came to the push, I found I had forgot all I intended to say, and he stood upon punctilios and would not speak first, and so we parted. Cole[4] has been examined by the proctors,[5] and took bachelors' degrees,[6] in order (he

7. HW's imitation of Horace, *Epist.* I. xii, addressed to Iccius, has not been found.

8. Not identified. The historical Iccius ca 27 B.C. joined Ælius Gallus in an expedition to Arabia (*Carm.* I. xxix. 1–2); he became caretaker of Agrippa's possessions in Sicily 20 B.C. In this epistle Horace advises him to be content with his lot.

1. That is, academic degrees. Gray wrote to West before 22 Dec. that he would leave college (*Gray's Corr.* i. 56). He was admitted a student at the Inner Temple 22 Nov. 1735 (*Eton Coll. Reg.*). Extended residence was not required (see *post* ca 12 Nov. 1737, n. 20), but the student had to keep his name on the books for seven years before he could be called to the bar (Sir Frank Mac-Kinnon in *Johnson's England*, ed. A. S. Turberville, Oxford, 1933, ii. 288). Gray

left Cambridge 14 Sept. 1738 without taking his B.A. (*Gray's Corr.* i. 90 and 'Chronological Table').

2. There is a list of suggested readings in the 'philosophical' studies for third-year students in Daniel Waterland's *Advice to a Young Student,* 1730, p. 25; see Christopher Wordsworth, *Scholæ Academicæ,* Cambridge, 1877, p. 333. A copy of Samuel Pufendorf's *De Officio hominis et civis juxta legem naturalem* is listed among the schoolbooks in Gray's MS catalogue of his library (W. P. Jones, *Thomas Gray, Scholar,* Cambridge, Mass., 1937, p. 154).

3. Probably Thursday 21 Oct. (see *ante* 26 Sept. 1736, n. 7).

4. William Cole, HW's correspondent.

5. Leonard Addison (ca 1699–1772), D.D., Fellow of Pembroke 1722, Senior Proctor 1736–7; and John Ferrar (d. 1739), Fellow

says), when he is Master of Arts, to assist a friend with his vote and interest;[7] he told me he would not be puzzled in philosophy, because he would not expose himself, but desired to be examined in classics, which he understood. He still talks of having his leg cut off, and then being married. I have not seen Ashton; he is at St Ives,[8] and I don't know when he comes back; Berkly[9] makes a speech the 5th of November;[10] I am dear, dear Horace,

Yours most truly,

T. G.

When d'ye come?

To WEST, October 1736

Missing. Mentioned *post* 31 Oct. 1736.

From WEST, Sunday 31 October 1736

Printed from MS now WSL.

Address: ⟨To the Honourable⟩ Horace Walpole Esq. ⟨in care of the⟩ Honourable Sir Robert ⟨Walpole⟩, Downing Street, Whitehall.

Postmark: OXFORD 1 NO.

of Clare 1722–39, Junior Proctor 1736–7 (Venn, *Alumni Cantab.*).

6. As a fellow-commoner of King's (Cole migrated from Clare in 1735) he was not subject to the Senate House examinations held in Lent term (*ante* 27 Jan. 1735, n. 7); consequently the last statutable exercise performed by Cole for the B.A. degree was his second act and opponency. 'These exercises began on the third Monday of each term' (Winstanley, *Unreformed Cambridge* 45), that is, on 25 Oct. this year. See also Adam Wall, *Account of the different Ceremonies observed in the Senate House of the University of Cambridge,* Cambridge, 1798, pp. 41–51; Wordsworth, op. cit. 32–43.

7. The proctors were elected by the regent masters of arts (Wall, op. cit. 7–12), and the proctors, meet in the vestry at St proctors and moderators in examinations (George Peacock, *Observations on the Statutes of the University of Cambridge,* 1841, p. 70). Cole took his M.A. in 1740.

8. Hunts. Ashton's relatives at St Ives

have not been traced. An Alpress Ashton (d. 1808) is buried in All Saints at St Ives. See *Vict. Co. Hist., Hunts* ii. 222.

9. Probably Samuel Barkley or Berkley (b. 1714, d. *post* 1750), at Eton 1727–33; admitted 1733, Fellow of King's 1736–50, B.A. 1738, M.A. 1741 (*Eton Coll. Reg.;* Venn, *Alumni Cantab.*).

10. On 5 Nov., the day after the vice-chancellor's election, 'at three o'clock, the vice-chancellor, noblemen, heads, doctors, and the proctors, meet in the vestry at St Mary's Church, and go from thence to the Senate House, preceded by the bedels, where a speech in Latin is delivered by a master of arts, a regent (who comes to the vestry in the regent's habit) appointed by the vice-chancellor of the preceding year' (Wall, op. cit. 36). Why Samuel Barkley, not even a B.A., should have been appointed orator is not clear; but the decree of 1606 ordering this speech did not require that the orator should be a regent master of arts, though he customarily was (ibid.).

Ch[rist] Ch[urch], Oct. 31, 1736.

Dearest Walpole,

I RETURN you ten thousand thanks for your late agreeable letter[1] about Antony and Cleopatra, *Cantaber* and Cymodoce.[2] I take your criticism on John Dryden,[3] servant to his Majesty, to contain a great deal of learning and sagacity. Bossu[4] himself nor Hédelin[5] could not have made a juster remark than yours about the divorce of Scribonia from Tiberius.[6] That was certainly an elegant circumstance in the tragedy, and might be made a second part to the divorce of Queen Catharine from Harry VIII.[7] The thought about the hiss has the true sting of an epigram, and deserves a clap. But, I protest, I forgot all this while and took you for your namesake;[8] not but that he is much obliged to you, since you have explained me the scheme of his drama with as much wit as he himself could. Pray, the next time you see him, give my humble service, and tell him nobody has a greater respect for him than,

R. WEST, Gent.

As for the Grotto-nymphs,[9] I desire my love to them, and would certainly send them an eclogue; but there is a sort of one ready-made for them in the 8 vol. *Spectators* No. 632[10] which is very much at their serv-

1. In the absence of HW's letter, West's allusions remain unexplained. Considering HW's fondness for allegory, and his proposal to carry on a classical correspondence (*ante* 9 Nov. 1735), his letter may perhaps have dealt with George II's rumoured affair with Madame Wallmoden, whose removal from Hanover to London would place Queen Caroline in a difficult position. During Oct. 1736 'pasquinades were stuck up in several quarters of the town, and some practical jokes and satires . . . were likewise exhibited' (Hervey, *Memoirs* ii. 610). The scandal which Madame Wallmoden's arrival would cause, and the possibility of a divorce between George II and Queen Caroline, would explain some of West's allusions. The parallels between George II's trips to Hanover and Antony's to Egypt, and between the implied neglect of Caroline and of Octavia, are obvious.

2. Cymodoce (see Virgil, *Æneid* v. 826) is one of the fifty Nereids who together with the rivers attend the marriage of the Thames and the Medway (*Faerie Queene* IV. xi. 50). Cantaber perhaps means a Cam-

bridge man. Since both the Cherwell and the Granta (Cam) attend the marriage (*F.Q.* IV. xi. 25 and 34), the allegory may refer to a meeting of Oxford and Cambridge (West and HW) in London.

3. Probably Dryden's *All for Love*.

4. René le Bossu (1631–80). His *Traité du poème épique* (1675) is often mentioned by Dryden.

5. François Hédelin (1604–76), Abbé d'Aubignac, critic; champion of the three unities.

6. It was not Scribonia (the wife of Augustus) whom Tiberius divorced, but Vipsania Agrippina.

7. George II's divorce would have been the first royal divorce in England since Henry VIII's in 1533.

8. Presumably the poet Horace, upon whom HW seems to have fathered his 'tragedy.'

9. See below, n. 16.

10. *The Spectator* No. 632 (13 Dec. 1714) contains a poem of forty lines 'To Mrs —— on her Grotto.'

ice. I had a great mind at first to have imitated Claudian's manner,[11] and have called absence[12] among the Naiads and Nereids from Deiopæa[13] down to Merdamante,[14] late of Fleetditch, and so have made them all bring in some little peppercorn towards finishing the grotto—
  I then thought of setting out in Pope's style[15] with a—

Thy grotto, Chelsea, and thy shell-retreats,[16] etc., etc.

At last (I beg pardon) I struck out this little *échantillon* of an attempt, which I desire you to keep warm in your bureau, as you did my late letter to Ashton—[17]

The Grotto

Authors of doubtless faith relate,
That Taste and Leisure met of late,
And formed a grotto fair and neat,
To deck the ministerial seat.[18]

Impossible! some others cried,
For they on Richmond Hill reside,
And there with our illustrious Queen
In Merlin's Cave[19] they oft are seen.

11. In *Epithalamium de nuptiis Honorii Augusti*, lines 159–71, where Venus is surrounded by Naiads and Nereids, each giving her a present.

12. An Eton term, meaning to call the roll.

13. See Virgil, *Georg.* iv. 343, *Æneid* i. 72.

14. A 'mud-nymph' in *Dunciad* ii. 334–5: 'Nigrina black, and Merdamante brown
Vied for his love in jetty bowers below.'

15. Cf. first line of 'Windsor Forest.'

16. Lady Walpole's grotto at Chelsea, which was the subject of two poems in the *Gentleman's Magazine*. One of them, entitled 'On the Presents of Shells to Lady Walpole' (GM 1735, v. 47), contains the lines:

'The fame of W-lp-le is above
Mean monuments of private love:
Let Chelsea grotto be bedeckt
With marks of *national* respect.'

See also GM 1734, iv. 697.

17. Perhaps West to Ashton July 1736

(*Gray-HW-West-Ashton Corr*. i. 91), which contained a paraphrase of Martial iii. 61.

18. 'In the year 1723 Sir Robert Walpole obtained from the Crown the lease of a house and garden in the stable-yard adjoining to the Royal Hospital. Here he himself occasionally resided, and enlarged and improved the premises by the purchase of part of the ground belonging to the Gough family' (Thomas Faulkner, *Historical and Topographical Description of Chelsea*, 1829, ii. 294).

19. Built in 1735. Toynbee's statement that it was the same as the Queen's Hermitage (see *post* ca Jan. 1748, n. 45) is erroneous. It was 'erected in Richmond Garden by Queen Caroline, . . . was designed by Kent, and was by no means a cave but a thatched house with small Gothic windows, and furnished with bookcases. At one end were six waxen figures large as life: Merlin and his secretary writing at a table,' etc. (HW in his notes to Mason's *Satirical Poems* ed. Paget Toynbee, Oxford, 1926, pp. 58–9).

Credit to both reports is due:
They long at Richmond dwelt, 'tis true:
But, from the downy lap of rest
When business called the royal breast,
Then straight to Chelsea-side in haste
Leisure retired, and with her Taste.

From GRAY, Wednesday 29 December 1736

Printed from MS in Waller Collection.

Dated by the postmark and the reference to Lord Townshend. Unless Gray mis-
wrote 'Wednesday' for 'Tuesday,' this is a rare example in the correspondence of
a letter stamped in London the same day it was posted in Cambridge (see also *post*
20 March 1738, and preliminary note to *ante* 16 April 1734).

Address: To the Honourable Horace Walpole Esq. at the Treasury, Westminster. *Postmark:* CAMBRIDGE 29 DE.

Wednesday [Dec. 29, 1736], Cambridge.

My dear Horace,

I THINK this is the first time I have had any occasion to find fault
with Sir Robert's mal-administration,[1] and if he should keep you in
town another week, I don't know whether I shan't change my side, and
write a *Craftsman;*[2] I am extreme sorry I could not dine with you last
Sunday, but I really was engaged at Peterhouse, and did not know of the
honour you intended me till night; if it had not been for a great cold I
had got, I certainly should have come post to supper. I engage myself to
drink tea with you at King's the day after tomorrow, for then we expect
you; I mean me, for Ashton is to try not to expect you then. I believe I
shall stay here till February, so pray come hither, if that can be any part
of a reason for it. The Moderator[3] has asked me to make the Tripos
verses[4] this year; they say the[5] University has sent a letter by the post to

1. MS, 'male-administration.' Such spellings were common in the eighteenth century. See OED.

2. The organ of the Opposition, founded
(Dec. 1726) and edited by Nicholas Am-
hurst (1697–1742) under the pseudonym of
'Caleb D'Anvers, of Gray's Inn, Esq.' Its
principal contributors were Bolingbroke,
Pulteney, and Thomas Cooke (*Cambridge
Bibliography of English Literature*, 1941,
ii. 698, 713).

3. Probably the Senior Moderator, James

Brown (ca 1709–84), D.D., Master of Pembroke 1770–84; friend and correspondent
of Gray.

4. Also called *carmina comitialia*; commissioned by the two moderators of the
year for distribution among the undergraduates on Thursday after Midlent Sunday (Thursday 24 March 1737), the day of
the second tripos (Christopher Wordsworth, *Scholæ Academicæ*, Cambridge,
1877, p. 19; Adam Wall, *Account of the different Ceremonies observed in the Senate*

thank my Lord Townsend[6] for the statue.[7] I have had a letter from West with an elegy of Tibullus translated in it,[8] t h u s l o n g ; I have wrote you a letter with fifty I's in it, besides me's and we's, and I am.

Ever yours,

T. GRAY

From WEST, ca December 1736

Missing. Probably written at Oxford. Implied *post* 3 Jan. 1736.

To WEST, Monday 3 January 1737

Printed from MS now WSL. Bequeathed in 1828 by Mrs Damer to Sir Wathen Waller, 1st Bt; Waller sale (5 Dec. 1921), lot 194, to Maggs; offered by Maggs, Cat. No. 439 (Summer, 1923), lot 1166; No. 473 (Spring, 1926), lot 697; Edgar A. Wells to WSL (Nov. 1930).

Misdated by HW 3 Dec. 1736 for 3 Jan. 1737. Dated by the postmark and *post* 12 Jan. 1737.

Address: To Mr Richard West at Christ Church College, Oxford.
Postmark: 4 IA.

London, Dec. [Jan.] 3d, 1736 [1737].

My dear West,

THAT poem[1] you mention went once under my name; but you commend it, and its praise, *cum recitas, incipit esse tuus:*[1a] Yet I assure you 'tis the last thing of your writing that I would commend. As to myself, I assure you I don't think I am at all a poet, but from lov-

---

House of the University of Cambridge, 1798, p. 56). For Gray's verses, 'Luna habitabilis,' see *post* 18 April 1737.

5. Gray first wrote 'my.'

6. Charles Townshend (1674–1738), 2d Vct Townshend, who married HW's aunt, Dorothy Walpole.

7. Lord Townshend in a letter to John Wilcox, the Vice-Chancellor, 2 Dec. 1736, offered to pay for the statue of George I in the Senate House; the offer was accepted 8 Dec. The statue, by John Michael Rysbrack (ca 1693–1770), was not erected until October 1739, and as Lord Townshend d. 21 June 1738, the costs were borne by his son, Charles. See Willis and Clark iii. 55–6; Nichols, *Lit. Illus.* iv. 525.

8. 'The reason I choose so melancholy a kind of poesy is because my low spirits and constant ill health (things in me not imaginary, as you surmise, but too real, alas! and, I fear, constitutional) "have tuned my heart to elegies of woe. . . ." As for this poor unlicked thing of an elegy, pray criticize it unmercifully, for I send it with that intent' (West to Gray 22 Dec. 1736; *Gray's Corr.* i. 58). The elegy is not extant.

---

1. Not identified.

1a. From Martial I. xxxviii, an epigram on a plagiarist (information from Dr R. W. Chapman).

ing verses, try to make some now and then: There are few but try in their lives, and most of us succeed alike. In short as naturalists account for insects in places, where they can't tell how they got there, but cry the wind wafts their eggs about into all parts, and some perish, and some, meeting with proper juices, thrive; so Nature, I believe, wafts about poetical eggs or seeds, and thence come poets, when the grain don't light upon a barren surface. But I'll give you some account of it, as far as my own experience goes, in verse; as the best way to describe a circle, is to draw it: You will perceive that my knowledge extends no farther than the miscarrying embryos.[2]

1.

Seeds of poetry and rhyme
    Nature in my soul implanted;
But the genial hand of Time,
    Still to ripen 'em is wanted:
Or soon as they begin to blow,
My cold soil nips the buds with snow.[3]

2.

If a plenteous crop arise,
    Copious numbers, swelling grain,
Judgment from the harvest flies,
    And careless spares to weed the plain:
Tares of similes choke the roots,
Or poppy-thoughts blast all the shoots.

3.

Youth, his torrid beams who plays,
    Bids the poetic spirit flourish;
But though flowers his ardour raise,
    Maggots[4] too 'twill form and nourish;
And variegated Fancy's seen
Vainly enamelling the green.[5]

4.

First when pastorals I read;
    Purling streams[6] and cooling breezes

2. See n. 9 below. Much of this reflection on poetry was inspired by Pope.

3. These six lines are perhaps the most revealing HW ever wrote upon himself.

4. See n. 9 below.

5. 'O'er the smooth enamel'd green' (Milton, *Arcades*, line 84).

6. See Pope, *Epistle to Dr Arbuthnot*, line 150.

I only wrote of; and my head
   Rhymed on, reclined beneath the treezes:7
In pretty dialogue I told
Of Phœbus' heat, and Daphne's cold.

5.

Battles, sieges, men and arms,
   If heroic verse I'm reading,
I burn to write, with Myra's charms
   In episodes, to show my breeding:
But if my Myra cruel be,
I tell her so in elegy.

6.

Tragic numbers, buskined strains,8
   If Melpomene inspire,
I sing; but fickle throw my trains
   And half an act into the fire:
Perhaps Thalia prompts a sonnet
On Chloe's fan or Cælia's bonnet.

7.

For one silk-worm thought that thrives,
   Twenty more in embryo die;
Some spin away their little lives
   In ductile lines of foolery:9
Then for one moiety of the year,
Pent in a chrysalis appear.

8.

Till again the rolling sun
   Bursts th' inactive shell, and thoughts

7. Pope, *Essay on Criticism*, lines 350–1: 'Where'er you find "the cooling western breeze," In the next line, it "whispers through the trees." '

8. See Milton, *Il Penseroso*, lines 97–102.

9. Pope, *Dunciad* i. 55–66:
'Here she beholds the chaos dark and deep,
Where nameless somethings in their causes sleep,
Till genial Jacob, or a warm third day,
Call forth each mass, a poem, or a play:
How hints, like spawn, scarce quick in embryo lie,
How new-born nonsense first is taught to cry,
Maggots half-formed in rhyme exactly meet,
And learn to crawl upon poetic feet.
Here one poor word a hundred clenches makes,
And ductile Dulness new meanders takes;
There motley images her fancy strike,
Figures ill-paired, and similes unlike.'

Like butterflies their prison shun,
    Buzzing with all their parent faults;
And springing from the sluggish mould
Expand their wings of flimsy gold.

9.

But, my dear, these flies, they say,
    Can boast of one good quality,
To Phœbus gratefully they pay
    Their little songs and melody:
So I to you this trifle give,
Whose influence first bid it live.

Excuse this extempore jumble and if you have not patience to read it
through, ⟨make⟩ a present of it to the man at the Physic Garden:[10]
'twould make a great figure at the front of a monthly calendar,[11] or sub-
joined to the prognostications in *Poor Robin's Almanac*.[12] Poor Dab!
Adieu! my dear,

Yours sincerely,

H. W.

From West, Wednesday 12 January 1737

Reprinted from *Works* iv. 412–14.

Christ Church, Jan. 12, 1736/7.

Dear Sir,

POETRY, I take it, is as universally contagious as the smallpox;
every one catches it once in their life at least, and the sooner the
better; for methinks an old rhymester makes as ridiculous a figure as
Socrates dancing at fourscore.[1] But I can never agree with you that
most of us succeed alike; at least I'm sure few do like you. I mean not to
flatter, for I despise it heartily, and I think I know you to be as much

---

10. The Botanic Garden, opposite Magdalen College, at Oxford, founded in 1632
by Henry Danvers, E. of Danby (see
Thomas Salmon, *The Present State of the
Universities*, 1744, pp. 44–5).

11. The calendars of several eighteenth-
century almanacs, such as Gadbury's,
Moore's, and Partridge's, have doggerel
verses prefixed to each month.

12. 'Poor Robin. 1737. A New Almanack

after both Old and New Fashion,' etc. It
was begun ca 1662 by William Winstanley
(ca 1628–98), originally a barber (DNB). The
second section of the almanac is entitled 'A
Prognostication for the Year of our Lord
God 1737,' and is written partly in verse.

---

1. For the source of this tradition see
Xenophon's *Symposium* ii. 15–20 (from information supplied by Mr E. A. Havelock).

above flattery as the use of it is beneath every honest, every sincere man. Flattery to men of power is analogous with hypocrisy to God, and both are alike mean and contemptible; nor is the one more an instance of respect than the other is a proof of devotion. I perceive I am growing serious, and that is the first step to dulness; but I believe you won't think that in the least extraordinary, to find me dull in a letter, since you have known me so often dull out of a letter.

As for poetry, I own, my sentiments of it are very different from the vulgar taste. There is hardly anywhere to be found (says Shaftesbury) a more insipid race of mortals than those whom the moderns are contented to call poets[2]—but methinks the true legitimate poet is as rare to be found as Tully's orator, *qualis adhuc nemo fortasse fuerit.*[3] Truly, I am extremely to blame to talk to you at this rate of what you know much better than myself; but your letter gave me the hint, and I hope you will excuse my impertinence in pursuing it. It is a difficult matter to account why, but certain it is that all people, from the duke's coronet to the thresher's flail,[4] are desirous to be poets; Penelope herself had not more suitors, though every man is not Ulysses enough to bend the bow. The poetical world, like the terraqueous, has its several degrees of heat from the line to the pole—only differing in this, that whereas the temperate zone is most esteemed in the terraqueous, in the poetical it is the most despised. Parnassus is divisible in the same manner as the mountain chimæra,

> —mediis in partibus hircum,
> Pectus et ora leæ, caudam serpentis habebat.[5]

The medium between the rampant lion and the creeping serpent is the filthy goat—the justest picture of a middling poet, who is generally very

2. Anthony Ashley Cooper (1671–1713), 3d E. of Shaftesbury, in 'Soliloquy: or, Advice to an Author' (the third treatise in *Characteristics of Men, Manners, Opinions, Times*): 'I must confess there is hardly anywhere to be found a more insipid race of mortals than those whom we moderns are contented to call poets, for having attained the chiming faculty of a language, with an injudicious random use of wit and fancy' (*Characteristics*, edn 1711, i. 207).

3. 'Atque ego in summo oratore fingendo talem informabo qualis fortasse nemo fuit' (Cicero, *Orator* 7).

4. Stephen Duck (1705–56). In the frontispiece to his *Poems on Several Subjects*, 2d edn, 1730, he is represented with a flail in the left hand and a copy of Milton in the right. The title-page explains that he was 'lately a poor thresher in a barn in the county of Wilts, at the wages of four shillings and sixpence per week.' *A Full and Authentic Account of Stephen Duck*, 1731, by Joseph Spence, had been prefixed to Duck's *Poems on Several Occasions*, 1736, of which extracts appeared in GM 1736, vi. 317–19.

5. Ovid, *Met.* ix. 646–7: modern texts read 'ignem' for 'hircum.'

bawdy and lascivious, and, like the goat, is mighty ambitious of climb-
ing up the mountains, where he does nothing but browse upon weeds.
Such creatures as these are beneath our notice. But whenever some
wondrous sublime genius arises, such as Homer or Milton, then it is
that different ages and countries all join in an universal admiration.
Poetry (I think I have read somewhere or other) is an imitation of nature; the poet considers all her works in a superior light to other mortals; he discerns every secret trait of the great mother, and paints it in
its due beauty and proportion. The moral and the physical world all
open fairer to his enthusiastic imagination; like some clear-flowing
stream, he reflects the beauteous prospect all around, and, like the
prism-glass, he separates and disposes nature's colours in their justest
and most delightful appearances. This sure is not the talent of every
dauber: art, genius, learning, taste, must all conspire to answer the full
idea I have of a poet, a character which seldom agrees with any of our
modern miscellany-mongers—but

> Quid loquor? aut ubi sum? quæ mentem insania mutat?[6]

I am got into enchanted ground, and can hardly get out again time
enough to finish my letter in a decent and laudable manner. Dear Sir,
excuse and pardon all this rambling criticism—I writ it out of pure
idleness, and, I can assure you, I wish you idle enough to read it
through. I am, my dear Walpole,

Yours most sincerely,

R. WEST

I wish you a happy New Year.

To GRAY, January 1737

Missing. Contained 'fragments' of 'the works of Cramputius' (see next letter).

From GRAY, Sunday 16 January 1737

Printed from MS in Waller Collection.
Dated by the postmark. The date of the year is conjectural. Gray was charged full
commons at Peterhouse during January in both 1737 and 1738, but since he wrote

6. Virgil, *Æneid* iv. 595.

to HW on 15 Jan. 1738, this letter is assigned to 1737. The Peterhouse records show no charges in 1736 before Jan. 23.

>   *Address:* To the Honourable Horace Walpole Esq. at the Treasury, Westminster. *Postmark:* CAMBRIDGE 17 IA.

[Cambridge, January 16, 1737.]

<   >

I HAVE a taste for the works of Cramputius,[1] and his scraps; if you can fill twelve baskets with such fragments, I have a stomach for 'em all.[2] One should have had a passion for Simplicia oneself, if one had lived in those days; she is so open and unreserved in her behaviour: the pleasure of having a mistress, that, when one made her a compliment and called her spider, should only cry ehe! I don't doubt but Portia behaved just so when Brutus made love to her (this was reckoned a scene of great gallantry I suppose at that time), and Q. Crassus Tubero[3] as pretty a fellow with the women as the Génie Jonquil.[4] I don't know whether you have forgot Cambridge or not; it's plain, you choose only to keep it in mind; it seems to be at this time of year that the humour usually takes you to tell us stories about your coming, but, however, I would rather be deceived than hear nothing at all of it; so say something of it, pray; everybody in Cambridge knows better than I, who remain

Yours to command,

PATIENT GRISSEL

For God's sake write often, if it be but two syllables.

To WEST, February 1737

Missing. Mentioned *post* 27 Feb. 1737.

1. This passage is unexplained, in the absence of HW's letter to which this is a reply.

2. Cf. *Othello* V. ii. 75.

3. This name was perhaps suggested by Orasius Tubero, the pseudonym of François de la Mothe le Vayer (1588–1672), an imitator of the classics. HW may have written 'Q. Orasius Tubero,' which Gray misread as Crassus.

4. Le Génie Jonquille, a voluptuous character in *L'Écumoire*, 1734, by Claude-Prosper Jolyot de Crébillon (1707–77). Those who opposed his desires and passions became objects of his wrath and were metamorphosed into moles, cormorants, monsters, etc. For Gray's copy (1735, 2 vols) see Gray's MS Catalogue of his library, f. 12 (W. P. Jones, *Thomas Gray Scholar*, Cambridge, Mass., 1937, p. 163).

From WEST, Sunday 27 February 1737

Reprinted from *Works* iv. 414–15.

Christ Church, February 27, 1736/7.

My dear Walpole,

IT seems so long to me since I heard from Cambridge, that I have been reflecting with myself what I could have done to lose any of my friends there. The uncertainty of my silly health might have made me the duller companion, as you know very well; for which reason, fate took care to remove me out of your way; but my letters, I am sure, at least carry sincerity enough in them to recommend me to any one that has a curiosity to know something concerning me and my amusements. As for Ashton, he has thought fit to forget me entirely;[1] and for Gray, if you correspond with him as little as I do (wherever he be, for I know not), your correspondence is not very great.—Full in the midst of these reflections came your agreeable letter.[2] I read it, and wished myself among you. You can promise me no diversion but the novelty of the place, you say, and a renewal of intimacies. Novelty, you must know, I am sick of; I am surrounded with it, I see nothing else. I could tell you strange things, my dear Walpole, of anthropophagi, and men whose heads do grow beneath their shoulders.[3] I have seen Learning dressed in old frippery, such as was in fashion in Duns Scotus's days; I have seen Taste in changeable [?garb],[4] feeding like the chameleon on air; I have seen Stupidity in the habit of Sense, like a footman in the master's clothes; I have seen the phantom mentioned in *The Dunciad*,[5] with a brain of feathers and a heart of lead:[6] it walks here, and is called Wit. Your other inducement you suggested had all its influence with me; and I had before indulged the thought of visiting you all at Cambridge this next spring—But *fata obstant*—I am unwillingly obliged to follow much less agreeable engagements. In the meantime I shall pester you

1. HW must have shown West's letter to Ashton, for Ashton soon afterwards wrote to West in a penitent manner. See *Gray-HW-West-Ashton Corr.* i. 126–7.
2. HW to West Feb. 1737, missing.
3. *Othello* I. iii. 144–5.
4. Word apparently omitted.
5. James Moore Smythe (1702–34), author of *The Rival Modes*, 1727.
'Never was dash'd out, at one lucky hit,

A fool, so just a copy of a wit;
So like, that critics said, and courtiers swore,
A wit it was, and call'd the phantom Moore.'
(*Dunciad* ii. 47–50.) See also *The Dunciad Variorum. With the Prolegomena of Scriblerus*, 1729, p. 25.
6. *Dunciad* ii. 44.

with quires of correspondence, such as it is; but remember, you were two letters in my debt—though indeed your last letter may fully cancel the obligation. You may recollect my last was a sort of a criticism upon poetry; and this will present you with a sort of poetry⁷ which nobody ever dreamt of but myself. I am, dear Sir,

Yours very sincerely,

R. WEST

To WEST, April 1737

Missing. Probably written at King's College. Mentioned *post* 18 April 1737.

From WEST, Monday 18 April 1737

Printed from MS now WSL.

H.G.,¹ April 18, [17]37.

Dear Sir,

METHINKS I need not doubt long who wrote either poem;² they sufficiently discover each their parent, the characteristic marks are upon them, and, this point settled, all prejudice of friendship apart, which is best may more easily be determined—*micat inter ignes* LUNA *minores*—³

I own the planetary poet's thoughts are sometimes as pretty as his expressions are easy, but I should apprehend his bent is more to humour than poetry. I wish too he were more correct. Perhaps there may be something laughable enough in his tale of the *gibbosus homuncio*,⁴

7. 'This poetry does not appear' (Berry).

1. Probably Highgate, London.
2. 'Planetæ sunt habitabiles' by Jacob Bryant (1717–1804), of King's (Fellow of King's, 1739), and 'Luna habitabilis' by Gray. On the basis of this letter Toynbee (*Gray-HW-West-Ashton Corr.* i. 132, n. 1) attributed the first poem to HW; but evidence to the contrary is supplied by an annotated copy of *Musæ Etonenses*, 1755, in the possession of Mr R. A. Austen-Leigh. The two poems are printed on pp. 48–52 and pp. 107–12 of vol. ii. of *Musæ Etonenses* (see also 'Authors' List for *Musæ Etonenses*, 1755,' *Etoniana* No. 21, 20 June 1917, pp. 334–6). These were the tripos verses for

1737, and were to be distributed among the undergraduates on the day of the second tripos, i.e., 24 March 1737 (see *ante* 29 Dec. 1736, n. 4; *Gray's Corr.* iii. 1198–9).
3. Horace, *Carm.* I. xii. 46–8, adapted. A compliment to Gray.
4. 'Planetæ sunt habitabiles,' lines 13–14. The hunch-backed manikin, the inhabitant of the moon, whose lips are frequently moistened by the cups of Bacchus:
'Si qua fides vulgo gibbosus homuncio
    Lunam
Incolit, et crebro cyathis uvescit Iacchi.'
For a reprint of the verses (mistakenly assigned to HW), see *Horace Walpole's Fugitive Verses*, ed. W. S. Lewis, New York, 1931, pp. 108–11.

in his reflection about Mercury's planet,⁵ *o felix senibus sedes,* and in
his thought about the solar inhabitants all bedewed with salamander-
water;⁶ but, to venture my opinion, is there not something wild, low,
and unphilosophical in those ideas, and I may say altogether unworthy
of the more serious spirit of his fellow-poet? The lines of his, which are
perhaps least taken notice of and which I like best, are these:

> In quibus halantes herbæ, fontesque sonori,
> Et sylvæ campos ditant; munitaque circum
> Oppida, cumque suis consurgunt mœnibus urbes⁷

which make a pretty group of images enough, and after them the final
lines about Galileo—*tu primus Olympi,*⁸ etc., where you may observe
the *et sine Thessalico,*⁹ etc., to be the same thought as Gray's *neu crede
ad magicas te invitum accingier artes.*¹⁰

The confidence I have in your discretion may excuse the great freedom of my criticism, so I will proceed with great sagacity and acuteness. Well then! in the lunar poem I find more of a design, and something besides a series of hexameters. I need not add, it is writ in quite a
different strain from the other piece—however, being so young a bard,
I would advise him not to fetch such midnight walks with his Goddess-
Muse;¹¹ scandal may ensue, and folks will talk: *dulce est per aperta—*
'tis so—*vere frui dulce est—*to be sure, but why *frui?* and *sub umbra*
too? O fie! nay his Muse grows jealous and calls him forsooth an
Endymion¹²—ah *infidele cavaliero della luna!* I am afraid your Cambridge criticasters (excuse the word)¹³ may again object to him his
bawdry and obscenity—but seriously, from *ecce autem* to *se vertere*

5. 'Planetæ sunt habitabiles,' lines 44–58.
6. Ibid. lines 59–63.
7. Ibid. lines 30–2.
8. Ibid. lines 80–4, which may be paraphrased, 'O illustrious Galileo! how many
thanks do we owe to you. You the first to
open the iron gates of Olympus; you the
first to unfold the lucid realms which once
would not endure mortal vision; you the
first to charm the moon without Thessalian
song.'
9. That is, with the telescope.
10. 'Luna habitabilis,' lines 21–2. Here
too the allusion is to the telescope. See Miss
Marjorie Nicolson's treatment of Gray's
poem in 'A World in the Moon,' *Smith College Studies in Modern Languages,* 1936,
xvii, No. 2, pp. 51–2, and her 'The Telescope and Imagination,' *Modern Philology,*
1934–5, xxxii. 233–60. For the classical allusions in the poem see the Aldine edition of
the *Poetical Works of Thomas Gray,* 1836,
pp. 177–82.
11. 'Luna habitabilis,' lines 6–9:
'Huc mihi, Diva veni; dulce est per aperta
    serena
Vere frui liquido, campoque errare silenti;
Vere frui dulce est; modo tu dignata pe-
    tentem
Sis comes, et mecum gelida spatiere sub
    umbra.'
12. Ibid. line 23.
13. The OED gives 1684 as the earliest use
of the word.

flammas[14] is very pretty and philosophical, and something better than the *gibbosus homuncio*. The next lines as far as *propriique crepuscula cœli*[15] I much admire and envy. The *et dubitas tantum*, etc., as far as *quin, uti nos*,[16] etc., brings Anchises to my mind in 6th *Æneid*,[17] and has that peculiar energy and conciseness of charming Virgil. Then down to *nostra se jactat in aula*[18] I no less like, especially *albescens pater Apenninus*[19] *ad auras*, and the *parvulus Anglia nævus, aliis longe fulgentior*,[20] alluding, I suppose, to our island's *late candentia saxa*.[21] And then the *certatimque suo cognomine signant*[22] is very concise and natural. The last thought, about our sending colonies to the *moon*,[23] I have some scruples about, as being a little satirical; at least it conveys satire to my apprehension, and his close of *victis dominabitur auris*[24] is at best a very squinting panegyric.[25]

I have thought of this subject so long, and the moon and planets have run in my head so much since I received yours,[26] that I deem it not improper to send you a dream I had concerning the lunar territory but the night before last.

Methought the angel Gabriel descended from heaven and carried me up out of my bed wherein I lay to the top of a high mountain. Then upon the spot he took a hatchet, aimed it at my skull, and cut my head in two; incontinently he scooped out my brains, and gave them me to

14. 'Luna habitabilis,' lines 30–41. Gray here describes the moon and her ocean as seen through the telescope; the waters greedily absorbing, and the islands reflecting the rays of the sun.

15. Ibid. lines 42–50. Continuing the topography of the moon: the glittering lands, snow-capped mountains, dark caves, shaded hills, etc.

16. Ibid. lines 51–5. The lunar inhabitants, cultivating their fields, building their fortifications, making wars, and honouring their triumphant victors. Here, too, Gray proceeds, praise has its reward—love and fear are not foreign to them, and mortal sorrows touch their hearts (Virgil, *Æneid* i. 461).

17. *Æneid* vi. 724–51.

18. 'Luna habitabilis,' lines 56–72. An account of the earth as seen from the moon.

19. In lines 64–5 Gray is speaking of France, Germany, and Italy.

20. Ibid. lines 66–7.

21. Horace, *Serm.* I. v. 26: 'saxis late candentibus Anxur.'

22. 'Luna habitabilis,' line 70. That is, eagerly calling England by its name. The spectators are the assembled lunar nobility.

23. Ibid. lines 80–91.

24. Ibid. line 95.

25. A free translation of the prophetic conclusion of the poem was printed in an advertisement in the *New Statesman and Nation* for 25 Jan. 1941:

'The time will come, when thou shalt lift thine eyes
To watch a long-drawn battle in the skies,
While aged peasants, too amazed for words,
Stare at the flying fleets of wondrous birds.
England, so long the mistress of the sea,
Where winds and waves confess her sovereignty,
Her ancient triumphs yet on high shall bear,
And reign, the sovereign of the conquered air.'

26. Missing.

swallow down into my belly; after that he stripped a solan-goose of all her feathers, buttered them, and crammed them into the ventricle of my brain-pan. Upon this I thanked him, and found myself so light that directly I mounted into the air, and in an hour's time was conveyed (by the force of attraction or of gravitation, which you like best) into the region of the moon. Upon inquiry I learned I was in the land of Galilæo, and soon after methought I was introduced to the king of the country, who, to give him his due, was as hospitable as any sublunary monarch; among other civilities, his lunātic[27] majesty showed me his cabinet of *lost things upon earth,*[28] which was so curious, and so useful besides, to an inhabitant of *terra firma,* that I could not refrain begging a catalogue of it, which he granted me with infinite humanity. What I remember ran thus—

1. Livy's *Decads.*[29] Complete. Best edition.
2. Mr Addison's poetical works.[30]
3. Astræa's pair of scales.
4. Foible in *The Way of the World.*[31]
5. A receipt to conserve mummies.
6. All the heroes of *The Dunciad.* Complete set.
7. A very fine Tibbalds.[32] Scarce, and to be had single.
8. The fountainhead of the river Nile.
9. Homer's country.
10. Æneas's nurse.[33]
11. Dido's reputation.
12. A large parcel of virginities. Of all sizes and something impaired by the keeping.

27. The significance of West's stress, as Dr Chapman points out, is doubtless etymological: West is indicating the classical pronunciation of 'lunatic'—introduced by pedants and still common in dialects—to distinguish it from the traditional (and Shakespearian) pronunciation.

28. *Rape of the Lock* v. 114; see also lines 115–22, and *Orlando Furioso* xxxiv. 48–92.

29. Of Livy's 'Annals'—sometimes called 'Decads' ('Decades') because of the traditional division of the books into groups of ten—only thirty-five out of the original 142 books have survived. For anecdotes concerning the supposed recovery, or near-recovery, of some of the lost books, see Isaac Disraeli's *Curiosities of Literature sub* 'Re-

covery of MSS,' 'Some Notices of Lost Works,' and 'Literary Impostures' (1868 edn, pp. 21, 59, 135).

30. Evidently West, like Gray, thought little of Addison's verses. See Gray to HW ca Jan. 1748.

31. Lady Wishfort of her maid-servant: 'Foible's a lost thing; has been abroad since morning, and never heard of since' (Congreve, *Way of the World* III. iv).

32. Lewis Theobald (1688–1744), the original hero ('piddling Tibbald') of *The Dunciad.* His Shakespeare, 'collated with the oldest copies and corrected. With notes explanatory and critical,' was published in 1734.

33. Caieta (Virgil, *Æneid* vii. 1–4).

13. *Lusus Westmonasterienses.*[34]
14. Several bundles of miscellany poems. A pennyworth.
15. Honour, Sincerity, Hospitality, Friendship, with several other virtues.
16. A Pylades and Orestes,[35] kept in spirits. A curious piece.
17. All the Dutch commentators,[36] very fair, never read but once.
18. Several Pindarics, Miltonics, Pastorals, etc. To be sold by the pound.
19. A great quantity of English gin, lately imported.
20. Most of the Eton play exercises, etc., etc., etc.[37]

I found, upon reading over the catalogue[38] of his majesty's cabinet, that he was intending a sale of his curiosities, and you may be sure, for the honour of our school, I should have bought up at any rate the things specified in the last article; but I must own I was so surprised to see it that the sudden anguish it put me in, made me awake. I am, dear Sir,

Yours sincerely,

R. W.

PS. My services to all: thanks to Gray and Ashton for their letters. Gray I intend to answer soon; I was afraid some fooleries of mine had offended him. My answer to Ashton I must defer till I have time to read *Leonidas* through with attention—[39] Some silly friend or cunning

34. The title of a collection of the verses, chiefly in Latin, recited at the two annual festivals at Westminster School. The collection was first published in 1730, ed. by Robert Prior; 2d edn 1734, 3d 1750 (BM Cat. *sub* Prior, Robertus). See also *Lusus alteri Westmonasterienses*, ed. James Mure, Henry Bull and C. B. Scott, 1863 (*pars secunda* 1867), pp. v–xx.

35. I.e., friendship.

36. On the classics: Joseph Scaliger, Grotius, the Gronovii, *et al.*

37. 'Exercises . . . were laid before the provost, by a time-honoured custom, as a claim for the weekly half-holiday called "play" ' (Farmer, op. cit. 151–2). William L. Collins, *Etoniana*, 1865, p. 116, defines play exercises as exercises in Attic Greek done by collegers of the sixth and a few of the upper divisions in the fifth form. The texts studied were Greek plays. For Gray's play exercises see Leonard Whibley, 'Thomas Gray at Eton,' *Blackwood's Magazine* 1929,

ccxv. 620; see also C. W. Brodribb, 'Gray's Eton Exercise and Pope,' N&Q 1921, ser. XII. viii. 101–2.

38. Probably suggested by *The Tatler* No. 42 (14–16 July 1709) (T), a satire on Christopher Rich, occasioned by the closing of Drury Lane by the Lord Chamberlain's orders, 6 June 1709 (*Genest* ii. 426). Rich's 'Inventory' includes 'A rainbow, a little faded. . . . A new moon, something decayed. . . . A setting sun, a pennyworth. . . . Roxana's night-gown. . . . Othello's handkerchief. . . . A serpent to sting Cleopatra. A mustard-bowl to make thunder with. Another of a bigger sort, by Mr D[enni]s's directions, little used.'

39. Ashton to West 5 April 1737 is a critique upon *Leonidas*, an epic poem in nine books by Richard Glover (1712–85), West's first cousin. It was published 1 April 1737 by Robert Dodsley (*Daily Adv.* 1 April 1737; *Gray-HW-West-Ashton Corr.* i. 129–31).

enemy,[40] I am afraid, has hurt Mr Glover extremely by panegyrizing him in such an extraordinary manner as he does in a new weekly paper, called *Common Sense, or the Englishman's Journal,* No. 10.[41] He prefers him, you must know, to Milton and Pope.[42]

> Of all mad creatures, if the learn'd say right,
> It is the slaver kills, and not the bite.[43]

Believe me, I long much to see you all; my spirit is often among you unseen; I mingle in your diversions; I have read two or three cantos in Tasso with Gray,[44] I have studied mathematics with Ashton, and am at present methinks learning music with you;[45] I often walk with you; I often drink tea with you; I laugh with you all, and smile at other people—Adieu.

I hope the length of my letter may excuse my long silence, if it does not tire you. I must desire you to read Shaftesbury's *Inquiry concerning Virtue;*[46] I dote on it. Mr Pope is much obliged to it in his *Essay.*[47]

From WEST, Tuesday 12 July 1737

Reprinted from *Gray-HW-West-Ashton Corr.* i. 146–9 (from Add. MS 32,562, folios 164 ff., a transcript by Mitford. See *ante* i. xxxv).
Address: To Horace Walpole Esquire at King's College, Cambridge.

[Oxford,] Tuesday, July 12, 1737.

My dearest Walpole,

I HAVE writ Ashton a long serious letter,[1] for which reason I intend to be very witty in this; I tell you so beforehand, for fear you should mistake me; you must expect a simile in every letter, and a metaphor

40. George Lyttelton (1709–73), cr. (1756) Bn Lyttelton. See *ante* i. 18 n. 121.

41. 9 April 1737. The first number appeared 5 Feb. 1737.

42. 'I can't help congratulating my own [country], that after having in the last age brought forth a Milton she has in this produced two more such poets as we have the happiness to see flourish now together, I mean Mr Pope and Mr Glover. . . . If the diction of *Leonidas* be softer, and the general flow of the numbers more harmonious than that of Milton himself, it may, in part, be ascribed to Mr Pope, as the great polisher and improver of our verse' (*Common Sense,* 2d edn, 1738, pp. 79–80).

43. Pope, 'Epistle to Dr Arbuthnot,' lines 105–6; in line 105 read 'the learn'd are right.'

44. 'I learn Italian like any dragon, and in two months am got through the 16th book of Tasso, whom I hold in great admiration. I want you to learn too, that I may know your opinion of him' (Gray to West March 1737, *Gray's Corr.* i. 61).

45. HW never 'learned' music.

46. 'An Inquiry concerning Virtue, or Merit,' in *Characteristics,* 1711, ii. 5–176.

47. *An Essay on Man,* 1734.

1. Missing. Ashton answered it 7 July (*Gray-HW-West-Ashton Corr.* i. 143–6).

in every syllable. Nay, you'll find a *je ne sais* in every comma, and something very surprising in every full stop. I don't intend to think neither, for I've heard your great wits never think—

> Critics indeed prescribe it as a rule
>   That you must think before you write;
> But I, who am, you know, no fool
>   Aver their judgment is not right.
> Now if you ask the reason why
>   I'll tell you truly by and by.
> Meantime if you should rashly think
>   My pen will drop a word of sense,
> Pray read no more, but with the rest dispense,
>   For faith, I send you nought but ink,
>   But if you deem the want of thought
>   A tolerable fault,
>   Prithee, proceed
> On that condition you may read.

I think these lines very much *à la française;* you can tell why.[2] And now I'll give you some in the English fashion.

> To thee, my thoughts magnetically roll,
> My heart the needle is, and thine the pole.[3]
> Since thou art gone no company can please,
> They rather show my want than give me ease.
> When Sol resigns our hemisphere to night
> Ten thousand stars but ill supply his light.
> Though to repay thy loss, enough there be,
> They're all a poor equivalent of thee.
> Like Ovid thus I stand, whose lines declare
> No inspiration like our native air.[3a]
> Banished from thee, I feel my notes decay,
> And miss the Muse to animate the lay.

Now, what Muse do you like best, French or English? In my opinion the first is in a consumption, and the latter in a dropsy. The French one is a pale slammekin[4] without any colour in her skin; and the English

2. Because of the metrical virtuosity shown in the lines.

3. Cf. Cowley, 'Resolved to be beloved,' lines 9–12:

'The needle trembles so, and turns about,
 Till it the northern point find out;

But constant then and fixt does prove
Fixt, that his dearest pole as soon may move.'

3a. An allusion to Ovid's poems written in exile; cf. *Epistolæ ex Ponto* I. iii. 35–6.

4. A slovenly female, a slattern (OED).

dab is a flushed dowdy, as full of pimples as she can stare. Had I time, I would rifle all Petrarca, but I would send you some

> Sonnetti, madrigaletti,
> Versi sciolti, vezzosetti
> Per Signor mio Valpoletti.

I would send you some Spanish too, not plain but mighty ampullated were I sufficiently versed in the *obras del*[5] *poetas Castellanos;* and then I'd tell you that the Italian and Spanish Muse both used a great deal of paint, only the last laid on in higher colours.

I dare say, after all, you'll tell me this is nothing to you. And yet so far it is, that I intended all this to divert you, and if it does not, at least the intention was good. If I knew as many languages as Briareus had hands, I should tell you a hundred ways only, how much I am—I know I might end my letter here, very conveniently, and end very prettily, but I won't; I'll write as far as my paper will let me, and then as Alexander wept heretofore that he had no more to conquer, or as the wild Indian[6] that galloped with full speed till he came to the sea, and then wondered that he could gallop no further, so I—. Apropos, an ode of Horace[7] lies before me, which I translated about three months ago—here it is.

Ad Pyrrham

> Say what dear youth his amorous rapture breathes
> Within thy arms beneath some grot reclined?
>   Pyrrha, for whom dost thou in wreaths
>   Thy golden tresses bind
> In plainness elegant? How oft shall he
> Complain, alas! upon the fickle skies,
>   And suddenly astonished see
>   The black'ning tempest rise;
> Who now enjoys thee, happy in conceit,
> Who fondly thinks thy love can never fail,
>   Never to him—unmindful yet
>   Of the fallacious gale.
> Wretch! to whom thou untried seemest fair,[8]

'Mrs Slammekin! as careless and genteel as ever! all you fine ladies, who know your own beauty, affect an undress' (Gay, *Beggar's Opera* II. iv).

5. So Mitford (Toynbee).

6. Allusion not found.

7. *Carm.* I. v.

8. This phrase is taken from Milton's version, the influence of which appears elsewhere in the lines.

For me, I've 'scaped the wreck; let yonder fane
Inscribed my gratitude declare
To him that rules the main.

I am, dear Sir, with all sincerity,

Your most humble servant and affectionate friend,

RICH. WEST

PS. I am afraid I cannot see you this summer, but I long to hear from you.

To GRAY, ca Thursday 14 July 1737

Missing. Mentioned as 'your little modicum' below. Probably written on HW's arrival at Houghton. HW, to whom Lord Hervey intended a visit at Cambridge on his way from Ickworth to London in late June or early July 1737, was at Cambridge 26 June, and left Cambridge for Norfolk Wednesday 13 July (Conyers Middleton to John, Lord Hervey 26 June, 17 July 1737, in the collection of autograph letters of Hervey and Middleton on the Roman Senate, vol. ii. pp. 86, 91, at Ickworth. Cited with the kind permission of the Marquess of Bristol, from a transcript made by Miss Dorothy Margaret Stuart).

From GRAY, ca Saturday 16 July 1737

Printed from MS in Waller Collection.

Dated by Mason, Aug. 1738 (*Mem. Gray*, p. 35). The above conjectural date is based on the address and Gray's allusion to his trip to London 'the week after next.' In 1738 Gray was in residence at Cambridge throughout the summer and did not leave it until ca 14 Sept. (*Gray's Corr.* i. 90–1). In 1737, on the other hand, he left Cambridge on or before 29 July (he was charged for commons up to 28 July). There is no record of HW's being at Houghton in 1738, but he was there in 1737 (see note on *ante* ca 14 July 1737, missing). The letter was written before 17 July, since otherwise Gray would have referred to his trip as 'the next week.'

Address: To the Honourable Horace Walpole Esq. at Houghton Hall, Norfolk.
Postmark: CAMBRIDGE.

[Cambridge, ca July 16, 1737.]

My dear Horace,

I WAS just going to write to you, in opposition to a couple of very weighty reasons: one, that you did not bid me, and t'other, that I had nothing to say; but, alas! what are reasons against one's inclinations! for you know in such a case a feather at any time will weigh down lead; but you, by instinct knowing my situation, were so good as to supply me with the cause, though not with materials. If you never were to tell me any fresher piece of news than that[1] with which you end your little modicum, I should be well enough content, for though I heard it every day, I should wonder as much as ever, and it would never be the less agreeable for repetition; I rely wholly upon you, my correspondent, for the truth of it, as the only person who can tell what passes in that little country where my concerns lie. My motions at present (which you ask after the particulars of) are much like those of a pendulum, or (Dr Longically[2] speaking) oscillatory;[3] I swing from Chapel or Hall home, and from home to Chapel or Hall; all the strange incidents that happen in my journeys and returns I shall be sure to acquaint you with; the most wonderful that I have been able to pick up as yet is, that it rains exceedingly; this has refreshed the prospect very agreeably, as the way for the most part lies between green fields on either hand, terminated with buildings at some distance; seats, I presume; and they seem of great antiquity. The roads are very good, being, as I suspect, the work of Julius Cæsar's army, for they still preserve in many places the appearances of a pavement in pretty good repair, and if they were not so near home, might perhaps be as much admired as the Via Appia, that we hear so much cried up. There are at present several rivulets to be crossed, and which serve to enliven the view all round; the country is exceeding fruitful in ravens, and such black cattle. But not to tire you with my travels, you must know Mr Turner[4] is come down, his list is vastly near being full, notwishstanding[5] which, and the great cares and duties attending his office,[6] he says he thinks to go to Paris every year. I think too to go to town the week after next, and am,

Yours eternally,
T. GRAY

PS. I have forgot my English, and can't spell.[7]

1. Doubtless an expression of his friendship.

2. Roger Long (1680–1770), D.D., astronomer and divine, Master of Pembroke 1733–70; F.R.S., 1729; Vice-Chancellor 1733–4; Lowndean Professor of Astronomy 1750–70. For his inventions, which he kept in his Lodge at Pembroke, see Edmund Carter, *History of . . . Cambridge*, 1753, p. 78; see also *Gray's Corr.* i. 314; Nichols, *Lit. Anec.* vi. 94–5, 639–40; Roger Long's *Astronomy*, 1742–64, ii. pp. iii–iv.

3. 'All that follows is a humorously hyperbolic description of the quadrangle at Peterhouse' (Mason, *Mem. Gray* 35).

4. Shallet Turner (1692–1762), Fellow of Peterhouse 1715–48; LL.D., 1728; Regius Professor of Modern History 1735–62; F.R.S., 1741 (Venn, *Alumni Cantab.*).

5. So in MS. See PS. below.

6. The Professorship of Modern History and Modern Languages, founded by George I in 1724, which Gray himself held 1768–71. Gray's comment is ironical, since Turner never lectured. The first to deliver lectures on this foundation was Gray's successor John Symonds (Winstanley, *Unreformed Cambridge* 155–60).

7. See n. 5 above. 'Agreeable' and 'Chapel' are also misspelled in the MS.

To Ashton, August 1737

Missing. Two letters, probably written at Chelsea, mentioned *post* 7 Aug. 1737.

From Ashton, Saturday 7 August 1737

Hitherto unpublished. Printed from photostat of the original, Add. MS 37,728 f. 42.

Endorsed by HW: From Thomas Ashton.

Address: To the Honourable Horatio Walpole at the Right Honourable Sir Robert Walpole's, Chelsea. *Postmark:* CAMBRIDGE 8 AV.

> The 7th after the 31st of July in the 37th
> year of the 18th century.

INDIFF'RENCE, Walpole, is the only art,
   To calm your passions and secure your heart:[1]
The source from whence your purest bliss must flow,
Uninterrupted stream, unstained with woe!

See we, unmoved, how these fair orbs of light,
Now glad the day, now dissipate the night;
How circling years in constant change repeat
Pleasing vicissitude of cold and heat?
And shall our servile spirits sink or rise
As clouds condense, or suns refine the skies?
Shall I curse Barnard[2] for my falling rent
If trade decay by stocks at three per cent?[3]
Or feel one mean emotion while I view
The native wealth of Ormus and Peru![4]
And can that praise, which Chartres's[5] self might hear,
Soothe my vain soul, or please my wanton ear!

1. Pope's influence is evident throughout these verses. E.g., cf. the 'Prologue to Mr Addison's Tragedy of Cato' 1–2 (lines 1–2), and the *Essay on Man* i. 18 ff. (lines 5–10).

2. Sir John Barnard (1685–1764), Kt, 1732; M.P. London 1722–61; Lord Mayor of London 1736–7.

3. On 14 March 1737 Sir John Barnard brought forth in the House his scheme of reducing the interest on the national debt to 3 per cent. The debate ended 14 April, and the motion was defeated 220 to 157 (Cobbett, *Parl. Hist.* x. 62–154; GM 1737, vii. 666–70, 712–46, 771–5).

4. For similar allusions to Peru see note on the first couplet of Johnson's 'The Vanity of Human Wishes' in *The Poems of Samuel Johnson,* ed. D. N. Smith and E. L. McAdam, Oxford, 1941, p. 30. Ormuz, on the Persian Gulf, was once a great trading centre.

5. Ashton may be alluding ironically to such 'praise' as the noted rake Col. Francis Charteris (ca 1660–1732) might have received from ruined maidens and fleeced noblemen. Pope, who often alludes to him with the greatest contempt (e.g., *Essay on Man* iv. 130, *Moral Essays* iii. 20), spells his

Who fears disgrace or poverty or shame,
Will sigh for dignity and wealth and fame:
Desire and fear in close embrace are laid;
Who shuns the heat, will ever seek the shade.
Excessive passion, whether grief or joy,
Alike, the springs of health and life destroy;
As frost or fire the body's force control,
So one congeals and one dissolves the soul.

The scale of justice held too strictly nice,
Will soon incline to pinching avarice:
If grave religion pass the golden rule
Her wisest votary becomes a fool.
On picture then, on sculpture fix your heart;
The dear remains of Greek and Roman art:
Admire how age improves the beauteous face,
Made doubly graceful by the loss of grace.

Be next on dress your chief attention plac'd;
And blend each colour by the rules of taste;
With sad delight survey your loaded side,
In all the tedious pomp, the pain of pride.

Or change your rings, canes, swords, brocards, and laces,
For statutes, judgments, acts, reports, and cases:
By quirk and quibble turn the doubtful cause,
And learn the licensed knavery of laws.
Early at Westminster, at Chelsea[6] late,
Forego your dear repose, your peace for state;
Lest some pert prentice, offspring of today,
Proud of his heiress stol'n, dispute the way.

The gold which now lies deep within the mine,
Our sons shall see with Fred'rick's[7] image shine:
While that which bears each George's sacred bust
Shall sink to earth and moulder in the dust.

name 'Chartres.' See E. B. Chancellor, *Col. Charteris and the Duke of Wharton*, 1925, p. 31 and *passim*.

6. Where HW was staying (see *'Address'* above; *ante* 31 Oct. 1736, n. 18). 'Westminster' refers of course to Downing Street.

7. Frederick, Prince of Wales, the patron of the leaders of the Opposition. Relations between him and George II were at this time approaching a complete break (see *post* 4 May 1742, n. 7).

And you, my friend, whom ev'ry tongue shall praise,
And hail triumphant through the public ways,
You too, ere long, must seek that distant shore,
Where York and Lancaster are gone before.

Your two letters[8] which I received last night refreshed me exceedingly. If you don't write before Thursday you may adorn the outside of your letter with a new title,[9] for that is the day on which I hope to receive a kiss from Mr Evans.[10]

Yours in haste,

T. A.

N.B. You have promised a long letter.

To WEST, ca August 1737

Missing. Mentioned *post* 1 Dec. 1737.

From GRAY, ca Monday 22 August 1737

Printed from MS in Waller Collection.
Dated by Gray to West 22 Aug. 1737 (*Gray's Corr.* i. 66), on which day **Gray** learned, in London, of Lady Walpole's death.

[London, ca Aug. 22, 1737.]

FORGIVE me, my poor dear Horace, if I intrude upon your grief[1] sooner possibly than I ought, yet hardly soon enough for the anxiety I am in upon your account; far from having any such confidence in myself as to imagine anything I can say should lighten your affliction, I fear your own good sense, and resignation to Him who has spared so long the best of mothers to you, is hardly able to support you

8. Missing.
9. Ashton became a Fellow of King's College in 1737 (Venn, *Alumni Cantab.*)
10. Probably John Evans (d. 1741), Fellow of King's, 1717 (Venn, *Alumni Cantab.*). He had been bursar of King's College ca 1735 when he absconded with funds which he seems to have restored, suffering no penalty. See Thomas Hearne, *Remarks and Collections*, Oxford, 1884–1918, xi. 412, 415. On 11 Aug. Ashton wrote a jubilant letter to West on becoming 'in a few minutes . . . a free agent' and of no

longer being 'led or drove at another's pleasure: the rein will presently be thrown upon my neck, and I may direct my coach as I please myself' (*Gray-HW-West-Ashton Corr.* i. 152).

1. Lady Walpole died at Chelsea on Saturday 20 Aug. 1737 at nine in the evening (*London Evening Post* 20–23 Aug. 1737). See HW to Lyttelton 18 Sept. 1737. She was Catherine Shorter (born ca 1682), m. (1700) Sir Robert Walpole. HW's devotion to his mother was a dominant element of his life.

under it; I can the easier imagine the situation you are in from the fears, which are continually before my eyes, of a like misfortune in my own case;[2] if that were really to happen, I know not the least shadow of comfort that could come to me, but what I perhaps might find in my dearest Horace's compassion, and that pity he never denies the unhappy. Would to God I might alleviate in some measure his sorrows, in the part I willingly would bear in them, and in that commiseration which I should feel for any one in such circumstances; how much more then for him whose friendship has been my greatest joy, and I hope shall continue so many years. For God's sake, as soon as melancholy reflection shall give you any intermission, let me hear of your welfare; let me have the pleasure of a line, or the sight of you, as soon as it can be proper. Believe, I shall not enjoy a moment's ease till I have some information of your condition. I am, my dearest Walpole, with the greatest truth,

Your faithful friend and servant,

T. G.

From GRAY, ca Saturday 12 November 1737

Printed from MS in Waller Collection.
Endorsed by (?)Mason: '1737.' Dated by Queen Caroline's illness, Caffarelli's début in *Arsaces* and Gray's return to Cambridge on 15 Nov.

[London, ca Nov. 12, 1737.]

<   >

WE were all here in mighty consternations this morning in imagination that the Queen was dead,[1] not out of a joke, as she died, you know, a while ago,[2] but seriously gone to the Stygian ferry; how-

2. Mrs Gray did not die until 11 March 1753. In 1766 Gray wrote to Nicholls, referring to her death, 'It is thirteen years ago, and seems but yesterday, and every day I live it sinks deeper into my heart' (*Gray's Corr.* iii. 926).

1. Caroline (1683–1737) of Brandenburg-Anspach, m. (1705) George II; she did not die till Sunday 20 Nov. 1737, 'of a rupture and mortification of the bowels' (*London Evening Post* 19–22 Nov. 1737), but 'on Saturday last [12 Nov.] about noon the whole Court was in the utmost consternation, and a perfect state of despondency, her Majesty's life being despaired of' (*London Evening Post* 12–15 Nov. 1737).

2. On 2 Oct. 1731 it was reported in London that the Queen had died the previous day 'of an apoplectic fit, which took its rise from the death of a woman at Court, whom the grooms and servants called Queen, on which account several dealers were considerable losers by buying up blacks for mourning' (GM 1731, i. 447).

ever, now they say she is only very bad, and in a fair way;[3] as we have been twice balked,[4] she will have much ado to persuade us that she's dead in earnest, and perhaps she will survive her funeral no small time in the breasts of her good subjects. I shall take care to be as sorry as one of my diminutiveness[5] ought to be, not for myself, but in charity to my superiors. I saw her a little while ago at the Opera[6] in a green velvet sack embroidered κατὰ the facings and sleeves with silver, a little French cap, a long black hood, and her hair in curls round her face; but you see, crowned heads and heads *moutonnées,* scald heads and lousy heads, quack heads and cane heads must all come together to the grave, as the famous Abou-saïd[7] has elegantly hinted in his Persian madrigals. For my part I shall wear her image long imprinted in my mind, though I hope for all this to refresh it frequently, and retouch it from the living original. I don't know whether I should not debase the dignity of my subject ⟨after this by⟩[8] telling you anything of Signor Cafarelli,[9] so leaving him, as all the world has done, to screech by himself, we shall descend more gradually, and talk of West, who is just gone to Oxford again. As soon as Ashton told me he was in town, I went to Mr Periam's[10] in Hatton Garden; but Mr Periam had left his house (and con-

---

3. For a detailed account of the Queen's illness see Hervey, *Memoirs* iii. 877–915; see also Hist. MSS Comm., *Diary of the First Earl of Egmont,* 1920–3, ii. 442–5.

4. Perhaps an allusion to the rumour on 25 Aug. about the Queen's death when 'a man on horseback having, in order to pass the turnpike on the King's private road from Fulham without paying, pretended he came express from Hampton Court with an account of the Queen's death' (GM 1737, vii. 513).

5. Gray was short (see *ante* 31 Oct. 1734 and 27 Jan. 1735), but he is here referring as much to his social as to his physical insignificance.

6. On 29 Oct. at the Haymarket. The opera was *Arsaces,* text by Paolo Antonio Rolli (fl. 1718–44), music by Giovanni Battista Pescetti (ca 1704–ca 1766), who conducted the performance (*Daily Adv.* 31 Oct. 1737; Grove's *Dictionary of Music*). The *Daily Advertiser* 31 Oct.–12 Nov. does not record any further visits by the Queen to the theatre.

7. A fictitious authority. HW attributes

the passage to 'St Jonathan Swift' (MONTAGU i. 199), but it has not been found.

8. Piece cut out; supplement in pencil by HW.

9. Gaetano Majorano (1703–83), called Caffarelli, a castrato brought to England in the autumn of 1737 to replace Farinelli. Caffarelli made his London début in *Arsaces.* Burney observes that Caffarelli arrived in England 'at an unfortunate period; besides the recent remembrance of Farinelli's wonderful powers, it is said that he was never well, or in voice, all the time he remained here' (Burney, *Hist. of Music* iv. 419; Grove's *Dictionary of Music*).

10. Probably John Periam (b. ca 1702) or his brother Zachary (ca 1703–38), sons of John Periam (d. 1711), of Milverton, Somerset. The brothers were admitted at St John's College, Oxford, 6 March 1719 (Foster, *Alumni Oxon.*), and at the Inner Temple between 16 Nov. 1718 and 21 Nov. 1719 (*Calendar of the Inner Temple Records,* vol. iv, ed. R. A. Roberts, 1933, p. 59), that is, at the time when West's father (see n. 11 below) became a bencher of the Inner

sequently Mrs West,[11] as a lodger) and was removed to Thavies Inn;[12] at Thavies Inn, instead of Mr Periam, I could find nothing but a note in the key-hole, directing me to Mr Greenaway's,[13] but Mr Greenaway's key-hole sent me to Mr Herriot,[14] and there I found one of the blood of the Periams, who was so good as to inform me he knew nothing of the matter, *ibi omnis effusus labor*,[15] but in a few days more he came to me himself; then I went to supper with him, where he entertained me with all the product of his brain, verses upon Stow,[15a] translations of Catullus and Homer, epic epigrams, and odes upon the New Year, wild ducks, and *petits pâtés*. We are to write to each other every post, if not oftener. He corresponds with Tozhy Cole[16] and Quid Prinsep.[17] The transactions of Mr Fleetwood[18] and Rich[19] I defer to my next,

Temple (31 Jan. 1719; ibid. 50). John Periam was Sheriff of Somerset 1737–8 (*Calendar of Treasury Books and Papers 1735–8*, pp. 447, 575); M.P. Minehead 1742–7. Zachary, d. 13 May 1738, was buried at St Michael's, Milverton, Somerset (John Collinson, *History . . . of the County of Somerset*, 1791, iii. 17).

11. West's mother, Elizabeth Burnet (b. 1692), younger dau. of Gilbert Burnet, Bp of Salisbury (by his second wife, Maria Scot or Mary Scott); m. (1714) Richard West, of the Inner Temple, barrister-at-law (George Burnett, *The Family of Burnett of Leys*, Aberdeen, 1901, p. 141; T. E. S. Clarke and H. C. Foxcroft, *Life of Gilbert Burnet*, Cambridge, 1907, p. 309; DNB).

12. Thavies Inn, Holborn Circus, an inn of chancery, purchased in 1551 by Lincoln's Inn for students' chambers, and leased 1717–68 by Nathaniel Brand, 'Principal of Thavies Inn,' for £100 (*Black Books of Lincoln's Inn*, vol. iii, 1899, p. 251; C. L. Kingsford, 'Historical Notes on Mediæval London Houses,' *London Topographical Record*, vol. xii, 1920, pp. 42–3).

13. Probably 'Rand[olph] Greenway, of Thavies Inn, Esq.' who d. 21 July 1754 (GM 1754, xxiv. 341).

14. Not identified.

15. Virgil, *Georg.* iv. 491–2.

15a. I.e. Stowe, Lord Cobham's seat in Bucks. The verses have not survived.

16. Crossed out in MS.

17. Crossed out in MS.

18. Charles Fleetwood (d. 1747), patentee

of Drury Lane 1734–45 (Benjamin Victor, *History of the Theatres of London and Dublin*, 1761–71, i. 40), only son of Thomas Fleetwood, of Gerard's Bromley, Staffs, by Frances, dau. of Richard Gerard, of Hilderstone, Staffs (N&Q 1909, ser. X. xi. 183; xii. 58). Fleetwood, who 'at the age of twenty-one . . . entered into a landed estate of six thousand a year' (Victor, op. cit. i. 33), lost the better part of his fortune by gambling, before he purchased the principal share of the Drury Lane patent from the actors on 9 March 1734 (Thomas Davies, *Memoirs of Garrick*, 1808, i. 67–8; Percy Fitzgerald, *New History of the English Stage*, 1882, i. 91). He died at Brussels, 1747 (*Daily Adv.* 22 Aug. 1747).

19. Fleetwood introduced pantomimes (heretofore the province of Rich) into Drury Lane, made attractive offers to Covent Garden actors without increasing the salaries of his own actors, and raised the prices of tickets. Both actors and audience rebelled, the latter staging tempestuous riots. On 18 Dec. 1735, however, Fleetwood and Rich made an agreement 'to divide all moneys at each playhouse . . . above fifty pounds . . . for the remainder part of this season, and to pay to each other so much money as shall be wanting to make up fifty pounds each night' (quoted by Henry Saxe Wyndham, *Annals of Covent Garden Theatre*, 1906, i. 49–50). This transaction caused much bitterness. See Victor, op. cit. i. 46–7, and HW to Mann 26 Nov. 1744.

or to word of mouth, for I shall be at Cambridge on Tuesday night,[20] though I fear my not meeting with you there. I am, Sir,

Yours most sincerely,

T. GRAY

From WEST, Thursday 1 December 1737

Printed from MS now WSL.
Address: To the Honourable Mr Horace Walpole at King's College, Cambridge.
Postmark: OXFORD 3 DE.

Christ Church, Dec. 1, [17]37.

Dear Sir,

IT is now above three months since I had the last letter[1] from you. My silence all this while has been too involuntary to need excuse. Give me leave to renew a correspondence, the loss of which at another time would have been a real affliction to me. At present I find a more melancholy subject[2] for my concern: I shall not dwell any longer upon it, for fear I should make my letter disagreeable when I least would have it so. Perhaps it may be some alleviation that the whole nation at present is in distress, nor are even royal families exempt from the common fatalities of human life—poor Mr Good![3] Forgive me, if I reflect here, how much he must feel for his late loss! Probably the same hearse that carried his wife may soon return for himself. Were I not as much convinced as any person living of your good sense, I should hardly write in this manner; but I protest I hardly know what manner to write in. Letters of consolation in form, you know, are, one or other, the most odious things upon earth; and yet I cannot write to you with

20. 15 Nov., the day of his return, as shown by his charges for commons. The reason for Gray's late return might have been his keeping a 'whole term' at the Inner Temple (*ante* 27 Oct. 1736, n. 1). Michaelmas term began 24 Oct. and ended 28 Nov. There were several ways of keeping a 'whole term': one was to attend the first day of 'grand week' (the week of the second Thursday in Michaelmas term), that is, Monday 31 Oct., and the four preceding days (26–29 Oct.); another was to attend the last day of 'grand week' (5 Nov.) and the four succeeding days (7–10 Nov.). See

Thomas Lane, *The Student's Guide through Lincoln's Inn,* 1823, pp. 72–6; William Andrews, *Ephemeris for . . . 1737.*

1. HW to West ca Aug. 1737 (missing).
2. Lady Walpole's death.
3. George II, who, after the Queen's death, 'showed a tenderness of which the world thought him before utterly incapable,' which 'made him for some time more popular and better spoken of than he had ever been before this incident' (Hervey, *Memoirs* iii. 916).

Dear Sir,   Christ Church. Dec. 1 – 37.

It is now above three months since I had the last letter from you: my silence all this while has been too involuntary to need excuse: give me leave to renew a correspondence, the loss of which at another time would have been a real affliction to me: at present I find a more melancholy subject for my concern: I shall not dwell any longer upon it, for fear I should make my letter disagreeable when I least would have it so. Perhaps it may be some alleviation, that the whole nation at present is in distress, nor are even Royal families exempt from the common fatalities of human life — poor Mr. Good! forgive me, if I reflect here, how much he must feel for his late loss! probably, the same hearse, that carried his wife, may soon return for himself.

WEST'S LETTER OF 1 DECEMBER 1737

the same easiness as I used to do. Were I with you I should know better what to say than I do now what to write. I intended more, but shall defer it; forgive my affection: I hope you are well and easy, and am impatient to hear from you. I am, dear Sir, very sincerely

Yours most affectionately,

R. WEST

From GRAY, Thursday 29 December 1737

Printed from MS in Waller Collection.

Dated by the postmark (indistinct), the reference to HW's appointment as Inspector General of Exports and Imports, and the allusion to Queen Caroline's funeral.

Address: To the Honourable Horace Walpole, Esq. at the Treasury, London.
Postmark: CAMBRIDGE 30 [DE].

[Cambridge, Dec. 29, 1737.]

My dear ——

I SHOULD say Mr Inspector General of the Exports and Imports,[1] but that appellation would make but an odd figure in conjunction with the two familiar monosyllables above written, for, *Non bene conveniunt, nec in una sede morantur majestas et amor,*[2] which is, being interpreted, 'Love does not live at the Custom-house.' However, by what style, title, or denomination soever you please to be dignified or distinguished hereafter, you'll never get rid of these two words, nor of your Christian name; it will stick like a bur, and you can no more get quit of it than St Anthony could of his pig.[3] We had no Queen to bury here, so I have no procession to tell you of,[4] but we are collecting our flowers, as fast as may be, to strew upon her tomb.[5] Mr Pemberton[6] of

1. See *ante* i. 7 n. 33.
2. Ovid, *Met.* ii. 846–7.
3. 'The famous St Antony of Padua . . . is always to be known in his pictures by a little pig which is running by his side, whence ⟨(in⟩ all probability) we have our expressi⟨on⟩ of a child's *doddling about one like a* ⟨*St*⟩ *Antony-pig'* (Joseph Spence to his mother, Rome, 21 Jan. 1741, N.S., BM Add. MS Egerton 2234 f. 239; see also Robert Chambers, *Book of Days*, Edinburgh, 1863, i. 126).
4. Queen Caroline was buried 17 Dec. in

Henry VII's Chapel at Westminster Abbey. The procession is described in *London Gazette* 20–24 Dec. 1737 and GM 1737, vii. 764–6.
5. The collection, entitled *Pietas Academiæ Cantabrigiensis in Funere Serenissimæ Principis Wilhelminæ Carolinæ et Luctu Augustissimi Georgii II Britanniarum etc. etc. Regis,* with the names and colleges of the authors at the end of the poems, was published 2 Feb. (*Daily Adv.* 2 Feb. 1738), and was presented to the King by Dr Richardson, the Vice-Chancellor, 26

Catharine Hall and one Ambrose[7] of Trinity Hall, a blind man, they say, will bear away the bell; both English. Mr Whitehead[8] does not shine vastly this time. The bellman[9] has paid his duty in the following epigram:

> O cruel death! how could'st be so unkind
> To snatch the Queen, and leave the King behind?

almost as laconic as Mr Conway's[10] letter,[11] who has wrote[12] to his sister[13] in the same style as one would write to the devil, whose ancient title has been 'Old Boy.' I am,

Yours ever,

T. GRAY

From GRAY, Tuesday 10 January 1738

Printed from MS in Waller Collection.
Dated by the postmark and the reference to the gale on 9 Jan. 1738.
Address: To the Honourable Horace Walpole Esq. at the Treasury, St. James's.
Postmark: CAMBRIDGE 11 IA.

Jan. 1738, together with the University's 'humble address on occasion of the death of her late Majesty, which his Majesty was pleased to receive very graciously' (*London Gazette* 24–28 Jan. 1738).

6. Henry Pemberton (d. 1741), son of Francis Pemberton, of Trumpington, Cambs; admitted pensioner (16 Dec. 1730), Fellow (1736–41) of St Catharine's (Venn, *Alumni Cantab.*). He contributed 101 lines of blank verse, beginning, 'Stay yet a while, blest Saint.'

7. No one of this name contributed to the published collection.

8. William Whitehead (?1715–85), Poet Laureate (1757), admitted sizar (25 Nov. 1735), Fellow (1742–6) of Clare (Venn, *Alumni Cantab.*). In 1733, while a scholar at Winchester, Whitehead had attracted the attention of Pope with a prize poem on Lord Peterborough's campaign of 1706. See William Mason, *Memoirs of the Life and Writings of William Whitehead*, 1788, p. 6; *Harcourt Papers* vii. 206; Nichols, *Lit. Anec.* iii. 193–4. His elegy in *Pietas* begins,

'Vain were the thought t'instruct the verse to flow.'

9. Bellmen, or public criers, traditionally composed doggerel verses. See MON-TAGU ii. 109, n. 7.

10. Crossed out in MS, but still legible. Henry Seymour Conway, HW's cousin and correspondent, entered the army in 1737 (he was commissioned lieutenant 27 June 1737 in Lord Viscount Molesworth's Regiment of Dragoons; *Army List of 1740*, 1931, p. 65).

11. Gray first wrote 'epigram,' which he smudged out and altered to 'letter.' This letter has not been traced.

12. MS, 'wrought.'

13. Either the Hon. Jane Seymour Conway (1716–49), Lord Conway's dau. by his 2d wife, or the Hon. Anne Seymour Conway (d. 1774), youngest dau. of Lord Conway by his 3d wife, m. (1755) John Harris (Burke, *Peerage*, 1928, *sub* Hertford; GM 1755, xxv. 138; HW to Lady Ossory 6 April 1774; *Miscellanea Genealogica et Heraldica* II Ser. iii. 2–3).

[Cambridge, Jan. 10, 1738.]

<   >

I AM in good hopes that by this time the eclipse[1] is over with you, and that your two satellites have recovered their usual light: the sublimity of which two metaphors, after you have taken them out of their pantoufles[2] and reduced 'em to their just value, will be found to amount to my wishes for your health, and that of your eyes, whose warmth I have been too sensible of, when they used to shine upon me, not to be very apprehensive of any damage that might befall 'em. I should have taken care to write upon green paper, and dipped my pen in copperas-water, if you had not assured me that they were on the mending hand, and pretty well able to sustain the white-making rays. Now as for the transactions here, you are to be ascertained that the man[3] at the Mitre has cut his throat, that one Mr White[4] of Emanuel a week ago drowned himself, but since that has been seen a few miles off,[5] having the appearance of one that had never been drowned; wherefore it is by many conjectured that he walketh. Dr Bouquet's[6] verses have been returned by Mr Vice-Chancellor[7] to undergo several corrections; the old man's invention is much ⟨admired as⟩[8] having found out a way to make bawdy verses upon a burying.[9] The wind was so high last night[10] that I every minute expected to pay you a visit at London perforce, which was the place I certainly should have directed the storm to, if I had been obliged to ride in the whirlwind.[11] If I

1. The nature of HW's ocular ailment is unknown. Gray's metaphor may have been suggested by the 'great' eclipse of 1737, an annular solar eclipse on 18 Feb.

2. 'Take sentiments out of their pantoufles, and reduce them to the infirmities of mortality, what a falling off there is!' (HW to Montagu 18 May 1749: MONTAGU i. 83).

3. Not identified.

4. Perhaps John White, admitted pensioner at Emmanuel 28 June 1732 (Venn, *Alumni Cantab.*).

5. MS reads 'of.'

6. Philip Bouquet (ca 1671–1748), Fellow of Trinity College, 1696; D.D.; Regius Professor of Hebrew 1712–48. He was 'an old miserly refugee who died rich in college, and left his money among the French refugees' (Cole, quoted by Venn, *Alumni Can-*

tab.). He contributed to *Pietas* (*ante* 29 Dec. 1737) four Hebrew stanzas, and a Latin poem of 42 lines.

7. William Richardson (1698–1775), D.D., Master of Emmanuel 1736–75; Vice-Chancellor 1737–8, 1769–70. He wrote a Latin dedication in meter to *Pietas*.

8. Piece cut out; emendation in pencil by HW.

9. George II, according to the Latin verses, tries to put his arms about the Queen's neck, but her ghost eludes him, leaving his bed deserted throughout the night.

10. See GM 1738, viii. 49.

11. Cf. Pope's *Dunciad* iii. 264: 'Rides in the whirlwind, and directs the storm.' The line is borrowed from Addison's *Campaign* (1704), line 292.

don't hear from you this week, I shall be in a thousand tirrits and frights[12] about you. I am, my dear Horace,

Yours most affectionately,

T. GRAY

To GRAY, ca Thursday 12 January 1738

Missing. Probably written in Downing Street in answer to *ante* 10 Jan. 1738. The letter must have also contained a ballad on Gillian of Croydon; see the following letter.

From GRAY, Sunday 15 January 1738

Printed from MS in Waller Collection.
Endorsed in an unknown hand: 'Send by wm Haselwod att the Green Dragon With in beeshops Gate on wensday be fore Noon.' Dated by Mason: '1737'; i.e., 1737/8. The date of the year is further determined by the reference to *Pietas Academiæ Cantabrigiensis* below.
Address: To the Honourable Horace Walpole Esq. at the Treasury, St. James's.

Jan. 15 [1738], Cambridge.

<   >

THE moving piece of ancient poetry[1] you favoured me with the sight of, would be sufficient, I must confess, to deter me, if I had any ambition of appearing among the *consolatores*,[2] from all pretence to writing at this time; so long as the sad catastrophe of the beautiful and never-to-be-enough-lamented Gillian dwells upon my memory. Those geniuses, my friend, those mighty spirits of antiquity! alas, what are we to 'em? mere tinsel! mere flash! and indeed (not to dwell upon the moral, so feelingly inculcated in this little elegiacal narration, which 'tis impossible should escape the acuteness of your penetration)

---

12. Mrs Quickly: 'Here's a goodly tumult! I'll forswear keeping house, afore I'll be in these tirrits and frights' (*2 Henry IV* II. iv).

---

1. Apparently a ballad, perhaps by HW himself, on Gillian of Croydon. No such ballad appears in the collections (Ambrose Philips, Percy, Child, Rollins, Fawcett, Roxburghe Ballads); but see N&Q 1897, ser. VIII. xii. 243; 1917, ser. XII. iii. 117; see also chapter i of the chap-book printed for Arthur Bettesworth in 1727, entitled *The Pleasant and Delightful History of Gillian of Croydon: containing, Her Birth and Parentage: Her first Amour, with the sudden Death of her Sweetheart: . . . The Whole done much after the same Method as those celebrated Novels by Mrs Eliza Haywood.*

2. Contributors to the Cambridge *Pietas* (*ante* 29 Dec. 1737). Gray was not a contributor.

what can be beyond the elegant simplicity of the language? In the ex-
ordium the poet lays down the groundwork and foundation, as it were,
of that beautiful fabric he intends to erect; he does not injudiciously
draw his inferences after he has recounted the story; at least he does not
expatiate much in the end; no! he leaves the mind then to ruminate at
its own leisure, and make its own applications, when it shall have recovered itself from that sorrow which every virtuous mind must feel
after so woeful a tale. He recommends to the ladies of his time a strict
observance of honour and chastity,[3] who, I doubt not, received his advice with reverence (our modern females would perhaps ⟨have
laug⟩hed[4] at his gravity); he also solemnly affirms the truth of it, as well
knowing the prevalence of truth over the mind; from whence his deep
insight into nature is sufficiently evidenced. At the beginning of his
narration, he fixes the place of his heroine's habitation in Surry;[5] he
had undoubtedly observed in Homer and the imitators of that poet,
how much we are engaged in the interest of any person who has the
misfortune of falling in battle, by being told the place of his birth and
abode, as

Ὑιὸν δὲ Στροφίοιο Σκαμάνδριον αἵμονα[6] θήρης, etc.[7]
—'Ορσίλοχόν τε,
τῶν ῥα πατήρ μὲν ἔναιεν ἐϋκτιμένῃ ἐνὶ Φηρῇ.[8]

'Tis true, he has not carried it quite so far as Homer in telling us
whether Gillian loved hunting or not, or whether her father's house
was well or ill built; he has showed, as he proceeds, his generous aversion and contempt for your cockneys and fluttering beaux of the town,
so agreeable to the simplicity of the age he lived in, and its uncorrupted
innocence, by making this ill-grounded passion of Gillian's the cause of
all her misfortunes,

—Hinc prima mali labes—[9]

3. 'The reader, therefore, may observe
through the course of this history that it
was not writ with a view to encourage per-
fidy, or the gratifying a brutish appetite in
either sex, but, on the contrary, rather to
excite constancy in affection and a chaste
enjoyment of each other, for which man
and woman were first formed in paradise'
(*Pleasant and Delightful History*, p. ii).

4. Piece cut out; emendation in pencil by
HW.

5. 'Gillian of Croydon (vulgarly so called
because that her mother, who was born in
Surrey, often resorted with this her daughter to Croydon markets and fairs) had for
her parents an honest farmer and a malt-
ster's daughter of Kent' (ibid. 1–2).

6. MS reads αἵμονα.

7. *Iliad* v. 49: 'Skamandrios, son of
Strophios, cunning in the chase.'

8. *Iliad* v. 542–3: 'And Orsilochos, whose
father dwelt in well-built Phere.' MS reads
τοῦ for τῶν.

9. Virgil, *Æneid* ii. 97: 'Hinc mihi prima
mali labes.'

I don't wonder at her innocence not being proof against so strong al-
lurements as are contained in those two unaffected lines,

> He said as how he would her carry
> To London, and her there would marry.

Then, how feelingly yet concisely is the main part of the story expressed—

> He did persuade her to his bed,
> And there he got her maidenhead:[10]
> —fulsere ignes, et conscius æther
> Connubiis, summoque ulularunt teastere nymphæ.[11]

What woman would not consent, when a man swears upon his life?
Then for the master-stroke,

> She sat down at his door, and cried,
> And broke her heart, and so she died.[12]

I suspect here some small imitation of the celebrated dragon of Wantley (provided that were really elder than this)

> So groaned, kicked, shit, and died.[13]

Only indeed the indecent circumstances are suppressed, though the
elegancy is still preserved. Pray excuse these little remarks, which
a⟨re⟩, however ill executed, designed to make more conspicuous the
⟨ex⟩cellencies of this amiable author, and believe me,

> Your faithful friend and humble servant,
>
> PHILOGILLIANUS

To Gray, February 1738

Missing. Probably written in Downing Street. Implied in the following letter.

10. Couplets similar to this are to be
found in Scottish ballads. See 'Bonny Dun-
dee; or, Jockey's Deliverance' in *A Collection of Old Ballads* (ed. [?] Ambrose
Philips), 1723–5 (reprint ?1872), i. 275, and
'An Excellent New Song called the Ruined
Virgin, or the Hard-hearted Young Man'
in *Broadside Ballads of the Restoration Period*, ed. F. Burlington Fawcett, 1930, p.
119.

11. Virgil, *Æneid* iv. 167–8, altered from

'vertice nymphæ.' 'Teastere' is evidently
formed from an old spelling of 'tester'; i.e.,
tester-bed (see OED).

12. In the chap-book (pp. 11–14) Gillian
survives.

13. The last line of 'An Excellent Ballad
of a most dreadful Combat, fought between
Moore of Moore Hall, and the Dragon of
Wantley,' in *A Collection of Old Ballads* i.
42 (see COLE i. 90).

From Gray, Thursday 23 February 1738

Printed from MS in Waller Collection.
Dated by the postmark and the reference to Thomson's *Agamemnon*.
Address: To the Honourable Horace Walpole Esq. at the Treasury, St. James['s].
Postmark: SAFFRON WALDEN 24 FE.

[Cambridge, Feb. 23, 1738.]

My best Horace,

I CONFESS, I am amazed: of all likely things this is the last I should have believed would come to pass.[1] However I congratulate you upon being able at this time to talk of Clytemnæstra and Mrs Porter.[2] I wish you have not admired this last-mentioned gentlewoman long enough to catch a little of her art from her, for if I'm not mistaken, you are a very different person behind the scenes, and whatever face you set upon the matter, I guess—but perhaps I guess wrong; I wish I may for your sake; perhaps you are as cool as you would seem: either way I may wish you joy; of your dissimulation, or philosophy. I long extremely to see you, but till I have that pleasure, methinks you might be a little more open in writing; have pity a little upon my curiosity. If you distrust my faith (I won't say honour; that's for gentlefolks) and imagine I would show your letters to any one, yet rely upon my vanity, which won't suffer me to do an ill thing; if you fear the common fate of loose papers, I give you my word to sacrifice to the fire immediately (no small sacrifice, I assure you) all I shall receive, if you desire it. I don't wonder at the new study[3] you have taken a liking to: first, because it

---

1. Perhaps Sir Robert Walpole's marriage to Maria Skerrett, whom he introduced at Court as his wife 3 March 1738. She was presented by Sir Robert's sister-in-law Mrs Horatio Walpole, 'to show that Sir Robert marrying his whore was by consent of his family' (Hist. MSS Comm., *Diary of the first Earl of Egmont*, 1920–3, ii. 469). Maria Skerrett (ca 1702–38) was the daughter of Thomas Skerrett (d. 1734), a wealthy London merchant, who left her £14,000 (Hervey, *Memoirs* i. 86). She had been Sir Robert's mistress for over thirteen years. One of their two daughters, born during the lifetime of Sir Robert's first wife, was Lady Maria Walpole, b. ca 1725 (BERRY i. 42. n. 4).

2. Thomson's *Agamemnon*, with Mrs Porter as Clytemnestra, was first performed 6 April 1738 at Drury Lane. HW had evidently heard that the play was in rehearsal, and wrote to Gray on the subject. This may be the 'essay' mentioned in the postscript, and also the 'ingenious paper' for which Mrs Porter thanked HW in her letter to him of ?1738. HW's respect for Mrs Porter's histrionic powers is further revealed by his lines to her printed at the beginning of T. E. Williams's edition (1807) of Hentzner's *Journey into England*. See Hazen, *SH Bibliography* 31.

3. See preceding note.

diverts your thoughts from disagreeable objects;⁴ next, because it particularly suits your genius; and lastly, because I believe it the most excellent of all sciences, to which in proportion as the rest are subservient, so great a degree of estimation they ought to gain. Would you believe it, 'tis the very thing I would wish to apply to myself? ay! as simple as I stand here.⁵ But then the apparatus necessary to it costs so much; nay, part of it is wholly out of one's own power to procure; and then who should pare one, and burnish one? for they would have more trouble and fuss with me, than Cinderaxa's⁶ sisters had with their feet, to make 'em fit for the little glass slipper. Oh yes! to be sure one must be licked; now to lick oneself I take to be altogether impracticable, and to ask another to lick one, would not be quite so civil. Bear I was born, and bear, I believe, I'm like to remain; consequently a little ungainly in my fondnesses, but I'll be bold to say, you shan't in a hurry meet with a more loving poor animal, than

Your faithful creature,

BRUIN

PS. I beg you to continue your essay.⁶ᵃ And tell Zeph[yrus]⁷ when you see him to expect a letter in rabbinical Hebrew from me,⁸ unless he writes directly.

From GRAY, Tuesday 7 March 1738

Printed from MS in Waller Collection.

Dated by Mason: '1738.' The date of the year is confirmed by the references to *Comus* and Swift's *Complete Collection of Genteel and Ingenious Conversation*.

Address: To the Honourable Horace Walpole Esq. at the Treasury, St James's.

Postmark: CAMBRIDGE 10 MR.

4. Sir Robert's marriage.

5. Slender, of Shallow: 'He's a justice of peace in his country, simple though I stand here' (*Merry Wives of Windsor* I. i).

6. A variant of Cinderella. It appears two years later in William Somerville's *Hobbinol or the Rural Games*, 1740.

6a. See *ante* n. 2.

7. Zephyrus or Zephyrille, West's pseu-donym. He was in London, expecting to be 'settled at the Temple very soon' (West to Gray 21 Feb. 1738; *Gray's Corr.* i. 79).

8. Gray to West 22 Jan. 1738 is in Latin, and West's reply, 21 Feb. 1738, was originally in French; but Mason, doubting 'whether it would stand the test of polite criticism,' chose to translate it into English (Mason, *Mem. Gray* 29).

<   >   March 7 [1738], Cantab.

I DID not allow myself time to rejoice with Ashton upon his good
fortune,[1] till after I had ransacked all his informations as to you,
and with him admired your judgment and conduct;[2] for these virtues
(I find you are resolved to show us) you are as well acquainted with, as
we knew you were with their sisters. What! will no less than the whole
family serve your turn? sure one of 'em might have contented any mod-
erate stomach! There's Miss Temperance, Miss Constance and the rest
of 'em; e'er a one, i'gad, a match for an emperor! These, it is well-
known (or the world much belies you) you have had; deny it if you can;
and must poor Miss Prue go to pot too? Well, I say no more, but it's too
much in all conscience, methinks, for one man to be fit equally for this
world and the next. They tell me you are to be here once more in a
little while; dear now, don't let it be much longer.[3] In the meantime
have you seen *Comus*,[4] and what figure does it make after cutting for
the simples?[5] Have you read yourself to sleep with Dr Swift's conversation,[6] as I did? That confounded Lady Answerall, though she says less
than anybody, is the devil to me! Pray did you ever see an elephant?[7] I
have. If you han't, you never saw an ugly thing. I would not be
Aurengzebe for the world; they say, he rid upon one.[8] That's all.

                                        Yours ever,
                                        T. G.

1. On becoming tutor (through HW's
agency) to Lord Plymouth, then aged six.
Ashton had been appointed in Sept. 1737
(Ashton to West Sept. 1737; *Gray-HW-
West-Ashton Corr.* i. 157; *post* 19 Sept.
1738). He assumed his duties ca 29 March
(*post* 28 March 1738). Presumably Gray had
not seen Ashton since his appointment.

2. In connection with Sir Robert Walpole's marriage. This explains Gray's allusions to HW's temperance, constancy, and
prudence ('Miss Prue').

3. The date of HW's going to Cambridge
is not known.

4. Adapted for the stage from Milton's
masque by John Dalton (1709–63), music by
Thomas Augustine Arne (1710–78); it was
first performed at Drury Lane 4 March and
published 6 March 1738 (*Daily Adv.* 4, 6
March 1738).

5. That is, after being adapted for 'persons in a humble or ordinary condition of
life' (OED). The idiom is Swift's, but in a
different sense (n. 6 below).

6. *A Complete Collection of Genteel and
Ingenious Conversation, according to the
Most Polite Mode and Method now used at
Court, and in the Best Companies of England. In Three Dialogues. By Simon Wag-
staff, Esq.*, published 28 Feb 1738 (*Daily
Adv.* 28 Feb. 1738). The idiom 'cut for the
simples,' in the sense of 'to be cured of
folly' (see OED), occurs in the first dialogue
(pp. 17–18).

7. Elephants were still a great curiosity
in England. In the *Daily Advertiser* 3 Jan.
1736 there appeared the following advertisement: 'To be seen at the Golden Cross
at Charing-Cross, during the holidays, a
noble large elephant, lately brought from
the Indies in the ship Lethieullier; he is
vastly grown since his arrival, fetches and
carries like a spaniel, and is the admiration
of the quality and gentry who resort daily
to see him. To be seen from eight in the
morning till eight at night.'

8. Aurangzíb Á'lamgír (1618–1707), Emperor of India, the hero of Dryden's

To Gray, March 1738

Missing. Probably written in Downing Street; answered *post* 20 March 1738.

From Gray, Monday 20 March 1738

Printed from MS in Waller Collection.
The date of the year is determined by the reference to Cornwallis's admission to his Fellowship at Christ's College.
Address: To the Honourable Horatio Walpole Esq. at the Treasury, St. James's.
Postmark: CAMBRIDGE 20 MR. (See preliminary note to *ante* 29 Dec. 1736).

Cam[bridge,] March 20 [1738].

<   >

THANK God, I had a very good night's rest, and am sufficiently awake to answer your letter,[1] though likely to be more dull than you that write in your sleep. And indeed I do not believe that you ever are so much asleep, but you can write to a relation, play a sober game at piquet, keep up a tête-à-tête conversation, sell a bargain, or perform any of the little offices of life with tolerable spirit; certain I am, there are many people in the world who in their top spirits are no better *éveillés,* than you are at four in the morning, reclined upon your pillow. I believe[2] I partly guess [what is] your hopeful branch; I fancy you may find the first letters of both somewhere between H and T inclusive,[3] if I interpret your hieroglyphs aright. As to my journey to London,[4] which you are so good as to press, alas! what can I do? If I come, it is for good and all, and I don't know how it is, I have a sort of reluctance to leave this place, unamiable as it may seem; 'tis true Cambridge is very ugly, she is very dirty, and very dull; but I'm like a cabbage: where I'm stuck I love to grow; you should pull me up sooner than any one, but I shall be never the better for transplanting. Poor

tragedy, *Aureng-Zebe* (1676). The allusion is to the battle of Samúgarh (7–10 June 1658), afterwards known as Fathábád, 'the place of victory,' where Aurangzíb, 'mounted . . . on an elephant,' defeated the superior forces of his brother, Dárá Shukóh (1615–59) (François Bernier's *History of the Late Revolution of the Empire of the Great Mogol,* 1671, pp. 102–26, which Gray probably read). See also Stanley Lane-Poole, *Rulers of India: Aurangzíb,* Oxford,

1893, pp. 21, 45–50. Dryden's tragedy does not mention the elephant.

———

1. Missing.
2. This sentence has been heavily scored through, possibly by HW. The meaning is obscure.
3. Unexplained.
4. Gray was in residence at Cambridge until ca 14 Sept. 1738 (see introductory note to *ante* ca 16 July 1737; *post* 19 Sept. 1738).

Mr Cornwallis[5] is here, sadly altered,[6] so that one can very hardly know him; Towers[7] still stands out, and refuses to admit him,[8] so that they have called in their visitors (that is, the Vice-Chancellor, Dr Bentley,[9] and Dr Ashton[10]), but nothing is yet determined. The assizes are just over;[11] I was there, but I an't to be transported. Adieu!

Yours sincerely,

T. GRAY

To GRAY, ca Sunday 26 March 1738

Missing. Probably written in Downing Street; mentioned *post* 28 March 1738.

From GRAY, Tuesday 28 March 1738

Printed from MS in Waller Collection.
Dated by the postmark and the reference to Ashton's departure from Cambridge.
Address: To the Honourable Horace Walpole Esq. at the Treasury, St James's.
Postmark: CAMBRIDGE 29 MR.

[Cambridge, March 28, 1738.]

⟨   ⟩

YOU can never weary me with repetition of anything that makes me sensible of your kindness, since that has been the only idea of any social happiness that I have ever received almost, and which (beg-

5. 'Afterwards Archbishop of Canterbury' (HW; *ante* 3 July 1735, n. 4).

6. 'He had the misfortune to have a stroke of the palsy, which took away the use of his right hand, and obliged him to write with his left, which he did very expeditiously' (Cole, quoted by Sir Egerton Brydges, *Restituta*, 1814–16, iv. 262).

7. William Towers (ca 1681–1745), D.D., Master of Christ's College 1723–45; Vice-Chancellor 1734–5 (Venn, *Alumni Cantab.*).

8. Cornwallis had been elected Fellow of Christ's 28 Jan. 1738, but Towers refused to admit him on the grounds that he was the son of a peer, and therefore ineligible to a fellowship under the statute '*De Sociorum qualitate*' ('Statutes of Christ's College, Cambridge,' cap. xxvi, *Documents Relating to the University and Colleges of Cambridge*, 1852, iii. 192–3), although the statute merely stipulates that the candi-

dates be poor, magnanimous, and learned. Cornwallis appealed to Richardson, the Vice-Chancellor, who on 24 April 1738 ordered Towers to admit Cornwallis. Towers complied the next day, adding to the usual form the statement that he acted under the Vice-Chancellor's mandate (*Gray's Corr.* i. 83, n. 5; John Peile, *Christ's College*, 1900, pp. 226–7).

9. Richard Bentley (1662–1742), D.D., Master of Trinity College 1700–42; Regius Professor of Divinity 1717–42; 'the great Bentley.'

10. Charles Ashton (1665–1752), D.D., Master of Jesus College 1701–52.

11. The Cambridge assizes (Norfolk circuit) were held at Cambridge Castle beginning 13 March by Lord Chief Justice Willes and Justice Denton (see MONTAGU i. 209, n. 10, 373, n. 3; *Daily Adv.* 1 Feb. 1738).

ging your pardon for thinking so differently from you in such cases) I would by no means have parted with for an exemption from all the uneasinesses mixed with it. But it would be injust[1] to imagine my taste was any rule for yours, for which reason my letters are shorter and less frequent than they would be had I any materials but myself to entertain you with. Love and brown sugar must be a poor regale for one of your *goût,* and alas! you know I am by trade a grocer.[2] Scandal (if I had any) is a merchandise you don't profess dealing in; now and then indeed and to oblige a friend you may perhaps slip a little out of your pocket, as a decayed gentlewoman would a piece of right Mechlin,[3] or a little quantity of run tea; but this only now and then, not to make a practice of it. Monsters, appertaining to this climate, you have seen already both wet and dry. So you see within how narrow bounds my pen is circumscribed, and the whole contents of my share in our correspondence may be reduced under the two heads of, 1: You, 2: I. The first is indeed a subject to expatiate upon, but ⟨you mig⟩ht laugh at me for talking of what I do not understand; the second is as tiny, as tiresome, wherefore you shall hear no more of it, till you come to finis. Ashton was here last night; he goes tomorrow,[4] he bid me farewell, and drank a health in ale and small to our meeting hereafter in a happy eternity. Mrs Ward[5] has bought her a silver chamberpot. Mademoiselle Quimbeau[5] (that was) is weary of her new husband, and has sent a *petit billet* to a gentleman to pray he would come and ravish her. There is a curious woman here that spins glass, and makes short aprons and furbelowed petticoats of it, a very genteel wear for summer, and discovers all the motions of the limbs to great advantage. She is a successor of Jack, the apple-dumpling spinner's: my duck has eat a snail, etc.: and I am,

Yours eternally,

T. G.

PS. I give you a thousand thanks for your characters.[6] If I knew whether West was in town,[7] I'd write to him.

---

1. So in the MS.

2. 'I.e., a man who deals only in coarse and ordinary wares: to these he compares the plain sincerity of his own friendship, undisguised by flattery, which, had he chosen to carry on the allusion, he might have termed the trade of a confectioner' (Mason, *Mem. Gray* 17).

3. Lace manufactured at Mechlin, Belgium (OED).

4. To Lord Plymouth (see *ante* 7 March 1738, n. 1).

5. Not identified.

6. HW to Gray ca 26 March 1738, missing.

7. *Ante* 23 Feb. 1738, n. 7.

From WEST, Thursday 7 September 1738

Printed from MS now WSL.

No address. Below the date West wrote, 'To be left at the posthouse here' (Epsom). HW was at this time at Tunbridge Wells, and was expected to return to London 12 Sept. (Ashton to West 9 Sept. 1738, *Gray-HW-West-Ashton Corr.* i. 197).

Epsom,[1] September 7, 1738.

My dear Horace,

'TIS now three weeks almost since I saw you at Richmond.[2] You desired me then to write something upon your thatched house, and I have done it. I believe you little expected that the consequence of a request made out of pure civility would have been so long a poem. As it is, I wish it may amuse you one half hour. I am going in about a fortnight's time to Oxford.

Yours,

R. W.

The View from the Thatched House.[3]

Stranger! whosoe'er you be,
Deign to enter: though you see
All above the moss-grown shed
With stubble vile and straw o'erspread,
Still beneath a mean outside
Inward graces oft reside.
Expect not here the glare of state,
No Persian loom, no splendid plate,
No polished pillar, no carved dome,
Rare ornaments of Greece or Rome:
But if such simple soft repose

1. 'I go tomorrow to Epsom where I shall be for about a month' (West to Gray 29 Aug. 1738 *Gray's Corr.* i. 89). According to Mason (*Mem. Gray* 39), West's mother and sister were at this time living at Epsom.

2. 'I was last week at Richmond Lodge with Mr Walpole for two days, and dined with Cardinal Fleury' (West to Gray 29 Aug. 1738, loc. cit.). This visit probably took place 19–20 Aug., since it was Sir Robert Walpole's practice to spend Saturdays and Sundays at Richmond New Park, hunting and resting from the business of government, 'or rather, as he said himself, to do more business than he could in town' (*Reminiscences Written by Mr Horace Walpole in 1788*, ed. Paget Toynbee, Oxford, 1924, pp. 16–17). There he erected several buildings, on which, together with other improvements, he spent £14,000 (ibid.).

3. 'In Richmond New Park' (HW).

A hermit in his grotto knows,
If calm philosophy, if ease,
And nature's rural face can please,
Awhile, from this rude spot of ground
Let us view the fair scene round.
      See! how wide the prospects lie,
Open all beneath the eye!
Fallows grey, and pastures green,
Where herds and flocks are grazing seen,
With many a woody park and hill
Hanging o'er some shadowy rill,
And villas glimm'ring through the glade,
And scattered towns half-wrapt in shade,
Each with their little spire in view
Pointing up the clear sky blue.
Old Thames the beauteous vale below
Gently bids his waters flow,
Pleased with his course. Down the pure stream
Moves the huge barge; the lab'ring team
Fast by, beside the winding shore,
To aid the sail, or ease the oar,
Tug the long cord, and slowly tread,
The driver whistling at their head.
Meantime, along the distant road,
From farm or field, with different load
Of country fare, the village swain
On panniered horse or jingling wain
To market drive; and often by
Gilt chariots, glitt'ring to the eye,
Roll nimbly on, toward some lone seat,
Descried afar, of aspect neat.
There oft, ere yet the grey-eyed Dawn
Has visited the dewy lawn,
The early chase with cheerful yell
Calls sleepy Echo from her cell.
Hark! the pack open on the scent;
Down that hoar hill the course is bent;
Within this brake the hare is hid—
—Ah me! the horn proclaims it dead.
      And now, the bright sun 'gins arise
Up the high zenith of the skies,
And all the hot horizon glows,

While not a breath of wind scarce blows.
Then underneath the elm-shade cool,
Or knee-deep in the wat'ry pool
Stand the mute herd: But where the plain
Waves high above with golden grain,
Observe the reapers' tawny band,
Each with his sickle in his hand;
Down fall the ripened stalks apace;
And now they wipe their weary face,
Till the glad bell for dinner call
The labourers to their master's hall.
Nor less, athwart the sultry way
Mark where the active sporters stray,
And, while the setter points the game,
Nimbly take their level aim.
Lo! the quick flash! anon is heard
The faint report: down drops the bird
In giddy circles wheeling round,
And marks with blood the guilty ground—
But turn the eye, and shift the scene
Down to yonder level green,
Where, through the meadow winding slow,
A little rivulet learns to flow;
There underneath a willow tree,
Beside the bank, the fisher see,
In musing posture silent stand,
(The long rod bending in his hand)
And, watching every minute bite,
Deftly catch with nimble sleight
The frequent prey, till his fell hook
Has nigh unpeopled half the brook:
Still further from the fountain-head,
As the stream begins to spread,
See! where some boys are met to play,
And wash 'em on a sunshine day:
All life and gaiety they seem;
They sport adown the merry stream,
And dash the water as they pass,
Or, naked, run along the grass:
The nymphs, at distance, eye the flood,
Concealed, and laugh behind the wood.

Now look, how vast a space the eye
Has journeyed thwart the ambient sky,
O'er grove and park and woody dale,
Up the high hill and down the vale,
Till we're come round th' horizon wide
Back to where Thames' fruitful tide
Through meadow, field, and garden fair
Winds its clear current, here and there
With town or village interlaid
Alternate on each bank, and shade
Of flowery lime, or elm tree green
Before some decent villa seen
In seemly row: Such yonder seat,
Fair Howard's elegant retreat!4
Such Twickenham to the Muses dear!5
And many a rural mansion near,
Some rising low the river by,
Some on a slope hill hanging high,
Whose different beauties ere I'd done
Repeating, the bright noonday sun
Would down the west have rolled his light,
And all the prospect sink in night.
    Thus could I ever change the view
To something pleasing still, and new,
Or something, which, perhaps, though seen
Before, would please the eye again:
For perfect Nature never cloys
The mind well taught to taste her joys.
But the Muse whispers in my ear,
'Tis time to close the rapture here,
Poets know seldom where to end,
And one may chance to tire a friend.
No longer now then let us stay:
Here's pleasure for another day.

4. Marble Hill near Twickenham, the residence of Henrietta Hobart (ca 1681–1767), m. (1) (1706) Charles Howard, 9th E. of Suffolk, 1731; (2) (1735) Hon. George Berkeley. She was the mistress of George II, who in 1724, when still Prince of Wales, contributed twelve thousand pounds towards the erection of Marble Hill, which was designed by Henry Herbert, 9th E. of Pembroke. For HW's description of her see *Reminiscences Written by Mr Horace Walpole in 1788*, ed. Paget Toynbee, Oxford, 1924, pp. 65–7, 101–2. See also R. S. Cobbett, *Memorials of Twickenham*, 1872, pp. 241–5.

5. Pope's villa at Twickenham.

From GRAY, Tuesday 19 September 1738

Printed from MS in Waller Collection.

Dated by the postmark and the reference to Ashton and Lord Plymouth.

Address: To the Honourable Horace Walpole Jun. Esq. at New Park,¹ Richmond. *Postmark:* 19 SE.

[London,] Tuesday night [Sept. 19, 1738].

<   >

I HAVE been in town a day or two, and in doubt where to direct to you, till Ashton, whom I saw today, told me you were at Richmond.² I have seen him and his Lordling,³ and am mightily pleased with 'em both; the boy kisses his eyes out, and had no sooner heard that I was Mr John Ashton⁴ but he climbed up to the top of my head, and came down again on the other side in half a second. I shall be glad to know when and where I may see you most alone, and am

Yours ever,

T. G.

From WEST, ca Wednesday 4 April 1739, O.S.

Missing. Probably written at the Inner Temple (*post* 15 May 1739, N.S.); implied *post* 21 April 1739, N.S. West's letter, together with Ashton's (probably of the same date), arrived at Paris 21 April, N.S. (Gray to Ashton 21 April 1739, N.S., *Gray's Corr.* i. 104). Mail for France left London Mondays and Thursdays (*Complete Guide to . . . London*, 1740, p. 80). West's and Ashton's letters probably went by the post of Thursday 5 April, O.S.

1. So called in the eighteenth century to distinguish it from the ancient park connected with the royal palace on the bank of the Thames. Today it is known as Richmond Park, and the latter as the Old Deer Park (H. M. Cundall, *Bygone Richmond*, 1925, p. 30).

2. On 2 Sept. 1738 Sir Robert Walpole had a fit of the ague at Richmond, and for some days his life was in danger (Francis Hare, Bp of Chichester to Francis Naylor 9 Sept. 1738; Hist. MSS Comm., XIVth Report, App. ix, 1895, p. 241). By 18 Sept. Sir

Robert had recovered sufficiently to go to his house in Chelsea. Accounts of his illness appeared in the *Daily Advertiser* 6, 19 Sept. 1738.

3. Other Lewis Windsor (1731–71), 4th E. of Plymouth, 1732.

4. (1721–59), Ashton's brother; Eton, ca 1739; St John's College, Cambridge, 1739; migrated to Trinity College, 1741; Fellow of Trinity College, 1745; rector of Aldingham, Lancs, 1749–59 (Venn, *Alumni Cantab.; Eton Coll. Reg.*). Why Ashton presented Gray as his brother is unexplained.

From ASHTON, ca Wednesday 4 April 1739, O.S.

Missing. Probably written in Hanover Square, London (see *post* July 1739). Gray wrote to Ashton 21 April 1739, N.S.: 'You and West have made us happy tonight in a heap of letters, and we are resolved to repay you tenfold' (*Gray's Corr.* i. 104; see also above note on West to HW).

To WEST, Tuesday 21 April 1739, N.S.

Reprinted from *Works* iv. 419–21.

Paris,[1] April 21, N.S., 1739.

Dear West,

YOU figure us in a set of pleasures,[2] which, believe me, we do not find: cards and eating are so universal, that they absorb all variation of pleasures. The operas indeed are much frequented three times a week;[3] but to me they would be a greater penance than eating *maigre:* their music resembles a gooseberry tart as much as it does harmony. We have not yet been at the Italian playhouse;[4] scarce any one goes there. Their best amusement, and which in some parts beats ours, is the comedy;[5] three or four of the actors[6] excel any we have: but then to this nobody goes, if it is not one of the fashionable nights, and then they go, be the play good or bad—except on Molière's nights, whose pieces they are quite weary of.[7] Gray and I have been at the *Avare* tonight: I cannot at all commend their performance of it. Last night I was in the

1. 'Mr Walpole left Cambridge towards the end of the year 1738, and in March 1739 began his travels by going to Paris, accompanied by Mr Gray' (Berry). HW and Gray left Dover Sunday 29 March, N.S., at noon; they reached Calais by five o'clock, and proceeded to Boulogne on the following afternoon. They arrived at Abbeville Tuesday 31 March, N.S., at Amiens Wednesday, and at Paris Saturday evening (Gray to Mrs Gray 1 April 1739, N.S.; Gray to West 12 April 1739, N.S., *Gray's Corr.* i. 99–102). In Paris they lodged at the Hôtel de Luxembourg, Rue des Petits Augustins (now part of Rue Bonaparte), Quartier Saint-Germain (Gray to Ashton 21 April 1739, N.S., *Gray's Corr.* i. 106).

2. An allusion to West to Gray and HW ca 4 April 1739, O.S., missing.

3. The Opera (Académie Royale de Musique) was at this time in Rue Saint-Honoré, near the Palais Royal (Le Sage, *Le Géographe Parisien*, 1769, ii. 83–4).

4. The Comédie-Italienne at the Hôtel de Bourgogne, Rue Mauconseil. 'Les spectâcles sont toujours très brillants, si vous en exceptez la Comédie-Italienne, aussi vide de sens que des spectateurs' (from an anonymous letter of Feb. 1736 in *Nouvelles de la cour et de la ville . . . 1734–1738*, ed. Édouard-Marie Barthélemy, 1879, p. 60).

5. The Comédie-Française, from 1689 to 1770 in the Rue des Fossés-Saint-Germain-des-Prés (now Rue de l'Ancienne Comédie) (see *Larousse Mensuel*, No. 291, May 1931, pp. 691–3).

6. For Gray's account of them see Gray to West 12 April 1739, N.S., *Gray's Corr.* i. 103–4.

7. Garrick wrote, 25 May 1751: 'Molière's comedies scarcely bring a house and are generally acted by the inferior actors; novelty is the greatest incitement to fill the house' (*Diary of David Garrick*, ed. R. C. Alexander, New York, 1928, p. 7).

Place de Louis le Grand[8] (a regular octagon, uniform, and the houses handsome, though not so large as Golden Square), to see what they reckoned one of the finest burials[9] that ever was in France. It was the Duke de Tresmes,[10] Governor of Paris, and Marshal of France.[11] It began on foot from his palace[12] to his parish-church,[13] and from thence in coaches to the opposite end of Paris, to be interred in the church of the Célestins,[14] where is his family vault. About a week ago we happened to see the grave digging, as we went to see the church, which is old and small, but fuller of fine ancient monuments[15] than any except St Denis,[16] which we saw on the road, and excels Westminster; for the windows are all painted in mosaic, and the tombs as fresh and well-preserved as if they were of yesterday. In the Célestins' church is a votive column[17] to Francis II which says, that it is one assurance of his being immortalized, to have had the martyr Mary Stuart[18] for his wife. After this long digression I return to the burial, which was a most vile thing. A long procession of flambeaux and friars; no plumes, trophies, banners, led horses, scutcheons, or open chariots;[19] nothing but

—friars,

White, black, and grey, with all their trumpery.[20]

8. Now Place Vendôme.

9. It cost his son, the Duc de Gesvres, 20,000 écus besides the damages caused by the fire (Charles-Philippe d'Albert, Duc de Luynes, *Mémoires*, ed. L. Dussieux and E. Soulié, 1860–5, ii. 413–14).

10. François-Bernard Potier de Gesvres (1655–12 April 1739), Duc de Tresmes; Gouverneur de Paris 1704 (La Chenaye-Desbois xvi. 241–2; Anatole, Marquis de Granges de Surgères, *Répertoire . . . de la Gazette de France*, 1902–6, iii. 871).

11. His name does not appear in the 'Chronologie critique des Maréchaux de France, 1047–1931,' in Gabriel le Barrois d'Orgeval's *Le Maréchalat de France*, 1932, ii. 173–308.

12. In the Rue Neuve-Saint-Augustin, near the Rue Saint-Anne (*Almanach Royal*, 1739, p. 80; Edmond-Jean-François Barbier, *Chronique de la régence et du règne de Louis XV*, 1866, iii. 170–1).

13. Saint-Roch in Rue Saint-Honoré (Barbier, op. cit. iii. 171).

14. In the Rue du Petit-Musc, near the Bastille. The church was sacked in the Revolution and demolished in 1849 (Marquis de Rochegude and Maurice Dumolin,

Guide pratique à travers le vieux Paris, 1923, pp. 135, 145).

15. Most of them are now in the Louvre (ibid. 135).

16. See Gray to West 12 April 1739, N.S., *Gray's Corr.* i. 101–2.

17. In the Chapelle d'Orléans, made of white marble, with a bronze urn on the top of it (Hurtaut and Magny, *Dictionnaire historique de la ville de Paris*, 1779, ii. 108).

18. (1542–87), m. (1) (1558) François II (1543–60), K. of France 1559–60. The inscription mentioned by HW is one of three on the pedestal of the votive column:

'. . . tanto veræ fidei assertori, generosam Christi martyrem Mariam Stuard conjugem habuisse, quædam fuit veræ immortalitatis assertio.'

The other two extol Francis' virtues and commemorate the erection of the monument by Charles IX, 1562 (Hurtaut and Magny, loc. cit.).

19. As in England. The accuracy of HW's description is borne out by Barbier's journal under 20 April (Barbier, op. cit. iii. 170–2).

20. *Paradise Lost* iii. 474–5.

This goodly ceremony began at nine at night,[21] and did not finish till three this morning; for, each church they passed, they stopped for a hymn and holy water. By the by, some of these choice monks,[22] who watched the body while it lay in state, fell asleep one night, and let the tapers catch fire of the rich velvet mantle lined with ermine and powdered with gold flower-de-luces, which melted the lead coffin, and burned off the feet of the deceased[23] before it wakened them. The French love show; but there is a meanness reigns through it all. At the house where I stood to see this procession, the room was hung with crimson damask and gold, and the windows were mended in ten or dozen places with paper. At dinner they give you three courses; but a third of the dishes is patched up with salads, butter, puff-paste, or some such miscarriage of a dish. None, but Germans, wear fine clothes; but their coaches are tawdry enough for the wedding of Cupid and Psyche. You would laugh extremely at their signs: some live at the Y grec,[24] some at Venus's Toilette,[25] and some at the Sucking Cat.[26] You would not easily guess their notions of honour: I'll tell you one: it is very dishonourable for any gentleman not to be in the army, or in the King's service as they call it, and it is no dishonour to keep public gaming houses: there are at least an hundred and fifty people of the first quality in Paris who live by it.[27] You may go into their houses at all hours of the

21. 'On est parti à huit heures et demie de l'hôtel. . . . La marche était composée de cent pauvres avec des flambeaux; les couvents des Carmes, Cordeliers, les trois maisons des Capucins, Petits-Pères de la Place des Victoires, Augustins et Jacobins, avec des cierges; une trentaine de ses Suisses, cinquante gentilshommes en manteau et rabat à cheval' (Barbier, op. cit. iii. 171).

22. The priests of Saint-Roch (ibid. 170).

23. 'Les cierges, qui étaient autour du lit, par la grande chaleur du luminaire, se sont fondus, des mèches sont tombées sur le drap mortuaire, y ont mis le feu de façon que le cercueil de plomb a fondu, et ledit seigneur mort a eu les pieds brûlés' (ibid. 170–1).

24. No. 14 Rue de la Huchette, a mercer's shop famed for its pins and needles. The sign 'Y' was actually a pair of breeches (grègues) upside down. See Nicolas de Blegny, Livre commode des adresses de Paris pour 1692, ed. Édouard Fournier, 1878, ii. 24; Édouard Fournier, Histoire des enseignes de Paris, 1884, p. 293; Gustave

Pessard, Nouveau dictionnaire historique de Paris, 1904, p. 530.

25. Perhaps the 'Toilette de Psyche,' 5 Rue Saint-Croix-de-la-Bretonnerie, a barber shop mentioned by Balzac in his Petit dictionnaire critique et anecdotique des enseignes de Paris (Œuvres complètes, ed. Marcel Bouteron and Henri Longnon, 1912–, vol. xxxviii, 1935, pp. 182–3). See also Fournier, Histoire 377.

26. Possibly Miss Berry's misreading of 'Sucking Calf,' since both Balzac (op. cit. 185) and Fournier (op. cit. 381) speak of restaurants at the sign of the 'Veau qui tette,' one in the Rue de la Vrillière and another in the Place du Châtelet.

27. 'It is to be lamented that this disgraceful circumstance is no longer peculiar to France' (Berry). Argenson remarks under March 1739: 'Paris est inondé de jeux publics, de maisons où on donne à jouer aux jeux de hasard, avec un mauvais souper. . . . On compte plus de trois cents de ces maisons dans Paris, où l'on joue au biribi et au pharaon: tous les jeunes gens s'y rui-

night, and find hazard, pharaoh,[28] etc. The men who keep the hazard-table at the Duke de Gesvres'[29] pay him twelve guineas each night for the privilege. Even the princesses of the blood are dirty enough to have shares in the banks kept at their houses. We have seen two or three of them;[30] but they are not young, nor remarkable but for wearing their red of a deeper dye than other women, though all use it extravagantly.

The weather is still so bad, that we have not made any excursions to see Versailles and the environs, not even walked in the Thuilleries; but we have seen almost everything else that is worth seeing in Paris, though that is very considerable. They beat us vastly in buildings, both in number and magnificence. The tombs of Richelieu[31] and Mazarine[32] at the Sorbonne and the Collège de Quatre Nations are wonderfully fine, especially the former. We have seen very little of the people themselves, who are not inclined to be propitious to strangers, espe-

nent' (René-Louis de Voyer de Paulmy, Marquis d'Argenson, *Journal et mémoires,* 1859–67, ii. 92; see also Gray to Ashton 21 April 1739, N.S., *Gray's Corr.* i. 105).

28. *Pharaon* (faro), as well as other games of chance, was prohibited by an *arrêt du conseil* 15 Jan. 1691; the prohibition was renewed by further ordinances of 12 Nov. 1731 and of 18 April 1741 (see *Recueil général des anciennes lois françaises,* 1821–33, xx. 115, xxi. 367, xxii. 144; Luynes, op. cit. iii. 374; see also GM 1739 ix. 362–4 for an act of Parliament forbidding hearts, faro, basset, and hazard.

29. The Hôtel de Gesvres (Hôtel de Tresmes), Rue Neuve-Saint-Augustin, the residence of François-Joachim-Bernard Potier (1692–1757), Duc de Gesvres (*Almanach Royal,* 1740, p. 82), son of the Duc de Tresmes. This and the Prince de Carignan's house, the Hôtel de Soissons, Rue des Deux Écus, were then the most notorious gambling places in Paris. Though games of hazard were prohibited by royal decree, in 1722 Cardinal Dubois authorized the establishment of public gaming houses, after which many of the nobility farmed out the privilege to gamesters, and turned their houses into 'académies de jeux.' Gesvres and Carignan received a monthly rent of 10,000 livres each from M. Thuret (or Thurette), director of the Opéra. Both 'académies' were closed upon Carignan's death 4 April 1741, though Thuret's lease at the Hôtel de Gesvres did not expire un-

til 1746. See Argenson, op. cit. ii. 92–4, 367; Barbier, op. cit. iii. 159–60, 270–1; Luynes, op. cit. iii. 363–4; Karl Ludwig, Freiherr von Pöllnitz, *Memoirs,* 1737–8, ii. 198–201; Henri Martin, *Decline of the French Monarchy,* tr. Mary L. Booth, Boston, 1866, i. 311–12.

30. HW's description would apply to at least two of the numerous *princesses du sang* living at the time: Louise-Anne de Bourbon-Condé (1695–1758), Mlle de Charolais, who was a notorious procuress and gambler, and Anne-Louise-Bénédicte de Bourbon-Condé (1676–1753), m. (1692) Louis-Auguste de Bourbon, Duc du Maine, of whom the Duc de Luynes (*Mémoires* xii. 345) says, 'Partout elle avait son jeu qui a été longtemps le biribi et depuis le cavagnole.'

31. Armand-Jean du Plessis (1585–1642), Duc de Richelieu; cardinal, 1622. The 'Tombeau du Cardinal de Richelieu,' a marble group (1694), is by François Girardon (1628–1715). See Hurtaut and Magny, op. cit. iv. 657–9; Stanislas Lami, *Dictionnaire des sculpteurs de l'école française sous le règne de Louis XIV,* 1906, p. 211.

32. Jules Mazarin (1602–61), cardinal, 1641. The 'Monument de Mazarin' (1689–93), now in the Louvre, is by Antoine Coyzevox (1640–1720), assisted by Étienne Le Hongre and Jean-Baptiste Tuby. See Hurtaut and Magny, op. cit. ii. 415; Lami, op. cit. 129; Gustave Masson, *Mazarin,* 1886, p. 144.

cially if they do not play, and speak the language readily. There are many English here: Lord Holderness,[33] Conway[34] and Clinton,[35] and Lord George Bentinck;[36] Mr Brand,[37] Offley,[38] Frederic,[39] Frampton,[40] Bonfoy,[41] etc. Sir John Cotton's son[42] and a Mr Vernon[43] of Cambridge passed through Paris last week. We shall stay here about a fortnight longer,[44] and then go to Rheims with Mr Conway[45] for two or three months. When you have nothing else to do, we shall be glad to hear from you; and any news. If we did not remember there was such a place as England, we should know nothing of it: the French never mention it, unless it happens to be in one of their proverbs. Adieu!

Yours ever,

H. W.

33. Robert Darcy (1718–78), 4th E. of Holdernesse. HW and Gray dined with him 5 April, N.S. (Gray to West 12 April 1739, N.S., *Gray's Corr.* i. 102).

34. Francis Seymour Conway (1718–94), 2d Bn Conway; cr. (1750) E. and (1793) M. of Hertford; HW's cousin and Eton friend (*Eton Coll. Reg.*). He set out 'on his travels into foreign parts' 17 June 1736 and returned to England at the end of April 1739 (*Daily Adv.* 16 June 1736, 1 May 1739).

35. Hugh Fortescue (1696–1751), 14th Bn Clinton; cr. (1746) E. Clinton (Montagu i. 33).

36. Lord George Bentinck (1715–59), son of the 1st D. of Portland; M.P. Droitwich 1742–7, Grampound 1747–54, Malmesbury 1754–9; colonel, 5th Regiment of Foot, 1754–9; HW's contemporary at Eton (*Eton Coll. Reg.*; *Army Lists*).

37. Thomas Brand (d. 1770), of The Hoo, Herts; M.P. New Shoreham 1741–7, Tavistock 1747–54, Gatton 1754–68, Okehampton 1768–70; HW's 'old schoolfellow' (Cole i. 198) and correspondent (*Vict. Co. Hist., Herts*, ii. 408, iii. 30; *Eton College Lists*, ed. R. A. Austen-Leigh, Eton, 1907, p. 28; HW to Mann 5 June 1754).

38. Perhaps Laurence (ca 1719–49), son of Crewe Offley, of Wichnor, Staffs; admitted fellow-commoner at Clare 11 Nov. 1736 (Venn, *Alumni Cantab.*), or his brother, John (d. 1784), M.P. and later Groom of the Bedchamber (Montagu i. 294).

39. Perhaps John Frederick (1708–83), 4th Bt 1770. 'Mr Frederick' is mentioned by

HW with Lord Holdernesse, Lord Conway, H. S. Conway, Brand, etc., as one of the directors of the opera in London (HW to Mann 5 Nov. 1741, O.S.).

40. James Frampton (1711–84), of Moreton, Dorset, High Sheriff of Dorset, 1744; HW's contemporary at Eton (*Eton Coll. Reg.*; Venn, *Alumni Cantab.*).

41. Probably Nicholas Bonfoy (d. 1775), of Abbots Ripton, Hunts, sergeant-at-arms to the House of Commons 1762–75 (Venn, *Alumni Cantab.*; *Court and City Register*). HW saw him at Chatsworth when visiting at the Duke of Devonshire's (Montagu i. 295). Gray sent him a copy of his *Odes*, 1757 (see Gray to Brown 25 July 1757, *Gray's Corr.* ii. 509; Hazen, *SH Bibliography* 27).

42. John Hinde Cotton (ca 1717–95), M.P., of Madingley Hall, Cambs; 4th Bt 1752; son of Sir John Hinde Cotton (ca 1688–1752), 3d Bt. The younger Cotton was admitted fellow-commoner of Emmanuel, 6 Jan. 1736 (Venn, *Alumni Cantab.*).

43. Henry Vernon (1718–65), of Hilton Park, Staffs; M.P. Lichfield 1753–61, Newcastle-under-Lyme 1761–2; commissioner of Excise; admitted fellow-commoner of Trinity, 17 May 1735 (Venn, *Alumni Cantab.*). He accompanied Cotton to Florence (HW to Mann 17 Nov. 1743, O.S.).

44. They did not leave Paris until 1 June, N.S. (Gray to Ashton 29 May 1739, N.S., *Gray's Corr.* i. 109).

45. Hon. Henry Seymour Conway, Lord Conway's brother.

Tomorrow we go to the *Cid*.⁴⁶ They have no farces, but *petites pièces* like our *Devil to Pay*.⁴⁷

From WEST, ca April 1739

Missing. Probably written at the Inner Temple in reply to *ante* 21 April 1739, N.S.

To WEST, ca Friday 15 May 1739, N.S.

Reprinted from *Works* iv. 421–3.
Dated by HW's and Gray's visit to Versailles on 'Wednesday' (13 May, N.S.) and by the reference to their going there again 'next Sunday' (17 May, N.S.) to witness the installation of the 'Knights of the Holy Ghost.'

From Paris [ca May 15], 1739.

Dear West,

I SHOULD think myself to blame not to try to divert you, when you tell me I can. From the air of your letter¹ you seem to want amusement, that is, you want spirits. I would recommend to you certain little employments that I know of, and that belong to you,¹ᵃ but that I imagine bodily exercise is more suitable to your complaint. If you would promise me to read them in the Temple Garden,² I would send you a little packet of plays and pamphlets³ that we have made up, and intend to dispatch to Dick's⁴ the first opportunity.—Stand by, clear the way, make room for the pompous appearance of Versailles le grand! But no: it fell so short of my idea of it, mine, that I have resigned to Gray the office of writing its panegyric.⁵ He likes it. They say I am to like it better next Sunday;⁶ when the sun is to shine, the King is to be

46. *Le Cid* (1636) by Pierre Corneille.
47. *The Devil to Pay; or, the Wives Metamorphosed* (1731), a ballad opera adapted from Thomas Jevon's *Devil of a Wife* (1686) by Charles Coffey (d. 1745) and John Mottley (1692–1750). It was very popular as an afterpiece.

---

1. West to HW ca April 1739, missing.
1a. That is, making verses.
2. West was admitted a student at the Inner Temple between 20 Nov. 1732 and 16 Nov. 1733, since his name appears in the

Treasurer's account for that period, under 'admittances into the house' (*Calendar of Inner Temple Records*, vol. iv, ed. R. A. Roberts, 1933, p. 279).
3. Acknowledged and described by West *post* 21 June 1739, O.S.
4. Dick's Coffee-house in Fleet Street (later No. 8), near Temple Bar (John Timbs, *Clubs and Club Life in London*, 1908, pp. 285–6).
5. See Gray to West ca 15 and 22 May 1739, N.S. (*Gray's Corr.* i. 106–8).
6. Whitsunday 17 May, N.S. (ibid.).

fine, the waterworks are to play,[7] and the new Knights of the Holy Ghost are to be installed![8] Ever since Wednesday, the day we were there, we have done nothing but dispute about it. They say, we did not see it to advantage, that we ran through the apartments, saw the garden *en passant,* and slubbered over Trianon. I say, we saw nothing. However, we had time to see that the great front[9] is a lumber of littleness, composed of black brick, stuck full of bad old busts, and fringed with gold rails. The rooms are all small, except the great gallery, which is noble, but totally wainscoted with looking-glass. The garden is littered with statues and fountains, each of which has its tutelary deity. In particular, the elementary God of Fire[10] solaces himself in one. In another, Enceladus,[11] in lieu of a mountain, is overwhelmed with many waters. There are avenues of water-pots, who disport themselves much in squirting up cascadelins. In short, 'tis a garden for a great child. Such was Louis Quatorze, who is here seen in his proper colours, where he commanded in person, unassisted by his armies and generals, and left to the pursuit of his own puerile ideas of glory.

We saw last week a place of another kind, and which has more the air of what it would be, than anything I have yet met with: it was the convent of the Chartreux.[12] All the conveniencies, or rather (if there

7. The fountains of the Petit Parc played from 10 A.M. to 8 P.M. during the summer, whenever the King was in residence, but the full display (*les grandes eaux*) was reserved for Whitsunday, St Louis' Day (25 Aug.), and visits of foreign ambassadors (Louis-Étienne Dussieux, *Le Château de Versailles,* Versailles, 1885, ii. 270).

8. At the Chapel Royal at Versailles, being the nineteenth promotion during the reign of Louis XV, with 'high mass, celebrated with music, great crowd, much incense, King, Queen, Dauphin, Mesdames, cardinals, and Court. Knights arrayed by his Majesty; reverences before the altar, not bows but curtsies; stiff hams; much tittering among the ladies; trumpets, kettledrums, and fifes' (Gray to West ca 15 and 22 May 1739, N.S., *Gray's Corr.* i. 108). The order was founded by Henri III in 1578, and was suppressed in 1830 (Comte de Colleville and François Saint-Christo, *Les Ordres du Roi,* n.d., pp. xii–xxii). For the names of the seven knights installed 17 May 1739, see ibid., p. 32.

9. The Château de Versailles facing the Cour de Marbre.

10. 'Le Statue de Feu' (1681) by Nicolas Dossier (fl. 1664–1701), near the Fontaine de Latone; No. 157 in Girard's *Plan général . . . du petit Parc de Versailles,* 1714 (Gilles de Mortain, *Plans . . . de Versailles,* 1714–15; see also Stanislas Lami, *Dictionnaire des sculpteurs de l'école française sous le règne de Louis XIV,* 1906, p. 160).

11. 'La Fontaine de l'Encelade' (1675–6) by André Le Nôtre (1613–1700), with sculpture by Gaspard Marsy (ca 1625–81) (Lami, op. cit. 355), on the right of the Bassin d'Apollon. It is No. 204 in Girard's *Plan général.* 'La figure de ce géant . . . est accablée sous les rochers des monts Ossa et Olympe. Il sort de sa bouche une gerbe d'eau de 78 pieds de haut et est environné de quantité de bouillons' (Girard's inscription, Gilles de Mortain, op. cit. plate xvii).

12. The entrance was on the Rue d'Enfer. The convent was demolished in 1796 for the expansion of the Jardin du Luxembourg (Alphonse de Gisors, *Le Palais du Luxembourg,* 1847, p. 78).

was such a word) all the *adaptments*[13] are assembled here, that melancholy, meditation, selfish devotion, and despair would require. But yet 'tis pleasing. Soften the terms, and mellow the uncouth horror that reigns here, but a little, and 'tis a charming solitude. It stands on a large space of ground,[14] is old and irregular. The chapel is gloomy: behind it, through some dark passages, you pass into a large obscure hall, which looks like a combination-chamber for some hellish council. The large cloister surrounds their burying-ground. The cloisters are very narrow, and very long, and let into the cells, which are built like little huts detached from each other. We were carried into one, where lived a middle-aged man not long initiated into the order. He was extremely civil, and called himself Dom Victor. We have promised to visit him often. Their habit is all white: but besides this, he was infinitely clean in his person; and his apartment and garden, which he keeps and cultivates without any assistance, was neat to a degree. He has four little rooms, furnished in the prettiest manner, and hung with good prints. One of them is a library, and another a gallery. He has several canary-birds disposed in a pretty manner in breeding-cages. In his garden was a bed of good tulips in bloom, flowers and fruit-trees, and all neatly kept. They are permitted at certain hours to talk to strangers, but never to one another, or to go out of their convent. But what we chiefly went to see was the small cloister, with the history of St Bruno,[15] their founder, painted by Le Sœur.[16] It consists of twenty-two pictures,[17] the

13. Given in OED as 'obsolete, rare,' with this passage as the sole illustration.

14. A triangle formed by the Rue Notre-Dame-des-Champs, the Rue de Vaugirard, and the Rue d'Enfer (Rochegude and Dumolin, *Guide pratique à travers le vieux Paris*, 1923, p. 510). Around the convent, with its large cells, each with a study, a bedroom, and a small garden, there were about 110 acres (90 *arpents*) of cultivated land. See Germain Brice, *Description de la ville de Paris*, 7th edn, 1717, ii. 449.

15. St Bruno (ca 1030–1101), founder of La Grande Chartreuse (1084), near Grenoble. See Max Heimbucher, *Die Orden und Kongregationen der katholischen Kirche*, Paderborn, 1933–4, i. 376.

16. Eustache Le Sueur (1616–55). He was known as 'le Raphael français' (Antoine-Nicolas Dezallier d'Argenville, *Voyage pittoresque de Paris*, 1752, pp. 309–10; *Archives de l'art français* 1853–5, v. 329).

17. 'La Vie de Saint-Bruno,' now in the Louvre, in the Salle Le Sueur (Louis Hourticq, *Les Tableaux du Louvre*, n.d., p. 102). They were painted 1645–8, while Le Sueur (according to tradition) was in sanctuary at the Chartreuse after killing a nobleman in a duel. Louis XVI bought the pictures in 1776 for 30,000 livres, and after restoration (n. 19 below) they were transferred to Versailles. They have been at the Louvre since 1793. See G. K. Nagler, *Neues allgemeines Künstler-Lexikon*, Munich, 1835–52; NBG; J. J. Guiffrey, 'Lettres et documents sur l'acquisition des tableaux d'Eustache Le Sueur pour la collection du Roi (1776–1789),' *Nouvelles archives de l'art français*, 1877, v. 277. Miss Berry wrote on this passage: 'Lord Orford always continued to think that in these pictures Le Sœur had rivalled, if not excelled, Raphael.' In his 'Book of Materials,' 1771, HW wrote: 'I met two Frenchmen, who had been in Italy,

figures a good deal less than life. But sure they are amazing! I don't know what Raphael may be in Rome, but these pictures excel all I have seen in Paris and England. The figure of the dead man[18] who spoke at his burial, contains all the strongest and horridest ideas, of ghastliness, hypocrisy discovered, and the height of damnation; pain and cursing. A Benedictine monk, who was there at the same time, said to me of this picture: *C'est une fable, mais on la croyait autrefois.* Another, who showed me relics in one of their churches, expressed as much ridicule for them. The pictures I have been speaking of are ill preserved,[19] and some of the finest heads defaced, which was done at first by a rival[20] of Le Sœur's.—Adieu! dear West, take care of your health; and some time or other we will talk over all these things with more pleasure than I have had in seeing them.

Yours ever.

To West, Thursday 18 June 1739, N.S.

Reprinted from *Works* iv. 423–4.

Rheims,[1] June 18, 1739, N.S.

Dear West,

HOW I am to fill up this letter is not easy to divine. I have consented that Gray shall give you an account of our situation and proceedings; and have left myself at the mercy of my own invention—a

walking in Le Sœur's cloister at Paris. They talked to me of Italian masters: I said there [these?] were works of one of their own painters equal to anything I had seen. One of them shook his head, and said, "You would not think so if you had ever been in Italy." ' See also HW to Gray 19 Nov. 1765, and to Chute 5 Aug. 1771.

18. 'Raymond Diocrès [(d. ca 1082), canon of Notre-Dame de Paris] répondant après sa mort.' The miracle of the dead man rising to pronounce the words inscribed on the funeral pall, 'Justo Dei judicio appellatus sum; justo Dei judicio judicatus sum; justo Dei judicio condemnatus sum,' takes place in the church, with the priests and the torch-bearers around the coffin. See Frédéric Villot, *Notices des tableaux . . . dans les galeries du . . . Louvre*, 1878, iii. 345; *Acta Sanctorum*, li (1868). 549, *sub* 6 Oct., *De S. Brunone Confessore*.

19. Because of the excessive humidity of the 'petit cloître.' The pictures, painted on wood, were transferred to canvas in 1777 (Guiffrey, op. cit. 295).

20. Charles Le Brun (1619–90), according to Guillet de Saint-Georges and Pierre-Jean Mariette. See Guillet de Saint-Georges, 'Mémoire historique des ouvrages d'Eustache Le Sueur,' in *Archives de l'art français*, 1852–3, iii. 23–4.

---

1. 'Mr Walpole was now removed to Rheims, where, with his cousin Henry Seymour Conway and Mr Gray, he resided three months, principally to acquire the French language' (Berry). HW and Gray left Paris 1 June (*ante* 21 April 1739, N.S., n. 44). They stayed at Rheims a little over three months, living at 'M. Hibert's, Rue Saint-Denis.' They set out for Dijon 7 Sept., N.S. (Gray's MS Journal 1739–1741; *post* 13 Dec. 1765; Gray to Philip Gray 11 Sept. 1739, N.S., *Gray's Corr.* i. 116).

most terrible resource, and which I shall avoid applying to, if I can possibly help it. I had prepared the ingredients for a description of a ball,[2] and was just ready to serve it up to you, but he has plucked it from me.[3] However, I was resolved to give you an account of a particular song and dance in it, and was determined to write the words and sing the tune just as I folded up my letter: but as it would, ten to one, be opened[4] before it gets to you, I am forced to lay aside this thought, though an admirable one. Well, but now I have put it into your head, I suppose you won't rest without it. For that individual one, believe me, 'tis nothing without the tune and the dance; but to stay your stomach, I will send you one of their vaudevilles[5] or ballads,[6] which they sing at the comedy after their *petites pièces.*

You must not wonder if all my letters resemble dictionaries, with French on one side, and English on t'other; I deal in nothing else at present, and talk a couple of words of each language alternately from morning till night. This has put my mouth a little out of tune at present; but I am trying to recover the use of it, by reading the newspapers aloud at breakfast, and by chewing the title-pages of all my English books. Besides this, I have paraphrased half the first act of your new *Gustavus,* which was sent us to Paris: a most dainty performance,[7] and

2. Perhaps the impromptu supper and dancing in a public garden until four in the morning, in the 'company of eighteen people, men and women of the best fashion,' which Gray describes in Gray to Mrs Gray 21 June 1739, N.S. (*Gray's Corr.* i. 113–14). 'Mr Walpole had a mind to make a custom of the thing, and would have given a ball in the same manner next week, but the women did not come into it, so I believe it will drop, and they will return to their dull cards and usual formalities' (ibid. 114).

3. In the first of two letters in French written to West. The letters (both missing) were suppressed by Mason in his *Memoirs of Gray,* on the advice of HW, who objected to the poor French (Mason to HW 28 June 1773; HW to Mason 5 July 1773).

4. See MONTAGU and DU DEFFAND indexes *sub* 'Post: lack of privacy of.'

5. This passage is the first given in OED to illustrate 'Vaudeville. 1. A light popular song . . . *spec.* a song of this nature sung on the stage.'

6. 'This ballad does not appear' (Berry).

7. Presumably sarcasm. *Gustavus Vasa, the Deliverer of his Country,* a five-act tragedy by Henry Brooke (ca 1703–83), was published 5 May 1739, O.S. (*Daily Adv.* 5 May 1739). The play was banned while in rehearsal, 16 March, by the Duke of Grafton, Lord Chamberlain (ibid. 29 March 1739). The title itself (which was presumably taken to refer to the Old Pretender) was sufficient to forbid the acting of the play (GM 1739, ix. 146), but it was evidently a scurrilous libel on George II, Sir Robert Walpole, and the Whig administration. It was first acted at the Smock Alley Theatre, Dublin, 3 Dec. 1744 (Nicoll, *Drama 1700–50,* p. 300; see also Herbert Wright, 'Henry Brooke's "Gustavus Vasa," ' *Modern Language Review,* 1919, xiv. 176; R. W. Chapman, 'Brooke's *Gustavus Vasa,*' *Review of English Studies,* 1925, i. 460–1, 1926, ii. 99; Gray to Ashton 29 May 1739, N.S., *Gray's Corr.* i. 110).

just what you say of it. Good night, I am sure you must be tired: if you
are not, I am.

Yours ever,

Hor. Walpole

From West, Thursday 21 June 1739, O.S.

Reprinted from *Works* iv. 424–7.

Temple, June 21, 1739.

Dear Walpole,

YOUR last letter puts me in mind of some good people who,
though they give you the best dinner in the world, are never satisfied with themselves, but—wish they had known sooner—quite
ashamed—a little unprepared—hope you'll excuse, and so forth; for
you tell me you only send me this to stay my stomach against you are
better furnished, and at the same time you treat me, *ut nunquam in
vita melius.*[1] Nor is it now alone I have room to say so, but 'tis always;
and I know I had rather gather the crumbs that fall from under your
table, than be a prime guest with most other people. Sincerely, Sir, nobody in Great Britain, nor, I believe, in France, keeps a more elegant
table than yourself. Mistake me not, I mean a metaphorical one, for
else I should lie confoundedly; for you know you did not use to keep a
very extraordinary one, at least when I had the honour to dine with
you—boiled chickens and roast legs of mutton were your highest ef-
fort.[2] But, with the metaphor, the case is quite altered; 'tis no longer
chapon toujours bouilli; 'tis *varium et mutabile semper*[3] enough, I am
sure; 'tis *Italo perfusus aceto;*[4] 'tis *tota merum sal.*[5] You see too it has a
particularity, which perhaps you did not know before, that it is of all
genders, and is masculine, feminine, or neuter, which you please.[6]
Your feasts are like Plato's; one feeds upon them for two or three days

1. Horace, *Serm.* II. viii. 3–4, adapted.
2. Referring to HW's later years William Beloe wrote, '[Lord Orford's] establishment at his villa was not very splendid; nor had his Lordship a very high character for hospitality. It was facetiously said
by an author, who went to dine at [Straw-
berry Hill], on invitation, that he returned
as he went—exceedingly hungry. . . . His

Lordship lived on the very humblest fare,
drinking only water' (William Beloe, *The
Sexagenarian,* 1817, i. 293; see also ibid. i.
277–9).
3. Virgil, *Æneid* iv. 569.
4. Horace, *Serm.* I. vii. 32.
5. Lucretius, *De Rer. Nat.* iv. 1158.
6. *Merum sal* is neuter, *varium* is neuter,
perfusus masculine, and *tota* feminine.

together, and *e convivio sapientiores resurgimus quam accubuimus.*[7]
So it is with me, and I never receive any of your tables, or *tabulæ* (for
you know 'tis the same thing) but I exclaim to myself:

Di magni! salicippium disertum![8]

If you don't understand this line, you must consult with Doctor Bentley's nephew,[9] who thinks nobody can understand it without him,
when, after all, it does not signify a brass farthing whether you understand it or no. But, Sir, this is not all; you not only treat me with a
whole bushel of Attic salt, and a gallon of Italian vinegar, but you give
me some English-French music—a vaudeville in both languages!

Docte sermones, utriusque linguæ—[10]

But now I talk of music at a feast; I'll tell you of a feast and music
too. About a fortnight ago, walking through Leicester Fields, I ran full-
butt against somebody. Upon examination, who should it be but Mr.
A——?[11] I mean the nephew of the Lord of ——. So we saluted very
amicably, and I engaged to sup with him Thursday next. To his lodgings I went on Thursday, and there I found Plato, Puffendorf, and
Prato[12] (can't you guess who they be?) A very good supper we had, and
Plato gave your health. I believe he is in love. Did you ever hear of
Nanny Blundel?[13] But I forget our music. We had, Sir, for an hour or
two, an Ethiopian, belonging to the Duchess of Athol,[14] who played to

7. Dr Chapman suggests that this may
be a quotation from Aulus Gellius, but it
has not been traced.

8. 'Di magni! salaputium disertum!'
(Catullus liii. 5). West's *salicippium*, a bar-
barism, is perhaps derived from *sal* and
cippus and means pillar or tombstone of
wit. It may, however, be merely a misreading by a previous transcriber.

9. Thomas Bentley (ca 1691–1742),
LL.D.; son of James Bentley, of Oulton,
Yorks, half-brother of Dr Richard Bentley;
librarian of Trinity 1721–9; classical
scholar. See Nichols, *Lit. Anec.* iv. 491–2,
and Pope's note on *Dunciad* ii. 205.

10. Horace, *Carm.* III. viii. 5.

11. Perhaps Joseph (1715–80), son of
Joseph Amphlett, of Clent, Staffs, by Anne
Lyttelton, sister of Sir Thomas Lyttelton,
4th Bt, who was lord of the manor of Hagley. Amphlett was a contemporary at Eton

1725–32; Worcester College, Oxford,
1735–9; D.C.L., 1750; vicar of Bampton,
Oxon 1757–80; Prebendary of Carlisle
1778–80 (*Eton Coll. Reg.*; Collins, *Peerage*,
1812, viii. 349).

12. Not identified: Eton contemporaries
of HW's.

13. Not identified. Perhaps a niece of
Nicholas Blundell (d. 1737), of Crosby Hall,
Lancs, or a member of the North Meols
(Lancs) branch of the same family (see
Burke, *Commoners* ii. 529).

14. Either Mary Ross (d. 1767), the
dowager Duchess, who m. (1710), as his 2d
wife, John Murray, 1st D. of Atholl; or Jane
(ca 1693–1748), dau. of Thomas Frederick,
of Westminster, m. (1) (ca 1723) James Lan-
noy; m. (2) (1726) James Murray, 2d D. of
Atholl (Sir James Balfour Paul, *Scots Peerage*, Edinburgh, 1904–14, i. 485–9).

us upon the French horn. A——— made me laugh about him very much,
I said, 'I suppose you give this Ethiopian something to drink?' Upon
which he ordered him half a crown. I said, 'So *much?*' 'Oh! he's only a
black,' answered he. Puffendorf (who you know says good things sometimes) said, not amiss, 'O Sir, if he had been a white, he'd have given
him a crown.' I don't pretend to compare our supper with your *partie
de cabaret* at Rheims, but at least, Sir, our materials were more sterling
than yours. You had a *goûté* forsooth, composed of *des fraises, de la
crême, du vin, des gâteaux,* etc. We, Sir, we supped *à l'anglaise. Im-
primis,* we had buttock of beef, and Yorkshire ham; we had chickens
too, and a gallon bowl of salad, and a gooseberry pie as big as anything.
Now, Sir, notwithstanding (do you know what this notwithstanding
relates to? I'll mark the cue for you—'tis—) notwithstanding, I say, I am
neither *solers citharæ, neque musæ deditus ulli,*[15] as you are; yet, as I
am very vain, and apt to have a high opinion of my own poetry, I have
a mind to treat you as elegantly as you have treated me—as you remember a certain doctor[16] at King's College did the Duke of Devonshire—
and so have prepared you a little sort of musical *accompagnamento* for
your entertainment. 'Tis true, I said to myself very often—

> An quodcunque facit Mæcenas, te quoque verum est,
> Tanto dissimilem, et tanto certare minorem?[17]

Then I reflected—

> Ut gratas inter mensas symphonia discors,
> Et crassum unguentum et Sardo cum melle papaver,
> Offendunt; poterat duci quia cœna sine illis;
> Sic animis natum inventumque poema juvandis,
> Si paulum summo discessit, vergit ad imum.[18]

Yet in spite of these two long quotations (which I made no other use of
than what you see) I still determined to scrape a little, and accordingly
have sent you, in lieu of your vaudeville, a miserable elegy.[19]

---

15. Horace, *Serm.* II. iii. 105, adapted.
16. Not identified.
17. Horace, *Serm.* II. iii. 312–13.
18. Horace, *Ars Poet.* 374–8 (in line 376 read 'istis' and in line 378 'decessit').
19. 'This elegy does not appear' (Berry). Tovey and Toynbee insert in the text at this point West's imitation of Propertius III. xvii (*Ad Bacchum*) which they print from the copy in Gray's hand in his Com-

monplace Books, inscribed by him 'Fav[on-ius] June 1739' (see Tovey, *Gray and His Friends,* pp. 127–8; *Gray-HW-West-Ashton Corr.* i. 229–31; also *post* 8 Feb. 1747, n. 20). There is no question that this is the imita-tion West wrote; but it was probably an enclosure rather than a part of the letter itself. The imitation is printed in Appen-dix 3.

I dare say you wish you could shake the pen out of my hand. But I don't know how it is, I am at present in a vein to make up for the dryness of most of my former letters since you have been abroad, and I can't tell but I may fill up this sheet, if not another, with more such trumpery. I forget all this while to thank [?you] for the packet[20] which I have received, and which was more welcome to me than an Amiens pie; for I can't help running on upon the metaphor I set out with, and you know I always was a *heluo librorum*. The first thing I pitched upon was Crébillon's love letters,[21] allured by the garnishing, I fancy; that is, the red leaves and the blue silk calendar.[22] 'Tis an ingenious account of the progress of love in a very virtuous lady's heart, and how a fine gentleman may first gain her approbation, then her esteem, then her heart, and then her—you know what. But don't you think it ends a little too tragically?[23] For my part, I protest, I was very sorry, the last letter made me cry. But the passions are charmingly described all through, and the language is fine. After this I would have read the *Amusement philosophique*,[24] but Ashton has run away with it—

> Callidus, quicquid placuit jocoso
> Condere furto.[25]

Very jocose indeed to rob a body! So I ha'n't seen it since. *Gustave*[26] is no bad thing, as far as I can judge. One may see the author was young when he wrote it, and it looks to me like a first play of an author.[27] But the language is natural, and in many places poetical. The plot is very entertaining, only I don't like the conclusion. It ends abrupt, and Leonor[28] comes in at last too much like an apparition. The rest of the pieces I have not read but from what I can discover by a transient view, I fancy they are better seen than read.

I am now at the eighth page; 'tis time to have done, and wish you

---

20. See *ante* ca 15 May 1739, N.S.

21. *Lettres de la Marquise de M*** au Comte de R****, 1732, by Crébillon *fils*.

22. Apparently the book was colourfully bound, with red end-papers, and a silk calendar to go with it perhaps for a bookmark.

23. Abandoned by her lover, the Marquise wastes away and presumably dies.

24. *Amusement philosophique sur le langage des bêtes*, 1739, by Guillaume-Hyacinthe Bougeant (1690–1743).

25. Horace. *Carm.* I. x. 7–8.

26. *Gustave*, 1733, a tragedy in five acts by Alexis Piron (1689–1773), first acted at the Comédie-Française 3 Feb. 1733. See Paul Chaponnière, *Piron*, Geneva, 1910, p. 69; Claude Parfaict, *Dictionnaire des théâtres de Paris*, 1756, iii. 54.

27. It was his third, besides numerous marionette plays written between 1722 and 1726. His first five-act play was *Les Fils ingrats*, 1728 (Chaponnière, op. cit. 33–51).

28. Gustave's mother who, together with Adélaïde, the heroine, is freed by Gustave.

adieu. I hear Sir Robert is very well.[29] My Lord Conway[30] is reckoned one of the prettiest persons about town.

Yours ever,

R. WEST

From ASHTON, ? July 1739

Missing. Probably written in Hanover Square, London. Implied *post* July 1739.

To ASHTON, July 1739

Printed from Mitford's transcript in the British Museum. See *ante* i. xxxv.

Written in collaboration with Gray. HW obviously wrote the second paragraph. The letter may be assigned approximately to the week of 19 July, N.S., from the reference to the visit of 'Messrs Selwyn and Montague.'

Address: To Mr Ashton at Mrs Lewis's,[1] Hanover Square, London. Franc à Paris. Pour l'Angleterre.

Rheims, July [1739].

My dear Ashton,

THE exceeding slowness and sterility of me, and this place, and the vast abundance and volubility of Mr Walpole and his pen will sufficiently excuse to you the shortness of this little matter. He insists that it is not him, but his pen that is so volubility, and so I have borrowed it of him; but I find it is both of 'em that is so volubility, for though I am writing as fast as I can drive, yet he is still chattering in vast abundance. I have desired me to hold his tongue, pho, I mean him, and his, but his pen is so used to write in the first person, that I have screwed my finger and thumb off, with forcing it into the third.

---

29. There appeared in the *Daily Adv.* 18–27 April 1739 reports of Sir Robert Walpole's illness. By 21 June he was well enough to hold 'a great levee at his house in Downing Street, Westminster' (ibid. 22 June 1739).

30. He returned to London from Paris at the end of April 1739 (*ante* 21 April 1739, N.S., n. 34).

---

1. Elizabeth Turnour (d. 1754), of London, m. (1709) Thomas Lewis (d. 1736) of Van, St Fagan's, and Soberton, Hants, and of Hanover Square. Their only daughter, Elizabeth, m. (1730) the 3d E. of Plymouth (George T. Clark, *Limbus Patrum Morganiæ et Glamorganiæ*, 1886, pp. 42, 52; his conjectures as to Elizabeth Turnour's identity, however, are inconsistent and erroneous. See also GM 1754, xxiv. 483). Since the Earl and Countess of Plymouth died in 1732 and 1733, respectively, Mrs Lewis was made one of the guardians of their child, Lord Plymouth, Ashton's pupil (see Private Act 17 Geo. II, 1744, c. 24). (Toynbee [*Gray-HW-West-Ashton Corr.* i. 157n], following Mitford [Tovey, *Gray and His Friends*, p. ix], erroneously identifies this Mrs Lewis as Anne Wright, wife of Thomas Lewis of Harpton Court, Radnor.)

After all this confusion of persons, and a little stroke of satire upon me, the pen returns calmly back again into the old *I*, and *me,* as if nothing had happened, to tell you how much I am tired, and how cross I am, that this cursed scheme of Messrs Selwyn and Montague should have come across all our measures,[2] and broke in upon the whole year, which, what with the month we have to wait for them, and the month they are to stay here, will be entirely slipped away, at least, the agreeable part of it, and if we journey at all, it will be through dirty roads, and falling leaves.

The man, whose arguments you have so learnedly stated,[3] and whom you did not think fit to honour with a confutation, we from thence conceive to be one who does us honour in thinking us fools, and so you see, I lay my claim to a share of the glory; we are not vastly curious about his name, first because it don't signify, secondly because we know it already: it is either Sir T.G.[4] himself, or your friend Mr Fenton,[5] if it's them, we don't care, and if it is not, we don't care neither, but if you care to convince the man, whoever he be, that we are in some points not altogether fools, you might [let] him know that we are most sincerely

Yours,

H. W.

T. G.

To West, Monday 20 July 1739, N.S.

Reprinted from *Works* iv. 427–9.

Rheims, July 20, 1739.

GRAY says, 'Indeed you ought to write to West.' Lord, child, so I would, if I knew what to write about. If I were at London and he at Rheims, I would send him volumes about peace and war, Spaniards, camps and conventions;[1] but d'ye think he cares sixpence to know who

2. HW and Gray had planned to leave Rheims 20 July (see *post* 20 July 1739, N.S.).

3. In Ashton to HW ?July 1739, missing.

4. Not identified. Perhaps a nickname.

5. James Fenton (1716–91), Ashton's Eton contemporary and fellow-townsman: son of James Fenton, vicar of Lancaster; Eton 1729–34; Queen's College, Oxford, 1734; barrister-at-law; recorder of Lancas-

ter (*Eton Coll. Reg.;* Foster, *Alumni Oxon.; Registers of the Parish Church of Lancaster 1691–1748,* ed. Henry Brierley, vol. ii, Cambridge, 1920, p. 38; GM 1791, lxi pt ii. 1069). Ashton, like Fenton, grew up at Lancaster, where Ashton's father was usher of Lancaster Royal Grammar School.

———

1. London was full of rumours about the

is gone to Compiègne,[2] and when they come back, or who won and lost four livres at quadrille last night at Mr Cockbert's?[3]—No, but you may tell him what you have heard of Compiègne; that they have balls twice a week after the play,[4] and that the Count d'Eu[5] gave the King a most flaring entertainment[6] in the camp, where the polygon[7] was represented in flowering shrubs. Dear West, these are the things I must tell you; I don't know how to make 'em look significant, unless you will be a Rhemois for a little moment. I wonder you can stay out of the city so long, when we are going to have all manner of diversions. The comedians return hither from Compiègne in eight days, for example; and in a very little of time one attends the regiment of the King, three battalions,[8] and an hundred of officers; all men of a certain fashion, very amiable, and who know their world. Our women grow more gay, more lively from day to day in expecting them; Mademoiselle la Reine[9] is brewing a wash of a finer dye, and brushing up her eyes for their arrival. La Baronne[10] already counts upon fifteen of them; and Madame

imminent war with Spain. On 25 May, Spain abrogated Article III of the Convention of the Prado of 14 Jan. 1739 (stipulating an indemnity of £95,000 for damages to British shipping) because the British refused to withdraw their fleet from the Mediterranean, as agreed upon in the Convention. Negotiations were broken off in June, and the order for reprisals against Spanish shipping, heretofore kept secret, was published in the London Gazette 10 July 1739; war was declared 23 Oct. 1739 (see The Annals of Europe for 1739, 1740–1, i. 58–60, 130–8; GM 1739, ix. 275, 330, 386).

2. The summer residence of the kings of France. The Court was there from 11 June to 2 Aug. (Mercure historique et politique, July and Aug. 1739, cvii. 108, 227; Charles-Philippe d'Albert, Duc de Luynes, Mémoires, ed. L. Dussieux and E. Soulié, 1860–5, iii. 2).

3. Probably Henri Coquebert, lieutenant des habitants de la ville de Reims 1757–63, 1770–6 (see Georges Boussinesq and Gustave Laurent, Histoire de Reims, Rheims, 1933, ii pt i. 185, ii pt ii. 936). A 'Monsieur and Madame Coqbert' appear in a list of names under Rheims in Gray's MS Journal 1739–1741.

4. The Comédie-Française ordinarily played at the Court Tuesdays and Thursdays, and part of the troupe followed the

Court whenever it left Versailles (Hurtaut and Magny, Dictionnaire historique de la ville de Paris, 1779, ii. 507, iv. 668).

5. Louis-Charles de Bourbon (1701–75), Comte d'Eu; lieutenant général des armées du Roi, 1735, in command of the camp at Compiègne (Jean-Baptiste-Pierre Jullien, Chevalier de Courcelles, Histoire généalogique et héraldique des pairs de France, 1822–33, i. 104–5, sub 'Maison de France'; NBG; Luynes, op. cit. ii. 448).

6. On 10 July (ibid. ii. 457–9).

7. 'On a construit près de cette ville [Compiègne] un fort poligone, pour donner à M. le Dauphin une juste idée de l'attaque d'une place. . . . Les ouvrages du fort sont minés . . . et on a jeté un pont sur la rivière d'Oise. Le 12 [juillet] on a ouvert la tranchée' (Mercure historique et politique, July 1739, cvii. 108–9; Luynes, op. cit. ii. 459).

8. 'Les quatre bataillons du Regiment du Roi partirent le 23 et le 24 [juillet] pour aller prendre leurs quartiers à Rheims' (Mercure historique et politique, Aug. 1739, cvii. 226).

9. Not identified.

10. Perhaps 'Madame la Baronne de Pouilly,' who is mentioned in the same list with 'Monsieur and Madame Lelue' in Gray's MS Journal 1739–1741 under Rheims. She might have been either Mar-

Lelu,[11] finding her linen robe conceals too many beauties, has bespoke one of gauze.

I won't plague you any longer with people you don't know, I mean French ones; for you must absolutely hear of an Englishman that lately appeared at Rheims. About two days ago, about four o'clock in the afternoon, and about an hour after dinner; from all which you may conclude we dine at two o'clock, as we were picking our teeth round a littered table, and in a crumby room, Gray in an undress, Mr Conway in a morning grey coat, and I in a trim white night-gown, and slippers, very much out of order, with a very little cold; a message discomposed us all of a sudden, with a service to Mr Walpole from Mr More, and that, if he pleased, he would wait on him. We scuttle upstairs in great confusion, but with no other damage than the flinging down two or three glasses, and the dropping a slipper by the way. Having ordered the room to be cleaned out, and sent a very civil response to Mr More, we began to consider who Mr More should be. Is it Mr More of Paris?[12] No. Oh, 'tis Mr More, my Lady Tenham's husband?[13] No, it can't be he. A Mr More[14] then that lives in the Halifax family? No. In short, after thinking of ten thousand more Mr Mores, we concluded it could be never a one of 'em. By this time Mr More[15] arrives; but such a Mr More! a young gentleman out of the wilds of Ireland, who has never been in England, but has got all the ordinary language of that kingdom; has been two years at Paris, where he dined at an ordinary with the refugee Irish, and learnt fortifications, which he does not understand at all, and which yet is the only thing he knows. In short, he is a

guerite de Chamisso, m. (1699) Albert, Baron de Pouilly, or her daughter-in-law, Lucie-Louise de Hézerques, m. (1719) Louis-Joseph, Baron de Pouilly (Achille-Ludovic, Vicomte de Rigon de Magny, *Nobiliaire universel de France*, 2d ser. vol. i, 1865, 'De Pouilly,' p. 15).

11. Probably Marguerite - Antoinette Maugras (d. 1756), 'la plus jolie femme de Reims,' who m. (1726) Henri Leleu, Seigneur d'Aubilly, Cernay, etc. 'Madame Leleu était une jolie brune à la peau blanche et aux beaux yeux; Lattaignant disait que l'Amour l'avait mille fois prise pour sa mère' (*Travaux de l'Académie nationale de Reims*, 1912, cxxxi. 290–1; see also ibid. 1902, cvi. 188).

12. Not identified.

13. Hon. Robert Moore (1688–1762), of

West Lodge, Enfield Chase, Middlesex; M.P. Belfast 1713–14, Louth 1715–27 (GEC, *sub* Dacre, is incorrect on his parliamentary career; see *Members of Parliament*, 1878, ii. 649, 654). He m. (1725), as her 3d husband, Lady Anne Lennard (1684–1755) (later Bns Dacre), who m. (1) (1716) Richard Barrett, of Belhus, Aveley, Essex; m. (2) (1718), as his 3d wife, Henry Roper, 8th Bn Teynham.

14. Not identified.

15. Not identified. He was at Florence in July 1740 (HW to Conway 5 July 1740, N.S.), and Mann wrote to HW 2 Sept. 1741: 'I cannot recollect who that Mr More is whom you speak of; I shall be glad to see him as you seem to mention him with some regard.'

young swain of very uncouth phrase, inarticulate speech, and no ideas. This hopeful child is riding post into Lorrain, or anywhere else, he is not certain; for if there is a war he shall go home again: for we must give the Spaniards another drubbing, you know; and if the Dutch do but join us, we shall blow up all the ports in Europe; for our ships are our bastions, and our ravelins, and our hornworks;[16] and there's a devilish wide ditch for 'em to pass, which they can't fill up with things—Here Mr Conway helped him to fascines.[17] By this time I imagine you have laughed at him as much, and were as tired of him as we were: but he's gone. This is the day that Gray and I intended for the first of a southern circuit; but as Mr Selwyn[18] and George Montagu[19] design us a visit here, we have put off our journey for some weeks.[20] When we get a little farther, I hope our memoirs will brighten: at present they are but dull, dull as

Your humble servant ever,

H. W.

PS. I thank you ten thousand times for your last letter:[21] When I have as much wit and as much poetry in me, I'll send you as good an one. Good night, child!

To West, Monday 28 September 1739, N.S.

Reprinted from *Works* iv. 429–31.

16. Ravelin and hornwork: a two-fronted and a single-fronted outwork in fortifications. Both words are used in the same context by HW in his letter to Conway 5 July 1740, N.S.

17. Cylindrical faggots or bundles of brush used in filling up ditches.

18. Selwyn and Montagu arrived at Rheims ca 4 Aug., N.S. (Gray to Ashton 25 Aug. 1739, N.S., *Gray's Corr.* i. 116), and stayed there until the beginning of Sept. (ibid.).

19. Montagu was Lord Conway's companion on his travels to Italy, and had been abroad since 1736 (*ante* 21 April 1739, N.S., n. 34; MONTAGU i. 9).

20. HW and Gray left Rheims ca 7 Sept., N.S., and in 'three short days' journey' (*Gray's Corr.* i. 116) arrived at Dijon, where they spent four days, lodging at the 'Croix d'Or.' On their journey they passed through 'Verzenay, famous for the best red wines in Champagne, and Sillery'; they dined at Châlons-sur-Marne 'à la poste,' and spent the night at Saint-Dizier. The next day they followed the valley of the Marne, and through Vignoris arrived at Langres. The third day they 'entered Burgundy at a village called Thil, passed through a fine fertile plain by an avenue of lime trees,' and came to Dijon, 'the capital of the duchy, a very small but beautiful city of an oval form, full of people of quality and a very agreeable society.' They left Dijon ca 13 Sept., N.S., for Lyons, which they reached the next day (Gray's MS Journal 1739–1741).

21. *Ante* 21 June 1739, O.S.

From a hamlet among the mountains of Savoy,[1]
Sept. 28, 1739, N.S.

PRECIPICES, mountains, torrents, wolves, rumblings, Salvator
Rosa[2]—the pomp of our park and the meekness of our palace! Here
we are, the lonely lords of glorious desolate prospects. I have kept a
sort of resolution which I made, of not writing to you as long as I stayed
in France: I am now a quarter of an hour out of it, and write to you.
Mind, 'tis three months since we heard from you. I begin this letter
among the clouds; where I shall finish, my neighbour heaven probably
knows: 'tis an odd wish in a mortal letter, to hope not to finish it on this
side the atmosphere. You will have a billet tumble to you from the stars
when you least think of it; and that I should write it too! Lord, how po-
tent that sounds! But I am to undergo many transmigrations before I
come to 'yours ever.' Yesterday I was a shepherd of Dauphiné;[3] today
an Alpine savage; tomorrow a Carthusian monk; and Friday a Swiss
Calvinist. I have one quality which I find remains with me in all worlds
and in all ethers; I brought it with me from your world, and am admired for it in this; 'tis my esteem for you: this is a common thought
among you, and you will laugh at it, but it is new here; as new to remember one's friends in the world one has left, as for you to remember
those you have lost.

Aix in Savoy,[4] Sept. 30th.

We are this minute come in here, and here's an awkward abbé this
minute come in to us. I asked him if he would sit down. *Oui, oui, oui.*
He has ordered us a radish soup for supper, and has brought a chess-
board to play with Mr Conway. I have left 'em in the act, and am set
down to write to you. Did you ever see anything like the prospect we
saw yesterday? I never did. We rode three leagues to see the Grande
Chartreuse;[5] expected bad roads, and the finest convent in the king-

1. Probably Les Échelles, where HW and
Gray spent two nights on their five and a
half days' journey to Geneva through Dauphiné and Savoy (Gray's MS Journal 1739–
1741).
2. Salvator Rosa (1615–73), whose 'bold-
ness in landscape' (HW to Mason 18 Feb.
1776), 'knowledge of the force of shade, and
his masterly management of horror and
distress, have placed him in the first class
of painters' (*Ædes Walpolianæ, Works* ii.
233). For HW's high opinion of Rosa see

HW to Bentley 18 Sept. 1755, HW to Mann
31 Oct. 1779 and 25 Feb. 1782, and HW to
Mary Berry 4 Dec. 1793 (BERRY ii. 78).
3. 'First night at La Verpillier, a poor
village. Second day entered Savoy at Pont-
Beauvoisin' (Gray's MS Journal 1739–1741).
4. Aix-les-Bains, where they spent the
night after leaving Les Échelles (ibid.).
5. For two accounts by Gray of this excursion, see *Gray's Corr.* i. 122–3 and i. 122
n. 1.

dom. We were disappointed pro and con. The building[6] is large and plain, and has nothing remarkable but its primitive simplicity: They entertained us in the neatest manner, with eggs, pickled salmon, dried fish, conserves, cheese, butter, grapes and figs, and pressed us mightily to lie there. We tumbled into the hands of a lay-brother, who, unluckily having the charge of the meal and bran, showed us little besides. They desired us to set down our names in the list of strangers,[7] where, among others, we found two mottoes of our countrymen for whose stupidity and brutality we blushed. The first was of Sir J—— D——,[8] who had wrote down the first stanza of *Justum et tenacem*,[9] altering the last line to *Mente quatit Carthusiana*.[10] The second was of one D——,[11] *Cælum ipsum petimus stultitia*,[12] and *Hic ventri indico bellum*.[13] The Goth!— But the road, West, the road! winding round a prodigious mountain, and surrounded with others, all shagged with hanging woods, obscured with pines or lost in clouds! Below, a torrent breaking through cliffs, and tumbling through fragments of rocks! Sheets of cascades forcing their silver speed down channelled precipices, and hasting into the roughened river at the bottom! Now and then an old foot-bridge, with a broken rail, a leaning cross, a cottage, or the ruin of an hermitage! This sounds too bombast and too romantic to one that has not seen it, too cold for one that has. If I could send you my letter post between two lovely tempests that echoed each other's wrath, you might have some idea of this noble roaring scene, as you were reading it. Almost on the summit, upon a fine verdure, but without any prospect, stands the Chartreuse. We stayed there two hours, rode back through this charming picture, wished for a painter, wished to be poets! Need I tell you we wished for you?

Good night!

6. Built in 1676, after the original buildings had been destroyed by fire (Adolphe Joanne, *Dauphiné et Savoie*, 1875, p. 160).

7. Extracts from the 'album,' beginning with Gray's Alcaic ode ('Oh tu, severi religio loci,' which he wrote in the visitors' album on his second visit to the Grande Chartreuse 21 Aug. 1741) are given in *The World* 15 Aug.—17 Nov. 1789, *passim*. In the introductory article on the inscriptions, *The World* 14 Aug. 1789 observes: 'That the inscriptions at the Chartreuse are various will be out of all doubt. . . . In some instances there are only names and dates. . . . Here and there with a name some good author's words are quoted—and with a few inscribers it may be wished there might have been any words but their own.' The album is apparently not extant. For Gray's second visit see *Gray's Corr*. ii. 867.

8. Possibly Sir James Dashwood.

9. Horace, *Carm*. III. iii.

10. The substitution of 'Carthusiana' makes the line unmetrical.

11. Not identified.

12. Horace, *Carm*. I. iii. 38.

13. Horace, *Serm*. I. v. 7–8.

'Hic ego, propter aquam, quod erat deterrima, ventri

    Indico bellum.'

Geneva, Oct. 2.

By beginning a new date, I should begin a new letter; but I have seen
nothing yet, and the post is going out: 'tis a strange tumbled dab, and
dirty too, I am sending you; but what can I do? There is no possibility
of writing such a long history over again. I find there are many English
in the town; Lord Brook,[14] Lord Mansel,[15] Lord Hervey's[16] eldest son,[17]
and a son[18] of—of Mars and Venus, or of Antony and Cleopatra, or in
short, of—. This is the boy in the bow of whose hat Mr Hedges[19] pinned
a pretty epigram: I don't know if you ever heard it: I'll suppose you
never did, because it will fill up my letter:

> Give but Cupid's dart to me,
> Another Cupid I shall be;
> No more distinguished from the other,
> Than Venus would be from my mother.

Scandal says, Hedges thought the two last very like; and it says too, that
she was not his enemy for thinking so.

Adieu! Gray and I return to Lyons in three days. Harry[20] stays here.

---

14. Francis Greville (1719–73), 8th Bn Brooke, cr. (1746) E. Brooke of Warwick Castle; cr. (1759) E. of Warwick. The *Daily Adv.*, 3 May 1740, speaks of him as 'lately arrived from his travels.'

15. Thomas Mansell (1719–44), 2d Bn Mansell of Margam.

16. John Hervey (1696–1743), cr. (1733) Bn Hervey of Ickworth (see *post* ca 19 Feb. 1747).

17. George William Hervey (1721–75), styled Lord Hervey of Ickworth; 2d Bn Hervey of Ickworth, 1743; 2d E. of Bristol, 1751; son of HW's friend and correspondent, Mary Lepell, Lady Hervey. He was at Florence in May 1741 (Mann to HW 9 May 1741, N.S.) on his way to England, where he arrived 17 June 1741, O.S. (*Daily Adv.* 19 June 1741).

18. Charles Churchill (ca 1720–1812), of Chalfont Park, Bucks, M.P. Stockbridge 1741–7, Milborne Port 1747–54, Great Marlow 1754–61; later (1746) the husband of HW's half-sister, Lady Maria Walpole. He was the natural son of Lt-Gen. Charles Churchill (d. 1745) and Anne Oldfield (1683–1730), the actress. Mrs Oldfield appeared as Cleopatra both in Dryden's *All for Love* (Drury Lane 3 Dec. 1718) and in

Cibber's *Cæsar in Egypt* (Drury Lane 9–15 Dec. 1724). Charles Churchill Jr was praised for his acting at Geneva by HW's Eton contemporary, Richard Aldworth Neville (William Coxe, *Literary Life and Select Works of Benjamin Stillingfleet*, 1811, i. 79; see also *Vict. Co. Hist., Bucks*, iii. 193, 196; *The Record of Old Westminsters, Supplementary Volume*, ed. J. B. Whitmore and G. R. Y. Radcliffe, n.d. [?1928], p. 33; GM 1746, xvi. 107, 1812, lxxxii pt i. 398; Genest ii. 639, iii. 161; Nicoll, *Drama 1700–50*, p. 312). A portrait of him, Lady Mary Churchill, and their son, Charles, hung in the Blue Room at SH ('Des. of SH,' *Works* ii. 436).

19. John Hedges (ca 1689–1737), of Finchley, Middlesex, M.P.; treasurer to Frederick, Prince of Wales 1728–37 (see MONTAGU i. 66; GM 1836, n.s. v pt i. 376). He was the reputed lover of Mrs Oldfield while she was the accepted mistress of Lt-Gen. Churchill, and was named with the General and Lord Hervey as an executor of her will (William Egerton, *Faithful Memoirs of . . . Mrs Anne Oldfield*, 1731, Appendix ii, p. 8). See also Venn, *Alumni Cantab.*

20. Henry Seymour Conway. He left Geneva for Paris (whither HW wrote to

Perhaps at our return we may find a letter from you: It ought to be very full of excuses, for you have been a lazy creature; I hope you have, for I would not owe your silence to any other reason.

Yours ever,

Hor. Walpole

From West, Monday 24 September 1739, O.S.

Printed from MS now wsl.
Address: To Horace Walpole Esq. au soin de Monsieur Alexander,[1] Banquier, à Paris, France. *Postmark:* RJ [unexplained].

Temple, Sept. 24 [1739].

Moi R. West.

COMME nous avons entendu par notre fidèle et bon ami Thomas Ashton, que vous, Thomas Gray et Horace Walpole, nos anciens et bien-aimés alliés, vous êtes fâché un peu, de ce que nous n'avons pas écrit ce longtemps, ni à l'un ni l'autre, et que vous le considerez tous deux comme un contravention de notre amitié, nous de notre bonne volonté promettons pour le futur d'être plus exact en notre correspondance, et, parce que nous avons envie de continuer la paix et la tranquillité, qui ont été de tout temps entre nous trois, nous sommes résolus en plein conseil de vous demander pardon, et, au lieu que nous pouvions nous plaindre de vous à notre tour, et rejeter la faute sur vous, à la mode espagnole, nous au contraire, pour donner à l'Europe un example de notre modération, avouons que nous sommes coupables, et vous prions, de nous continuer votre amitié, et correspondance.

Signé.   Moi R. W.

Soussigné.   Grimalkin, premier chat.

I hope this silly, unmeaning thing won't be opened and stopped at the post. Adieu! mes chers.

him 6 March 1740, N.S.), and returned to London in or before June 1740 (HW to Conway 5 July 1740, N.S.).

———

1. Alexandre Alexander (fl. 1727–51). In the *Almanach Royal*, 1739, p. 349, he is listed among the 'banquiers pour les traites et remises de place en place.' From 1729 until 1741 Alexander's address was the Rue Saint-Apolline. In 1741 he went into partnership with Denis Despueches and moved to Rue Saint-Roch; in 1746 the firm moved to the Rue Thérèse, Butte Saint-Roch, where it stayed until Alexander left it in 1751 (see *Almanach Royal*, 1727, p. 311, 1729, p. 339, 1742, p. 364, 1746, p. 349, 1751, p. 334).

From WEST, Monday 15 October 1739, O.S.

Printed from MS now WSL.
Dated by the allusions to *ante* 28 Sept. 1739, N.S.

[London,] October 15 [1739].

Dear Walpole,

NOTHING can be more obliging than your last letter; 'tis so obliging that you must forgive me if I impute a good part of what you
say to complaisance; I should be vain if I didn't. You tell me you had
made a kind of resolution not to write to me as long as you stayed in
France: If you always make me such amends, I don't care how many of
those resolutions you make, though in the mean time I should be a
loser, so that I might very well have spared my compliment. But it is
not so easy for me to make you amends. I have often accused myself for
my negligence in writing, but never yet could excuse myself. Perhaps I
should never have known how to do it if you had not prevented me by
doing it for me. I believe you lay the fault on a very right cause. I confess my laziness. It has such an ascendancy over me that, I'm pretty
sure, if I were divided into two persons one half would forget t'other
very quickly. Would you have me say any more after that?

You seem to take it for granted that I'm a poet, I find; but you never
dream all this while of another quality I have, which is that I'm a
prophet. For I told Ashton, before I received your letter, that you
would go into Savoy and come back again; which you have done. Your
description of the Alps made me shudder, but I don't see any occasion
you have to wish you were a poet, or to wish for your humble servant
at least in that capacity, since you can give such a description so very
poetically. Nay, there is a couple of verses, which perhaps you did not
take notice of when you writ it—

> Others all shagged with hanging woods,
> Obscured in pines, or lost in clouds.

They are so good that I could wish they had not been alone; as they are,
I shall consider them as a fragment.

The epigram of Hedges I have seen before, but if you'll give me leave
I'll copy down some things which I fancy you never did. I take 'em
from a new book or an old book just come out. 'Tis a collection of

Prior's relicts,[1] which the editor[2] has scraped together good and bad, and has swelled them out into a couple of large volumes in octavo. The first volume contains an account of his negotiations, and consists chiefly of letters, treaties, instructions, journals, and so forth.[3] There is the examination of Prior before the Committee of Secrecy[4] (in which Sir Robert was chairman) which is curious enough. The second volume contains several epigrams and *petites pièces,* very few of which seem intended for publication.[5] Some of them are very pretty, and have that easy air of the world which is so visible in Prior's poetry. I'll pick you out some and fill my paper with them.

Yours ever,

R. W.

I hope you received my manifesto[6] and a letter since.[7]

Cupid Turned Plowman. Imitation of Moschus.[8]

His lamp, his bow, and quiver laid aside,
A rustic wallet o'er his shoulders tied,
Sly Cupid always on new mischief bent,
To the rich field, and furrowed tillage went.
Like any plowman toiled the little god,
His tune he whistled, and his wheat he sowed:

1. *Miscellaneous Works of his late Excellency Matthew Prior, Esq.,* published 11 Oct. 1739 (*Daily Adv.* 11 Oct. 1739).

2. Adrian Drift (b. ca 1709), Prior's secretary and literary executor (G. F. Russell Barker and Alan H. Stenning, *The Record of Old Westminsters,* 1928, i. 285; *Admissions to the College of St John . . . Cambridge,* ed. Robert F. Scott, Cambridge, pt iii, 1903, p. 48; Francis Bickley, *Life of Matthew Prior,* 1914, pp. 186, 281).

3. 'This work, pursuant to Mr Prior's last will and testament, contains a full account of his political life, viz. his negotiations, commissions, warrants, and letters, from his first entrance into public business to his death' (from the title-page).

4. Ibid. i. 417–35. Prior, who had been Minister Plenipotentiary to France 24 Sept. 1712 to 25 March 1715, was examined 16 June 1715 by the Committee of Secrecy, appointed 13 April 1715 to 'inquire into the late peace [of Utrecht, 1713] and the management of the late Queen's ministry.'

Prior, suspected of being a Jacobite, was expected to furnish the Whig ministry with evidence to be used in the approaching impeachment proceedings against Bolingbroke and the Earl of Oxford. See Charles K. Eves, *Matthew Prior,* New York, 1939, pp. 348–56; Cobbett, *Parl. Hist.,* vii. 53–7, 68; *British Diplomatic Representatives 1689–1789,* ed. D. B. Horn, 1932, pp. 13–14.

5. 'Volume the second, containing a new collection of poems: consisting of epistles, tales, satires, epigrams, etc., with some select Latin performances written by Mr Prior while at St John's College, Cambridge. Now first published from his original manuscripts. Revised by himself, and copied fair for the press by Mr Adrian Drift, his executor' (from the title-page).

6. *Ante* 24 Sept. 1739, O.S.

7. Probably West to Gray 28 Sept. 1739, O.S. (*Gray's Corr.* i. 120–1).

8. 'Cupid turned Plowman. From the Greek of Moschus' (Prior, op. cit. ii. 88–9).

Then sat and laughed, and to the skies above
Raising his eye, he thus insulted Jove:
'Lay by your hail, your hurtful storms restrain,
And, as I bid you, let it shine or rain.
Else you again beneath my yoke shall bow,
Feel the sharp goad, and draw the servile plow,
What once Europa was, Nannette[9] is now.'

'Tis pretty. But don't you think it a little like one of Quarles' *Emblems?*[10]

To Fortune.[11]

Whilst I in prison on a court look down,
Nor beg thy favour, nor deserve thy frown,
In vain, malicious Fortune, hast thou tried
By taking from my state to quell my pride:
Insulting girl! thy present rage abate;
And wouldst thou have me humble, make me great.

I writ this down for the sentiment. Prior seems to have writ it in his confinement.[12]

Human Life.[13]

What trifling coil do we poor mortals keep:
Wake, eat, and drink, evacuate, and sleep.

To My Lord Harley.[14] Extempore.
For My Lady Harley.[15]

Pen, ink, and wax, and paper send
To the kind wife, the lovely friend:
Smiling bid her freely write
What her happy thoughts indite,

9. Anne Durham, one of Prior's mistresses (Eves, op. cit. 217, 406).

10. If West had a particular 'Emblem' in mind, it was probably ii. 9, in which Jove is mentioned as having been 'vanquished by [Cupid's] greater might.'

11. Prior, op. cit. ii. 91.

12. On 9 June 1715, by motion of Sir Robert Walpole, Spencer Compton (later E. of Wilmington), the Speaker of the House of Commons, was ordered to issue a warrant to Thomas Wibergh, sergeant-at-arms, to apprehend Prior. For a week Prior was kept prisoner at his own house in Duke Street, but on 17 June he was ordered to be taken in 'close custody,' and was removed to Wibergh's house in Brownlow Street, Longacre. He was not released until 26 June 1716 (Cobbett, *Parl. Hist.* vii. 64–5, 68; Eves, op. cit. 357, 363).

13. Prior, op. cit. ii. 124.

14. Ibid. ii. 132. Edward Harley (1689–1741), 2d E. of Oxford, Prior's friend, and (with Adrian Drift) his literary executor. The first volume of Prior's *Miscellaneous Works* contains a dedication to him by John Banks (1709–51).

15. Added by West. She was Lady Henri-

Of virtue, goodness, peace, and love,
Thoughts which angels might approve.

If I remember, I think you told me this extempore once, so I'm
afraid you know it.

A Letter

To the Honourable Lady Miss Margaret Cavendish Holles Harley.[16]

My noble, lovely, little Peggy,
Let this my first epistle beg ye,
At dawn of morn and close of even
To lift your hands and heart to heaven,
In double duty[17] say your prayer,
Our Father, first, then *Notre Père;*
And, dearest child, along the day
In everything you do and say
Obey and please my Lord and Lady,
So God shall love, and angels aid ye.
    If to these precepts you attend
No second letter need I send,
And so I rest your constant friend.
                                        M. P.

Can one write better to a child of five year old? I would send you two
or three more, but I have not room, as you see, without a fresh sheet—
Adieu!

To WEST, Wednesday 11 November 1739, N.S.

Reprinted from *Works* iv. 431–3.

Turin,[1] Nov. 11, 1739, N.S.

SO, as the song[2] says, we are in fair Italy! I wonder we are; for, on the
very highest precipice of Mount Cenis,[3] the Devil of Discord in the
similitude of sour wine had got amongst our Alpine savages, and set

etta Cavendish Holles (ca 1693–1755), dau.
of John Holles, 1st D. of Newcastle; m.
(1713) Edward Harley, 2d E. of Oxford.

16. Prior, op. cit. ii. 133–4. Lady Margaret Cavendish Harley (1715–85), only dau.
of Lord Harley, m. (1734) William Bentinck, 2d D. of Portland. The poem was
written on her sixth birthday (11 March
1721). See Eves, op. cit. 366–7, and GEC.

17. West's marginal note: ' 'Tis printed

"beauty." It must be wrong.' All editions of
Prior, however, read 'beauty.'

1. On Saturday 7 Nov. HW and Gray
reached Turin, where they stayed until 18
Nov. at 'l'Auberge Royale' (Gray's MS Journal 1739–1741; *Gray's Corr.* i. 125, 129).

2. Not identified.

3. They crossed it 7 Nov. (*Gray's Corr.* i.
126).

them a-fighting, with Gray and me in the chairs: they rushed him by me on a crag where there was scarce room for a cloven foot. The least slip had tumbled us into such a fog, and such an eternity, as we should never have found our way out of again. We were eight days in coming hither from Lyons; the four last in crossing the Alps. Such uncouth rocks and such uncomely inhabitants! my dear West, I hope I shall never see them again! At the foot of Mount Cenis we were obliged to quit our chaise, which was taken all to pieces and loaded on mules; and we were carried in low arm-chairs on poles, swathed in beaver bonnets, beaver gloves, beaver stockings, muffs, and bear-skins. When we came to the top,[4] behold the snows fallen! and such quantities, and conducted by such heavy clouds that hung glouting, that I thought we could never have waded through them. The descent is two leagues, but steep, and rough as O[ldham's] father's face, over which, you know, the Devil walked with hobnails in his shoes.[5] But the dexterity and nimbleness of the mountaineers is inconceivable; they run with you down steeps and frozen precipices, where no man, as men are now, could possibly walk. We had twelve men and nine mules to carry us, our servants and baggage, and were above five hours in this agreeable jaunt! The day before, I had a cruel accident, and so extraordinary an one, that it seems to touch upon the traveller.[5a] I had brought with me a little black spaniel,[6] of King Charles's breed; but the prettiest, fattest, dearest creature! I had let it out of the chaise for the air, and it was waddling along close to the head of the horses, on the top of one of the highest Alps, by the side of a wood of firs. There darted out a young wolf, seized poor dear Tory by the throat, and, before we could possibly prevent it, sprung up the side of the rock and carried him off. The postilion jumped off and struck at him with his whip, but in vain. I

4. 'It was six miles to the top' (ibid.).

5. Mitford points out the source of this allusion in John Oldham (1653–83), 'Character of a Certain Ugly Old P[riest]': 'His filthy countenance looks like an old chimney-piece in a decayed inn, sullied with smoke and the sprinkling of ale-pots. 'Tis dirtier than an ancient thumbed record, greasier than a chandler's shop-book. . . . It has more furrows than all Cotswold. . . . I believe the Devil travels over it in his sleep with hob-nails in his shoes' ('Remains,' in *Works*, 1684, pp. 115–16. HW's copy, 1692 edn, was sold SH iii. 158). For a refutation of the tradition that Oldham

was portraying his father, John Oldham, a non-conformist minister, see A. W. Ward in DNB *sub* Oldham.

5a. I.e., it sounds like a traveller's 'tall' tale. West echoes the expression in *post* 13 Dec. 1739 O.S. (The emendation 'marvellous' has been suggested by Mr Pottle, but it seems unlikely that Miss Berry or the printer of the *Works* would have misread the word in both HW's and West's hand.)

6. Tory, given to HW by Lord Conway in Paris. Lord Conway had it as a present from Mrs Parsons, the widow of Humphrey Parsons, Lord Mayor of London, an 'incorruptible Tory' (COLE i. 379).

saw it and screamed, but in vain; for the road was so narrow, that the servants that were behind could not get by the chaise to shoot him.[7] What is the extraordinary part is, that it was but two o'clock, and broad sunshine. It was shocking to see anything one loved run away with to so horrid a death.

Just coming out of Chamberri, which is a little nasty old hole,[8] I copied an inscription, set up at the end of a great road,[9] which was practised[10] through an immense solid rock by bursting it asunder with gunpowder: the Latin is pretty enough,[11] and so I send it you:

Carolus Emanuel II.[12] *Sab. dux, Pedem. princeps, Cypri rex, publica felicitate parta, singulorum commodis intentus, breviorem securioremque viam regiam, natura occlusam, Romanis intentatam, cæteris desperatam, dejectis scopulorum repagulis, æquata montium iniquitate, quæ cervicibus imminebant precipitia pedibus substernens, æternis populorum commerciis patefecit. A.D. 1670.*

We passed the Pas de Suze,[13] where is a strong fortress[14] on a rock, between two very neighbour mountains; and then, through a fine avenue of three leagues, we at last discovered Turin.

> E l'un[o] a l'altro [il] mostra, e in tanto oblia
> La noia, e'l mal de la passata via.[15]

'Tis really by far one of the prettiest cities I have seen—not one of your large straggling ones that can afford to have twenty dirty suburbs, but clean and compact, very new and very regular.[16] The King's pal-

---

7. See also Gray to Mrs Gray 7 Nov. 1739, N.S. (*Gray's Corr.* i. 125–6), which furnished Edward Burnaby Greene with materials for his 'Ode on the Death of a Favourite Spaniel,' published in *The Universal Magazine*, 1775, lvii. 374–5.

8. HW's unfavourable impression of Chambéry persisted for fifty years. See BERRY i. 138.

9. At Les Échelles, 14¼ miles SW of Chambéry.

10. I.e., constructed. OED quotes only this example and one by Shelley.

11. See *Mémoires lus à la Sorbonne dans les séances extraordinaires du Comité Impérial des travaux historiques et des sociétés savantes*, 1863, i. 315–17.

12. Charles Emmanuel II (1634–75), Duke of Savoy.

13. Suse (Susa) in Piedmont, 33 miles W

of Turin, between Mont Cenis and Mont Genevre.

14. La Brunetta, a fortress of eight bastions, the outworks of which were hewn of solid rock; it was razed by order of Napoleon in 1796. See Anton F. Büsching, *Erdbeschreibung*, 8th edn, Hamburg, 1787–92, iv. 62; Stefano Grande, *Piemonte*, Turin, 1925, pp. 219–20.

15. Tasso, *Gerusalemme liberata* III. iv.

16. 'The straightness of the streets, which in the new quarter are wholly laid out by the line, as it contributes much to the beauty of this city, so it makes it appear much smaller than it really is, for at your first entrance you see quite through it. . . . The buildings here in general are of brick, either plastered or intended to be so (for in those that are not, the holes of the scaffolding are all left unstopped), and generally of

ace[17] is not of the proudest without, but of the richest within; painted, gilt, looking-glassed, very costly, but very tawdry; in short, a very popular palace. We were last night at the Italian comedy—the devil of a house, and the devil of actors! Besides this, there is a sort of an heroic tragedy, called *La Rappresentazione dell' anima dannata*.[18] A woman, a sinner, comes in and makes a solemn prayer to the Trinity: Enter Jesus Christ and the Virgin: he scolds, and exit: she tells the woman her son is very angry, but she don't know, she will see what she can do. After the play, we were introduced to the assembly, which they call the *conversazione*:[19] There were many people playing at ombre, pharaoh, and a game called taroc,[20] with cards so *high*,[21] to the number of seventy-eight. There are three or four English here; Lord Lincoln,[22] with Spence,[23] your Professor of Poetry; a Mr B——,[24] and a Mr C——,[24] a man that never utters a syllable. We have tried all stratagems to make him speak. Yesterday he did at last open his mouth, and said *Bec*.[25] We all laughed so at the novelty of the thing, that he shut it again, and will never speak more. I think you can't complain now of my not writing to you. What a volume of trifles! I wrote just the fellow to it from Geneva; had it you? Farewell!

> Thine,
>
> Hor. Walpole

some regular order, four story high, for the length of whole streets: the windows are oiled paper, which is often torn and has a very ill effect to the eye. Many great houses; the architecture but indifferent, but altogether makes a good appearance enough' (Gray's MS Journal 1739–1741; see also *Gray's Corr.* i. 127).

17. Charles Emmanuel III (1701–73), Duke of Savoy and King of Sardinia.

18. Enrico Furno treats of this literary type (*sacre rappresentazioni*) in his *Il dramma allegorico nelle origini del teatro italiano*, Arpino, 1915, pp. 83 ff. See also Spence's *Anecdotes*, ed. Singer, 1820, pp. 397–400.

19. At the Marquise de Cavaillac's (Gray to West 16 Nov. 1739, N.S., *Gray's Corr.* i. 128).

20. In French and English 'tarot,' played with 78 cards, of which 52 are ordinary whist cards, 22 are tarocchi (tarots) or

trumps, and four, cavaliers or mounted valets. The size of the cards is usually 2½ by 5 inches. See Catherine Perry Hargrave, *History of Playing Cards*, Boston, 1930, pp. 31–9; see also *Gray-HW-West-Ashton Corr.* i. 257n; *Gray's Corr.* i. 128.

21. 'In the MS, the writing of this word is extraordinarily tall' (Berry).

22. Henry Fiennes-Clinton (after 1768 Pelham-Clinton) (1720–94), 9th E. of Lincoln, 1730; 2d D. of Newcastle, 1768.

23. Rev. Joseph Spence (1699–1768), Lord Lincoln's tutor, with whom he set out on his travels from London 1 Sept. 1739, O.S., and arrived at Turin 11 Oct. 1739, N.S. (Spence to his mother 13 Oct. 1739, N.S., BM Add. MS Egerton 2234, f. 135). Spence was a Fellow of New College, Oxford, and professor of poetry 1728–38 (Foster, *Alumni Oxon*).

24. Not identified.

25. See *post* 13 Dec. 1739, O.S., n. 1.

To West, Monday 14 December 1739, N.S.

Reprinted from *Works* iv. 435–7.
Dated by the reference to HW's and Gray's departure for Florence.

From Bologna,¹ [Dec. 14] 1739.

I DON'T know why I told Ashton I would send you an account of what I saw; don't believe it, I don't intend it. Only think what a vile employment 'tis, making catalogues!² And then one should have that odious Curl³ get at one's letters, and publish them like Whitfield's *Journal*,⁴ or for a supplement to the *Traveller's Pocket Companion*.⁵ Dear West, I protest against having seen anything but what all the world has seen; nay, I have not seen half that, not some of the most common things; not so much as a miracle. Well, but you don't expect it, do you? Except pictures and statues, we are not very fond of sights; don't go a-staring after crooked towers and conundrum staircases. Don't you hate too a jingling epitaph of one Procul and one Proculus that is here?⁶ Now and then we drop in at a procession, or a High Mass,

1. 'Bologna. 12 days, al Pelegrino' (Gray's MS Journal 1739–41, f. 21). HW and Gray left Turin 18 Nov., spent the night at Asti, the next day passed through Alexandria to Novi, and arrived at Genoa 20 Nov. They stayed at Genoa for a week at the 'Santa Martha,' visiting galleries (ibid. ff. 9–14). Their itinerary from Genoa to Bologna: 28 Nov. Tortona; 29 Nov. through the 'vast plains of Lombardy' to Castel S. Giovanni; 30 Nov. 'passed the famous river Trebia . . . and arrived very late at night at Parma . . . stayed there one day'; 2 Dec. 'passed through Reggio without stopping . . . came in the afternoon to Modena . . . stayed there one day' (ibid. ff. 14, 17). They arrived at Bologna 3 Dec. in the afternoon. See Gray to Mrs Gray 19 Dec. 1739, N.S., *Gray's Corr.* i. 134; see also ibid. i. 131–3.

2. Perhaps an allusion to Gray, whose observations on Bologna alone run to 20 pages in his MS journal (ff. 21–31), and include a catalogue of the contents of some two dozen palaces and churches.

3. Edmund Curll (1675–1747), the notorious publisher of Pope's *Literary Correspondence*, 1735.

4. George Whitefield (1714–70), the

Methodist preacher. His *Journal of a Voyage from Gibraltar to Georgia* was published 3 Aug 1738 by Thomas Cooper (fl. 1732–40). James Hutton, subsequently Whitefield's exclusive publisher, denounced Cooper's edition the next day as surreptitious (*Daily Adv.* 4 Aug. 1738). The bitter exchange of advertisements concluded with Hutton's publishing his own edition on 21 Aug. See George L. Lam and Warren H. Smith, 'Two Rival Editions of George Whitefield's *Journal*, London, 1738,' in *Studies in Philology*, 1944, xli. 86–93.

5. Not identified, but doubtless similar to *The Gentleman's Pocket Companion, for travelling into foreign parts: being a . . . description of the Roads from London to all the Capital Cities in Europe. . . . Illustrated with maps. With three Dialogues in six European languages*, 1722 (BM Cat.).

6. 'Si procul a Proculo Proculi campana fuisset,
Jam [nunc] procul a Proculo Proculus ipse foret.
A.D.1392 [1393].
Epitaph on the outside of the wall of the church of St Proculo' (Berry), 'upon a

hear the music, enjoy a strange attire, and hate the foul monkhood. Last week was the Feast of the Immaculate Conception. On the eve we went to the Franciscans' church to hear the academical exercises.[7] There were moult and moult[8] clergy, about two dozen dames, that treated one another with *illustrissima* and brown[8a] kisses, the Vice-Legate,[9] the gonfalonier,[10] and some senate.[11] The Vice-Legate, whose conception was not quite so immaculate, is a young personable person, of about twenty, and had on a mighty pretty cardinal-kind of habit; 'twould make a delightful masquerade dress. We asked his name: Spinola. What, a nephew of the Cardinal-Legate?[12] *Signor, no: ma credo che gli sia qualche cosa.* He sat on the right-hand with the gonfalonier in two purple *fauteuils*. Opposite was a throne of crimson damask, with the device of the Academy [of] the Gelati;[13] and trimmings of gold. Here sat at a table, in black, the head of the Academy, between the orator and the first poet. At two semicircular tables on either hand sat three poets and three; silent among many candles. The chief made a little introduction, the orator a long Italian vile harangue. Then the chief, the poet, the poets, who were a Franciscan, an Olivetan, an old abbé, and three lay, read their compositions; and today they are pasted up in all parts of the town. As we came out of the church, we found all the convent and neighbouring houses lighted all over with lanthorns of red and yellow paper, and two bonfires. But you are sick of this foolish ceremony; I'll carry you to no more: I will only mention, that we found the Dominicans' church here in mourning for

young man who always rose in the night time, when that bell tolled, to go to study, which he loved so much that it killed him' (De Blainville, *Travels*, 1757, vol. ii, tr. William Guthrie, p. 193). Guthrie's translation of the inscription (ibid.) reads: 'If the bell of Proculus had been far from Proculus, Proculus himself would have been far from Proculus.' The emendations in brackets are from Johann Caspar Goethe, *Viaggio in Italia (1740)*, ed. Arturo Farinelli, Rome, 1932–3, ii. 53.

7. For an account similar to HW's see Edward Wright, *Some Observations made in Travelling through France, Italy, etc., in the Years 1720, 1721, and 1722*, 1730, ii. 450.

8. Old French for 'many,' perhaps with a pun on the English word.

8a. *Sic.* Perhaps we should read 'thrown.'

9. Girolamo Spinola (1713–84), vice-legate to Bologna, 1738 (Charles Berton, *Dic-*

tionnaire des cardinaux, 1857, p. 1541; Ranfft iv pt i. 161–3).

10. Count Caprara (not further identified) (Gray's MS Journal 1739–41, f. 24), gonfaloniere di giustizia. The gonfaloniere is the third officer of Bologna (he is preceded in rank by the legate and the vice-legate) and presides in all civil causes (Lady Pomfret to Lady Hertford, Bologna, 2 June 1741, N.S., *Hertford Corr.* iii. 172).

11. The senators were fifty in number (ibid.).

12. Giorgio Spinola (1667–1739), nuncio at Vienna, 1713; cardinal, 1719; papal secretary of state, 1721; legate to Bologna, 1727 (Ranfft ii. 237–41; Berton, op. cit. 1540–1).

13. Accademia dei Gelati, founded in 1588 by Melchiorre Zoppio (Michele Maylender, *Storia delle accademie d'Italia*, Bologna, 1926–30, iii. 81–2).

the inquisitor;[14] 'twas all hung with black cloth, furbelowed and fes-
tooned with yellow gauze. We have seen a furniture here in a much
prettier taste; a gallery of Count Caprara's:[15] In the panels between the
windows are pendant trophies of various arms taken by one of his ancestors[16] from the Turks. They are whimsical, romantic, and have a
pretty effect.[17] I looked about, but could not perceive the portrait of
the lady at whose feet they were indisputably offered. In coming out of
Genoa we were more lucky; found the very spot where Horatio and
Lothario were to have fought, 'west of the town a mile among the
rocks.'[18]

My dear West, in return for your epigrams of Prior, I will transcribe
some old verses too, but which I fancy I can show you in a sort of a new
light. They are no newer than Virgil, and, what is more odd, are in the
second *Georgic*. 'Tis, that I have observed that he not only excels when
he is like himself, but even when he is very like inferior poets:[19] You
will say that they rather excel by being like him: but mind: they are all
near one another:

> Si non ingentem foribus domus alta superbis
> mane salutantum totis vomit ædibus undam:[20]

And the four next lines; are they not just like Martial? In the following he is as much Claudian;

> Illum non populi fasces, non purpura regum
> flexit, et infidos agitans discordia fratres;
> aut conjurato descendens Dacus ab Istro.[21]

14. Not identified.
15. 'The Palazzo Caprara is one of the most magnificent for architecture; it is built round a court, of which a large stair-case with a double ascent takes up one side. A gallery runs along the opposite side, furnished with spoils taken from the Turks by a general of this family' (Wright, op. cit. ii. 443). See also *Hertford Corr.* iii. 174–5.
16. Enea Silvio (1631–1701), Conte Caprara, general, who took Érsekujvár, in Hungary, from the Turks in 1685; from 1674 he was commander of Leopold I's forces against the Turks.
17. They may have been the inspiration of a similar arrangement, the Armoury at SH.
18. Nicholas Rowe, *The Fair Penitent* II. ii:

'*Lothario*. West of the town a mile, among the rocks,
Two hours e'er noon tomorrow I expect thee,
Thy single hand to mine.
Horatio. I'll meet thee there.'
19. The late Leonard Whibley, Professor G. L. Hendrickson of Yale University, and Dr Chapman are in agreement that the resemblances are general rather than specific.
20. *Georg*. ii. 461–2.
21. *Georg*. ii. 495–7. Both Dacia (east of the Tisza, a tributary of the Danube, including Transylvania, Rumania, and the eastern part of Hungary) and Ister (the lower part of the Danube) are frequently mentioned by Claudian.

Then who are these like?

> —nec ferrea jura,
> insanumque forum, aut populi tabularia vidit.
> Sollicitant alii remis freta cæca, ruuntque
> in ferrum, penetrant aulas et limina regum.
> Hic petit excidiis urbem miserosque penates,
> ut gemma bibat, et Sarrano indormiat ostro.[22]

Don't they seem to be Juvenal's?—There are some more, which to me resemble Horace; but perhaps I think so from his having some on a parallel subject.[23] Tell me if I am mistaken; these are they:

> Interea dulces pendent circum oscula nati:
> casta pudicitiam servat domus—

inclusively to the end of these:

> Hanc olim veteres vitam coluere Sabini;
> hanc Remus et frater: sic fortis Etruria crevit,
> scilicet et rerum facta est pulcherrima Roma.[24]

If the imagination is whimsical, why at least 'tis like me to have imagined it. Adieu, child! We leave Bologna tomorrow.[25] You know 'tis the third city in Italy for pictures: knowing that, you know all. We shall be three days crossing the Appenine to Florence; would it were over!

My dear West, I am yours from St Peter's to St Paul's!

Hor. Walpole

From West, Thursday 13 December 1739, O.S.

Reprinted from *Works* iv. 434.

Temple, Dec. 13, 1739.

Dear Walpole,

BEC!¹ for I have not spoke today, and therefore I am resolved to speak to you first. Asheton is of opinion you have read Herodotus, but I imagine no such thing, and verily believe the gentleman to be a

22. *Georg.* ii. 501–6.
23. *Epod.* ii, especially lines 39–48.
24. *Georg.* ii. 523–34.
25. See Gray to Mrs Gray 19 Dec. 1739, N.S. (*Gray's Corr.* i. 134)

1. See *ante* 11 Nov. 1739, N.S. Herodotus II. 2 relates how Psammetichus, King of Egypt (fl. 671–617 B.C.), in order to determine the relative antiquity of the Egyptian and Phrygian nations, selected two infants

Phœnician. I can't forgive Mont Cenis poor Tory's death! I can assure her I'll never sing her panegyric, unless she serves all her wolves as Edgar the Peaceable² did. It did touch a little upon the traveller. What do you think it put me in mind of? Not a bit like, but it put me in mind of poor Mrs Rider in Cleveland,³ where she's tore to pieces by the savages. I can't say I much like your Alps by the description you give, but still I have a strange ambition to be where Hannibal was; it must be a pretty thing to fetch a walk in the clouds, and to have the snow up to one's ears. But I am really surprised at your going two leagues in five hours. A'n't it prodigious quick, to go down such a terrible descent? The inscription you mention is very pretty Latin. I see already you like Italy better than France and all its works. When shall you be at Rome? Middleton,⁴ I think, says you find there everything you find everywhere else. I expect volume upon volume there. Do you never write folios as well as quartos? You know I am a *heluo* of everything of that kind, and I am never so happy as when—*verbosa et grandis epistola venit*—.⁵ We have strange news here in town, if it be but true. We hear of a sea-fight between six of our men-of-war and ten Spanish; and that we sunk one and took five.⁶ I should not forget that Mr Pelham⁷

and forbade their nurse, a shepherd, ever to speak in their presence. When the children, at the age of two, began to talk, the first word they uttered was βεκός, which in Phrygian means bread (see Tovey, *Gray and His Friends* 134).

2. Edgar (944–75), King of the English, called 'pacificus' by Adelard and Florence of Worcester, imposed ca 968 an annual tribute of three hundred wolves' heads for four years on Judwall, King of the Welsh. The payment was discontinued after three years because no more wolves were left. See William of Malmesbury, *De gestis Regum Anglorum* ii. 155 (ed. William Stubbs, 1887–9, i. 177); see also Adelard, *De vita Sancti Dunstani* lectio iii (*Memorials of St Dunstan*, ed. William Stubbs, 1874, p. 56); Florence of Worcester, *Chronicon ex chronicis*, ed. Benjamin Thorpe, 1848–9, i. 143.

3. Correctly 'Mrs Riding,' a character in *Le Philosophe anglais, ou histoire de Monsieur Cleveland, fils naturel de Cromwel*, 1731–9, by Antoine-François Prévost d'Exiles (1697–1763). The hero, after Mrs Riding's capture by the savage 'Rouintons'

of the 'Désert de Drexara,' sees 'la flâme qui s'élevait au-dessus du cercle des sauvages,' and concludes that she and his daughter 'servissent alors de proies aux flâmes, pour servir ensuite de pâture à nos cruels ennemis' (quoted from London edn, 1777, ii. 375–80).

4. Middleton says, in *A Letter from Rome, showing an exact conformity between Popery and Paganism*, etc., 1729: 'Rome, . . . of all the places that I have yet seen, or ever shall see, is by far the most delightful, since all those very things which had recommended any other place to me, and which I had been admiring before, single and dispersed, in the several cities through which I passed, may be seen in Rome, as it were in one view, and not only in greater plenty but in greater perfection' (Conyers Middleton, *Miscellaneous Works*, 1752, iii. 63; see also HW to Middleton 22 Nov. 1741).

5. Juvenal, *Sat.* x. 71.

6. 'But little credit is given to a report which was current yesterday at 'Change that Admiral Haddock with part of his squadron had had an engagement with six

has lost two only children at a stroke. 'Tis a terrible loss; they died of a sort of sore throat. To muster up all sort of news: Glover has put out on this occasion a new poem, called *London, or the Progress of Commerce*,[8] wherein he very much extols a certain Dutch poet, called Janus Douza,[9] and compares him to Sophocles. I suppose he does it to make interest upon 'Change. Plays we have none, or damned ones. Handel has had a concerto this winter.[10] No opera, no nothing. All for war and Admiral Haddock.[11] Farewell and adieu!

Yours,

R. WEST

From WEST, Wednesday 23 January 1740, O.S.

Reprinted from *Works* iv. 437–8.

[London,] Jan. 23, 1740.

IT thaws, it thaws, it thaws! A'n't you glad of it? I can assure you we are. We have been this four weeks a-freezing; our Thames has been in chains, our streets almost unpassable with snow and dirt and ice, and

Spanish men-of-war off the Bay of Cadiz, wherein he took four Spanish ships and sunk two, and that the admiral had the misfortune to lose two, which were sunk, but the crews saved, because the last letters from Spain particularly mention that the ships in the Spanish ports were unrigged, and that they were in the greatest necessity for men to man them' (*Daily Adv.* 4 Dec. 1739). The report was untrue. See also *post* 7 May 1740, N.S., n. 1.

7. Hon. Henry Pelham (1696–1754) who succeeded Sir Robert Walpole as First Lord of the Treasury in 1743. His sons, Thomas (b. 1729) and Henry (b. ca 1736) d. 27 and 28 Nov. 'of sore throats at their father's house at Whitehall' (*Daily Adv.* 29 Nov. 1739).

8. It was published 7 Nov. by Thomas Cooper (*Daily Adv.* 7 Nov. 1739).

9. Johan van der Does (1545–1604), poet and historian, who wrote principally Latin verse, and is remembered for his *Annales rerum a priscis Hollandiæ comitibus per CCCXLVI annos gestarum*, The Hague,

1599 (A. J. van der Aa, *Biographisch Woordenboek der Nederlanden*, Haarlem, 1852–76). Glover wrote (*London*, lines 364–7):

'Brave Æschylus and Sophocles, around
Whose sacred brows the tragic ivy twined,
Mixed with the warrior's laurel; all surpassed
By Douza's valour.'

In a footnote to line 347 Glover describes Douza as 'a famous poet, and the most learned man of his time.'

10. The day West was writing, Handel's *Acis and Galatea*, 'with two new concertos for several instruments' (perhaps two of the twelve *Concerti Grossi*, subscription proposals for which had been published in the *Daily Adv.* 29 Oct. 1739) together with the *Ode for St Cecilia's Day* 'and a concerto on the organ' (*Daily Adv.* 13 Dec. 1739), were to be performed. See also Friedrich Chrysander, *G. F. Händel*, 2d edn, Leipzig, 1919, ii. 430–3, iii. 110–11.

11. Nicholas Haddock (1686–1746), admiral; commander of the fleet in the Mediterranean 1738–42.

all our vegetables and animals in distress. Really, such a frost as ours has been is a melancholy thing.¹ I don't wonder now that whole nations have worshipped the sun; I am almost inclined myself to be a Guebre,² tell Orosmades. I believe you think I'm mad, but you would not if you knew what it was to want the sun as we do; 'tis a general frost delivery. Heaven grant the thaw may last! for 'tis a question.

Your last letter,³ my dear Walpole, is welcome. I thank you for its longitude, and all its parallel lines. You have rather transcribed too many lines out of Virgil, but your criticism I agree with, without any hesitation. Whimsical, quotha: 'tis just and new. You might have added Ovid—*quos rami fructus,*⁴ *quos ipsa*—and Statius: *At secura quies*—and what follows down to *non absunt*—⁵

But what do you think? Your observations have set me a-translating, and Asheton has told me it was worth sending.⁶ Excuse it, 'tis a tramontane. I shall certainly publish your letters. But now I think on't, I won't. I should make Pope quite angry.⁷ *Addio, mio caro, addio! Dove sei? Ritorna, ritorna, amato bene!*

Yours from St Paul's to St Peter's!

R. WEST

I believe you must send my translation to the Academy of the Gelati. My love to Gray, and pray tell him from me—

Ψῦχος δὲ λεπτῷ⁸ χρωτὶ πολεμιώτατον.⁹

1. 'This month the frost, which began the 26th of last [December], grew more severe than has been known since the memorable winter of 1715–16. . . . The streets of London were so clogged with snow and ice that hackney coaches went with three or four horses, and coal carts up the streets from the wharfs with eight horses. . . . 'Twould be endless to mention all the calamities, distresses, and accidents occasioned by the severe weather' (GM Jan. 1740, x. 35). West wrote some verses on the hard winter, beginning 'Ipse Pater Thamisinus aquas jam frigore vinci ingemit,' which Gray copied in his Commonplace Book with the note, 'Favonius, the hard winter 1740.' The verses are printed in Tovey, *Gray and His Friends* 137.

2. A Zoroastrian or Parsee, a fire-worshipper (OED). See ante 17 Nov. 1734, n. 8.

3. *Ante* 14 Dec. 1739, N.S.

4. Virgil, *Georg.* ii. 500.

5. *Georg.* ii. 467–71.

6. 'This translation does not appear' (Berry). It is the translation (of which the MS is now WSL) of Virgil, *Georg.* ii. 458–542, beginning 'Hail happy swains!' At the end HW added 'R. West.' The verses were printed by Toynbee in *Gray-HW-West-Ashton Corr.* ii. 310–12.

7. *Ante* 14 Dec. 1739, N.S.

8. Berry: 'λέπτῳ.'

9. 'Cold is extremely inimical to thin habits of body' (Berry). As Miss Berry points out, this passage, from a lost tragedy by Euripides, is preserved by Cicero in *Epistolæ ad Familiares* XVI. viii.

To West, Sunday 24 January 1740, N.S.

Reprinted from *Works* iv. 438–9.

Florence, Jan. 24, 1740, N.S.

Dear West,

I DON'T know what volumes I may send you from Rome; from Florence[1] I have little inclination to send you any. I see several things that please me calmly, but *à force d'en avoir vu* I have left off screaming, Lord! this! and Lord! that! To speak sincerely, Calais surprised me more than anything I have seen since. I recollect the joy I used to propose if I could but once see the Great Duke's gallery;[2] I walk into it now with as little emotion as I should into St Paul's. The statues are a congregation of good sort of people, that I have a great deal of unruffled regard for. The farther I travel, the less I wonder at anything: a few days reconcile one to a new spot, or an unseen custom; and men are so much the same everywhere, that one scarce perceives any change of situation. The same weaknesses, the same passions that in England plunge men into elections, drinking, whoring, exist here, and show themselves in the shapes of Jesuits, cicisbeos,[3] and *Corydon ardebat Alexin's*.[4] The most remarkable thing I have observed since I came abroad, is, that there are no people so obviously mad as the English. The French, the Italians, have great follies, great faults; but then they are so national, that they cease to be striking. In England, tempers vary so excessively, that almost every one's faults are peculiar to himself. I take this diversity to proceed partly from our climate, partly from our government: the first is changeable, and makes us queer; the latter permits our queernesses to operate as they please. If one could avoid contracting this queerness, it must certainly be the most entertaining to live in England, where such a variety of incidents continually amuse. The incidents of a week in London would furnish all Italy with news for a twelvemonth. The only two circumstances of moment in the life

1. Where HW and Gray arrived 16 Dec., N.S., after a two days' journey from Bologna across the Apennines (*Gray's Corr.* i. 134–5).

2. The Uffizi (1560–74) by Vasari, built during the reign of Cosimo de' Medici, the first Grand Duke of Tuscany. The Grand Duke at the time of HW's visit was Francis II (1708–65), Duke of Lorraine, the husband (1736) of Maria Theresa of Austria; Grand Duke of Tuscany, 1737; elected Emperor, 1745.

3. Gallants and escorts of Italian noblewomen. See John Moore, *A View of Society and Manners in Italy*, 6th edn, 1795, ii. 373–84. See also R. S. Charnock, 'Del Cicisbeismo.' N&Q 1882, ser. VI. vi. 105.

4. Virgil, *Ecl.* ii. 1.

of an Italian, that ever give occasion to their being mentioned, are, being married, and in a year after taking a cicisbeo. Ask the name, the husband, the wife or the cicisbeo of any person, *et voilà qui est fini.* Thus, child, 'tis dull dealing here! Methinks your Spanish war is little more lively. By the gravity of the proceedings, one would think both nations were Spaniard. Adieu! Do you remember my maxim, that you used to laugh at? *Everybody does everything, and nothing comes on't.* I am more convinced of it now than ever. I don't know whether S———'s[5] was not still better, *Well, 'gad, there is nothing in nothing.* You see how I distil all my speculations and improvements, that they may lie in a small compass. Do you remember the story of the prince, that after travelling three years brought home nothing but a nut? They cracked it: in it was wrapped up a piece of silk, painted with all the kings, queens, kingdoms, and everything in the world: After many unfoldings, out stepped a little dog, shook his ears, and fell to dancing a saraband.[6] There is a fairy tale for you. If I had anything as good as your old song,[7] I would send it too; but I can only thank you for it, and bid you good night.

Yours ever,

HOR. WALPOLE

PS. Upon reading my letter, I perceive still plainer the sameness that reigns here; for I find I have said the same things ten times over. I don't care; I have made out a letter, and that was all my affair.

To WEST, Saturday 27 February 1740, N.S.

Reprinted from *Works* iv. 440–1.

Florence, February 27, 1740, N.S.

WELL, West, I have found a little unmasked moment to write to you; but for this week I have been so muffled up in my domino, that I have not had the command of my elbows. But what have you been doing all the mornings? Could you not write then? No, then I was masked too; I have done nothing but slip out of my domino into bed,

---

5. Perhaps Selwyn.
6. There is a similar episode in the Comtesse d'Aulnoy's fairy tale *La Chatte blanche* (*Contes de fées*, 1882, p. 242).
7. Not explained.

HORACE WALPOLE, BY JONATHAN RICHARDSON, ca 1734

and out of bed into my domino. The end of the Carnival[1] is frantic, Bacchanalian; all the morn one makes parties in mask to the shops and coffee-houses, and all the evening to the operas and balls. *Then I have danced, good gods, how I have danced!*[2] The Italians are fond to a degree of our country dances:[3] *Cold and raw*[4] they only know by the tune; *Blowzy-Bella*[5] is almost Italian, and *Buttered Peas*[6] is *Pizelli al buro*. There are but three days more; but the two last are to have balls all the morning at the fine unfinished palace of the Strozzi;[7] and the Tuesday night a masquerade after supper: they sup first, to eat *gras*, and not encroach upon Ash Wednesday. What makes masquerading more agreeable here than in England, is the great deference that is showed to the disguised. Here they do not catch at those little dirty opportunities of saying any ill-natured thing they know of you, do not abuse you because they may, or talk gross bawdy to a woman of quality. I found the other day by a play of Etheridge's,[8] that we have had a sort of Carnival ever since the Reformation; 'tis in *She Would if She Could,* they talk of going a-mumming in Shrove-tide.[9]—After talking so much of diver-

1. Ash Wednesday fell on 2 March.

2. Statira in Lee's *Rival Queens* I. i: 'Then he will talk, good gods, how he will talk!'

3. Lady Pomfret to Lady Hertford 25 Sept. 1740, N.S. (*Hertford Corr.* ii. 105–6) describes a Florentine wedding breakfast at the Contessa Galli's, after which the Marchesa Corsi 'took her place in the country dances that the lady of the house might not think her entertainment slighted.' The popularity of country dances, 'transplanted into almost all the courts of Europe,' is mentioned by John Weaver in *An Essay towards an History of Dancing*, 1712, p. 170.

4. 'Cold and raw the North did blow,' the first line of 'The Farmer's Daughter,' a song by Thomas D'Urfey (1653–1723), printed with music as the 'last new Scotch song' in *Comes Amoris, or the Companion of Love*, 1688. The tune to which this poem gave its name is a variant of 'Stingo,' first printed in Playford's *English Dancing Master*, 1651 (see reprint, ed. Hugh Mellor and Leslie Bridgewater, 1933, p. 10). See also Cyrus L. Day, *Songs of Thomas D'Urfey*, Cambridge, Mass., 1933, pp. 104–5, 147–8.

5. 'Blowzabel,' a song with words by 'Mr Baker' (?Henry Baker, 1698–1774, poet and

naturalist) was set to the tune of 'Sally in our Alley,' ?1715, by Henry Carey (d. 1743) (see W. Barclay Squire, *Catalogue of Printed Music . . . in the BM*, 1912, i. 229; William Chappell, *Popular Music of the Olden Time* [1859], ii. 646). In *The Beggar's Opera* III. xiii, the tune is sung to the words 'Of all the friends in time of grief.'

6. For tune and choreography see Thomas Wilson, *Companion to the Ball Room*, 1816, p. 87; see also Earl of Buckinghamshire to Countess of Suffolk 13 Sept. 1763, Hist. MSS Comm., *Lothian*, 1905, p. 177.

7. Built 1489–1536 for Filippo Strozzi (d. 1491). The cornice by Cronaca (Simone del Pollaiolo, 1457–1508) runs only half way around the palace. See Giorgio Vasari, *Vite*, Milano, 1807–11, viii. 175; Karl Baedeker, *Northern Italy*, Leipzig, 1930, pp. 621–2.

8. Sir George Etherege (ca 1635–91). His *Works . . . Containing his Plays and Poems*, 1704 (MS Cat. K.4.10–12) was sold SH iii. 162.

9. 'Rampant is a mad wench; she was half a dozen times a-mumming in private company last Shrovetide, and I lay my life she has put 'em all upon this frolic' (*She wou'd if she cou'd* III. iii, *Dramatic Works,*

sions, I fear you will attribute to them the fondness I own I contract for Florence; but it has so many other charms, that I shall not want excuses for my taste. The freedom of the Carnival has given me opportunities to make several acquaintances; and if I have not found them refined, learned, polished, like some other cities, yet they are civil, good-natured, and fond of the English. Their little partiality for themselves, opposed to the violent vanity of the French, makes them very amiable in my eyes. I can give you a comical instance of their great prejudice about nobility; it happened yesterday. While we were at dinner at Mr Mann's,[10] word was brought by his secretary,[11] that a cavalier demanded audience of him upon an affair of honour. Gray and I flew behind the curtain of the door. An elderly gentleman, whose attire was not certainly correspondent to the greatness of his birth, entered, and informed the British minister that one Martin[12] an English painter had left a challenge for him at his house, for having said Martin was no gentleman. He would by no means have spoke of the duel before the transaction of it, but that his honour, his blood, his etc. would never permit him to fight with one who was no cavalier; which was what he came to inquire of His Excellency. We laughed loud laughs, but unheard: his fright or his nobility had closed his ears. But mark the sequel; the instant he was gone, my very English curiosity hurried me out of the gate St Gallo;[13] 'twas the place and hour appointed. We had not been driving about above ten minutes, but out popped a little figure, pale but cross, with beard unshaved and hair uncombed, a slouched hat, and a considerable red cloak, in which was wrapped, under his arm, the fatal sword that was to revenge the highly injured Mr Martin, painter and defendant. I darted my head out of the coach, just ready to say 'Your servant, Mr Martin,' and talk about the architecture of the triumphal arch[14] that was building there; but he

ed. H. F. B. Brett-Smith, Oxford, 1927, ii. 136).

10. Horace Mann (ca 1706–86), chargé d'affaires at the court of the Grand Duke of Tuscany; HW's correspondent and host in Florence. His date of birth is variously given, but HW in a note to his letter to Mann of 2 Oct. 1747 says that Horace was twin brother of Galfridus Mann, who, according to the inscription on his monument, died 20 Dec. 1756, '*ætatis suæ* 50.' Mann to HW 8 July 1786 says he is reaching 'the age of 80, which I think the next month will complete, for I have not any precise memorandum about it.'

11. Palombo. Mann became dissatisfied with him in 1741, and asked HW to find him a new secretary in England. See Mann to HW 30 July, 8 Oct. 1741, N.S.; HW to Mann 22 Oct. 1741, O.S.

12. Not identified. Mann to HW 1 July 1741, N.S., speaks of him as the constant companion in Florence of Sir Erasmus Philipps, 5th Bt 1737, HW's distant cousin.

13. Porta San Gallo (erected 1284) in the present Piazza Cavour.

14. By Jean Nicolas Jadot (1710–61),

would not know me, and walked off. We left him to wait for an hour, to grow very cold and very valiant the more it grew past the hour of appointment. We were figuring all the poor creature's huddle of thoughts, and confused hopes of victory, or fame, of his unfinished pictures, or his situation upon bouncing into the next world. You will think us strange creatures; but 'twas a pleasant sight, as we knew the poor painter was safe. I have thought of it since, and am inclined to believe that nothing but two English could have been capable of such a jaunt. I remember, 'twas reported in London that the plague was at a house in the city, and all the town went to see it.

I have this instant received your letter.[15] Lord! I am glad I thought of those parallel passages, since it made you translate them. 'Tis excessively near the original; and yet, I don't know, 'tis very easy too.—It snows here a little tonight, but it never lies but on the mountains. Adieu!

> Yours ever,
>
> Hor. Walpole

PS. What is the history of the theatres this winter?

From Ashton, March 1740

Missing. Probably written in Hanover Square, London, early in March (see *post* i. 209).

To West, Tuesday 22 March 1740, N.S.

Reprinted from *Works* iv. 442–3.

> Siena, March 22d, 1740, N.S.

Dear West,

PROBABLY now you will hear something of the Conclave;[1] we have left Florence,[2] and are got hither on the way to a Pope. In three hours time we have seen all the good contents of this city: 'tis

Baron de Ville-Issey, commemorating the entry of Francis II on 19 Jan. 1739 (Antonio Zobi, *Storia civile della Toscana*, Firenze, 1850–2, i. 186–7; Thieme and Becker).

15. *Ante* 23 Jan. 1740, O.S., containing West's translation of Virgil, *Georg.* ii. 458–542.

1. Clement XII d. 6 Feb. 1740, N.S. The Conclave formally opened 18 Feb. (*London Gazette* 4–8 March 1740) and ended 17 Aug. with the election of Benedict XIV (Ludwig Freiherr von Pastor, *Geschichte der Päpste*, vol. xvi, pt i, Freiburg, 1931, pp. 5, 16).

2. 21 March, N.S. (*Gray's Corr.* i. 143).

old, and very smug, with very few inhabitants. You must not believe Mr Addison about the wonderful Gothic nicety of the dome:[3] the materials are richer, but the workmanship and taste not near so good as in several I have seen. We saw a college of the Jesuits,[4] where there are taught to draw above fifty boys: they are disposed in long chambers in the manner of Eton, but cleaner. N.B. We were not *bolstered*,[5] so we wished you with us. Our cicerone, who has less classic knowledge and more superstition than a colleger, upon showing us the she-wolf,[6] the arms of Siena, told us that Romulus and Remus were nursed by a wolf, *per la volontà di Dio, si può dire;* and that one might see by the arms, that the same founders built Rome and Siena.[7] Another dab of Romish superstition, not unworthy of Presbyterian divinity, we met with in a book of drawings: 'twas the Virgin standing on a tripod composed of Adam, Eve and the Devil, to express her immaculate conception.

You can't imagine how pretty the country is between this and Florence; millions of little hills planted with trees, and tipped with villas or convents. We left unseen the Great Duke's villas and several palaces in Florence till our return from Rome: the weather has been so cold, how could one go to them? In Italy they seem to have found out how hot their climate is, but not how cold; for there are scarce any chimneys, and most of the apartments painted in fresco; so that one has the additional horror of freezing with imaginary marble. The men hang little earthen pans of coals[8] upon their wrists, and the women have portable stoves under their petticoats to warm their nakedness and carry silver shovels in their pockets, with which their cicisbeos stir

3. That is, *duomo.* See Addison, *Remarks on Several Parts of Italy,* edn 1726, p. 225 (HW's copy is now WSL).

4. Founded by Celso Tolomei in 1628 (though not opened until 1676) for the education of the sons of the Sienese nobility, and later attended by both Italians and foreigners. See Pacifico Provasi, 'Relazioni di cultura fra Siena e Palermo dal 1723 al 1729,' *Bullettino senese di storia patria,* n.s., v (1934). 317.

5. 'An Eton phrase' (HW), meaning to be pelted with pillows (OED).

6. The she-wolf with the twins (1429–30), of gilt bronze, on a column in the Via Giovanni Dupré, near the Palazzo Pubblico, by Giovanni and Lorenzo Turino (Corrado Ricci, *Il Palazzo Pubblico di Siena,* Bergamo, 1904, p. 14 and fig. 14, p.

28; Thieme and Becker *sub* Turino; *Enciclopedia italiana*).

7. The legends relating to Siena's Roman origin belong to the Renaissance. According to Agostino Patrizi (d. 1496), Bishop of Pienza, as summarized by Langton Douglas (*History of Siena,* New York, 1902, pp. 6–9), 'Senio and Aschio, sons of Remus, fleeing from their cruel uncle, bore away with them from Rome the image of the wolf and the twins. . . . On reaching the banks of the Tressa . . . on the spot now known as Castelvecchio [the highest hill in Siena], they built a strong castle to which they gave the name of Castel Senio.' See also Narciso Mengozzi, 'Il Monte dei Paschi,' *Arte antica senese* ii. 442n, in *Bullettino senese di storia patria,* vol. xi, 1904–5.

8. Called *scaldini.*

them—hush! by them, I mean their stoves. I have nothing more to tell you; I'll carry my letter to Rome and finish it there.

Re di Coffano,[9] March 23, where lived one of the three kings.

The King of Coffano carried presents of myrrh, gold, and frankincense: I don't know where the devil he found them, for in all his dominions we have not seen the value of a shrub. We have the honour of lodging under his roof tonight. Lord! such a place, such an extent of ugliness! A lone inn[10] upon a black mountain, by the side of an old fortress![11] no curtains or windows, only shutters! no testers to the beds! no earthly thing to eat but some eggs and a few little fishes! This lovely spot is now known by the name of Radicofani. Coming down a steep hill with two miserable hackneys, one fell under the chaise; and while we were disengaging him, a chaise came by with a person in a red cloak, a white handkerchief on its head, and black hat: We thought it a fat old woman; but it spoke in a shrill little pipe, and proved itself to be Senesini.[12]

I forgot to tell you an inscription I copied from the portal of the dome of Siena:

> Annus centenus Romæ semper est jubilenus;
> crimina laxantur si pœnitet ista donantur;
> sic ordinavit Bonifacius[13] et roboravit.

Rome, March 26.

We are this instant arrived, tired and hungry! Oh! the charming

---

9. Radicofani, 43½ miles SE of Siena. See also HW to Conway 5 July 1740, N.S., for an elaboration of the same pun.

10. The 'Osteria grande della Posta,' built as a hunting-seat by Ferdinand I of Tuscany, but later 'converted into an inn. It is the shell of a large fabric, but such an inside, such chambers and accommodations that your cellar is a palace in comparison, and your cat sups and lies much better than we did, for, it being a saint's eve, there was nothing but eggs. We devoured our meagre fare, and, after stopping up the windows with the quilts, were obliged to lie upon the straw beds in our clothes' (Gray to Mrs Gray 2 April 1740, N.S., Gray's Corr. i. 145; see also O. Bicchi, 'Radicofani,' Bullettino senese di storia patria, 1912, xix. 160).

11. Originally a monastery, it was fortified against the Sienese by Adrian IV in 1154–8. The fortress was virtually demolished 13 Sept. 1735 by an explosion of powder. See Bicchi, op. cit. 127–30, 157.

12. Francesco Bernardi (ca 1680–ca 1750), called Senesino, the celebrated castrato, who was one of Handel's leading singers in London between 1720 and 1736 (see Daily Adv. 23 June 1736 for his intended return to Italy). Senesino was returning from Naples to his native Siena (Gray's Corr. i. 145). For his relations with Handel see L. Cellesi, 'Un poeta romano e un sopranista senese,' Bullettino senese di storia patria, n.s. i (1930). 320–3.

13. 'The jubilee was instituted by Boniface VIII in 1300' (Toynbee).

city—I believe it is—for I have not seen a syllable yet,[14] only the Pons Milvius[15] and an obelisk. The Cassian and Flaminian ways were terrible disappointments; not one Rome tomb left; their very ruins ruined. The English are numberless. My dear West, I know at Rome you will not have a grain of pity for one; but indeed 'tis dreadful, dealing with schoolboys just broke loose, or old fools that are come abroad at forty to see the world, like Sir Wilful Witwoud.[16] I don't know whether you will receive this, or any other I write: but though I shall write often, you and Ashton must not wonder if none come to you; for, though I am harmless in my nature, my name has some mystery in it.[17] Good-night! I have no more time or paper. Ashton, child, I'll write to you next post. Write us no treasons, be sure!

To West, Saturday 16 April 1740, N.S.

Reprinted from *Works* iv. 444–6.
Written in collaboration with Gray; HW wrote the first four paragraphs, and Gray the concluding one.

Rome, April 16, 1740, N.S.

I'LL tell you, West, because one is amongst new things, you think one can always write new things. When I first came abroad, everything struck me, and I wrote its history;[1] but now I am grown so used to be surprised, that I don't perceive any flutter in myself when I meet with any novelties; curiosity and astonishment wear off, and the next thing is, to fancy that other people know as much of places as one's self; or, at least, one does not remember that they do not. It appears to me as odd to write to you of St Peter's, as it would do to you to write of Westminster Abbey. Besides, as one looks at churches, etc. with a book of

14. See Appendix 4. HW's lodging was 'close by the Villa Medici' (Chute to HW 26 June 1745, N.S.).
15. Now Ponte Milvio (Molle, Mollo) on the Tiber, rebuilt in 109 B.C.; it connects the Via Cassia with the Via Flaminia.
16. Congreve, *The Way of the World*, I. v:
'*Fainall.* He [Sir Wilfull] is expected today. . . . He comes to town in order to equip himself for travel.
Mirabell. For travel! Why the man that I mean is above forty.

Fainall. No matter for that; 'tis for the honour of England that all Europe should know we have blockheads of all ages.'
17. Since HW was the prime minister's son, his correspondence might have been suspected of containing information concerning the Old Pretender and his Jacobite entourage then living at Rome. See HW to Mann 23 April 1740, N.S., *et passim.*
———
1. I.e., in letters to his friends.

Rome. I forget Porto Bello[19] all this while; pray let us know where it is, and whether you or Ashton had any hand in the taking of it. Duty to the admiral.[20] Adieu!

Ever yours,

T. Gray

From West, April 1740

Missing. A letter, containing poetical 'fragments,' probably written at the Inner Temple, is mentioned in HW to Ashton 28 May 1740, N.S.

From Ashton, ca 27 April 1740, O.S.

Missing. Probably written in Hanover Square, London; answered *post* 28 May 1740, N.S.

To West, Saturday 7 May 1740, N.S.

Reprinted from *Works* iv. 446–8.

Rome, May 7, 1740, N.S.

Dear West,

'TWOULD be quite rude and unpardonable in one not to wish you joy upon the great conquests that you are all committing all over the world. We heard the news last night from Naples, that Admiral Haddock had met the Spanish convoy going to Majorca, and taken it all, all; three thousand men, three colonels, and a Spanish grandee.[1] We conclude it is true, for the Neapolitan majesty[2] men-

Inner Temple Records, vol. iv, ed. R. A. Roberts, 1933, pp. 76, 348; *Gray-HW-West-Ashton Corr.* i. 287.

19. On the Isthmus of Darien, about 40 miles NW of Panama, taken from the Spaniards by Admiral Vernon 22 Nov. 1739. The news of the victory reached Mann by 10 April (Mann to Earl Waldegrave 10 April 1740, N.S., in the Waldegrave Papers at Chewton Priory, Bath), and he probably communicated it to HW in Mann to HW April 1740, missing (see HW to Mann 16 April 1740, N.S.). London had no news of the taking of Porto Bello until 13 March, O.S. (24 March, N.S.), the date of the arrival of Captain Rentone with letters from Admiral Vernon and the articles of capitu-

lation. See *London Gazette* 11–15 March 1740; GM 1740, x. 124–7, 142–6; Douglas Ford, *Admiral Vernon and the Navy*, 1907, pp. 132–44.

20. Edward Vernon (1684–1757).

———

1. 'Yesterday advice came that Admiral Haddock's squadron had intercepted the Spanish troops designed against Minorca, had taken two men-of-war and five transports, and sunk, burnt, and destroyed the rest' (*Daily Adv.* 26 March 1740). This report appears to have been false. W. Laird Clowes, in *The Royal Navy*, 1897–1903, iii. 314, lists two Spanish ships captured in April, but none in March.

2. Charles IV (1716–88) of Naples and the

tioned it at dinner. We are going thither in about a week[3] to wish him joy of it too. 'Tis with some apprehensions we go too, of having a Pope chosen in the interim: that would be cruel, you know. But, thank our stars, there is no great probability of it. Feuds and contentions run high among the Eminences.[4] A notable one happened this week. Cardinal Zinzendorff[5] and two more[6] had given their votes for the General of the Capucins:[7] he is of the Barberini family, not a cardinal, but a worthy man. Not effecting anything, Zinzendorff voted for Coscia,[8] and declared it publicly. Cardinal Petra[9] reproved him; but the Ger-

Two Sicilies, 1734 (Charles III of Spain, 1759).

3. They did not leave for Naples until 12 June ('Gray's Notes of Travel,' Tovey, *Gray and His Friends* 223).

4. The College of Cardinals at the opening of the Conclave (18 Feb.) consisted of sixty-eight cardinals; thirteen were absent throughout, and four died in the Conclave. At this time there were two major factions: the 'Collegio Vecchio,' including the 'Benedictines' and the 'zelanti,' consisting mostly of the cardinals created by Clement XI, Innocent XIII, and Benedict XIII, and headed by Annibale Albani, nephew of Clement XI; and the 'new college,' mostly created by Clement XII, whose nephew, Corsini, headed it (HW to Ashton 28 May 1740, N.S.). In addition there were minor political factions, the Austrian and Spanish factions being in an apparently irreconcilable conflict. Subsequently the Austrians combined with the French under Corsini against the Spanish, who were forced into Albani's camp. See Ludwig Freiherr von Pastor, *Geschichte der Päpste* xvi pt i (Freiburg, 1931). 6–12; Benedict XIV's diary (*Briefe Benedicts XIV*, ed. Franz Xaver Kraus, 2d edn, Freiburg, 1888, pp. 154–63); Maurice Boutry, 'Le Cardinal de Tencin au conclave de Benoit XIV,' *Revue d'histoire diplomatique*, 1897, xi. 263–75, 387–96; Maurice Boutry, *Intrigues et missions du Cardinal de Tencin*, 1902, pp. 176–236; Gabriel de Mun, 'Un conclave de six mois,' *Revue des deux mondes*, 1914, 6th ser., xxiv. 490–519.

5. Philipp Ludwig (1699–1747), Count von Sinzendorff; cardinal, 1727, of the creation of Benedict XIII (*Allgemeine deutsche Biographie*, Leipzig, 1875–1912).

6. The ballots were unsigned, and while the number of ballots cast for the several cardinals in the course of the Conclave might be ascertained, the names cannot be, since the voting was secret (information kindly supplied by Giovanni, Cardinal Mercati, Archivist of the Biblioteca Apostolica Vaticana).

7. Mgr Bonaventura Barberini (1674–1743), Ministro Generale di tutto l'Ordine de' Capuccini, 1733; Archbishop of Ferrara, 1740. On 26 April he received three, and on the 27th four votes (*Conclave doppo la morte del Pont. Clemente XII*, a week-by-week account of the Conclave of 1740, Bayerische Staatsbibliothek MS, Cod. ital. 323, f. 43; information from Dr Albert Hartmann, director of the Department of Manuscripts, Bavarian State Library, Munich). See also *Cenni biografici e ritratti di padri illustri dell' Ordine Capuccino*, ed. Carlo Felice da Milano, Rome, 1850, i. 84–90; Pius Bonifacius Gams, *Series episcoporum Ecclesiæ Catholicæ*, Ratisbon, 1873, p. 695; Petruccelli della Gattina, *Histoire diplomatique des conclaves*, 1866, iv. 121.

8. Niccolo Coscia (1682–1755), cardinal, 1725. During the pontificate of Benedict XIII he enriched himself through simony, bribery, and embezzlement of papal funds to such an extent that in the pontificate of Clement XII he was excommunicated, fined, deprived of his vote in the Conclave, and sentenced to prison (1733). His prison sentence was suspended and his vote restored by the Conclave of 1740. See Pastor, op. cit. xv (Freiburg, 1930). 479–87, 634–8; xvi pt i (Freiburg, 1931). 5; Ranfft iii. 196–237; Charles de Brosses, *Lettres*, ed. R. Colomb, 1861, ii. 401; see also *post* 14 May 1740, N.S.

9. Vincenzo di Petra (1662–1747), cardinal, 1724, of the creation of Benedict XIII.

man replied, he thought Coscia as fit to be Pope as any of them. It seems, his pique to the whole body is, their having denied a daily admission of a pig into the Conclave for His Eminence's use; who being much troubled with the gout, was ordered by his mother to bathe his leg in pig's blood every morning.[10]

Who should have a vote t'other day but the *Cardinalino* of Toledo?[11] Were he older, the Queen of Spain[12] might possibly procure more than one for him, though scarcely enough.

Well, but we won't talk politics; shall we talk antiquities? Gray and I discovered a considerable curiosity lately. In an unfrequented quarter of the Colonna Garden lie two immense fragments of marble, formerly part of a frieze to some building;[13] 'tis not known of what. They are of Parian marble; which may give one some idea of the magnificence of the rest of the building, for these pieces were at the very top. Upon inquiry, we were told they had been measured by an architect, who declared they were larger than any member of St Peter's. The length of one of the pieces is above sixteen feet.[14] They were formerly sold to a stone-cutter for five thousand crowns;[15] but Clement XI[16] would not permit them to be sawed, annulled the bargain, and laid a penalty of twelve thousand pounds upon the family if they parted with them. I think it was a right judged thing. Is it not amazing that so vast a structure should not be known of, or that it should be so entirely destroyed? But indeed at Rome this is a common surprise; for, by the remains one sees of the Roman grandeur in their structures, 'tis evident that there must have been more pains taken to destroy those piles than to raise them. They are more demolished than any time or chance could have

10. This refusal, it is said, infuriated Sinzendorff so much that he swore he would leave the Conclave and not return until the day of election (Cardinal Ferrerio to Charles Emanuel I of Sardinia 16 April 1740, quoted by Petruccelli della Gattina, op. cit. iv. 118–19).

11. Luis Antonio Santiago (1727–85), son of Philip V of Spain by Elizabeth Farnese; cardinal, 1735 (aged eight); Archbishop of Toledo, 1736, of Seville, 1742. On 18 Dec. 1754 he resigned all his ecclesiastical offices (*Enciclopedia universal ilustrada*, Barcelona, 1905–33, *sub* Borbon; Mario Guarnacci, *Vitæ . . . pontificum romanorum et S.R.E. cardinalium a Clemente X usque ad Clementem XII*, Rome, 1751, ii. 695–8).

12. Elizabeth Farnese (1692–1766), of Parma, m. (1714), as his 2d wife, Philip V of Spain.

13. The Templum Solis Aureliani, the columns of which (shaft and capital) measured approximately 65 feet and the entablature 16 feet (S. B. Platner and Thomas Ashby, *Topographical Dictionary of Ancient Rome*, 1929, p. 492).

14. See Gray's 'Criticisms on architecture and painting,' in Mitford, 1835–43, iv. 248–9.

15. By Filippo Colonna (1663–1714), Gran Contestabile del Regno di Napoli (Litta ii, 'Colonna di Roma,' table xi; Mitford, loc. cit.).

16. Clement XI (Gianfrancesco Albani) (1649–1721), Pope 1700–21.

effected. I am persuaded that in an hundred years Rome will not be worth seeing; 'tis less so now than one would believe. All the public pictures are decayed or decaying; the few ruins cannot last long; and the statues and private collections must be sold, from the great poverty of the families. There are now selling no less than three of the principal collections, the Barberini,[17] the Sacchetti,[18] and Ottoboni: the latter belonged to the Cardinal[19] who died in the Conclave. I must give you an instance of his generosity, or rather ostentation. When Lord Carlisle[20] was here last year, who is a great virtuoso, he asked leave to see the Cardinal's collection of cameos and intaglios. Ottoboni gave leave, and ordered the person who showed them to observe which my Lord admired most. My Lord admired many: they were all sent him the next morning. He sent the Cardinal back a fine gold repeater; who returned him an agate snuff-box, and more cameos of ten times the value. *Voilà qui est fini!* Had my Lord produced more golden repeaters, it would have been begging more cameos.

Adieu, my dear West! You see I write often and much, as you desired it. Do answer one now and then with any little job that is done in England. Good night.

Yours ever,

Hor. Walpole

To Ashton, Saturday 14 May 1740, N.S.

Printed from MS in the possession of C. C. Auchincloss, Esq., of New York City. Sold by Hodgson, 9 March 1904, lot 211; offered for sale by Quaritch, Cat. No. 253 (Nov. 1906), lot 181a; No. 286 (March 1910), lot 1261a; No. 344 (June 1916), lot 273a; sold by Sotheby's 12 July 1921, lot 244, to Maggs; Maggs to Mr Auchincloss.

17. The effects of Francesco Barberini (1662–1738), cardinal, 1690; eldest son of Maffeo, Principe di Palestrina, and great-grandnephew of Urban VIII (who built the Palazzo Barberini 1626–38). See Ranfft ii. 223–5, 231–2; *Ædes Walpolianæ, Works* ii. 225; Litta ii, 'Colonna di Roma,' table x.

18. 'The Sacchetti collection has been since purchased by Pope Benedict XIV, and placed in the Capitol' (HW's note, *Ædes Walpolianæ,* loc. cit.).

19. Pietro Ottoboni (1667–1740), cardinal, 1689, of the creation of Alexander VIII, his great-uncle. He d. 28 Feb. 1740. A 'man of great courtesy and generosity,' he made 'all his entertainments *da gran principe*,' and arranged a contest between his protégé Handel and Domenico Scarlatti in 1708. See Edward Wright, *Some Observations made in Travelling through France, Italy, etc., in the Years 1720, 1721, and 1722, 1730,* i. 281–2; Friedrich Chrysander, *G. F. Handel,* 2d edn, Leipzig, 1919, i. 224–9; Ranfft ii. 268–81; see also *post* 2 Oct. 1740.

20. Henry Howard (1694–1758), 4th E. of Carlisle. For his opinion of Rome see Lady Mary Wortley Montagu, *Letters,* ed. Lord Wharncliffe, 3d edn [?1861], ii. 44–5.

Written in collaboration with Gray; probably written 13 May and the date added by HW the following day, since the reference to his going to the assembly of the Marchese Patrizi 'tonight' is contradicted by the fuller account in HW to Mann 14 May 1740, N.S., where he refers to the assembly as of 'last night.'

Rome, May 14, 1740, N.S.

BOILEAU'S Discord dwelt in a college of monks;[1] at present the lady is in the Conclave. Cardinal Corsini has been interrogated about certain millions of crowns[2] that are absent from the Apostolic Chamber; he refuses giving account, but to a Pope: However he has set several arithmeticians to work, to compose sums, and flourish out expenses, which probably never existed. Cardinal Cibo[3] pretends to have a banker at Genoa, who will prove that he has received three millions on the part of the eminent Corsini. This Cibo, is a madman, but set on by others. He had formerly some great office in the government, from whence they are generally raised to the cardinalate. After a time, not being promoted as he expected, he resigned his post and retired to a mountain, where he built a most magnificent hermitage. There he inhabited for two years; grew tired, came back and received the hat.[4]

Other feuds have been between Cardinal Portia[5] and the faction[6] of Benedict the Thirteenth;[7] by whom he was made cardinal.[8] About a month ago he was within three votes of being Pope.[9] He did not apply

1. An allusion to *Le Lutrin* i. 25–6 by Nicolas Boileau-Despréaux (1636–1711) (*Œuvres complètes,* ed. A. C. Gidel, 1870–3, ii. 416):
'Quand la Discorde encor toute noire de crimes,
Sortant des Cordeliers pour aller aux Minimes,' etc.
2. The contemporary *Genealogisch-his-torische Nachrichten,* ed. J. S. Heinsius, mentions this 'borrowing' (pt xix, Leipzig, 1741, p. 618).
3. Camillo Cybo (Cibo) (1681–1743), son of Carlo II, Duca di Massa e Carrara, and grandnephew of Innocent X; cardinal, 1729 (Ranfft ii. 343–8).
4. In 1718 he was appointed Auditor General of the Apostolic Chamber, which office he resigned in Oct. 1721 to retire to a mountain near Spoleto (Ranfft ii. 344–5); he returned to Rome in Nov. 1723. In 1725 he was appointed majordomo. Because Cybo sought to stop the corrupt practices of Coscia, Benedict XIII's favourite, Coscia

induced Benedict to create Cybo cardinal (23 March 1729) and to relieve him of his post of majordomo (Ludwig Freiherr von Pastor, *Geschichte der Päpste,* xv [Freiburg, 1930]. 485; see also Mario Guarnacci, *Vitæ . . . pontificum romanorum et S.R.E. cardinalium a Clemente X usque ad Clementem XII,* Rome, 1751, ii. 548–9).
5. Leandro (1673–1740), Conte di Porcia e Brugnera, Benedictine monk of Monte Cassino, 1693; cardinal, 1728 (Guarnacci, op. cit. ii. 533–4; *Enciclopedia storico-nobiliare italiana,* ed. Vittorio Spreti, Milan, 1928–36, v. 461; Ranfft ii. 284–9).
6. Toynbee (*Gray - HW - West - Ashton Corr.* i. 294), following Mitford's transcript, reads 'father.'
7. Pietro Francesco Orsini (1649–1730), pope 1724–30.
8. 30 April 1728, N.S.
9. On 8 April he proposed himself as a candidate, and received thirty votes (Gabriel de Mun, 'Un conclave de six mois,'

to any party, but went gleaning privately from all, and of a sudden burst out with a number; but too soon, and that threw him quite out. Having been since left out of their meetings, he asked one of the Benedictine cardinals[10] the reason; who replied, that he never had been their friend, and never should be of their assemblies; and did not even hesitate to call him apostate. This flung Portia into such a rage, that he spit blood, and instantly left the Conclave with all his baggage.[11] But the great cause of their antipathy to him, was his having been one of the four, that voted for putting Coscia to death;[12] who now regains his interest, and may prove somewhat disagreeable to his enemies; whose honesty is not abundantly heavier than his own. He met Corsini t'other day, and told him, he heard his Eminence had a mind to his cell: Corsini answered he was very well contented with that he had. 'Oh,' says Coscia, 'I don't mean here in the Conclave; but in the Castle St Angelo.'[13]

With all these animosities, one is near having a Pope; Cardinal Gotti,[14] an old, inoffensive Dominican, without any relations, wanted yesterday but two voices; and is still most likely to succeed.[15] Cardinal Altieri[16] has been sent for from Albano, whither he was retired upon

Revue des deux mondes, 1914, 6th ser. xxiv. 516).

10. That is, of the creation of Benedict XIII.

11. On 26 April, N.S., Porcia found posted in the Sistine Chapel an anonymous satirical broadside attacking him. Annibale Albani, the Papal Chamberlain, promised to seek out the culprit, and Porcia withdrew to his cell, where he secluded himself for two weeks during Albani's fruitless investigation. On 11 May, 'under pretence of indisposition, but it is said the disappointment he has met with, and the great disagreements in the Conclave' (*London Gazette* 31 May–3 June 1740), he left the session. He died 10 June, N.S., of, so it was said, the 'rabbia papale.' See Benedict XIV's diary (*Briefe Benedicts XIV*, Franz Xaver Kraus, Freiburg, 1888, pp. 162–3); Pastor, op. cit. xvi pt i. 12; Mun, op. cit. 518; Charles de Brosses, *Lettres*, ed. R. Colomb, 1861, ii. 429–31.

12. For the punishment actually inflicted on Coscia see *ante* 7 May 1740, N.S., n. 8. The congregation 'de nonnullis' con-

sisted of ten members, not four (see Pastor, op. cit. xv. 634).

13. Where Coscia was imprisoned 1733–40 (see *ante* 7 May 1740, N.S., n. 8).

14. Vincenzo Luigi Gotti (1664–1742), cardinal, 1728 (Guarnacci, op. cit. ii. 525–6 *bis*; Ranfft ii. 332–7; A. Touron, *Histoire des hommes illustres de l'ordre de Saint Dominique*, Paris, 1749, vi. 640–87).

15. He was the candidate of the 'zelanti' (*post* 28 May 1740, N.S.), but lacked the support of the French cardinals (Mun, op. cit. 520). The number of votes he received 13 May is not recorded in *Conclave doppo la morte del Pont. Clemente XII*, but the following week he received 30 and 22 (Bayerische Staatsbibliothek MS, Cod. ital. 323, f. 53v; information from Dr Albert Hartmann). The *Mercure historique et politique* for June 1740 records 33 votes for Cardinal Gotti (cviii. 605, 616).

16. Lorenzo Altieri (1671–1741), cardinal, 1690, nephew of Clement X. Because of illness he was absent during the entire Conclave (Benedict XIV's diary, ed. Kraus, op. cit. 171; see also Guarnacci, op. cit. i. 377–80; Ranfft ii. 307–11).

account of his brother's death[17] and his own illness; and where he was to stay till the election drew nigh. There! there's a sufficient competency of Conclave news, I think.

We have miserable weather for the season; could you think I was writing to you by my fireside at Rome in the middle of May? The common people say 'tis occasioned by the Pope's soul, which cannot find rest.

How goes your war?[18] We are persuaded here of an additional one with France.[19] Lord! it will be dreadful to return through Germany. I don't know who cooks up the news here, but we have some strange piece every day. One that is much in vogue, and would not be disagreeable for us, is, that the Czarina[20] has clapped the Marquis de la Chétardie[21] in prison. One must hope till some months hence 'tis all contradicted.

I am balancing in great uncertainty, whether to go to Naples or stay here; you know 'twould be provoking to have a Pope chosen just as one's back was turned; and if I wait, I fear the heats may arrive. I don't know what to do.

We are going tonight to a great assembly at one of the villas[22] just out of the city, whither all the English are invited; amongst the rest, Mr Stuard and his two sons.[23] There is one lives with him called Lord Dun-

17. Giambattista Altieri (1673–1740), cardinal, 1724, died of an apoplectic stroke 12 March in the Conclave (Ranfft ii. 281–4; Guarnacci, op. cit. ii. 434).

18. The Spanish war.

19. 'France was arming in all her ports, which did not seem consistent with the neutrality she had promised' (GM 1740, x. 205–6).

20. Anne (1693–1740), Empress of Russia 1730–40; she was Peter the Great's niece, and succeeded his grandson, Peter II.

21. Joachim-Jacques Trotti (1705–59), Marquis de la Chétardie, the first French ambassador to Russia (23 April 1739, N.S.–1742). He arrived at St Petersburg 16 Dec., and presented his credentials 27 Dec. 1739, O.S. (London Gazette 22–26 Jan. 1740). Rumours of his amour with Peter the Great's daughter, the Grand Duchess Elizabeth (whose coup d'état of 6 Dec. 1741 he actively promoted), might have been exaggerated into a story of his disgrace, although no evidence of his imprisonment at this time is available. See Recueil des

instructions données aux ambassadeurs et ministres de France . . . Russie, ed. Alfred Rambaud, 1890, i. 339–64; R. Nisbet Bain, The Daughter of Peter the Great, 1899, pp. 43–7, 84–5, 111–13; Mercure historique et politique, 1740, cviii. 202–3, 555.

22. The 'Villa Patrizzi' (HW to Mann 14 May 1740, N.S.) where the (?) Marchese Giovanni Chigi Montoro Patrizi (Spreti, op. cit. v. 209–10) gave a 'great ball' in honour of the Prince and Princesse de Craon (Marc de Beauvau-Craon, 1679–1754, who m. in 1704 Anne-Marguerite de Ligniville, ca 1687–1772), on the occasion of the Prince de Craon's formal installation into the Order of the Golden Fleece 1 May at Rome (Gray's Corr. i. 158, 166; La Chenaye-Desbois ii. 740; Mercure historique et politique, 1740, cviii. 611–16).

23. James Francis Edward (Stuart) (1688–1766), the Old Pretender, and his two sons: Charles Edward (1720–88), the Young Pretender, and Henry Benedict (1725–1807), Cardinal York (cr. 1747).

bar,[24] Murray's[25] brother, who would be his minister if he had any occasion for one: I meet him frequently in public places, and like him. He is very sensible, very agreeable and well-bred. Good-night, child; by the way I have had no letters from England these two last posts.

Yours ever.

I am by trade a finisher of letters. Don't you wonder at the Conclave? Instead of being immured every one in his proper hutch as one used to imagine, they have the liberty of scuttling out of one hole into another, and might breed if they were young enough. I do assure you everything one has heard say of Italy is a lie, and am firmly of opinion that no mortal was ever here before us. I am writing to prove there never was any such people as the Romans, that this was anciently a colony of the Jews, and that the Coliseum was built on the model of Solomon's Temple. Our people have told so many stories of them, that they don't believe anything we say about ourselves; Porto Bello is still said to be impregnable, and it is reported the Dutch have declared war against us. The English Court here brighten up on the news of our conquests, and conclude all the contrary has happened. You do not know perhaps that we have our little good fortune in the Mediterranean, where Admiral Haddock has overturned certain little boats carrying troops to Majorca, drowned a few hundreds of them, and taken a little grandee of Spain that commanded the expedition; at least so they say at Naples.[26] I'm very sorry, but methinks they seem in a bad condition. Is West dead to the world in general, or only so to me? For you I have not the impudence to accuse, but you are to take this as a sort of reproof, and I hope you will demean yourself accordingly. You are hereby authorized to make my very particular compliments to my Lord Plymouth, and return him my thanks *de l'honneur de son souvenir*. So I finish my postscript with

Yours ever,

T. G.

24. Hon. James Murray (ca 1690–1770), 2d son of the 5th Vct Stormont; cr. (1721) titular E. of Dunbar; he was governor to the Young Pretender (GEC), and (according to Spence) to Cardinal York (Spence to his mother 8 Dec. 1740, N.S., BM Add. MS Egerton 2234, f. 227v).

25. Hon. William Murray (1705–93), Vct Stormont's 4th son, cr. (1756) Bn and (1776) E. of Mansfield; Lord Chief Justice of the King's Bench 1756–88.

26. See *ante* 7 May 1740, N.S., n. 1.

To Ashton, Saturday 28 May 1740, N.S.

Printed from photostat of Mitford's transcript, Add. MS 32,562, ff. 135–9.

Rome, May 28, 1740, N.S.

Dear Child,

I HAVE just received your letter of news;[1] I had heard before of Symphony's[2] affair, with Lady ——.[3] But they called it a report: but I find, like many stories of that kind 'tis true. What are we to be appear[4] before the House of Lords? are there to be damages? or is it to be blown over, with only a separate maintenance for the fair one? I am sorry he has already established such a character. 'Tis too soon to be arrived at one's *ne plus ultra*. I doubt 'tis all the fame he ever will be master of, and 'tis horrid to begin where one must end.

By a considerable volume of charts and pyramids, which I saw at Florence, I thought it threatened a publication.[5] His travels have really improved him; I wish they may do the same for any one else.

West has sent me a letter of fragments,[6] which not being antique, I am extremely angry, are not complete.

> Nor cease the maiden Graces from above
> To shower their fragrance on the field of love.

I desire, you will set him to digging in the same spot, where he found these verses, for the other parts of the poem. I took them for his own; but upon showing them to a great virtuoso[7] here, he assures me they are undoubtedly ancient, by one of the best hands, and in the true Greek taste.

This is the first day, we have had, that one can call warm; they say, in England you have not a leaf yet on the trees.

I have made a vow against politics, or I would wish you joy of your West Indian conquests.[8] One shall not know you again. You will be so martial all. Here one should not know, if there had ever been such a

1. Ashton to HW ca 27 April 1740, O.S., missing.
2. This suggests a close friend at Eton, but he is unidentified.
3. Not identified.
4. So in Mitford's transcript. HW doubtless intended to write: 'What! are we to appear,' etc.

5. No doubt Gray's MS Journal 1739–41.
6. West to HW April 1740, missing. The verses are not identified.
7. Gray.
8. The taking of Porto Bello (*ante* 16 April 1740, N.S., n. 19).

thing as war, if it were not now and then from seeing a scrap of a soldier on an old bas-relief. 'Tis comical to see a hundred and twenty thousand inhabitants in a city where you scarce can see one, that has not taken a vow never to propagate; but they say there are larger parsley beds[9] here, than in other countries. Don't talk of our coronation; 'tis never likely to happen. The divisions are so great between the Albani and Corsini factions,[10] that the Conclave will probably be drawn out to a great length. With Albani,[11] are his uncle's creatures,[12] the Spanish and Neapolitan factions,[13] and the *zelanti;*[14] a set of cardinals, who always declare against any party, and profess being solely in the interest of the Church. With Corsini are the late Pope's creatures,[15] and the dependants of France.[16]

Mrs G.[17] writes me word how much goodness she met with in Hanover Square. Poor creature! You know, how much it obliges me, my

9. 'That phrase which we use to little children, when we tell them they were born in their mothers' parsley-bed' (Mabbe, quoted in OED; see also MONTAGU i. 176).

10. See *ante* 7 May 1740, N.S., n. 4.

11. Annibale Albani (1682–1751), cardinal, 1711, who was a nephew of Clement XI; Papal Chamberlain, 1719; 'grand génie dans les affaires, inépuisable en ressources dans les intrigues, la première tête du collège et le plus méchant homme de Rome' (Charles de Brosses, *Lettres*, ed. R. Colomb, 1861, ii. 399; see also Ranfft iii. 39–62).

12. Nine of the cardinals had been created by Clement XI. See Benedict XIV's diary (*Briefe Benedicts XIV*, ed. Franz Xaver Kraus, Freiburg, 1888, p. 171). HW is borrowing the Italian *creature:* in this context, 'the creations of.'

13. Headed by Trajano Acquaviva (1695–1747), cardinal, 1732, of the creation of Clement XII, himself a Neapolitan; and by Tomaso Ruffo (1663–1753), cardinal, 1706, of the creation of Clement XI, also a Neapolitan (Ranfft ii. 473, 480–1, iii. 137–43; Ludwig Freiherr von Pastor, *Geschichte der Päpste*, xvi pt i, Freiburg, 1931, pp. 6–11). Both Spain and Naples were under the rule of the Bourbons.

14. 'Les *zelanti* forment la troisième faction, composée de ceux qui font profession de ne suivre que l'inspiration du Saint-Esprit, et sans vouloir se mêler ni entendre aucune brigue, se déclareront pour celui qu'ils croiront n'avoir point intrigué pour parvenir au pontificat' (Brosses, op. cit. ii. 418).

15. Twenty-seven cardinals of the creation of Clement XII attended the Conclave (Benedict XIV's diary, Kraus, op. cit. 172–3).

16. Cardinal Rohan of the creation of Clement XI; Henri Oswald de la Tour d'Auvergne (1671–1747), cardinal, 1737, and Pierre Guérin de Tencin (1680–1758), cardinal, 1739, both of the creation of Clement XII (Ranfft ii. 489, iii. 282; NBG).

17. Presumably Anne Grosvenor (1679–1750), Lady Walpole's friend; aunt of Grosvenor Bedford, Deputy Usher of the Receipt of the Exchequer 1755–71 (see HW to Bedford 21 Aug. 1755). In two childhood letters, HW calls her 'Mrs Gravenner' and 'Grave' (HW to Lady Walpole ?1725, 30 Sept. 1733). Mrs Lewis, a friend and possibly a connection of the Walpole family, apparently took Miss Grosvenor into her household about this time. Ashton, as tutor to Mrs Lewis's grandson, Lord Plymouth, was then living at Mrs Lewis's house in Hanover Square. Miss Grosvenor, through Sir Robert Walpole's influence, was appointed Under Housekeeper (1738) and Housekeeper (1739) of Somerset House (Record Office, L.C. 3. 65, p. 77; GM 1739, ix. 384; see also *post* 25 July 1741; Paget Toynbee, 'Horace Walpole and "Mrs G.",' *Times Literary Supplement* 16 Dec. 1920, p. 858; Mann to HW 10 Jan. 1742, N.S.).

dear Ashton, and if that can give you any satisfaction as I believe it does, be assured, it touches me in the strongest manner. It obliges me in a point that relates to my mother, and that is all I can say in this world! You must make my particular [compliments] to Mrs Lewis: her kindness to Mrs G. is adding to the several great obligations I have to her. 'Tis a pleasure to receive such from one who acts from no motives, but innate goodness and benevolent virtue. You must not tell that poor woman, what I am now going to mention; I fear we shall not see Naples. We have been setting out for some time; and if we do not, to be back by the end of this month, it will be impracticable from the heats, and the bad air,[18] in the Campania. But we are prevented by a great body of banditti, soldiers deserted from the King of Naples, who have taken possession of the roads, and not only murdered several passengers, but some *sbirri* who were sent against them. Among others was a poor hermit, who had a few old medals which he had dug up, that they took for money.

The poverty of the Roman State and the mutinous humour of the inhabitants, who grow desperate for want of a Pope, through decay of trade, and a total want of specie are likely to increase the bands, while the Conclave sits, so that I fear, we are prisoners at Rome, till the election. I should not at all dislike my situation, if I were entirely at liberty and had nothing to call me to England. I shall but too soon miss there the peace I enjoy here; I don't mention the pleasures I enjoy here, which are to be found in no other city in the world, but them I could give up to my friends with satisfaction. But I know the causes that drove me out of England, and I don't know that they are remedied.[19] But adieu! When I leave Italy, I shall launch out into a life, whose colour I fear, will have more of black than of white.

Yours ever.

18. 'At Rome there is what they call the *mala aria* (and what we should call a bad air) at a particular part of the summer. They have great superstition about it, and are so exact as to name the very day that it comes in. The country about Rome is almost a desert. . . . This is one great occasion of the *mala aria* which lies over Rome in July and August, and in some parts for forty mile round it' (Spence to his mother 23 Aug. 1732, N.S., quoted from an early MS copy in the possession of Mr James M. Osborn of New Haven). See also HW to Conway 5 July 1740, N.S.

19. It has been suggested that this refers to a love affair, but it is more likely that 'the causes' had to do with HW's relations with his father following Sir Robert's marriage to Miss Skerrett.

From WEST, June 1740

Missing. Probably written from Bond Street, London (see West to Gray 5 June 1740, O.S., *Gray's Corr.* i. 164); answered *post* 31 July 1740, N.S.

To WEST, Tuesday 14 June 1740, N.S.

Reprinted from *Works* iv. 448–50.

Naples,[1] June 14, 1740, N.S.

Dear West,

ONE hates writing descriptions that are to be found in every book of travels; but we have seen something today that I am sure you never read of, and perhaps never heard of. Have you ever heard of the subterraneous town? a whole Roman town with all its edifices remaining under ground? Don't fancy the inhabitants buried it there to save it from the Goths: they were buried with it themselves; which is a caution we are not told they ever took. You remember in Titus's time[2] there were several cities destroyed by an eruption of Vesuvius, attended with an earthquake.[3] Well, this was one of them, not very considerable, and then called Herculaneum. Above it has since been built Portici, about three miles from Naples, where the King has a villa. This underground city is perhaps one of the noblest curiosities that ever has been discovered. It was found out by chance about a year and half ago.[4] They began digging, they found statues; they dug farther, they found more. Since that they have made a very considerable progress, and find continually. You may walk the compass of a mile; but by the misfortune of the modern town being overhead, they are obliged to proceed with great caution, lest they destroy both one and t'other. By this occasion the path is very narrow, just wide enough and high enough for one man to walk upright. They have hollowed as they found it easiest to work, and have carried their streets not exactly

1. See *ante* 7 May 1740, N.S., n. 3. They stayed 'about nine days' (*Gray's Corr.* i. 169).
2. Titus Flavius Vespasianus (41–81 A.D.), Roman Emperor, 79 A.D.
3. 1 Nov. 79 A.D.
4. Excavations were begun 22 Oct. 1738 by Roque Joaquin de Alcubierre (d. 1780), on the site (purchased by Charles IV of Naples in 1736) where the Prince d'Elbœuf had excavated marble for his villa together with sculptures in 1711. See Michele Ruggiero, *Storia degli scavi di Ercolano*, Naples, 1885, pp. xiii–xiv, 2; Niccolò Marcello Venuti (later Marchese Venuti), *A Description of the First Discoveries of the Ancient City of Herculaneum* [?1750], p. 50.

were on the dawn of a schism. Aldovrandi [*sic*][15] had thirty-three voices[16] for three days, but could not procure the requisite two more;[17] the Camerlingo having engaged his faction to sign a protestation against him, and each party were inclined to elect. I don't know whether one should wish for a schism or not; it might probably rekindle the zeal for the Church in the powers of Europe, which has been so far decaying.

On Wednesday we expect a third she-meteor. Those learned luminaries the Ladies P[omfret][18] and W[alpole][19] are to be joined by the Lady M[ary] W[ortley] M[ontagu].[20] You have not been witness to the rhapsody of mystic nonsense which these two fair ones debate incessantly, and consequently cannot figure what must be the issue of this

15. Pompeo Aldrovandi (1668–1752), cardinal, 1734, of the creation of Clement XII (Mario Guarnacci, *Vitæ . . . pontificum romanorum et S.R.E. cardinalium*, Rome, 1751, ii. 669).

16. For three successive weeks (10–30 July) he commanded thirty-one votes, but not until 11 Aug. did he attain thirty-three (*Conclave doppo la morte del Pont. Clemente XII*, Bayerische Staatsbibliothek MS, Cod. ital. 323, ff. 91r, 95v, 100r, 113r, 114v; information from Dr Albert Hartmann. See also Benedict XIV's diary, *Briefe Benedicts XIV*, ed. Franz Xaver Kraus, Freiburg, 1888, pp. 168–9).

17. Aldrovandi, Corsini's candidate, had the support of the heretofore irreconcilable Austrian, French, and Spanish factions (*ante* 7 May 1740, N.S., n. 4). His candidature was violently opposed by the Camerlingo (Annibale Albani) who controlled nineteen of the fifty-two votes of the Conclave. A deadlock ensued, and, to expedite the close of the Conclave, Aldrovandi on 30 July wrote to Corsini offering to withdraw as a candidate. It was not until 17 Aug., however, that Lambertini (Benedict XIV) was unanimously elected. See *Acta Historico-ecclesiastica*, Weimar, iv (1740–1), Appendix, pp. 1054–6, for the text of Aldrovandi's letter; see also Benedict XIV's diary, ed. Kraus, loc. cit.; Ludwig Freiherr von Pastor, *Geschichte der Päpste*, xvi pt i (Freiburg, 1931). 4–7, 14–16; Maurice Boutry, 'Le Cardinal de Tencin au conclave de Benoît XIV,' *Revue d'histoire diplomatique*, 1897, xi. 404–7;

Gabriel de Mun, 'Un conclave de six mois,' *Revue des deux mondes*, 1914, 6th ser., xxiv. 523–7.

18. The Hon. Henrietta Louisa Jeffreys (d. 1761), dau. of the 2d Bn Jeffreys of Wem, m. (1720) Thomas Fermor, 2d Bn Leominster, cr. (1721) E. of Pomfret. She stayed at Florence from 20 Dec. 1739, N.S. to 13 March 1741 with Lord Pomfret and her two eldest daughters (*Hertford Corr.* i. 175, ii. 284; see also *post* 2 Oct. 1740, N.S.; Appendix 5; HW to Mann 16 May 1756; E. M. Symonds, *Little Memoirs of the Eighteenth Century*, 1901, pp. 17–23).

19. Margaret Rolle (1709–81), dau. of Samuel Rolle of Heanton Satchville, Devon, m. (1) (1724) Robert Walpole, 1st Bn Walpole, 2d E. of Orford 1745; m. (2) (1751) Hon. Sewallis Shirley; *suo jure* Bns Clinton 1760. In 1734 she had eloped with Thomas Sturges, Fellow of King's College, Cambridge, with whom she was living at this time in Florence. The wits of the Sublime Society of Beefsteaks celebrated her departure in a toast (Lady Mary Wortley Montagu, *Letters*, ed. Lord Wharncliffe, 3d edn [?1861], ii. 82). For her return to England in 1745 and her separations from her husbands in 1746 and 1754 see HW to Mann 6 Sept. 1745, 17 Jan., 6 March 1746, 5 July 1754; see also HW to Mann ?Aug. 1741.

20. Lady Mary Wortley Montagu, who had left England 26 July 1739, was in Florence 22 Aug.–16 Oct. 1740, N.S. (Lady Mary Wortley Montagu, op. cit. ii. 41, 70; *Hertford Corr.* ii. 82, 134). See Appendix 5.

triple alliance: we have some idea of it. Only figure the coalition of prudery, debauchery, sentiment, history, Greek, Latin, French, Italian, and metaphysics; all, except the second, understood by halves, by quarters, or not at all. You shall have the journals of this notable academy. Adieu, my dear West!

Yours ever,

Hor. Walpole

Though far unworthy to enter into so learned and political a correspondence, I am employed *pour barbouiller une page de sept pouces et demie en hauteur et cinq en largeur,* and to inform you that we are at Florence, a city of Italy, and the capital of Tuscany. The latitude I cannot justly tell, but it is governed by a prince called Great Duke; an excellent place to employ all one's animal sensations in, but utterly contrary to one's rational powers. I have struck a medal upon myself: the device is thus ○, and the motto *Nihilissimo,* which I take in the most concise manner to contain a full account of my person, sentiments, occupations, and late glorious successes. If you choose to be annihilated too, you cannot do better than undertake this journey. Here you shall get up at twelve o'clock, breakfast till three, dine till five, sleep till six, drink cooling liquors till eight, go to the bridge[21] till ten, sup till two, and so sleep till twelve again.

> Labore fessi venimus ad larem nostrum,
> Desideratoque acquiescimus lecto:
> Hoc est, quod unum est, pro laboribus tantis.
> O quid solutis est beatius curis?[22]

We shall never come home again; a universal war is just upon the point of breaking out;[23] all outlets will be shut up. I shall be secure in

21. The Ponte S. Trinità, destroyed by the retreating German army 4 Aug. 1944. HW and Gray were living near it (*post* 4 Dec. 1740, N.S.). 'We are settled here with Mr Mann in a charming apartment; the river Arno runs under our windows, which we can fish out of. The sky is so serene, and the air so temperate, that one continues in the open air all night long in a slight nightgown without any danger; and the marble bridge is the resort of everybody, where they hear music, eat iced fruits, and sup by moonlight' (*Gray's Corr.* i. 167).

22. Catullus xxxi. 9–11, 7.

23. The rumours about France's assembling her fleet were confirmed by the sailing of four men-of-war from Brest 28 July, commanded by André, Chevalier de Nesmond; the rest of the squadron of eighteen ships under the Marquis d'Antin left Brest towards the end of August, and the squadron of fifteen ships at Toulon, under Gaspard de Goussé, Chevalier de Roche-Allard, left on 25 Aug. British interference with French transatlantic shipping was said to have been the reason. See *The Annals of Europe for . . . 1740,* 1742, pp. 393–400; *Daily Adv.* 22 Oct. 1740.

my nothingness, while you, that will be so absurd as to exist, will envy me. You don't tell me what proficiency you make in the noble science of defence.[24] Don't you start still at the sound of a gun? Have you learned to say 'Ha! ha!' and is your neck clothed with thunder?[25] Are your whiskers of a tolerable length? And have you got drunk yet with brandy and gunpowder? Adieu, noble captain!

T. Gray

From West, ca August 1740

Missing. Probably written at Tunbridge Wells, Kent; answered *post* 2 Oct. 1740, N.S. From Spence's letters to his mother, dated at Florence 29 Oct. and 7 Nov. 1740, N.S., and postmarked on arrival at London 8 NO. (O.S., 19 Nov., N.S.) and 15 NO. (O.S., 26 Nov., N.S.) it would appear that on the average it took three weeks for a letter written at Florence to reach London, and vice versa.

To West, Sunday 2 October 1740, N.S.

Reprinted from *Works* iv. 452–6.

Florence, Oct. 2, 1740, N.S.

Dear West,

T'OTHER night as we (you know who *we* are) were walking on the charming bridge, just before going to a wedding assembly, we said, 'Lord, I wish, just as we are got into the room, they would call us out, and say, West is arrived! We would make him dress instantly, and carry him back to the entertainment. How he would stare and wonder at a thousand things, that no longer strike us as odd!' Would not you? One agreed that you should have come directly by sea from Dover, and be set down at Leghorn, without setting foot in any other foreign town, and so land at *Us*, in all your first full amaze; for you are to know, that astonishment rubs off violently; we did not cry out 'Lord!' half so much at Rome as at Calais, which to this hour I look upon as one of the most surprising cities in the universe. My dear child, what if you were to take this little sea-jaunt? One would recommend Sir John Norris's convoy to you, but one should be laughed at now for supposing that he is

24. 'West had thoughts of entering the army' (Toynbee). See *post* 22 June 1741.

25. An allusion to Job xxxix. 19, 25. Cf. Gray's *Progress of Poesy*, l. 106.

ever to sail beyond Torbay.[1] The Italians take Torbay for an English town in the hands of the Spaniards, after the fashion of Gibraltar, and imagine 'tis a wonderful strong place, by our fleet's having retired from before it so often, and so often returned.

We went to this wedding that I told you of; 'twas a charming feast: a large palace finely illuminated; there were all the beauties, all the jewels, and all the sugar-plums of Florence. Servants loaded with great chargers full of comfits heap the tables with them, the women fall on with both hands, and stuff their pockets and every creek and corner about them. You would be as much amazed at us as at anything you saw: instead of being deep in the liberal arts, and being in the Gallery[2] every morning, as I thought of course to be sure I would be, we are in all the idlenesses and amusements of the town. For me, I am grown so lazy, and so tired of seeing sights, that, though I have been at Florence six months, I have not seen Leghorn, Pisa, Lucca, or Pistoia; nay, not so much as one of the Great Duke's villas.[3] I have contracted so great an aversion to inns and postchaises, and have so absolutely lost all curiosity, that, except the towns in the straight road to Great Britain, I shall scarce see a jot more of a foreign land; and trust me, when I return, I will not visit Welsh mountains, like Mr Williams.[4] After Mount Cenis, the Bocchetto,[5] the Giogo,[6] Radicofani, and the Appian Way, one has mighty little hunger after travelling. I shall be mighty apt to set up my staff at Hyde Park Corner: The alehouse-man there at Hercules's Pillars[7] was certainly returned from his travels into foreign parts.

1. On the Devonshire coast. Sir John Norris sailed 29 July, O.S., from Torbay, but in a few days was obliged to put back into harbour; he sailed again 4 Aug. and 22 Aug. but failed to get out of the Channel. His squadron, windbound for nearly six weeks, returned to Spithead 13 Sept. (*London Gazette* 23–26 Aug., 26–30 Aug., 13–16 Sept. 1740; *Daily Adv.* 1, 7, 25, 26, 29 Aug., 12, 15 Sept. 1740; GM 1740, x. 466–7; *ante* 31 July 1740, n. 12).

2. The Uffizi.

3. There were eight in the immediate vicinity of Florence. See Giuseppe Conti, *Firenze dopo i Medici*, Florence, 1921, pp. 99–104.

4. John Williams (*ante* 16 April 1740, N.S.).

5. La Bocchetta, a pass in the Ligurian Apennines, between Novi and Genoa. HW and Gray crossed it 20 Nov. 1739, N.S., on their way to Genoa (Gray's MS Journal 1739–1741, f. 9; *ante* 14 Dec. 1739, N.S.; *Gray's Corr.* i. 136).

6. Giogo della Scarperia in the Etruscan Apennines, 6 miles from Firenzuola. HW and Gray crossed it 16 Dec. 1739, N.S., on their way from Bologna to Florence (ibid. i. 134–5).

7. A tavern west of Hamilton Place, where Squire Western stopped on his arrival in London (Fielding, *Tom Jones* XVI. ii). It probably took its name from the more famous Hercules' Pillars in Fleet Street, mentioned by Pepys (*Diary, sub* 11 Oct. 1660, *et passim*) and by Wycherley in *The Plain Dealer* II. i (edn 1691, p. 31). See *London Past and Present* ii. 211.

Now I'll answer your questions.[8]

I have made no discoveries in ancient or modern arts. Mr Addison travelled through the poets, and not through Italy; for all his ideas are borrowed from the descriptions, and not from the reality. He saw places as they were, not as they are. I am very well acquainted with Doctor Cocchi;[9] he is a good sort of man, rather than a great man; he is a plain honest creature with quiet knowledge, but I dare say all the English have told you, he has a very particular understanding: I really don't believe they meant to impose on you, for they thought so. As to Bondelmonti,[10] he is much less; he is a low mimic; the brightest cast of his parts attains to the composition of a sonnet: he talks irreligion with English boys, sentiments with my sister,[11] and bad French with any one that will hear him. I will transcribe you a little song that he made t'other day; 'tis pretty enough; Gray turned it into Latin, and I into English; you will honour him highly by putting it into French, and Ashton into Greek. Here 'tis:

> Spesso amor sotto la forma
> D'amista ride, e s'asconde;
> Poi si mischia, e si confonde
> Con lo sdegno e col rancor.
>
> In pietade ei si trasforma,
> Par trastullo e par dispetto;
> Ma nel suo diverso aspetto,
> Sempre egli e l'istesso amor.

8. In West to HW ca August 1740, missing.

9. Antonio Cocchi (1695–1758), Florentine physician; Professore di Medicina Teorica, Pisa, 1726; Lettore di Anatomia e Filosofia Naturale nello Studio Fiorentino, 1731; Lettore di Anatomia e Maestro di Chirurgia nell' Arcispedale di S. Maria Nuova, Florence, 1745; F.R.S., 1735; HW's friend who attended him in his illness at Reggio (G. L. Targioni's 'Elogio di Antonio Cocchi' in *Serie di ritratti d'uomini illustri Toscani con gli elogj istorici dei medesimi*, Florence, 1766–73, vol. iv; *post* 22 June 1741, O.S.). Among HW's collection of tracts (now WSL) were Cocchi's *Lettera critica sopra un manoscritto in cera*, Florence, 1746; *Del Vitto Pitagorico*, Florence, 1743; *Le Lodi d'Isacco Newton, Poema del Signore Giovanni Tompson tradutto dall'*

Inglese in versi Toscani . . . dedicato all' illustriss. signore Orazio Mann, Florence, 1741. His *Dei Bagni di Pisa*, Florence, 1750, was also in HW's library (MS Cat. L.3.1). See also *ante* i. 10 n. 62.

10. Giuseppe Maria Buondelmonte (1713–57), Florentine nobleman, called 'Abate' from the ecclesiastical habit he wore. According to Litta, Buondelmonte was respected as a poet and orator; his poems are printed in Antonio Filippo Adami, *Poesie*, Florence, 1755. He made a prose translation of Pope's *Rape of the Lock* on which Andrea Bonducci based his translation in verse (1739). See Litta i, 'Buondelmonte di Firenze,' table xii. He appears in a conversation piece at Mann's house by Patch, now WSL.

11. Lady Walpole, HW's sister-in-law.

Risit[12] amicitiæ interdum velatus amictu,
    Et bene composita veste fefellit amor:
Mox iræ assumpsit cultus faciemque minantem,
    Inque odium versus, versus et in lacrymas:
Ludentem[13] fuge; nec lacrymanti aut crede furenti;
    Idem est dissimili semper in ore deus.

Love often in the comely mien
Of friendship fancies to be seen;
Soon again he shifts his dress,
And wears disdain and rancour's face.

To gentle pity then he changes;
Through wantonness, through piques he ranges;
But in whatever shape he move,
He's still himself, and still is love.

See how we trifle! But one can't pass one's youth too amusingly; for one must grow old, and that in England; two most serious circumstances, either of which makes people grey in the twinkling of a bed-staff;[14] for know you, there is not a country upon earth where there are so many old fools, and so few young ones.

Now I proceed in my answers.

I made but small collections, and have only bought some bronzes and medals, a few busts, and two or three pictures: One of my busts is to be mentioned; 'tis the famous Vespasian in touchstone,[15] reckoned the best in Rome except the Caracalla[16] of the Farnese:[17] I gave but

12. So Miss Berry. In Gray's own version which he sent to West, in Gray to West 21 April 1741, N.S., 'Lusit amicitiæ' (Gray's Corr. i. 183).

13. Corrected from Miss Berry's 'Sudentem.'

14. Toynbee traced the allusion to Thomas Shadwell's Virtuoso, I. i: 'Sir Samuel Hearty: Gad, I'll do't instantly, in the twinkling of a bed-staff' (edn 1676, p. 11).

15. A bust of Vespasian, with head of basalt and shoulders of agate marble, stood at the right of the fireplace in the Gallery at SH. It was sold SH xxiii. 73 for £220 10s. to William Beckford, through whose daughter it came into the possession of the Dukes of Hamilton. In 1882 it was sold to T. Agnew and Sons for £336 ('Des. of SH,' Works ii. 461, 465; Adolf Michaelis, An-

cient Marbles in Great Britain, Cambridge, 1882, pp. 68–9, 300; Hamilton Palace Collection, Illustrated Priced Catalogue, 1882, p. 31).

16. The bust of M. Aurelius Antoninus (Caracalla) (A.D. 186–217), now in the Museo Nazionale, Naples, No. 6033 (J. J. Bernoulli, Römische Ikonographie, Stuttgart, 1882–94, ii pt iii. 50; Pauly's Real-Encyclopädie der classischen Altertumswissenschaft, Stuttgart, 1894–, ii. 2439, sub Aurelius No. 46; Domenico Monaco, A Complete Handbook to the National Museum in Naples, 1883, p. 39).

17. HW is mistaken about the location of the Farnese collection, which was moved from Rome to Naples in 1734. See Catalogo del Museo Nazionale di Napoli, Naples, 1867, i. Preface.

twenty-two pounds for it at Cardinal Ottoboni's sale.[18] One of my medals is as great a curiosity: 'tis of Alexander Severus, with the amphitheatre in brass; this reverse is extant on medals of his,[19] but mine is a *medagliuncino,* or small medallion, and the only one with this reverse known in the world: 'Twas found by a peasant while I was in Rome, and sold by him for sixpence to an antiquarian, to whom I paid for it seven guineas and an half: but to virtuosi 'tis worth any sum.

As to Tartini's musical compositions,[20] ask Gray:[21] I know but little in music.

But for the Academy,[22] I am not of it, but frequently in company with it: 'tis all disjointed. Madam ———,[23] who, though a learned lady, has not lost her modesty and character, is extremely scandalized with the other two dames, especially with Moll Worthless,[24] who knows no bounds. She is at rivalry with Lady W[alpole] for a certain Mr ———,[25] whom perhaps you knew at Oxford. If you did not, I'll tell you: He is a grave young man by temper, and a rich one by constitution; a shallow creature by nature, but a wit by the grace of our women here, whom he deals with as of old with the Oxford toasts. He fell into sentiments with my Lady W[alpole] and was happy to catch her at Platonic love:

18. See *ante* 7 May 1740, N.S.

19. Struck in 223 A.D. on the restoration of the Coliseum. On the obverse a draped and cuirassed bust of M. Aurelius Severus Alexander (208–235), with the legend Imp. Cæs. M. Aur. Sev. Alexander Aug.; on the reverse the Coliseum. Mattingly lists three varieties of coins representing the Coliseum: bronze (No. 411 *sub* Severus Alexander), gold (No. 410), and silver (No. 33, with a slightly different legend and reverse). See Harold Mattingly, E. A. Sydenham, and C. H. V. Sutherland, *The Roman Imperial Coinage* iv pt ii (1938). 64, 73, 104, plate viii. No. 2. HW's medallion was among those which he gave to Lord Rockingham in Feb. 1772, in exchange for the Cellini bell. See HW to Mann 12 Feb. 1772.

20. Giuseppe Tartini (1692–1770), maestro di capella of S. Antonio, Padua, 1721–3, 1725–70, celebrated virtuoso and teacher of the violin. For a list of his works see Robert Eitner, *Biographisch-Bibliographisches Quellen-Lexikon der Musiker und Musikgelehrten,* Leipzig, 1900–4, ix. 356–8. His sonata known as the 'Devil's Trill' is still a favourite of violinists.

21. While in Italy Gray made a collection of the works of Arrigoni, Bernasconi, Farinelli, Galuppi, Hasse, Lampugnani, Latilla, Leo, Mazzoni, Pergolesi, Rinaldo di Capua, Sarro, Vinci, and others, bound in ten volumes (now wsl). See Mason, *Mem. Gray* 342, and C. F. Bell's 'Thomas Gray and the Fine Arts' in *Essays and Studies by Members of the English Association,* vol. xxx, 1944, pp. 50–81.

22. See *ante* 31 July 1740, N.S.

23. Lady Pomfret.

24. Lady Mary Wortley Montagu.

25. Perhaps George Pitt (1721–1803), of Stratfield-Say, Hants; M.P. Shaftesbury 1742–7, Dorset 1747–74; cr. (1776) Bn Rivers. He matriculated at Magdalen College, Oxford, 26 Sept. 1737; M.A. 1739. Lady Pomfret to Lady Hertford ca 5 Nov. 1740 (undated in *Hertford Corr.* ii. 159–61) calls 'Mr Pitt of Hampshire' a 'very agreeable young man,' and HW in notes on his letter to Mann 24 June 1742 says that while in Florence 'he had been in love with Lady Charlotte Fermor, second daughter of Lord Pomfret' and that he was 'very handsome, and Lady Mary Wortley Montagu had liked him extremely, when he was in Italy.'

but as she seldom stops there, the poor man will be frightened out of his senses, when she shall break the matter to him; for he never dreamt that her purposes were so naught. Lady Mary[26] is so far gone, that to get him from the mouth of her antagonist, she literally took him out to dance country dances last night at a formal ball, where there was no measure kept in laughing at her old, foul, tawdry, painted, plastered personage. She played at pharaoh two or three times at Princess Craon's,[27] where she cheats horse and foot. She is really entertaining: I have been reading her works, which she lends out in manuscript,[28] but they are too womanish; I like few of her performances. I forgot to tell you a good answer of Lady P[omfret] to Mr ——, who asked her if she did not approve Platonic love? 'Lord, Sir,' says she, 'I am sure any one that knows me, never heard that I had any love but one, and there sit two proofs of it'; pointing to her two daughters.[29]

So I have given you a sketch of our employments, and answered your questions, and will with pleasure as many more as you have about you.

Adieu! Was ever such a long letter? But 'tis nothing to what I shall have to say to you. I shall scold you for never telling us any news, public or private, no deaths, marriages, or mishaps; no account of new books: Oh, you are abominable! I could find in my heart to hate you, if I did not love you so well; but we will quarrel now, that we may be the better friends when we meet: there is no danger of that, is there? Good night, whether friend or foe! I am most sincerely

Yours,

Hor. Walpole

From West, Monday 10 November 1740, O.S.

Printed from MS now wsl.

Address: Al Illustrissimo Signor Il Signor Horazio Walpole, Signor Inglese a Firenze.

26. See HW to Conway 25 Sept. 1740, N.S.

27. Anne-Marguerite de Ligniville (ca 1687–1772), m. (1704) Marc de Beauvau, Prince de Craon, President of the Council of Regency to Francis II of Tuscany at Florence (La Chenaye-Desbois xii. 138; de Granges de Surgères, *Répertoire . . . de la Gazette de France*, Paris, 1902, i. 283). See HW to Conway 5 July 1740, N.S.

28. See *post* ca Jan. 1748, n. 40.

29. Lady Sophia Fermor (1721–45), m. (1744) John Carteret, 2d E. Granville, and Lady Charlotte Fermor (1725–62), m. (1746) Hon. William Finch, son of Daniel Finch, 7th E. of Winchilsea (Collins, *Peerage*, 1812, iii. 402, iv. 206). 'Lady Sophia is still, nay she must be, the beauty she was: Lady Charlotte is much improved, and is the cleverest girl in the world; speaks the purest Tuscan, like any Florentine' (HW to Conway 5 July 1740, N.S.).

Old Bond Street,[1] Nov. 10, 1740.

My dear Walpole,

I DID not long for the King's arrival[2] so much as I do for yours. Ashton never sees me but he tells me you are coming, and so he has prevented my writing two or three times. But now I mind him no longer, and I begin not to expect you till you have completed your two year. But, be that as it will, 'tis high time you should return, for, in the first place, you seem a little tired of seeing sights and in the next place you have a great inclination to represent Steyning,[3] and in the third place, you long prodigiously to see me and Miss Conway.[4] I beg Miss Conway's pardon for putting her so close to me, but I intended it merely to give this last reason for your coming home its proper weight, and besides, with all your kindness for me, I began to be a little doubtful whether you would think it worth while to come over purely to see me; and so upon this account I pressed Miss Conway's name into my assistance.

You and Gray have done Bondelmonte a great deal of honour by turning his Italian into Latin and English. I begun it in French, but miscarried—I begun thus:

L'amour c'est un vrai protée.

But I could not go on, for fear I should spoil Love in his French dress, and so make it too evident that he was not *sempre l'istesso*—by the by

1. 'I lived at the Temple till I was sick of it: I have just left it' (West to Gray, 'Bond Street, June 5, 1740,' *Gray's Corr.* i. 164).

2. George II left for Hanover 13 May 1740, O.S., and returned to London 13 Oct. (*Annals of Europe for . . . 1740*, 1742, pp. 257–8; GM 1740, x. 260, 522).

3. 'We hear from Steyning in Sussex that Hitch Younge, Esq., stands candidate for that borough at the ensuing [by] election . . . upon the interest of the friends of Horatio Walpole [HW's uncle] and Charles Eversfield, Esqrs, who have declared themselves candidates for the said borough at the next General Election' (*Daily Adv.* 18 Nov. 1740). A garbled account of this may have reached West. For HW's parliamentary career see *post* 4 Dec. 1740, N.S., n. 11.

4. Either the Hon. Anne Seymour Con-

way, HW's cousin, or her half-sister, the Hon. Jane Seymour Conway (see *ante* 29 Dec. 1737); probably the latter. That HW felt anything more than a cousinly affection for either of the sisters is unlikely. West's remark, however, has been coupled with a line ('While Seymour's look supplies the absent Nine') in a poem addressed to HW by John Whaley, to show HW's supposed sentimental attachment to Anne (see Toynbee's note on Whaley to HW 4 Dec. 1744 in Toynbee *Supp.* iii. 121). But in HW's copy (now in the Dyce Collection, Victoria and Albert Museum) of Whaley's *Collection of Poems*, 1745, in which the verses were printed (pp. 83–5), HW has identified the lady as 'Miss J. Conway.' Little is known of Jane Conway other than that she was uncommonly handsome, and seems at one time to have engaged the affections of the Prince of Wales.

Ashton translated this part into Greek—αἰεὶ αὐτότατός μεν ἔρως[4a]—but I believe he never begun it no more than I finished it.

The part of my last letter[5] you don't understand, I don't understand neither. I doubt not however but it had a meaning when I writ it. After that it is not my fault if my readers don't understand it.

What news have I to tell you? Humphrey Parsons[6] is Lord Mayor, and the Pope, the King of Prussia,[7] the Emperor,[8] and the Czarina[9] are all dead. Admiral Vernon's birthday has been kept all over the globe two or three times over—[10]

My dear Walpole, I have done. Everything I write is nonsense but only this, that I am ever

Yours entirely,

R. W.

To WEST, Sunday 4 December 1740, N.S.

Reprinted from *Works* iv. 456–8. Dated by Miss Berry: Nov. 1740. The correct date is determined by the reference to the flood in Florence on Saturday 3 Dec. 1740, N.S.

From Florence, Nov. [Dec. 4], 1740.

CHILD, I am going to let you see your shocking proceedings with us. On my conscience, I believe 'tis three months since you wrote to either Gray or me. If you had been ill, Ashton would have said so; and if you had been dead, the gazettes would have said it. If you had been angry,—but that's impossible; how can one quarrel with folks three thousand miles off? We are neither divines nor commentators, and consequently have not hated you on paper. 'Tis to show that my charity for you cannot be interrupted at this distance, that I write to

4a. MS reads ἀιει ἀυτοτατος μεν ἐρῶς.
5. West to HW ca Aug. 1740, missing.
6. Sir Humphrey Parsons (ca 1676–1741), twice Lord Mayor of London (1730–1, 1740–1). He succeeded George Heathcote 22 Oct. 1740 (GM 1740, x. 523).
7. Frederick William I (1688–1740), King of Prussia, 1713, d. 31 May 1740, N.S., at Berlin.
8. Charles VI (1685–1740), Emperor, 1711, d. 20 Oct. 1740, N.S., at Vienna.
9. Anne (1693–1740), Empress of Russia, 1730, d. 28 Oct. 1740, N.S., at St Petersburg.
10. 'Wednesday 12 [Nov. 1740, O.S.].

This being the brave Admiral Vernon's birthday, it was distinguished in a very extraordinary manner by ringing of bells and public dining in many places. . . . The day was celebrated also in most of the chief places of the kingdom, as also in Ireland, as was likewise the 1st instant in the borough of Southwark and other places, there being then some uncertainty whether that or the 12th was the anniversary of the birth of that great man' (*London Magazine* 1740, ix. 558; see also HW to Mann 9 Feb. 1758).

you; though I have nothing to say, for 'tis a bad time for small news; and when emperors and czarinas are dying all up and down Europe, one can't pretend to tell you of anything that happens within our sphere. Not but that we have our accidents too. If you have had a great wind in England,[1] we have had a great water at Florence.[2] We have been trying to set out every day, and pop upon you. . . .[3] It is fortunate that we stayed, for I don't know what had become of us! Yesterday, with violent rains, there came flouncing down from the mountains such a flood, that it floated the whole city. The jewellers on the Old Bridge removed their commodities, and in two hours after the bridge was cracked. The torrent broke down the quays, and drowned several coach-horses, which are kept here in stables under ground. We were moated into our house[4] all day, which is near the Arno, and had the miserable spectacles of the ruins that were washed along with the hurricane. There was a cart with two oxen not quite dead, and four men in it drowned: but what was ridiculous, there came tiding along a fat hay-cock, with a hen and her eggs, and a cat. The torrent is considerably abated; but we expect terrible news from the country, especially from Pisa, which stands so much lower and nearer the sea. There is a stone here, which when the water overflows, Pisa is entirely flooded. The water rose two ells yesterday above that stone. Judge!

For this last month we have passed our time but dully; all diversions silenced on the Emperor's death,[5] and everybody out of town. I have

1. 1 Nov. 1740, O.S. (*Hertford Corr.* ii. 185; see also GM 1740, x. 569).

2. 'We had here yesterday [3 Dec. 1740, N.S.] a very new and surprising scene, for the whole city of Florence was full of water. . . . Vast quantities of oil, wine, and wood were spoiled in the cellars, or carried down the Arno—whose unusual rise occasioned this inundation' (*Hertford Corr.* ii. 187–8; see also the contemporary accounts of Morozzi and Giovanni Berti in *Narrazioni istoriche delle più considerevoli inondazioni dell' Arno*, Florence, 1845, pp. 43–8; Antonio Zobi, *Storia civile della Toscana*, Florence, 1850–2, i. 214–17).

3. 'A line of the manuscript is here torn away' (Berry).

4. Mann had two houses in Florence at this time: the Casa Ambrogi (Mann to HW 17 June 1741, 27 Nov. 1742, N.S.), where HW and Gray were lodged, in the Via de' Bardi; and the Casa Manetti, Via S. Spirito 23/25, which Mann had leased 1 Aug.

1740, and where HW and Gray subsequently stayed (HW to Mann 4 Jan. 1745, 2 Oct. 1746, O.S.; Mann to HW 10 Sept. 1751, N.S.; Archivio di Stato di Firenze: *Decime Granducali: Giustificazioni di città dell' anno 1740*, No. 210). The Casa Ambrogi is described in *idem*, *Arroti della communità di Firenze dell' anno 1783*, No. 649 (information from Dott. Ferdinando Sartini of Florence). Alfredo Reumont in 'Il Principe e la Principessa di Craon . . . ,' *Archivio storico italiano*, 1877, III ser., xxv. 258, shows Mann's tenure of the Casa Ambrogi in the autumn of 1740. A note in BERRY (i. 154 n. 49) erroneously identifies the Casa Ambrogi as the Casa Manelli, and confuses the Casa Manetti with another house of the same name.

5. Charles VI d. 20 Oct., though his obsequies were not celebrated publicly at Florence until 16 Jan. 1741, N.S. (*Gray's Corr.* i. 180). He was succeeded by his

seen nothing but cards and dull pairs of cicisbeos. I have literally seen so much love and pharaoh since being here, that I believe I shall never love either again as long as I live. Then I am got into a horrid lazy way of a morning. I don't believe I should know seven o'clock in the morning again, if I was to see it. But I am returning to England, and shall grow very solemn and wise! Are you wise? Dear West, have pity on one, who have done nothing of gravity for these two years, and do laugh sometimes. We do nothing else, and have contracted such formidable ideas of the good people of England, that we are already nourishing great black eyebrows, and great black beards, and teasing our countenances into wrinkles. Then for the common talk of the times we are quite at a loss, and for the dress. You would oblige us extremely by forwarding to us the votes of the Houses, the King's speech,[6] and the magazines;[7] or if you had any such thing as a little book called the Foreigner's Guide through the City of London and the Liberties of Westminster;[8] or a Letter to a Freeholder; or the Political Companion:[9] then 'twould be an infinite obligation if you would neatly bandbox up a baby dressed after the newest Temple fashion[10] now in use at both playhouses. Alack-a-day! We shall just arrive in the tempest of elections![11]

As our departure depends entirely upon the weather, we cannot tell you to a day when we shall say, 'Dear West, how glad I am to see you!' and all the many questions and answers that we shall give and take. Would the day were come! Do but figure to yourself the journey we are to pass through first! But you can't conceive Alps, Apennines, Ital-

daughter, Maria Theresa, the wife of Francis II of Tuscany.

6. 18 Nov., O.S., on the opening of the seventh session of parliament.

7. *The Gentleman's Magazine* (1740, x. 562–3) and *The London Magazine* (1740, ix. 558–60), both of which carried the King's speech.

8. Cf. *The Foreigner's Guide: or Companion both for the Foreigner and Native, in their Tour through . . . . London and Westminster*, 1729, in English and French (BM Cat.).

9. Pamphlets with such titles flourished on the eve of a general election. HW is doubtless alluding to them in general and not to any particular pamphlets which these titles might fit.

10. HW is suggesting that a doll be sent

to him, dressed in the fashion current among the Temple beaux who frequented the playhouses. See also *post* ca Jan. 1748, n. 25.

11. Parliament was dissolved 27 April 1741. On 14 May 1741 HW was returned M.P. for Callington, for which he also sat in the next Parliament (1747–54). The manor of Callington, Cornwall, came into the Walpole family through Lady Walpole, HW's sister-in-law. HW was subsequently M.P. for Castle Rising 1754–7, King's Lynn 1757–68 (W. T. Lawrence, *Parliamentary Representation of Cornwall*, Truro [1925], pp. 316–19; C. S. Gilbert, *An Historical Survey of . . . Cornwall*, Plymouth Dock, 1817–20, i. 490; L. B. Namier, *Structure of Politics*, 1929, i. 178, ii. 375, n. 3).

ian inns and postchaises. I tremble at the thoughts. They were just sufferable while new and unknown, and as we met them by the way in coming to Florence, Rome, and Naples; but they are passed, and the mountains remain! Well, write to one in the interim; direct to me addressed to Monsieur Selwyn,[12] *chez Monsieur Alexandre, Rue St Apolline à Paris.* If Mr Alexandre is not there, the street is, and I believe that will be sufficient. Adieu, my dear child!

> Yours ever,
> Hor. Walpole

From West, ca January 1741

Missing. A letter, containing the first part of Act I of *Pausanias,* is implied in *post* 29 March 1741, O.S., *post* 10 May 1741, N.S.

To West, ca February 1741

Missing. Implied in *post* 29 March 1741, O.S.

From West, Sunday 29 March 1741, O.S.

Printed from MS now WSL.
For the *Pausanias* fragment, which is a part of this letter, see Appendix 6.

March 29, 1741.

My dear Walpole,

SINCE I had finished the first act, I send you now the rest of it. Whether I shall go on with it is to me a doubt. I find you all make the same objections to my style; but change my manner now I can't, for it would not be all of a piece, and to begin afresh goes against my stomach; so I believe I must e'en break it off, and bequeath it to my grandchildren to be finished, with other old pieces of family work.

12. Charles Selwin (ca 1716–94), Paris banker, at this time apparently a member of the Alexandre Alexander banking firm, Rue Saint-Apolline (*ante* 24 Sept. 1739, O.S.). In 1741 he went into business under his own name, appearing in the *Almanach Royal,* 1742, p. 365, among the 'Banquiers pour les traités et remises de place en place.' In 1749 he formed a partnership with his brother Richard, and in 1755 with Robert Foley. He apparently retired in 1763 (ibid. 1750, p. 371; 1756, p. 351; 1764, p. 440). See also Laurence Sterne, *Letters,* ed. L. P. Curtis, Oxford, 1935, p. 177, n. 3; HW to Miss Pitt 10 Dec. 1763; HW to Hertford 16 Dec. 1763; J. H. Jesse, *George Selwyn and His Contemporaries,* 1882, i. 38; GM 1794, lxiv pt ii. 865; Boswell's *Johnson,* ed. Hill and Powell, Oxford, 1934–, iv. 488.

I have another objection to it, and that is, the unlucky affair of an impeachment in the play. For, supposing the thing public, which it was never intended to be, every blockhead of the faction would swear Pausanias was Greek for Sir R[obert], though it may as well stand for Bolingbroke;[1] but the truth is, the Greek word signifies neither one, nor t'other, as you may find in Scapula,[2] Suidas,[3] and other lexicographers.

Since I have mentioned Sir R[obert], I might make you a compliment upon his late victories,[4] but you must not expect it; 'tis a national thing, and every Englishman was as much concerned in the success as you were; if ever Sir R[obert] triumphed, he did that day. He stood the trial, and came off with honour, with honour to himself, but with confusion to his adversaries. I am not versed enough in politics to judge of your father's administration, but 'tis very evident that no minister could have stood such an attack as he did, if his administration had been such as his enemies would represent it. In short, I believe, his enemies now repent what they've done most heartily, since, instead of hurting him, they have only confirmed him ten times stronger than ever he was.

Mr Chute's[5] reply to my Lady Countess[6] was good; nevertheless I must dissent about the Latin translation, not that I adore it any more than the original, but, I think, the Latin is to the full as far off from the extreme of Worst, as the French is from that of Best—I'll send you what came into my head, as I read them; if it will bear once reading, excuse it—

How can you doubt if the new King
Means what he writes, or feigns,

1. Bolingbroke was impeached for high treason on motion of Sir Robert Walpole 10 June 1715 (Cobbett, *Parl. Hist.* vii. 66, 128–37, 143, 214).

2. Johann Scapula (fl. 1572–9).

3. Suidas (fl. 970–1000), the Byzantine lexicographer. His account of Pausanias follows that of Thucydides.

4. On 13 Feb. 1741, O.S., a motion was introduced in both Houses of Parliament for Sir Robert's removal from 'his Majesty's presence and councils forever.' In the Commons the debate continued 'from eleven o'clock in the morning till past three the next morning,' but the motion was lost; in

the Lords the debate lasted eleven hours. See Cobbett, *Parl. Hist.* xi. 1085, 1215, 1242, 1303; for the debate see ibid. xi. 1047–1388; for Sir Robert's speech in his own defence see ibid. xi. 1284–1303.

5. John Chute (1701–76), of the Vyne; HW's correspondent. He was evidently in Florence at this time: see also Mann to HW 21 Aug. 1741 and Chute to HW 22 Aug. 1741 (both N.S.). The allusions in this paragraph cannot be explained, since they evidently refer to a missing letter (HW to West ca Feb. 1741).

6. Perhaps Lady Pomfret: see *ante* 2 Oct. 1740, N.S.

Since what his learned pen conceals,
His honest sword explains?[7]

I hear Mr Selwyn[8] is better, though he still keeps his chamber. I always loved him. There's a sweetness in his temper and a justness in his understanding that please me. Adieu, dear Sir, I have room for no more.

To West, Wednesday 10 May 1741, N.S.

Reprinted from *Works* iv. 458–60.

Reggio,[1] May 10, 1741, N.S.

Dear West,

I HAVE received the end of your first act, and now will tell you sincerely what I think of it. If I was not so pleased with the beginning as I usually am with your compositions, believe me the part of Pausanias has charmed me. There is all imaginable art joined with all requisite simplicity; and a simplicity, I think, much preferable to that in the scenes of Cleodora and Argilius. Forgive me, if I say they do not talk laconic but low English; in her, who is Persian too, there would admit more heroic. But for the whole part of Pausanias, 'tis great and well worked up, and the art that is seen seems to proceed from his head, not from the author's. As I am very desirous you should continue, so I own I wish you would improve or change the beginning: those who know you not so well as I do, would not wait with so much patience for the entrance of Pausanias. You see I am frank; and if I tell you I do not approve the first part, you may believe me as sincere when I tell you I admire the latter extremely.

My letter has an odd date. You would not expect I should be writing

---

7. Evidently an epigram on Frederick the Great (1712–86), who succeeded Frederick William I as King of Prussia 31 May 1740, N.S.

8. George Augustus Selwyn.

---

1. For the usual route from Florence to Reggio see Thomas Nugent, *The Grand Tour*, 2d edn, 1756, iii. 303, 423. HW and Gray, apparently in company with Chute and Whithed (see Mann to HW 9 May 1741, N.S.), planned to leave Florence 24 April, 'and not stop above a fortnight at any place in . . . [their] way' (Gray to West 21 April 1741, N.S., *Gray's Corr.* i. 181). Their route was to be: 'First to Bologna for a few days . . . next to Reggio, where is a fair . . . next to Venice by the 11th of May. . . . Then to Verona, so to Milan, so to Marseilles, so to Lyons, so to Paris' (ibid. 182). They reached Bologna (a two days' journey from Florence) ca 26 April, and stayed until ca 4 May. At Reggio, which they reached ca 5 May, HW and Gray quarrelled (see *ante* i. 9 n. 59). Gray, Chute, and Whithed must have left Reggio by 8 May in order to reach Venice by the 11th.

in such a dirty little place as Reggio: but the fair is charming; and here come all the nobility of Lombardy, and all the broken dialects of Genoa, Milan, Venice, Bologna, etc. You never heard such a ridiculous confusion of tongues. All the morning one goes to the fair undressed, as to the walks at Tunbridge: 'tis just in that manner, with lotteries, raffles, etc. After dinner all the company return in their coaches, and make a kind of *corso,* with the ducal family, who go to shops, where you talk to 'em, from thence to the opera,[2] in mask if you will, and afterwards to the *ridotto.*[3] This five nights in the week. Fridays there are masquerades, and Tuesdays balls at the Rivalta,[4] a villa of the Duke's.[5] In short, one diverts oneself. I pass most part of the opera in the Duchess's[6] box, who is extremely civil to me and extremely agreeable. A daughter of the Regent's,[7] that could please him, must be so. She is not young, though still handsome, but fat; but has given up her gallantries cheerfully, and in time, and lives easily with a dull husband, two dull sisters[8] of his, and a dull court. These two princesses are woefully ugly, old maids and rich. They might have been married often; but the old Duke[9] was whimsical and proud, and never would consent to any match for them, but left them much money, and pensions of three thousand pounds a year apiece. There was a design to have given the eldest to this King of Spain,[10] and the Duke was to have had the Parmesan Princess;[11] so that now he would have had Parma and Placentia,[12] joined to Modena, Reggio, Mirandola, and Massa. But there

2. The 'new' theatre (Teatro della cittadella dal luogo) which opened 29 April 1741. The 'old' theatre (Teatro Vecchio, 1645) burned down 6 March 1740 (*Enciclopedia italiana,* Rome, 1929–38, xxviii. 997; Andrea Balletti, *Storia di Reggio nell' Emilia,* 1925, p. 488; Spence to his mother 22 May 1741, N.S., Add. MSS Egerton 2234, f. 265).

3. The Président de Brosses from Modena 2 March 1740, N.S.: 'On va masqué à la cour, aux promenades, aux spectacles, aux ridotti, qui sont des galeries près de l'Opéra où l'on s'assemble pour jouer' (Charles de Brosses, *Lettres,* ed. R. Colomb, 1861, ii. 466).

4. The Palazzo ducale di Rivalta, built (1724–30) by Francis III of Modena, in imitation of Versailles (Balletti, op. cit. 482–4).

5. Francis III (Francesco Maria d'Este) (1698–1780), D. of Modena, 1737 (Isenburg,

Stammtafeln ii. table 125; Litta iii. 'Este' table xvii).

6. Charlotte-Aglaé de Bourbon d'Orléans (1700–61), m. (1720) Francesco Maria d'Este (Francis III of Modena) (La Chenaye-Desbois xv. 240).

7. Philippe de Bourbon (1674–1723), Duc d'Orléans (ibid. xv. 238–9).

8. Benedetta Ernestina (1697–1777) and Amalia Giuseppina (1699–1778), daughters of Rinaldo III of Modena (Isenburg, loc. cit.; Litta, loc. cit.; see also *Hertford Corr.* iii. 183).

9. Rinaldo III (Rinaldo d'Este) (1655–1737), D. of Modena, 1694.

10. Philip V (1683–1746), K. of Spain, 1700.

11. Elizabeth Farnese of Parma, Philip V's second wife.

12. Parma and Piacenza, which Elizabeth inherited upon the death without

being a Prince of Asturias,[13] the old Duke Rinaldo broke off the match, and said his daughter's children should not be younger brothers: and so they mope old virgins.

I am going from hence to Venice,[14] in a fright lest there be a war with France, and then I must drag myself through Germany. We have had an imperfect account of a sea-fight in America;[15] but we are so out of the way, that one can't be sure of it. Which way soever I return, I shall be soon in England, and there you will find me again as much as ever,

Yours,

H. W.

To Ashton, ca Saturday 27 May 1741, N.S.

Missing. *Post* 25 July 1741 mentions a letter from HW received seven weeks earlier. The letter probably reached London ca 6 June, O.S., and assuming that it took about three weeks for a letter to reach England, it might conjecturally be dated ca 27 May, N.S.

From West, Monday 22 June 1741, O.S.

Reprinted from *Works* iv. 460–1.

London, June 22, 1741.

Dear Walpole,

I HAVE received your letter from Reggio, of the 10th of May, and have heard since that you fell ill there, and are now recovered and returning to England through France. I heard the bad and good news both together, and so was afflicted and comforted both in a breath. My

issue (1731) of her uncle, Antonio Francesco Farnese, Duke of Parma and Piacenza (Litta iii. 'Farnese' table xxi).

13. Louis I (1707–24), son of Philip V of Spain by his first wife; Prince of Asturias, 1709. Upon the abdication of his father, 15 Jan. 1724, he succeeded as King of Spain, but d. 31 Aug. 1724.

14. In 'Short Notes' *ante* i. 10 HW states that he went to Venice with Lord Lincoln and Spence; but this is an error, as is shown by Spence to his mother 29 May and 9 June 1741, N.S., Add. MS Egerton 2234, ff. 264, 267 (see also Mann to HW 3 June and 10 June 1741, N.S., and *Hertford Corr.* iii. 203, 209, 221, 233). HW travelled with Lincoln and Spence from Venice to Paris, but evidently did not accurately recollect at what city he joined their party.

15. 'I was in hopes of sending you some tolerable assurances of a victory in America. It has been wrote by many from London, and is credited at Leghorne and at Genoa' (Mann to HW 2 May 1741, N.S.). The taking of Cartagena 1 April, ?N.S., was not officially confirmed until 17 May, O.S. (*Daily Adv.* 18 May 1741).

joy now has got the better, and I live in hopes of seeing you here again. The author of the first act of *Pausanias* desires his love to you, and, in return for your criticism, which seems so severe to him in some parts, and so prodigious favourable in others that if he were not acquainted with your unprejudiced way of thinking he should not know what to say to it, has ordered me to acquaint you with an accident that happened to him lately, on a little journey[1] he made. It seems, he had put all his writings, whether in prose or rhyme, into a little box, and carried them with him. Now, somebody imagining there was more in the box than there really was, has run away with them; and, though strict inquiry has been made, the said author has learnt nothing yet, either concerning the person suspected or the box. Since I am engaged in talking of this author, and as I know you have some little value for him, I beg leave to acquaint you with some particulars relating to him, which perhaps you will not be so averse to hear.

You must know then, that from his cradle upwards he was designed for the law,[2] for two reasons: first, as it was the profession which his father followed, and succeeded in, and consequently there was a likelihood of his gaining many friends in it; and secondly, upon account of his fortune, which was so inconsiderable that it was impossible for him to support himself without following some profession or other. Nevertheless, like a rattle as he is, he has hitherto fixed on no profession; and for the law in particular, upon trial he has found in himself a natural aversion to it. In the mean while, he has lost a great deal of time, to the great diminution of his narrow fortune and to the no little scandal of his friends and relations. At length, upon serious consideration, he has resolved that something was to be done, for that poetry and Pausanias would never be sufficient to maintain him. And what do you think he has resolved upon? Why, apprehending that a general war in Europe was approaching, and, therefore, that there might be some opportunity given, either of distinguishing himself or being knocked of the head; being convinced besides that there was little in life to make one over fond of it, he has chosen the army; and being told that it was a much cheaper way to procure a commission by the means of a friend than to buy one,[3] to do which he must strip himself of what fortune he has left,

1. West wrote to Ashton from Paris 8 May 1741, N.S. (now WSL) (*Gray-HW-West-Ashton Corr.* ii. 8). The duration and circumstances of his trip are not known.

2. West was admitted to the Inner Temple in 1732 or 1733 (*ante* ca 15 May 1739, N.S., n. 2).

3. The practice of selling commissions in the army was confirmed by royal warrant 36 Charles II (7 March 1684), and was not

he desired me to use what little interest I had with my friends to procure him what he wanted.

At first I objected to him the weakness of his constitution, which
might render him incapable of military service, and several other
things, but all to no purpose. He told me, he was neither knave nor
fool enough to run in debt, and that he must either abscond from
mankind, or do something to enable him to live as he would upon a
decent rank, and with dignity; and that what he chose was this.[4]

I perceived there was nothing to reply, so I submitted; and as I have
some sort of regard for the man, I promised him I would use what interest I had, and frankly told him I would venture to ask for him what
I should hardly ask for myself.

Excuse my freedom, dear Walpole, and whether I succeed or not,
assure yourself that I shall always be

Yours most affectionately,

R. WEST

From ASHTON, June–July 1741

Two letters missing; mentioned *post* 25 July 1741, O.S.

To ASHTON, July 1741

Missing. Enclosed in Anne Grosvenor to Ashton (missing), and mentioned *post*
25 July 1741. The letter probably reached London Wednesday 22 July or Saturday
25 July, and allowing three weeks for passage, it might conjecturally be dated ca 19
or 22 July, N.S. HW was at that time in Genoa, bound for England.

discontinued until 1871. The prices of
commissions have from time to time been
changed and re-adjusted by the Crown, as
the circumstances of the Service seemed to
demand. Major Henry Cope's commission,
for instance, was sold in 1721 for £900.
But in addition to purchase, commissions
were obtained through political influence,
a practice condemned by the Duke of
Argyll in the debate in the Lords on the
state of the army, 9 Dec. 1740: 'Preferments in the army, instead of being considered as proofs of merit, are looked on
only as badges of dependence; nor can anything be inferred from the promotion of
an officer but that he is, in some degree or
other, allied to some member of Parliament, or the leading voters of a borough'
(Cobbett, *Parl. Hist.* xi. 904; see also C. M.
Clode, *The Military Forces of the Crown*,
1869, i. 470–1, ii. 79, 607, *et passim*; Johnson's England, ed. A. S. Turberville, Oxford, 1933, i. 66).

4. 'The answer to this letter does not appear; but Mr West's increasing bad health
must probably have obliged him to drop
all thought of going into the army' (Berry).

From ASHTON, Saturday 25 July 1741, O.S.

Printed from MS now WSL. Misdated by Mitford (Add. MS. 32,562, ff. 210–12) 'Acton, July 5, 1741.' See *Gray-HW-West-Ashton Corr.* ii. 15–16.

Acton, July 25th, 1741.

My dearest Walpole,

SINCE the last letter[1] I received from you, which though it gave me the pleasure of your recovery did not however rid me from the fear of a relapse, I have not been able till this week to pick up one syllable relating to you—judge you what I have felt. An interval of seven weeks without one word of intelligence after so dangerous an indisposition in so remote a place, unattended, as I feared, with physician or friend. I went from Somerset House[2] to Downing Street[3] and from Downing Street to Somerset House—but still nothing. I would fain have persuaded poor Mrs Gr.[4] and myself that if anything ill had happened we must have heard.[5] But that was (at best) conjecture. It might be so, but my apprehensions would have it otherwise. So dexterously did we impose a cruel deceit upon ourselves by admitting no probability that would make for us and by swelling every possibility of the contrary into a demonstration. In short we feared and felt the worst. If one had told me you were actually dead it would have been no news to me. I had already attended you to the grave and was become as lifeless as if I had been laid there with you. I do solemnly protest to you that I would not feel again what I have done on this occasion, no, not for the inexpressible satisfaction of knowing the contrary. My senses were so benumbed with so long a concern that it was almost beyond the power of any pleasure to recall 'em. Dear Mrs Gr., I thank her, did all she could; I am infinitely obliged to her. She enclosed your letter[6] to me the moment she received it. I trembled when I opened hers, but

1. HW to Ashton ca 27 May 1741, N.S., missing.
2. At this time a royal palace, where Anne Grosvenor was Under Housekeeper (*ante* 28 May 1740, N.S., n. 17).
3. Sir Robert Walpole's residence. It is possible that Ashton was already living there as Sir Robert's chaplain (*post* 4 May 1742, n. 12).
4. Anne Grosvenor.
5. On 30 May 1741, N.S., Mann had written his brother Galfridus that HW 'had been ill of a cold at Reggio' but that

he 'was then much better, which he might tell Mr Oswald [George Oswald, Sir Robert Walpole's steward], in case by other means Sir Robert might be alarmed.' To avoid creating unnecessary anxiety in England, Mann decided not to visit HW at Reggio, since the departure of a diplomatic representative from Tuscany, even for a private visit, might be interpreted in London as an indication that HW's illness was extremely serious. See Mann to HW 30 May 1741, N.S.
6. HW to Ashton, July 1741, missing.

when I saw the jewel within I do not know or cannot tell you what I did. This is the third letter I have wrote to you since I had yours. My dear Walpole I speak sincerely to you. I would not for the world go over that time again which I have passed since you left England. I would not, I do assure you. I am like a man who has been tossed about a long winter's night in uneasy dreams. I have been dragged through rivers and thrown down precipices—oh it has been a weary night! Come dear Walpole and bring the day. I could say a thousand things to you, but I will think of nothing but yourself. Tell me, for God['s] sake, all your intended motions and let 'em be homeward all. Trifle not with a constitution which carries more lives in it than your own.

I have not been able to see Mrs Gr. since your letter; I will go on purpose next week to rejoice with her. Believe me I am much obliged to her.

West is *hic et ubique*—at Paris, at London,[7] in the country. I never see him. He talks of the army,[8] the law, and the ministry. He suspects some disagreement between you and ———.[9] I hope the broken bone will be stronger when set. Mrs ———[10] came to me in such a manner as makes me believe she knows the whole.

From WEST, April 1742

Missing. Written at Popes, near Hatfield, Herts, probably before 15 April 1742; mentioned *post* 4 May 1742. In the postscript to West to Ashton 15 April 1742 West says: 'My compliments to Walpole. I wish he would write and comfort the sick. 'Tis a Christian duty.' Ashton was at this time living at Lord Orford's house in Downing Street (n. 12 below).

To WEST, Tuesday 4 May 1742

Reprinted from *Works* iv. 462–3.

London, May 4, 1742.

Dear West,

YOUR letter[1] made me quite melancholy, till I came to the postscript of fine weather. Your so suddenly finding the benefit of it, makes me trust you will entirely recover your health[2] and spirits with

7. West to HW 22 June 1741, O.S., was written from London.

8. See *ante* 22 June 1741, O.S.

9. Gray.

10. Perhaps Gray's mother.

———

1. West to HW April 1742, missing.

2. West, who was troubled with a severe

the warm season: Nobody wishes it more than I: nobody has more reason, as few have known you so long.

Don't be afraid of your letters being dull. I don't deserve to be called your friend, if I were impatient at hearing your complaints. I do not desire you to suppress them till their causes cease; nor should I expect you to write cheerfully while you are ill. I never design to write any man's life as a stoic, and consequently should not desire him to furnish me with opportunities of assuring posterity what pains he took not to show any pain.

If you did amuse yourself with writing anything[3] in poetry, you know how pleased I should be to see it; but for encouraging you to it, d'ye see, 'tis an age most unpoetical! 'Tis even a test of wit, to dislike poetry; and though Pope has half a dozen old friends that he has preserved from the taste of last century, yet I assure you, the generality of readers are more diverted with any paltry prose answer to old Marlborough's secret history of Queen Mary's robes.[4] I do not think an author would be universally commended for any production in verse, unless it were an ode to the Secret Committee,[5] with rhymes of liberty and property, nation and administration.

cough, wrote to Gray in April: 'And now you must know that my body continues weak and enervate. And for my animal spirits, they are in perpetual fluctuation: some whole days I have no relish, no attention for anything; at other times I revive, and am capable of writing a long letter' (*Gray-HW-West-Ashton Corr.* ii. 32). West also sent Gray a Latin poem of eleven lines on his cough, beginning 'Ante omnes morbos importunissima tussis' (see West to Gray 4 April 1742, ibid. ii. 24).

3. West must have been working on his translation of Catullus, *Carm.* v and vii, which he sent to Gray in his last extant letter, that of 11 May (see *post* 8 Feb. 1747, n. 27).

4. Sarah Jennings (1660–1744), m. (1678) John Churchill, cr. (1702) D. of Marlborough; the intimate friend of Queen Anne until she was dismissed from the Household in 1711. HW refers to *An Account of the Conduct of the Dowager Duchess of Marlborough, from her first coming to Court, to the Year 1710. In a Letter from herself to My Lord ——*, written by Nathaniel Hooke (d. 1763) on behalf of the Duchess of Marlborough

(W. T. Lowndes, *Bibliographer's Manual*, 1864, iii. 1478; W. L. Cross, *History of Henry Fielding*, New Haven 1918, i. 360–1). It was published before 9 March, the date of Samuel Johnson's review in GM 1742, xii. 128–31. HW's copy was sold SH i. 18. The *Account* precipitated a pamphlet war, in which the Duchess was defended by Henry Fielding (GM 1742, xii. 224).

5. Following a series of defeats in the House of Commons throughout December 1741 and January 1742, Sir Robert Walpole was created Earl of Orford 6 Feb., and on 11 Feb. resigned his offices of first lord of the Treasury and chancellor of the Exchequer. On 29 March, following a motion by Lord Limerick, a Committee of Secrecy was appointed 'to inquire into the conduct of Robert Earl of Orford during the last ten years.' Its report was first read 13 May, and a further report was read 30 June, dealing with the payment of troops, the freedom of elections, 'the quantity as well as manner and consequence of issuing and receiving the public money, supposed to be employed for secret services of the State,' etc., etc. See HW to Mann 10 March, 24 March, 1 April 1742, *et passim*; Cobbett,

Wit itself is monopolized by politics; no laugh but would be ridiculous if it were not on one side or t'other. Thus Sandys[6] thinks he has spoken an epigram, when he crinkles up his nose, and lays a smart accent on *ways and means*.

We may indeed hope a little better now to the declining arts. The reconciliation between the royalties is finished, and £50,000 a year more added to the Heir Apparent's revenue.[7] He will have money now to tune up Glover,[8] and Thomson,[9] and Dodsley[10] again.

Et spes et ratio studiorum in Cæsare tantum.[11]

Ashton is much yours.[12] He has preached twice at Somerset Chapel[13] with the greatest applause. I do not mind his pleasing the generality, for you know they ran as much after Whitfield[14] as they could after

Parl. Hist. xii. 404–5, 448–590, 625–734, 788–827. Both reports were printed.

6. 'Samuel Sandys [(1695–1770), cr. (1743) Bn Sandys], a republican, raised on the fall of Sir R.W. to be chancellor of the Exchequer, then degraded to a peer and cofferer, and soon afterwards laid aside' (HW's note on HW to Mann 24 Dec. 1741; see also HW to Mann 9 Feb. 1742, O.S.).

7. On 17 Feb. Frederick, Prince of Wales, attended George II for the first time after having been forbidden to come to Court 10 Sept. 1737. On 29 April 1742 his allowance was increased from £50,000 per annum to £100,000, thus removing the principal cause of the difference between the King and the Prince of Wales. Pulteney negotiated the reconciliation, although Sir Robert Walpole had made an unsuccessful attempt to arrange it shortly before his resignation (Hist. MSS Comm., *Diary of the First Earl of Egmont*, 1920–3, iii. 253–5, 256, 264). For the reasons for the disagreement between the King and the Prince, see Sir George Young, *Poor Fred*, 1937; Hervey, *Memoirs* ii. 614–18, iii. 661–705, 756–845; Philip C. Yorke, *Life and Correspondence of Philip Yorke Earl of Hardwicke*, Cambridge, 1913, i. 162–82; Cobbett, *Parl. Hist.* ix. 1352–1454; *Diary of the First Earl of Egmont* ii. 352–6.

8. Richard Glover, West's cousin, and author of *Leonidas* (*ante* 18 April 1737). He was a protégé of the Prince, who once sent him £500 (Arthur S. Collins, *Author-*

ship in the Days of Johnson, 1927, pp. 167–8). For HW's low opinion of Glover see HW to Mann 8 March 1742.

9. James Thomson dedicated his poem *Liberty* (1735) and his tragedy *Agamemnon* (1737) to the Prince of Wales, but the dedications produced no patronage until Aug. 1737 when Thomson's friend, George Lyttelton (later Bn Lyttelton), became secretary to the Prince of Wales, and procured for Thomson a pension of £100 per annum. See Collins, op. cit. 156–8; Léon Morel, *James Thomson*, Paris, 1895, pp. 163–4; Hervey, *Memoirs* iii. 838.

10. Robert Dodsley printed the works of several of the Prince's protégés, and also pamphlets of the Opposition, which Frederick supported.

11. Juvenal, *Sat.* vii. 1.

12. Ashton was living in Downing Street with HW, in the capacity of 'chaplain to the Right Hon. the Earl of Orford' (*Daily Adv.* 19 June 1742). The fact of his living with HW is mentioned in HW to Pelham 17 May 1742, when HW asked Pelham to obtain for Ashton the Crown living of Aldingham, Lancs, worth £200 per annum. Ashton was appointed rector of Aldingham 7 June (*Daily Adv.* 9 June 1742), and was installed 12 July (*Vict. Co. Hist., Lancs*, 1906–14, viii. 327).

13. The Chapel Royal at Somerset House.

14. Whitefield after an absence of four weeks at Bristol returned 24 Feb. to London and had 'preached twice every day

Tillotson;[15] and I do not doubt but St Jude converted as many honourable women as St Paul. But I am sure you would approve his compositions, and admire them still more when you heard him deliver them. He will write to you himself next post, but is not mad enough with his fame to write you a sermon. Adieu, dear child! Write me the progress of your recovery,[16] and believe it will give me a sincere pleasure; for I am

Yours ever,

Hor. Walpole

since at the New Tabernacle, and intends to continue so doing for some time before he goes to Scotland and Ireland' (*Daily Adv.* 1 March 1742). In 1739 the churches began to refuse their pulpits to him and he took to open-air preaching. His audiences at times reached twenty thousand at Moorfields, Kennington Common, and Blackheath (John Gillies, *Memoirs of Rev. George Whitefield*, New Haven, 1834, p. 43).

15. John Tillotson (1630–94), Abp of Canterbury 1691–4.

16. 'Mr West died in less than a month from the date of this letter . . .' (Berry). He died of consumption, according to HW to Mann July 1742, which contains Ashton's elegy 'On the Death of Richard West, Esq.' The poem was reprinted in *The London Magazine* June 1742, xi. 305, with the title 'To the Memory of Richard West, Esq., who died at Popes in Hertfordshire, June 1, 1742, after a tedious and painful indisposition, in the 26th year of his age.' Gray's sonnet to West is well known. See also *Gray's Corr.* i. 213–14.

THE YALE EDITION

OF

HORACE WALPOLE'S

CORRESPONDENCE

EDITED BY W. S. LEWIS

VOLUME FOURTEEN

HORACE WALPOLE'S
CORRESPONDENCE

WITH

THOMAS GRAY

II

EDITED BY W. S. LEWIS

GEORGE L. LAM
AND
CHARLES H. BENNETT

NEW HAVEN
YALE UNIVERSITY PRESS
LONDON · GEOFFREY CUMBERLEGE · OXFORD UNIVERSITY PRESS
1948

TABLE OF CONTENTS

VOLUME II

LIST OF ILLUSTRATIONS

VOLUME II

Grateful acknowledgment is made to the British Museum, the National Portrait Gallery, Pembroke College, Cambridge, and the Toledo Museum of Art, for permission to reproduce illustrations listed here.

From GRAY, Thursday 7 November 1745

Missing. Gray wrote to Wharton 14 Nov. 1745 (*Gray's Corr.* i. 226): 'I wrote a note [to HW] the night I came [to London] and immediately received a very civil answer.'

To GRAY, ca Friday 8 November 1745

Missing: HW's answer to the preceding.

From GRAY, Monday 3 February 1746

Printed from MS in Waller Collection.

Cambridge,[1] February 3, 1746.

Dear Sir,

YOU are so good to inquire after my usual time of coming to town: it is at a season when even you, the perpetual friend of London, will I fear hardly be in it, the middle of June,[2] and I commonly return hither in September, a month when I may more probably find you at home.[3] I do not imagine that anything farther can be done with Mr Turner,[4] but you only, who saw the manner of his promising, can judge of that. What he calls the College is the Master[5] and his party of Fellows, among which he himself has been reckoned latterly. But, I know, it must be from some other influence than that of the Master merely, if he vote with them; which, if Mr Brudenel[6] could stand,

1. Gray, who had resumed residence at Peterhouse as a fellow-commoner, had proceeded to the degree of Bachelor of Laws 16 Dec. 1743 (*Gray's Corr.* iii. 1203–6). Except for his customary summer holidays he resided at Cambridge until his death (see 'Chronological Table,' *Gray's Corr.*).

2. Gray left for London 13 July 1746, and returned 10 Oct. ('Chronological Table,' *Gray's Corr.*).

3. Early in August 1746, HW rented a house at Windsor (see *post* 15 Dec. 1746).

4. Shallet Turner, Fellow of Peterhouse. 'What follows evidently refers to a fellowship election at Peterhouse' (*Gray's Corr.* i. 228, n. 2).

5. John Whalley (ca 1699–1748), D.D., Master of Peterhouse 1733–48; Regius Professor of Divinity 1742–8 (Venn, *Alumni Cantab.*).

6. George Bridges Brudenell (1725–1801) (MONTAGU i. 184). He was a friend of the Earl of Lincoln, HW's travelling companion on his return journey from Italy.

might very likely be made use of (as he is nearly related to several people of condition),[7] but he is disqualified at present[8] in every sense. 'Tis likely indeed he is intended for next year, and Mr Turner has had some application made already, by his knowing anything about him; but he mistakes the time.

Our defeat[9] to be sure is a rueful affair for the honour of the troops, but the Duke is gone,[10] it seems, with the rapidity of a cannon-bullet to undefeat us again. The common people in town at least know how to be afraid, but we are such *uncommon* people here as to have no more sense of danger than if the battle had been fought when and where the Battle of Cannæ was. The perception of these calamities and of their consequences, that we are supposed to get from books, is so faintly impressed that we talk of war, famine, and pestilence with no more apprehension than of a broken head, or of a coach overturned between York and Edinburgh. I heard three people, sensible middle-aged men (when the Scotch were said to be at Stamford, and actually were at Derby),[11] talking of hiring a chaise to go to Caxton[12] (a place in the high road) to see the Pretender and the Highlanders as they passed.

I can say no more for Mr Pope (for what you keep in reserve may be worse than all the rest). It is natural to wish the finest writer, one of them, we ever had should be an honest man. It is for the interest even of that virtue whose friend he professed himself, and whose beauties he sung, that he should not be found a dirty animal.[13] But however this is

7. Brudenell's father, James (d. 1746), of Ayston, Rutland, M.P., was the younger brother of George, 3d E. of Cardigan, and the uncle of George (1712–90), 4th E. of Cardigan, cr. (1766) D. of Montagu.

8. Brudenell was admitted 7 April 1743 a pensioner at Peterhouse, and consequently was not eligible for a fellowship until he became a resident B.A. His family, however, probably pressed for an exception, but without success. The Probationer Fellow of Peterhouse who was elected at this time, and confirmed Foundation Fellow 14 April 1747, was Pyers Libanus (*Gray's Corr.* i. 228, n. 2).

9. By the Young Pretender at Falkirk 17 Jan. 1746. See *London Gazette* 23 Jan. 1746; GM 1746, xvi. 27–8, 41–2; HW to Mann 28 Jan. 1746; 'Itinerary of Prince Charles Edward Stuart,' ed. W. B. Blaikie, *Scottish History Society* xxiii, Edinburgh, 1897, p. 37.

10. William Augustus (1721–65), D. of Cumberland, George II's younger son, left London for Edinburgh 25 Jan., to assume the command of the British forces (*London Gazette* 21–25 Jan., 5 Feb. 1746; Evan Charteris, *William Augustus Duke of Cumberland*, 1913, pp. 246–8).

11. After the surrender of Carlisle 14 Nov. 1745, the rebels resolved (18 Nov.) 'to march through Lancashire towards London.' They reached Manchester 30 Nov. and Derby 4 Dec. The Duke of Cumberland's forces at Meriden Common and Coventry frightened them into retreating northwards 6 Dec. (*London Gazette* 19–26 Nov., 6–9 Dec. 1745; 'Itinerary,' ed. Blaikie, 26–30).

12. Nine miles west of Cambridge.

13. An allusion to Pope's alleged double-dealing in his savage lines on 'Atossa' (which, beginning with the edition of 1751, appeared in *Moral Essays* ii. 115–50), first published at about this time (listed in

Mr Warburton's[14] business, not mine, who may scribble his pen to the stumps and all in vain, if these facts are so. It is not from what he told me about himself[15] that I thought well of him, but from a humanity and goodness of heart, ay, and greatness of mind, that runs through his private correspondence,[16] not less apparent than are a thousand little vanities and weaknesses mixed with those good qualities, for nobody ever took him for a philosopher.

If you know anything of Mr Mann's state of health and happiness, or the motions of Mr Chute homewards,[17] it will be a particular favour to inform me of them, as I have not heard this half year from them. I am

Sincerely yours,

T. Gray

Daily Adv. 12 Feb. 1746) as *Verses upon the late D——ss of M——*, with a note stating that 'the D——ss gave Mr P. £1000 to suppress' the lines. We are indebted to Mr F. W. Bateson for sending us Cole's report of HW's version of the story, inscribed in Cole's copy of Pope's *Works* (lately *penes* B. H. Newdigate, Boars Hill, Oxford): 'The following verses [i.e., the lines on 'Atossa'], made by Mr Pope upon Sarah late Duchess of Marlborough, and shown to her by one who was employed by him for that purpose, had such an effect upon her that she sent him a present of a thousand pounds, upon which he never printed them; but they were found in his study after his death. It is moreover said that he showed them alternately to the Duchesses of Buckingham and Marlborough, and pretended that they were designed [?for] the different character to whom he at that time showed them. They are authentic and I had them from the Hon. Horatio Walpole, Esq., 3d son to the late Earl of Orford, 1745.' A briefer version of the same story is given in HW's 'Reminiscences,' *Works* iv. 318.

Later gossip tended to accept the rumour of bribery as a fact, as well as to assume unquestioningly that the lines were intended for the Duchess of Marlborough. C. W. Dilke, however, in *The Papers of a Critic* (1875, i. 166–8, 226–33, 269–87),

undertook Pope's defence, and, taking up the hints dropped by both HW and Joseph Warton, attempted to prove that it was Katherine, Duchess of Buckingham, whom Pope was attacking. Mr Bateson accepts this theory, and supports it with new evidence, in an Appendix to the forthcoming third volume of the Twickenham edition of Pope (information from Mr Bateson and Mr Maynard Mack).

14. William Warburton (1698–1779), Bp of Gloucester 1759–79, Pope's literary executor. Gray refers to Warburton's projected edition of Pope's works, published 1751.

15. The date of Gray's interview with Pope is not known. It is possible that it was arranged by Spence after Gray's return from Italy, while he was staying in London.

16. Both Curll's edition of Pope's *Literary Correspondence*, 3 vols, and Pope's own edition (*Letters of Mr Pope, and Several Eminent Persons*, 2 vols) were published in 1735.

17. Chute and Whithed left Florence 26 May, having been delayed by Chute's gout (Mann to HW 24 May, 31 May 1746, N.S.). HW saw them in London during the week of 22–28 Sept. 1746, shortly after their arrival from abroad (HW to Mann 2 Oct. 1746, O.S.).

To Gray, March 1746

Missing. Implied in *post* 28 March 1746.

From Gray, Friday 28 March 1746

Printed from MS in Waller Collection.
Dated in part by the postmark. The date of the year rests on the assumption that Gray refers to George Bridges Brudenell's candidature for a fellowship at Peterhouse (*ante* 3 Feb. 1746), and that 'T.' stands for Shallet Turner.
Address: To the Honourable Horace Walpole Esq. at his house in Arlington Street,[1] Westminster. *Postmark:* ROYSTON 29 MR.

[Cambridge, March 28, 1746.]

Dear Sir,

I HAVE expected some time what you tell me.[2] If T.[3] can be prevailed upon to stay away it is all I desire,[4] for he is mistaken in imagining that will leave still an equality among the Fellows. It is all an idle tale the Master for his own interest would propagate about the party of his antagonists. Whatever some of the people who give us their vote may have been, I may confidently affirm no one so young as my friend[5] can be more rationally and zealously well-affected to the government[6] than he. The hurry I write in does not permit to return you the thanks I ought for your steadfastness and resolution in obliging me. I am

Yours sincerely,

T. Gray

1. Later No. 5 Arlington Street, where HW lived from 1742 until 1779 (see HW to Mann 1 Nov. 1742, O.S., and HW to Lady Ossory 14 Oct. 1779).
2. In HW to Gray March 1746, missing.
3. Presumably Shallet Turner. It is assumed that Gray is again referring to the candidature of George Brudenell. For a suggestion that Henry Tuthill is the 'young friend' referred to, see *Gray's Corr.* i. 231, n. 3, iii. 1206–10.
4. Turner was of Whalley's faction, opposed to Brudenell, and thus his abstaining

from voting would have reduced the opposition.
5. Brudenell was twenty.
6. The fact that Brudenell had Jacobite connections may have hindered his election. His first cousin, Charlotte Maria Livingston, Countess of Newburgh, had married as her second husband the attainted 5th Earl of Derwentwater who was beheaded 8 Dec. 1746 (*post* Jan. 1747, n. 11). Another Jacobite cousin was John Middleton (1683–1746), titular 2d E. of Monmouth.

To Gray, April–June 1746

Missing. Mentioned *post* 7 July 1746.

From Gray, Monday 7 July ?1746

Printed from MS in the Charles Roberts Autograph Collection, presented to Haverford College in 1902. The date of the year is conjectural. Gray left Cambridge ca Monday 13 July ('Chronological Table,' *Gray's Corr.*).

Endorsed by Pinkerton:[1] 'Original letter from Mr Gray, the poet, to Mr Walpole. Given me by Mr W.'

Cambridge, July 7 [?1746].

My dear Sir,

I COULD make you abundance of excuses, as indeed I have reason, but they would be bad and false ones, such as my respect for you will not permit me to use. Attribute then this long interval of silence to whatever motive you please besides; only don't imagine it neglect, or want of sensibility to the many expressions of kindness you bestowed upon me in your last letter. My sentiments are nothing altered since that time, however tardy I may have been in telling you so. I well remember how little you love letters, when all the materials are drawn out of oneself; yet such mine must have been from a place where nothing ever happens but trifles that it would be mere impertinence to think of entertaining you with. However I am apt to suspect you have been a little angry, for Dr Middleton,[2] though often with you in town, did not bring me the least compliment to show you remembered me. Do you mean to continue so, or shall you see me the less willingly next week, when I mean to call at your door some morning? I hope you are still in town.[3] Believe me, dear Sir,

Very sincerely yours,

T. Gray

1. John Pinkerton (1758–1826), Scottish antiquary and historian; HW's correspondent.

2. Conyers Middleton (1683–1750), D.D., Fellow of Trinity College, Cambridge, 1706; Librarian of the Cambridge University Library 1721; HW's correspondent.

3. HW wrote to Henry Fox 19 July 1746 from Mistley Hall, Essex, the seat of Richard Rigby, secretary to the Duke of Bedford (MONTAGU i. 14). When he left London is not known.

From GRAY, Monday 20 October 1746

Printed from MS in Waller Collection.
Dated by Mason: 1746.

Camb[ridge], Oct. 20 [1746].

My dear Sir,

I FOUND (as soon as I got hither) a very kind letter from Mr Chute,[1] from whence I have reason to hope we may all meet in town about a week hence.[2] You have probably been there since I left you, and consequently have seen the Mr Barry[3] you desired some account of; yet as I am not certain of this, and should be glad to know whether we agree about him, I will nevertheless tell you what he is, and the impression he made upon me.[4] He is upwards of six foot in height, well and proportionably made, treads well, and knows what to do with his limbs; in short a noble graceful figure. I can say nothing of his face but that it was all black, with a wide mouth and good eyes. His voice is of a clear and pleasing tone, something like Delane's, but not so deep-mouthed, not so like a passing-bell. When high-strained, it is apt to crack a little and be hoarse, but in its common pitch, and when it sinks into any softer passion, particularly expressive and touching. In the first scenes, especially where he recounts to the Senate the progress of his love, and the means he used to win Desdemona, he was quite mistaken, and I took a pique against him: instead of a cool narration he flew into a rant of voice and action, as though he were relating the circumstances of a battle that was fought yesterday. I expected nothing more from him,

1. Missing. Gray received Chute's letter 10 Oct. and answered it on the 12th (*Gray's Corr.* i. 248–9.

2. HW was living at Windsor (*post* 15 Dec. 1746) where he spent 'the greatest part of every week,' with frequent 'jaunts to town' (HW to Mann 21 Aug. 1746, O.S.).

3. Spranger Barry (1719–77), the Dublin actor, who made his London début as Othello at Drury Lane 4 Oct. (*Daily Adv.* 1 Oct. 1746).

4. Contemporary witnesses bear out Gray's favourable criticism. There appeared in the *Daily Advertiser* 7 Oct. 1746 a letter by an 'impartial admirer, A.B.,' who comments: 'Your attitudes were often masterly, particularly where you kneel, and in the bed scene (which from the elegance and grandeur of your figure seem[s] to me inimitable by any other actor at present on the stage), your gait and deportment were easy, natural, and graceful; but you were too frequent in your bows; your voice is such as the present age hath not heard in any other actor. . . . Therefore it must be your own fault if you are not the greatest player in time that this nation has seen.'

but was deceived: in the scenes of rage and jealousy he was seldom inferior to Quin; in the parts of tenderness and sorrow far above him. These latter seem to be his peculiarly: his action is not very various, but rarely improper, or without dignity, and some of his attitudes are really fine. He is not perfect to be sure, but I think may make a better player than any now on the stage in a little while. However to see a man in one character, and but once, is not sufficient, so I rather ask your opinion by this, than give you mine.

I annex (as you desired) another ode.[5] All it pretends to with you is, that it is mine, and that you never saw it before, and that it is not so long as t'other.[6]

> Lo, where the rosy-bosomed hours,
> Fair Venus' train, appear,
> Disclose the long-expecting flowers,
> And wake the purple year!
> The Attic warbler pours her throat
> Responsive to the cuckoo's note,
> The untaught harmony of spring:
> While whisp'ring pleasure as they fly
> Cool zephyrs through the clear blue sky
> Their gathered fragrance fling.
>   Where'er the oak's thick branches stretch
> A broader browner shade;
> Where'er the rude and moss-grown beech
> O'ercanopies the glade;[7]
> Beside some water's rushy brink
> With me the muse shall sit, and think
> (At ease reclined in rustic state)
> How vain the ardour of the crowd,
> How low, how indigent the proud,
> How little are the great![8]

5. 'Ode on the Spring,' originally called 'Noontide, an Ode.' Gray enclosed it in the letter he wrote to West (not knowing that he was already dead) ca 3 June 1742 (*Gray's Corr*. i. 213, 250).

6. *An Ode on a Distant Prospect of Eton College* (*post* ca 15 June 1747), which Gray sent to HW before 3 Oct., since a copy was sent by HW to Conway in his letter of 3 Oct. 1746.

7.   '—— a bank [. . .]
      O'ercanopied with luscious woodbine—
      Shakesp: Mids: Night's Dream' (Gray's
         marginal note).

The reference is to Act II, Scene i, lines 249–51.

8. In the 1768 edn of Gray's *Poems* the lines were changed to:
      'How low, how little are the proud,
      How indigent the great!'

Still is the toiling hand of care:
The panting herds repose.
Yet hark, how through the peopled air
The busy murmur glows!
The insect-youth are on the wing
Eager to taste the honeyed spring,
And float amid the liquid noon:9
Some lightly o'er the current skim,
Some show their gaily-gilded trim
Quick-glancing to the sun.

To contemplation's sober eye
Such is the race of man:
And they that creep, and they that fly,
Shall end where they began.
Alike the busy and the gay
But flutter through life's little day,
In fortune's varying colours dressed:
Brushed by the hand of rough mischance,
Or chilled by age, their airy dance
They leave, in dust to rest.

Methinks I hear in accents low
The sportive kind reply.
Poor moralist! and what are thou?
A solitary fly!
Thy joys no glittering female meets,
No hive hast thou of hoarded sweets,
No painted plumage to display:
On hasty wings thy youth is flown,
Thy sun is set; thy spring is gone:
We frolic, while 'tis May.

My compliments to Ashton.10 Adieu, I am

Sincerely yours,

T. G.

9. 'Nare per æstatem liquidam. Virg.' (Gray's marginal note). The reference is to *Georg.* iv. 59.

10. Ashton, through the influence of Sir Robert Walpole, was as early as 10 Dec. 1745 Fellow of Eton College (see letter of 'old' Horace Walpole to Edward Weston, *Etoniana* 1 May 1925, No. 38, p. 607). Ashton was perhaps in residence (he preached in Eton Chapel 10 Aug., see Montagu i. 44), and since HW was living at Windsor he was Ashton's neighbour.

crowd of dramatical performances coming upon the stage.[11] Agrippina[12] can stay very well, she thanks you, and be damned at leisure. I
hope in God you have not mentioned or showed to anybody that scene
(for, trusting in its badness, I forgot to caution you concerning it), but
I heard the other day that I was writing a play, and was told the name
of it, which nobody here could know, I'm sure. The employment[13] you
propose to me much better suits my inclination. But I much fear our
joint stock would hardly compose a small volume; what I have is less
considerable than you would imagine, and of that little we should not
be willing to publish all. There is an epistle *Ad Amicos*[14] (that is, to us
all at Cambridge) in English, of above fourscore lines;[15] the thoughts
are taken from Tibullus and from a letter of Mr Pope's in prose.[16] It
begins

> While you, where Camus rolls his sedgy tide, etc.[17]

 2. An imitation of Horace,[18] *Trojani belli scriptorum,* etc., about
120 lines, wrote to me. Begins

> While haply you (or haply not at all)
> Hear the grave pleadings in the Lawyers' Hall, etc.[19]

11. The newspapers carried advertise-
ments of Drury Lane, Haymarket, Good-
man's Fields, the 'New Theatre in James
Street, near the Haymarket,' and the 'Cole-
Hole' in Red Lion Street, Holborn. See
Daily Adv. 13 Jan.—8 Feb. 1747.

12. Gray's tragedy (*ante* 15 Dec. 1746).

13. A book of Gray's and West's poems.
In Gray's Commonplace Books (see below)
at Pembroke College there are transcripts
of ten of West's poems, both Latin and
English. The text of Gray's transcripts differs from the text of the poems as printed
by Mason. It has been suggested (*Gray's
Corr.* iii. 1199–1200) that Gray made corrections and improvements, and that Mason printed Gray's version of the poems.

14. Written at Oxford during West's illness, and sent in West to Gray 4 July 1737
(*Gray's Corr.* i. 61–4). First printed by Mason, *Mem. Gray* 18–22.

15. I.e., 86 lines.

16. 'Do you remember Elegy 5th, Book
the 3d, of Tibullus, *Vos tenet,* etc. and do

you remember a letter of Mr Pope's, in
sickness, to Mr Steele [Pope to Steele 15
July 1712]? This melancholy elegy and this
melancholy letter I turned into a more
melancholy epistle of my own, during my
sickness, in the way of imitation; and this
I send to you and my friends at Cambridge,
not to divert them, for it cannot, but
merely to show them how sincere I was
when sick' (West to Gray 4 July 1737,
Gray's Corr. i. 61).

17. So in Gray's Commonplace Books i.
91 (lines 1–32; lines 33–86, ibid. i. 104). In
Mason, *Mem. Gray* 18: 'Yes, happy youths,
on Camus' sedgy side.' See Tovey, *Gray and
His Friends* 95–8; *Gray's Corr.* iii. 1199.

18. *Epist.* I. ii. Dated by Gray in his Commonplace Books i. 273, 'Fav. from Epsome,
before I went to France, in 1739' (*Gray's
Corr.* i. 95–9). First printed in Tovey, *Gray
and His Friends* 119–23.

19. Westminster Hall (*Gray's Corr.* i.
164).

3. A translation from Propertius L[iber] III. El[egia] xv,[20] 50 lines.[21] Begins

Now prostrate, Bacchus, at thy shrine I bend, etc.

4. An elegy, Latin.[22] 34 lines. Begins, *Quod mihi tam gratæ* etc.

5. Another, sent to Florence.[23] 36 lines. *Ergo desidiæ videor*, etc.

6, 7, 8, 9, 10, 11. Translation from Posidippus,[24] an epigram. Some lines on the hard winter.[25] Long verse. On himself, a little before his death.[26] Long verse. Two imitations of Catullus' *Basia*.[27] English. A little ode of five stanzas, to the spring.[28]

This is all I can anywhere find. You, I imagine, may have a good deal more. I should not care how unwise the ordinary sort of readers might think my affection for him, provided those few that ever loved anybody, or judged of anything rightly, might from such little remains be moved to consider what he would have been, and to wish that heaven had granted him a longer life and a mind more at ease. I can't help fancying that if you could find out Mrs West, and ask her for his papers of that kind[29] (Ashton might do it in your name), she would be ready

20. Propertius III. xvii ('Ad Bacchum'). Some early editions, as Leyden, 1603, and Utrecht, 1680, number the elegy III. xvi, but no edition giving it as III. xv has been found. Sent in *ante* 21 June 1739, O.S.; printed in Appendix 3.

21. 'Sent to me at Rheims' (Gray).

22. Written at Epsom and sent to Gray at Cornhill (where he was staying with his father) in West to Gray 17 Sept. 1738 (*Gray's Corr.* i. 91–2). First printed by Mason, *Mem. Gray* 38–9.

23. Dated by Gray in his Commonplace Books, 'Fav. sent from London to Florence, April, 1740' (*Gray's Corr.* i. 151). The verses were printed by Mason, *Mem. Gray* 76–7, with the note, 'The letter which accompanied this little elegy is not extant. Probably it was only enclosed in one to Mr Walpole.'

24. *Anthol. Græc.* vii. 170. West's translation begins 'Perspicui puerum ludentem.' It was entered by Gray in his copy of *Anthol. Græc.*, ed. Stephanus, Paris, 1566, p. 220, with the comment, 'Descriptio pulcherrima et quæ tenuem illum græcorum spiritum mirifice sapit' (see Mason, *Mem. Gray* 27). Written at Oxford and sent in

West to Gray (?)2 Dec. 1737 (*Gray's Corr.* i. 70–1).

25. Twenty-one lines, beginning, 'Ipse Pater Thamisinus' (see *ante* 23 Jan. 1740, O.S., n. 1).

26. Perhaps West's poem on his cough, which, like 'Ipse Pater Thamisinus,' is in Latin hexameters ('long verse') (see *ante* 4 May 1742, n. 2).

27. *Carm.* v and vii ('Ad Lesbiam'), beginning, 'Lesbia, let us' and 'You ask how often you must kiss.' Written at Popes, and dated by Gray in his Commonplace Books, 'Fav. wrote, May 11, 1742. He died the first of June following.' Sent in West to Gray 11 May 1742, West's last extant letter (*Gray's Corr.* i. 203). Printed by Tovey, *Gray and His Friends* 167–8.

28. It begins, 'Dear Gray, that always in my heart.' Written at Popes, and sent in West to Gray 5 May 1742. Printed by Mason, *Memoirs* 147–8. For variants in Gray's Commonplace Books see *Gray's Corr.* iii. 1200; Tovey, *Gray and His Friends* 165–6.

29. HW acquired at some unknown date a number of MS verses by West (now wsl), both Latin and English, not mentioned in Gray's list. It may be that, in accordance

enough to part with them, and we might find something more; at least it would be worth while to try, for she had 'em in a great box altogether, I well know.

I send you a few lines, though Latin (which you don't like), for the sake of the subject. It makes part of a large design,[30] and is the beginning of the fourth book, which was intended to treat of the passions. Excuse the three first verses; you know vanity (with the Romans) is a poetical licence.

> Hactenus haud segnis naturæ arcana retexi
> Musarum interpres, primusque Britanna per arva
> Romano liquidum deduxi flumine rivum.
>
>   Cum tu opere in medio, spes tanti et causa laboris,
> Linquis, et æternam fati te condis in umbram!
> Vidi egomet duro graviter concussa dolore
> Pectora, in alterius non unquam lenta dolorem;
> Et languere oculos vidi et pallescere amantem
> Vultum, quo nunquam pietas nisi rara, fidesque,
> Altus amor veri, et purum spirabat honestum.
> Visa tamen tardi demum inclementia morbi
> Cessare est, reducemque iterum roseo ore salutem
> Speravi, atque una tecum, dilecte Favoni,
> Credulus heu longos, ut quondam, fallere soles.
> Heu spes nequicquam dulces, atque irrita vota,
> Heu mæstos soles, sine te quos ducere flendo
> Per desideria, et questus iam cogor inanes!
>   At tu, sancta anima, et nostri non indiga luctus
> Stellanti templo, sincerique ætheris igne
> Unde orta es, fruere. Atque oh si secura, nec ultra
> Mortalis, notos olim miserata labores
> Respectes, tenuesque vacet cognoscere curas:
> Humanam si forte alta de sede procellam
> Contemplere, metus, stimulosque cupidinis acres,
> Gaudiaque et gemitus, parvoque in corde tumultum
> Irarum ingentem, et sævos sub pectore fluctus:
> Respice et has lachrymas, memori quas ictus amore

---

with Gray's suggestion, he got them from Mrs West. They were printed by Toynbee in *Gray-HW-West-Ashton Corr.* ii. 301–14 (see also ibid., 'Chronological List of Poems and Translations by Richard West,' ii. 323–6).

30. *De Principiis cogitandi*, of which the only other surviving fragment was sent in a letter to West 21 April 1741 (see *Gray's Corr.* i. 183, n. 6).

Fundo; quod possum, propter lugere sepulchrum
Dum juvat, et mutæ vana hæc jactare favillæ.

*   *   *   *   *

PS. My love to the Chutheds.[31] Pray tell 'em I am learning whisk,[32] and have sent one of my old gowns to be made up into full-bottomed hoods. Compliments to Mrs Tr[a]cy.[33] Adieu, Sir, I am

Yours ever,

T. G.

From GRAY, ca Thursday 19 February 1747

Printed from MS in Waller Collection.

Dated by the reference to Middleton's *Treatise on the Roman Senate,* published 18 Feb. (*Daily Adv.* 18 Feb. 1747). It appears likely that Middleton's presentation copies were dispatched on the publication day, since HW thanks Middleton for the book, 'which I received this week from Manby,' on Saturday 21 Feb.

[Cambridge, ca Feb. 19, 1747.]

I HAVE abundance of thanks to return to you for the entertainment Mr Spence's book[1] has given me, which I have almost run over already; and I much fear (see what it is to make a figure) the breadth of the margin, and the neatness of the prints, which are better done than one could expect, have prevailed upon me to like it far better than I did in manuscript. For I think it is not the very genteel deportment of Polymetis nor the lively wit of Mysagetes[2] that have at all corrupted me.

There is one fundamental fault from whence most of the little faults

31. John Chute (1701–76), of the Vyne, Hants, HW's friend and correspondent, and Francis Whithed. Chute and Whithed were inseparable friends. Francis Whithed (1719–51), of Southwick Park, Hants, M.P. Southampton 1747–51, formerly Francis Thistlethwayte, of Norman Court, Hants, was the sole heir of his uncle, Richard Whithed (d. 1733) (GM 1733, iii. 663–4), of Southwick Park, and took the name Whithed by Private Act 14 Geo. II (1741) c. 17.

32. I.e., whist.

33. Probably Anne Atkyns (1683–1761), dau. of Sir Robert Atkyns, of Sapperton, Glos, who m. (1699) John Tracy (d. 1735), of Stanway, Glos, Chute's half-brother. See Roland Austin, 'Some Account of Sir Robert Atkyns the Younger and Other Members of the Atkyns Family,' *Bristol and Gloucestershire Archæological Society,* 1912, xxxv. 91–2; John Lodge and Merwyn Archdall, *Peerage of Ireland,* 1789, v. 12; GM 1761, xxxi. 538. See also Appendix 1.

1. *Polymetis.* HW must have sent one of his subscription copies to Gray (*ante* 8 Feb. 1747, n. 8).

2. One of the three persons in the dialogues; the others are Polymetis and Philander.

throughout the whole arise. He professes to neglect the Greek writers,[3] who could have given him more instruction on the very heads he professes to treat than all the others put together. Who does not know that upon the Latin, the Sabine, and Hetruscan mythology (which probably might themselves at a remoter period of time owe their origin to Greece too) the Romans engrafted almost the whole religion of Greece to make what is called their own? It would be hard to find any one circumstance that is properly of their invention. In the ruder days of the republic, the picturesque part of their religion (which is the province he has chose, and would be thought to confine himself to) was probably borrowed entirely from the Tuscans, who, as a wealthy and trading people, may be well supposed (and indeed are known) to have had the arts flourishing in a considerable degree among them. What could inform him here, but Dionysius Halic[arnasseus] (who expressly treats of those times[4] with great curiosity and industry) and the remains of the first Roman writers? The former he has neglected as a Greek, and the latter he says were but little acquainted with the arts, and consequently are but of little authority.[5] In the better ages, when every temple and public building in Rome was peopled with imported deities and heroes, and when all the artists of reputation they made use of were Greeks, what wonder if their eyes grew familiarized to Grecian forms and habits (especially in a matter of this kind, where so much depends upon the imagination), and if those figures introduced with them a belief of such fables as first gave them being, and dressed them out in their various attributes? It was natural then, and (I should think) necessary, to go to the source itself, the Greek accounts of their own religion. But, to say the truth, I suspect he was little conversant in those books and that language, for he rarely quotes any but Lucian,[6] an author that falls in everybody's way, and who lived at the very extremity of that period[7] he has set to his inquiries, later than any of the

3. 'My confining myself to the Roman writers only, or such of the Greeks as were quite Romanized, has been of great use to me toward making the whole work the less perplexed' (*Polymetis*, Preface, p. v).

4. Dionysius of Halicarnassus (ca 62–7 B.C.) in his *Roman Antiquities* treats the history of Rome from the beginnings to the First Punic War (265 B.C.).

5. 'My chief stock was laid in from all the Roman poets, quite from Ennius down to Juvenal, and from several of their prose writers, from Varro down to Macrobius. Had I gone lower, the authorities would have grown still weaker and weaker, and my subject would have been the more liable to have been confused' (*Polymetis*, Preface, p. v).

6. Lucian is quoted fourteen times, Homer three times, three other Greek writers and the Greek Anthology twice, and nine writers once.

7. Born ca 120, living 180 A.D.

poets he has meddled with, and for that reason ought to have been regarded as but an indifferent authority, especially being a Syrian too. As he says himself, his book, I think, is rather a beginning than a perfect work; but a beginning at the wrong end; for if anybody should finish it by inquiring into the Greek mythology, as he proposes, it will be necessary to read it backward.

There are several little neglects that any one might have told him of, I minded in reading it hastily, as page 311, a discourse about orange trees occasioned by Virgil's *inter odoratum lauri nemus*,[8] where he fancies the Roman *laurus* to be our laurel, though undoubtedly the bay tree, which is *odoratum*, and (I believe) still called *lauro* or *alloro* at Rome; and that the *pomum Medicum*[9] in the *Georgic* is the orange, though Theophrastus, whence Virgil borrowed it, or even Pliny, whom he himself quotes, might convince him it is the *cedrato*,[10] which he has often tasted at Florence. Page 144 is an account of Domenichin's Cardinal Virtues,[11] and a fling at the Jesuits,[12] neither of which belong to them. The painting is in a church of the Barnabiti,[13] dedicated to Santo Carlo Borromeo,[14] whose motto is *Humilitas*. Page 151, in a note he says: the old Romans did not regard Fortune as a deity,[15] though Servius Tullius[16] (whom she was said to be in love with; nay there was actually an affair between them)[17] founded her temple in Foro Boario.[18] By the way, her worship was Greek, and this King was

8. *Æneid* vi. 658–9. See Dialogue XX of *Polymetis*, 'The Defects of our Translators of the Ancient Poets . . . instanced from Mr Dryden's Translation of Virgil.'

9. The *malum felix* of *Georg.* ii. 127.

10. Gray is following the Delphin Virgil (ed. C. Ruæus, The Hague, 1723, pp. 107–8; for Gray's copy see W. Powell Jones, *Thomas Gray, Scholar*, Cambridge, Mass., 1937, p. 152), where it is asserted that *pomum Medicum*, i.e., Virgil's *malum felix*, is properly *citreum* (Italian *cedrato*).

11. The four Cardinal Virtues (1630) on the pendentives below the dome of S. Carlo ai Catinari, Rome, by Domenico Zampieri (1581–1641), called Domenichino.

12. 'Prudence he paints as supported by Time, and holding a looking glass in her hand . . . and by her is a boy, holding a serpent and a dove (in compliment, possibly, to the Jesuits who employed him, and to signify that they are wise as serpents, and innocent as doves)' (*Polymetis* 144).

13. S. Carlo ai Catinari at Rome, erected in 1612 by Cardinal Leni (d. 1627) on plans of Rosato Rosati (1560–1622); architect, Giovanni Battista Soria (1581–1651). See A. Nibby, *Itinerario di Roma*, 1830, ii. 536. The Barnabiti were a religious order founded at Milan about 1530 by St Antonio Maria Zaccaria.

14. S. Carlo Borromeo (1538–84), Archbishop of Milan, 1560.

15. The words 'regard Fortune as a deity' are underlined in the MS, but in what appears to be another hand.

16. Servius Tullius (fl. 578–534 B.C.), 6th King of Rome.

17. See Ovid, *Fasti* vi. 569–80.

18. The Ædes Fortuna in the Forum Boarium at Rome. In the eighteenth century it was identified with S. Maria Egiziaca (Dion. Halic. IV. xxvii. 7; Thomas Nugent, *The Grand Tour*, 2d edn, 1756, iii. 279; S. B. Platner and Thomas Ashby, *Dictionary of Ancient Rome*, 1929, p. 214).

educated in the family of Tarquinius Priscus[19] whose father[20] was a Corinthian. So it is easy to conceive how early the religion of Rome might be mixed with that of Greece, etc., etc.

Dr Middleton has sent me today a book on the Roman Senate,[21] the substance of a dispute between Lord Hervey[22] and him, though it never interrupted their friendship,[23] he says, and I dare say not.[24] Mrs Lætitia Pilkington is a name under certain recommendatory verses in the front of Cibber's book,[25] that seem designed to laugh at him. They were in a loose sheet, not sewed in. How does your comedy[26] succeed? I am told, very well. Adieu! I am

Yours ever,

T. G.

My respects to the Chutheds. I am much theirs, though to no purpose.

From Gray, ca Sunday 22 February 1747

Reprinted from Mason, *Mem. Gray*, p. 188. Dated conjecturally. As Cole observed in a marginal note in his copy of the *Memoirs* (formerly in the possession of Samuel Rogers), Mason 'clumsily joined together' two letters, and printed them as one, with the date 'Cambridge, March 1, 1747' (see Mitford, 1835–43, i. pp. xii and cvii). This date is here retained for the second part of the letter, while the first part is assigned to 22 February because of the references to the cat and to Walpole's election to the Royal Society.

19. Tarquinius Priscus (d. ?578 B.C.), 5th King of Rome.

20. Demaratus (Dion. Halic. III. xlvi. 3).

21. See introductory note above. In the 'Catalogue of Dr Middleton's Works' (HW, Waldegrave MSS 1.61) HW wrote: 'A Treatise on the Roman Senate. 1747. This was originally an amicable dispute carried on by letters between the Doctor and Lord Hervey, whose part in it was much the greater, though wrote in Kensington Palace in the heart [*sic*] and hurry of the Court. Lord Bristol [Hervey's son] would not give Dr M[iddleton] leave to publish Lord Hervey's letters, upon which he threw his own into this form.'

22. John Hervey (1696–1743), cr. (1733) Bn Hervey of Ickworth, Vice-Chamberlain of the Household 1730–40, Pope's 'Sporus' (*Epistle to Dr Arbuthnot*, lines 304–33),

memoir-writer, and HW's occasional correspondent.

23. The words 'interrupted their friendship' are underlined in the MS by a later hand.

24. The conclusion of the letter, beginning here, has been underscored with a wavy line, perhaps by Mason.

25. See *ante* 8 Feb. 1747, n. 3.

26. HW's *Terræ Filius; or, Harlequin Candidate. A Farce*, published anonymously in *Old England: or, The Broad-bottom Journal* 16 May 1747. The death of the 6th D. of Somerset, Chancellor of the University of Cambridge, was eagerly awaited by his would-be successors, Frederick, Prince of Wales, and the D. of Newcastle, the objects of HW's satire. HW's MS is now WSL.

Cambridge, [ca Feb. 22] 1747.

AS one ought to be particularly careful to avoid blunders in a compliment of condolence, it would be a sensible satisfaction to me
(before I testify my sorrow, and the sincere part I take in your misfortune) to know for certain, who it is I lament. Zara I know and Selima I
know[1] (Selima,[2] was it, or Fatima?) or rather I knew them both together; for I cannot justly say which was which. Then as to your handsome cat, the name you distinguish her by, I am no less at a loss, as well
knowing one's handsome cat is always the cat one likes best; or, if one
be alive and the other dead, it is usually the latter that is the hand-
somest. Besides, if the point were never so clear, I hope you do not
think me so ill-bred or so imprudent as to forfeit all my interest in the
survivor: Oh no! I would rather seem to mistake, and imagine to be
sure it must be the tabby one that had met with this sad accident. Till
this affair is a little better determined, you will excuse me if I do not
begin to cry:

Tempus inane peto, requiem, spatiumque doloris,[3]

which interval is the more convenient, as it gives time to rejoice with
you on your new honours.[4] This is only a beginning; I reckon next
week we shall hear you are a Freemason, or a Gormogon[5] at least.

From Gray, Sunday 1 March 1747

Reprinted from Mason, *Mem. Gray* 188-9.

1. So Gray wrote, but Mason, objecting
to the 'idle allusion in it to Scripture' (Acts
xix. 15), altered it in *Mem. Gray* 188 to 'I
knew Zara and Selima.' See Mason to Edward Bedingfeld 22 Dec. 1773, quoted in
Gray's Corr. i. 271.

2. In Rowe's *Tamerlane* she is the
daughter of Bajazet. Zara is the heroine of
Voltaire's *Zaïre* (Zara in Aaron Hill's translation); but Mason may have misread Zara
for Zama, the name of a general in *Tamerlane*. HW had recently written an 'Epilogue to Tamerlane,' published 5 Nov.
1746 (*Daily Adv.* 4, 5 Nov. 1746; see also
post ca Jan. 1748, n. 26).

3. Virgil, *Æneid* iv. 433, adapted.

4. 'Mr Walpole was about this time [19
Feb.] elected a Fellow of the Royal Society'
(Mason). See also *The Record of the Royal
Society of London*, 3d edn, 1912, p. 343.

5. A secret society which flourished for
a few years only, established in England in
1724 in opposition to Freemasonry. In ridicule of the Freemasons it claimed descent
from an ancient Chinese society (see A. G.
Mackey, *Encyclopædia of Freemasonry*, ed.
W. J. Hughan and E. L. Hawkins, New
York, 1920, i. 303–4; William Pinkerton,
'Decoration of Honour: Gormogons: Freemasons,' N&Q 1869, ser. IV. iv. 441–2). Gray's
allusion was probably suggested by *Dunciad* iv. 565–76.

THOMAS GRAY, BY JOHN GILES ECCARDT, 1748

Cambridge, March 1, 1747.

HEIGH HO! I feel (as you to be sure have done long since) that I have very little to say, at least in prose. Somebody will be the better for it; I do not mean you, but your cat, *feue Mademoiselle Selime*, whom I am about to immortalize for one week or fortnight as follows:[1]

[On the Death of a Favourite Cat, Drowned in a Tub of Gold Fishes.[2]

I.

'Twas on a lofty vase's[3] side,
Where China's gayest art had dyed
　　The azure flowers that blow;
The pensive Selima reclined,
Demurest of the tabby kind,[4]
　　Gazed on the lake below.

II.

Her conscious tail her joy declared,
The fair round face, the snowy beard,
　　The velvet of her paws,
Her coat that with the tortoise vies,
Her ears of jet, and emerald eyes,
　　She saw; and purred applause.

III.

Still had she gazed: but 'midst the tide
Two beauteous forms[5] were seen to glide,
　　The genii of the stream:

1. Mason omitted the ode. In printing it in his edition of Gray's poems (pp. 6–8), Mason followed Gray's own edition (1768), which agrees with the text of the ode in *Designs by Mr R. Bentley, for six Poems by Mr T. Gray* (1753). The text here printed is taken from the first edition, in Robert Dodsley's *Collection of Poems by Several Hands*, 1748, ii. 267–9, which seems to have been based on an earlier version of the ode. What is apparently an intermediate version was sent by Gray in a letter to Wharton ca 17 March 1747 (*Gray's Corr.* i. 277–8).

2. The editions of 1753 and 1768 both follow Dodsley's title. In the Wharton letter, the title is 'On a Favourite Cat, called Selima, that fell into a China Tub with Gold-Fishes in it and was drowned.'

3. It was sold SH xix. 32 for £42 to the Earl of Derby: 'The celebrated large blue and white oriental china cistern, on Gothic carved pedestal, in which Horace Walpole's cat was drowned; this gave occasion to Mr Gray, the poet, to write his beautiful ode.' See illustration in MONTAGU i. 134; see also Hazen, *SH Bibliography* 209–10.

4. This line and the preceding one are transposed in the Wharton letter and the editions of 1753 and 1768.

5. 'Angel-forms' (Wharton letter and editions of 1753 and 1768).

Their scaly armour's Tyrian hue
Through richest purple to the view
   Betrayed a golden gleam.

IV.

The hapless nymph with wonder saw:
A whisker first and then a claw,
   With many an ardent wish,
She stretched in vain to reach the prize.
What female heart can gold despise?
   What cat's a foe to fish?[6]

V.

Presumptuous maid! with looks[7] intent
Again she stretched, again she bent,
   Nor knew the gulf between.
(Malignant fate sat by and smiled.)
The slipp'ry verge her feet beguiled:
   She tumbled headlong in.

VI.

Eight times emerging from the flood
She mewed to ev'ry wat'ry God
   Some speedy aid to send.
No dolphin came, no Nereid stirred
Nor cruel Tom, nor Harry heard.
   What fav'rite has a friend?[8]

VII.

From hence, ye beauties undeceived
Know, one false step is ne'er retrieved,
   And be with caution bold.
Not all, that tempts[9] your wand'ring eyes,
And heedless hearts, is lawful prize:
   Nor all, that glisters, gold.]

There's a poem for you, it is rather too long for an epitaph.

6. 'What cat's averse to fish?' (ibid.)

7. So in the editions of 1753 and 1768, but 'eyes' in the Wharton letter.

8. 'A fav'rite has no friend!' (Wharton letter and editions of 1753 and 1768.)

9. So in the editions of 1753 and 1768, but 'strikes' in the Wharton letter.

To Gray, ca May 1747

Missing. Probably written in Arlington Street; implied in *post* 12 May 1747.

From Gray, Tuesday 12 May 1747

Printed from MS in Waller Collection.
Dated by the postmark and the reference to Lyttelton.
Address: To the Honourable Horace Walpole Esq. at his house in Arlington Street, Westminster. *Postmark:* [1]3 MA.

Stoke[1] [May 12, 1747].

I AM not dead, neither sleep[2] I so sound as not to feel the jog you give me, or to forget that I ought to have wrote before. But I have been on the confines of that land where all things are forgotten,[3] and returned from thence with a loss of appetite and of spirits that has made me a very silly gentleman, and not worth your correspondence. However I am tolerable well again, and came post hither on Friday[4] to see my mother[5] < >[6] she was then at the extremity, but is far better at present. I have no business to regale you with all <t>his, but it is only by way of excuse. On Monday next I hope to return home,[7] and in my way (probably on Tuesday morning) to call at your door, and that of the Chutheds,[8] if possible.

I am obliged to you for transcribing Voltaire[9] and Mr Lyttleton.[10]

1. West End Cottage (now Stoke Court or West End House) in Stoke Park, the 'compact neat box of red brick with sash windows' (*Gray's Corr.* ii. 586) which Mrs Rogers, Gray's aunt, leased from the Salter family, of Stoke Poges, Bucks (*Vict. Co. Hist., Bucks* iii. 303-4).

2. An echo of Matthew ix. 24.

3. Probably the Plain of Oblivion or Lethe's Plain (Plato, *Republic* x. 16; Aristophanes, *Frogs*, 186).

4. 8 May. Gray was charged half-commons at Peterhouse the week of 3 May.

5. Dorothy Antrobus (1685-1753), m. (1709) Philip Gray. Mrs Gray had been living with her sisters Mary and Anne at Stoke since 1741 (*Gray's Corr.* iii. 1306-8).

6. Piece cut out, with the loss of perhaps six words.

7. Gray's commons charges resume 22 May.

8. Gray to Chute 23 Nov. 1746 is addressed 'To John Chute Esq. at the house of Francis Whithed Esq. in New Bond Street, Westminster' (*Gray's Corr.* i. 254).

9. Probably *Stances VII*, 'Au Roi de Prusse 2 Dec. 1740,' as Roger Martin suggests (*Gray's Corr.* i. 281, n. 6).

10. George Lyttelton, brother of HW's friend Charles Lyttelton. He commemorated his deceased wife in an *Inscription to be engraved on the Monument of the Lady of the Hon. George Lyttelton, Esq.*, published in GM July 1747, xvii. 338, and in a monody *To the Memory of a Lady Lately Deceased* (*post* ca 10 Nov. 1747), published 30 Oct. It was probably the former which HW had seen in MS and of which he sent Gray a transcript. It begins in prose and concludes with twelve lines of verse, the last six of which might be called 'prettyish.'

The last has six good prettyish lines. The other I do not much admire:

Ni sa flûte,[11] ni son épée.

The thought is Martial's,[12] and many others after him; and the verses frippery enough, as his easy poetry usually is. Nobody loves him better than I in his grander style. Adieu, dear Sir, I am ever

Yours,

T. GRAY

From GRAY, ca Monday 15 June 1747

Reprinted from Mitford, 1835–43, v. 217–21. Dated by the allusion to the *Ode on a Distant Prospect of Eton College* (published 30 May 1747).

[Cambridge, ca June 15, 1747.]

WHEN I received the testimonial of so many considerable personages to adorn the second page of my next edition,[1] and (adding them to the *testimonium auctoris de seipso*) do relish and enjoy all the conscious pleasure resulting from six pennyworths of glory, I cannot but close my satisfaction with a sigh for the fate of my fellow-labourer in poetry, the unfortunate Mr Golding,[2] cut off in the flower or rather

---

11. Voltaire's fourth stanza reads:
'Adieu, vous dont l'auguste main,
Toujours au travail occupée,
Tient, pour l'honneur du genre humain
La plume, la lyre et l'épée.
Frederick the Great studied the flute under Johann Joachim Quantz (1697–1773) and developed into a very proficient player. The popularity of the 'German flute' (*flauto traverso*) in England in the eighteenth century is perhaps attributable to Frederick's hobby. See Robert Eitner, *Biographisch-Bibliographisches Quellen-Lexikon der Musiker und Musikgelehrten*, Leipzig, 1900–4, *sub* Quantz.
12. Book VIII of Martial's epigrams, dedicated to Domitian, contains several epigrams in praise of the Emperor, to which Gray may allude. Martial VIII. lxxxii. 3–4, in particular, 'has the suggestion that the Emperor could at once govern the State and honour the Muses' (*Gray's Corr.* i. 282, n. 6).

1. *An Ode on a Distant Prospect of Eton College* was published by Robert Dodsley, price sixpence, 30 May (*Daily Adv.* 30 May 1747). A missing letter from HW doubtless reported favourable comments on the *Ode*.
2. Probably William Goldwin (ca 1684–1747), a baker's son, Fellow of King's 1703–10, of Eton 1733–47; Master of Bristol Grammar School 1710–17; vicar of St Nicholas, Bristol, 1717–47. He was born at Windsor, where he died 1 June 1747 (*Eton Coll. Reg.*). He may have been related to John Goldwin or Golding (d. 1719), organist and choirmaster of the Chapel Royal at Windsor (DNB). Goldwin published in 1706 *Musæ Juveniles* which contains *Certamen Pilæ Anglice*, an early account of a cricket match (see *Etoniana* 30 Dec. 1922, No. 31, pp. 481–3), and in 1712 *A Poetical Description of Bristol*. No poem by him on Windsor has been found.

the bud of his honours, who, had he survived but a fortnight more, might have been by your kind offices as much delighted with himself as I. Windsor and Eton might have gone down to posterity together, perhaps appeared in the same volume,[3] like Philips and Smith,[4] and we might have set at once to Mr Pond[5] for the frontispiece; but these, alas! are vain reflections. To return to myself. Nay! but you are such a wit! sure the gentlemen an't so good, are they? and don't you play upon the word. I promise you, few take to it here at all, which is a good sign (for I never knew anything liked here, that ever proved to be so anywhere else), it is said to be mine, but I strenuously deny it, and so do all that are in the secret, so that nobody knows what to think; a few only of King's College gave me the lie, but I hope to demolish them; for if I don't know, who should? Tell Mr Chute I would not have served him so, for any brother in Christendom, and am very angry.[6] To make my peace with the noble youth[6] you mention, I send you a poem that I am sure they will read (as well as they can): a masterpiece, it is said, being an admirable improvement on that beautiful piece called *Pugna Porcorum*,[7] which begins:

Plangite[8] porcelli porcorum pigra propago;

but that is in Latin, and not for their reading, but indeed this is worth a thousand of it, and unfortunately it is not perfect, and it is not mine.[9]

The Characters of the Christ-Cross Row,[10] By a Critic, to Mrs ——.

＊   ＊   ＊   ＊   ＊[11]

3. If, as Gray implies, HW had proposed to publish Goldwin's poem, nothing came of the project.

4. Gray refers to the practice of binding into one volume *Poems on Several Occasions* by John Philips (1676–1709) and *The Works of Mr Edmund Smith* (1672–1710), both of Christ Church, Oxford.

5. Arthur Pond (ca 1705–58), painter and engraver, F.R.S. 1752; known at this time for his *Imitations of the Italian Masters*, 1734–5, and several of the engravings in Thomas Birch's *Heads of Illustrious Persons*, 1743–51.

6. Unexplained.

7. *Pugna Porcorum per P. Porcium Poetam*, Antwerp, 1530, by Johannes Leo Placentius (ca 1500–ca 1550), a poem of 249 lines, besides the dedication and post-

script, consisting entirely of words beginning with 'p' (see *Nugæ Venales, sive Thesaurus ridendi et iocandi*, 1648).

8. 'Plaudite' in 1648 edn (*Nugæ Venales*, 1648).

9. The author, it appears from Mason to HW 20 March 1773, was William Trollope (d. 1749), Fellow of Pembroke College, Cambridge, 1731–49 (Venn, *Alumni Cantab.*). But see n. 11 below.

10. The alphabet (OED).

11. Mitford omitted some of the verses, probably because of indecency. In his edition of the *Walpole-Mason Corr.*, i. 412, he observes that he printed the poem on the alphabet in his edition of Gray's *Works*, 1835–43, from 'Gray's autograph in the Strawberry Hill Collection, in which Horace Walpole asserted that though Gray

Great D draws near—the Duchess sure is come,
Open the doors of the withdrawing-room;
Her daughters decked most daintily I see,
The dowager grows a perfect double D.
E enters next, and with her Eve appears,
Not like yon dowager deprest with years;
What ease and elegance her person grace,
Bright beaming, as the evening star, her face;
Queen Esther next—how fair e'en after death,
Then one faint glimpse of Queen Elizabeth;
No more, our Esthers now are nought but Hetties,
Elizabeths all dwindled into Betties;
In vain you think to find them under E,
They're all diverted into H and B.
F follows fast the fair—and in his rear,
See Folly, Fashion, Foppery, straight appear,
All with fantastic clews, fantastic clothes,
With fans and flounces, fringe and furbelows.
Here Grub Street geese presume to joke and jeer,
All, all, but Grannam Osborne's Gazetteer.[12]
High heaves his hugeness H, methinks we see,
Henry the Eighth's most monstrous majesty,
But why on such *mock* grandeur should we dwell,
H mounts to heaven, and H descends to hell.

*   *   *   *   *

As H the Hebrew found, so I the Jew,
See Isaac, Joseph, Jacob, pass in view;

never owned it, he was convinced it was his'; he adds that 'a few omissions deemed necessary were made in printing the poem. . . . Gray's MS copy was destroyed by the gentleman who bought it at Strawberry Hill; and the transcript which I made, and from which I printed the poem, is probably the only one existing.' Gray's MS does not appear in the SH sale catalogue (1842).

12. The *Daily Gazetteer* (1735–48), commonly called the *Gazetteer* (see GM 1736, vi. 248, 250), in which James Pitt (ca 1680–1763: GM 1763, xxxiii. 46) under the pseudonym of Francis Osborne defended Sir Robert Walpole's administration against the attacks of the *Craftsman*. Pitt is said to have been a Norwich schoolmaster be-

fore coming to London (GM 1733, iii. 91). He started writing for the *London Journal* in the issue of 31 May 1729 (see K. L. Joshi, 'The London Journal, 1719–1738,' *Journal of the University of Bombay*, new ser., 1940, ix pt ii. 58), though his first article signed 'F. Osborne' did not appear until 4 April 1730 (*London Journal* No. 557). In the bitter controversy between the *Craftsman* and the *London Journal*, rich in personal abuse, Pitt earned the nickname 'Mrs Osborne' or 'Mother Osborne' (*Craftsman* No. 346, 17 Feb. 1733; No. 366, 7 July 1733), and as 'Mother Osborne' was introduced into the 1743 edition of *The Dunciad* (ii. 312).

The walls of old Jerusalem appear,
See Israel, and all Judah thronging there.

*   *   *   *   *

P pokes his head out, yet has not a pain;
Like Punch, he peeps, but soon pops in again;
Pleased with his pranks, the pisgies¹³ call him Puck,
Mortals he loves to prick, and pinch, and pluck;
Now a pert prig, he perks upon your face,
Now peers, pores, ponders, with profound grimace,
Now a proud prince, in pompous purple drest,
And now a player, a peer, a pimp, or priest;
A pea, a pin, in a perpetual round,
Now seems a penny, and now shows a pound;
Like perch or pike, in pond you see him come,
He in plantations hangs like pear or plum,
Pippin or peach; then perches on the spray,
In form of parrot, pie, or popinjay.
P, Proteus-like all tricks, all shapes can show,
The pleasantest person in the Christ-Cross Row.

*   *   *   *   *

As K a King, Q represents a Queen,
And seems small difference the sounds between;
K, as a man, with hoarser accent speaks,
In shriller notes Q like a female squeaks;
Behold K struts, as might a King become,
Q draws her train along the drawing-room,
Slow follow all the quality of state,
Queer Queensbury¹⁴ only does refuse to wait.

*   *   *   *   *

Thus great R reigns in town, while different far,
Rests in retirement, *little* rural R;
Remote from cities lives in lone retreat,
With rooks and rabbit burrows round his seat—
S, sails the swan slow down the silver stream.

*   *   *   *   *

13. I.e., pixies (OED).
14. Lady Catherine Hyde (1701–77), m. (1720) Charles Douglas, 3d D. of Queensberry. She is the 'Prior's Kitty, ever fair' of HW's verses 'Left on the Duchess of Queensberry's Toilet' (HW to Mann 26 April 1771). She was dismissed from Court, 27 Feb. 1729, for soliciting subscriptions in the royal apartments, at a guinea each, for the printing of Gay's *Polly,* 'a thing which the King had forbid being recited' (Hervey, *Memoirs* i. 99). See HW to Mann 3 Jan. 1746, O.S. For her letter to George II on the occasion of her dismissal (Waller MS) see *Gray-HW-West-Ashton Corr.* ii. 84, n. 14.

So big with weddings, waddles W,
And brings all womankind before your view;
A wench, a wife, a widow, and a w[hor]e,
With woe behind, and wantonness before.

When you and Mr Chute can get the remainder of *Mariane*,[15] I shall
be much obliged to you for it—I am terribly impatient.

To Gray, August 1747

Missing. Probably written at SH and addressed to Gray at Cambridge. Mentioned *post* 9 Sept. 1747; answered *post* 19 or 26 Aug. 1747.

From Gray, Wednesday 19 or 26 August 1747

Printed from MS in Waller Collection.
The month is determined by Gray's intended visit to SH in Sept. 1747, referred
to below as 'next month' and *post* 9 Sept. 1747 as 'this month.' The date of the
year is ascertained by the reference to Middleton's third marriage. Since Gray did
not leave Cambridge until ca 16 Aug. (n. 1 below), 'Wednesday' must be either 19
or 26 Aug.

[Stoke,] Wednesday [Aug. 19 or 26, 1747].

I CAME to town the day that you went out of it,[1] and am now at Stoke
very hot, and very well, thank ye. I embrace your invitation,[2] and
shall be glad to make you a visit at Strawberry Hill.[3] The week I leave
to you; it is indifferent to me what time next month it shall be; Mr
Walpole and Comp[any][4] will settle it among them. You must inform
me what place on the Windsor Road is nearest Twickenham, for I am

15. *La Vie de Marianne, ou les Aventures
de Madame la Comtesse de* ✳ ✳ ✳ by Pierre
Carlet de Chamblain de Marivaux (1688–
1763) was published in Paris in eleven
parts 1731–41. In 1745 a spurious twelfth
part appeared in an edition published at
Amsterdam. Gray probably refers to this
French continuation, but he may be alluding to one of the several English translations which appeared between 1736 and
1746 (see Jean Fleury, *Marivaux et le marivaudage*, 1881, p. 195; Helen S. Hughes,
'Translations of the *Vie de Marianne* and
Their Relation to Contemporary English
Fiction,' *Modern Philology*, 1917–18, xv.
127). Gray sent three parts (probably parts

ix–xi, about Mlle de Tervire) to Chute in
July 1742 (*Gray's Corr.* i. 217–18).

———

1. Gray left Cambridge 16 Aug., or a day
or two earlier (he was charged half-commons at Peterhouse the week of 14 Aug.).
2. Contained in HW to Gray Aug. 1747,
missing. In HW to Mann 1 Sept. 1747, O.S.,
written in Arlington Street, HW speaks of
going to Twickenham with Chute 'tomorrow for the rest of the season.'
3. At this time merely 'a small house
near Twickenham,' which HW leased from
Mrs Chenevix in May 1747 (*ante* i. 17).
4. John Chute.

no geographer; there I will be at the appointed day, and from thence you must fetch me.

Nicolini[5] with a whole coach full of the Chattichees[6] has been at Cambridge in an equipage like that of Destiny and his comrades in the *Roman comique*.[7] They said they had been in the meridional parts of Great Britain, and were now visiting the oriental. Your friend Dr Middleton has married really a pretty kind of woman[8] both in figure and manner, which is strange methinks. Adieu, I am

Yours ever,

T. GRAY

From GRAY, Wednesday 9 September 1747

Printed from MS in Waller Collection.

Memoranda by HW:[1] 'Lord Sandw.[2] acting plays.

Battering ram.'

Address: To the Honourable Horace Walpole Esq. at his house in Arlington Street, Westminster. *Postmark:* WINDSOR 11 SE.

---

5. Antonio Niccolini (1701–69), Marchese di Ponsacco, Florentine ecclesiastic and man of letters. See Vittorio Spreti, *Enciclopedia storico-nobiliare Italiana*, Milan, 1928–36, iv. 816–17, and *The Record of the Royal Society of London*, 3d edn, 1912, p. 343; see also HW's correspondence with Mann, where Niccolini is frequently mentioned.

6. 'Panciatici, Nicolini, and Pandolfini, Florentines then in England' (HW). Giovanni Gualberto Panciatichi (1721–50), Imperial Chamberlain (1746) to Maria Theresa and Francis I (Litta, 'Panciatichi,' table xv); Roberto Pandolfini (living 1750), Florentine senator, cr. (1748) Cavaliere, with title of Conte (Spreti, op. cit. v. 99; Giuseppe Conti, *Firenze dopo i Medici*, Florence, 1921, p. 329). Niccolini and Pandolfini arrived in Nov. 1746 and Panciatichi in Feb. 1747 (HW to Mann 4 Nov. 1746, 23 Feb. 1747, O.S.).

7. *Le Roman comique* (1651) by Paul Scarron (1610–60). Gray refers to the 'charrette . . . pleine de coffres, de malles et de gros paquets de toiles peintes qui faisaient comme une pyramide' in which 'une troupe de comédiens arrive dans la ville du

Mans' (I. i). The 'nom de théâtre' of the leader is 'Le Destin' (see ed. Émile Magne, Paris, n.d., pp. 3, 5).

8. 'His 3d wife' (HW). Anne Powell (d. 1760), dau. of John Powell, of Boughrood, Radnor, m. (1) —— Wilkins, merchant at Bristol; m. (2) (5 June 1747) Conyers Middleton (Nichols, *Lit. Anec.*, v. 412; GM 1747, xvii. 296; 1760, xxx. 347). The following character is taken from HW, Waldegrave MSS 1.59: 'His second wife dying without any surviving issue, he married Mrs Wilkins, a widow. . . . The new Mrs Middleton was an accomplished woman and well skilled in music, of which Dr Middleton was very fond, and played himself on the bass viol.'

---

1. These words, which are scribbled on the letter in pencil, appear to be notes for the year 1751 in *Mem. Geo. II:* 'Lord Sandwich had been hoisted to the head of the Admiralty by the weight of the Duke of Bedford, into whose affection he had worked himself by intrigues, cricket-matches, and acting plays' (edn 1847, i. 2).

2. John Montagu (1718–92), 4th E. of Sandwich.

Stoke, at Mrs Rogers's.[3]
Wednesday, Sept. 9 [1747].

IF I am mistaken, you will have the trouble of reading a few unnecessary lines, but I imagine a letter[4] I wrote to you (about a week after
I received yours)[5] has never come to your hands. It was to say that I
should be glad to make you a visit as you propose, and left it to you
what time this month it should be; only desired that you would inform
me a little beforehand, and tell me (who am too fine a person to know
where any English place lies) whether Hounslow or Brentford be nearest Twickenham,[6] where I would be on a certain day, and you must
fetch me from thence. Adieu! I am

Yours ever,

T. GRAY

To GRAY, Nov. 1747

Missing. Probably written in Arlington Street soon after HW's return from SH
during the week of 1 Nov. From the following letter it appears that it contained an
account of HW's disagreement with Ashton and remarks on Lyttelton's *Monody*.

From GRAY, Tuesday ? 10 November 1747

Reprinted from *Works* v. 388–9. The date of the year is ascertained by the references to Lyttelton's *Monody* and Dodsley's *Collection of Poems*. The day of the
month is conjectural. Tuesdays in Nov. 1747 fell on the 3d, 10th, 17th, and 24th.
HW probably read Lyttelton's *Monody* within a few days of its publication 30 Oct.,
and wrote Gray upon his return to London (probably the latter part of the week of
1 Nov.). Gray, it is assumed, answered within a few days.

Nov. [?10, 1747], Tuesday, Cambridge.[1]

IT is a misfortune to me to be at a distance from both of you at present.[2] A letter[3] can give one so little idea of such matters! * * * *[4] I
always believed well of his heart and temper, and would gladly do so

3. Gray's aunt, Anne Antrobus (1677–
1758), who m. (1710) Jonathan Rogers, attorney (H. P. Stokes, 'Thomas Gray and
His Cambridge Relatives,' *Cambridge Review*, 1917, xxxviii. 165–6).
4. *Ante* 19 or 26 Aug. 1747.
5. HW to Gray Aug. 1747, missing.
6. Hounslow is three miles, and Brentford four miles, from Twickenham.

1. Gray returned ca 23 Oct., the day on
which his commons charges at Peterhouse
were resumed.
2. This doubtless refers to HW's quarrel
with Ashton. See Introduction, *post* 12
June 1750, n. 4, and HW to Mann 25 July
1750, O.S.
3. HW to Gray Nov. 1747, missing.
4. The asterisks are in Miss Berry's text.

still. If they are as they should be, I should have expected everything from such an explanation; for it is a tenet with me (a simple one, you'll perhaps say), that if ever two people, who love one another, come to breaking, it is for want of a timely *éclaircissement,* a full and precise one, without witnesses or mediators, and without reserving any one disagreeable circumstance for the mind to brood upon in silence.

I am not totally of your mind as to Mr Lyttelton's Elegy,[5] though I love kids and fawns as little as you do. If it were all like the fourth stanza,[6] I should be excessively pleased. Nature and sorrow, and tenderness, are the true genius of such things, and something of these I find in several parts of it (not in the orange tree);[7] poetical ornaments are foreign to the purpose, for they only show a man is not sorry—and devotion worse, for it teaches him that he ought not to be sorry, which is all the pleasure of the thing. I beg leave to turn your weathercock the contrary way. Your Epistle[8] I have not seen a great while, and Doctor M[iddleton][9] is not in the way to give me a sight of it, but I remember enough to be sure all the world will be pleased with it, even with all its *faults upon its head,* if you don't care to mend them. I would try to do it myself (however hazardous), rather than it should remain unpublished. As to my Eton Ode, Mr. Dodsley is *padrone.*[10] The second[11] you

5. *To the Memory of a Lady Lately Deceased. A Monody,* 15 pp. fol., published by Andrew Millar 30 Oct. 1747 (*Daily Adv.* 30 Oct. 1747). See *ante* 12 May 1747, n. 10. It was reprinted in Dodsley's *Collection of Poems* (*post* ca Jan. 1748, n. 1), 2d edn, 1748, ii. 69–80.

6. The stanza (p. 3) begins:
'In vain I look around
 O'er all the well-known ground
My Lucy's wonted footsteps to descry;
 Where oft we us'd to walk,
 Where oft in tender talk
We saw the summer sun go down the sky.'

7. 'The verdant orange lifts its beauteous
     head:
   From ev'ry branch the balmy flow'rets
     rise,
   On ev'ry bough the golden fruits are
     seen;
   With odours sweet it fills the smiling
     skies' (p. 10).

8. 'From Florence to Thomas Ashton' (Berry). The 'Epistle from Florence to Thomas Ashton, Esq., Tutor to the Earl of

Plimouth,' according to HW's MS note in HW, Waldegrave MSS 2.12, was 'wrote 1739/40,' and was sent to Ashton before 16 July 1740, N.S. (*Gray's Corr.* i. 170). Both the original MS and the letter in which it was sent are missing. The text of HW's autograph copy of the verses in HW, Waldegrave MSS 2.11–26 differs but slightly from that in his *Fugitive Pieces,* SH, 1758 (see also *Works* i. 4–16), but the notes are much fuller and more numerous than those in the printed editions. The following note was added by HW in HW, Waldegrave MSS 2.11: 'Mr. Ashton left Lord Plimouth in about a year after this was wrote, and went into orders. . . . This "Epistle" was not published till January 1748, in the second volume of a miscellany of poems printed by Dodsley in three volumes.'

9. HW had evidently sent Middleton a copy of the 'Epistle,' perhaps from Italy.

10. 'To publish in his collection of poems' (Berry). See *post* ca Jan. 1748, n. 1.

11. 'The Ode to Spring' (Berry). See *ante* 20 Oct. 1746.

had, I suppose you do not think worth giving him; otherwise, to me it seems not worse than the former. He might have Selima[12] too, unless she be of too little importance for his patriot-collection, or perhaps the connections you had with her may interfere. *Che so io?* Adieu!

I am yours ever,

T. G.

To GRAY, January 1748

Missing. Probably written in Arlington Street shortly after the publication of Dodsley's *Collection of Poems* on 14 Jan. 1748. Answered *post* ca Jan. 1748.

From GRAY, ca January 1748

The MS of the original is incomplete; the missing first part is reprinted from *Works* v. 393–5, and the remainder (see n. 44, below) printed from MS in Waller Collection.

Dated approximately, with reference to the publication of Dodsley's *Collection*.

[Cambridge, ca Jan. 1748.]

I AM obliged to you for Mr Dodsley's book,[1] and, having pretty well looked it over, will (as you desire) tell you my opinion of it. He might, methinks, have spared the Graces[2] in his frontispiece, if he chose

---

12. 'The Ode on Mr Walpole's cat drowned in the tub of gold-fish' (Berry). See *ante* 1 March 1747.

---

1. *A Collection of Poems. By Several Hands. In Three Volumes*, published by Robert Dodsley (1703–64) 14 Jan. (*Daily Adv.* 14 Jan. 1748). The poems in the *Collection* are for the greater part reprints, though several poems were here published for the first time, including HW's, Gray's (except the *Eton Ode*), and West's. For studies of the *Collection* see W. P. Courtney, *Dodsley's Collection of Poetry, Its Contents and Contributors*, 1910, also published serially in N&Q 1906–9; and R. W. Chapman, 'Dodsley's Collection of Poems by Several Hands,' *Oxford Bibliographical Society Proceedings*, 1933, iii. 268–316. Courtney observes: 'Most of the pieces composing the first three volumes (January 1748) were

submitted to the judgment of George, the first Lord Lyttelton, before they were passed for printing. Some of them were suggested by Horace Walpole. Among these are the six Town Eclogues of Lady Mary Wortley Montagu, the poems of Gray, the monody of their friend Richard West, and, I would add, Seward's "Female Right to Literature." ' HW's set, 6 vols, 1748–58 (vols i–iii are the 2d edn), with his MS notes supplying names and other information, was sold SH vi. 20 to John Mitford; after his death it was acquired by the British Museum.

2. A vignette of the Three Graces, engraved by Charles Mosley (d. 1770), fills half the title-page. In the second (1748) and subsequent editions the vignette was changed to one of Apollo and the Nine Muses.

to be economical, and dressed his authors in a little more decent rai-
ment—not in whited-brown paper and distorted characters like an old
ballad.[3] I am ashamed to see myself,[4] but the company keeps me in
countenance; so, to begin with Mr. Tickell.[5] This is not only a state-
poem (my ancient aversion), but a state-poem on the Peace of Utrecht.[6]
If Mr Pope had wrote a panegyric on it, one could hardly have read
him with patience, but this is only a poor short-winded imitator of Addison who had himself not above three or four notes in poetry, sweet
enough indeed, like those of a German flute, but such as soon tire and
satiate the ear with their frequent return. Tickell has added to this a
great poverty of sense, and a string of transitions that hardly become a
schoolboy. However, I forgive him for the sake of his ballad,[7] which I
always thought the prettiest in the world. All there is of M. Green[8] here
has been printed before:[9] there is a profusion of wit everywhere; reading would have formed his judgment and harmonized his verse, for
even his wood-notes often break out into strains of real poetry and
music. *The Schoolmistress*[10] is excellent in its kind and masterly, and
(I am sorry to differ from you, but) *London*[11] is to me one of those few
imitations that have all the ease and all the spirit of an original. The
same man's verses at the opening of Garrick's theatre[12] are far from bad.
Mr Dyer[13] (here you will despise me highly) has more of poetry in his
imagination than almost any of our number, but rough and injudi-

3. The typography of the first edn of the *Collection*, though undistinguished, is not actually crude.

4. 'An Ode on a Distant Prospect of Eton College,' 'Ode' (i.e. the 'Ode on the Spring'), and 'Ode on the Death of a Favourite Cat, Drowned in a Tub of Gold-Fishes' (Dodsley, *Collection* ii. 261–9). The poems, like most of the others in the second and third volumes of the *Collection*, were printed anonymously.

5. Thomas Tickell (1685–1740; see R. E. Tickell, *Thomas Tickell*, 1931, p. 15, for proof that his birth was in 1685, not, as in DNB, in 1686).

6. 'A Poem, To His Excellency the Lord Privy-Seal, on the Prospect of Peace,' 1712 (Dodsley, *Collection* i. 1–24).

7. 'Colin and Lucy,' 1725 (ibid. i. 24–7; see R. E. Tickell, op. cit. 194).

8. Matthew Green (1696–1737).

9. He is represented by six poems (Dodsley, *Collection* i. 28–71), first printed posthumously in the 3d edn (1738) of *The Spleen* (see *The Spleen and Other Poems by Matthew Green*, ed. R. K. Wood, Kensington, 1925, p. 8).

10. 'The Schoolmistress, A Poem, in Imitation of Spencer,' 1742, by William Shenstone (1714–63) (Dodsley, *Collection* i. 211–22).

11. 'London: A Poem, In Imitation of the Third Satire of Juvenal,' 1738, by Samuel Johnson (ibid. i. 101–15).

12. 'Prologue Spoken by Mr Garrick, at the Opening of the Theatre in Drury Lane, 1747' (ibid., iii. 150–2).

13. John Dyer (1699–1757) is represented by 'Grongar Hill,' 1727, and 'The Ruins of Rome,' 1740 (ibid. i. 72–100). Dyer's dates have been established by Ralph M. Williams in 'Life and Works of John Dyer,' an unpublished Yale dissertation, 1938.

cious. I should range Mr Bramston[14] only a step or two above Dr King,[15] who is as low in my estimation as in yours. Dr Evans[16] is a furious mad-man, and *Pre-existence* is nonsense in all her altitudes. Mr Lyttelton[17] is a gentle elegiac person. Mr Nugent[18] sure did not write his own ode.[19] I like Mr Whitehead's little poems, I mean the ode on a tent,[20] the verses to Garrick,[21] and particularly those to Charles Townshend,[22] better than anything I had seen before of him. I gladly pass over H. Brown[23] and the rest, to come at you. You know I was of the publish-ing side, and thought your reasons against it none; for though, as Mr Chute said extremely well, the *still small voice* of Poetry was not made to be heard in a crowd, yet Satire will be heard, for all the audience are by nature her friends; especially when she appears in the spirit of Dry-den, with his strength and often with his versification, such as you have caught in those lines on the royal unction, on the papal dominion and convents of both sexes, on Henry VIII and Charles II, for these are to me the shining parts of your Epistle.[24] There are many lines I could

14. James Bramston (ca 1694–1744), vicar of Lurgashall, Sussex, 1723, and of Hart-ing, Sussex, 1725 (G. F. Russell Barker and A. H. Stenning, *Record of Old Westmin-sters*, 1928). Dodsley included his 'The Art of Politics,' 1729 and 'The Man of Taste,' 1733 (*Collection* i. 115–59).

15. William King (1663–1712), D.C.L., is represented by eight pieces (ibid. i. 223–63).

16. Abel Evans (1679–1737), D.D., vicar of Kirtlington, Oxon, 1700, of Great Staughton, Hunts, 1723; rector of Cheam, Surrey, 1724–37 (Foster, *Alumni Oxon.*). Dodsley included his 'The Apparition . . . a Dialogue . . . concerning a Book falsely called, The Rights of the Christian Church,' 1710, and 'Pre-existence' (*Collec-tion* i. '238–83' [pagination repeated]).

17. George (later Bn) Lyttelton, the patron of the *Collection*, is represented by eighteen pieces (ibid. ii. 3–61), to which twelve more were added in the second edi-tion.

18. Robert Nugent (ca 1702–88), cr. (1767) Bn and (1776) E. Nugent.

19. 'An Ode to William Pultney, Esq.' (Dodsley, *Collection* ii. 203–5), published as *An Ode on Mr Pultney* in 1739. HW called it a 'glorious ode on religion and liberty' (MONTAGU i. 65). 'It was addressed to Lord Bath upon the author's change of his religion; but was universally believed

to be written by Mallet, who was tutor to Newsham, Mrs Nugent's son, and improved by Mr Pulteney himself and Lord Chester-field' (*Mem. Geo. II* i. 46, n. 2). Besides the 'Ode,' Dodsley printed thirteen other poems and fourteen epigrams by Nugent (*Collection* ii. 155–202, 205–33).

20. William Whitehead, 'An Ode to a Gentleman, on his pitching a Tent in his Garden' (ibid. ii. 255–9).

21. Ibid. ii. 246–50.

22. 'To the Honourable * * *' (ibid. ii. 244–6). According to William Mason (*Memoirs of . . . William Whitehead*, 1788, p. 39) this was the Hon. Charles Townshend (1725–67), 2d son of Charles, 3d Vct Townshend; Chancellor of the Ex-chequer, 1766. Townshend and Whitehead were at Clare College, Cambridge, between 1742 and 1745, as Fellow-Commoner (ad-mitted 23 July 1742) and Fellow (1742–6) respectively (Venn, *Alumni Cantab.*, has apparently transposed the admission dates at Clare of this Charles Townshend and his namesake, who became Lord Bayning; see *Eton Coll. Reg.*).

23. Isaac Hawkins Browne (1705–60), a friend of Dr Johnson. Dodsley included his 'A Pipe of Tobacco,' 1736, and four other poems (*Collection* ii. 276–91).

24. 'An Epistle from Florence' (ibid. ii. 305–20). See *ante* ? 10 Nov. 1747, n. 8. The

wish corrected, and some blotted out, but beauties enough to atone for a thousand worse faults than these. The opinion of such as can at all judge, who saw it before in Dr Middleton's hands, concurs nearly with mine. As to what any one says since it came out: our people (you must know) are slow of judgment; they wait till some bold body saves them the trouble, and then follow his opinion, or stay till they hear what is said in town (that is, at some bishop's table, or some coffee-house about the Temple).[25] When they are determined, I will tell you faithfully their verdict. As for the Beauties,[26] I am their most humble servant. What shall I say to Mr Lowth,[27] Mr Ridley,[28] Mr Rolle,[29] the Reverend Mr Brown,[30] Seward,[31] etc.? If I say, Messieurs! this is not the thing; write prose, write sermons, write nothing at all; they will disdain me and my advice. What then would the sickly peer[32] have done, that

passages to which Gray refers are lines 136–57, 204–20, 299–316, and 349–58.

25. Gray elsewhere refers to the summary literary judgments of young lawyers as criticism 'à la mode du Temple' (Gray to Wharton 26 April 1744, *Gray's Corr.* i. 224).

26. HW's 'The Beauties. An Epistle to Mr Eckardt the Painter' (Dodsley, *Collection* ii. 321–7). The poem was transcribed by HW in HW, Waldegrave MSS 2.153–60. According to his MS note, it was written in July 1746, and 'some copies of [it] having got about, it was printed without the author's knowledge, with several errors.' It was published anonymously by Mary Cooper 23 Sept. 1746 (*Daily Adv.* 23 Sept. 1746; see also *Horace Walpole's Fugitive Verses*, ed. W. S. Lewis, New York, 1931, pp. 28–33), and was 'reprinted more correctly . . . by Dodsley 1748' (HW, Waldegrave MSS 2.153).

Gray is silent about HW's third contribution to Dodsley's *Collection* (ii. 327–30), viz. the 'Epilogue to Tamerlane, On the Suppression of the Rebellion. Spoken by Mrs Pritchard, in the Character of the Comic Muse, Nov. 4, 1746.'

27. Robert Lowth (1710–87), Professor of Poetry, Oxford, 1741–51; Bp of St Davids, 1766, of Oxford 1766–77, of London 1777–87. Dodsley included his 'The Choice of Hercules' (first printed by Spence in his *Polymetis*, 1747, pp. 155–62) and 'Ode to the People of Great Britain . . . Written in 1746' (Dodsley, *Collection* iii.

1–18). Both appear anonymously, but Lowth's authorship apparently was generally known. HW attributes 'The Choice of Hercules' to Lowth in a MS note in his copy of Dodsley (*Gray's Corr.* i. 297, n. 24).

28. Glocester Ridley (1702–74), D.D., Fellow of New College, Oxford, 1724–34; a prebendary of Salisbury (see Foster, *Alumni Oxon.*). Dodsley included two of Ridley's poems anonymously (*Collection* iii. 18–54).

29. Edward Rolle (ca 1705–91), another clergyman (see Foster, *Alumni Oxon.*). Dodsley included five of his pieces anonymously (*Collection* iii. 58–68, 222–6).

30. John Brown (1715–66), author of the *Estimate* (1757), vicar of Morland, Westmorland, 1743–56 (for his other livings see Venn, *Alumni Cantab.*). He is represented by two pieces (Dodsley, *Collection* iii. 99–136).

31. Thomas Seward (1708–90), rector of Eyam, Derby, 1740, and of Kingsley, Staffs, 1747 (see Venn, *Alumni Cantab.*); father of Anna Seward. Four poems by him are included in the *Collection* (ii. 295–304), of which 'The Female Right to Literature, in a Letter to a young Lady, from Florence' may have been recommended to Dodsley by HW (n. 1 above). HW met Seward at Lyons in Sept. or Oct. 1739 (HW to Conway 26 Dec. 1774).

32. 'Lord Hervey' (Berry). He was always in poor health, 'suffering from violent and recurrent paroxysms of pain due to an affection of the gall-bladder, probably gallstones' (Hervey, *Memoirs* i. p. xviii; see also

spends so much time in admiring everything that has four legs,[33] and
fretting at his own misfortune in having but two, and cursing his own
politic head and feeble constitution that won't let him be such a beast
as he would wish? Mr S. Jenyns[34] now and then can write a good line or
two—such as these—

> Snatch us from all our little sorrows here,
> Calm every grief, and dry each childish tear, etc.

I like Mr Aston Hervey's[35] fable and an ode (the last of all) by Mr
Mason,[36] a new acquaintance of mine, whose *Musæus*[37] too seems to
carry with it the promise at least of something good to come. I was glad
to see you distinguished who poor West was, before his charming ode,[38]
and called it anything rather than a Pindaric. The town is an owl if it
don't like Lady Mary,[39] and I am surprised at it; we here are owls
enough to think her eclogues[40] very bad, but that I did not wonder at.

'An Account of my own Constitution and
Illness . . . Written in the Year 1731,' ibid.
iii. 961–87). Gray's allusion is to the verses
'To Mr Fox, written at Florence' (in 1728 or
1729) and 'To the Same. From Hampton
Court, 1731' (Dodsley, *Collection* iii. 240–
50).

33. In 'To the Same' (ibid. iii. 245–9). Cf.
the following lines (p. 246):

> 'Will the wise elephant desert the wood,
> To imitate the whale and range the flood?
> Or will the mole her native earth forsake,
> In wanton madness to explore the lake?
> Yet man, whom still ideal profit sways,
> Than those less prudent, and more blind
>   than these,
> Will quit his home, and vent'rous brave
>   the seas.'

34. Soame Jenyns (1704–87), of Botti-
sham Hall, Cambs; M.P. Ten of his poems,
without the author's name, are given (ibid.
iii. 153–208). The couplet quoted by Gray
is from 'An Essay on Virtue' (ibid. iii. 206).

35. Hon. Henry Hervey Aston (ca 1702–
48), son of the 1st E. of Bristol, and younger
brother of John Lord Hervey. He assumed
the family name of his wife Catherine Aston by Private Act 17 Geo. II (1744) c. 22.
Aston was rector of Shotley, Suffolk, 1743
(Venn, *Alumni Cantab.*; Burke, *Peerage*,
1928, *sub* Bristol; Collins, *Peerage*, 1812, iv.
153–4). His only piece in the *Collection*

(iii. 232–6) is 'The Female-Drum: Or, the
Origin of Cards.'

36. William Mason (1725–97), Gray's correspondent and biographer, whom Gray
first met ca 1747 (Mason, *Memoirs* 172).
The poem Gray alludes to is 'Ode to a
Water-Nymph' (Dodsley, *Collection* iii.
330–3), printed anonymously.

37. 'Musæus,' first published 17 April
1747 (*Daily Adv.* 17 April 1747), appears in
the *Collection* iii. 136–48.

38. 'A Monody On the Death of Queen
Caroline. By Richard West, Esq; Son to
the Chancellor of Ireland, and Grandson to
Bishop Burnet' (ibid. ii. 269–75).

39. Lady Mary Pierrepont (1689–1762),
dau. of the 1st D. of Kingston, m. (1712)
Edward Wortley Montagu. See Appendix
5.

40. 'Six Town Eclogues. By the Right
Hon. L.M.W.M.' (ibid. iii. 274–98). HW
noted in his copy of the *Collection*: 'These
eclogues Lady M. Wortley allowed me to
transcribe from a volume of her poems in
MS at Florence in 1740 [see *ante* 2 Oct.
1740, N.S.], and from my copy Dodsley
printed them [published 14 Nov. 1747] and
the "Epistle from A[rthur] Grey," "The
Lover," and the "Epilogue"; and her Ladyship told me all the persons alluded to. Bp
Warburton has printed the second eclogue
as Pope's, who might correct or at least

From Gray, Sunday 3 March 1751

Reprinted from *Works* v. 387–8.

Cambridge, March 3, 1751.

ELFRIDA (for that is the fair one's name) and her author are now
in town together. He has promised me that he will send a part of it
to you some morning while he is there, and (if you shall think it worth
while to descend to particulars) I should be glad you would tell me
very freely your opinion about it, for he shall know nothing of the
matter that is not fit for the ears of a *tender* parent—though, by the
way, he has ingenuity and merit enough (whatever his drama may have)
to bear hearing his faults very patiently. I must only beg you not to
show it, much less let it be copied;[1] for it will be published, though not
as yet.[2]

I do not expect any more editions,[3] as I have appeared in more magazines than one.[4] The chief errata[5] were *sacred* bower for *secret;*[6] *hidden*
for *kindred*[7] (in spite of dukes and classics);[8] and *frowning* as in scorn
for *smiling.*[9] I humbly propose, for the benefit of Mr Dodsley and his
matrons,[10] that take *awake* for a verb,[11] that they should read *asleep,*
and all will be right. *Gil Blas*[12] is *The Lying Valet*[13] in five acts. *The*

1. An allusion to HW's handling of the *Elegy.*

2. It was published 21 March 1752 by J. and P. Knapton, Ludgate Street (*Daily Adv.* 21 March 1752).

3. The second quarto had appeared 25 Feb.; and see below, n. 11.

4. As Whibley believed, Gray may be playing on the title, *Magazine of Magazines,* or he may even have thought that the *Elegy* had been printed in other magazines, though no other appearances of the poem at this time have been discovered. See F. G. Stokes, *An Elegy written in a Country Churchyard,* Oxford, 1929, pp. 38–42. The 'Epitaph' only was printed in the *True Briton* for 6 Mar. 1751 (p. 234).

5. In the first quarto edition.

6. Line 11.

7. Line 96.

8. Since the original MS is missing, Miss Berry's reading cannot be verified.

9. Line 105.

10. See *ante* 20 Feb. 1751, where Gray refers to Dodsley as 'Nurse.'

11. In the first quarto edition, line 92 reads: 'Awake, and faithful to her wonted fires.' But Gray is unjust in blaming Dodsley for the comma which makes 'Awake' look like an imperative, for Gray himself inserted it in the line he sent to HW (*ante* 11 Feb. 1751). The comma was deleted in the third quarto (14 March) and the whole line changed in the eighth quarto (1753). See Stokes, op. cit. 29, 33, 76.

12. A five-act comedy by Edward Moore (1712–57), based on Smollett's translation of Le Sage's *Gil Blas.* It opened 2 Feb. 1751 at Drury Lane, where it had a run of nine nights (J. H. Caskey, *Life and Works of Edward Moore,* New Haven, 1927, pp. 73–85); and it was published 15 Feb. (*Daily Adv.* 15 Feb. 1751).

13. In the GM for Feb. 1751 the failure of *Gil Blas* is attributed to the fact that Moore had 'widely mistaken the character of Gil Blas, whom he has degraded from a man of sense, discernment, true humour, and great knowledge of mankind . . . to an impertinent, silly, conceited coxcomb, a mere *Lying Valet,* with all the affectation of a fop, and all the insolence of a coward'

Fine Lady[14] has half a dozen good lines dispersed in it. *Pompey*[15] is the hasty production of a Mr Coventry[16] (cousin to him you knew),[17] a young clergyman: I found it out by three characters, which once made part of a comedy that he showed me of his own writing. Has that miracle of *tenderness and sensibility* (as she calls it) Lady Vane[18] given you any amusement? Peregrine,[19] whom she uses as a vehicle, is very poor indeed with a few exceptions. In the last volume[20] is a character of Mr Lyttelton, under the name of Gosling Scrag,[21] and a parody of part of his *Monody,* under the notion of a pastoral on the death of his grandmother.[22] I am

Ever yours,

T. GRAY

(xxi. 78). Gray's allusion was probably suggested by this article. Garrick's farce, *The Lying Valet,* was first performed at Goodman's Fields 30 Nov. 1741 (Nicoll, *Drama 1700–50,* p. 329).

14. *The Modern Fine Lady,* a satire by Soame Jenyns, was published by Robert Dodsley 2 Feb. (*Daily Adv.* 2 Feb. 1751). It was a sequel to his *The Modern Fine Gentlemen,* 1746.

15. *Pompey the Little: or, the Life and Adventures of a Lap-Dog,* published 12 Feb. (*Daily Adv.* 12 Feb. 1751).

16. Francis Coventry (ca 1725–59), son of Thomas, of Mill End, Bucks, younger brother of the 5th E. of Coventry; Magdalene College, Cambridge (B.A. 1749); vicar of Edgware, Middlesex (DNB; Nichols, *Lit. Anec.* v. 569; Venn, *Alumni Cantab.;* Collins, *Peerage,* 1812, iii. 758; *Vict. Co. Hist., Bucks* iii. 49–50).

17. Henry Coventry (ca 1709–52), son of Henry, youngest brother of the 5th E. of Coventry; Fellow of Magdalene College, Cambridge, 1730, where HW had apparently been acquainted with him. See MONTAGU i. 7; see also Collins, loc. cit.; *Eton Coll Reg.;* GM 1753, xxiii. 51.

18. Frances Hawes (ca 1718–88), m. (1) (1733) Lord William Hamilton; m. (2) (1735) William Holles Vane, 2d Vct Vane. Smollett, who 'received a very handsome reward' (GM 1788, lviii pt i. 368), inserted her *Memoirs of a Lady of Quality* as chapter lxxxviii of *The Adventures of Peregrine Pickle* (edn 1751, iii. 66–237). The GM for 1751 suggests that the 'Lady of Quality' is

Lady Vane (xxi. 95; see also HW to Mann 13 March 1751, O.S.). The *Memoirs* were probably revised for the press by Dr John Shebbeare (H. S. Buck, *A Study in Smollett, Chiefly 'Peregrine Pickle,'* New Haven, 1925, p. 47; see also pp. 20–52).

19. *The Adventures of Peregrine Pickle. In which are included the Memoirs of a Lady of Quality.* It was published 25 Feb. (*Daily Adv.* 25 Feb. 1751). The *Daily Advertiser* 9 Feb. 1751 adds to its advertisement: 'That the public may not be imposed on, we are authorized to assure them that no memoirs of the above Lady that may be obtruded on the world under any disguise whatever are genuine, except what is comprised in this performance.'

20. Vol. iv, pp. 116–23.

21. 'The universal patron . . . the famous Gosling Scrag, Esq., son and heir of Sir Marmaduke Scrag, who seats himself in the chair of judgment, and gives sentence upon the authors of the age' (ibid. iv. 120). See also *Mem. Geo. II* iii. 259 and Buck, op. cit. 100–12.

22. Smollett makes 'Mr. Spondy' (Fielding) the author of his parody of Lyttelton's *Monody (ante* ca 10 Nov. 1747). It begins:
'Where wast thou, wittol Ward, when hapless fate
From these weak arms mine aged grannam tore?'
(Smollett, op. cit. iv. 117).
In the second revised edition of *Peregrine Pickle,* 1758, the attack on Lyttelton was suppressed (see also Buck, op. cit. 198–202).

To GRAY, April 1751

Missing. Probably written in Arlington Street. Answered *post* 16 April 1751.

From GRAY, Tuesday 16 April 1751

Printed from MS in Waller Collection.

The date of the year, added by Mason, is confirmed by the references to the deaths of Whithed and Lord Orford.

Address: To the Honorable Horace Walpole Esq. in Arlington Street, London.

Postmark: CAMBRIDGE 17 AP.

Cambridge, April 16 [1751].

I AM ashamed, but not astonished at poor Mr Whithed's insensi- bility.[1] Yet I had settled it with myself before that he would give Mr Chute £500 a year, which I thought at least by half too little. But this was just the thing in which Mr Chute neither would, nor could, sug- gest to him what he ought to do, and so he has done accordingly. I hope it was only negative ingratitude, but (I own to you) I do suspect there was a little reflection in it, and that his conversations with Mr L.,[2] and perhaps with another person[2] who knows the value of money better than that of friendship, might have had their effect upon his mind. I do not wonder that Mr Chute is satisfied with everything; I even be- lieve that when time shall convince him that Whithed has fallen ex- tremely short in his acknowledgments to him, it will rather add to his concern than diminish it. My best wishes always accompany him; and I can only *wish* that they were of more consequence. What a change this loss will make in his future life! I can only guess at the extent of it. The brothers are nasty people,[3] that don't deserve mentioning. I see *Alexander* sets himself up in his brother's room, which (I hope in God) will considerably reduce his share in the inheritance.[4]

1. Whithed died 29 March 1751 at the Vyne, Chute's country-seat (30 March in the *London Magazine* 1751, xx. 189, but see HW to Mann 1 April 1751, O.S.). By his will, dated 30 Aug. 1748, proved 15 April 1751 (P.C.C. Busby 128), Whithed divided his landed estates and the residue of his personal property between his brothers Alexander and Robert Thistlethwayte. He left £1000 to 'my cousin John Chute, Esq.'
2. Not identified.
3. Alexander Thistlethwayte (ca 1718–

71), of Winterslow, Wilts (subsequently of Southwick Park, Hants), M.P. Southamp- ton 1751–61 (as successor to Whithed); and Robert Thistlethwayte (ca 1721–67), D.D., rector of Tytherley, Hants (Foster, *Alumni Oxon.*). 'His [Whithed's] youngest brother, the clergyman, . . . is the greatest brute in the world, except the elder brother, the layman' (HW to Mann 1 April 1751, O.S.).

4. Alexander inherited the large Norton estate which had come to Whithed from his great-grandfather, Richard Norton,

You surprise me with the account you give me of the alteration in your own family. What a man must my Lord O.[5] have been, who might so easily have prevented it! I am heartily concerned for the share you must bear in it.[6] Sure your uncle[7] and Mrs H.[8] have it in their power, if not to retrieve, at least much to alleviate this misfortune, for from the mother nobody would expect anything. Perhaps the good qualities you mention in your nephew[9] may go farther in repairing his loss[10] than any of his relation could have done. From the little I had seen and heard of him, it did not seem probable that he could continue long in the thoughtless ways of folly. You were very good when you found time to let me know what I am interested in, not barely from curiosity, but because it touches you so nearly. I can return that kindness no otherwise than by not taking up your attention longer, when it is so fully employed on your own affairs. Adieu, my dear Sir, I am

Ever yours,

T. G.

To GRAY, September 1751

Missing. Probably written in Arlington Street. Implied *post* 29 Sept. 1751.

through his uncle, Richard Whitehead (Whithed's will; *Vict. Co. Hist., Hants* iii. 144–6, 161–72).

5. Robert Walpole (1701–51), 2d E. of Orford, HW's eldest brother, who had died 'Sunday night [31 March] between eleven and twelve o'clock . . . of an abscess in his back, at his house in the Exchequer' (*Daily Adv.* 2 April 1751). See also HW to Mann 21 March, 1 April 1751, O.S. Lord Orford did not make his will until Saturday 30 March. 'His spoils are prodigious—not to his own family! Indeed I think his son the most ruined young man in England' (HW to Mann 1 April 1751, O.S.). His will merely appointed his son George as executor, and recommended financial provision for a mistress and an illegitimate son, and a year's wages for his servants. Except for Houghton, which was entailed, the second Earl of Orford had little besides debts to leave.

6. 'My loss, I fear, may be considerable, which is not the only motive of my concern. . . . It is no small addition . . . to foresee that Houghton and all the remains of my father's glory will be pulled to pieces' (HW to Mann 1 April 1751, O.S.) Sir Robert Walpole at his death left debts amounting to more than £40,000 ('Account of my Conduct,' *Works* ii. 365). HW's own legacy from his father had not been paid.

7. Horatio, Sir Robert Walpole's younger brother.

8. Mrs Harris, Lady Orford's mother. She was Margaret Tuckfield (d. 1754), dau. of Roger Tuckfield, of Thorverton, Devon; m. (1) (before 1709) Samuel Rolle, of Heanton Satchville, Petrockstow, Devon; m. (2) (after 1719) John Harris, of Hayne, Devon, M.P. Helston 1727–41, Ashburton 1741–67 (GEC *sub* Orford; Thomas Wotton, *English Baronetage*, 1741, ii. 268; HW to Mann 28 March 1754).

9. George Walpole (1730–91), 3d E. of Orford. According to the *Daily Advertiser* 2 April 1751 he was still 'on his travels in foreign parts.'

10. Lady Orford 'triumphs in advancing her son's ruin by enjoying her own estate and tearing away great part of his' (HW to Mann 1 April 1751, O.S.).

From GRAY, Sunday 29 September 1751

Printed from MS in Waller Collection.

Dated in pencil, by HW or Mason: 1751.

Address: To the Honourable Horace Walpole Esq. in Arlington Street, London.

Postmark: SAFFRON WALDEN 30 SE.

Memoranda by HW: ⟨Ad⟩m[iral] Vernon who had much more reputation than courage and more courage than sense. One should ⟨h⟩ave thought his head light enough ⟨to⟩ have buoyed up his heart in any extremity.[1]

Mr Mann

Etoffe[2]

Donne[3]

Graham[4]

Camb[ridge], Sept. 29 [1751], Sunday.

I ASK your pardon for not having immediately informed you that I received the parcel very safe; but I was in Huntingdonshire[5] when it arrived, and did not return hither till Friday evening. The Sionites,[6] I am sorry to say, are just where they were. So is Mr Bentley,[7] having had cold water thrown upon him,[8] which stunted his growth. The other[9] I will send you in a few days, as you desire. I am going to see three of Dr M[iddleton]'s little works, that *were burnt.*[10] Adieu! I am

Ever yours,

T. G.

1. See *Mem. Geo.* II i. 100.

2. HW wrote to Mann 14 Oct. and to Henry Etough 12 Oct.

3. Not identified.

4. Perhaps Josiah Graham (fl. 1737–57), bookseller, on the corner of Craven Street in the Strand, publisher (1757) of HW's *Letter from Xo Ho.* In 1754 HW employed him to bid at an auction (HW to Bentley 13 Dec. 1754; H. R. Plomer *et al., Dictionary of . . . Printers and Booksellers . . . 1726–1775,* Oxford, 1932).

5. Probably visiting Nicholas Bonfoy at Abbots Ripton, Hunts, about twenty miles from Cambridge. See *ante* 21 April 1739, N.S., n. 41.

6. Toynbee suggests that Gray alludes to Mason and Lord Holdernesse, later Mason's patron. Holdernesse, HW's Eton contemporary, had a seat at Syon Hill, Middlesex (*Times Literary Supplement* 7 July

1927, p. 472; *Gray's Corr.* i. 417, n. 9; J. W. Draper, *William Mason,* New York, 1924, pp. 17, 45).

7. Richard Bentley (1708–82), son of the Master of Trinity College, Cambridge; HW's correspondent.

8. Perhaps by Gray himself, through criticism of his drawings for Gray's poems, published subsequently as *Designs by Mr R. Bentley for Six Poems by Mr T. Gray.* HW to Montagu 13 June 1751 mentions that Bentley 'is drawing vignettes' for Gray's odes (MONTAGU i. 116.) See also *post* 8 July 1752, n. 2, and 13 Feb. 1753.

9. Gray's 'Hymn to Adversity' (*post* 8 Oct. 1751).

10. See ibid., nn. 9 and 14. Evidently there had been an exaggerated report of the number of Middleton's MSS which Dr Heberden had burned.

From GRAY, Tuesday 8 October 1751

Printed from MS in Waller Collection.

Apparently misdated by Gray 'Sept. 8. Camb.'; 'Sept.' altered to 'Oct.,' and '1751' added, probably by HW. See preceding letter.

Memoranda by HW: Mr Spence Oct. 10.

Mrs Talbot——11.

Mr Conway——12.[1]

Sept. [Oct.] 8 [1751], Camb[ridge].

Hymn to Adversity

DAUGHTER of Jove, relentless power,
Thou tamer of the human breast!
Whose iron scourge, and torturing hour,
The bad affright, afflict the best,
Bound in thy adamantine chain
The proud are taught to taste of pain
And purple tyrants vainly groan
With pangs unfelt before, unpitied and alone.

When first thy sire, to send on earth
Virtue, his darling child, designed,
To thee he gave the heav'nly birth
And bade to form her infant mind.
Stern rugged nurse! thy rigid lore
With patience many a year she bore:
What sorrow was thou bad'st her know,
And from her own she learned to melt at other's woe.

Scared at thy frown terrific, fly
Self-pleasing folly's idle brood,
Wild laughter, noise, and thoughtless joy,
And leave us leisure to be good:
Light they disperse, and with them go
The summer friend, the flatt'ring foe;
By vain prosperity received,
To her they vow their truth, and are again believed.

Wisdom in sable garb arrayed,
Immersed in rapturous thought profound,

---

1. These notes probably refer to missing letters.

And melancholy, silent maid,
With leaden eye that loves the ground,
Still on thy solemn steps attend:
Warm charity, the general friend,
And pity, dropping soft the sadly-pleasing tear.

   Oh, gently on thy suppliant's head
Dread goddess lay thy chast'ning hand,
Not in thy gorgon-terrors clad,
Nor circled with the vengeful band,
As by the impious thou art seen,
With thund'ring voice, and threat'ning mien,
With screaming horror's funeral cry,
Despair, and fell disease, and ghastly poverty.

   Thy form benign, O goddess, wear,
Thy milder influence impart;
Thy philosophic train be there
To soften, not to wound, my heart.
The generous spark extinct revive,
Teach me to love and to forgive,
Exact my own defects to scan,
What others are, to feel, and know myself a man.

I send you this (as you desire) merely to make up half a dozen,[2] though it will hardly answer your end in furnishing out either a head- or tail-piece. But your own fable[3] may much better supply the place. You have altered it to its advantage, but there is still something a little embarrassed here and there in the expression. I rejoice to find you apply (pardon the use of so odious a word) to the history of your own times.[4] Speak, and spare not. Be as impartial as you can; and after all, the world will not believe you are so, though you should make as many protestations as Bishop Burnet.[5] They will feel in their own breast, and

2. The 'Hymn to Adversity' became No. 5 in the *Designs*. The others were: 1. 'Ode on the Spring,' 2. 'Ode on the Death of a Favourite Cat,' 3. 'Ode on a distant Prospect of Eton College,' 4. 'A Long Story,' 6. 'Elegy written in a Country Churchyard.'
3. Miss Berry mistakenly calls this 'The Entail,' which was not written until July

1754 (see *ante* i. 25). Gray alludes to 'The Funeral of the Lioness: A Fable. Imitated from La Fontaine' (printed in *Works* iv. 377–80 with head- and tail-pieces by Bentley), which HW wrote this year (see *ante* i. 24).
4. *Memoirs of the Reign of King George II*, which HW began this year.

find it very possible to hate fourscore persons, yea, ninety and nine; so you must rest satisfied with the testimony of your own conscience. Somebody has laughed at Mr Dodsley or at me, when they talked of the *Bat*:[6] I have nothing more, either nocturnal or diurnal, to deck his miscellany with.[7] We have a man here that writes a good hand, but he has two little failings that hinder my recommending him to you:[8] he is lousy, and he is mad. He sets out this week for Bedlam; but if you insist upon it, I don't doubt he will pay his respects to you. I have seen two of Dr M[iddleton's] unpublished works.[9] One is about 44 pages in quarto against Dr Waterland, who wrote a very orthodox book on *The Importance of the Doctrine of the Trinity*,[10] and insisted that Christians ought to have no communion with such as differ from them in fundamentals.[11] M[iddleton] enters no farther into the doctrine itself than to show that a mere speculative point can never be called a fundamental, and that the earlier Fathers, on whose concurrent tradition Wat[erlan]d would build, are so far, when they speak of the three Persons, from agreeing with the present notion of our Church, that they declare for the inferiority of the Son, and seem to have no clear and distinct idea of the H[oly] Ghost at all. The rest is employed in expos-

5. 'I writ with a design . . . to lay open the good and bad of all sides and parties as clearly and impartially as I myself understood it . . . without any regard to kindred or friends, to parties or interests. For I do solemnly say this to the world, and make my humble appeal upon it to the great God of truth, that I tell the truth on all occasions, as fully and freely as upon my best inquiry I have been able to find it out' (*Bishop Burnet's History of His Own Time*, ed. Sir Thomas Burnet, 1724–34, i. 2–3). HW's Postscript to the memoirs for 1751 is strongly influenced by Burnet's Preface. See *Mem. Geo. II* i. pp. xxix–xxxvii.

6. Apparently someone had told Dodsley that Gray had written a poem about a bat, which Dodsley wished to print in his *Collection*.

7. Dodsley was about to publish the third edition of his *Collection of Poems* (vols i–iii), which appeared 29 Jan. 1752. Vol. iv of the *Collection*, containing Gray's *Elegy* and the 'Hymn to Adversity,' did not appear until 18 March 1755 (Ralph Straus, *Robert Dodsley*, 1910, pp. 343, 356).

8. 'As an amanuensis' (Berry). This was probably 'Lawman, the mad attorney,' Christopher Smart's copyist, mentioned in Gray to Wharton 17 March 1747 (*Gray's Corr.* i. 274). See D. C. Tovey in N&Q 1905, ser. X. iii. 221–2.

9. Middleton had died 28 July 1750. His widow had left his papers to Dr William Heberden.

10. *The Importance of the Doctrine of the Holy Trinity Asserted*, 1734, by Daniel Waterland (1683–1740), Master of Magdalene College, Cambridge. Middleton's answer, 'An Expostulatory Letter to the Reverend Dr Waterland,' etc., is Add. MS 32,459, folios 52ff.

11. 'In short, all parties and denominations of Christians, who appear to have had the truth of the doctrine [of the Trinity] at heart, or any degree of zeal for it, have contended equally for the necessity of believing it, and have refused communion with the impugners of it' (Waterland, op. cit. 7–8).

ing the folly and cruelty of stiffness and zealotism in religion, and in showing that the primitive ages of the Church, in which tradition had its rise, were (even by confession of the best scholars and most orthodox writers) the *era of nonsense and absurdity*. It is finished, and very well wrote, but has been mostly incorporated into his other works, particularly the *Inquiry*,[12] and for this reason I suppose he has writ upon it, *This wholly laid aside*. The second is in Latin, on miracles,[13] to show that of the two methods of defending Christianity, one from its intrinsic evidence (the holiness and purity of its doctrines), the other from its external (the miracles said to be wrought to confirm it): the first has been little attended to by reason of its difficulty; the second much insisted upon because it appeared an easier task, but that it can in reality prove nothing at all. 'Nobilis illa quidem defensio' (the first) 'quam si obtinere potuissent, rem simul omnem expediisse, causamque penitus vicisse viderentur. At causæ huius defendendæ labor cum tanta argumentandi cavillandique molestia conjunctus ad alteram, quam dixi, defensionis viam, ut commodiorem longe et faciliorem, plerosque adegit—ego vero istiusmodi defensione religionem nostram non modo non confirmari, sed dubiam potius suspectamque reddi existimo.' He then proceeds to consider miracles in general, and afterwards those of the pagans compared with those of Christ. I only tell you the plan, for I have not read it out (though it is short), but you will not doubt to what conclusion it tends. There is another thing, I know not what, I am to see. As to the treatise on prayer, they say it is burnt[14] indeed. Adieu, I am ever

Yours,

T. G.

To GRAY, November 1751

Missing. Probably written in Arlington Street. Mentioned *post* 26 Nov. 1751.

12. *A Free Inquiry into the Miraculous Powers which are supposed to have subsisted in the Christian Church from the earliest ages, through several successive centuries*, etc., 1749, advertised in *Daily Adv.* 23 Dec. 1748 as published 'this day.'

13. 'On the Power of Miracles to prove a Religion,' now Add. MS 32,459, folios 21ff.

14. 'Dr Middleton had left . . . a discourse on prayer, which had raised great curiosity; but it was burnt by advice of Lord Bolingbroke, and with the consent and opinion of Dr Heberden, a young phy-sician of note, who had the care of Dr M.'s posthumous writings. On Lord Bolingbroke's death, there was found among his papers, a copy of the treatise on prayer, which he had taken privately' (HW, Waldegrave MSS 1. 89). See also William Seward's *Anecdotes*, 4th edn, 1798, ii. 344–5 (quoted in Nichols, *Lit. Anec.* v. 423), where it is said that Bolingbroke recommended publication of the treatise. Walter Sichel in *Bolingbroke and His Times*, 1901–2, ii. 395, supports HW's assertion that Bolingbroke at least kept a copy of it.

From GRAY, Tuesday 26 November 1751

Printed from MS in Waller Collection.

Dated by Mason: 'Nov. 1751.' The day of the month is determined by the postmark.

Address: To the Honourable Horace Walpole Esq. in Arlington Street, London.
Postmark: SAFFRON WALDEN 27 NO.
Memoranda by HW: 'The —— who began to feel flaws in his divinity.

'H[arry] V[ane] the centurion of their spies, who when he was drunk told all he knew, and when he was sober more than he knew.'[1]

On the margin, next to the address, is a profile in ink, probably sketched by HW.

Tuesday [Nov. 26, 1751], Camb[rid]ge.

IF Etoughe had any such paper[2] trusted to his hands, I don't at all doubt but it has been showed to someone here. It is about three weeks ago that he was here with his budget of libels (for it is his constant practice twice in a year to import a cargo of lies and scandalous truths mixed), but his confidants are cautioned against me, who have had more squabbles than one either with him or about him, so that *directly* it would be impossible for me to come at it, or even to hear any of the contents. But I have a roundabout way or two in my head: if I succeed, you shall be sure to know immediately; but this will take up a week or a fortnight, for I must not seem too eager about it. I am amazed at the impudence of the fiend (as much a fiend as I knew him).[3] You say you took him to task;[4] I am impatient to know in what manner. For I imagine you sent to him, and that this has given him an opportunity of writing those impudent letters[5] you mention, to you. There are three methods of taking him properly to task: the cudgel, the blanket, and the horse-pond. If you are present at the operation, you may venture to break a leg or an arm *en attendant,* and when I see you, I may possibly give you some reasons why you ought to have broke t'other leg and t'other arm also; for it is too long to stay till he is a bishop.

I do not wonder at their rage venting itself on Mr Chute.[6] They think him easier to come at, and more open to injury. I am glad he

1. For the second of these notes see *Mem. Geo. II* i. 117; the first has not been located, but was probably also intended for use in the *Memoirs.*

2. Missing. The paper evidently described Chute's interview with Margaret Nicoll, 21 June 1751, at Francis Capper's house (see Appendix 1).

3. See *ante* ca Jan. 1748.

4. In HW to Etough 12 Oct. 1751.

5. Missing.

6. See Appendix 1.

hears so little of the matter. What my insipid Lord H . . . on⁷ could poke out of his memory against him, I don't conceive. Would to God anything I could do might make all the world think of him as I do. But the way you propose would signify very little. Adieu, Sir, I am

Yours ever,

T. G.

From GRAY, Tuesday 31 December 1751

Printed from MS in Waller Collection.
The date of the year is determined by the allusion to the Nicoll affair.

[Cambridge,] Dec. 31 [1751].

YOU have probably before now met with the paper¹ I enclose, it-self, though when you wrote last, you had only heard of it from others. It must not be known on any account that it came from me, for by that means it might be easily discovered whom I had it from, which might be the ruin of a gentleman.² I do not see any one end it can an-swer but that of putting Mr C[hute] in a silly light to such as do not know him. The exactness of dates, hours, and minutes with the obser-vation of his different tones of voice, betray it to be the work of a lis-tener, placed on purpose.³ I am told that old H[orace] does not deny his design of getting her⁴ for D[ick] W[alpole],⁵ after my Lord O[rford] had refused her. He insists he was not once at C[appe]r's⁶ chambers while she was in his hands, and that the story of the £10,000⁷ is a manifest lie. He affects to treat it as a fact asserted by Mr C[hute],

7. This name is partly deleted in the MS. Not identified.

1. An account of the interview of 21 June 1751 between Miss Nicoll and Chute, evidently based on Miss Nicoll's own ac-count. For this account, and an explana-tion of the other allusions in this letter, see Appendix 1.
2. Not identified.
3. See Appendix 1 for HW's accusation of espionage. Gray evidently did not know of the existence of Miss Nicoll's account,

from which the details he mentions could have been learned.
4. I.e., Miss Nicoll.
5. 'Old' Horace's third son: the Hon. Richard Walpole (1728–98), M.P. for Great Yarmouth 1768–84; m. (1758) Margaret Vanneck (d. 1818) (Burke, *Peerage*, 1928, pp. 1265, 1785; *Members of Parliament*, 1878, ii. 141, 153, 179; GM 1758, xxviii. 556).
6. Francis Capper. See Appendix 1, n. 18.
7. See *post* ii. 217.

though no such thing appears even in the paper itself. I can't find for certain that Et[ough] (though he has been here a second time with his budget) has given any copies of this paper about, yet I do not doubt but he has. This I know: he has showed your letter to him and his own answers[8] to a few people here, though I have not seen them. I am in haste, but shall write again soon. Pray tell me as soon as you receive this.

From GRAY, Thursday 28 May 1752

Reprinted from *The Times* (London) 15 May 1922, p. 16, col. 7. The original, which had been owned by Mr Henry G. Bohn, was sold to Maggs by Knight, Frank and Rutley (lot 98), 12 May 1922. In 1924 it was offered for sale by Myers and Co., Cat. No. 241, lot 135. Toynbee in *SH Accounts,* p. 62, says that on the back of the MS (which the editors have not seen) HW drew a shield of arms and wrote 'Palmer,' probably referring to a glazier employed at SH.

Address: To the Honourable Horace Walpole Esq. in Arlington Street, London.

Cambridge, May 28, 1752.

I AM sorry I am forced to tell you that I cannot have the satisfaction of seeing you now at Strawberry. Here is a Dr Wharton[1] (whose name you remember), a particular friend of mine, that I have not seen in several years;[2] his errand hither has been chiefly to see me,[3] and till he leaves the place it will be impossible for me to stir.

I wish your invitation had been some weeks later, but as it is, I must be content to lose that pleasure, as I do most others, and only send my love to Mr Chute and compliments to Mr Bentley.[4] I am

Yours ever,

T. GRAY

To GRAY, ca July 1752

Missing. Mentioned *post* 8 July 1752.

8. Missing.

1. Thomas Wharton (1717–94), of Old Park, Durham, physician; Gray's intimate friend and correspondent (*Gray's Corr.* i. 141–2, n. 8).

2. Wharton, on his marriage, vacated his fellowship at Pembroke, and Gray had seen him last at Stilton, Hunts, before Wharton

and his bride left for London on their honeymoon (*Gray's Corr.* i. 280).

3. Wharton came to Cambridge to take his M.D., and signed the Registrar's book as M.D. on 14 April. Gray, on a fortnight's visit to London, returned to Cambridge 15 April (*Gray's Corr.* i. 360–1).

4. He was at SH 'finishing the drawings for Gray's *Odes*' (MONTAGU i. 134).

BENTLEY'S FRONTISPIECE TO HIS DESIGNS

FOR GRAY'S POEMS, 1753

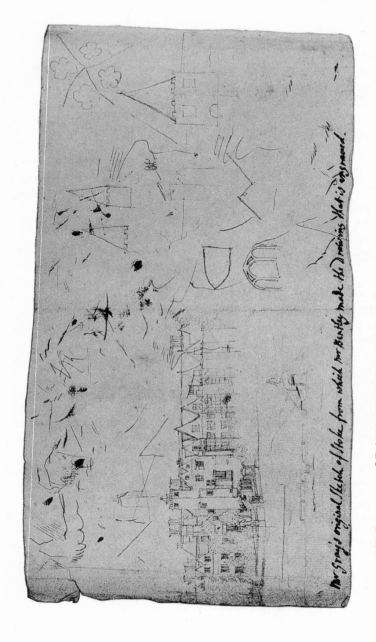

GRAY'S SKETCH OF STOKE MANOR HOUSE

From GRAY, Wednesday 8 July 1752

Printed from MS in Waller Collection.
Dated by Mason: 1752.
Address: To the Honourable Horace Walpole Esq. in Arlington Street, London.
Postmark: 9 IY.

Wednesday [July 8, 1752], Stoke.

I AM at present at Stoke, to which I came at half an hour's warning upon the news I received of my mother's illness, and did not expect to have found her alive; but, as I found her much better, and she continues so, I shall be very glad to make you a visit at Strawberry, whenever you give me notice of a convenient time. I am surprised at the print,[1] which far surpasses my idea of London graving. The drawing itself was so finished that I suppose it did not require all the art I had imagined to copy it tolerably.[2] My aunts[3] just now, seeing me open your letter, take it to be a burying ticket enclosed, and ask whether anybody has left me a ring? and so they still conceive it to be, even with all their spectacles on. Heaven forbid they should suspect it to belong to any verses of mine: they would burn me for a poet. Mr Bentley (I believe) will catch a better idea of Stoke House[4] from any old barn he sees, than from my sketch,[5] but I will try my skill. I forbid no banns, but am satisfied if your design succeed so well as you intend it. And yet I know it will be accompanied with something not at all agreeable to me. Adieu! I am

Yours ever,

T. G.

1. The *cul-de-lampe* for the *Elegy*, representing 'a country burial. At bottom, a torch fallen into an ancient vault' ('Explanation of the Prints' in *Designs*, 1753). It was engraved by Charles Grignion (1717–1810).

2. Bentley's pen and ink drawings (sold London 1044, now WSL) are executed in such detail, and with such scrupulous care, as to make it hard to distinguish them from engravings. See illustration and *post* 20 Feb. 1753.

3. Mrs Rogers and her sister Jane Antrobus (1681–1771), m. William Olliffe. Mrs Olliffe, who on Mrs Rogers's death in 1758 became with Gray her joint executor, is called by Gray 'an old harridan, who is the spawn of Cerberus and the Dragon of Wantley' (*Gray's Corr.* ii. 592; see also ii. 593, iii. 1308).

4. Stoke Manor House, the 'ancient pile of building' of Gray's 'A Long Story,' to the north of the church at Stoke Poges, was completed in 1555 by the 2d Earl of Huntingdon. His son Henry Hastings (ca 1536–95), the 3d Earl, in 1594 sold the manor to Richard Branthwaite, who in turn sold it in 1599 to Sir Edward Coke, lord chief justice (*Vict. Co. Hist., Bucks* iii. 302, 306–7).

5. Gray's original pencil drawing of Stoke Manor House is now WSL. Bentley followed it in his head-piece for 'A Long Story.' See illustration.

To Gray, July–August 1752

Missing. HW apparently sought information on the furniture in Stoke Manor House. Answered *post* ca Aug. 1752.

From Gray, ca August 1752

Reprinted from *Works* v. 392–3. The date of the year is supplied by the allusions to *Designs*, 1753. From the reference to *The Progress of Poesy* as being too late for inclusion in the *Designs*, it would seem that Bentley had nearly finished his drawings, a fact likewise implied in HW to Montagu 28 Aug. 1752 (Montagu i. 143).

[Stoke, ca August 1752.]

YOUR pen was too rapid to mind the common form of a direction, and so, by omitting the words *near Windsor*, your letter has been diverting itself at another Stoke near Ailesbury,[1] and came not to my hands till today. The true original chairs were all sold when the Huntingdons broke;[2] there are nothing now but Halsey[3] chairs, not adapted to the squareness of a Gothic dowager's rump. And by the way I do not see how the uneasiness and uncomfortableness of a coronation chair can be any objection with you: every chair that is easy is modern, and unknown to our ancestors. As I remember, there were certain low chairs, that looked like ebony, at Esher,[4] and were old and pretty. Why should not Mr Bentley improve upon them?[4a]—I do not wonder at Dodsley. You have talked to him of six *odes,* for so you are pleased to call everything I write, though it be but a receipt to make apple-dumplings. He has reason to gulp when he finds one of them only 'a long story.'[5] I don't know but I may send him very soon (by your hands) an ode to his own tooth, a high Pindaric upon stilts,[6] which one must be a better scholar than he is to understand a line of, and the very best scholars will understand but a little matter here and there. It wants

1. Stoke Mandeville, Bucks, three miles SE of Aylesbury.

2. See *ante* 8 July 1752, n. 4.

3. Anne Halsey (d. 1760), m. Sir Richard Temple, Bt, of Stowe, Bucks, cr. (1714) Bn and (1718) Vct Cobham. Stoke Manor was purchased in 1724 by her father, Edmund Halsey, a London brewer, from Robert Gayer for £12,000 (*Vict. Co. Hist., Bucks* iii. 307). On Halsey's death (1729) the manor was inherited by Lady Cobham.

4. Esher Place, Surrey, the seat of Henry Pelham. Gray probably visited it with HW in 1748 (Montagu i. 71).

4a. Among Bentley's drawings (now wsl) for the 'improvements' at SH are several designs for Gothic chairs.

5. Gray finished the poem thus titled ca 10 Oct. 1750 (*Gray's Corr.* i. 330–1, n. 1).

6. *The Progress of Poesy. A Pindaric Ode.* It was not published until 1757 (*post* 11 July 1757.)

but seventeen lines of having an end, I don't say of being finished. As it is so unfortunate to come too late for Mr Bentley, it may appear in the fourth volume of the *Miscellanies*,[7] provided you don't think it execrable and suppress it. Pray, when the fine book is to be printed, let me revise the press, for you know you can't,[8] and there are a few trifles I could wish altered.

I know not what you mean by hours of love,[9] and cherries, and pineapples. I neither see nor hear anything here, and am of opinion that is the best way. My compliments to Mr Bentley, if he be with you. I am

Your ever,

T. GRAY

I desire you would not show that epigram[10] I repeated to you as mine. I have heard of it twice already as coming from you.

From GRAY, Sunday 17 December 1752

Printed from MS in Waller Collection.
Dated by Mason: 1752.
Address: To the Honourable Horace Walpole Esq. in Arlington Street, London.
Postmark: SAFFRON WALDEN 18 DE.

Camb[rid]ge, Dec. 17 [1752], Sunday.

I SENT to Dodsley some time since, who wrote to me by your order, what little alterations I had to make, and should be glad to know whether you thought them for the better or the worse. He tells me now he could finish in a fortnight if I were in town, but this would be very inconvenient to me at present, so I must have the sheets sent me to correct hither, and I suppose it may come out in less than a month[1] . . . .[2]

7. See *ante* 8 Oct. 1751, n. 7.
8. A frequent reproach of Gray's, according to HW. See HW to Mason 15 May 1773.
9. HW probably was alluding to Gray's meetings with Lady Cobham's niece, Henrietta Jane Speed (1728–83), m. (1761) Francesco Maria Giuseppe Giustino di Viry, Barone de la Perrière, Conte di Viry, 1766 (Vittorio Spreti, *Enciclopedia storico-nobiliare italiana*, Milan, 1928–36, vi. 924). She had been living at Stoke with Lady Cobham since 1747, and in Sept. 1750, in company with Lady Schaub, she called on Gray at Mrs Rogers's house. Gray was absent, but soon returned the visit, and composed for the occasion 'A Long Story,' of which Miss Speed and Lady Schaub are the 'heroines.' He became intimate with Miss Speed and on Lady Cobham's death (1760) there were rumours of their impending marriage (*Gray's Corr.* i. 330–3, ii. 704).
10. Not identified.

1. *Designs* was published 29 March 1753 (*Daily Adv.* 27–29 March 1753).
2. A piece containing about five lines of the text has been cut from the MS.

. . . you may imagine I do not expect anything very particular on either of these subjects,[3] but some sort of satisfaction you will easily know how to give me in a letter, as it will be a good while before I can see you. Adieu, I am ever

Yours,

T. G.

Have you read Madame Maintenon's Letters?[4] or the *Micromégas*,[5] or the dull *Life of Dr Tillotson*?[6] I have gone through the third volume of the *Biographia*,[7] which will be a great relief to you after Bayle's[8] pedantic bawdy. All the 'Lives' marked with an 'E'[9] or a 'C'[10] have something curious in them, those with a 'G'[11] are abominable foolish.

I have just received the first proofs from Dodsly. I thought it was to be a quarto, but it is a little folio.[12] The stanzas are numbered,[13] which I do not like.

3. Not explained.

4. Françoise d'Aubigné (1635–1719), Marquise de Maintenon, m. (1) (1652) Paul Scarron; m. (2) (1684) Louis XIV. Two editions of her *Lettres* were printed this year, one at Nancy and the other at Paris, edited by Laurent Angliviel de la Baumelle (BM Cat.; Bibl. Nat. Cat.). HW's copy, Paris, 1752, was sold SH ii. 147 and is now WSL. For Gray's opinion of the *Lettres* see *Gray's Corr.* i. 369.

5. *Le Micromégas de M. de Voltaire* was published by Jacob Robinson 16 Nov. 1752 (*Daily Adv.* 16 Nov. 1752). An English translation was published 21 Nov. (ibid. 20, 21 Nov. 1752). A French edition was reviewed in the April 1752 number (pp. 751–61) of *Mémoires pour l'histoire des sciences et des beaux arts.*

6. *The Life of the Most Reverend Dr John Tillotson, Lord Archbishop of Canterbury* by Thomas Birch (1705–66) was published 28 Nov. (*Daily Adv.* 28 Nov. 1752). Birch's *Life* was also prefixed to a new edition in 3 vols folio of Tillotson's *Works*, published by J. and R. Tonson the following day (*Daily Adv.* 29 Nov. 1752).

7. *Biographia Britannica: or, the Lives of the most eminent Persons who have flourished in Great Britain and Ireland. . . . Digested in the Manner of Mr Bayle's Historical and Critical Dictionary*, 7 vols folio,

1747–66. The third volume was published 17 May 1751 (*Daily Adv.* 17 May 1751).

8. Pierre Bayle (1647–1706), author of *Dictionnaire historique et critique.*

9. E and X were the initials used by John Campbell (1708–75), miscellaneous writer, author of the *Lives of the Admirals*, 1742–4. He contributed 49 articles to the third volume (see *Biographia Britannica*, 2d edn, ed. Andrew Kippis, vol. i, 1778, p. xx; DNB).

10. The initial used by Philip Morant (1700–70), antiquary; he wrote 48 articles for the third volume (Nichols, *Lit. Anec.* ii. 205; Kippis, loc. cit.).

11. The initial used by William Oldys (1696–1761), antiquary, co-editor with Dr Johnson of the *Harleian Miscellany*. He wrote 22 articles for the *Biographia*, six of which are in the third volume (Kippis, loc. cit.).

12. *Designs*, 1753, was actually imperial quarto printed in half-sheets, but so cut that it looks like a folio. The text comprises thirty-six leaves, printed on one side only. The type-page measures 9½ inches, but because of the engravings (11½ by 8¾) a larger format was employed: HW's copy (now WSL) measures 14¾ by 10½; an untrimmed copy (also WSL) measures 15½ by 11.

13. The numbering was omitted from the published book.

To Gray, ca January 1753

Missing. Probably written in Arlington Street (the 'long letter' mentioned in *post* 13 Feb. 1753).

To Gray, ca Sunday 11 February 1753

Missing. Probably written in Arlington Street. Answered *post* 13 Feb. 1753.

From Gray, Tuesday 13 February 1753

Printed from MS in Waller Collection.

Camb[rid]ge, Feb. 13, 1753.

SURE you are not out of your wits! This I know, if you suffer my head[1] to be printed, you infallibly will put me out of mine. I conjure you immediately to put a stop to any such design. Who is at the expense of engraving it I know not, but if it be Dodsley, I will make up the loss to him. The thing as it was, I know, will make me ridiculous enough, but to appear in proper person at the head of my works, consisting of half a dozen ballads in thirty pages,[2] would be worse than the pillory. I do assure you, if I had received such a book with such a frontispiece without any warning, I believe it would have given me a palsy. Therefore I rejoice to have received this notice, and shall not be easy till you tell me all thoughts of it are laid aside. I am extremely in earnest, and can't bear even the idea!

I had wrote to Dodsley[3] to tell him how little I liked the title[4] he

1. Dodsley proposed as a frontispiece to *Designs*, 1753, a print of John Giles Eccardt's portrait of Gray (painted for HW in 1748, now in the National Portrait Gallery; see *ante* facing ii. 22). The engraving was more than half completed when suppressed at Gray's request (Mason, *Mem. Gray* 225). The proof of the unfinished head, which Mason found among Gray's prints, was returned by Mason to HW (Mason to HW 5 Nov. 1772), and in 1944 was in the hands of Dr A. S. W. Rosenbach of New York. It bears the following note in HW's hand: 'Mr Gray, from the picture at Strawberry Hill, the plate of which Mr Gray destroyed v. p. 225' (referring to Mason, *Mem.*

Gray). The engraver was Johann Sebastian Müller (ca 1715–ca 1790). If HW is right in saying that the plate was destroyed, Müller evidently engraved another one, since many prints of his engraving of the portrait survive (*Gray's Corr.* i. 372, n. 1; *BM Cat. of Engraved British Portraits* ii. 376).

2. See *ante* 17 Dec. 1752, n. 12.

3. On 12 Feb. (*Gray's Corr.* i. 371).

4. The title proposed by Dodsley was probably 'Poems by Thomas Gray, with Designs by Richard Bentley.' The advertisement in *Daily Adv.* 27–31 March, 2–5 April reads 'Poems by Mr Gray, with Designs by Mr Bentley'; but one of Gray's complaints concerned the use of their 'plain

had prefixed, but your letter has put all that out of my head. If you think it necessary to print these explanations[5] for the use of people that have no eyes, I could be glad they were a little altered. I am to my shame in your debt for a long letter,[6] but I cannot think of anything else till you have set me at ease. Adieu, I am

Yours ever,

T. G.

To GRAY, ca Thursday 15 February 1753

Missing. A 'note,' probably written in Arlington Street, in answer to *ante* 13 Feb. 1753; mentioned *post* 20 Feb. 1753.

From GRAY, ca Saturday 17 February 1753

Missing. Probably written at Cambridge. Answered *post* 20 Feb. 1753.

To GRAY, Tuesday 20 February 1753

Printed from MS now WSL. In 1828 it was bequeathed by Mrs Damer to Sir Wathen Waller, 1st Bt; sold at Sotheby's, 5 Dec. 1921, lot 20, to Maggs; offered by Maggs, Cat. No. 421 (April 1922), lot 836; bought by Frank B. Bemis, of Boston, Mass.; sold by his trustees to Goodspeed; Goodspeed to WSL, Sept. 1944.

Arlington Street, Feb. 20, 1753.

I AM very sorry that the haste I made to deliver you from your uneasiness the first moment after I received your letter,[1] should have made me express myself in a manner to have the quite contrary effect from what I intended. You well know how rapidly and carelessly I always write my letters; the note[2] you mention was written in a still greater hurry than ordinary, and merely to put you out of pain. I had not seen Dodsley, consequently could only tell you that I did not doubt but he would have no objection to satisfy you, as you was willing

Christian and surnames without a "Mr" before them' (*Gray's Corr.* i. 371). As the result of Gray's objections, the title was changed to read: *Designs by Mr R. Bentley for six Poems by Mr T. Gray.*

5. At the end of *Designs* there are four pages of 'Explanations of the Prints.'
6. HW to Gray ca Jan. 1753, missing.

---

1. *Ante* 13 Feb. 1753.
2. HW to Gray ca 15 Feb. 1753, missing.

to prevent his being a loser by the plate. Now, from this declaration how is it possible for you to have for one moment put such a construction upon my words, as would have been a downright stupid brutality, unprovoked? It is impossible for me to recollect my very expression, but I am confident that I have repeated the whole substance.

How the bookseller would be less a loser by being at more expense, I can easily explain to you: He feared the price of half a guinea[3] would seem too high to most purchasers; if by the expense of ten guineas more he could make the book appear so much more rich and showy (as I believe I said) as to induce people to think it cheap, the profits from selling many more copies would amply recompense him for his additional disbursement.

The thought of having the head engraved was entirely Dodsley's own, and against my opinion, as I concluded it would be against yours, which made me determine to acquaint you with it before its appearance.

When you reflect on what I have said now, you will see very clearly, that I had and could have no other possible meaning in what I wrote last. You might justly have accused me of neglect, if I had deferred giving you all the satisfaction in my power, as soon as ever I knew your uneasiness.

The head I give up. The title I think will be wrong, and not answer your purpose, for as the drawings are evidently calculated for the poems, why will the improper disposition of the word *Designs* before *Poems,* make the edition less yours? I am as little convinced that there is any affectation in leaving out the *Mr* before your names; it is a barbarous addition; the other is simple and classic, a rank I cannot help thinking due to both the poet and painter. Without ranging myself among classics, I assure you, were I to print anything with my name, it should be plain Horace Walpole: *Mr* is one of the Gothicisms I abominate. The explanation was certainly added for people who have not eyes—such are almost all who have seen Mr Bentley's drawings, and think to compliment him by mistaking them for prints.[4] Alas! the generality want as much to have the words *a man, a cock,* written under his drawings, as under the most execrable hieroglyphics of Egypt or of sign-post painters!

3. The book was advertised: 'Elegantly printed in royal quarto, price sewed 10s. 6d.' (*Daily Adv.* 27 March 1753).

4. See *ante* 8 July 1752, n. 2.

I will say no more now, but that you must not wonder if I am partial to you and yours, when you can write as you do and yet feel so little vanity. I have used freedoms enough with your writings to convince you I speak truth: I praise and scold Mr Bentley immoderately as I think he draws well or ill; I never think it worth my while to do either, especially to blame, where there are not generally vast excellencies. Good night—don't suspect me when I have no fault but impatience to make you easy.

Yours ever,

H. W.

From Gray, Tuesday 27 February 1753

Printed from MS in Waller Collection.
The year is determined by the reference to the title of *Designs*, 1753.
Address: To the Honourable Horace Walpole Esq. in Arlington Street, London.
Postmark: 1 MR.

Stoke, Feb. 27 [1753].

I AM obliged on the sudden to come hither to see my poor mother, who is in a condition between life and death,[1] though (I think) much nearer the latter. Yet I could not help telling you I had received your letter, and am pleased to find I was in the wrong. You may be sure, I was not willing to think you so. Do what you please about the title, if it is time; but it seems to me the less of puff or ostentation it has, the better it will be, even for Dodsley. Excuse my brevity, adieu, I am ever

Yours,

T. G.

To Gray, January 1754

Missing. Probably written in Arlington Street. Implied *post* 15 Feb. 1754. HW to Mann 28 Jan. 1754 shows that it must have been written in January.

1. Mrs Gray died Sunday 11 March, and was buried in Stoke Poges churchyard in the same tomb with her sister, Mary Antrobus (d. 5 Nov. 1749), where Gray also was subsequently buried. To Mary Antrobus's epitaph on the tombstone Gray added: 'In the same pious confidence, / beside her friend and sister, / here sleep the remains of / Dorothy Gray, / widow, the careful tender mother / of many children, one of whom alone / had the misfortune to survive her. / She died March XI. MDCCLIII. / Aged LXVII.' (Mason, *Mem. Gray* 229).

From GRAY, Friday 15 February 1754

Printed from MS in Waller Collection.
Dated by HW: Feb. 15, 1754.
Address: To the Honourable Horace Walpole Esq. in Arlington Street, London.
Postmark: ROYSTON 16 FE.

Friday [Feb. 15, 1754], Cambridge.

Dear Sir,

I SEND you my story,[1] that you may not wait longer for it, though it does not at all satisfy me, but I do not know how to make it intelligible in fewer words.[2]

Bianca Capello,[3]

Veneta, adolescenti nupsit nobili Florentino,[4] quem ideo a patre[5] domo expulsum uxor sua opera diu sustentabat, donec Franciscus Mediceus[6] M[agnus] Hetruriæ Dux, mulieris forma captus eam in aulam perduxit,

1. HW had asked Gray to compose in Latin an account of Bianca Cappello, short enough to fit in a 'label' at the bottom of the frame of her picture by Vasari, which later hung in the Round Drawing Room at SH, and was sold SH xx. 92 (see also MONTAGU ii. 54). The picture was 'bought out of the Vitelli Palace at Florence by Sir Horace Mann and sent to Mr Walpole' ('Des. of SH,' *Works* ii. 469), and the story 'in a cartouche on the frame,' as quoted in the 'Description,' is a free English translation of Gray's Latin.

2. Gray's source has not been identified. In Florence, he might have read Bianca's story in a manuscript version. There is hardly an Italian library without a collection of *fatti tragici,* i.e. seventeenth and early eighteenth century manuscript accounts of murder, rape, and incest, concerning the Medici, the Farnese, the Cenci, etc. (see Guglielmo E. Saltini, 'Della morte di Francesco I de' Medici e di Bianca Cappello,' *Archivio storico italiano,* 1863, 2d ser. xviii pt i. 22). The Yale Library owns several such manuscripts, one of which is 'Istoria della Signora Bianca Cappello, Gran Duchessa di Toscana, e di Pietro Buonaventuri suo marito.' Gray probably wrote his account from memory, since he omits

important facts, such as Bonaventuri's name and the date of Bianca's marriage to Francis I.

3. Bianca (1548–87), dau. of Bartolomeo Cappello by Pellegrina Morosini, m. (1) (1563) Pietro Bonaventuri; m. (2) (1578) Francis I (Francesco de' Medici), Grand Duke of Tuscany (Samuele Romanin, *Storia documentata di Venezia,* Venice, 1912–21, vi. 371–87).

4. Pietro Bonaventuri (d. 1572), not a nobleman but a clerk in the banking house of the Salviati in Venice. See Romanin, op. cit. vi. 371–5; Riguccio Galluzzi, *Istoria del Granducato di Toscana sotto il governo della Casa Medici,* Florence, 1781, ii. 83–8; see also Celio Malespini's *novella* 'Come peruenisse la Signora Bianca Cappello Gran Duchessa di Toscana,' *Ducento novelle,* Venice, 1609, ii. 275b–278a (pt ii, *novella* lxxxiv).

5. Bartolomeo Cappello, Venetian senator. See Francesco Sansovino, *Venetia città nobilissima,* Venice, 1581, dedication to 'Bianca Cappello de' Medici,' also p. 178a, and the appendix ('Cronica Veneto') p. 38a.

6. Francis I (Francesco de' Medici) (1541–87), Grand Duke of Tuscany, 1574 (Litta, 'Medici di Firenze' table xiii).

maritum ad summos honores⁷ extulit, qui potestate insolenter usus cum
sæpe in crimina incurrisset, sæpe conjugis gratia (quam tamen asperius
tractaverat) supplicium effugisset, novissime sua manu hominem confodit.
Bianca ducis clementiam implorante, juravit Franc[is]cus se de marito
pœnas non sumpturum, sed nec de illis, qui eum ipsum occidissent. Quo
audito, vir ab inimicis interfectus est.⁸ Viduam Franciscus justum in matrimonium duxit.⁹ Hos ambos uno in convivio Ferdinandus¹⁰ Cardinalis,
Fr[ancis]ci frater, veneno sustulit,¹¹ ipse deinceps Hetruriæ Dux, cogno-
mento Maximus.

   I am collecting what I can about the two marriages¹² and will send it
you next week,¹³ though I find the chronicles of latter times do little

7. He was made 'guardaroba' in the ducal household (Galluzzi, op. cit. ii. 86).

8. In 1572 by Roberto de Ricci and twelve assassins. See Malespini, op cit. ii. 278a–280b (pt ii, *novella* lxxxv).

9. They were married secretly 5 June 1578. The marriage was announced publicly 10 June 1579, and Bianca, who had previously been in disgrace, was declared at a meeting of the Venetian Senate, 16 June 1579, '*particolar figliuola della Repubblica*,' a distinction conferred on royalty (Romanin, op. cit. vi. 377–9; Galluzzi, op. cit. ii. 312–20).

10. Ferdinand I (Ferdinand de' Medici) (1549–1609), Grand Duke of Tuscany, 1587; cardinal 1563–89 (Litta, 'Medici di Firenze' table xv).

11. A more common version of the story has it that Bianca, in an attempt to poison Ferdinand, accidentally poisoned her husband, Francis, and then in despair committed suicide ('Istoria della Signora Bianca Cappello,' cited in n. 2 above). But according to medical testimony Francis and Bianca both died of chills and fever, on 19 and 20 Oct. 1587 (Saltini, op cit. 19–81; see also Clifford Bax, *Bianca Cappello*, 1927, pp. 87–8).

12. HW had recently purchased two fifteenth-century pictures painted on wood, one an anonymous painting supposedly of the marriage of Henry VI to Margaret of Anjou, and the other, wrongly attributed to John Mabuse, supposedly of the marriage of Henry VII to Elizabeth of York. The former hung over the chimney in the Library at SH, and was sold SH xx. 25 to the Duke of Sutherland; it is now in the Toledo Museum of Art, Toledo, Ohio (see COLE i. 305). The latter, which HW bought at Lord Pomfret's sale for £84, hung at the east end of the Long Gallery, and was sold SH xxi. 52 to John Dent of Sudeley Castle, Winchcombe, Glos, where it now is (COLE i. 32; for engravings by Charles Grignion and description see *Anecdotes, Works* iii. 37–9, 50–1; 'Des. of SH,' *Works* ii. 442–3, 461; see also HW to Bentley 18 Sept. 1755, and HW to Mann 21 July 1753).

HW's identification of the subject of the 'Henry VI' painting has been categorically denied by John Gough Nichols (N&Q 1866, ser. III. x. 61) and Alfred Woltmann (*Fortnightly Review* 1866, vi. 152–3), both of whom believed it to portray the marriage or betrothal of the Virgin. Neither, however, attempted to dispute HW's statement (*Works* iii. 37–9) that the cardinal in the picture is very like the image on the tomb of Henry Beaufort, Cardinal of Winchester, or to deny the still more positive 'authentication' of Duke Humphrey and Archbishop Kemp by the altar-piece which HW had in his own possession. (The altar-piece was also bought by the Duke of Sutherland, but its present whereabouts has not been ascertained.) If the bride were the Virgin it is remarkable that she did not, like the bridegroom (see *post* 3 March 1754 and nn. 91–5), have a nimbus; but Mr Blake-More Godwin, Director of the Toledo Museum of Art, is confident that one was never there.

13. *Post* 3 March 1754. HW had sought Gray's assistance in identifying the figures in the paintings.

'THE MARRIAGE OF HENRY VI'

more than copy Fabian.¹⁴ They are excellent writers, and I thank you
for bringing us acquainted. I am ever

Yours,

T. G.

From GRAY, Sunday 3 March 1754

Printed from MS in Waller Collection.

[Cambridge,] March 3d, 1754.

YOU are to dispatch forthwith an express to Angers to fetch the
windows of St Bonaventure's Chapel¹ in the church of the Corde-
liers² there; in them are painted Margaret of Anjou³ herself kneeling;
her mother, Isabella,⁴ Duchess of Lorraine, first wife of René,⁵ King of
Sicily; Joan de la Val,⁶ his second wife; Yolande,⁷ his eldest daughter,
also Duchess of Lorraine; and John,⁸ Duke of Calabria, his eldest son.
These are not mobled queens⁹ upon a tomb, but fair and flourishing
figures with entire faces; the hair of the four women is disheveled below their girdle, which one would think was a fashion peculiar to
them, for no other cotemporary lady have I ever seen that did not wear
hers trussed up and plaited, or quite hid. To stay your stomach till

14. Robert Fabyan (d. 1513). See *post* 3 March 1754, nn. 15–16.

1. Gray here follows Bernard de Mont-faucon (1655–1741), *Les Monuments de la monarchie française,* 1729–33, iii. 345. 'Chapelle de S. Bonaventure' is apparently Montfaucon's slip for Chapelle de Saint-Bernardin (Célestin Port, *Dictionnaire historique . . . de Maine-et-Loire,* 1874–8, i. 71). See also Louis de Farcy, *Monographie de la cathédrale d'Angers,* Angers, 1901–10, ii. 297.
2. Saint-Sébastien, built in 1294 (Port, loc. cit.).
3. (1429–82), m. (1445) Henry VI of England. See Montfaucon, op. cit. iii. 346, plate lxiii, fig. 3; Port, op. cit. ii. 593–4.
4. Isabelle (1410–53), dau. of Charles II, Duc d'Anjou, m. (1420) René I, Duc d'Anjou; Duchesse de Lorraine, 1431. See Montfaucon, op. cit. iii. 255, plate xlvii, fig. 11.
5. René I (1409–80), Duc de Bar, 1419, de

Lorraine, 1431, d'Anjou, 1435; Comte de Provence, 1435; King of Sicily 1435–42. See Montfaucon, op. cit. iii. 254; Port, op. cit. iii. 237–43.
6. Jeanne de Laval (1433–98), dau. of Gui (XIV), Comte de Laval, m. (1454) René I (Port, op. cit. ii. 465–6). See Montfaucon, op. cit. iii. 255, plate xlvii, fig. 12.
7. Yolande d'Anjou (1428–83), dau. of René I by Isabelle, m. (1444) Ferry (II) de Lorraine, Comte de Vaudemont. Upon her nephew's death in 1473, she became in her own right Duchesse de Lorraine (La Chenaye-Desbois, xii. 394; *L'art de vérifier les dates,* Paris, 1818–44, xiii. 408–10). See Montfaucon, op. cit. iii. 345–6, plate lxiii, fig. 2.
8. Jean II (1425–70), Duc de Calabre; Duc de Lorraine, 1453 (Isenburg, *Stammtafeln* i. table 13; *L'art de vérifier les dates,* loc. cit.). See Montfaucon, op. cit. iii. 345, plate lxiii, fig. 1.
9. *Hamlet,* II. ii.

the return of the courier, you may see them all in Montfaucon's *Antiquities*[10] (tom. 3, plates 47 and 63). I think you have the book;[11] and pray observe if the mother does not resemble that figure[12] in the picture with the large sleeves and hair at length on the foreground. Now for the time, place, and circumstances of the marriage, here begins Wyllyam Wyrcester (p. 462).[13] 'A.D. 1444, et anno Regis Hen[rici] VIti XXIIImo, Rex accepit in uxorem dominam juvenem, filiam Regis Neapolis, Ceciliæ, et Jerusalem, quæ desponsata erat in abbacia de Tycchefield in comitatu Suthampton. . . . A.D. 1445. Coronacio uxoris Henr[ici] VIti apud Westmonast[eriu]m XXXmo Maii.'[14] Next comes Mr Alderman Fabian.[15] 'A.D. 1444.[16] The Marquess of Suffolke[17] soon after with his wyfe[18] and other honourable Personages as well of men as of women with great Apparayll of chayris and other costious ordenaunce for to convey the forenamed Lady Margerete into Englande sayled into Fraunce, and so tarryed there all this Mayres year.[18a] . . . A.D. 1445. This 23d Year (of Henry VI) and monthe of . . . the foresayd Lady Margerete came over into Englande, and in the monthe of . . . following she was maryed at a towne called Southwyke in the countre of Hamshyre, and from thence she was conveyed by the Lordes and Estates of this Lande, which mette with her in sundry places with

10. Gray's slip for *Monuments,* etc. (n. 1 above). Montfaucon is also the author of *L'Antiquité expliqué et représentée en figures* . . ., Paris, 1716.

11. MS Cat. B.1.8, 3 vols. The French edition of Montfaucon's *Monuments* was in five vols, folio. Possibly HW had the five volumes bound in three.

12. At the extreme right of HW's picture supposedly representing the marriage of Henry VI is a female figure which HW took for 'Margaret Richmond, mother of Henry VII' (*Anecdotes, Works* iii. 38). She however was only two years old at the time of the marriage, and could only have been included as a compliment to Henry VII, during whose reign the picture was perhaps painted.

13. Gray quotes Thomas Hearne's edition of William of Worcester's *Annales rerum Anglicarum,* printed in vol. ii, pp. 424–521, of *Liber Niger Scaccarii,* Oxford, 1728.

14. Ibid. ii. 463. Gray's transcript contains a few unimportant contractions and omissions.

15. In the *Calendar of Letter Books* . . .

of the City of London . . . *Letter-Book L.* Temp. *Edward IV-Henry VII,* ed. R. R. Sharpe, 1912, Robert Fabyan appears among the aldermen 21 Nov. 1495 (11 Hen. VII) and 21 Sept. and 13 Oct. 1496 (12 Hen. VII) (pp. 310, 317–18).

16. Gray, as appears from his page references, quotes from the first edition of Fabyan's *The newe Cronycles of Englande and of Fraunce,* 1516. He tried to follow Fabyan's spellings (not his punctuation or capitalization), but his transcription is unexpectedly careless.

17. William de la Pole (1396–1450) 4th E. of Suffolk, cr. (1444) M. and (1448) D. of Suffolk.

18. Alice Chaucer (ca 1404–75), dau. of Thomas Chaucer (? the poet's son), by Matilda Burghersh; m. (as her third husband, before 1436) William de la Pole, 4th E. of Suffolk, later D. of Suffolk (GEC; M. B. Ruud, *Thomas Chaucer,* Minneapolis, 1926, p. 2).

18a. The Mayor of London at this time was Thomas Catworthe (Fabyan, op. cit.).

great retynewe of men in sundry Lyveryes with their slevys browderyd and some betyn with goldsmythes werkes in most costly maner, and specyally (of) the D. of Glouceter[19] mette with her with 500 Men in one lyverye, and so was conveyed unto Black-hethe, where upon the 18th of Maye she was mette with the Mayer, Aldermen and Sheryffes of the Citie and the Craftes of the same in *Browne* blew with brawderyd slevys, that is to meane, every maister or crafte with the conysaunce of his *maister* (read, *mystery*) and red hoodes upon eyther of their heddes, and so the same day brought her unto London, where for her were ordeyned sumptuous and costly Pagentes and resemblaunce of dyverse old hystories to the great comfort of her and such as came with her— and so with great triumphe she was brought unto Westminstre, where upon the 30th of May, the day after Trinitie Sonday she was solemply crowned' (fol. 199). As to Grafton,[20] Hall,[21] Speed,[22] Hollingshed,[23] and other chroniclers of Queen Elizabeth's time, I transcribe nothing from them, because they add nothing new to Fabian's account, indeed only copy him, or one another; Stow[24] only, as he is more particular, I shall make use of.[25] 'This noble Company (Lord Suffolk, and others not named) came to the City of Towers[26] in Touraine, where they were honourably received and entertained both of the French King[27] and Duke Reiner, where the Marquess of Suffolke, as Procurator to K. Henry, espoused the said Lady in the Church of St Martin. At which marriage were present the Father and Mother of the Bride, the French King who was Uncle[28] to Duke Reiner, and the French Queen[29] Aunt[30] to the Duchess his Wife.[31] Also the Dukes of Orleans,[32] of Ca-

19. Humphrey (1390 – 1447), D. of Gloucester; 4th son of Henry IV.

20. Richard Grafton (d. ca 1572), *A Chronicle at Large and Meere History of the Affayres of England*, 1568-9, ii. 591. He follows Hall.

21. Edward Hall (d. 1547), *The Union of the two noble and illustre Famelies of Lancastre and Yorke*, 1548, fol. cxlviii recto.

22. John Speed (ca 1552–1629), *The Historie of Great Britaine*, 1611; 2nd edn 1623, p. 845. Speed's account differs from those of his predecessors in being more concise and in citing authorities.

23. Raphael Holinshed (d. ca 1580), *Chronicles of England, Scotlande, and Irelande*, 1577, ii. 1270. His account of the marriage contains facts not to be found in the other chronicles.

24. John Stow (ca 1525–1605), *The Annales of England . . . 1592.*

25. Gray probably followed the 1st edn, 1592, pp. 623–4 but the carelessness of his transcript makes this uncertain.

26. I.e., Tours.

27. Charles VII (1403–61).

28. 'This is a mistake. He was indeed uncle to King Henry VI, but cousin only to René, King of Sicily, etc.' (Gray).

29. Marie d'Anjou (1404–63), René I's sister, m. (1422) Charles VII.

30. 'Another mistake. She was René's own sister, and aunt to the bride' (Gray).

31. Isabelle, Duchesse de Lorraine, was Marie d'Anjou's sister-in-law.

32. 'Charles, who had been prisoner twenty-five years in England, and returned home about four years before this marriage'

labre,[33] of Alanson[34] and of Brytaine,[35] 7 Earls, 12 Barons, 20 Bishops, besides Knights and Gentlemen. When the feast, triumphs, banquets, and justs were ended, the Lady was delivered to the Marquess of Suffolk, which in great estate conveied her thorow Normandy unto Diepe, where awhile they remained.[36] The Lady, being transported from Diepe, landed at Portchester, from whence she was conveyed by water to Hampton, and rested there in a place called Gods-House;[37] from thence she went to Southwicke,[38] and was married to the King in the Abbey of Tichfield[39] on the 22d of April,' etc.

Now you are to determine whether the picture represent the marriage at Tours (which may be; and yet Henry VI may be introduced, though not there in person). This must be the case, if one of those women be the Queen of Sicily, for neither she, nor any of the family accompanied Margaret to England. They took leave of her at Bar-le-Duc with abundance of tears, and at Rouen she was consigned to her English attendants, who made their entry with great pomp into that city. I can tell you exactly who they were, and what they did there. Shall I? If it is nothing to your purpose, you may pass it over.[40]

Le Roy Henry envoya plusieurs Seigneurs et Dames de son pays au dit lieu de Rouën fort hautement et richement habilléz, c'est a sçavoir le Duc d'Jorcq,[41] le Comte de Suffort,[42] le Seigneur de Tallebot,[43] le Marquis de

(Gray). Charles (1391–1465), Duc d'Orléans, Comte d'Angoulême, was Charles VII's first cousin. He was taken prisoner at Agincourt in 1415, and set at liberty 3 Nov. 1440 (Thomas Rymer, Fœdera, 1703–35, x. 823).

33. 'Brother to the bride' (Gray). See n. 8 above.

34. 'John, the second of the name' (Gray). Jean II (1409–76), Duc d'Alençon, Comte de Perche (NBG; Isenburg, Stammtafeln ii. table 33).

35. 'Francis, first of the name. He had married Margaret's aunt' (Gray). François I (1414–50), Duc de Bretagne, 1442, m. (1) (1431) Yolande d'Anjou (1412–40), dau. of Louis II, Duc d'Anjou, titular King of Naples, by Yolande d'Aragon (NBG; Isenburg, Stammtafeln ii. tables 29, 34).

36. Gray here omits three sentences.

37. 'An hospital for poor folks at Southampton (Leland. v. iii. p. 92)' (Gray). Gray's reference is to The Itinerary of John Leland the Antiquary, ed. Thomas Hearne, 2d edn, Oxford, 1744–5. God's House was

founded ca 1197 by Gervase le Riche, burgess of Southampton (Vict. Co. Hist., Hants ii. 202–5).

38. 'It is a good big thoroughfare, but no celebrate market. The fame of it stood by the priory of the Black Chanons there, and a pilgrimage to our Lady (Leland. ib. p. 98)' (Gray). Southwick was founded by Henry I in 1133 (Vict. Co. Hist., Hants ii. 164–8).

39. 'It was a monastery of Prémontrés founded by Henry III, given at the Reformation to Mr Wriothesley, who pulled it down and built a "right stately house" there (Leland, p. 95)' (Gray). See also Vict. Co. Hist., Hants ii. 181, 185–6, iii. 222–3.

40. The following passage is from Godefroy's edition of Mathieu d'Escouchy. See below, nn. 60–1.

41. Richard (1411–60), 3d D. of York, father of Edward IV.

42. Suffolk.

43. John Talbot (1390–1453), 7th Lord

Susalby (Salisbury),[44] le Seigneur de Clif (Lord Clifford),[45] le Baron de Gruisot,[46] Messires Jamet d'Ormont,[47] Jean Bolledit,[48] Guil. Bonnechille,[49] Rich. Rios,[50] Jean Secaley,[51] Ed. Hoult,[52] Rob. de Willeby,[53] Rob. de Harcourt,[54] et plusieurs autres Chevaliers et Ecuyers de grand etat. Au regard des Dames y estoient la Comtesse de Suffort, la Dame de Talbot,[55] la Dame de Salsebery,[56] la Dame Marguerite Hoult,[57] et autres en grand nombre. Il y avoit aussi des chariots couverts et plusieurs haquenées houssées de si riches habillemens, que peu avoient eté veus de pareils, venans du susdit royaume d'Angleterre; sur tout a leur entrée de Rouën, ou ils pouvoient bien etre 1500 chevaux. Or faut il declarer la maniere comment les Seigneurs et Dames devant dits et leurs gens entrerent en bel ordre en ladite ville. Premierement pour l'Estat de la Reyne y estoient les premiers entrans les dessus nommez (here he names all the men again but the three first) et avec eux Messire Huy Coquesin,[58] lesquels tous en leur compagnie avoient quelque 400 Archers pour l'estat de la maison d'icelle Reyne, tous vestus d'une meme parure de gris. Aprés lesquels suivoient les Ecuyers et Officiers d'icelui Estat; et outre ce il y avoit avec les dessusdits 200 Archers de la grande Garde du Roi d'Angleterre, portans ses couleurs et livrées, c'est a scavoir,

Talbot; cr. (1442) E. of Shrewsbury, (1446) E. of Waterford.

44. Sir Richard Nevill (1400–60), 5th E. of Salisbury, 1428.

45. Thomas de Clifford (1414–55), 8th Lord Clifford.

46. Probably Ralph de Greystoke (ca 1414–87), 5th Lord Greystoke. See George L. Lam, 'Margaret of Anjou's English Escort,' in N&Q, 1943, clxxxiv. 7–9.

47. Sir James Butler (1420–61), 5th E. of Ormond, 1452. He was commonly called Sir James Ormond.

48. Not identified. See, however, George L. Lam, op. cit.

49. In Godefroy's text: 'Guillaume Bonneclulle.' Sir William Bonville (1393–1461), cr. (before 1417) Kt, (1449) Lord Bonville of Chewton, (1461) K.G. See ibid.

50. Probably Sir Richard Roos (fl. 1438–46), 5th son of William de Ros (Roos), 7th Lord Ros (see Lam, op. cit.).

51. 'Iean Scalay' in the second list of names in Godefroy's text (see ibid.). He was probably Sir John Clay (d. before 1465), of Cheshunt, Herts, Treasurer of the Household of Richard, Duke of York.

52. Sir Edward Hull (d. 1453) of Enmore, Somerset; M.P. Somerset, 1447; cr. (before 1445) Kt, (1453) K.G. (Calendar of Patent

Rolls, 1441–1446, p. 420; W. A. Shaw, Knights of England, 1906, i. 13). For his official career see Lam, op. cit.

53. Sir Robert Willoughby (ca 1385–1452), 6th Lord Willoughby de Eresby, 1409; K.G., 1416; styled E. of Vendosme and Beaumont, Lord Willoughby in 1424; at Agincourt 25 Oct. 1415 (GEC; Collins, Peerage, 1812, vi. 601–7).

54. Sir Robert Harcourt (d. 1470), cr. (1463) K.G. (Lam, op. cit.)

55. Lady Margaret Beauchamp (d. 1467), dau. of the 13th E. of Warwick, m. (after 1433) John Talbot, 7th Lord Talbot, cr. (1442) E. of Shrewsbury, and (1446) E. of Waterford.

56. Lady Alice de Montacute (d. before 1463), dau. of the 4th E. of Salisbury, m. (1424) Sir Richard Nevill, later 5th E. of Salisbury; suo jure Cts of Salisbury, 1428.

57. Margery, dau. of Sir Thomas Lovell, Kt, m. (before 1441) Sir Edward Hull, of Enmore, Somerset (Calendar of Close Rolls, 1441–1447, pp. 9–10; Francis Blomefield and Charles Parkin, An Essay towards a Topographical History of . . . Norfolk, 1805–10, x. 395–6).

58. Sir Hugh Cokesey (fl. 1413–45), Kt, 1419 (W.A. Shaw, Knights of England, 1906. i. p. lx; see also Lam, op. cit.).

sur chacune de leurs manches une couronne d'or, lesquels estoient trés
richement habillez: aprés les Chevaliers dessusdits venoient 6 Pages montéz
sur six haquenées, richement vestus de robes et de chaperons noirs, chargez
d'orfevrerie d'argent doré, qui estoient tous fils de Chevaliers; et menoit le
premier Page par la main une haquenée de son costé dextre, que ledit Roy
d'Angleterre envoyoit a la Reyne sa femme, ornée d'une selle et de paremens, tels que le tout en etoit de fin or, et les paremens des autres haquenées estoient tous d'argent doré. Aprés suivoit le chariot, que le dit, Roy
lui envoyoit, lequel estoit le plus richement orné et paré que depuis trés
long tems il n'en estoit party du Royaume d'Angleterre un pareil; car il
estoit couvert d'un trés riche drap d'or et armoyé des armes de France et
d'Angleterre: lequel chariot estoit tiré par 6 chevaux blancs de grand prix,
et estoit icelui chariot figuré par dedans et dehors de plusieurs et diverses
couleurs, dans lequel estoient la Comtesse de Suffort, les Dames de Talbot,
et de Salsebery, et estoit ladite Comtesse en l'estat de la Reyne pareil au
jour qu'elle espousa. Les autres dames ensuivans de degré en degré venoient
aprés ce chariot montées sur haquenées au plus prés d'icelui chariot estoit le
Duc d'Jorcq d'un costé, et le Seigneur de Talbot de l'autre, tenant maniere
et contenance, comme si la Reyne eust eté dedans. Le Comte de Suffort alloit
chevauchant devant le chariot representant la personne du Roy d'Angleterre, et aprés luy il y avoit 36 tant chevaux qu'haquenées de grand parage
tous housséz de vermeil armoyé de ses armes. Aprés icelui chariot il y
avoit encore 5 chevaux richement ornéz, dont 2 estoient couverts de velours
vermeil battu à or, semez de roses d'or dedans, et les autres estoient couverts de drap de damas cramoisy. Aprés tout ce que dit est, venoit encore
un chariot richement orné, dedans lequel estoient la Dame de Talbot la
jeune,[59] la Dame Marguerite Hoult, et autres, lesquelles estoient toutes
ordonnées et destinées pour recevoir icelle nouvelle Reyne d'Angleterre
(Matthieu de Coucy,[60] a cotemporary, p. 553).[61]

Out of these, if the scene of the picture lies in England, you may pick
and choose, for it is likely they all waited upon her to Southwick. I am
sorry Duke Humphrey could not be there, but you see he did not meet
her till after the marriage in her way to London. Much less could his
wife Jaqueline[62] appear, as that marriage was set aside eighteen years

59. For alternative identifications see
Lam, op. cit.

60. Mathieu d'Escouchy (ca 1420–ca
1483), chronicler, who continued Monstrelet's Chroniques from 1444 to 1461 (for his
biography see Chronique de Mathieu d'Escouchy, ed. Gaston du Fresne, Marquis de
Beaucourt, Paris, 1863–4, i. pp. i–xli).

61. Gray quotes Histoire de Charles VII,

Roy de France, par Jean Chartier . . .
Mathieu de Coucy, et autres autheurs . . .
depuis l'an 1421 jusques en 1461, ed. Denys
Godefroy, Paris, 1661, p. 554. Gray's transcript contains many small inaccuracies.

62. Jacqueline (1401–36), dau. of William
II, D. of Bavaria; Cts of Holland, Zeeland,
and Hainault. She married as her third
husband (ca 1423) Humphrey, D. of

before; indeed his Duchess Eleanor Cobham[63] was now in prison,[64] and had been so (in spite of Shakespear)[65] three or four years before Margaret came over. The Cardinal Beaufort, then at least seventy years old,[66] one would think should have the honour of joining their hands, especially in his own diocese; but I recollect no marks of a cardinal, and what I take for the pallium, which he holds over their hands, is (I believe) peculiar to archbishops; so it may be John Stafford,[67] Archbishop of Canterbury, who certainly crowned her the next month.[68] I could tell you many small particulars, as the name of the ship she came over in, which was *Coq Johan de Cherburgh,* Thomas Adams, Master.[69] The ring she was married with, which was a *fair Ruby,*[70] *sometime yeven unto us* (says the King) *by our bel Oncle the Cardinal of Englande, with the which we were sacred in the day of our Coronacion at Parys, and which was broke, thereof to make another ring for the Quene's wedding.* The jewels[71] he gave for New Year's gifts before the marriage, to the Duke of Gloucester, the Cardinal, the Duke of Exeter,[72] the Archbishop, Duchess of Buckingham,[73] Earl of Warwick,[74] etc.; the George[75] he wore himself, which cost 2000 marks; *the Puson*[76] *of*

Gloucester, the marriage being annulled in 1428 (GEC; Isenburg, *Stammtafeln,* i. table 27; K. H. Vickers, *Humphrey Duke of Gloucester,* 1907, pp. 127–8.

63. (d. 1454), dau. of Sir Reynold Cobham, of Sterborough, Surrey, *de jure* Lord Cobham; m. (1428) Humphrey, D. of Gloucester.

64. She was tried for necromancy, witchcraft, etc., in St. Stephen's Chapel at Westminster in Aug. 1441; was committed in Nov. 1441 to Chester Castle, transferred 26 Oct. 1443 to Kenilworth Castle, and in 1446 to Peel Castle, Isle of Man, where she died (Stow, *Annales,* 1592, pp. 618–19; GEC *sub* Gloucester; *Calendar of Patent Rolls, 1441–1446,* p. 206; Rymer, *Fœdera,* xi. 45).

65. In 2 *Henry VI,* II. iii she is made to receive sentence in a hall of justice with King Henry and Queen Margaret present. Margaret did not arrive in England until 9 April 1445.

66. Henry Beaufort (ca 1375–1447), illegitimate son of John of Gaunt; Bp of Lincoln 1398–1404, of Winchester 1404–47; cardinal 1426. For theories concerning the date of his birth, see L. B. Radford, *Henry Beaufort,* 1908, p. 2.

67. (d. 1452), Abp of Canterbury 1443–52.

68. 30 May 1445.

69. Thomas Adam, according to Rymer (*Fœdera* xi. 85). He was probably Thomas Adam (fl. 1433–65) of Polruan, Cornwall, master of a Fowey vessel. See *Calendar of Patent Rolls, 1429–1436,* p. 352; ibid. *1446–1452,* p. 449; ibid. *1461–1467,* p. 412.

70. The quotation is taken, with some alteration, from Thomas Rymer's *Fœdera* xi. 76. The *Fœdera* was published in 20 vols folio, 1703–35. Vol. xi, published in 1710, treats of the years 1440–74.

71. See Rymer, *Fœdera* xi. 76–7.

72. John Holand (1395 or 1396–1447), cr. (1444) D. of Exeter.

73. Lady Anne Nevill (d. 1480), dau. of the 1st E. of Westmorland, m. (1) (1424) Sir Humphrey Stafford, D. of Buckingham; m. (2) (1467) Walter Blount, Bn Mountjoy.

74. Henry Beauchamp (1425–46), 14th E. of Warwick; cr. (1445) D. of Warwick.

75. The jewel belonging to the insignia of the Order of the Garter. Gray alludes to Rymer, *Fœdera* xi. 82.

76. Pisane, 'a piece of armour to protect the upper part of the chest and neck' (OED).

Golde, called Iklyngton[77] *Coler, garnished with 4 Rubees, 4 greet*
Saphurs, 32 greet Perles and 53 other Perles; and the Pectoral of Golde
garnished with rubees, perles and diamondes; and also the great
Owche[78] *garnished with diamondes, rubees and perles, that cost 2000*
Marcs, which the Quene wore at the solempnitee of hir Coronation.[79]
If these suit your palate, you may see them all, and many other curious
papers, in Rymer's *Fœdera*, vol. xi, some dated from the Priory of
Southwyk, and witnessed[80] by the Marquess of Suffolk, the Tresorer of
Englande (which was Sir Ralph Boteler, Lord Sudeley),[81] and the Privy
Seal (Adam Moleyns,[82] Dean of Salisbury, afterwards Bishop of Chi-
chester, and murdered by the mob at Southampton).

Now I shall set down the ages[83] of the parties concerned. The King
was barely 23 years old. (What shall we do with this stubborn date?)
The Queen was in her 15th year. Her mother Isabella was probably
about 35. René, her father, was 36 (see his picture, when old, done by
himself, in Montfaucon).[84] Mary, Queen of France, her aunt, was 40
(see her, ibid.[85] with a very odd face, an odder coif, and high, but not
pointed bonnet, from an original). Charles VII of France was 41 (see
him in the same plate).[86] John, her brother, Duke of Calabria, was
about 19. Yolande, her sister, was not a year older than herself.

There is so particular a description of the dresses in use about the
middle of the fifteenth century extant, that (long as it is) I must send it
you.[87]

En ceste année delaisserent les dames et damoiselles les queues a porter a
leurs robes: et en ce lieu meirent bordures a leurs robbes de gris de lestices,
de martres, de veloux et d'autres choses si larges, comme d'un veloux de
haut ou plus. Et si meirent sur leurs tetes bourrelets a maniere de bonnet

77. Ickleton, Benedictine nunnery in
Cambridgeshire, founded 1140 or 1190 (Sir
William Dugdale, *Monasticon Anglicanum*,
ed. John Caley, *et al.*, 1849, iv. 439). Why
this pisane was called 'Ickleton collar' is
unexplained.

78. Clasp or buckle (OED; MONTAGU i. 25).

79. Rymer, *Fœdera* xi. 83. Gray's transcript is very inaccurate.

80. Ibid. xi. 83-4.

81. Sir Ralph Boteler (d. 1473), 6th Lord
Sudeley; Lord High Treasurer 1444-7.

82. Adam de Molyneux (Moleyns) (d.
1450), Bp of Chichester 1445-50; Keeper of
the Privy Seal 1444-9 (DNB; John Le Neve

and T. D. Hardy, *Fasti Ecclesiæ Anglicanæ*,
Oxford, 1854, i. 247).

83. In 1444.

84. Plate xlvii, fig. 8. For an explanation
see Montfaucon, iii. 254-5.

85. Plate xlvii, fig. 6; explanation, iii.
254.

86. Plate xlvii, figs 1-2; explanation, iii.
253.

87. The following passage is from En-
guerrand de Monstrelet (d. 1453), *Chroniques*, 3 vols fol., Paris, 1752, iii. f. 130
verso. Gray's transcript has been collated
with the original: the variants are for the
most part normalized spellings, with a few
unimportant omissions and transpositions.

rond, qui s'amenuisoient par dessus de la hauteur de demie aulne, ou de trois quartiers de long tels y avoit: et aucunes les portoient moindres, et deliez couvrechess par dessus pendans par derriere jusques a terre, les aucuns et les autres: et prindrent aussi a porter leurs ceintures de soye plus larges beaucoup qu'elles n'avoient accoutumé et de diverses façons; et les ferrures plus somptueuses assez, et coliers d'ors a leurs cols autrement et plus cointement beaucoup qu'elles n'avoient accoutumé. Et en ce temps aussi les hommes se prindrent a vestir plus court, qu'ils n'eurent oncques fait; tellement que l'on veoit la façon de leurs culs et de leurs genitoires, ainsi comme l'en souloit vestir les singes qui estoit chose tres malhonnête et impudique. Et si faisoient les manches fendre de leurs robbes et de leurs pourpoints pour monstrer leurs chemises deliées, larges, et blanches. Portoient aussi leurs cheveux si longs, qu'ils leur empêchoient leurs visages, mesmement leurs yeux. Et sur leur testes portoient bonnets de drap hauts et longs d'un quartier ou plus. Portoient aussi, comme tous indifferemment, chaines d'or moult somptueuses chevaliers et escuyers: les varlets mêmes pourpoints de soye, de satin et de veloux. Et presque tous, especiallement és cours des Princes, portoient poulaines á leurs souillers d'un quartier de long; et a leurs pourpoints gros mahoitres á leurs espaules pour monstrer, qu'ils fussent larges par les espaules; qui sont choses moult vaines, et par adventure fort haineuses a Dieu. Et qui estoit huy court vestu, il estoit le lendemain long vestu jusques a terre.

(Monstrelet, vol. iii. après p. 130.)

The date he assigns to these new fashions is 1467. Yet it is sure the sugar-loaf caps, the long close hose, and long pointed shoes are seen in paintings a good while before. As in Montfaucon (vol. iii, plate 46), where one of the lords has a hawk on his fist, *marque d'une grande qualité dans ces tems là*. Charles VI used to go to council, *l'épervier sur le poing* (ibid. p. 189). Mary, the heiress of Burgundy,[88] is the last lady with a high cap[89] that I meet with. She died 1481,[90] and from what I recollect of the dresses in your picture, they are all older than that date, for about this time very different fashions came in. I even believe it was painted soon after 1445, and the glory[91] about the King's head

88. Marie (1457–82), dau. of Charles the Bold, Duke of Burgundy, m. (1477), as his first wife, Maximilian I of Austria; Duchess of Burgundy, 1477 (Isenburg, *Stammtafeln* ii. table 26).

89. No picture of her is given by Montfaucon. Gray perhaps refers to Montfaucon, op. cit. iii. plate xxix, fig. 2, which repre-

sents Marie (d. 1463), dau. of John the Fearless, Duke of Burgundy, m. (1406) Adolf I, Duke of Cleves.

90. 27 March 1482, according to Isenburg, *Stammtafeln* ii. table 26.

91. Now very faint in the original painting.

might be added afterwards;[92] though Jo[hn] Blackman,[93] a Carthusian, who has wrote a short account, as an eyewitness, of Henry VI's private life,[94] treats him already as a sort of a saint.[95] The pomegranates[96] are only a fashionable pattern for embroidery and brocades about that time. Philip, Duke of Burgundy,[97] made his entry into Ghent in such a robe, and Charles VII into Paris (vol. iii, plates 39 and 45), etc.

This is what I have yet met with to your purpose at all, though perhaps little to your satisfaction, with regard to that picture. Now for the other, I must tell you my disappointment, which has been the reason why I have made you and *the world* wait so long for this first volume of my Antiquities. A Senior Fellow of Trinity,[98] I was told, had got a MS, in which were painted Henry VII and many of his court. He was absent, and I have stayed with impatience for a sight of it. I have now met with him, but the painting is at his living in Cheshire. It is not a MS, but a roll of vellum as long as the room (he says), in which are represented that King and all his Lords going to Parliament. This must be a great curiosity, but we are not like to be the better for it. Another disappointment! In reading Thomas of Otterbourne's *Chronicle*[99] I found mention of a *sainte-ampoule*[100] kept in Westminster Abbey. He speaks of Henry IV's being *inunctus sancto oleo, quod S. Thomæ martyri dedit beatissima Virgo Maria in exilio ejus.*[101] This seemed to account for St Thomas' attending Elizabeth of York as the future

92. So HW in *Anecdotes, Works* iii. 38.

93. John Blakman (fl. 1436–48), Fellow of Merton College, Oxford, 1436, of Eton, 1447.

94. His account of Henry VI was printed by Thomas Hearne as *Collectarium mansuetudinum et bonorum morum Regis Henrici VI*, Oxford, 1732, pp. 285–307.

95. In the section entitled *Timor Domini inerat ei* (p. 289) Blakman exclaims: 'O! quanta diligentia placendi Deo in tam sublimi et juvenili persona reperta est! Attendite reges et principes universi, juvenes et virgines et populi quique, et laudate Dominum in sanctis ejus.'

96. On the Queen's gown.

97. Philippe III (1396–1467), called Philip the Good, father of Charles the Bold.

98. Presumably John Allen (1699–1778), Fellow of Trinity College, Cambridge, 1724, rector of Tarporley, Cheshire 1752–78. Of the nine senior fellows at Trinity in 1754, Allen was the only one with a living in Cheshire (information from Mr H. McLeod Innes, Fellow of Trinity College, Cambridge). See COLE i. 4.

99. Thomas Otterbourne, rector of Chingford, Essex, 1393. His *Chronica regum Angliæ*, extending to 1420, was printed by Hearne, together with Blakman's *Collectarium*, in *Duo rerum Anglicarum scriptores veteres*, 1732, pp. 1–283.

100. The ampulla, part of the coronation regalia, is a vessel 'in the shape of an eagle, the head of which screws off in order to allow the oil to be put in; and the oil is poured out through the beak' (*English Coronation Records*, ed. L. G. Wickham Legg, 1901, p. xxxvii).

101. Gray is apparently paraphrasing Otterbourne's account of Henry IV's coronation. See his *Chronica*, ed. Hearne, p. 221.

anointed Queen of England. But alas! on second thoughts these words must mean St Thomas Becket.[102]

Immediately after the battle of Bosworth, Aug. 22, 1485, the King sent Sir Robert Willoughby[103] to the Castle of Sheriff Hutton in Yorkshire with orders to conduct the Princess Elizabeth to her mother[104] at London. He himself entered the city five days after;[105] was crowned Oct. 30 by Cardinal Thomas Bourchier, Archbishop of Canterbury,[106] and married Jan. 18, 1486, at Westminster, being then in his 31st year, and Elizabeth turned of 20.[107] He (you see) is in his kingly ornaments; but he would not suffer her to be crowned[108] till almost two years after, when she had brought him a son.[109] If you are sure the person who accompanies the King is a cardinal, it must be Bourchier, who died very soon after this marriage, for the writ, *de custodia commissa* to Jo[hn] Morton, Bishop of Ely,[110] who succeeded him, is dated July 13, 1486.[111] Bourchier was not Legate *de latere*, but perhaps may bear the Legatine double cross, as Archbishop of Canterbury, for both our archbishops were styled *Apostolicæ Sedis Legati* (see Rymer, vol. xii, pp. 208 and 245); but I take the person there represented to be James, Bishop of Imola,[112] who granted the dispensation for this marriage (they being in the fourth degree of consanguinity[113] to one another), and was then *orator et commissarius cum potestate Legati de latere in regnis Angliæ*

102. (ca 1118–70), Abp of Canterbury 1162–70. According to a fifteenth-century MS (Legg, op. cit. 169–71), the Virgin, with an eagle of gold in her bosom and a small phial of stone in her hand, appeared to Becket while he was in exile at Sens (1164–70). After putting the phial into the eagle's neck, she told Becket to hide the eagle at the Abbey of Poitiers. The subsquent history of the eagle is given by Thomas Walsingham, *Historia Anglicana*, ed. H. T. Riley, 1863–4, ii. 239–40 (Rolls Ser.).

103. (ca 1452–1502), cr. (1488) K.G., (1491) Lord Willoughby de Broke.

104. Elizabeth (1437–92), dau. of Sir Richard Woodville (Wideville, Widwille), cr. (1466) E. Rivers. She m. (1) (ca 1452) Sir John Grey; m. (2) (1464) Edward IV of England. See David MacGibbon, *Elizabeth Woodville*, 1938, pp. 6, 17, 35.

105. See Stow, *Annales*, 1592, pp. 784–5.

106. Thomas Bourchier (ca 1404 or 1405–86), Abp of Canterbury 1454–86.

107. Gray probably followed James Anderson (*Royal Genealogies*, 1735, p. 748)

who gives Henry VII's date of birth as 1455. The generally accepted date is 28 Jan. 1456/7 (DNB; James Gairdner, *Henry the Seventh*, 1889, p. 3; Gladys Temperley, *Henry VII*, Boston, 1914, p. 1). Elizabeth was born 11 Feb. 1466 (MacGibbon, op. cit. 57).

108. 25 Nov. 1487.

109. Arthur (1486–1502), Prince of Wales. He was born 19 Sept. 1486 (DNB). Gray evidently followed Anderson, op. cit. 748, where Arthur is said to have been born in Sept. 1487.

110. John Morton (ca 1420–1500), Bp of Ely 1479–86, Abp of Canterbury 1486–1500; cardinal, 1493; Lord Chancellor, 1487.

111. Rymer, *Fœdera* xii. 302–3.

112. Iacopo Pasarella (d. 1495), Bp of Imola 1479–88, of Rimini 1488–95 (P. B. Gams, *Series episcoporum ecclesiæ catholicæ*, Ratisbon, 1873, pp. 702, 722).

113. Edward III was both Henry VII's and Elizabeth's great-great-great-grandfather.

et Scotiæ (see the Bull,[114] in Rymer, vol. xii, p. 313); and somewhere,[115] though I cannot turn to the place, I found the King returning the Pope[116] thanks for honouring the solemnity with the presence of his *ambassador.* 'Tis true, this legate was no cardinal, but (I believe) as legate he might wear the purple, though I am not sure his dress is anything more than a Doctor in Divinity's scarlet robe, and the hood, as usual, lined with minever. It is certain there is no hat, though this was the distinction of a cardinal long before these times.[117]

This is all at present compyled by the paynful hand and symple engyne of Your Honour's pour bedesman,   T. G.

My love to Mr C[hute], pray tell me about him,[118] and about the Vine. I have not found his Dugdale[119] yet; it is not in Emanuel, nor the Public Library.[120]

From GRAY, Sunday 17 March 1754

Printed from MS in Waller Collection.
Dated by the postmark and the reference to the year 1754.
Address: To the Honourable Horace Walpole Esq. in Arlington Street, London.
Postmark: SAFFRON WALDEN 18 MR.

Dear Sir,   [Cambridge, March 17, 1754.]

I DO not [at] all wonder at you for being more curious about an interesting point of modern history[1] than a matter that happened three hundred years ago.[2] But why should you look upon me as so

114. 'Bulla de Matrimonio inter Henricum Septimum et Elizabetham Filiam Edwardi Quarti.' It is dated at Rome, 'Decimo Kal. Augusti [23 July]' 2 Innocentius VIII (1486).

115. Probably Francis Bacon, *The History of the Reign of King Henry the Seventh,* 1622, p. 38.

116. Innocent VIII (1432–92), elected Pope, 1484.

117. Their use was authorized by Innocent IV's decree of 1245, given at the Council of Lyons (X. Barbier de Montault, *La Costume et les usages ecclésiastiques selon la tradition romaine,* Paris [1897–1901], ii. 348).

118. Chute visited HW 1 March for the first time after an illness of thirteen weeks (HW to Bentley 2 March 1754).

119. See *post* 11 April 1754.

120. The University Library. The expression seems to have been common: Edmund Carter, *History of the University of Cambridge,* 1753, pp. 13–14, speaks of the 'Public Library of the University.' George III, talking to Dr Johnson, called the Bodleian the 'public library' (Boswell, *Johnson,* ii. 35).

————

1. Hon. Henry Pelham, first lord of the Treasury and chancellor of the Exchequer 1743–54, died 6 March. 'On the 12th of March at night, only six days after the death of Mr Pelham, to the astonishment of all men, yet only to their astonishment, it was settled that the Duke of Newcastle [Pelham's brother] should take the Treasury' (*Mem. Geo. II* i. 381).

2. The marriages of Henry VI and Henry VII.

buried in the dust of an old chronicle that I do not care what happens in George II's reign? I am still alive (I'd have you to know), and, though these events are indeed only subjects of speculation to me, feel some difference still between the present and the past. You are desired therefore to look in the annals of Strawberry, March . . . 1754.³ And when you can find time, please to transcribe me a little paragraph or two, that when I come, like the rest of my brethren here, to ask for some little thing, I may know at least what door to knock at. Adieu, I am ever

Yours,

T. G.

To GRAY, April 1754

Missing. Answered *post* 11 April 1754.

From GRAY, Thursday 11 April 1754

Printed from MS in Waller Collection.
Address: To the Honourable Horace Walpole Esq. in Arlington Street, London.
Postmark: CAMBRIDGE 12 AP.

Camb[rid]ge, April 11, 1754.

Dear Sir,

I AM very glad my objections serve only to strengthen your first opinion about the subject of your picture;[1] if I casually meet with anything more, I shall send it you. The reason I trouble you at present is to tell you that I have got in my hands the Dugdale[2] Mr Chute inquired after. A great number of the arms are blazoned in the margin, not very neatly, but (I suppose) they are authentic; though in it I find written in an old hand[3]

> This volume no errata's has;
> The whole may for errata's pass.
> If to correct them you intend,
> You'll find it labour without end.

3. This is doubtless an allusion to HW's *Memoirs.*

1. The 'Marriage of Henry VI.'
2. John Knight's copy, with his arms and autograph notes, of *The Baronage of England*, 1676, 2 vols fol., by Sir William Dugdale (1605–86), in the library of Caius College. (Information from Mr G. T. Griffith, Fellow of Gonville and Caius College, Cambridge.)
3. On verso of leaf of vol. ii which bears the dedication to Charles II.

'Tis therefore better let them go.
God only 'tis knows, who gets who.

Whether this is wit only, or a censure upon Dugdale's work, or upon
the heraldry added to it, I leave you to judge. The arms were done
by a sergeant-surgeon[4] to King Charles II, who made this art his
particular study, and the book belongs to Caius College. You are desired to send your queries forthwith, for I cannot keep it a great while.

I return you thanks for the civilities you have showed Mason,
who is here, and speaks much of your politeness to him. Adieu, I am

Ever yours,

T. G.

To GRAY, ca Tuesday 21 May 1754

Missing. Answered *post* 23 May 1754. Writing to Chute 21 May 1754 on the
death of Anthony, Chute's brother, HW says: 'I am going to notify it to Gray.'

From GRAY, Thursday 23 May 1754

Printed from MS in Waller Collection.
The date of the year is determined by the reference to Anthony Chute's death.

May 23 [1754], Cambridge.

My dear Sir,

I HAVE scarce time to thank you for your kindness in immediately
telling me the unexpected good news.[1] I must trouble you to send
this[2] to the Vine, as I do not rightly know the direction. Adieu, I am

Ever yours,

T. G.

4. John Knight (1600–80). He was a
student at Caius 1619–25, was ordained
priest in 1625, and later accompanied
Charles II into exile as a surgeon. On the
Restoration, his loyalty was rewarded by
an appointment March 1661 as principal
surgeon (*Calendar of State Papers, Domestic, 1660–1661*, p. 556). He left his collection
of heraldic manuscripts to his college (Caius
Coll. MSS 515–78, 794–9). See Venn, *Alumni
Cantab.;* M. R. James, *A Descriptive Catalogue of the Manuscripts in the Library of
Gonville and Caius College, Cambridge,*
1907–8, i. p. viii, ii. 585–618, and *Supplement* (Cambridge, 1914) 43.

1. Anthony Chute (1691–1754), of the
Vyne, Hants, died intestate 20 May (GM
1754, xxiv. 244; HW to Chute 21 May 1754),
and 'by his death an estate of £4,000 a year,
and a very considerable personal estate,
devolves to his only brother John Chute,
Esq. of Argyle Buildings' (*Daily Adv.* 28
May 1754). See MONTAGU i. 161.
2. Missing.

To Gray, July 1755

Missing. Mentioned *post* 22 July 1755.

From Gray, Tuesday 22 July 1755

Printed from MS in Waller Collection.
The date of the year is supplied by Gray's pocket-diary for 1755 (see n. 1 below).
Address: To the Honourable Horace Walpole Esq. in Arlington Street, London.
Postmark: BASINGSTOKE 23 IY.

Dear Sir,   The Vine, Tuesday, July 22 [1755].

I SHALL be very sorry if I have been the occasion of interrupting any party or design of yours. When Mr C[hute] thought to carry me to the Vine, I was hardly recovered from a fit of the gout,[1] and was obliged to delay my journey thither till the week afterwards;[2] and the uncertainty of my own motions has made me defer answering your message without reflecting that it might be troublesome to you. My intention is to wait upon you tomorrow sennight at Strawberry;[3] if you go to Colonel Conway's,[4] or have any other design that makes mine inconvenient to you at present, be so good to let me know at this place, where I shall stay till the end of this week.[5] We returned yesterday night from Portsmouth,[6] Southampton, and Winchester. I leave to Mr Ch[ute] (who will write next post)[7] to display to you all the beauties of Netley Abbey.[8] The two views of this house[9] go on apace, and grow every day under our eyes. Adieu, I am ever

Yours,

T. G.

1. Gray had been in poor health all the year, and particularly since his arrival at Stoke on 7 June, as is shown by his pocket-diary for 1755 (now at Pembroke College, Cambridge), extracts from which were published by Mitford (GM 1845, n.s. xxiv. 229–33). On 26 June he speaks for the first time of the gout: 'Noctes inquietæ et quasi febriculosæ, quas nunc primum excepit podagra sub articulo pollicis dextri pedis.' He was confined to the house until 13 July (GM 1845, n.s. xxiv. 232).

2. 'July 15. Went into Hampshire to the Vine' (ibid.).

3. See *post* 8 Aug. 1755.

4. At Park Place, Berks. Conway had returned from Ireland shortly before this time (HW to Bentley 17 July 1755).

5. 'Thursday [31 July]. Returned to Stoke' (GM 1845, n.s. xxiv. 232).

6. 'Saturday [19 July] go to Portsmouth' (ibid.).

7. Missing.

8. 6 miles SE of Southampton. The ruins of this Cistercian abbey, founded 1239 by Henry III, were in particular favour with eighteenth-century romantics. See *Gray's Corr.* ii. 843; see also i. 428.

9. By Johann Heinrich Müntz (1727–98), a Swiss painter in HW's employ (MONTAGU

From Gray, Friday 8 August 1755

Printed from MS in Waller Collection.
Address: To the Honourable Horace Walpole Esq. in Arlington Street, London.
Postmark: 9 AV.

Aug. 8, Stoke, 1755.

I INTEND to be at Strawberry on Monday before dinner.[1] But as saints have the diabetes,[2] you will not wonder if a miserable sinner cannot answer a day beforehand for his own constitution. Seriously it has not been fair weather within me,[3] ever since I came into this country. At Mr Chute's I was not quite right, and since my return, particularly this morning, I am sensible of a feverish disposition, and little wandering pains[4] that may fix into the gout, and confine me again. If so, you will excuse the caprices of my distemper, and conclude that it came upon me too suddenly for me to give you notice in time. I am

Yours ever,

T. G.

From Gray, Sunday 10 August 1755

Printed from MS in Waller Collection.
Address: To the Honourable Horace Walpole Esq. in Arlington Street, London.
Postmark: 11 AV.

Aug. 10, 1755, Stoke.

A S they have ordered me to bleed presently,[1] I write to you, while I can make use of my arm, to desire you would excuse me. I have had advice,[2] as they call it, and am still as uncertain as ever,

i. 187). One of his drawings, 'View of the Vine in Hampshire, the seat of John Chute, Esq.,' later hung in HW's bedchamber at SH (Des. of SH,' *Works* ii. 452). See also Montagu i. 259 and *ante* i. 34.

1. HW himself was ill of a fever and a rash, and was unable to go to Twickenham. Early Monday morning (11 Aug.) he sent a messenger to Gray at Stoke asking him to defer his visit (*Gray's Corr.* i. 430–1). Gray eventually visited HW at SH 11–16 Sept. (GM 1845, n.s., xxiv. 232).
2. See HW to Bentley 4 Aug. 1755: 'St Swithin's diabetes.'

3. On 7 Aug. Gray complains of the consequences of excessive use of butter and citrus fruits (GM loc. cit.).
4. 'Friday [8 Aug.]. Redit febricula, non belle habet stomachus, ponderis semper [? sensus] in femoribus et lenis interdum dolor in pedum amborum articulis' (GM loc. cit.).

1. 'Sunday [10 Aug.] Sanguinis 10 unc. traxi. Nox inquieta et turbida' (GM 1845, n.s., xxiv. 232).
2. From Dr Cherry Hayes. See Gray to Wharton 21 Aug. 1755 (*Gray's Corr.* i. 433; see also i. 431).

whether I am to expect the gout or rheumatism. One thing is certain, that I am to expect medicines enough,[3] and as I do not think it civil to bring an apothecary's shop to Strawberry, and am told besides that it is not very safe, I hope you will forgive

Yours ever,

T. G.

To GRAY, ca Tuesday 12 August 1755

Missing. Probably written at SH. Mentioned *post* 14 Aug. 1755.

From GRAY, Thursday 14 August 1755

Printed from MS in Waller Collection.
Address: To the Honourable Horace Walpole Esq. in Arlington Street, London.
Postmark: 15 AV.

Stoke, Aug. 14, 1755.

WHEN you name a fever and rash in the middle of August, I cannot but inquire (as soon as I am able) what you are doing to get rid of them, and how you are since I heard from you. I do not at all expect an answer from yourself, but should be much obliged to you if you would order Harry[1] or Louis[2] to write me a line of information. I myself am a little better and a little worse for my *advice*. The heats I felt in a morning are abated, if not gone, and in their room I have got the headache, which with me is a very unusual thing. Adieu! I hope to hear a better account of you. I am ever

Yours,

T. G.

If you easily get rid of your fever, pray do not think of going so soon near the coast of Essex.[3]

3. Gray mentions draughts of salt of wormwood, lemon juice, alexiteric water, peppermint, tincture of guaiacum, etc. (GM loc. cit.; *Gray's Corr.* i. 431, 433).

1. Henry Jones, HW's servant 1752–62 (MONTAGU i. 132).

2. (d. 1767), HW's Swiss valet (DU DEFFAND i. 201).

3. 'I am going to Mr Rigby's for a week or ten days' (HW to Bentley 15 Aug. 1755). Richard Rigby lived at Mistley Hall, Manningtree, Essex.

To Gray, ca Friday 15 August 1755

Missing. A letter telling Gray that HW was 'well again' is mentioned in Gray to
Wharton 21 Aug. 1755 (*Gray's Corr.* i. 433). The letter was written probably on 15
Aug. in Arlington Street, before HW's departure for Mistley.

From Gray, Tuesday 14 October 1755

Printed from MS in Waller Collection.
Address: To the Honourable Horace Walpole in Arlington Street, London.
Postmark: 15 OC.

[Stoke,] Oct. 14, 1755.

I DO not think of leaving this place till about a fortnight hence,[1]
and as I doubt if you will continue at Twickenham so late in the
year,[2] shall then call upon you at your house in town. I heartily
pity poor G. Montagu, who never was made for solitude, and who
begins to feel it at a time of life when everybody grows unfit for it.[3]
Pray tell Mr Chute I have been tolerably well[4] ever since I saw him.
I am ever

Yours,

T. G.

To Gray, Thursday 25 December 1755

Printed from MS now wsl. In 1828 it was bequeathed by Mrs Damer to Sir
Wathen Waller, 1st Bt; sold at Sotheby's 5 Dec. 1921, lot 21, to Maggs; offered by
Maggs, Cat. No. 421 (Spring, 1922), lot 837; No. 459 (Spring, 1925), lot 749; No. 522
(Summer, 1929), lot 1274; Maggs to wsl, 1931.

1. 'Came to town Saturday November 1'
(GM 1845, n.s., xxiv. 233).
2. HW stayed at SH until 11 Nov. (MON-
TAGU i. 178).
3. George Montagu (ca 1713–80), HW's
Eton friend and correspondent. His sister
Henrietta (Harriet), who had been living
with him at Greatworth, Northants, had
just died (MONTAGU i. 174–5).
4. See HW to Chute 20 Oct. 1755.

Arlington Street, Christmas Day, 1755.

Advice of Dr Oliver[1] to Sir John Cope[2] on his
getting St Anthony's fire[3] by drinking the Bath waters
out of Miss Molly's[4] hand.
By Lord Bath.[5]

See gentle Cope with gout[6] and love opprest,
Alternate torments raging in his breast,
Tries at his cure, but tampers still in vain;
What lessens one, augments the other pain.
    The charming nymph, who strives to give relief,
Instead of comfort, heightens all his grief:
For health he drinks, then sighs for love, and cries,
Health's in her hand, destruction in her eyes.
She gives us water, but each touch alas!
The wanton girl electrifies the glass.
To cure the gout, we drink large draughts of love,
And then, like Ætna, burst in flames above.

The }
Advice } Sip not, dear knight, the daughter's liquid fire,
But take the healing bev'rage from the sire:
'Twill ease thy gout—for love no cure is known;
The god of physic could not cure his own.

On Lord Darl——'s being made Joint Paymaster.[7]

Wonders, Newcastle, mark thy ev'ry hour;
But this last act's a plenitude of pow'r:

1. William Oliver (1695–1754), M.D., Bath physician 1725–64, originator of the 'Bath Oliver' biscuit and author of a *Practical Essay on the Use and Abuse of Warm Bathing in Gouty Cases*, 1751.
2. (d. 1760), Col. 7th Dragoons 1741–60; Lt-Gen., 1743; K.B., 1743; M.P. Queenborough 1722–7, Liskeard 1727–34, Orford 1738–41; defeated at Prestonpans by the Young Pretender.
3. Erysipelas.
4. Not identified. Lines 13–14 suggest that she may have been a daughter of Dr Oliver.
5. William Pulteney (1684–1764), cr. (1742) E. of Bath, Sir Robert Walpole's antagonist. For another version of his lines on Cope, printed from a MS belonging to

Mrs Stopford Sackville, see Hist. MSS Comm., 9th Report, Appendix, pt iii (1884), p. 132.
6. Chesterfield in a letter to Newcastle 8 Feb. 1746 refers to Cope as 'an incurable cripple of the gout, and absolutely incapable of ever serving.' See Chesterfield's *Letters*, ed. Bonamy Dobrée, 1932, iii. 726.
7. Henry Vane (ca 1705–58), 3d Bn Barnard, 1753, cr. (1754) E. of Darlington. He had been granted, together with Vct Dupplin 16 Dec. 1755, 'the office of receiver and paymaster-general of all His Majesty's guards, garrisons, and land forces . . . in the room of . . . William Pitt' (*London Gazette* 13–16 Dec. 1755).

Naught but the force of an almighty reign
Could make a *paymaster* of Harry V——.

On Splitting the Pay Office.

Holles,[8] not past his childhood yet, retains
The maxims of his nurse or tutor's pains:
Thence did the mighty babe this truth derive,
Two negatives make one affirmative:
But ah! Two dunces never made a wit,
Nor can two Darlingtons[9] compose a Pitt.[10]

To draw poetry from you I send you these mediocre verses, the only ones in fashion. The first lines indeed are pretty, when one considers they were writ by a man of seventy, Lord Bath. The first epigram was a thought of George Selwyn,[11] rhymed; the last is scarce a thought at all.

Ministers, patriots, wits, poets, paymasters, all are dispersed and gone out of town. The changes are made, and all preferments given away:[12] you will be glad to hear that our Colonel Montagu[13] has got a regiment. Lord Waldgrave[14] last night hearing them talk over these histories, said with a melancholy tone, alas! they talk so much of giving places for life, I wish they don't give me mine[15] for life!

8. The Duke of Newcastle.

9. Darlington and his colleague, Thomas Hay (1710–87), styled Vct Dupplin, 9th E. of Kinnoull, 1758.

10. William Pitt (1708–78), cr. (1766) E. of Chatham, paymaster-general of the forces 1746–55, dismissed for his opposition to Newcastle and for his speech 13 Nov. in the House of Commons opposing the 'treaties of subsidy with the Landgrave of Hesse and the Empress of Russia for the defence of Hanover' (HW's note on HW to Conway 15 Nov. 1755; see also *Mem. Geo. II* ii. 55–62).

11. George Augustus Selwyn (1719–91) of Matson, Glos; HW's lifelong friend and occasional correspondent. 'George Selwyn says, that no act ever showed so much the Duke of Newcastle's absolute power as his being able to make Lord Darlington a *paymaster*' (HW to Bentley 17 Dec. 1755; see also *Horace Walpole's Fugitive Verses*, ed. W. S. Lewis, New York, 1931, pp. 121–2).

12. For a list of changes in the Newcastle-Fox administration see MONTAGU i. 180–1; HW to Mann 21 Dec. 1755.

13. Charles Montagu (d. 1777), K.B., 1771, George Montagu's youngest brother (MONTAGU i. 31). His commission as colonel of the 61st Regiment of Foot was dated 30 Dec. 1755 (*Army Lists*, 1756, p. 81).

14. James Waldegrave (1715–63), 2d E. Waldegrave.

15. 'Of governor to the Prince of Wales' (HW). Waldegrave was appointed, 18 Dec. 1752, 'Governor and Keeper of the Privy Purse to George, Prince of Wales and to Prince Edward' (GEC; *Daily Adv.* 20 Dec. 1752). He accepted the office with reluctance (HW to Mann 11 Dec. 1752; *Mem. Geo. II* i. 291), and never gained the Prince's confidence. For the relations between the rival courts of the King and the Prince of Wales see introduction to *Letters from George III to Lord Bute 1756–1766*, ed. Romney Sedgwick, 1939; see also James, Earl Waldegrave, *Memoirs, from 1754 to 1758*, 1821, pp. 63–80.

Adieu! I expect prodigious interest for my pômes.

Yours ever,

H. W.

From GRAY, Friday 30 July 1756

Printed from MS in Waller Collection.

Memorandum by HW: Great poets have a right to command and none are so much their subjects as great men. I know you think Mr Gr[ay] the greatest poet we have and I know he thinks you the greatest man we have; judge if you can disobey him.[1]

July 30, Friday, 1756, Stoke.

Sir,

IT is a good number of years since I applied to you on a like occasion.[2] Your ready compliance with my desire at that time gives me confidence to do so at present, but how far it is practicable or proper for you to satisfy me in this case I leave entirely to your own judgment.

Dr Long, the Master of Pembroke Hall, (I am told) is either dying or dead.[3] Mr Brown,[4] the President[5] and Senior Fellow, is a person entirely unknown to the world, whom those few that know, love and esteem; and to whom I myself have a thousand obligations. His interest in the college is considerable,[6] but, as among eleven or twelve Fellows who elect, there are (you will not doubt) some that will regard their own interest rather more than his, a word from you to Mr F[ox],[7] or the Duke of B[edfor]d,[8] or any other great man, may contribute to recommend him, and incline these doubtful people to vote for him.

1. Presumably a draft of an unsent letter to Henry Fox, 31 July 1756 (see n. 7 below). Gray's opinion of Fox, if correctly given by HW, had greatly altered by 1766, when he wrote the lines beginning 'Old and abandoned by each venal friend,' etc.

2. To support Brudenell's election to a Peterhouse fellowship (*ante* 3 Feb. 1746).

3. Dr Long did not die, however, until 1770 (Venn, *Alumni Cantab.*).

4. James Brown (see *Gray's Corr.* i. 222 *et passim*).

5. 'The title borne by the Vice-Master at Pembroke' (ibid. ii. 468, n. 5).

6. He had been a Fellow for 21 years.

7. Henry Fox (1705–74), cr. (1763) Bn Holland; secretary of state (25 Nov. 1755) in the Newcastle administration. He was on friendly terms with HW until Nov. 1762, when a rift occurred (MONTAGU ii. 68; see also *Gray's Corr.* ii. 468, n. 6). HW's influence with him had been much overestimated by both Montagu (MONTAGU i. 136) and Gray. For HW's portrait of Fox, written at SH in 1748, see *Works* i. 192–4.

8. John Russell (1710–71), 4th D. of Bedford. For a brief portrait, see *Mem. Geo. II* i. 186.

Mr Mason, who is himself qualified to be Master,[9] and might probably enough succeed, I am fully persuaded (though you will think there is not common sense in the assertion) will do everything to further Mr Brown's election.[10] He (if you will let him know when you are at home) will wait upon you,[11] and give you any necessary information. I can answer for Mr B[rown]'s principles in government, as I can for my own, that they are those of every true and rational Whig. Perhaps you may hear the contrary said; and I ought not to conceal from you that he is one of the plainest, worthiest and most honest men I ever met with, but this ought to be a secret. The antagonist I apprehend is a Mr Addison,[12] a *creature* of your uncle[13] and preferred by him[14] (do not think I say this to add a spur to you, for I flatter myself it is not necessary). He will have the Bishop of Chester's[15] assistance, and that of the Heads of Colleges (who know him for a staunch man), and consequently, of the Duke of Newc[ast]le.[16] The thing (supposing Dr L. dead) must be decided in eight or ten days, I believe. The obligation you will lay upon me by this will be as great or greater than if I myself were the immediate object of your kindness. But I repeat, that you only are to judge, how far it can answer the end I propose. Mason comes to town[17] from Tunbridge today and will stay there, I imagine, some days. I am ever

Yours,

T. G.

9. Mason was ordained priest 24 Nov. 1754, became a Fellow of Pembroke College in 1749, and received his M.A. the same year. See *Gray's Corr.* ii. 473, n. 5.

10. Mason had considerable interest with the Earl of Holdernesse, his patron and distant connection.

11. He proposed to call on HW in Arlington Street on Monday 2 Aug. (Mason to HW 1 Aug. 1756).

12. Leonard Addison. See Gray to Mason 30 July 1756 (*Gray's Corr.* ii. 470–2) on Addison's supporters.

13. 'Old' Horace.

14. Addison held, among others, three Norfolk livings: Saxthorpe, Cawston, and Salle. The advowson of all three livings was held by Pembroke College, but Old Horace, as the most influential neighbouring landowner, may have been consulted as to the nomination, which would account for

Gray's expression 'preferred by him.' See *History and Antiquities of . . . Norfolk,* Norwich, 1781, iii pt ii. 278, iii pt iii (Eynsford). 78; Francis Blomefield and Charles Parkin, *An Essay towards a Topographical History of . . . Norfolk,* 1805–10, vi. 264, 500, viii. 274; *Gray's Corr.* ii. 471.

15. Edmund Keene (1714–81), Bp of Chester, 1752, of Ely, 1771; Master of Peterhouse 1748–54; Vice-Chancellor 1749–51. HW to Mann 11 Dec. 1752 calls Keene 'Newcastle's tool at Cambridge, which university he has half turned Jacobite, by cramming down new ordinances to carry measures of that Duke.'

16. Chancellor of Cambridge 1748–68.

17. Gray to Mason 30 July 1756 is addressed to Mason 'at the Right Honourable the Earl of Holderness's in Arlington Street, London' (*Gray's Corr.* ii. 473).

When I mentioned the Duke of B[edfor]d, I forgot that Mr Franklyn[18] may have some weight there. He is a mortal enemy of my Mr Brown.[19]

To GRAY, ca Monday 2 August 1756

Missing. Implied *post* 4 Aug. 1756.

From GRAY, Wednesday 4 August 1756

Printed from MS in Waller Collection.

Wednesday, Aug. 4, 1756, Stoke.

Dear Sir,

I SEE and feel the very natural unwillingness you must have to apply to those persons[1] for anything that may imply a sort of obligation, and I more strongly see and feel the obligation I have to you for being so ready to conquer that reluctance on my account. I could not at this distance do otherwise than refer you to Mr M[ason] (who, I hope, has seen you) for particulars, which he is better informed of than I am. I have heard since that Dr L[ong] is alive, and thought to be out of danger; but he is a very old man,[2] and though I am glad to see we may probably spare you this trouble for the present, I can only look upon it as deferred for a time. Mr B[row]n so little knew of my intention that the good man has wrote to acquaint me of Dr L.'s illness, and (if I will qualify myself by taking orders,[3] and I know not what) offers me his utmost endeavours to serve me in the same way, and make me his *Master*. You will know before now from M[aso]n, whether the man be dead, or dying, or alive and well at last. My zeal (indeed gratitude) to Mr B. only could have forced me to put you upon a disagreeable task, and I shall be glad to hear there

18. Thomas Francklin (ca 1721–84), D.D. 1770, Fellow of Trinity College, Cambridge, 1745–58; Regius Professor of Greek 1750–9; translator of the classics. He sought Bedford's patronage by publishing, 1755, *Truth and Falsehood,* a panegyric on the Duchess of Bedford.

19. Their feud began in the Three Tuns tavern at Cambridge on 17 Nov. 1750, in an affair which resulted in public humiliation of Francklin and a pamphlet war. For a detailed account, see D. A. Winstanley,

The University of Cambridge in the Eighteenth Century, Cambridge, 1922, pp. 211–22.

———

1. Fox and the Duke of Bedford (*ante* 30 July 1756).

2. He was in his 77th year.

3. Gray was trebly ineligible for the mastership of Pembroke: he was not in orders, and was neither a Fellow of the college nor an M.A.

is no farther occasion for doing anything. If you find there is not, you will be so good to mention nothing of what has passed, for I am aware too that my desire to serve him may chance to do hurt, yet was unwilling to omit anything that might possibly do good.

I put the thing in the strongest light to you (being obliged to be concise) and I don't wonder it appeared somewhat desperate to your foresight. But in reality Mr B. has a pretty strong natural interest among his own society, and might possibly be chose without any *brigue* at all, and in spite of opposition. Only I would wish to bring it to a certainty. Nobody calls him Jac[obi]te; I only mean, in case of disputes he might be called that, or something as absurd, for want of other abuse.

I will go to town on Friday to see poor Mr Ch[ute],[4] and at your return[5] hope to thank you at Strawberry for your kindness. If I made you no excuse before, it was because I thought you might have forgot the occasion of it. I am ever

Yours,

T. G.

To GRAY, August 1756

Missing. Mentioned *post* 29 Aug. 1756.

From GRAY, Sunday 29 August 1756

Printed from MS in Waller Collection.
Address: To the Honourable Horace Walpole in Arlington Street, London.
Postmark: 30 AV.

Stoke, Aug. 29, 1756.

NOT exactly knowing the time of your return, I had the day before I received your letter accepted an invitation from Mr Chute to come to the Vine. He is now actually at Windsor expecting to carry me thither tomorrow and insists upon his priority. As soon as ever I come back I shall send to know if you are *visible,* and am ever

Yours,

T. G.

4. Chute was suffering from gout. See *post* 8 Sept. 1756.
5. HW set out 'the first week in August into Yorkshire' (MONTAGU i. 192) and returned to SH 25 Aug. (ibid. i. 195).

From GRAY, Wednesday 8 September 1756

Printed from MS in Waller Collection.
Address: To the Honourable Horace Walpole in Arlington Street, London.
Postmark: BASINGSTOKE 8 SE.

Sept. 8, 1756, the Vine.

POOR Mr Chute has now had the gout for these five days, with such a degree of pain and uneasiness as he never felt before. Whether to attribute it to Dr La Cour's[1] forcing medicines, or to a little cold he got as soon as he came hither, I know not, but for above forty hours it seemed past all human suffering, and he lay screaming like a man upon the rack. The torture was so great that (against my judgment and even his own) he was forced to have recourse to the infusion of poppy-heads, which Cocchi used to give him,[2] and in half an hour's time was easy, fell into a gentle perspiration, and slept many hours. This was the night before last, and all yesterday he continued cheerful and in spirits. At night (as he expected) the pain returned, not so violent but in more places, for now it is in one foot, both knees, and one hand; and I hourly dread it will increase again to its former rage. If anything sudden happen, who can I send to? Here is no assistance nearer than a Dr Langrish[3] at Winchester, of whom he has no great opinion. As to Lacour he is enraged against him, and looks upon him as the cause of all he suffers. I cannot think there is any danger, for though with all this he is at times in a high fever, yet it seems to depend upon the gout entirely, increasing and abating with the pain. But if anything unexpected happen, here are nobody but myself and Muntz in the house, would you advise to send to Mrs Pawlet,[4] or to whom? You will oblige me, if you will answer

---

1. Philip de la Cour (ca 1710–80), M.D. (Leyden, 1733), licentiate of the Royal College of Physicians, 1751 (William Munk, *Roll of the Royal College of Physicians of London*, 1878, ii. 178). He is the 'Jew-Physician' mentioned in Gray to Wharton ca 20 June 1760 (*Gray's Corr.* ii. 678), who lived in Bury Street (*Court and City Register*, 1760, p. 226).

2. Chute had had attacks of the gout in Florence in 1742, 1743, 1744, and 1746. Cocchi presumably attended him then. See Mann correspondence.

3. Browne Langrish (d. 1759), M.D., extra licentiate of the Royal College of Physicians, 1734; F.R.S., 1734; author of *A New Essay on Muscular Motion*, 1733, and *Modern Theory and Practice of Physic*, 1735.

4. Not identified. She was probably related to Harry Powlett, 4th D. of Bolton, whose brother Charles (d. 1754), the 3d Duke, was a friend and neighbour of Chute's brother, Anthony (Chaloner W. Chute, *A History of the Vyne*, Winchester, 1888, p. 83). Bolton's seat, Hackwood Park, Hants, is 4½ miles south of the Vyne.

me in a loose paper, for he must see your letter. It will be a charity too to insert anything of news, or whatever you please to tell us, for when he gets any respite from pain, he is capable and desirous of entertainment, and talks with an eagerness of spirits, that seems to make part of his distemper. Pray tell us how Mr Man⁵ does. I am ever

Yours,

T. G.

To GRAY, ca Friday 10 September 1756

Missing. Mentioned *post* 12 Sept. 1756. Possibly a second letter is implied *post* 19 Sept. 1756.

From GRAY, Sunday 12 September 1756

Printed from MS in Waller Collection.
Misdated. Sunday fell on 12 Sept. The date of the year is determined by the references to Chute's gout and to *ante* 8 Sept. 1756.
Address: To the Honourable Horace Walpole at Strawberry Hill near Twickenham, Middlesex. *Postmark:* [B]A[SINGS]TO[KE] 13 SE.

The Vine, Sept. 11 [12], Sunday [1756].

I HAVE the pleasure to tell you that after repeating once again his infusion of poppies, which caused each time an entire cessation from pain and an easy perspiration for near twenty-four hours, Mr Chute has had no return of his tortures, but for these four days has continued in a very tolerable state, cheerful enough and in good spirits in the day-time, his appetite beginning to return, and all last night passed in quiet and natural sleep. But he is (as you may imagine) still nailed to his bed, and much weakened. God knows when he will be able to get up or bear any motion, and the least cold, as autumn is coming on, will certainly bring it all back again. I am quite of your opinion about going to town as soon as it is possible, and had of

5. Galfridus Mann (ca 1706–56), Horace Mann's twin brother, was suffering from asthma and consumption (HW to Mann 25 Jan., 5 Feb. 1756). After a summer at Bristol his health improved, and HW thought him 'much mended' but not recovered (HW to Mann 19 Sept. 1756). He died 21 Dec. (HW to Mann 8 Dec., 23 Dec. 1756).

my own accord talked about it, but he seems rather set against it; however I hope to prevail. As to the Tracies,[1] I think he told me just before this illness that they were all coming, and he had wrote to hinder it on some pretence or other.[2] What you say about Mrs P.[3] is very true. I only mentioned her because she was more within reach than anybody else, but I have now no farther thought of danger.

We are much obliged to you for your news, and hope, when you have leisure, again to hear from you. I am

Yours ever,

T. G.

From GRAY, Sunday 19 September 1756

Printed from MS in Waller Collection.
Dated by the postmark and the references to Chute's gout.
Address: To the Honourable Horace Walpole in Arlington Street, London.
Postmark: BASINGSTOKE 20 SE.

The Vine, Sept. [19], Sunday [1756].

MR CHUTE'S proceedings are as follows. Soon after I wrote to you, being very easy, he got up and sat in a chair for two days, where having caught cold, he proceeded to go to bed again. However as he has felt no great matter of pain, today he is to be seen once more sitting by the fireside. He won't hear of London, but talks of Bath, so I am easy about it, as that seems full as well. Yet I wish he would hasten his journey. I think of returning in four or five days to Stoke,[1] as he is now no longer alone in the house. We are much obliged to you for your packets and newses, particularly for your old news. I, who deal in sequels and second parts, am anxious to know what be-

1. Chute's sister-in-law, Mrs. John Tracy (see *ante* 8 Feb. 1747), had four married sons: Robert (1706–67), John (1706–73), Anthony (d. 1767), and Thomas (ca 1717–1770) (*Bristol and Gloucestershire Archæological Society*, 1912, xxxv. 91–2; ibid. 1905, xxviii. 465; ibid. 1900, xxiii. 22; ibid. 1928, l. 256; GM 1767, xxxvii. 331). See Appendix 1.
2. Chute was on particularly bad terms with Robert and John Tracy, who had both applied for the guardianship of Margaret Nicoll. See Appendix 1.
3. Presumably Mrs Pawlet (*ante* 8 Sept. 1756).

1. Gray apparently stayed at the Vyne until the first week in October (*Gray's Corr.* ii. 482). Following this visit he and Chute seem to have become estranged for some unknown reason (ibid. n. 1).

came of my Lady Sundon.[2] Whether she sunk into the ground, or flew through the window after this thunderclap.[3] Adieu, I am ever

Yours,

T. G.

From GRAY, Tuesday 21 September 1756

Printed from MS in Waller Collection.
Dated by the postmark and the reference to Chute's gout.
Address: To the Honourable Horace Walpole in Arlington Street, London.
Postmark: BASINGSTOKE 22 SE.

The Vine, Tuesday [Sept. 21, 1756].

IF you continue your intention of coming hither,[1] Mr Chute desires you would give yourself the trouble of looking among your prints (of Hollar[2] or others) for an inside view of St George's Chapel at Windsor,[3] and be so good to bring it with you. I have a notion there is such a print in Ashmole's book of the Garter.[4]

We have been up a second time for two days in our chair, but are forced to lie in bed again today with the gout in one ankle, yet with no great pain. I am ever

Yours,

T. G.

2. Charlotte (d. 1742), dau. of John Dyve, clerk of the Privy Council; m. (before 1714) William Clayton, cr. (1735) Bn Sundon; Bedchamber woman to Queen Caroline 1714–37 (John Chamberlayne, *Magnæ Britanniæ Notitia*, 1723, p. 567; 1737, 'List,' p. 245). She was a friend of the Duchess of Marlborough. Sir Robert Walpole called her a 'bitch' (Hervey, *Memoirs* ii. 605), and HW an 'absurd and pompous simpleton' (*Reminiscences,* ed. Paget Toynbee, Oxford, 1924, p. 71). For Hervey's sympathetic portrait, see his *Memoirs* i. 67; see also *Memoirs of Viscountess Sundon,* ed. Katherine B. Thompson, 1847.

3. HW has anecdotes about her in his letter to Mann 7 Jan. 1742, O.S., and others in his *Reminiscences* 71–2, 74, 91.

1. 'Poor Mr Chute . . . has been grievously ill with the gout—he is laid up at his own house, whither I am going to see him' (HW to Mann 19 Sept. 1756).

2. Wenceslaus (Vaclav) Hollar (1607–77), engraver, a native of Prague, came to England in 1635, and later was appointed drawing teacher to the future Charles II. Over 2700 prints by him are known (DNB; see also Arthur M. Hind, *Wenceslaus Hollar and his Views of London and Windsor in the Seventeenth Century,* 1922). HW's fine collection of Hollar was sold London 807–80, 899.

3. Hollar did six interiors, besides an elevation of the choir-screen and organ from the west (Hind, op. cit. 86–8).

4. *The Institution, Laws and Ceremonies of the Most Noble Order of the Garter,* 1672, by Elias Ashmole (1617–92), antiquary and astrologer, founder of the Ashmolean Museum at Oxford. Several of Hollar's views of St George's are inserted between pp. 154 and 161 of the 1672 edition. HW's copy (edn 1693) is in MS Cat. E.2.23.

From GRAY, Friday 11 March 1757

Printed from MS in Waller Collection.
Dated by HW: 1757.
Address: To the Honourable Horace Walpole in Arlington Street.

[London,] Friday morning, March 11 [1757].

Sir,

I CALLED at your door this morning between eleven and twelve,
and was told you were gone out. As I am, while I stay in town,[1] in
the City at a great distance from you, I shall take it as a favour if you
will inform me what day I may find you at home, having a particular
reason for desiring to see you.[2] I am

Yours ever,

T. G.

PS. Will tomorrow or Monday morning suit you? I am at Dr
Wharton's in King's Arms Yard, Coleman Street.

From GRAY, Monday 11 July 1757

Reprinted from *Works* v. 397–8.

Stoke, July 11, 1757.

I WILL not give you the trouble of sending your chaise for me. I
intend to be with you on Wednesday in the evening. If the press[1]
stands still all this time for me,[2] to be sure it is dead in childbed.

1. Gray arrived 5 March and stayed till
2 April as Wharton's guest (*Gray's Corr.* ii.
496; see also 'Chronological Table').

2. Gray was much disturbed by the predicament of his friend Henry Tuthill (b. ca
1722), Fellow of Pembroke 1749–57, who on
5 Feb. 1757 was deprived of his fellowship
for 'having been absent from the college
above a month contrary to the statutes.'
The true reason appears to have been some
scandalous reports which 'laid him under
violent suspicion of having been guilty of
great enormities' (*Pembroke College Register* under 5 Feb. 1757, quoted in *Gray's
Corr.* iii. 1208). These 'enormities' are not
explained, and Mason mutilated all letters
that even casually allude to Tuthill, while
those discussing the scandal have apparently all been destroyed. See the Appendix
'Henry Tuthill' in *Gray's Corr.* iii. 1206–10.

1. The 'Officina Arbuteana,' the SH
Press, erected 25 June 1757 (*Journal of
the Printing-Office* 3; MONTAGU i. 208, 214;
see also Hazen, *SH Bibliography*).

2. 'July 16th. Began to print. The first
work was an edition of two new odes by Mr
Gray: one, on the power and progress of
poetry; the other, on the destruction of
the Welsh bards by Edward I' (*Journal of
the Printing-Office* 3; Hazen, *SH Bibliography* 22–31).

I do not love notes,[3] though you see I had resolved to put two or three. They are signs of weakness and obscurity. If a thing cannot be understood without them, it had better be not understood at all.[4] If you will be vulgar, and pronounce it *Lunnun*[5] instead of London, I can't help it. Caradoc I have private reasons against, and besides it is in reality Carādoc,[6] and will not stand in the verse.[7]

I rejoice you can fill all your *vides:* the Maintenon could not, and that was her great misfortune.[8] Seriously though, I congratulate you on your happiness, and seem to understand it. The receipt is obvious: it is only 'Have something to do,'[9] but how few can apply it!—Adieu! I am ever

Yours,

T. GRAY

3. See Gray's comments on the 'Explanation of the Prints' in *Designs (ante* 13, 20 Feb. 1753). In the SH edition of the two odes there were only four notes (all to 'The Bard'), but in the 1768 edition of *Poems by Mr Gray* the number of notes was increased to 21 to 'The Progress of Poesy' and 35 to 'The Bard.' The original notes for the 1768 edition were written by Gray as marginalia in his copy of the *Odes,* now in the Pierpont Morgan Library, New York.

4. Gray prefixed an advertisement to 'The Progress of Poesy' in the 1768 edition, in which he apologized for the notes. The original draft of this advertisement in the Morgan Library copy of Gray's *Odes* reads: 'These odes were published Aug. 8, 1757. The author was at first advised (even by his friends) to subjoin some few explanatory notes, but had then too much respect for the understanding of his readers to take that liberty.' The last clause is an insertion; Gray first wrote, and then deleted: 'but chose to leave both his writings and the world to themselves. The words of Pindar prefixed to them (vocal to the intelligent alone) were prophetic of their fate: very few understood them; the multitude of all ranks called them unintelligible' (quoted by permission of the Trustees of the Pier-

pont Morgan Library). See also W. Powell Jones, *Thomas Gray, Scholar,* 1937, p. 16.

5. 'Ye towers of Julius, London's lasting shame' ('The Bard,' line 87).

6. Mason, in his notes to Gray's *Poems* 104, quotes a fragment translated from the Welsh, which he found among Gray's papers, in which the word is so scanned.

7. In the final copy of lines 57–144 of 'The Bard,' sent to Wharton before 11 June 1757, line 102 reads:

me unbless'd, unpitied here
'Leave [your despairing Caradoc] to mourn!'

The brackets and the interlinear correction are Gray's (see *Gray's Corr.* i. 436). In the printed text of 'The Bard' the words in brackets were omitted.

8. 'Je suis venue à la faveur, et je vous proteste, ma chère fille, que tous les états laissent un vide affreux' (from a letter of Mme de Maintenon to Mme de la Maisonfort, *Lettres de Madame de Maintenon,* Amsterdam, 1756, ii. 211. HW's copy of this edition, with the *Mémoires,* 1755, is now wsl).

9. 'To be employed is to be happy. This principle of mine, and I am convinced of its truth, has, as usual, no influence on my practice' (Gray to Hurd 25 Aug. 1757, *Gray's Corr.* ii. 520; see also ibid. 665–6).

From GRAY, Wednesday 10 August 1757

Printed from MS in Waller Collection.
Memorandum by HW: Testaceous powder or sal volatile.[1]

Stoke, Aug. 10, 1757.

I AM extremely sorry to hear of poor Mr Bentley's illness.[2] What I cannot account for is that you or he should trust such a dog of an apothecary,[3] after he had showed himself, to do anything, even to sell medicines, when it is just as easy for him to put in a grain of slow poison as to administer a dose of pure and innocent brown paper.

Dodsley sent me some copies last week.[4] They are very pleasant to the eye, and will do no dishonour to your press; as you are but young in the trade, you will excuse me if I tell you that some little inaccuracies have escaped your eye, as in the ninth page *Lab'rinth's*[5] and *Echo's*[6] (which are nominatives plural), with apostrophes after them, as though they were genitives singular; and p. 16, *sorrow* and *solitude*[7] without capital letters. Besides certain commas here and there omitted. If you do not commit greater faults in your next work, I shall grow jealous of Hentznerus.[8]

I am going to add to the trouble I have given you by desiring you would tell me what you hear anybody say[9] (I mean, if anybody says anything). I know you will forgive this vanity of an author, as the vanity of a printer is a little interested in the same cause. The Garricks[10] have been here for three days, much to my entertainment. If

1. Probably medicines intended for Bentley.

2. 'Poor Mr Bentley has been at the extremity with a fever and inflammation in his bowels; but is so well recovered that Mr Müntz is gone to fetch him hither to-day' (HW to Montagu 25 Aug. 1757, from SH, MONTAGU i. 216).

3. Not identified.

4. The *Journal of the Printing-Office* (p. 3) under 3 Aug. 1757 records, '1000 copies of the *Odes* finished,' and under 8 Aug., '2000 copies published by Dodsley.' They were sold at one shilling (*Daily Adv.* 8 Aug. 1757). See Hazen, *SH Bibliography* 23–9, for the complex bibliographical history of the *Odes*.

5. 'The Progress of Poesy,' line 70. It was corrected in the 1768 edition.

6. Ibid. line 71. It remained unchanged in the 1768 edition.

7. 'The Bard,' line 62. The two words remained uncapitalized in the 1768 edition.

8. See *ante* i. 28.

9. Gray asked the same question of Edward Bedingfield and James Brown (*Gray's Corr.* ii. 515–16). For the public's response to the *Odes*, see Gray to Wharton 17 Aug., to Mason 7 Sept. (ibid. 518, 522–4); see also W. Powell Jones in *Modern Philology* xxviii (1930), pp. 61–82, and Robert Halsband, 'A Parody of Thomas Gray,' *Philological Quarterly* xxii (1943), pp. 255–66.

10. David Garrick m. (1749) Eva Maria Violette (1725–1822), Viennese dancer who came to England in 1746. The Garricks were visiting Lady Cobham at Stoke manor house (Gray to Brown 14 Aug. 1757,

you see him, do not fail to make him tell you the story of *Bull and Poker*.[11] Adieu, I am ever

Yours,

T. G.

From GRAY, Thursday 13 October 1757

Address: To the Honourable Horace Walpole in Arlington Street, London.
Postmark: 15 OC.

Stoke, Oct. 13, 1757.

IT will be three weeks or more before I can come to town. I have had, almost ever since I was here,[1] a much worse state of health than I have been used to, and particularly of late; they advise me to force a fit of the gout, but methinks it is better to bear with a number of lesser maladies.[2] I am not, however, at present confined by them, and therefore leave you to weigh my infirmities against your own impatience. If it won't stay till I see you in London, and you will hazard the sending your chaise on Wednesday next, to be sure I will come,[3] if I am able.

I begin at this distance with telling you that though I admire rapidity in writing, and perseverance in finishing, being two talents that I want, yet I do not admire rapidity in *printing*,[4] because this is a thing that I, or anybody, can do. I am

Yours ever,

T. G.

Gray's Corr. ii. 516). See *post* 13 Oct. 1757, n. 4.

11. Not traced.

———

1. Gray left Cambridge 17 June ('Chronological Table,' *Gray's Corr.*).
2. It was commonly believed in the eighteenth century that the gout drove out all other ailments.
3. To SH.
4. HW seems to have boasted of the activity of his Press. The *Journal of the Printing-Office* 5–6 records: 'Oct. 13th. Fifty copies of Hentznerus finished. 17.

The whole number, being 220 copies, completed. Printed two dozen copies of Mr Garrick's stanzas to Mr Gray, occasioned by his odes being but moderately well received by the public. . . . The same day, Oct. 17th, began to print the catalogue of Royal and Noble Authors.' Garrick's verses 'To Mr Gray on his Odes' were published in the *London Chronicle* 29 Sept.–1 Oct. 1757, and in his letter to HW of 6 Oct. Garrick gave permission to HW to print them (Toynbee, *Supp.* iii. 146). See Hazen, *SH Bibliography* 164–70.

From GRAY, Friday 21 October 1757

Printed from MS in Waller Collection.
So dated by Whibley, on the assumption that it alludes to Garrick's verses to Gray.
Address: To the Honourable Horace Walpole, Arlington Street.

[Stoke,] Friday [Oct. 21, 1757].

I HAVE looked with all my eyes, and cannot discover one error, which is the greatest misfortune that can befall a critic.

T. G.

From GRAY, Tuesday 17 January 1758

Printed from MS in Waller Collection.
Address: To the Honourable Horace Walpole in Arlington Street, London.
Postmark: ROYSTON 19 IA.

Jan. 17, 1758, Pemb[roke] Hall.

Sir,

I OUGHT sooner to have thanked you for the *reverend* packet you were so good to convey to me.[1] It was (as you guessed) nine pages of criticism written with much freedom, full of rough (and sometimes ill-grounded) censures, but seasoned with high-flown compliments. It is all about 'The Bard' alone. If I think it worth my while to hear what he has to say about the other ode, I am told to direct to A. B., enclosed to the postmaster at Andover. After what I have said, you will think it strange that I have thought it worth while to write a line to this A. B.; nevertheless I have done so, for it is a merit with me that he has taken the pains to read and certainly does understand me, though his judgment about what he reads is not always

1. Gray wrote to Wharton on 8 Dec. 1757: 'Somebody has directed a letter to the *Rev.* Mr G. at Strawberry Hill, which was sent me yesterday hither. It is anonymous, consists of above nine pages, all about the *Bard,* and if I would hear as much more about his companion, I am to direct to the post-house at Andover' (*Gray's Corr.* ii. 542). Gray's correspondent was J. Butler (ibid. iii. 1001), who has not been further identified. Excerpts from his criticism were printed by Mason in 'Poems' 86, 88–9, 91–2, in Mason, *Mem. Gray.* See also N&Q 28 July 1945, clxxxix. 40.

superlative. I have taken the liberty to desire he would direct his packet as before,[2] which I hope you will forgive, as I am ever

Yours,

T. G.

To GRAY, July 1758

Two missing letters mentioned *post* 22 July 1758.

From GRAY, Saturday 22 July 1758

Printed from MS in Waller Collection.
Address: To the Honourable Horace Walpole, at the Honourable Mr Bateman's,[1] Old Windsor.

July 22, 1758, Stoke.

I HAVE been in town at your house, and left a note there for you; on my return hither I have received your second letter. On Monday I am going with the Cobhams to Hampton,[2] and propose to come from thence to Strawberry on Wednesday evening, or Thursday before dinner. I am sorry to hear of Mr C[hute]'s[3] illness; it is likely he will not be able to go into the country, but if he does, I shall be glad to attend you thither, and *back again,* if you will take that trouble upon you. I am

Yours ever,

T. G.

2. 'Now I have got six pages more, and his name (for that I insisted upon), yet am not much the wiser; however he is a man of letters and a good sensible person, and depends upon nobody, and has a little garden. This is all that I know about him' (Gray to Bedingfield 31 Jan. 1758, *Gray's Corr.* ii. 559–60; see also ibid. ii. 563).

1. Richard Bateman (ca 1705–73), col-

lector. HW speaks of his 'cloister at Old Windsor' in COLE i. 90. See also illustration, ibid.

2. Where Gray stayed for two days (Gray to Wharton 9 Aug. 1758, *Gray's Corr.* ii. 578).

3. This is the only reference to Chute in any extant letter of Gray's after October 1756. See *ante* 19 Sept. 1756, n. 1.

From GRAY, Wednesday 14 February 1759

Printed from MS in Waller Collection.
Dated by HW: 1759.
Address: To the Honourable Horace Walpole.

[London,] Wednesday, Feb. 14 [1759].

I HAVE been confined at home for this last fortnight[1] with a fit of the gout, and was but just got out again in a great shoe when I called on you. I go to Cambridge early tomorrow morning, and cannot (I'm afraid) today have it in my power to see you. If you will write to me, I shall be glad. Early in March I must of necessity be again in town.[2] I am

Yours,

T. G.

The Dean of Lincoln (Dr Green)[3] who is Master of Benet College,[4] Cambridge, offers his service with great civility, if you choose to have any letter or paper in their library (which, you know, abounds[5]) transcribed for you.

To GRAY, Thursday 15 February 1759

Bequeathed by Mrs Damer to Sir Wathen Waller, 1st Bt, in 1828; printed from MS now WSL.

Arlington Street, Feb. 15, 1759.

THE enclosed[1] which I have this minute received from Mr Bentley, explains much that I had to say to you—yet I have a question or two more.

1. He came to London ca 12 Dec., and was probably staying at his 'old lodgings' in Gloucester Street (*Gray's Corr.* ii. 601).

2. Gray left Cambridge ca 4 March (ibid. ii. 617, n. 1).

3. John Green (ca 1707–79), D.D., Fellow of St John's 1731–50; Master of Corpus Christi 1750–64; Regius Professor of Divinity 1749–56; Dean of Lincoln 1756–61; Bp of Lincoln 1761–79 (Venn, *Alumni Cantab.*).

4. Corpus Christi, referred to in the eighteenth century as Benet College, from its proximity to St Benedict's Church in Free School Lane. See Edmund Carter, *History of the University of Cambridge,* 1753, p. 84.

5. I.e. in ancient manuscripts.

———

1. Missing.

Who and what sort of man is a Mr Sharp[2] of Bennet? I have received a most obliging and genteel letter from him,[3] with the very letter of Edward VI[4] which you was so good as to send me. I have answered his,[5] but should like to know a little more about him. Pray thank the Dean of Lincoln too for me; I am much obliged to him for his offer, but had rather draw upon his *Lincolnship* than his *Cambridgehood*.[6] In the library of the former are some original letters of Tiptoft,[7] as you will find in my *Catalogue*.[8] When Dr Greene is there, I shall be glad if he will let me have them copied.

I will thank you if you will look in some provincial history of Ireland for Odo (Hugh) Oneil King of Ulster;[9] when did he live? I have got a most curious seal[10] of his, and know no more of him than of Ouacraw King of the Paw-waws.

I wanted to ask you whether you or anybody that you believe in, believe in the Queen of Scots' letter to Queen Elizabeth—[11] If it is

2. John Sharp (ca 1729–72), D.D. (Cantab. 1766), Fellow of Corpus Christi College 1753–72 (Venn, *Alumni Cantab.*).

3. Dated 9 Feb. 1759, in which Sharp compliments HW on his *Catalogue of the Royal and the Noble Authors*, the 2d edn of which was published 5 Dec. 1758 (*Daily Adv.* 5 Dec. 1758). Sharp's letter, together with his copy of Edward VI's letter (both now WSL), were printed by Toynbee in *Gray-HW-West-Ashton Corr.* ii. 179–80, n. 2.

4. His letter of 30 May 1547 to Catherine Parr, among the Parker MSS in the library of Corpus Christi College (MS 119 No. 8: see M. R. James, *Descriptive Catalogue of the Manuscripts in the Library of Corpus Christi College Cambridge*, Cambridge, 1912, i. 278). The letter had already been printed by Thomas Hearne in his *Sylloge epistolarum a variis Angliæ principibus scriptarum* (see Hearne's edition of 'Titus Livius Foro-Juliensis': *Vita Henrici Quinti*, Oxford 1716, p. 116) and by John Strype in *Historical Memorials* ii (1721) pt. i. 37. For an English translation see *Letters of the Kings of England*, ed. J. O. Halliwell, 1846, ii. 33–4.

5. HW's letter is missing.

6. See postscript to preceding letter.

7. John Tiptoft (ca 1427–70), 2d Lord Tiptoft, cr. (1449) E. of Worcester.

8. 'In the manuscripts belonging to the cathedral of Lincoln is a volume of some twenty epistles, of which four are written by our Earl, and the rest addressed to him' (*Royal and Noble Authors*, 2d edn, 1759, i. 66). HW's authority is Thomas Tanner, *Bibliotheca Britannico-Hibernica*, 1748, pp. 716–17. For Tiptoft's correspondents see R. J. Mitchell, *John Tiptoft*, 1938, pp. 188–94. Canon W. H. Kynaston, vice-chancellor of Lincoln Cathedral, informs us that 'no such letters are now in the library of Lincoln Cathedral.'

9. Hugh O'Neill (d. 1230). Both his name and his titles are disputed. See *Annals of the Kingdom of Ireland, by the Four Masters*, ed. John O'Donovan, Dublin, 1848–51, i [iii]. 257; *The Annals of Ulster*, ed. B. MacCarthy, Dublin, 1887–1901, ii. 285; *The Annals of Loch Cé*, ed. W. M. Hennessy, 1871, i. 305, Rolls Ser. His life was apparently spent in continuous wars against the English. The earliest mention of him in the chronicles occurs under the year 1198 (O'Donovan, op. cit. i [iii]. 115–17).

10. Sold SH xv. 10 for £29 8s.: described as 'a curious antique silver seal, extremely ancient; this remarkable relic once belonged to Hugh O'Neil, King of Ulster. Brought from Ireland by Mr William Bristow' (for Bristow see MONTAGU i. 169).

11. Called the 'scandal letter,' written to Elizabeth while Mary was a prisoner at Wingfield Castle, conjecturally dated Nov.

genuine, I don't wonder she cut her head off—but I think it must be some forgery[12] that was not made use of.

Now to my distress—you must have seen an advertisement, perhaps the book itself, the villainous book itself, that has been published to defend me against the *Critical Review*.[13] I have been childishly unhappy about it, and had drawn up a protestation or affidavit of my knowing nothing of it, but my friends would not let me publish it. I sent to the printer[14] who would not discover the author—nor could I guess. They tell me nobody can suspect my being privy to it, but there is an intimacy affected that I think will deceive many—and yet I must be the most arrogant fool living if I could know and suffer anybody to speak of me in that style—For God's sake do all you can for me, and publish my abhorrence. Today I am told that it is that puppy Dr Hill,[15] who has chosen to make war with the magazines through my sides. I could pardon him any abuse, but I never can forgive this *friendship*. Adieu!

Yours ever,

H. W.

From GRAY, ca April 1760

Printed from HW's copy of Gray's letter transcribed in HW to Sir David Dalrymple 4 April 1760 (now WSL). The letter is also printed in *Works* v. 398; the original is missing. Gray had been living in London, in his friend Wharton's old chambers in Southampton Row, since early July 1759 (he left Cambridge 9 July). See *Gray's Corr.* ii. 624.

1584. The letter discusses frankly Elizabeth's several lovers, and alludes to her deficiencies as a woman. It was printed, in French and English, in the *London Chronicle* 30 Jan.–1 Feb. 1759, based on the text as printed by William Murdin, editor of *A Collection of State Papers . . . from the Year 1571 to 1596*, 1759, pp. 558–60 (published *ante* 12 Feb., according to the *Daily Adv.* HW's copy was sold SH i. 174).

12. A doubt introduced into the 1770 printing (see Hazen, *SH Bibliography* 89) of *Royal and Noble Authors* (*Works* i. 496). The letter, which is discussed in *Lettres . . . de Marie Stuart*, ed. Prince Alexandre

Labanoff, London, 1844, vi. 50–8, may have been authentic. For a defence of its genuineness based on an analysis of the handwriting, see C. Ainsworth Mitchell, 'Mary Stuart's Scandal Letter to Queen Elizabeth,' *Discovery* vi. 368–73 (Oct. 1925).

13. See *ante* i. 30–1.

14. Henry Woodgate (d. 1766), at the Golden Ball, Paternoster Row. He went bankrupt in 1766 (H. R. Plomer, *Dictionary of . . . Printers and Booksellers . . . from 1726 to 1775*, Oxford, 1932, pp. 35–6, 270).

15. John Hill (?1716–75), M.D., apothecary and miscellaneous writer.

[London, ca April 1760.]

I AM so charmed with the two specimens of Erse poetry,[1] that I cannot help giving you the trouble to inquire a little farther about them, and should wish to see a few lines of the original that I may form some slight idea of the language, the measures and the rhythm.[2]

Is there anything known of the author or authors, and of what antiquity are they supposed to be?

Is there any more to be had of equal beauty, or at all approaching to it?

I have been often told that the poem called *Hardicnute* (which I always admired, and still admire) was the work of somebody[3] that lived a few years ago. This I do not at all believe, though it has evidently been retouched in places by some modern hand: but, however, I am authorized by this report to ask whether the two poems in question are certainly antique and genuine. I make this inquiry in quality of an antiquary, and am not otherwise concerned about it: for if I were sure that any one now living in Scotland had written them to divert himself and laugh at the credulity of the world, I would undertake a journey into the Highlands only for the pleasure of seeing him.[4]

To GRAY, August 1760

Printed from MS now WSL: offered for sale by Maggs, Cat. No. 536 (1930), lot 2408; Maggs to WSL, June 1932. The letter to which this is the postscript is missing.

1. In Jan. 1760 Sir David Dalrymple had sent to HW some of James Macpherson's Ossianic 'fragments,' which were acknowledged in HW to Dalrymple 3 Feb. 1760. Allusions in that letter and in HW to Dalrymple 20 June 1760 show that the specimen included at least a portion of Fragment XI (so numbered in *Fragments*, published June 1760: see *post* 2 Sept. 1760, n. 56) and the 'six descriptions of night' (first published as a footnote to 'Croma': *Works of Ossian*, 3d edn, 1765, i. 350–4). It is not known whether HW received other specimens, or which ones he sent to Gray. Gray's doubts concerning the authenticity of the 'fragments' led him to correspond with Macpherson, who wrote him two letters (now missing: see *Gray's Corr.* ii. 672; see also ii. 680).

2. Macpherson, in a letter of 24 April

1760, sent to Dalrymple 'two short specimens of the Irish versification' (see *Gray's Corr.* ii. 665, n. 3) and Dalrymple shortly thereafter wrote again to HW on the subject, as is shown by HW to Dalrymple 15 May, in which HW thanks him for his 'obliging kindness' in sending him 'for Mr Gray the account of Erse poetry.'

3. Elizabeth (1677–1727), dau. of Sir Charles Halkett, of Pitfirrane, co. Fife, 1st Bt; m. (1696) Sir Henry Wardlaw, of Pitreavie, co. Fife, 4th Bt. Her *Hardyknute: a Fragment*, was first published in folio, Edinburgh, 1719, and again in quarto, London, 1740 by Allan Ramsay with the subtitle 'Being the First Canto of an Epic Poem; with General Remarks, and Notes.'

4. For HW's comment on this passage see his letter to Dalrymple 4 April 1760.

Dated approximately by Gray's acknowledgment (2 Sept. 1760) of the anecdote about Sir Walter Ralegh.

[August, 1760.]

*   *   *   *   *

PS. I forgot to tell you the only thing I had worth telling you, that in a pocket-book of Vertue,[1] who you know was a rigid Catholic and who would no more have invented a falsehood on that side, than he could invent,[2] there is an extract from a copy taken by Martin Folkes[2] of a letter in the possession of the late Duke of Montagu;[3] it was to the Duke's ancestor Sir Ralph Winwood[4] from the Duke of Buckingham,[5] telling him how important the King[6] was, and how much he complained that Winwood had not yet disclosed to Gondomar[7] the purport and design of Sir Walter Raleigh's expedition to the West Indies![8]

From GRAY, Tuesday 2 September 1760

Edited from photostat of the MS at Eton College. It was included in the sale of Gray's papers at Sotheby's 4 Aug. 1854 (lot 258).

1. George Vertue (1684–1756) engraver and antiquary, most of whose notebooks HW had bought in 1758. See *ante* i. 33. The notebook mentioned here cannot be identified in the lists of extant Vertue MSS in the Walpole Society volumes iii and xviii.

2. (1690–1754), numismatist and antiquary; D.C.L.; P.R.S. 1741–53; President of the Society of Antiquaries 1750–4.

3. John Montagu (1690–1749), 2d D. of Montagu.

4. (?1563–1617), of Ditton, Bucks, Kt, 1607; secretary of state 1614–17. His daughter Anne was grandmother of the Duke of Montagu.

5. George Villiers (1592–1628), cr. (1617) E. and (1623) D. of Buckingham; James I's favourite. The letter, dated 28 March 1617, is in Hist. MSS Comm. (Buccleuch and Queensberry MSS), i (1899). 189.

6. James I.

7. Diego Sarmiento de Acuña (1567–1626), Conde de Gondomar; Spanish Ambassador to England 1613–18, 1619–22.

8. On 19 March 1616 Ralegh was re-leased from the Tower to make 'provisions' for his 'intended voyage' to the Orinoco, the stated aim of which was the rediscovery of the Caroni gold mine near San Tomás, which he had failed to chart on his first expedition in 1595. On 28 July 1616 he was officially given a commission to 'command an expedition to South America, for promotion of trade and conversion of the heathen' (*Calendar of State Papers. Domestic, 1611–1618*, pp. 387–8; see also *Acts of the Privy Council. Colonial, 1613–1680*, i. 9–10). In Aug. 1616 Gondomar 'lodged a protest in which he claimed that the whole of Guiana belonged to his master, and also stated his conviction that Ralegh had no intention of confining himself to the Orinoco, but would turn pirate and either seize the Mexico fleet or plunder the towns of the Spanish Main' (V. T. Harlow, *Ralegh's Last Voyage*, 1932, p. 24). Ralegh sailed from Plymouth 12 June 1617. The expedition was a failure, and in the summer of 1618 he returned to England, where, in compliance with the demands of Gondomar, he was beheaded 29 Oct. 1618.

Cambr[idge], Sept. 2, 1760.

MY inquiries, and the information I am able to give you in consequence of them, are as follows (if they amount to but little,
thank yourself for applying to a sucking antiquary):

Mr Vertue's MSS (as I do not doubt you have experienced) will often
put you on a false scent. Be assured that Occleve's portrait of Chaucer[1]
is not, nor ever was, in St John's Library.[2] They have a MS of the
Troilus and Cressida[3] without illuminations, and no other part of his
works. In the University Library indeed there is a large volume with
most of his works on vellum,[4] and by way of frontispiece is (pasted in)
a pretty old print taken (as it says) by Mr Speed[5] from Occleve's original painting in the book *De Regimine Principum*. In the middle is
Chaucer, a whole length, the same countenance, attitude, and dress
that Vertue gives you in the two heads[6] which he has engraved of him.
The border is composed of escutcheons of arms, all the alliances of the
Chaucer family,[7] and at bottom the tomb of Thomas Chaucer and
Maud Burghersh at Ewelm.[8] The print and all the arms are neatly

1. The miniature portrait of Chaucer which appears in the margin, opposite stanza 714, of several MSS of *De Regimine Principum* by Thomas Hoccleve (?1370–?1450). See G. L. Lam and W. H. Smith, 'George Vertue's Contributions to Chaucerian Iconography,' *Modern Language Quarterly*, 1944, v. 303–22, for the various replicas of this miniature. Gray was studying Hoccleve at the British Museum in the summer of 1759 (*Gray's Corr.* ii. 646).

2. I.e., St John's, Cambridge. There was a painting of Chaucer on canvas at St John's, Oxford (see Lam and Smith, op. cit.), perhaps a copy of Hoccleve's portrait. Vertue's reference is not in his published notebooks.

3. MS St John's Coll. Camb., No. 235, on vellum (M. R. James, *A Descriptive Catalogue of the Manuscripts in the Library of St John's College, Cambridge*, Cambridge, 1913, p. 274).

4. MS Camb. Univ. Gg iv. 27. Vellum. 12⅜ by 7⅜ inches. 516 leaves. Early 15th century (E. P. Hammond, *Chaucer: A Bibliographical Manual*, New York, 1908, pp. 189–91).

5. John Speed (?1552–1629), historian, whose monogram is on the right-hand corner of the print. This engraving, originally uncoloured, was executed as a frontispiece to Speght's edition of Chaucer's *Works*, 1598. The MS volume at Cambridge 'has, at some time, been rebound, and the portrait of Chaucer now comes after the text of the poems: it was originally at the beginning of the volume. Prefixed to the portrait is the following statement: "Thomas Occleve of the Office of the privye Seale sometime Chaucer's Scoller for the love that he bare to his Master caused his picture to be truly drawen in his booke *De Regimine Principum* dedicated to King Henry the fift according to the which this following was made by John Spede"' (*Gray's Corr.* ii. 696–7, n. 3). Speed himself does not say that his source was Hoccleve's miniature in *De Regimine Principum*; he more probably copied the Cottonian miniature of Chaucer (see Lam and Smith, op. cit.).

6. Four heads, actually (see ibid.).

7. The print is entitled 'The Progenie of Geffrey Chaucer.'

8. Thomas Chaucer (ca 1367–1434), of Ewelme, Oxon, probably son of Geoffrey, the poet; M.P. Oxon 1400–31; Speaker of the House of Commons; m. (ca 1394) Maud (Matilda) (ca 1379–1437), dau. of (?) Sir John Burghersh, of Ewelme, Oxon. For a

coloured.[9] I only describe this because I never took notice of such a print anywhere else, though perhaps you may know it, for I suppose it was done for some of Speed's works. About the painting I have a great puzzle in my head between Vertue, Mr D'Urry,[10] and Bishop Tanner.[11] Vertue (you know) has twice engraved Chaucer's head, once for D'Urry's edition of his works, and a second time in the set of Poets' Heads.[12] Both are done from Occleve's painting, but he never tells us where he found the painting, as he generally uses to do. D'Urry says there is a portrait of Chaucer (doubtless a whole length, for he describes his *port and stature* from it), in possession of *George Greenwood, Esq.* of Chastleton in Gloucestershire.[13] A little after he too mentions the picture by Occleve,[14] but whether the same, or not, does not appear. Tanner in his *Bibliotheca* (article Chaucer, see the notes) speaks of Occleve's painting too, but names another work of his (not the *De Regim[ine] Principum*) and adds that it is in the *King's Library at Westminster;*[15] if so, you will certainly find it in the Museum, and Casley's *Catalogue*[16] will direct you to the place.

description of the tomb at Ewelme see Russell Krauss, *Chaucerian Problems*, 1932, pp. 31–56; M. B. Ruud, *Thomas Chaucer*, Minneapolis, 1926, pp. 116–18; see also Krauss pp. 9–30, 131–69, Ruud pp. 68–86, and GEC *sub* William de la Pole, 1st D. of Suffolk, for Thomas Chaucer's parentage. For Maud Burghersh's date of birth see *Poetical Works of Geoffrey Chaucer*, ed. Richard Morris, i (1891). 86.

9. No other coloured example of this print is known.

10. *The Works of Geoffrey Chaucer, compared with the former Editions and many valuable MSS*, 1721, folio, edited by John Urry (1666–1715). Vertue's engraving of Chaucer, executed in 1717, is at the beginning of the book, after the frontispiece of Urry (Lam and Smith, op. cit.).

11. Thomas Tanner (1674–1735), Bp of St Asaph 1732–5, antiquary.

12. The second in a series of 'Twelve Heads of Poets,' 1730 (the Chaucer head was probably made by 1726; see Lam and Smith, op. cit.; Vertue's probable sources for his Chaucer engravings are given ibid.).

13. Chaucer, *Works*, ed. Urry, 1721, signature b₁ verso. The passage is not by Urry (see Lam and Smith, op. cit.). The George Greenwood portrait has not been

traced. Chastleton is in Oxfordshire, not Gloucestershire.

14. Chaucer's *Works*, ed. Urry, signature e₁ recto.

15. 'Thomas Occleve in Consolatione sua servili meminit imaginis magistri sui Chauceri depicti in margine libri MS. bibl. reg. Westmon. 17. D.VI.i. ubi effigies similis est Chauceri picturæ in bibl. Bodl.' (Thomas Tanner, *Bibliotheca Britannico-Hibernica*, 1748, i. 167). The allusion is probably to Hocclove's stanza 714 of *De Regimine Principum*, which says that to perpetuate Chaucer's memory, Hocclove had ordered his likeness to be painted in the margin of the MS. The MS to which Tanner refers is now BM MS Royal 17 D VI. See Lam and Smith, op. cit.

16. David Casley (ca 1682–*post* 1754), deputy keeper of the Cottonian and Royal Libraries ca 1719–ca 1754. He was deputy to three librarians: Richard Bentley, the classical scholar, Richard Bentley the younger, and Claudius Amyand (Venn, *Alumni Cantab.*; Sir George F. Warner and J. P. Gilson, *British Museum Catalogue of Western MSS in the Old Royal and King's Collections*, 1921, i. pp. xxx–xxxii; Nichols, *Lit. Anec.* vi. 78). For Casley's *Catalogue* see n. 64 below.

Of the profile of Dr Keys[17] there is only a copy in his College;[18] but there is a portrait of him (not in profile), a good picture, and undoubtedly original, a half-figure upon board, dated *Anno 1563, æt. suæ 53*.[19] There are fourteen Latin verses inscribed on it,[20] containing a character of him, as a scholar and excellent physician, and thus much more:

> Qui Cantabrigiæ Gonvilli incæpta minuta
>   auxit, et e parvo nobile fecit opus;
> Et qui Mausoleum Linacro donavit in æde,
>   quæ nunc de Pauli nomine nomen habet, etc.
> Talis erat Caius, qualem sub imaginis umbra
>   Pæne hic viventem picta tabella refert.

At the corners is written *Vivit Virtus*, and *Virtus Vivit*, but no *painter's name*.[21] In the same room hangs an old picture (very bad at first, and now almost effaced by cleaning) of a man[22] in a slashed doublet, dark curled hair and beard, looking like a foreigner, holding a pair of compasses, and by his side a polyhedron, made up of twelve pentagons. No name, or date. You will see presently why I mention it.

The Vice-Chancellor (Burroughs,[23] Master of Keys) tells me he very well knew Vertue. That in a book belonging to the Board of Works[24] he had discovered John of Padua[25] to be the architect of Somerset

17. John Caius (1510–73), M.D., second founder of Gonville and Caius College, Cambridge (charter of foundation 1557); Fellow 1533–45, Master 1559–73. See John Venn, 'Memoir of John Caius,' *Works of John Caius*, ed. E. S. Roberts, Cambridge, 1912, pp. 1–78.

18. It is described by John Venn in a 'Note on the Portraits of Dr Caius,' *The Caian*, 1898–9, viii. 264.

19. See ibid. 263.

20. The verses are in the top right corner. Gray quotes lines 5–8 and 13–14. All fourteen appear in a photogravure of the painting in John Venn, *Biographical Dictionary of Gonville and Caius College*, Cambridge, 1897–1912, iii. 30.

21. Thieme and Becker xvi. 163 attribute the portrait to Theodore Haveus (see n. 41, below).

22. 'Undoubtedly Theodore Haveus himself' (*Anecdotes, Works* iii. 143). Andrew Ducarel, the antiquary, writing to Lethieullier 24 Oct. 1750, speaks of the picture as representing John of Padua (see

J. E. Jackson, 'John of Padua,' *Wiltshire Archæological . . . Magazine*, 1887, xxiii. 17).

23. Sir James Burrough (1691–1764), architect, Master of Gonville and Caius College 1754–64; Vice-Chancellor, 1759 (Venn, *Alumni Cantab.*).

24. Now the Ministry of Works and Buildings. Mr G. H. Chettle informs us that the book Gray mentions cannot be traced.

25. (fl. 1542–9). Little is known of him beyond a grant of 2s. per diem, 30 June 1544, for his services to the King in architecture and to others in music (Rymer, *Fœdera*, vol. xv, 1713, pp. 34, 189). J. E. Jackson (op. cit.) tentatively identifies him with Giovanni Padovani (Paduani) of Verona (b. 1516), musician, mathematician, and author; and suggests as an alternative identification Giovanni Maria Padovani of Venice, sculptor and medallist, who was employed by the King of Poland in 1548 to 'construct a magnificent mausoleum' (ibid. 24).

House,[26] and had found that he likewise built Longleat[27] for Sir John Thynne.[28] That it was from the similitude of style in those buildings, and in the *four gates* of Keys College, he had imagined the latter to be also the work of John of Padua, and this was *all the proof* he had of it. Upon looking at these gates I plainly see that they might very well be the work of one man. From the College books[29] I find that the east side, in which are the *Portæ Virtutis* and *Sapientiæ*,[30] was built in 1566 and 1567.[31] These are joined by two long walls to the *Porta Humilitatis*, opening to the street, and in the two walls are two little Doric frontispieces,[32] leading into gardens. All these are (I dare say) of one time, and show the Roman architecture reviving amongst us with little columns and pilasters, well enough proportioned in themselves, and neatly executed, but in no proportion to the building they were meant to adorn. In the year 1575 are these words, 'Porta (quæ Honoris dicitur et ad scholas publicas aperit) a lapide quadrato duroque extruebatur, ad eam scilicet formam et effigiem, quam Doctor Caius (dum viveret)

26. In the Strand, demolished in 1775 to make room for the present building. The old Somerset House was built ca 1549 by the Duke of Somerset. The name of the architect is not known. Vertue (ca 1727) queries whether John of Padua built Somerset House, Longleat, and Burleigh House (*Walpole Society* xx. 32).

27. Longleat, in Wilts, the residence of Sir John Thynne, was built 1567–79, supposedly from Thynne's own plans (see J. E. Jackson, op. cit. 26–30), though he is said to have been assisted by Robert Smithson, builder of Wollaton (Charles Latham, *In English Homes*, 1904, i. 181). See also COLE i. 25; J. P. Neale, *Views of the Seats of Noblemen and Gentlemen*, 1st ser., 1818–23, vol. v, art. 28.

28. (d. 1580), secretary to the Duke of Somerset.

29. *Annalium Collegii de Gonville et Caius a Collegio condito libri duo. Per Joannem Caium unum fundatorum et custodem ejusdem. Anno Domini 1563*, continued by Caius' successor, Thomas Legge, to 1603. The original MS on vellum, and a paper copy (*Annales . . . a fundatione ad annum 1648*) by Moses Horne are both preserved in the Gonville and Caius College Library. See John Caius, *Annals*, ed. John Venn, Cambridge, 1904, pp. vii–ix (Cambridge Antiquarian Society); Venn,

Biographical Dictionary of Gonville and Caius College i. 322; J. J. Smith, *Catalogue of the Manuscripts in the Library of Gonville and Caius College*, Cambridge, 1849, pp. 282–3.

30. The gates are thus named from the inscriptions on the frieze on either side: the eastern (Tree Court) side has the word 'Virtutis,' the western (Caius Court) 'Io. Caius posuit Sapientiæ 1567' (Willis and Clark i. 177).

31. Under 1567, the *Annals* (ed. Venn, p. 124) record the building of a wall dividing Caius Court from the garden of St Mary's Hostel on School Street (later Senate House Passage), 'super fundum Collegii nostri, a parte ulteriori versus orientem, et super monumentum fundi Hospitii beatæ Mariæ . . . a parte occidentali proxima portæ honoris.' The references to the east side of Caius Court and to the Porta Honoris suggest that both were finished by 1567, although Porta Honoris is generally dated 1575 (see below).

32. Venn (*Biographical Dictionary of Gonville and Caius College* iii. 49), referring to this passage in the *Anecdotes* (see *Works* iii. 141–2), says: 'I have never seen any other reference to these "frontispieces," which were apparently small "shrines" built by Dr Caius in the style of the Gate of Honour.'

Architecto præscripserat, elaborata.'[33] This is the gate (more orna-
mented than the rest, but in the same style) which you remember; it
cost £128 9s. 5d.[34] in building. N.B. Dr Caius died July 29, 1573.

In the same year, 1575, are these words:[35] 'Positum est Joh[anni]
Caio ex alabastro monumentum summi decoris et artificii eodem in
sacelli loco, quo corpus ejus antea sepeliebatur: cui præter insculpta
illius insignia et annotatum ætatis obitusque diem et annum (uti vivus
executoribus ipse præceperat) duas tantummodo sententias has in-
scripsimus, Vivit post funera virtus—Fui Caius.' This monument[36]
(made to stand upon the ground, but now raised a great deal above the
eye on a heavy ugly base projecting from the wall) is a sarcophagus with
ribbed work and mouldings (somewhat antique), placed on a base-
ment, supporting pretty large Corinthian columns of fine alabaster,
which bear up an intablature, and form a sort of canopy over it. The
capitals are gilt, and the upper part both gilt and painted with ugly
scrolls and compartments, à l'Élisabet; the rest is simple and well
enough.

Charge of the Founder's tomb finished in 1575:[37]

For alabaster and carriage	£10	10s.	0d.
To *Theodore*,[38] and others, for carving .	33	16	5
To labourers	0	18	1
Charges extraordinary	2	0	2

Then in Anno 1576 are these words:[39] 'In atrio Doctoris Caii co-
lumna erecta est, eique lapis miro artificio elaboratus, atque in se LX
horologia complexus imponitur, quem Theodorus Haveus Claviensis
artifex egregius et insignis architecturæ professor fecit et insigniis
(*read*, insignibus) eorum generosorum qui tum in Collegio moraban-
tur depinxit, et velut monumentum suæ erga Collegium benevolentiæ
eidem dedicavit. Hujus in summitate lapidis constituitur ventilabrum
ad formam Pegasi formatum.'

This column is now destroyed, with all its sun-dials. But when Log-

33. *Annals*, ed. Venn, p. 189.
34. This figure represents the expendi-
ture for the Porta Honoris and the Chapel
tower (*Annals*, ed. Venn, p. 187).
35. See ibid. 189.
36. In Caius College Chapel. See illustration in Venn, *Biographical Dictionary of*
Gonville and Caius College iii, plate facing
p. 168.
37. See *Annals*, ed. Venn, p. 187.
38. Haveus (see below, n. 41).
39. See *Annals*, ed. Venn, p. 190. As usual
there are some slight errors in transcription.

gan[40] did his views of the colleges, the pillar (though not the dials) was still standing.

From all this I draw, that Theodore Haveus of Cleves,[41] the architect, sculptor, painter, and dialist, did probably build the Porta Honoris[42] (if not all the others), and having worked many years for Dr Caius and the College, in gratitude left behind him his *own picture*.

In the Gallery at Emanuel are several pictures worth remarking, but not one name of a painter to be found.

1. Archbishop Cranmer,[43] head and hands (on board), in his tippet of martens, and seal-ring of his arms, æt. 57.

2. Sir Walter Mildmay[44] (the Founder), whole length, black cap and long gown, book of statutes in his hand, pale and old. 1588. Tolerably well done.

3. Sir Antony Mildmay[45] (his son), 1596. Whole length, doublet of gold tissue, black cloak, many jewels, high-crowned hat hanging on a chair, armour lying on the floor, and a fine damasked long pistol. Letters on a table directed to 'hir Majestie's Ambassador.' A carpet mightily finished.

4. Mrs Joyce Franklin[46] (a benefactress), jolly woman above forty, with an enamelled watch open in her hand. No date; dress of about Queen Mary's time. A head and hands.

40. David Loggan (1635–1693 or 1700). His *Cantabrigia Illustrata,* containing thirty engravings, was published at Cambridge in 1690.

41. Theodore Haveus of Cleves (fl. 1575–6). Lionel Cust, 'Foreign Artists of the Reformed Religion Working in London from about 1560 to 1660,' *Proceedings of the Huguenot Society of London,* 1905, vii. 57–8, suggests a possible identification with Theodoric de Have of Delft. HW embodied the whole of Gray's notes on Thodeus Haveus and Caius College in the *Anecdotes of Painting,* 1st edn, 1762–3, i. 166–8, where he acknowledges his indebtedness 'to the same hand to which this work owes many of its improvements' (identified in the second edition, 1765, i. 179, as 'Mr Gray').

42. Willis and Clark iii. 527–8 find no evidence to support the tradition that Haveus built anything but the sun-dial.

43. Thomas Cranmer (1489–1556), Abp of Canterbury, 1533. From Gray's dating of

the portrait it would seem that this is a copy of the original (dated 1547) in the Combination Room of Jesus College, Cambridge. It is no longer at Emmanuel (*Gray's Corr.* ii. 700, n. 19a; see also C. H. Cooper, *Athenæ Cantabrigienses,* Cambridge, 1858–61, i. 154).

44. (Ca 1522–89), of Apthorpe, Northants, Kt, 1547; M.P.; chancellor of the Exchequer, 1566 (Venn, *Alumni Cantab.*). The portrait described by Gray is by Marcus Gheeraerts (1561–1636) the younger (see *Walpole Society* iii. 11, 36, and plate xxi).

45. Sir Anthony Mildmay (d. 1617), of Apthorpe, Northants, Kt, 1596; ambassador to France 1596–8. His portrait is also by Gheeraerts (ibid.; Venn, *Alumni Cantab.*).

46. Joyce (Jocosa) Trapps (1531–87), dau. of Robert Trapps, London goldsmith, m. (1) (before 1558) Henry Saxey; m. (2) William Frankland (d. 1577). She left considerable legacies to Caius and Emmanuel Col-

5. Dr Hall,[47] Bishop of Exeter, the great gold medal (representing the Synod of Dort)[48] hanging in a chain about his neck. A head miserably done.

6. *Effig[ies]: Rodulphi Simons,*[49] *architecti sua ætate peritissimi, qui (præter plurima ædificia ab eo præclare facta) duo collegia, Emanuelis hoc, Sidneii illud, extruxit integre: magnam etiam partem Trinitatis reconcinnavit amplissime.* Head and hands with a great pair of compasses.

In St John's Library is what I take for the original of Lady Margaret,[50] kneeling at her oratory under a state. It is hung at a great height, and spoiled by damp and neglect, while the Master keeps very choicely in his lodge a miserable copy of it. In the same Library is a very good whole length of Bishop Williams[51] (while Lord Keeper), standing, and *a carpet* in it finished with great care; perhaps therefore by the same hand with that of Sir Ant[hony] Mildmay. In the lodge is a very good old picture, that used to be called Bishop Fisher,[52] but Dr

leges, Cambridge, and to Lincoln and Brasenose Colleges, Oxford, in memory of her son William (d. 1581) (Venn, *Biographical Dictionary of Gonville and Caius College* iii. 229–30; DNB).

47. Joseph Hall (1574–1656), Bp of Exeter, 1627; Bp of Norwich, 1641.

48. The Synod of Dordrecht (3 Nov. 1618–9 May 1619) was called by the States General of Holland, James I, and other Protestant princes, to deal with the Arminian heresies. Hall, then Dean of Worcester, was one of four English delegates. Because of illness he was forced to leave on 8 Jan. 1619, when the Synod presented him with a gold medal. It is described by E. S. Shuckburgh, quoted by George Lewis in his *Life of Joseph Hall*, 1886, pp. 213–14. An engraving by P. de Zetter of Hall's portrait at Emmanuel is listed in *BM Cat. of Engraved British Portraits* iii. 415 (see also George Lewis, op. cit. 199–218; DNB; *Acta synodi nationalis . . . Dordrechti habitæ anno 1618 et 1619*, Dordrecht, 1620, pt i, p. 11).

49. Ralph Symons (Simons) (fl. 1584–1612) built Emmanuel (1584–6), Sidney Sussex (1596–8), the great court of Trinity (1593, 1598–9), the second court of St John's (1598–1602), and designed the hall

of Trinity College (1604). See Willis and Clark iii. 709 (Index).

50. Lady Margaret Beaufort, Cts of Richmond, Henry VII's mother, foundress of Christ's (1505) and St John's (1511), Cambridge, and of the Lady Margaret professorships of divinity at Cambridge and Oxford. St John's has three portraits of her. Gray describes the one which was originally in the Hall, later in the Library, and now (1946) in the hall of the Master's Lodge (information from Mr Hugh Gatty, Librarian of St John's College).

51. John Williams (1582–1650), Fellow of St John's, 1603; Bp of Lincoln, 1621; Abp of York, 1641; Lord Keeper 1620–5; founder of the Library of St John's. The picture, Mr Gatty tell us, is signed and dated 1625 by Gilbert Jackson, and is now in the Hall.

52. John Fisher (1469–1535), Bp of Rochester, 1504; Chancellor of the University of Cambridge 1504–35; Lady Margaret Professor of Divinity 1502–3. See A. H. Lloyd, *Early History of Christ's College*, Cambridge, 1934, p. 391; see also *post* 13 Dec. 1765, n. 7. As Lady Margaret's spiritual adviser and executor, he was largely responsible for her founding Christ's and St John's.

Taylor[53] has told them, it is *Sir Antony Brown*.[54] What his reasons are, I cannot tell, as he is not here; 'tis surely of Henry VIII's time, and a layman, on board split from top to bottom.

I sympathize with your gout;[55] it would be strange if I did not, with so many internal monitors as I carry about me, that hourly bid me expect it myself this autumn. Yet it frights me to hear of *both feet*. What did you do, and in the night too, which one foot only can make of equal duration with a night in Greenland?

I thank you for your anecdote about Sir Walter Raleigh, which is very extraordinary.

What do you think of the Erse poems,[56] now they are come out? I suppose your suspicions are augmented; yet (upon some farther inquiries I have made) Mr David Hume (the historian) writes word[57] that 'their authenticity is beyond all question; that Adam Smith,[58] the celebrated professor at Glasgow, has assured him (who doubted too) that he had heard the *Piper of the Argyleshire militia* repeat all these and many more of equal beauty. That Major Mackay,[59] the Laird and Lady of Macleod,[60] and the Laird of Macfarline,[61] the greatest anti-

---

53. Probably John Taylor (1704–66), LL.D., Fellow of St John's 1726–52; University Librarian 1732–4; Registrar 1734–51; prebendary and canon residentiary of St Paul's 1757–66; F.S.A., 1756 (Venn, *Alumni Cantab.*; Nichols, *Lit. Anec.* iv. 490–535).

54. Sir Anthony Browne (d. 1548), K.G., 1540, Ambassador to France. A whole-length portrait of him at Cowdray, Sussex, is mentioned by Vertue in 1739 (*Walpole Society* xxiv. 162).

55. On 12 Aug. HW complained to Montagu of his being 'pinned' to his chair (MONTAGU i. 292).

56. *Fragments of Ancient Poetry*, Edinburgh, 1760, with a preface by Hugh Blair affirming their authenticity. The name of the 'translator,' James Macpherson (1736–96), appears neither on the title-page nor in the preface. The *Fragments* were published before 28 June (see HW to Dalrymple 28 June 1760).

57. In his letter to Mason ca 31 Aug. 1760 Gray gives extracts from the letter he 'got . . . from Mr David Hume' (1711–76) (*Gray's Corr.* ii. 694–6). Hume's letter is missing, but it was probably written at the same time as one to an unidentified cor-

respondent (assumed to be Sir David Dalrymple), 16 Aug. 1760, which contains passages almost identical with Gray's extracts (see *Letters of David Hume*, ed. J. Y. T. Greig, Oxford, 1932, i. 328–31; *Gray's Corr.* iii. 1223–9).

58. (1723–90), professor of moral philosophy 1752–63 at the University of Glasgow, author of *The Wealth of Nations*.

59. Hugh Mackay (d. 1770), of Bighouse, Sutherlandshire, son of the 3d Lord Reay; Major (26 Aug. 1759) in the Earl of Sutherland's Battalion of Highlanders; Lieut. Col, 1762. See Angus Mackay, *The Book of Mackay*, Edinburgh, 1906, pp. 192–3, 306; *Army Lists*, 1760, p. 153, 1763, p. 197.

60. Norman Macleod (1706–72), 19th laird of Macleod; M.P. Inverness 1741–54; m. (ca 1726) Janet, dau. of Sir Donald Macdonald, Bt; m. (2) Ann, dau. of William Martin, of Inchture (Alexander Mackenzie, *History of the Macleods*, Inverness, 1889, pp. 122, 128, 153–5; Burke, *Landed Gentry*, 1939, p. 1494).

61. Walter Macfarlane (d. 1767), of Macfarlane, genealogist and antiquary (Sir James Balfour Paul, *Scots Peerage*, Edinburgh, 1904–14, v. 89; Mrs C. M. Little,

quarian in all their country, and others, who live in the Highlands very remote from each other, remember them perfectly well, and could not be acquainted with them if they were not spread into every one's mouth there, and become in a manner national works.' This is certainly the only proof that works preserved merely by tradition, and not in manuscript, will admit of.

Adieu, I have done at last. Oh no! My defence of Sir T. Wyat[62] is much at your service, but as it was the first thing I transcribed (when I was little versed in old hands), there probably may be mistakes, which I could correct by comparing it with the MS, were I in town. I have also four long letters of his to the King[63] (while he was ambassador), but I doubt you will scarce think them worth printing, as they contain no very remarkable facts, yet they help to show the spirit, vigilance, and activity of the man.

Look in Casley's *Catalogue of the King's Library* at 17. D. 4to. VI.i., and you will find the MS of Occleve and painting of Chaucer.[64]

From GRAY, ca Tuesday 28 October 1760

Printed from MS in Waller Collection.
Approximately dated by the allusion to George III's accession.
Address: To the Honourable Horace Walpole.

History of the Clan Macfarlane, Tottenville, N. Y., 1893, pp. 62–3).

62. Sir Thomas Wyatt (ca 1503–42), Kt, 1537, Henry VIII's ambassador to Charles V 1537–40. While working in the Reading Room of the British Museum (which was opened to the public 15 Jan. 1759) Gray made a transcript of MS Harl. 78, No. 7, described in his letter to Wharton 18 Sept. 1759 as 'Sir Tho. Wyat's defence at his trial, when accused by Bishop Bonner of high treason' (Gray's Corr. ii. 642; cf. Catalogue of the Harleian Collection of Manuscripts . . . in the British Museum, 1759, vol. i, item 78, nos 6 and 7). Wyatt's 'Defence' was printed by HW 21 Sept.–10 Dec. 1772 at SH as Miscellaneous Antiquities, Number II, with this prefatory note: 'The following papers of Sir Thomas Wyat were copied by Mr Gray from the originals in the Harleian collection, now in the British Museum. The Parnassian flame that had prophesied from the mouth of the bards, could condescend to be a transcriber. In this instance his labour was the homage

of justice paid to a genius, his predecessor. What Mr Gray thought worth copying, who will not think worth reading?' (p. 3). See also *ante* i. 47.

63. There are eleven letters from Wyatt to Henry VIII (written between 2 Dec. 1539 and 16 April 1540: see *Letters and Papers, Henry VIII, 1539*, xiv pt ii and ibid. *1540*, xv) in 'A Book consisting of Original Papers and Letters relating to the Negotiations of Sir Thomas Wyatt, Ambassador from K. Henry VIII to the Emperor,' viz. MS Harl. 282, Nos 21, 23–32 (*Cat. of the Harl. Collection of MSS*, 1759, vol. i). Which of the letters Gray copied is not known; HW did not print them.

64. 'Thomas Occleve's heroic poem of the Government of a Prince: wherein is a picture of G. Chaucer' (David Casley, *Catalogue of the Manuscripts of the King's Library: An Appendix to the Catalogue of the Cottonian Library*, 1734, p. 269; see also n. 16 above). HW's copy of the catalogue was sold SH i. 152.

Southampt[on] Row,[1] Anno 1[mo] Geo. III[ii].[2]
[London, ca 28 Oct. 1760.]

Sir,

I HAVE called two or three times at your house, but had not the luck to find you. I had in my pocket half a dozen artisans for your book[3] (though perhaps you may be already acquainted with them): they are Susan Hurembout,[4] Levina Benich,[5] two paintresses in miniature, Torreggiano Torreggiani,[6] Girolamo da Trevigi,[7] Benedetto da Rovezzano,[8] and Toto del Nunziata,[9] architects, sculptors, and painters, all of them employed in England by Henry VIII.

I wanted to ask also, if you would have the Wyatt papers now, as they are, that is, uncompared with the originals, and perhaps incorrect. I am

Yours,

T. G.

I hope the new reign agrees with you.

1. Wharton's old chambers, where Gray had been living since July 1759 (ante ca April 1760).

2. George II had died 25 Oct.

3. The *Anecdotes of Painting*. HW had finished the MS of the second volume on 23 Oct. (see ante i. 35). The original MS of Gray's notes (which were used by HW in vol. i of the *Anecdotes*, edn 1762–3, i. 55–7, 96–9, 102–3, 116) is now at Eton College. They are headed 'From Vasari,' and are extracts rather inaccurately transcribed from the Bologna, 1647, edition of Vasari's *Vite*, a copy of which was in Gray's library (W. P. Jones, *Thomas Gray, Scholar*, Cambridge, Mass., 1937, p. 156). Gray's MS notes were printed in Mitford, 1835–43, v. 214–16, and in *Gray-HW-West-Ashton Corr.* ii. 203–6.

4. Susanna Hornebolt (1503–45), m. (1) (before 1532) John Parker, yeoman of the robes in the Royal Household; m. (2) —— Worsley, sculptor. She came from Ghent to England ca 1528 with her parents and brother. See *Letters and Papers, Henry VIII, 1531–1532*, v. 303, 327; *Biographie na-

tionale . . . de Belgique*, Brussels, 1866–, ix. 474; DNB.

5. Lievine Bening (fl. 1546–70), dau. of Simon Bening of Bruges, m. George Teerling. She is first mentioned as 'Mrs Levyna Terling, paintrix' in a grant of £40 per annum, Nov. 1546 (*Letters and Papers, Henry VIII, 1546*, xxi pt ii. 227; *Biographie nationale . . . de Belgique* ii. 159; Thieme and Becker).

6. Pietro Torrigiani (1472–1528), sculptor, Bertoldo's pupil, worked in England 1512–22 (André Michel, *Histoire de l'art*, Paris, 1905–29, v. 337, 366–9; Thieme and Becker).

7. Girolamo Pennacchi da Trevigi (1497–1544) (Thieme and Becker).

8. Benedetto da Rovezzano (1474–1552), according to Thieme and Becker, was one of Torrigiani's successors on Wolsey's monument.

9. Antonio del Nunziata, called Anthony Toto (1498–1556), was engaged by Torrigiani in 1519 to come to England (Thieme and Becker).

From GRAY, ca Friday 2 January 1761

Reprinted from *Works* v. 399.

Dated approximately by the reference to *Julie, ou La Nouvelle Héloïse* and by Gray's reference to it in his letter to Mason, 22 Jan. 1761, in which he speaks of going through the 'six volumes of the *Nouvelle Eloïse*' while he 'was confined for three weeks at home by a severe cold, and had nothing better to do' (*Gray's Corr.* ii. 722).

[London, ca Jan. 2, 1761.]

I HAVE been very ill this week with a great cold and a fever, and though now in a way to be well, am like to be confined some days longer; whatever you will send me that is new, or old, and *long*, will be received as a charity. Rousseau's people[1] do not interest me; there is but one character and one style in them all, I do not know their faces asunder. I have no esteem for their persons or conduct, am not touched with their passions, and, as to their story, I do not believe a word of it— not because it is improbable, but because it is absurd. If I had any little propensity, it was to Julie; but now she has gone and (so hand over head) married that Monsieur de Wolmar, I take her for a *vraie Suissesse*, and do not doubt but she had taken a cup too much, like her lover.[2] All this does not imply that I will not read it out, when you can spare the rest of it.

From GRAY, Wednesday ca May 1761

Printed from MS in Waller Collection.

Dated conjecturally. Gray saw Edward Southwell after Southwell's return from the Grand Tour (Gray to Mason 10 Dec. 1760, *Gray's Corr.* ii. 716), and probably again before his trip to Ireland in May or June 1761 (Gray to Brown 26 May 1761, ibid. ii. 738).

Address: To Mr Walpole.

Wednesday morning [ca May 1761].

THERE is a little party going to see Strawberry on Friday before dinner, and it was asked of me whether I thought they should get in. What may I answer?

1. Gray had been reading the first two volumes of HW's set of Rousseau's *Julie, ou La Nouvelle Héloïse*, 6 vols, Amsterdam, 1761 (sold SH ii. 15). *La Nouvelle Héloïse* went on sale in London 20 Dec. 1760 (Rey to Rousseau 31 Dec. 1760, *Correspondance générale de J.-J. Rousseau*, ed. Théophile Dufour, Paris, 1924–34, v. 309).

2. Saint-Preux: see *Partie* i, *Lettre* 50, and *Partie* ii, *Lettre* 26.

They are *anonymous,* but their names are Mr and Mrs Southwell,[1] and Mrs Boscawen.[2]

From GRAY, Thursday 10 September 1761

Printed from MS in Waller Collection.
This note was probably written the day after HW's presentation to Queen Charlotte (9 Sept.). Gray left Cambridge 8 Sept. to attend the coronation on the 22nd ('Chronological Table,' *Gray's Corr.*)
Address: To Mr Walpole.

[London,] Thursday [Sept. 10, 1761].

I WAS hindered yesterday till I thought it would be too late to send for the papers.[1]

If you are alone and not busy, I should hope for a miniature of the Queen[2] in three strokes, excessively like.

To GRAY, Saturday ca 12 September 1761

Missing. Probably written in Arlington Street, in answer to *ante* 10 Sept. 1761. It contained a description of Queen Charlotte (see *ante* 10 Sept. 1761, n. 2).

From GRAY, Thursday 11 February 1762

Printed from MS in Waller Collection.
Memoranda by HW. (Many of the items are scored through. Most of the names are probably those of recipients of presentation copies of the first two volumes of

1. Probably Edward Southwell (1738–77), 20th Bn Clifford, 1776, and his mother (sister of the 2d and 3d Earls of Rockingham), Hon. Catherine Watson (d. 1765), m. (1729) Edward Southwell. Gray knew Southwell at Pembroke while the latter was a fellow-commoner there (he was admitted in 1754 and left in 1758 without taking a degree). See *Gray's Corr.* ii. 470–1; Collins, *Peerage,* 1768, ii. 394; Lodge and Archdall, *Peerage of Ireland,* 1789, vi. 12–13.
2. Probably Frances Evelyn Glanville (1719–1805), m. (1742) Edward Boscawen, admiral. See BERRY i. 34, n. 32.
———
1. The newspapers printed long ac-

counts of the arrival of the Queen on 8 Sept., the marriage ceremony the same night, and the King's levee, drawing room, and ball the following day. See *London Gazette* 5–8 Sept. 1761, *London Chronicle* 8–10 Sept. 1761.
2. Charlotte Sophia (1744–1818) of Mecklenburg-Strelitz. HW, who was presented to the Queen at the drawing room on 9 Sept., describes her as 'not tall, nor a beauty; pale, and very thin . . . looks sensible and is genteel,' etc. (HW to Mann 10 Sept. 1761). HW sent to Gray a similar description ca 12 Sept. (missing), a paraphrase of which Gray sent to Brown in his letter of ca 19 Sept. 1761 (*Gray's Corr.* ii. 752).

the *Anecdotes of Painting,* published 15 Feb. The other memoranda are probably notes for letters. See HW to Mann 25 Feb. 1762.)

Mr Pennicot[1]
Mr Gray
Mr Partridge[2]
Mr Zouch[3]
Sir D. Dalrymple[4]

———

Mr Chute
Lady Hervey[5] Lord Waldegrave

———

Bathoe[6] Lord Lyttelton
    Mr Mann

Morell[7]
vol. for Antiq. Soc. bound
Médailles non publiées.[8]

———

Mr Onslow?[9]   Mrs Vertue[10]
Lady Brown.[11]   Mrs Selwyn.[12]
Mrs Shirley[13]
Bunbury and wedn.[14] **Mr F.**
Lady Sarah[15]
Lady Romney[16]
Lord Tyrawley.[17]   Waldegrave.[18]   Sir

1. Probably the Rev. William Pennicott (1726–1811), rector of Long Ditton, Surrey, 1758–1811, who gave HW a portrait of John Rose, Charles II's gardener (see COLE ii. 200).

2. Probably John Partridge (ca 1719–1809), clerk of Stationers' Company 1759–76 (Nichols, *Lit. Anec.* iii. 606).

3. The Rev. Henry Zouch (ca 1725–95), antiquary; HW's correspondent. See HW to Zouch 13 Feb. 1762.

4. Sir David Dalrymple (1726–92), Lord Hailes, HW's correspondent.

5. Mary Lepell (1700–68), m. (1720) Hon. John Hervey, cr. (1733) Bn Hervey of Ickworth; HW's friend and correspondent. The first two volumes of the *Anecdotes* are dedicated to her.

6. William Bathoe (d. 1768: *London Magazine,* 1768, xxxvii. 704), bookseller, publisher of the *Anecdotes.*

7. Thomas Morell (1703–84), D.D., rector of Buckland, Herts, 1737–84; F.S.A., 1737; F.R.S., 1768. Morell's name is followed in the MS by two or three words of which only a few letters can be made out.

8. Perhaps a reference to Ducarel to HW 27 Feb. 1762, which informed HW that the first number of Francis Perry's *Series of English Medals* had not yet been published.

9. Doubtless Arthur Onslow (1691–1768), Speaker of the House of Commons 1728–61.

10. Margaret Evans (ca 1700–76), m. (1720) George Vertue (COLE ii. 8).

11. Margaret Cecil (ca 1698–1782), m.

Sir Robert Brown, 1st Bt; HW's neighbour and correspondent (MONTAGU i. 15).

12. Mary Farrington (ca 1691–1777), m. Col. John Selwyn; George Selwyn's mother (MONTAGU i. 104).

13. Probably Mary Sturt (d. 1800), m. (1749) Hon. George Shirley, of Twickenham. HW mentions her in *Paris Journals* (DU DEFFAND v. 277, *et passim*).

14. Sir Thomas Charles Bunbury (1740–1821), 6th Bt, 1764, M.P. Suffolk 1761–84, 1790–1812. The meaning of this item is doubtful. 'Wedn.' may be a contraction of 'wedding': Bunbury's approaching marriage to Lady Sarah Lennox (see next item) is discussed in HW to Mann 25 Feb. 1762.

15. Lady Sarah Lennox (1745–1826), m. (1) (1762) Sir Thomas Charles Bunbury (divorced, 1776); m. (2) (1781) Hon. George Napier.

16. Probably Priscilla (1724–71), dau. of Charles Pym, of Old Road, Island of St Kitts, m. (1742) Robert Marsham, 2d Bn Romney.

17. James O'Hara (1690–1773), 2d Bn Tyrawley, general, 1761. He was named commander of the Belle-Isle troops for the relief of Portugal (*London Chronicle* 16–18 Feb. 1762, xi. 167). See HW to Mann 25 Feb. 1762.

18. HW's information is probably based on the list of 'General officers who are to go to Portugal with Lord Tyrawley: Lieutenant-General Waldegrave, Lord Robert Bertie, Sir Harry Erskine . . .' (*London Chronicle* 16–18 Feb. 1762, xi. 168). John Waldegrave (1718–84), 3d E. Waldegrave,

H. Erskine[19]

Lord G. Lenox, aide de camp.[20]

Lord G. Sackville, peer.[21]

Duchess of Richm[ond] ?Saturd[ay]

club.[22]

Epigram.[23]

[Cambridge,] Thursday, Feb. 11, 1762.

I HAVE been in impatience ever since I saw your advertisement,[24] and should have reminded you of your promise, had I not believed you would not forget me. I beg my copy may not be sewed (or at least not bound) because I intend to interleave it.

The fly sets out for Cambridge every day from the Queen's Head in Gray's Inn Lane, and I am afraid there is no other conveyance that comes from any place nearer to your house.[25] I am

Yours ever,

T. GRAY

To GRAY, February 1762

Missing. A letter probably accompanied the parcel which contained the first two volumes of *Anecdotes of Painting*. Implied *post* 28 Feb. 1762.

From GRAY, Sunday 28 February 1762

Reprinted from *Works* v. 399–403.

1763, brother of the 2d Earl; Lt-Gen., 1759; M.P. Oxford 1747–54, Newcastle under Lyme 1754–63.

19. Sir Henry Erskine (d. 1765), 5th Bt; Maj.-Gen., 1759; Col. 25th Foot, 1761 (*Army Lists, sub* 67th Foot; GM 1761, xxxi. 285; *London Chronicle* 30 May–2 June 1761, ix. 522).

20. Lord George Henry Lennox (1737–1805), Lady Sarah's brother; Lt-Col. 33d Foot, 1758; Col. 20 Feb. 1762. His appointment as aide-de-camp to the King was announced in the *London Chronicle* 20–23 Feb. 1762, xi. 182.

21. Lord George Sackville (after 1770, Sackville-Germain) (1716–85), cr. (1782) Vct Sackville. HW had doubtless heard a rumour that Sackville was to receive a peerage at this time.

22. Unexplained. The Duchess of Richmond, one of HW's favourites, was Lady Mary Bruce (1740–96), who m. (1757) Charles Lennox, 3d D. of Richmond.

23. Unexplained. Doubtless a topical effusion, possibly on Lord Pembroke's elopement with Kitty Hunter (see MONTAGU ii. 17) or on Lady Sarah Lennox's marriage with Sir Charles Bunbury (see *London Chronicle* 18–20 Feb. 1762, xi. 176).

24. *Daily Adv.* Tuesday 9 Feb. 1762 (repeated 10, 11 Feb.): 'Next Monday will be published in small quarto, price £1 10s., printed at Strawberry Hill, *Anecdotes of Painting in England*. . . . Vol. I and II. . . . To be had of W. Bathoe, bookseller, in the Strand, near Exeter Exchange.'

25. See *post* 27 Jan. 1764.

[Cambridge,] Sunday, February 28, 1762.

I RETURN you my best thanks for the copy of your book which you sent me, and have not at all lessened my opinion of it since I read it in print, though the press has in general a bad effect on the complexion of one's works. The engravings look, as you say, better than I had expected, yet not altogether so well as I could wish. I rejoice in the good dispositions of our Court, and in the propriety of their application to you;[1] the work is a thing so much to be wished, has so near a connection with the turn of your studies and of your curiosity, and might find such ample materials among your hoards and in your head, that it will be a sin if you let it drop and come to nothing,[2] or worse than nothing, for want of your assistance. The historical part should be in the manner of Hénault,[3] a mere abridgment, a series of facts selected with judgment, that may serve as a clue to lead the mind along in the midst of those ruins and scattered monuments of art that time has spared. This would be sufficient, and better than Montfaucon's more diffuse narrative.[4] Such a work (I have heard) Mr Burke is now employed about,[5] which though not intended for this purpose might be applied perhaps to this use. Then at the end of each reign should come a dissertation explanatory of the plates, and pointing out the turn of thought, the customs, ceremonials, arms, dresses, luxury, and private

1. HW had apparently written to Gray about Bute's note (ca 13 Feb. 1762) acknowledging HW's *Anecdotes* and urging HW to undertake a work on old English manners, customs, etc., in imitation of Montfaucon. In Dec. 1760, 'having heard that his Majesty was curious about his pictures,' HW had sent to the King through Bute annotated copies (now in the Royal Library at Windsor) of catalogues of Charles I's and James II's collections of pictures, published by William Bathoe, 1757 and 1758, the advertisements of which were written by HW (see HW to Bute Dec. 1760, Bute to HW 17 Dec. 1760).

2. Shortly after receiving Bute's note HW drew up a plan for 'Collections for a History of the Manners, Customs, Habits, Fashions, Ceremonies, etc., etc., etc. of England, begun February 21, 1762,' indicated the chapter-heads, and made some preliminary notes (see *Works* v. 400–2). Further unpublished notes are contained in HW's 'Books of Materials' (now Folger Shakespeare Library).

3. Charles-Jean-François Hénault (1685–1770), HW's Paris friend and correspondent (see DU DEFFAND), whose *Abrégé chronologique de l'histoire de France* is discussed by HW in his letter to Mann 10 Jan. 1750. HW's copy (Paris, 2 vols, 1749) was sold SH ii. 143 (MS Cat. F.5.30).

4. See *ante* 3 March 1754, nn. 1, 10.

5. Edmund Burke (1729–97). Gray alludes to the unfinished 'Essay towards an Abridgement of the English History,' 1757, commissioned by Robert Dodsley. The printing was discontinued after the first six sheets in quarto (pp. 1–48), apparently because of Hume's *History of England*, the second volume of which was published the same year. The complete MS (Books I–III), carrying the history down to King John, was first printed in vol. x, pp. 163–566 of Burke's *Works*, 16 vols, 1801–27 (information from Mr R. H. Haynes of the Widener Library, Harvard University).

life, with the improvement or decline of the arts during that period. This you must do yourself, beside taking upon you the superintendence, direction, and choice of materials. As to the expense, that must be the King's own entirely, and he must give the book to foreign ministers and people of note, for it is obvious no private man can undertake such a thing without a subscription, and no gentleman will care for such an expedient; and a gentleman it should be, because he must have easy access to archives, cabinets, and collections of all sorts. I protest I do not think it impossible but they may give in to such a scheme: they approve the design, they wish to encourage the arts and to be magnificent, and they have no Versailles or Herculaneum.[6]

I hope to see you toward the end of March.[7] If you bestow a line on me, pray tell me whether the Baronne de la Peyrière[8] is gone to her castle of Viry, and whether *Fingal*[9] be discovered or shrewdly suspected to be a forgery. Adieu! I am

Yours ever,

T. Gray

To Gray, ca Monday 3 January 1763

Printed from MS in Waller Collection.

Dated conjecturally. The verses, probably written 23 Dec. 1762 (in 'Short Notes' they are entered under 1761, but see Hazen, *SH Bibliography*, pp. 175, 178), may have been sent to Gray the day after Granville's death, 2 Jan. 1763.

Portrait of Lord Granville.[1]

Commanding beauty, smoothed by cheerful grace,
Sat on each opening feature of his face:

6. The third volume of the sumptuous five-volume edition of *Le Pitture antiche d'Ercolano*, Naples, 1757–79, was published this year by the Reale Accademia Ercolanese di Archeologia of Naples. The edition, under the patronage of Charles III of Spain, is commonly called *Le Antichità di Ercolano esposte*, from the engraved title-page of vol. i. HW's copy of the 1762 volume is listed in SH Cat. under viii. 60, and was sold, with eight other volumes, London 999.

7. Gray went to London 22 March (*Gray's Corr.* ii. 778).

8. Miss Speed, who m. the Baron de la Perrière, later Conte di Viry, 12 Nov. 1761 in London (ibid. ii. 770).

9. Macpherson's *Fingal* was published ca 1 Dec. (Montagu i. 407; see also *Daily Adv.* 4 Dec. 1761). HW, who had seen it in MS, believed it then to be genuine (HW to Dalrymple 14 April 1761), but after he had read it in published form he pronounced it a forgery (see Montagu i. 407–8).

1. John Carteret (1690–1763), cr. (1744) E. Granville; statesman. 'His person was handsome, open, and engaging; his eloquence at once rapid and pompous, and by the mixture, a little bombast. He was an

Bold was his language, rapid, glowing, strong;
And science flowed spontaneous from his tongue.
With genius, seizing systems, slighting rules,
And, void of gall, with boundless scorn of fools.
Ambition dealt her flambeau to his hand,
And Bacchus aided to illume the brand.
His wish, to counsel monarchs or control;
His means?—th' impetuous ardour of his soul;
For Prudence, daring not to eye his aim,
Lent not a pop-gun to bring down the game.
Swift too the scaffold of his airy pride
Fell—but slight-built, diffused no ruin wide.
Unhurt, undaunted, undisturbed, he fell;
Could laugh the same, and the same stories tell:
And more a sage than he, who bade await
His revels, till his conquests were complete,
Our jovial statesman either sail unfurled,
And drank his bottle, though he missed the world.

From GRAY, ca Wednesday 5 January 1763

Printed from MS in Waller Collection.
Dated conjecturally (assigned by Mr Whibley to Dec. 1761, but see introductory
note to preceding letter). Gray probably returned HW's 'Portrait of Lord Granville' within a day or two after its receipt, together with the rough draft of the corrected version (headed in HW's hand: 'Mr Gray's correction of my lines on Lord
Granville'), and a clean copy which formed part of his letter. Both the rough draft
and HW's copy of the verses are folded as enclosures.
Address: To the Honourable Horace Walpole in Arlington Street.

[Cambridge, ca Jan. 5, 1763.]

Commanding beauty smoothed by cheerful grace
Sat on each open feature of his face.
Bold was his language, rapid, glowing, strong,
And science flowed spontaneous from his tongue:

extensive scholar, master of classic criticism, and of all modern politics. He was
precipitate in his manner, and rash in his
projects. . . . It is difficult to say whether
he was oftener intoxicated by wine or ambition: in fits of the former, he showed contempt for everybody; in rants of the latter,
for truth. His genius was magnificent and
lofty; his heart without gall or friendship,
for he never tried to be revenged on his
enemies, or to serve his friends' (*Mem.
Geo. II* i. 168–9). See also *Mem. Geo. III* i.
186.

Mr Grays correction of my lines on D Granville.

Commanding beauty smooth'd by cheerful grace
Sat on each open feature of his face.
Bold was his language, rapid, glowing, strong,
And Science flow'd spontaneous from his tongue.
A Genius big with systems, slighting rules;
Gall he had none, but boundless scorn of fools
Ambition's flambeau sparkled in his hand,
And Bacchus sprinkled fuel on the brand
His wish to counsel Monarchs, or controul;
His only means —— the ardour of his soul;
Soon fell the airy scaffold of his pride,
Yet (slightly-built) diffused no ruin wide.
Unhurt, undaunted, undisturb'd he fell,
Could laugh the same, & the same stories tell

And headlong from his airy scaffold hurl'd
He held his bottle fast, & drop'd the World
He hug'd his bottle, tho' he drop'd the World

GRAY'S COPY OF WALPOLE'S LINES ON LORD GRANVILLE

A genius big with system,[1] slighting rules!
Gall he had none, but boundless scorn of fools.
Ambition lent her flambeau to his hand,[2]
And Bacchus sprinkled fuel on the brand.
His wish to counsel monarchs or control;
His only means—the ardour of his soul!
Down came at once the fabric of his pride,[3]
Yet slightly-built diffused no ruin wide;
Unhurt, undaunted, undisturbed, he fell,
Could laugh the same, and the same stories tell:
Though headlong from his airy scaffold hurled,[4]
He held his bottle fast, and dropped the world.[5]

I make no excuses for the four lines I have omitted.[6] There are two more[7] I could not find in my heart to omit (good reason why!) and yet think it would be better, if they were not there.

To GRAY, ca September 1763

Missing. Probably written at SH. Answered *post* 12 Sept. 1763.

From GRAY, Monday 12 September 1763

Printed from MS in Waller Collection.

Gray's notes below were, with a few exceptions, inserted by HW in his edition of *The Life of Edward Lord Herbert of Cherbury, written by himself*, Strawberry Hill, 1764, the printing of which was begun 23 Sept. 1763 (200 copies) and finished 27 Jan. 1764 (*Journal of the Printing-Office* 12). The MS was lent to HW by Lady Hertford, who borrowed it from Lady Powis (wife of Lord Herbert of Cherbury's great-great-grandson). HW and Gray read it together at SH during Lady Waldegrave's visit there 9–18 April 1763 (MONTAGU ii. 59, 67, 129–30).

1. In the rough draft: 'systems.'

2. Gray first wrote in his rough draft: 'Ambition's flambeau sparkled in his hand.'

3. Gray first wrote: 'Soon fell the airy scaffold of his pride.'

4. Gray first wrote: 'And headlong from his airy scaffold hurled.'

5. Besides the final version of this line, with 'Still' interlined over 'He,' Gray wrote another version in his rough draft: 'He hugged his bottle, though he dropped the world.'

6. In the printed version of the 'Portrait' a few of Gray's corrections were adopted, but for the most part HW adhered to what he had written. HW 'printed about 30 copies' at his private press on 10 Jan. See *Journal of the Printing-Office* 10, 41; *Horace Walpole's Fugitive Verses*, ed. W. S. Lewis, New York, 1931, pp. 51–2; Hazen, *SH Bibliography* 175–8.

7. Probably the couplet beginning 'Unhurt, undaunted,' which, in the MS, is marked with crosses.

Pembroke Hall, Sept. 12, 1763.

SIR W. Herbert's book[1] I can learn nothing about.
Milium solis[2] (with a single *l*) is the plant we call *gromwell*, or
graymill, in Italian *miglio del sole*.

Antidotaries usually make a part of the old dispensatories; for, when
poisons were in fashion, antidotes were equally so.[3]

Joseph[us] Quercetanus published a *Pharmacopœa Dogmaticorum
Restituta*, 1607, 4to, Paris.[4]

Bricius Bauderonus: *Pharmacopœa*, and *Praxis Medica*, 1620,
Paris.[5]

Joannes Renadæus: *Dispensatorium Medicum et Antidotarium*,
1609, 4to, Paris.[6]

Valerius Cordus:[7] *Dispensatorium*, Antw[erpiæ], 1568.

Joannes Fernelius (physician to Henry II of France, I think): *Opera
Medicinalia*, and *Universa Medicina*, 1564, 4to, and 1577, folio.[8]

Ludov[icus] Mercatus (physician to Philip II and III of Spain):
Opera Medica et Chirurgica. Folio. Francof[urti], 1620.[9]

1. *A Letter written by a true Christian
Catholike to a Romaine pretended Catholike, uppon occasion of Controversie touching the Catholike Church*, 1586, by Sir William Herbert (ca 1553–93), of St Julians,
Monmouthshire, and Castle Island, co.
Kerry, Kt, 1578; Lord Herbert's father-in-
law. Lord Herbert, *Life*, 1764, p. 26, alludes
to the book as his 'Exposition upon the
Revelations.'

2. Ibid. 28.

3. This sentence was printed by HW as a
note on Lord Herbert's passage insisting
upon medical knowledge as necessary for a
young gentleman's education (ibid. 34–5).

4. Joseph Duchesne (ca 1544–1609), physician to Henri IV, 1593, is said to have
been the first to use mercury for venereal
diseases. His *Pharmacopœa*, together with
the works of Bauderonus, Renadæus, and
Cordus, is cited by HW in a footnote (ibid.
35).

5. Brice Bauderon (ca 1540–1623), physician of Mâcon. His *Pharmacopœa* was
first published in French, Lyons, 1588, as
Pharmacopée, and was translated into
Latin by Philemon Holland and published
in London in 1639. His *Praxis* [*medica*] *in
duos tractatus distincta* appeared in Paris,
1620.

6. Jean de Renou (fl. 1600), one of the
first to question popular beliefs concerning
the virtues of plants and minerals.

7. (1515–44), son of Euricius Cordus,
poet and physician; studied at Wittenberg
and Padua (*Biographisches Lexikon der
hervorragenden Ärzte*, Berlin, 1929–35).
His *Dispensatorium pharmacorum omnium* was first published in Nuremberg,
1535. The title of the 1568 (Antwerp) edition is *Valerii Cordi Dispensatorium sive
pharmacorum conficiendorum ratio* (Bibl.
Nat. Cat.).

8. See *Life*, 1764, p. 35 for HW's footnote
on Fernelius, Mercatus, Sennertus, and
Heurnius. Jean Fernel (1497–1558) was
physician to Henri II and professor of
medicine at the University of Paris, 1534.
The *Index-Catalogue of the Library of the
Surgeon-General's Office*, Washington, 1st
ser., vol. iv, 1883, lists a Venice, 1555, edition of his *Opera medicinalia nempe
phisiologia, pathologia et therapeutica, seu
medendi ratio*, etc. (p. 655). His *Universa
Medicina* was published in Frankfort in
1577 (Sir William Osler, *Bibliotheca Os-
leriana*, Oxford, 1929, p. 234).

9. Luis Mercado (1520–1606), physician
to Philip II and Philip III of Spain; professor of medicine at the University of Val-

Daniel Sennertus: *Institutiones Medicinæ*, 1620.[10]

Joannes Heurnius: (same title), 1597, Lugduni.[11]

The word wanting is *disease*[12] (I imagine), lest *it* (the making the body proof to any one distemper) should be thought to have made *it* (the body) *no less than a prison to the soul*, which would thereby have one way the less to escape from its confinement. This, you will say, is nonsense; that is not our fault but my Lord Herbert's,[13] who had learned from the Platonists.

Galeteus is *Il Galateo*,[14] a famous little work of Monsignore Giov[anni] della Casa[15] on the rules of good manners, that is, good breeding and behaviour.

What *St Islée*[16] should be, I know not, and you do not tell in what part of France it seems to lie. *Alet*[17] belonged (I believe) to the Montmorencies, but it runs in my head that they had an estate at St Hilaire;[18] perhaps you may find it in Sully's *Mémoires*.[19] After all, I guess it is *Chantilly*,[20] which was theirs.

Rees[21] lies in the Duchy of Cleve very near Emerick.

ladolid (*Enciclopedia universal ilustrada*, Barcelona, 1905–33). For the full title of his work see Bibl. Nat. Cat.

10. Daniel Sennert (1572–1637), professor of medicine at Wittenberg 1602–37. Gray lists the second edition, Wittenberg, 1620.

11. Johan van Heurne (1543–1601), professor of medicine at Leyden 1581–1601 (A. J. van der Aa, *Biographisch Woordenboek der Nederlanden*, Haarlem, 1852–76, which lists editions published at Leyden, 1592, 1596, and 1609).

12. 'I must no less commend the study of anatomy, which whosoever considers, I believe will never be an atheist; the frame of man's body and coherence of his parts being so strange and paradoxal, that I hold it to be the greatest miracle of nature; though when all is done, I do not find she hath made it so much as proof against one disease, lest it should be thought to have made it no less than a prison to the soul' (*Life*, 1764, p. 37).

13. Sir Edward Herbert (1583–1648), K.B., 1603, cr. (1624) Bn Herbert of Castle Island; cr. (1629) Bn Herbert of Cherbury.

14. *Galateo* was first printed at Venice in 1558. Lord Herbert's reference to 'Galateus de Moribus' (*Life*, 1764, p. 52) con-

cludes his discussion of the education of a gentleman.

15. (1503–56), Abp of Benevento, 1544; poet and essayist.

16. 'St Ilee' (*Life*, 1764, p. 67). 'Sic orig. But it is probably a blunder of the transcriber for Chantilly' (HW's note).

17. Not Alet on the Aude, south of Carcassonne, but Alais in Gard which Montmorency obtained from Jean de Montboissier in 1584, in exchange for Saint-Ciergues and other estates in Auvergne (La Chenaye-Desbois i. 188). Gray might have had one of the Duc de Montmorency's subsidiary titles in mind, among which was 'Comte de Dammartin, et d'Alets (André Duchesne, *Histoire de la maison de Montmorency*, Paris, 1624, i. 440).

18. Possibly Saint-Hilaire in Aude, between Carcassonne and Alet.

19. Maximilien de Béthune (1559–1641), Duc de Sully, Henri IV's prime minister. His *Mémoires*, 1634–62, were translated into English, and the 4th edn in 6 vols was published in 1763. St Hilaire does not appear in them.

20. It belonged to the Montmorency family until 1633, when it passed to the Prince de Condé (La Chenaye-Desbois v. 167).

21. Spelled 'Rice' (*Life*, 1764, p. 96.)

Do I know any more Spanish than you? *No ay* is what I doubt about; the rest should be *fuerça por las reynas.*[22]

The other bit of Spanish[23] seems right, for *cada uno* (so written separate) is *chacun, haga* is *fasse,* and *amo* is *maître.*

I cannot find *Tieleners*[24] or any name like it in the list of Grotius'[25] friends or correspondents. If anywhere, you will find it in Burigny's[26] life of him, not long since published,[27] and which, I conclude, you have.

If you are well and good-humoured, you will tell me a little news. How comes Lord Sh.[28] to resign? Is the tragical speech, that concluded a late conference,[29] anything like truth? The present times are so little like anything I remember, that you may excuse my curiosity. Besides I really interest myself in these transactions, and cannot persuade myself,

22. Gray is referring to a sentence (ibid. 158) which HW, apparently disregarding Gray's emendation, printed 'No ay feurce por las a reynas; there is no force for queens.' Gray's Spanish is at least better than that which HW printed, for he omits the meaningless *a* and corrects *fuerza* (*fuerça, ay,* and *reynas* are old spellings); but *por,* which is correctly used in the passage quoted in the following note, should here be *para.* Whether the errors were HW's or Lord Herbert's cannot be determined, since the MS from which HW printed is lost. It may be worth mentioning that in Sir Sidney Lee's 1886 edition of the *Autobiography,* the sentence is printed (p. 231) just as HW has it; and in only two of the numerous editions in the Yale Library has even partial emendation been made (Boston, 1877, and London, 1888) (note written with the assistance of Professor R. Selden Rose).

23. *'Que cada uno haga lo que pudiere por su amo:* Let every man do the best he can for his master' (ibid. 139), a remark made in 1619 by Don Fernando Giron, Spanish ambassador to France 1618–20 (see *Archivo General de Simancas: Catálogo IV. . . . Capitulaciones con Francia y negociaciones diplomáticas de los embajadores de España en aquella corte . . . ,* ed. Julián Paz, Madrid, 1914, pp. 739–41).

24. Daniel Tilenus (*post* 19 Sept. 1763). Lord Herbert, upon finishing his *De Veritate* (Paris, 1624), showed the MS to Tilenus and Hugo Grotius (*Life,* 1764, pp. 169–70).

25. Hugo Grotius (1583–1645). He lived with Tilenus in Paris in 1622. See Jean Lévesque de Burigny, *Vie de Grotius,* 1752, i. 204.

26. Jean Lévesque de Burigny (1692–1785), whom HW met 18 Nov. 1765 at Mme Geoffrin's ('Paris Journals,' DU DEFFAND v. 273).

27. First published in Amsterdam, 1750–4. An English translation, 1 vol. 8vo, was published by Andrew Millar in 1754. HW's copy (French edn, Paris, 1752) was sold SH iv. 42.

28. William Petty (1737–1805), 2d E. of Shelburne, cr. (1784) M. of Lansdowne. Bute, who employed Shelburne to negotiate for Pitt's return, in order to overthrow the unpopular Grenville administration, considered Pitt's demands so exorbitant as to justify George III in turning them down. On 2 Sept. 1763 Shelburne resigned as the result of his failure in this affair, though his ostensible reason was his distaste for the office. See *London Chronicle* 6–8, 8–10 Sept. 1763, xiv. 233, 248; HW to Mann 1, 13 Sept. 1763; *Grenville Papers,* ed. W. J. Smith, 1852–3, ii. 90; Edmond, Bn Fitzmaurice, *Life of William, Earl of Shelburne,* 1875–6, i. 281–92.

29. Pitt's audience with George III 27 Aug. 1763, in which Pitt insisted on the dismissal of the entire Grenville ministry. The King gave his answer in a second audience on Monday 29 Aug. The newspapers printed conflicting accounts of what they termed the 'late conference' (*London Chronicle* 10–13 Sept. 1763, xiv. 253; see also GM 1763, xxxiii. 451–4; *Grenville Papers* ii. 93–7; *Mem. Geo. III* i. 228–31).

that *quæ supra nos, nihil ad nos.*[30] I shall be in town the middle of October, I believe.[31] I am

Yours ever.

To GRAY, ca Thursday 15 September 1763

Missing. Probably written at SH. Answered *post* 19 Sept. 1763.

From GRAY, Monday 19 September 1763

Printed from MS in Waller Collection.
Dated by the postmark and the subject-matter.
Address: To the Honourable Horace Walpole in Arlington Street, London.
Postmark: ROYSTON 20 SE.

[Cambridge, Sept. 19, 1763.]

POSITIVELY I can make nothing of *St Islée,* and thought myself sure it was Chantilly; and even believe so still, not having the book before me.

To be sure I looked in Grotius' *Epistles*[1] the first thing I did; he writes to nobody with a name at all similar. But in the little book of this Lord Herbert's verses,[2] published by the *divine Herbert*[3] after his death, is a thing addressed 'to *Tilenus after the fatal defluxion upon my arm.'*[4] Now *Daniel Tilenus*[5] was a great theological writer of that time. He wrote about *Antichrist,*[6] and *Animadversions on the Synod of Dort,*[7] etc., and some of his works were published (I see) at Paris. He

30. Romans viii. 31, adapted.
31. 4 Nov. ('Chronological Table,' *Gray's Corr.*).

———

1. Grotius's *Epistolæ ad Gallos* (Leyden, 1648).
2. *Occasional Verses of Edward Lord Herbert, Baron of Cherbery and Castle-Island, deceased in August, 1648,* 1665.
3. The Rev. George Herbert (1593–1633), poet, Lord Herbert's younger brother. Gray is mistaken: the volume was not published by George Herbert but by another brother, Sir Henry Herbert (1595–1673).
4. 'In Answer to Tilenus, when I had

that fatal Defluxion in my Hand' (*Occasional Verses,* 1665, p. 90). It is a Latin epigram of four lines.
5. (1563–1633), Protestant divine, professor of theology at Sedan 1602–19. A remonstrant, he fell into disgrace after the Synod of Dordrecht, and, like Grotius, fled to Paris.
6. *Speculum Antichristi,* Rostock, 1605, and *Antichristus,* Amberg, 1610 (see *Catalogus librorum impressorum Bibliothecæ Bodleianæ,* Oxford, 1843).
7. *Canones Synodi Dordracenæ: cum notis et animadversionibus D. Tileni . . . ,* Paris, 1622 (BM Cat.).

was however a Silesian,[8] and his true name might well be *Tieleners;* and as Grotius was also a deep divine, he might well be acquainted with him, as well as Lord Herbert.

Do not lay your learning upon me, for I no more desire the title of *clarissimus* and *celeberrimus* than you do. A collector of antiquities,[9] whose work (yet unpublished) I have before me, cites you under the name of *the lively Editor of the Catalogue of Noble Authors.* Will that satisfy you better?

I give you many thanks for your political riddles.[10] Before I print them, I shall send you a list of my doubts and difficulties, for I don't understand a word of the matter. I wonder you should think folly less entertaining than wisdom. You, who live next door to the Theatre, may be as fastidious as you please, and disdain to cast an eye on Garrick above once in a year. I, who live in the country, am excusable if I go every night to see a troop of strollers in a barn, as long as they stay. Adieu, I am ever

Yours.

From GRAY, Friday 27 January 1764

Printed from MS in Waller Collection.
Address: To the Honourable Horace Walpole in Arlington Street, London.
Postmark: ROYSTON 28 IA.

[Cambridge,] Jan. 27, 1764.

I THANK you for remembering me, and am impatient for the books.[1] The nearest place you can send them to is the Queen's Head Inn in Gray's Inn Lane, from whence the Cambridge fly sets out, and brings parcels (I believe) daily.

Kidgell (I hear), to my sorrow, has escaped baiting.[2] I comfort myself

8. He was born at Goldberg in Silesia (NBG).

9. Not identified.

10. Probably having to do with Lord Shelburne's resignation: see *ante* 12 Sept. 1763. The reference to printing is of course an allusion to HW's having sent Gray 'doubts and difficulties' before printing Lord Herbert's *Life.*

---

1. The third volume of *Anecdotes of Painting* and the *Catalogue of Engravers* (see *ante* i. 37, 38).

2. John Kidgell (1722–?90), rector of Godstone and Horne 1762; chaplain to the Earl of March; 'a dainty priggish parson, much in vogue among the old ladies for his gossiping and quaint sermons' (*Mem. Geo. III* i. 247). He played the part of informer against John Wilkes, and the evidence furnished by him enabled Lord Sandwich to move in the Lords that Wilkes be voted the author of an obscene libel (ibid. i. 245–82). Gray's remark that Kidgell 'escaped baiting' probably alludes to the fact that public indignation over the affair

with the thoughts that he will soon have some prebend or more conspicuous dignity in the Church,[3] for I am persuaded the worst thing that can befall a rascal (and especially a parson) is to attain the height of his wishes.

The Bishop[4] has vanity enough to make him feel, at some time or other, what posterity will think of him. But who can damn the Devil?[5] He continues his temptations here with so much assiduity that I conclude he is not absolutely sure of success yet. His leading partisans,[6] though not ashamed of themselves, are yet heartily ashamed of him, and would give their ears it were any other devil but he. Yet he would be chose at present, I have little doubt, though with strong opposition, and in a dishonourable way for him. Yet I have some gleams of hope, for it is in the power of one man[7] to prevent it, if he will stand the brunt; and ——

Do oblige me with a change in the ministry. I mean, something one may tell, that looks as if it were near at hand; or if there is no truth to be had, then a good likely falsehood for the same purpose. I am sorry to be so reduced.

To Gray, January 1764

Missing. Implied *post* 27 Jan. 1764.

was directed chiefly against Sandwich, who had been Wilkes's friend (see *post* ?18 March 1764, n. 10). Kidgell however became involved in a pamphlet war. For the story of how he obtained four pages of the original 'black proof,' the revised proofs of the first 94 lines of Wilkes's *Essay on Woman,* and three smaller parodies equally blasphemous and obscene, see *Journals of the House of Lords* (1760–4), xxx. 416; *Essay on Woman,* 1871, printed by J. C. Hotten, pp. 59–64; HW's letter to Mann and to Hertford, 17 Nov. 1763; N&Q 1914, ser. XI. ix. 121–3, *et passim,* especially pp. 241–2; and Charles Johnstone, *Chrysal,* 1760–5, iv. 201–20.

3. Kidgell expected to become rector of St James's, Piccadilly, succeeding Dr Samuel Nicolls (d. 18 Nov. 1763), by Sandwich's recommendation. Bishop Osbaldeston, however, appointed his own chaplain, Dr Parker (Nichols, *Lit. Anec.* ix. 659). Kidgell, abandoned by his friends, was forced to flee his creditors, and died in Flanders (ibid. ix. 114).

4. Probably Edmund Keene, Bp of Chester (see Cole ii. 371–2).

5. Sandwich. The Earl of Hardwicke, High Steward of the University of Cambridge, had been reported as 'very ill' (*Daily Adv.* 22 Nov. 1763), and Sandwich immediately asked George III's 'approbation for his being candidate for Steward of the University . . . in case it should be vacant by Lord Hardwicke's death' (*Grenville Diary, sub* 22 Nov. 1763, *Grenville Papers,* ed. W. J. Smith, 1852–3, ii. 227). Bishop Keene was consulted by Grenville about Sandwich's candidacy (ibid.).

6. At Cambridge. For their names see Gray to Wharton 21 Feb. 1764 (*Gray's Corr.* ii. 832). For a full account of the election see ibid., Appendix P, iii. 1236–42; see also *post* ?18 March 1764.

7. The Duke of Newcastle, Chancellor of the University, who organized the campaign for Lord Royston (2d E. of Hardwicke 6 March 1764).

From GRAY, Tuesday 31 January 1764

Printed from MS in Waller Collection.
Dated by the postmark and the instructions for sending books (see *ante* 27 Jan. 1764).
Address: To the Honourable Horace Walpole in Arlington Street, London.
Postmark: SAFFRON WALDEN 1 FE.

[Cambridge,] Tuesday [Jan. 31, 1764].

AND so I must stay two if not three days longer for my books! They are to come by the *Cambridge fly,* which sets out from the *Queen's Head in Gray's Inn Lane.* Mr Mason is here, but talks of going to London tomorrow, where he will be at Lord Delaware's[1] house.

All letters to and from this place, that seem to promise anything, are opened (I hear) at the General Post Office.[2]

To GRAY, ca February 1764

Two letters missing. Probably written in Arlington Street. Mentioned *post* ?18 March 1764.

From GRAY, Sunday ?18 March 1764

Printed from MS in Waller Collection.
Dated by the reference to the election contest at Cambridge.

[Cambridge,] March [?18], Sunday [1764].

YOU had received an answer to your last letter[1] sooner, had I been able to write; but I have been very ill for near a month,[2] and this is the first day that I have breathed the open air. I do not believe I can give you any satisfaction as to the Provençal poetry.[3] Italy and France

1. John West (1693–1766), 7th Bn de la Warr, cr. (1761) E. de la Warr. He lived in Hanover Square (*Court and City Register,* 1764, p. 19).
2. In Lombard Street, London.

———

1. Missing.
2. With hæmorrhoids. Gray aggravated his illness by taking 'soap in large quantities,' and had to be operated on during the

summer (Gray to Wharton 10 July 1764, *Gray's Corr.* ii. 837).
3. HW's interest in Provençal poetry seems to have started with his search for Richard I's alleged Provençal poems (see HW to Mann 20 Nov. 1757) for the *Catalogue of Royal and Noble Authors.* HW made additions to the *Catalogue* as late as 1787 (*Journal of the Printing-Office* 20; see also Hazen, *SH Bibliography* 135).

abound in such manuscripts, but we (I believe) have little of the kind among us left; at least I remember no such article in our libraries. As to Eglisham's pamphlet,[4] I have formerly read it here, and think I know where it is; Baker's extract[5] is only a part of it, relating to King James's death,[6] but there is more of it (as I remember) about the Marquess Hamilton[7] worth transcribing. If the facts are true, it is curious, and you shall have it soon.

I received your books[8] and former letter[9] unrifled, and thank you much for them. The anti-Twitcherites[10] are numerous and sanguine, and make themselves sure of throwing him out, whatever becomes of their own candidate;[11] but as they are nearly equal,[12] I doubt his Lordship has some trick left to turn the scale.

4. George Eglisham (fl. 1612–42), James I's physician (see COLE i. 62). His *Prodromus vindictæ in Ducem Buckinghamiæ*, etc., (?) Delft, 1626 (BM Cat.), was translated as *The Fore-runner of Revenge upon the Duke of Buckingham*, etc., Frankfort, 1626. Gray may have read the copy which is at Emmanuel College (see *Hand-List of English Books in the Library of Emmanuel College, Cambridge, printed before 1641*, Cambridge, 1915, p. 53). The pamphlet is mentioned by HW in a footnote to the second edition of the *Anecdotes of Painting* ii. 61 (which HW began reprinting 30 Jan. 1764: *Journal of the Printing-Office* 12), but he cites the London 1642 edition.

5. Thomas Baker (1656–1740), antiquary, whose life was written by HW in 1778 (COLE ii. 129–30). Baker made his transcript (MS Camb. Mm. 1. 43, Baker 32, pp. 149–52) from a MS copy of the Frankfort 1626 text (see *Catalogue of Manuscripts preserved in the Library of the University of Cambridge*, Cambridge, 1856–67, ii. 51, v. 353). HW had been reading Cole's index to the Baker MSS in one of Cole's commonplace books, and wrote to Cole on 3 March 1764. 'This piece [Eglisham's pamphlet] I must get transcribed by Mr Gray's assistance' (COLE i. 62).

6. 27 March 1625.

7. James Hamilton (1589–2 March 1625), 2d M. of Hamilton. At the end of the pamphlet (which is in the form of two petitions accusing Buckingham of murder) are two sections entitled (in the 1642 edition) 'Concerning the poisoning of the Lord Marquess Hamelton' and 'Concern-

ing the poisoning of King James of happy memory,' etc.

8. See *ante* 27 Jan. 1764, n. 1.

9. Missing.

10. Newcastle's party at Cambridge (D. A. Winstanley, *The University of Cambridge in the Eighteenth Century*, Cambridge, 1922, pp. 77, 104). Sandwich acquired the nickname 'Jemmy Twitcher' at a performance of the *Beggar's Opera*, when the audience burst into applause on hearing Macheath's utterance, 'That Jemmy Twitcher should peach me, I own surprises me' (*Mem. Geo. III* i. 249). Gray, in 'The Candidate,' written about this time, makes use of Sandwich's nickname, which, HW observes, 'stuck by the Earl so as almost to occasion the disuse of his title' (ibid.). See also BM, *Satiric Prints* iv. 334–5, No. 4098.

11. Philip Yorke (1720–90), styled Vct Royston, who had just become 2d E. of Hardwicke (6 March 1764).

12. The Bishop of Lincoln told Newcastle, 17 March, that, allowing Sandwich all the doubtful votes, Hardwicke would be defeated in the Regents by one vote (Winstanley, op. cit. 91). The prediction came true: at the election, 30 March, Hardwicke was defeated in the Regents by the fraudulent vote of Thomas Pitt. Newcastle then filed suit, and after much delay and disputation, the King's Bench declared Hardwicke elected on 25 April 1765. See ibid. 106–37; Charles H. Cooper, *Annals of Cambridge*, 1842–52, iv. 334–5; Gray to Wharton 29 April 1765, *Gray's Corr.* ii. 871.

You are very perverse and mysterious about your discoveries,[13] but I hope to be satisfied next month.[14] You never said a word about Mr B[entle]y's *Patriotism;*[15] I hope nobody found out how good some of it is.[16] Has he made his market by it?

To Gray, April 1764

Missing. Probably written in Arlington Street. Mentioned *post* 25 April 1764.

From Gray, Wednesday 25 April 1764

Printed from MS in Waller Collection.
The date of the year is determined by the reference to the *Life of Lord Herbert of Cherbury.*

Pembroke Hall, April 25 [1764].

I AM obliged to you for your inquiries after me. I am indeed not well, though recovered in a great degree, and able to go about as usual. It will be about a fortnight before I can come to town;[1] therefore if Lord Herbert should be ripe within a week or ten days,[2] I could wish to see him at Cambridge, for I am impatient to be better acquainted with him, and by this long delay should expect additions to the manuscript, though of what kind I cannot imagine. I am ever

Yours,

T. G.

By the Cambridge fly, Queen's Head, Grey's Inn Lane.

13. Unexplained.

14. Gray went to London in the middle of May (*post* 25 April 1764).

15. *Patriotism, a Mock Heroic in Five Cantos,* published 10 Nov. (*Daily Adv.* 10 Nov. 1763), satirizing the Opposition, especially Newcastle, Pitt, and Wilkes. It contains panegyrics on Halifax (ii. 125–48) and George III (v. 93–106). HW calls it a 'servile poem . . . rewarded with £160 a year in the Post Office' (MONTAGU ii. 128). For the second edition see *post* 14 April 1765.

16. See HW's criticism in *Mem. Geo. III*

iii. 119. He praises Bentley's poetic spirit, sense, and imagination, but censures other aspects of the poem.

———

1. Gray went to London 16 May ('Chronological Table,' *Gray's Corr.*).

2. Though the printing was finished 27 Jan. (*ante* 12 Sept. 1763) HW did not send copies to his friends until after 16 July (see MONTAGU ii. 129; COLE i. 66). Publication was probably delayed by the preparation of Lord Herbert's genealogy (MONTAGU ii. 130).

To Gray, July 1764

Missing. Probably written at Strawberry Hill. Implied in *post* 10 July 1764 and in Gray to Wharton 10 July 1764 (*Gray's Corr.* ii. 840).

From Gray, Tuesday 10 July 1764

Printed from MS in Waller Collection.
Address: To the Honourable Horace Walpole in Arlington Street, London, M.P.
Postmark: SAFFRON WALDEN [?] IY. FREE.[1]

[Cambridge,] July 10, 1764.

I SEND you the list[2] you desired, which now perhaps signifies little, but I could not procure it sooner. Harding[3] is Nicholas Harding's[4] son. His uncle Pratt[5] has taken him away, and written a proper letter to Dr Smith[6] on the occasion.

1. For HW's franking privileges as M.P., see MONTAGU i. 51. Though Gray's letters to HW must have been delivered free ever since 1741, when HW first entered Parliament, this is the first to be stamped 'Free' —a requirement probably necessitated by the 'Act for preventing frauds and abuses in relation to the sending and receiving of letters and packets free from the duty of postage' (4 Geo. III, c. 24), which became effective 1 May 1764.

2. Probably a list of voters in the election of the High Steward (*ante* ?18 March 1764, n. 12).

3. George (1743–1816), Nicholas Hardinge's 3d son, M.P. Old Sarum 1784–1802; senior justice of Brecon, Glamorgan, and Radnor 1787–1816; HW's and Burke's correspondent. Hardinge was admitted as a pensioner at Trinity 14 Jan. 1761; M.A. 1769.

4. Nicholas Hardinge (1699–1758), of Canbury, Surrey, M.P. Eye 1748–58; chief clerk of the House of Commons 1731–48; secretary of the Treasury 1752–8 (Venn, *Alumni Cantab.*; DNB).

5. Sir Charles Pratt (1714–94), Kt, 1761, cr. (1765) Bn and (1786) E. Camden; chief justice of the Common Pleas, 1761, Lord Chancellor, 1766. His sister, Jane, married Nicholas Hardinge in 1738 (DNB *sub* Hardinge).

6. Robert Smith (ca 1690–1768), LL.D., D.D.; Master of Trinity College 1742–68; Plumian Professor of Astronomy 1716–60 (Venn, *Alumni Cantab.*); Sandwich's most ardent supporter. On 6 April, Sandwich having been invited to dine at Trinity as Smith's guest, the undergraduates stayed away from dinner and congregated in the court outside, cheering Sandwich's rival, Hardwicke. Smith drew up a document to be signed by the undergraduates, confessing that they had 'knowingly and wilfully' conspired 'to be absent from the hall . . . in open contempt and defiance of all decency, discipline, and government' (quoted by D. A. Winstanley, *The University of Cambridge in the Eighteenth Century,* Cambridge, 1922, p. 116). Only five undergraduates signed. Pratt, in a letter to Stephen Wisson, Fellow of Trinity, written before 23 June, said that he could not wish his nephew 'to sign so base a submission as is proposed, nor suffer him to stay in the college exposed to the future vengeance of the Master and seniors, to be wreaked upon him at a time when they can most essentially hurt him' (Lynford Caryl, Master of Jesus, to Newcastle 23 June 1764, quoted in ibid. 118–19). An act of oblivion was passed by the seniority on 23 June.

Has Lord Herbert drowned himself in his own purling stream, or has he only wetted his ruff, and discomposed his mustachios?[7] And what has the man-mountain been doing at Court?[8] Adieu, I am ever

Yours,

T. G.

From GRAY, Friday 17 August 1764

Printed from MS in Waller Collection.
Address: To the Honourable Horace Walpole in Arlington Street, London, M.P.
Postmark: ROYSTON 18 AV. FREE.

[Cambridge,] Aug. 17, 1764.

I RETURN you abundance of thanks for Lord Herbert and for the pamphlet.[1] The first is exceedingly defective in its commas and semicolons. The latter has a misfortune attends it (not at all in your power to remedy) that few or none had read the *Address*[2] which occasioned it. If they do now, it is your doing.

I shall probably be in town in about a fortnight,[3] where I hope to have the pleasure of seeing you. I am ever

Yours,

T. G.

From GRAY, Sunday 30 December 1764

Printed from MS in Waller Collection.
Address: To the Honourable Horace Walpole in Arlington Street, London.
Postmark: CAMBRIDGE 31 DE. FREE.
HW has added pencil memoranda which are partly illegible and wholly unintelligible.

7. Gray had evidently seen the frontispiece of Lord Herbert's *Life,* which shows him reclining by a stream.
8. 'Quinbus Flestrin,' the 'Great Man-Mountain,' the name given to Gulliver by the Lilliputians. Gray is probably alluding to Bute, whose 'frequent interviews with the King' and 'constant attendance when in town at Carlton House' were interpreted as an indication of changes in the ministry (see Lord George Sackville to Charles Townshend April–Aug. 1764, Hist. MSS Comm., *Stopford-Sackville* i. 62). Because of his supposed 'secret influence' at Court,

Bute was often represented in satirical prints as a Colossus. One such print, of the year 1767, shows Pitt standing between his feet (BM, *Satiric Prints,* iv, No. 4178: see also Nos. 3939, 4000).

1. HW's *A Counter Address to the Public, on the late Dismission of a General Officer.* See *ante* i. 40.
2. *An Address to the Public, on the late Dismission of a General Officer,* by William Guthrie (1708–70).
3. 3 Sept. (*Gray's Corr.* ii. 841, n. 4).

[Cambridge,] Sunday, Dec. 30, 1764.

I HAVE received *The Castle of Otranto*,[1] and return you my thanks for it. It engages our attention here, makes some of us cry a little, and all in general afraid to go to bed o' nights. We take it for a translation, and should believe it to be a true story, if it were not for St Nicholas.[2]

When your pen was in your hand, you might have been a little more communicative; for, though disposed enough to believe the Opposition rather consumptive, I am entirely ignorant of all the symptoms. Even what the Yorks[3] have been doing for themselves, or attempting to do, is to me a secret. Your canonical book[4] I have been reading with great satisfaction. He[5] speaketh as one having authority.[5a] If English-

1. Expanded by Miss Berry from Gray's 'C. of O.' 'This day is published, printed on a fine writing paper, in one volume, twelves, price 3s. sewed, The Castle of Otranto. A Story. Translated by William Marshal, Gent., from the original Italian of Onuphrio Muralto, canon of the church of St Nicolas, at Otranto. Printed for T. Lownds in Fleet Street' (*Daily Adv.* 24 Dec. 1764; see also Cole i. 85). HW showed the MS to Gray in August, and Gray encouraged HW to print it (ibid. i. 88; HW to Mason 17 April 1765). 'At first it was universally believed to be Mr Gray's' (HW to Hertford 26 March 1765).

2. He appears in the clouds to receive Alfonso's shade (*Works* ii. 88).

3. Lord Hardwicke and his brothers Charles, John, and James Yorke (see *ante* ?18 March 1764). Hon. Charles Yorke (1722–70), after resigning (2 Nov. 1763) as attorney-general, joined the Opposition, and assisted Newcastle in his efforts to secure the high-stewardship of Cambridge for Lord Hardwicke. With the battle won, Yorke deserted Newcastle, made peace with the ministry, and was given (30 Nov.) a patent of precedence to succeed Fletcher Norton as attorney-general. See D. A. Winstanley, *The University of Cambridge in the Eighteenth Century*, Cambridge, 1922, pp. 130–9; DNB *sub* Yorke, Charles; HW to Hertford 3 Dec. 1764.

4. *An Inquiry into the Doctrine, lately propagated, concerning Libels, Warrants, and the Seizure of Papers . . . In a Letter to Mr Almon from the Father of Candor*, published 29 Nov. (*Daily Adv.* 29 Nov.

1764). HW's copy with MS notes and identifications, bound in vol. ix of HW's 'Tracts of Geo. 3,' is now WSL. The second and subsequent editions were published with a different title: *A Letter concerning Juries, Libels, Warrants, etc.* (for date of the 2d edn see *Daily Adv.* 24 Dec. 1764). HW considered the *Inquiry* 'the finest piece . . . written for liberty since Lord Somers' (HW to Hertford 3 Dec. 1764).

5. HW suggests (ibid.) that the author was John Dunning (1731–83), cr. (1782) Bn Ashburton. John Almon, publisher of the *Inquiry*, says in his *Biographical, Literary, and Political Anecdotes*, 1797, i. 80, that the pamphlet 'was very generally ascribed to Lord Camden [Sir Charles Pratt] and Mr Dunning, sometimes distinctly, and sometimes united. But a learned and respectable Master in Chancery was not entirely ignorant of the composition.' William J. Smith in his essay on 'Lord Temple and the Authorship of Junius' (*Grenville Papers*, 1852–3, iii. p. clix) identifies the 'Master in Chancery' as Sir Charles Pratt's nephew, Robert Pratt (d. 1775), of Coscomb, Glos, M.P. Horsham 1763–74; Master of Chancery 1767–73 (Robert Beatson, *Political Index*, 1806, ii. 324; see also N&Q 1858, ser. II. v. 121–3, 141, 161–3 for Robert Pratt's authorship). Smith, however (op. cit. pp. clv–clxxvi), argues that the 'Father of Candor' was Lord Temple (see also Smith's article in N&Q 1858, ser. II. v. 240–2, 278–80, 397).

5a. An echo of Matthew vii. 29 and Mark i. 22.

men have any feeling left, methinks, they must feel now; and if the ministry have any feeling (whom nobody will suspect of insensibility), they must cut off the author's ears, for it is in all the forms a most wicked libel. Is the Old Man[6] and the Lawyer[7] put on, or is it real? or has some real lawyer furnished a good part of the materials, and another person employed them? This I guess, for there is an uncouthness of diction in the beginning, which is not supported throughout, though it now and then occurs again, as if the writer was weary of supporting the character he had assumed, when the subject[8] had warmed him beyond dissimulation.

Rousseau's letters[9] I am reading heavily, heavily! He justifies himself,[10] till he convinces me, that he deserved to be burnt, at least that his book[11] did. I am not got through him, and you never will. Voltaire I detest, and have not seen his book;[12] I shall in good time. You surprise me when you talk of going in February;[13] pray, does all the minority[14] go too? I hope you have a *reason. Desperare de republica* is a deadly sin in politics.

Adieu! I will not take my leave of you, for (you perceive) this letter means to beg another, when you can spare a little.

From GRAY, Sunday 14 April 1765

Printed from MS in Waller Collection.

Dated by the postmark and the reference to the second edition of Bentley's *Patriotism*.

6. The author of the *Inquiry*, 'Father of Candor.' The pseudonym refers to a pamphlet by 'Candor,' published 22 Sept. 1764 (*Grenville Papers* iii. p. clv). The identity of both 'Candor' and the 'Father of Candor' remains unsolved, notwithstanding the arguments (in *Grenville Papers*, loc. cit., and N&Q, loc. cit.), based on internal evidence, in favour of the common authorship of the two pamphlets.

7. 'For my own part, I shall endeavour to offer what I have to say with clearness, and according to law, although it is long since I have quitted the bar' (*Inquiry* 2).

8. The legal basis of the constitution.

9. *Lettres écrites de la montagne*, Amsterdam, 1764. The printing was finished by 5 Nov. (J.-J. Rousseau, *Correspondance générale*, ed. Dufour, Paris, 1924–34, xii.

34). For Gray's opinion of the letters see *Gray's Corr.* ii. 859.

10. Rousseau was defending his *Émile* against Jean-Robert Tronchin's *Lettres écrites de la campagne*, Geneva, 1763.

11. *Émile, ou de l'éducation*, Amsterdam and The Hague, 1762. It was ordered 'à être lacéré et brûlé' by decree of the Parlement de Paris 9 June 1762 (Rousseau, *Correspondance*, ed. Dufour, vii. 367).

12. *Dictionnaire philosophique portatif*, published with a London imprint at Geneva in July 1764 (Georges Bengesco, *Voltaire: Bibliographie*, 1882–90, i. 413).

13. To Paris (see HW to Hertford 12 Feb. 1765; MONTAGU ii. 140). HW did not leave until 9 Sept.

14. HW voted with the minority on the issue of general warrants (Cobbett, *Parl. Hist.* xv. 1405; *ante* i. 40 n. 268).

Address: To the Honourable Horace Walpole in Arlington Street, London.
Postmark: SAFFRON WALDEN 15 AP. FREE.

Pembroke College, Sunday [April 14, 1765].

I EXIST, though it is but of late that I walk again on two legs after a gentle fit of the gout that held me for six weeks.[1] In about a fortnight[2] I shall be in town, but had rather not stay so long for a sight of your new edition,[3] and should wish, if you have a copy to spare, that you would send it me hither.

Mr B[entley], since he was in the ministry,[4] has taken advice of no one, but perhaps his brother ministers. *Patriotism* appears again[5] with all its old faults on its head, even to the Duchess of Marlborough's striped gown.[6] Don't you reckon that there is a little flirt aimed at you[7] in it?

I see the Bishop[8] and you are destined to come together;[9] however, I make my protestation beforehand that I never will believe you had an eye to the Eleusinian mysteries,[10] or that you have demonstrated the truth of the Copernican system by making no mention of it[11] in any part of your writings. Adieu! I am

Ever yours,

T. G.

1. See Gray to Wharton 29 April 1765 (*Gray's Corr.* ii. 870).

2. 30 April ('Chronological Table,' *Gray's Corr.*).

3. Of *The Castle of Otranto.* 'The second edition with a new preface,' described as 'A Gothic Story,' was published by William Bathoe 11 April (*Daily Adv.* 11 April 1765). In the preface HW acknowledged his authorship.

4. Ironical: Bentley had a place in the Post Office (see *ante* ?18 March 1764, n. 15).

5. The second edition was published, according to HW's MS note in his copy of *Patriotism* (now WSL), 'March 19.' A new canto was added, and additions were made in other parts of the poem.

6. '. . . Down your perfect form in rainbow rows,
    The lutestring stripe with gay confusion flows . . .'
(*Patriotism,* 2d edn, canto iii, lines 97–8.)

7. I.e., at Sir Robert Walpole (ibid. canto v, lines 159–60).

8. William Warburton, Bp of Gloucester.

9. This is unexplained, but must be somehow connected with HW's quarrel with Warburton in 1762. See *ante* i. 38–9.

10. *Divine Legation,* Book II, sect. iv (edn 1755, i pt i. 136–329; see especially the examination of Book VI of the *Æneid* 210–96).

11. An allusion to the title of the orginal edition: *The Divine Legation of Moses demonstrated, on the Principles of a religious Deist, from the Omission of the Doctrine of a Future State of Reward and Punishment in the Jewish Dispensation,* 1738–41 (BM Cat.).

To GRAY, Sunday 20 October 1765

Missing. Written at Paris. Sent 'by Colonel Barré' (HW's list of letters in 'Paris Journals,' DU DEFFAND v. 377).

From GRAY, ca Tuesday 12 November 1765

Printed from MS in Waller Collection.

Dated approximately by the references to Gray's Scottish tour and the death of the Duke of Cumberland, and by an entry in Cole's 'Paris Journal' under 17 Nov. 1765: 'He [HW] received a letter from . . . Mr. Thomas Gray of Pembroke Hall in Cambridge' (William Cole, *Journal of my Journey to Paris in the Year 1765*, ed. F. G. Stokes, 1931, p. 266). The London-Paris mail took approximately four to five days (see DU DEFFAND, *passim*). The letter was evidently sent by a messenger.

Address: To the Honourable Horace Walpole.

[London, ca Nov. 12, 1765.]

AT my return from Scotland,[1] instead of seeing you I find an empty house, and an uncomfortable account of your situation: that you have been very ill with the gout in both feet, that you have been some time in France[2] for your health, that you have got no farther than Paris, have again been confined there, and are just beginning to go abroad again. At the hazard of being called an old woman I will take upon me to desire, when the fit is actually upon you, that you will make no sudden changes in your diet; I do not say in quantity, but in quality. That when you are recovering and the pain is gone, but has left behind it a weakness in the joint, you will not be too indulgent to that weakness, but give yourself so much of motion and exercise as you can well endure. Above all, keep your legs warmer at all times, whether you are well or ill, in bed or up, than you have commonly used to do, and as far as may be, always in the same temperature. The quantity of wine you have commonly used has been so inconsiderable, that I do not believe it ever did, or will hurt you; but if you leave it off, mix a little quantity of spirit, brandy or whatever else is palatable to

1. 30 Oct. (*Gray's Corr.* ii. 897). Gray made a tour in Scotland with Lord Strathmore, a former Pembroke undergraduate (whom he visited at Glamis Castle), Strathmore's brother the Hon. Thomas Lyon, of Hetton House, Durham, and 'Major Lyon' (? Charles Wilson Lyon, Capt. 19th Dra-

goons, 1759; Maj. 4th Light Dragoons, 1766) (*Army Lists*). They set out from Old Park, where Gray was visiting Wharton, 19 Aug. (*Gray's Corr.* ii. 883–4).

2. HW reached Paris on 13 Sept. ('Paris Journals,' DU DEFFAND v. 258–60).

you, with your water. Remember, it is only the wine-drinking nations
that know what the gout is; whereas those that even indulge themselves in distilled liquors, as well the laborious and hard-faring people
as the indolent and luxurious, though subject to many other disorders,
are utter strangers to this. My prescriptions are simple, but they are
such as I use myself, who am a fellow-sufferer with you, about your
own age, have (unhappily for me) a better right to this malady than
you,[2a] begun to feel it earlier, and yet have hitherto felt it mildly, and
never in my stomach or head. I only say they are better than French
nostrums or people of quality's receipts. You will do me pleasure (if
you are able) in telling me yourself how you do, for I have nobody but
your servants to inform me.

I am come back from the Highlands very much the better for my
journey and (what I little expected) very much pleased with what I
have seen.[3] I would send you *English news,* but that I know you receive
it from much better hands. They tell me *our* ministry[4] will stand upon
its legs, though they have lost the Duke.[5] There are three separations I
hear talked of in the married world: the Bolingbrokes,[6] the Shel-
burnes,[7] and the Warkworths;[8] the last I believe may be true. Adieu!
Take care of yourself! I am ever

Yours.

2a. Because it was in his family and not
in HW's.

3. See Gray's account of his tour in his
letter to Wharton from Glamis ca 30 Sept.
1765 (*Gray's Corr.* ii. 887–95).

4. Headed by Charles Watson-Went-
worth (1730–82), 2d M. of Rockingham.
The new ministry was sworn in 8 July
(*Mem. Geo. III* ii. 137; MONTAGU ii. 161).
HW had taken an active part in its forma-
tion.

5. Of Cumberland, who d. 31 Oct.

6. Lady Diana Spencer (1734–1808), who
m. (1757) Frederick St John (1734–87), 2d
Vct Bolingbroke, was divorced by her husband 10 March 1768 for crim. con. (Private
Act 8 Geo III, 1768, c. 70; *Journals of the
House of Lords* xxxii. 143). Two days later
she married Topham Beauclerk.

7. A false report. Lady Sophia Carteret
(1745–71), dau. of the Earl Granville, m.
(3 Feb. 1765) William Petty, 2d E. of Shelburne, cr. (1784) M. of Lansdowne. She was
an 'amiable, virtuous woman' (GEC *sub*
Lansdowne).

8. Lady Anne Stuart (b. 1746), 3d dau.
of the 3d E. of Bute, m. (1) (1764) Hugh
Percy (1742–1817), styled Lord Warkworth
1750–66, E. Percy 1766–86, 2d D. of
Northumberland. Many years later her
husband divorced her for crim. con. with
William Byrd, by Private Act 19 Geo. III,
1779, c. 20. She m. (2) (March 1780) Friedrich Karl Hans Bruno, Baron von Poellnitz
(GEC *sub* Northumberland; Charles Durn-
ford and E. H. East, *Term Reports in the
Court of King's Bench,* 1817, i. 5; information from Mr C. S. Belsterling).

To Gray, Tuesday 19 November 1765

Reprinted from *Works* v. 356–9 and from *Gray-HW-West-Ashton Corr.* ii. 238–44. The present location of the MS, which was bought by Messrs Maggs in the Waller sale (1921), is unknown.

Paris, Nov. 19, 1765.

YOU are very kind to inquire so particularly after my gout: I wish I may not be too circumstantial in my answer; but you have tapped a dangerous topic; I can talk gout by the hour. It is my great mortification, and has disappointed all the hopes that I had built on temperance and hardiness. I have resisted like a hermit, and exposed myself to all weathers and seasons like a smuggler; and in vain. I have however still so much of the obstinacy of both professions left, that I think I shall continue, and cannot obey you in keeping myself warm. I have gone through my second fit under one blanket, and already go about in a silk waistcoat with my bosom unbuttoned. In short, I am as prejudiced to my regimen, though so ineffectual, as I could have been to all I expected from it. The truth is, I am almost as willing to have the gout as to be liable to catch cold; and must run upstairs and down, in and out of doors when I will, or I cannot have the least satisfaction. This will convince you how readily I comply with another of your precepts, walking as soon as I am able—I have had little indulgence for myself on that head. Wine I drink with my water, because I cannot drink the filthy water here by itself; I began with brandy, but soon grew to nauseate it. The greatest change I have made, is in leaving off tea—I doubt, only because I took an aversion to it. I own I am much better since. This is the detail: the general history is, that I was seized with the gout in one foot at the end of June,[1] soon had it in both, with great torment, and then without its going out of my feet, in head, stomach, both wrists and both shoulders. Nine weeks passed before I could even walk without a stick; yet the state of convalescence, as it has been in my second fit, was much worse and more uneasy than the height of the pain, from the constant sickness at my stomach. I came hither, mended miraculously with the sea and the journey, but caught cold[2] in a fortnight, and have had six weeks more of pain in both feet, and such sickness that I have been very near starved: besides such

1. See HW to Montagu 6 July 1765 (MONTAGU ii. 159).

2. 4 Oct. ('Paris Journals,' DU DEFFAND v. 266).

swelled legs,[3] that they were as much too big for my body, as before
they would have been too little for any other person's alive. I have now
got the better of everything but the weakness, and am only thrown or
tumble down ten times a day. For receipts, you may trust me for making use of none; I would not see a physician at the worst, but have
quacked myself as boldly, as quacks treat others. I laughed at your
idea of quality receipts, it came so apropos: there is not a man or
woman here that is not a perfect old nurse, and who does not talk gruel
and anatomy with equal fluency and ignorance. One instance shall
serve; Madame de Bouzols,[4] Marshal Berwick's[5] daughter, assured me
there was nothing so good for the gout as to preserve the parings of
my nails in a bottle close stopped. When I try any illustrious nostrum,
I shall give the preference to this.

So much for the gout! I told you what was coming. As to the ministry, I know and care very little about them. I told you and told them
long ago, that if ever a change happened, I would bid adieu to politics
forever. Do me the justice to allow that I have not altered with the
times. I was so impatient to put this resolution in execution, that I
hurried out of England, before I was sufficiently recovered. I shall not
run the same hazard again in haste; but will stay here till I am perfectly well, and the season of warm weather coming on or arrived,
though the charms of Paris have not the least attraction for me, nor
would keep me here an hour on their own account. For the city itself,
I cannot conceive where my eyes were: it is the ugliest, beastly town in
the universe. I have not seen a mouthful of verdure out of it, nor have
they anything green but their treillage and window-shutters. Trees cut
into fire-shovels and stuck into pedestals of chalk, compose their
country. Their boasted knowledge of society is reduced to talking of
their suppers, and every malady they have about them, or know of.
The Dauphin[6] is at the point of death; every morning the physicians
frame an account of him, and happy is he or she who can produce a
copy of this lie, called a *bulletin*. The night before last, one of these was

3. HW complained of the gout in both
feet 7 Oct., and he was confined indoors
until 19 Oct. (ibid. v. 267–8).

4. Laure-Anne Fitzjames (1710–66), m.
(1732) Joachim-Louis de Montaigu, Marquis de Bouzols. HW visited her 17 Sept.
(ibid. v. 261; see also La Chenaye-Desbois
viii. 70; *Répertoire . . . de la Gazette de*

France, ed. Marquis de Granges de Surgères, 1902–6, iii. 620).

5. James Fitzjames (1670–1734), James
II's natural son, cr. (1687) D. of Berwick;
Maréchal de France, 1706 (GEC; La Che-
naye-Debois viii. 66–9).

6. Louis (1729–65). He died 19 Dec.

produced at supper where I was;[7] it was read, and said, he had had *une
évacuation fétide*—I beg your pardon, though you are not at supper.
The old lady of the house, who by the way is quite blind, was the Regent's mistress for a fortnight,[8] and is very agreeable, called out, 'Oh!
they have forgot to mention that he threw down his chamberpot, and
was forced to change his bed.' There were present several women of
the first rank, as Madame de la Valière,[9] who you remember Duchesse
de Vaujour, and who is still miraculously pretty though fifty-three, a
very handsome Madame de Forcalquier,[10] and others—nor was this
conversation at all particular to that evening. They talk of a *chienne
chaude,* or the *dangerous* time of a woman's age, as they would talk of
a knotting bag.

Their gaiety is not greater than their delicacy—but I will not expatiate. In short, they are another people from what they were. They
may be growing wise, but the intermediate passage is dulness. Several
of the women are agreeable, and some of the men; but the latter are
in general vain and ignorant. The *savants,* I beg their pardons, the
philosophes, are insupportable. Superficial, overbearing, and fanatic;
they preach incessantly, and their avowed doctrine is atheism; you
would not believe how openly—Don't wonder therefore, if I should
return a Jesuit. Voltaire himself does not satisfy them: One of their
lady devotees said of him, *il est bigot; c'est un déiste.*

I am as little pleased with their taste in trifles. Crébillon is entirely
out of fashion, and Marivaux a proverb; *marivauder,* and *marivaudage* are established terms for being prolix and tiresome. I thought
that we were fallen, but they are ten times lower.

7. At Mme du Deffand's 17 Nov. (DU
DEFFAND v. 272).

8. Probably in 1721, after Mme du Deffand's separation from her husband (ibid.
vi. 30). She is mentioned by Marais, 20
July, as present with Mme d'Averne at a
'fête magnifique à la Maréchale d'Estrées'
given by the Regent at Saint-Cloud
(*Journal et mémoires de Mathieu Marais,*
ed. M. F. A. de Lescure, 1863–8, ii. 181),
and by Buvat as one of the guests at the
'grande fête à Saint-Cloud,' 30 July, which
introduced Mme d'Averne, the Regent's
new mistress (*Journal de la Régence . . .
par Jean Buvat,* ed. Émile Campardon,
1865, ii. 277).

9. Anne - Julie - Françoise   de   Crussol

(1713–93), m. (1732) Louis-César de la
Baume le Blanc, Duc de Vaujour, 1732,
Duc de la Vallière, 1739 (La Chenaye-Desbois iii. 326). HW saw her at Mme du Deffand's 17 Sept. (DU DEFFAND v. 261). No allusion to the earlier meeting during HW's
and Gray's Paris visit in 1739 has been
found.

10. Marie-Françoise-Renée de Carbonnel
de Canisy (1725–ca 1796), m. (1) (1737) Antoine-François de Pardaillan de Gondrin,
Marquis d'Antin; m. (2) (1742) Louis-
Bufile de Brancas, Comte de Forcalquier;
Mme du Deffand's 'belle Comtesse,' 'la
Bellissima' (DU DEFFAND). HW describes
her in his 'Paris Journals' under 17 Sept.
(ibid. v. 261).

Notwithstanding all I have said, I have found two or three societies[11] that please me; am amused with the novelty of the whole, and should be sorry not to have come. The Dumenil[12] is, if possible, superior to what you remember;[13] I am sorry not to see the Clairon,[14] but several persons whose judgments seem the soundest, prefer the former. Préville[15] is admirable in low comedy: The mixture of Italian comedy and comic operas prettily written, and set to Italian music, at the same theatre,[16] is charming, and gets the better both of their Operas[17] and French Comedy, the latter of which is seldom full, with all its merit. *Petit maîtres* are obsolete, like our Lords Foppington[18]—*Tout le monde est philosophe*—when I grow very sick of this last nonsense, I go and compose myself at the Chartreuse,[19] where I am almost tempted to prefer Le Sœur to every painter I know—yet what new old treasures are come to light, routed out of the Louvre, and thrown into new lumber-rooms at Versailles!—but I have not room to tell you what I have seen! I will keep this and other chapters for Strawberry. Adieu! and thank you.

Yours ever

H. W.

Old Mariette[20] has shown me a print by Diepenbecke[21] of the Duke

11. Mme du Deffand's, Mme de Rochefort's, and Mme Geoffrin's.

12. Marie-Françoise Marchand (1713–1803), called Dumesnil (see the baptismal certificate cited by Charles Gueullette, *Acteurs et actrices du temps passé*, 1881, p. 274), of the Comédie-Française, 1737–76 (ibid. 275, 294). HW saw her act 'Hermione in the highest perfection' in Racine's *Andromaque* on 28 Sept. (DU DEFFAND v. 265).

13. Gray saw her in Racine's *Phèdre* in May 1739, and wrote to Ashton 29 May 1739 that he was 'affected . . . strongly' by 'a Mademoiselle Duminie, whose every look and gesture is violent nature; she is passion itself incarnate' (*Gray's Corr.* i. 110).

14. Claire-Joseph-Hippolyte Legris de Latude (1723–1803), called Mlle Clairon, of the Comédie-Française 1743–66 (NBG; DU DEFFAND i. 146).

15. Pierre-Louis Dubus (1721–99), called Préville, of the Comédie-Française 1753–86 (Alexandre Ricord, *Les Fastes de la Comédie-Française*, 1821–2, i. 184–8). HW

first saw him 30 Sept. (DU DEFFAND v. 265).

16. The Comédie-Italienne (merged with the Opéra-Comique in 1762) at the Hôtel de Bourgogne (*Larousse du XX Siècle*). For HW's visits to it see DU DEFFAND v. 260, 262, 272.

17. After the fire of 1763 at the Palais-Royal, operas were performed (1764–70) at the Salle des Machines in the Tuileries (*Larousse du XX Siècle*). HW attended 15, 17, 22 Sept. and 14 Nov. (for the operas, see DU DEFFAND v. 260–1, 263, 271).

18. 'Sir Novelty Fashion . . . Lord Foppington,' character in Vanbrugh's *Relapse*.

19. See *ante* ca 15 May 1739, N.S.

20. Pierre-Jean Mariette (1694–1774), collector. For HW's visit to him 2 Nov. and his comments on Mariette's collection, see DU DEFFAND v. 269.

21. Abraham van Diepenbeek (ca 1607–75), Dutch painter (A. J. van der Aa, *Biographisch Woordenboek der Nederlanden*, Haarlem, 1852–78). The print is by Peeter Clouwet (1629–70) (see *post* 13 Dec. 1765).

and Duchess of Newecastle[22] at dinner with their family:[23] You would oblige me if you would look into all their Graces' folios, and see if it is not a frontispiece to some one of them. Then he has such a Petitot[24] of Madame d'Olonne![25] The Pompadour[26] offered him fifty louis for it— Alack! so would I![27]

From GRAY, Friday 13 December 1765

Reprinted from *Works* v. 359–61.

Cambridge, December 13, 1765.

I AM very much obliged to you for the detail you enter into on the subject of your own health; in this you cannot be too circumstantial for me, who had received no account of you but at second hand—such as, that you were dangerously ill, and therefore went to France; that you meant to try a better climate, and therefore stayed at Paris; that you had relapsed, and were confined to your bed, and extremely in vogue, and supped in the best company, and were at all public diversions. I rejoice to find (improbable as it seemed) that all the wonderful part of this is strictly true, and that the serious part has been a little exaggerated. This latter I conclude not so much from your own account of yourself, as from the spirits in which I see you write; and long may they continue to support you! I mean in a reasonable degree of elevation; but if (take notice) they are so volatile, so flippant, as to suggest any of those doctrines of health which you preach with all the zeal of a French atheist, at least, if they really do influence your practice, I utterly renounce them and all their works. They are *evil spirits,* and will lead you to destruction. You have long built your hopes on temperance, you say, and hardiness. On the first point we are agreed. The

22. Hon. Margaret Lucas (1617–74), m. (ca 1645) as his second wife William Cavendish (1593–1676), cr. (1620) Vct Mansfield, (1628) E., (1643) M., and (1665) D. of Newcastle-upon-Tyne.

23. See *post* 13 Dec. 1765.

24. Jean Petitot (1607–91), miniature-painter.

25. Catherine - Henriette d'Angennes (1634–1714), m. (1652) Louis de la Trémoïlle, Comte d'Olonne (Louis de Rouvroy, Duc de Saint-Simon, *Mémoires,* ed. A. de Boislisle, 1879–1928, xxiv. 199). The

miniature is described in Mariette's *Abecedario* (ed. P. de Chennevières and A. de Montaiglon, *Archives de l'art français* viii. 132–3).

26. Jeanne-Antoinette Poisson (1721–64), cr. (1745) Marquise de Pompadour; mistress of Louis XV.

27. Mme du Deffand, commissioned by HW, purchased it for 3,200 livres in 1775 (DU DEFFAND iv. 245). It was sold SH xiv. 53 for £141 15s. to Colnaghi for Robert Holford. See also 'Des. of SH,' *Works* ii. 475.

second has totally disappointed you, and *therefore* you will persist in
it, by all means. But then be sure to persist too in being young, in stopping the course of time, and making the shadow return back upon
your sun-dial. If you find this not so easy, acquiesce with a good grace
in my *anilities,* put on your under-stockings of yarn or woollen, even
in the night-time. Don't provoke me! or I shall order you two night-
caps (which by the way would do your eyes good), and put a little of
any French liqueur into your water; they are nothing but brandy and
sugar, and among their various flavours some of them may surely be
palatable enough. The pain in your feet *I can* bear, but I shudder at
the sickness in your stomach, and the weakness that still continues. I
conjure you, as you love yourself, I conjure you by Strawberry not to
trifle with these edge-tools. There is no cure for the gout, when in the
stomach, but to throw it into the limbs. There is no relief for the gout
in the limbs, but in gentle warmth and gradual perspiration.

I was much entertained with your account of our neighbours. As an
Englishman and an anti-Gallican, I rejoice at their dulness and their
nastiness, though I fear we shall come to imitate them in both. Their
atheism is a little too much, too shocking to rejoice at. I have been long
sick at it in their authors, and hated them for it, but I pity their poor
innocent people of fashion. They were bad enough when they believed
everything!

I have searched where you directed me; which I could not do sooner,
as I was at London[1] when I received your letter, and could not easily
find her Grace's works.[2] Here they abound in every library. The print
you ask after is the frontispiece to *Nature's pictures drawn by Fancy's
pencil.*[3] But lest there should be any mistake, I must tell you the family
are not at dinner, but sitting round a rousing fire and telling stories.
The room is just such a one as we lived in at Rheims; I mean, as to the
glazing and ceiling. The chimney is supported by caryatids; over the
mantelpiece the arms of the family. The Duke and Duchess are
crowned with laurel. A servant stands behind him, holding a hat and
feather. Another is shutting a window. Diepenbecke *delineavit* and
(I think) S. Clouwe[4] *sculpsit.* It is a very pretty and curious print,[5]

1. From 28 Oct. to 2 Dec. ('Chronological Table,' *Gray's Corr.*).
2. The Duchess of Newcastle's.
3. *Nature's Pictures drawn by Fancie's
Pencil to the Life,* 1656.

4. Peeter Clouwet (1629–70). See *Catalogue of the Huth Collection,* 1911–22, pp.
1505–6.
5. HW's copy of the print was sold London 168 for £5.

and I thank you for the sight of it. If it ever was a picture, what a picture to have!

I must tell you, that upon cleaning an old picture here at St John's Lodge,[5a] which I always took for a Holbein,[6] on a ring which the figure wears, they have found H.H. It has been always called B[isho]p Fisher, but is plainly a layman, and probably Sir Anthony Denny,[7] who was a benefactor to the College.[8]

What is come of your Sévigné curiosity? I should be glad of a line now and then, when you have leisure. I wish you well, and am ever

Yours,

T. GRAY

To GRAY, Saturday 25 January 1766

Reprinted from *Works* v. 361–7.

Paris, January 25, 1766.

I AM much indebted to you for your kind letter and advice; and though it is late to thank you for it, it is at least a stronger proof that I do not forget it. However, I am a little obstinate, as you know, on the chapter of health, and have persisted through this Siberian winter in not adding a grain to my clothes, and in going open-breasted without an under-waistcoat. In short, though I like extremely to live, it must be in my own way, as long as I can: it is not youth I court, but liberty; and I think making one's self tender, is issuing a *general warrant*[1] against one's own person. I suppose I shall submit to confinement, when I cannot help it; but I am indifferent enough to life not to care if it ends soon after my prison begins.

I have not delayed so long to answer your letter, from not thinking

5a. The residence of the Master of the College.

6. Mr Hugh Gatty says that the portrait, which came originally from Longleat, is probably not by Holbein.

7. (1501–49), of Cheshunt, Herts, Kt ca 1545; M.P.; King's Remembrancer; Groom of the Stole. Since the picture bears the inscription '*Anno ætatis* 74,' it cannot represent Denny, or Fisher (see A. H. Lloyd, *Early History of Christ's College*, Cambridge, 1934, p. 391; information from Mr

Gatty). Gray (*ante* 2 Sept. 1760) identifies it as Sir Anthony Browne, on Dr Taylor's authority, but this is a mere conjecture.

8. He rebuilt the school of Sedbergh, Yorks to which St John's has power of appointing a governor, and recovered the estates constituting its endowment.

1. The legality of general warrants had been debated in the courts 1763–5, in various cases arising out of the publication of No. 45 of Wilkes's *North Briton*.

of it, or from want of matter, but from want of time. I am constantly occupied, engaged, amused, till I cannot bring a hundredth part of what I have to say into the compass of a letter. You will lose nothing by this: you know my volubility, when I am full of new subjects; and I have at least many hours of conversation for you at my return. One does not learn a whole nation in four or five months; but, for the time, few, I believe, have seen, studied, or got so much acquainted with the French as I have.

By what I said of their religious or rather irreligious opinions, you must not conclude their people of quality, atheists—at least not the men—Happily for them, poor souls! they are not capable of going so far into thinking. They assent to a great deal, because it is the fashion, and because they don't know how to contradict. They are ashamed to defend the Roman Catholic religion, because it is quite exploded; but I am convinced they believe it in their hearts. They hate the parliaments and the philosophers, and are rejoiced that they may still idolize royalty. At present too they are a little triumphant: the Court has shown a little spirit, and the parliaments much less: but as the Duc de Choiseul,[2] who is very fluttering, unsettled, and inclined to the philosophers, has made a compromise with the Parliament of Bretagne,[3] the parliaments might venture out again, if, as I fancy will be the case, they are not glad to drop a cause, of which they began to be a little weary of the inconveniencies.

The generality of the men, and more than the generality, are dull and empty. They have taken up gravity, thinking it was philosophy and English, and so have acquired nothing in the room of their natural levity and cheerfulness. However, as their high opinion of their own country remains, for which they can no longer assign any reason, they are contemptuous and reserved, instead of being ridiculously, consequently pardonably, impertinent. I have wondered, knowing my own countrymen, that we had attained such a superiority.—I wonder

2. Étienne-François de Choiseul-Stainville (1719–85), Duc de Choiseul; minister of foreign affairs (DU DEFFAND).

3. On 22 May 1765, all but twelve of the Breton magistrates resigned their seats in protest against Louis XV's absolute measures. This defiance of the Crown was supported by the other six parliaments. A flood of pamphlets and anonymous verses followed, and the affair culminated in the arrest and trial of La Chalotais, the *pro-cureur général*. See Bathélemy Pocquet, *Le Duc d'Aiguillon et La Chalotais*, 1900–1, vols i–ii; Marcel Marion, *La Bretagne et le Duc d'Aiguillon*, 1898, pp. 333–40; *Recueil des délibérations, arrestes, remonstrances et représentations du parlement, sur les affaires de Bretagne*, 1767; DU DEFFAND v. 371. Choiseul's 'compromise' involved reorganization of the parliament (see Aiguillon to Montbourcher 26 Dec. 1765, quoted by Pocquet, op. cit. ii. 164).

no longer, and have a little more respect for English *heads* than I had.

The women do not seem of the same country: if they are less gay than they were, they are more informed, enough to make them very conversable. I know six or seven with very superior understandings; some of them with wit, or with softness, or very good sense.

Madame Geoffrin,⁴ of whom you have heard much, is an extraordinary woman, with more common sense than I almost ever met with. Great quickness in discovering characters, penetration in going to the bottom of them, and a pencil that never fails in a likeness—seldom a favourable one. She exacts and preserves, spite of her birth⁵ and their nonsensical prejudices about nobility, great court and attention. This she acquires by a thousand little arts and offices of friendship; and by a freedom and severity which seems to be her sole end of drawing a concourse to her; for she insists on scolding those she inveigles to her. She has little taste and less knowledge, but protects artisans and authors, and courts a few people to have the credit of serving her dependents. She was bred under the famous Madame Tencin,⁶ who advised her never to refuse any man; for, said her mistress, though nine in ten should not care a farthing for you, the tenth may live to be an useful friend. She did not adopt or reject the whole plan, but fully retained the purport of the maxim. In short, she is an epitome of empire, subsisting by rewards and punishments. Her great enemy,⁷ Madame du Deffand, was for a short time mistress of the Regent, is now very old and stone blind, but retains all her vivacity, wit, memory, judgment, passions and agreeableness. She goes to operas, plays, suppers, and Versailles; gives suppers twice a week; has everything new read to her; makes new songs and epigrams, ay, admirably, and remembers every one that has been made these fourscore years. She corresponds with Voltaire, dictates charming letters to him, contradicts him, is no bigot to him or anybody, and laughs both at the clergy and the philosophers.

4. Marie-Thérèse Rodet (1699–1777), m. (1713) François Geoffrin (DU DEFFAND i. 178).

5. Mme Geoffrin's father, Pierre Rodet, was *valet de garde-robe* to the Dauphine Marie-Anne; her mother, Angélique-Thérèse Chemineau (Rodet's second wife), was the daughter of a Paris banker (see Pierre-Marie-Maurice-Henri, Marquis de Ségur, *Le Royaume de la Rue Saint-Honoré*, 1898, pp. 3–4).

6. Claudine-Alexandrine Guérin (1681–1749), Marquise de Tencin (DU DEFFAND).

7. Because of Mme Geoffrin's friendship with Mlle de Lespinasse after the latter's rupture with Mme du Deffand in 1764. A further cause for enmity was the popularity of Mme Geoffrin's own salon (see *Letters to and from Madame du Deffand and Julie de Lespinasse*, ed. W. H. Smith, New Haven, 1938; Marquis de Ségur, *Julie de L'Espinasse*, [1905,] pp. 167–183).

In a dispute, into which she easily falls, she is very warm, and yet scarce ever in the wrong: her judgment on every subject is as just as possible; on every point of conduct as wrong as possible: for she is all love and hatred, passionate for her friends to enthusiasm, still anxious to be loved, I don't mean by lovers, and a vehement enemy, but openly. As she can have no amusement but conversation, the least solitude and ennui are insupportable to her, and put her into the power of several worthless people, who eat her suppers when they can eat nobody's of higher rank; wink to one another and laugh at her; hate her because she has forty times more parts—and venture to hate her because she is not rich. She has an old friend whom I must mention, a Monsieur Pondevelle,[8] author of the *Fat puni,*[9] and the *Complaisant,*[10] and of those pretty novels, the *Comte de Cominge,*[11] the *Siege of Calais,*[12] and *Les Malheurs de l'amour.*[13] Would not you expect this old man to be very agreeable? He can be so, but seldom is: yet he has another very different and very amusing talent, the art of parody, and is unique in his kind. He composes tales to the tunes of long dances:[14] for instance, he has adapted the Regent's *Daphnis and Chloé*[15] to one, and made it ten times more indecent; but is so old and sings it so well, that it is permitted in all companies. He has succeeded still better in *Les Caractères de la danse,*[16] to which he has adapted words that express all the characters of love. With all this, he has not the least idea of cheerfulness in conversation; seldom speaks but on grave subjects, and not often on them; is a humourist, very supercilious, and wrapped up in admiration of his own country, as the only judge of his merit. His air and

8. Antoine Ferriol (1697–1774), Comte de Pont-de-Veyle (DU DEFFAND).

9. *Le Fat puni, comédie avec un divertissement . . . ,* 1738 (Bibl. Nat. Cat.). First performed at the Comédie-Française 7 April 1738.

10. *Le Complaisant, comédie en 5 actes et en prose, représentée par les Comédiens français ordinaires du Roi, le 29 décembre 1732 . . . , 1733* (ibid.).

11. *Mémoires du Comte Comminge,* The Hague, 1735, written in collaboration with Pont-de-Veyle's brother Charles-Augustin Ferriol (1700–88), Comte d'Argental (DU DEFFAND) and Mme de Tencin (Bibl. Nat. Cat.).

12. *Le Siège de Calais,* The Hague, 1739, written in collaboration with Mme de Tencin (ibid.).

13. Amsterdam, 1747, written in collaboration with Mme de Tencin (ibid.).

14. I.e., country-dances danced 'longways' (the word used in Playford's *The Dancing-Master*), as distinguished from rounds (information from Professor Curt Sachs of New York University; see his *Eine Weltgeschichte des Tanzes,* Berlin, 1933, pp. 105, 107, for 'Langtanz').

15. Not identified. They were verses to a dance (see DU DEFFAND v. 288–9). HW heard Pont-de-Veyle's parody 22 Dec. 1765 at Mme du Deffand's (ibid.).

16. Perhaps Pont-de-Veyle parodied Collin de Blamont's ballet *Les Caractères de l'amour* (1738). In 'Paris Journals' under 9 Dec. 1765 HW speaks of 'M. d'Ussé, an old man who sung the characters of love, parodied by Pont-de-Veyle' (ibid. v. 283).

look are cold and forbidding; but ask him to sing, or praise his works, his eyes and smiles open and brighten up. In short, I can show him to you: the self-applauding poet in Hogarth's Rake's Progress, the second print, is so like his very features and very wig, that you would know him by it, if you came hither—for he certainly will not go to you.

Madame de Mirepoix's[17] understanding is excellent of the useful kind, and can be so when she pleases of the agreeable kind. She has read, but seldom shows it, and has perfect taste. Her manner is cold, but very civil; and she conceals even the blood of Lorrain, without ever forgetting it. Nobody in France knows the world better, and nobody is personally so well with the King. She is false, artful, and insinuating beyond measure when it is her interest, but indolent and a coward. She never had any passion but gaming, and always loses. Forever paying court, the sole produce of a life of art is to get money from the King to carry on a course of paying debts or contracting new ones, which she discharges as fast as she is able. She advertised devotion to get made Dame du Palais[18] to the Queen[19] and the very next day this Princess of Lorrain was seen riding backwards with Madame Pompadour in the latter's coach. When the King was stabbed[20] and heartily frightened, the mistress took a panic too, and consulted d'Argenson,[21] whether she had not best make off in time. He hated her, and said, 'By all means.' Madame de Mirepoix advised her to stay. The King recovered his spirits, d'Argenson was banished,[22] and *la Maréchale* inherited part of the mistress's credit.—I must interrupt my history of illustrious women with an anecdote of Monsieur de Maurepas,[23] with whom I am much acquainted, and who has one of the few heads that approach to good ones, and who luckily for us was disgraced,[24] and the marine dropped, because it was his favourite object

17. Anne-Marguerite-Gabrielle de Beauvau-Craon (1709–91), m. (1) (1721) Jacques-Henri de Lorraine, Prince de Lixin; m. (2) (1739) Charles-Pierre-Gaston-François de Lévis de Lomagne, Duc de Mirepoix, Maréchal de France (MONTAGU; DU DEFFAND).

18. She was appointed 19 Aug. 1753, and was presented to the Queen the same day (see Charles Philippe d'Albert, Duc de Luynes, *Mémoires*, ed. L. Dussieux and E. Soulié, 1860–5, xiii. 34).

19. Marie Leszczyńska (1703–68), m. (1725) Louis XV.

20. By Damiens at Versailles, 5 Jan. 1757 (NBG; Luynes, op. cit. xv. 355–8).

21. Marc-Pierre de Voyer de Paulmy (1696–1764), Comte d'Argenson (La Chenaye-Desbois xix. 950).

22. Louis XV's order to Argenson, 1 Feb. 1757, is in Luynes, op. cit. xv. 395.

23. Jean-Frédéric Phélypeaux (1701–81), Comte de Maurepas (DU DEFFAND). For HW's acquaintance with him see HW to Selwyn 2 Dec. 1765, and 'Paris Journals' *sub* 30 Nov. 1765 (ibid. v. 278).

24. 24 April 1749. The cause of his disgrace was an epigram on Mme de Pompa-

and province.[25] He employed Pondevelle to make a song on the Pompadour:[26] it was clever and bitter, and did not spare even Majesty. This was Maurepas absurd enough to sing at supper at Versailles. Banishment ensued; and lest he should ever be restored, the mistress persuaded the King that he had poisoned her predecessor Madame de Châteauroux.[27] Maurepas is very agreeable, and exceedingly cheerful; yet I have seen a transient silent cloud when politics are talked of.

Madame de Boufflers,[28] who was in England, is a *savante,* mistress of the Prince of Conti,[29] and very desirous of being his wife. She is two women, the upper and the lower. I need not tell you that the lower is *galante,* and still has pretensions. The upper is very sensible too, and has a measured eloquence that is just and pleasing—but all is spoiled by an unrelaxed attention to applause. You would think she was always sitting for her picture to her biographer.

Madame de Rochfort[30] is different from all the rest. Her understand-

dour ('Par vos façons nobles et franches,' etc.; *Journal et mémoires du Marquis d'Argenson,* ed. E. J. B. Rathery, 1859–67, v. 456; for variants see *Mémoires du Comte de Maurepas,* 1792, iv. 265; *Chansonnier historique du XVIIIᵉ siècle,* 1879–84, i. p. lxv).

25. He was appointed *secrétaire d'État* in 1715 (aged 14), and took office in 1718. In 1723 he was charged with the *departement de la marine,* and in 1738 became *ministre d'État de la maison du Roi* (La Chenaye-Desbois xv. 792; *Répertoire . . . de la Gazette de France,* 1902–6, iii. 824–5). On his banishment, the office of *ministre d'État* was divided between the Comte de Saint-Florentin and the Comte d'Argenson; his place of *secrétaire d'État de la marine* was given by the King, 25 April, to Antoine-Louis Rouillé, Comte de Jouy (ibid. iv. 108; La Chenaye-Desbois xvii. 792; Luynes, op. cit. ix. 394–5).

26. 'Les Poissonnades' (beginning, 'Les grands seigneurs s'avilissent'), usually attributed to Maurepas (*Chansonnier historique* vii. 135–9). Collé, however, supports HW's statement that Pont-de-Veyle was the author (Charles Collé, *Journal et mémoires,* 1868, i. 51).

27. Marie-Anne de Mailly-Nesle (1717–44), Duchesse de Châteauroux, m. (1734) Louis, Marquis de la Tournelle; Louis XV's mistress 1738–44. She died 8 Dec. 1744

after a two weeks' illness, but her physician, Vernage, told Mme du Hausset that the rumours of poison were untrue, and that Mme de Châteauroux died of 'une fièvre putride avec le transport au cerveau' (*Mémoires de Madame du Hausset,* 1824, pp. 223–4). Under 30 May 1749, the Marquis d'Argenson wrote in his journal: 'L'on ne doute pas présentement que la cause du renvoi de M. de Maurepas ne soit pour la crainte du poison qu'en avait la Marquise de Pompadour. . . . La Marquise dit continuellement au roi qu'elle aurait ce sort de la même main qui avait empoisonné Mme de Châteauroux' (d'Argenson, op. cit. v. 485–6).

28. Marie-Charlotte-Hippolyte de Camps de Saujon (1725–1800), m. (1746) Édouard, Comte (Marquis, 1751) de Boufflers-Rouverel (DU DEFFAND). She visited England in 1763 (HW to Mann 30 April 1763).

29. Louis-François de Bourbon (1717–76), Prince de Conti (DU DEFFAND). Mme de Boufflers became his mistress in 1752 (P.-E. Schazmann, *La Comtesse de Boufflers,* 1933, pp. 14–15).

30. Marie-Thérèse de Brancas (1716–82), m. (1) (1736) Jean-Anne-Vincent de Larlan de Kercadio, Comte de Rochefort; m. (2) (1782) Louis-Jules-Barbon Mancini-Mazarini (1716–98), Duc de Nivernais (DU DEFFAND).

ing is just and delicate; with a finesse of wit that is the result of reflection. Her manner is soft and feminine, and though a *savante,* without any declared pretensions. She is the *decent* friend of Monsieur de Nivernois, for you must not believe a syllable of what you read in their novels. It requires the greatest curiosity, or the greatest habitude, to discover the smallest connection between the sexes here. No familiarity, but under the veil of friendship, is permitted, and love's dictionary is as much prohibited, as at first sight one should think his ritual was. All you hear, and that pronounced with nonchalance, is, that *monsieur un tel* has had *madame une telle.* The Duc de Nivernois has parts, and writes at the top of the mediocre,[31] but, as Madame Geoffrin says, is *manqué par tout; guerrier manqué,*[32] *ambassadeur manqué, homme d'affaires manqué,* and *auteur manqué*—no, he is not *homme de naissance manqué.* He would think freely, but has some ambition of being governor to the Dauphin,[33] and is more afraid of his wife[34] and daughter,[35] who are ecclesiastic fagots. The former out-chatters the Duke of Newcastle; and the latter, Madame de Gisors, exhausts Mr Pitt's eloquence in defence of the Archbishop of Paris.[36] Monsieur de Nivernois lives in a small circle of dependent admirers, and Madame de Rochfort is high priestess for a small salary of credit.

The Duchess of Choiseul,[37] the only young one of these heroines, is not very pretty, but has fine eyes, and is a little model in wax-work, which not being allowed to speak for some time as incapable, has a hesitation and modesty, the latter of which the Court has not cured, and the former of which is atoned for by the most interesting sound of voice, and forgotten in the most elegant turn and propriety of expression. Oh! it is the gentlest, amiable, civil, little creature that ever came out of a

31. Most of his works remained unpublished until 1796, the date of his *Œuvres,* 8 vols. For his translation (1785) of HW's *Essay on Modern Gardening,* see Hazen, *SH Bibliography* 129–30, and Berry ii. 259.

32. He took part in Belle-Isle's Bohemian campaign 1741–2 as colonel of the Limousin regiment. He was advanced to brigadier des armées du Roi 20 Jan. 1743, but resigned his commission in 1744 (Lucien Perey, *Un Petit-neveu de Mazarin,* 1899, pp. 13, 29–36; Luynes, op. cit. v. 381, under 8 April 1744; La Chenaye-Desbois xiii. 97).

33. (1754–93), subsequently Louis XVI.

34. Hélène-Angélique-Françoise Phély-

peaux de Pontchartrain (1715–82), whom he married in 1730 (du Deffand).

35. Hélène-Julie-Rosalie Mancini-Mazarini (1740–80), m. (1753) Louis-Marie Fouquet, Duc de Gisors (La Chenaye-Desbois xiii. 98).

36. Christophe de Beaumont du Repaire (1703–81), Duc de Saint-Cloud, Abp of Paris 1746–81 (du Deffand). For his dispute with the Parliament of Paris over the administration of the last rites to those who had not confessed, see ibid. v. 284.

37. Louise-Honorine Crozat du Châtel (1735–1801), m. (1750) Étienne-François de Choiseul-Stainville, Duc de Choiseul (du Deffand).

fairy egg! So just in its phrases and thoughts, so attentive and good-natured! Everybody loves it, but its husband,[38] who prefers his own sister the Duchesse de Grammont,[39] an Amazonian, fierce, haughty dame, who loves and hates arbitrarily, and is detested. Madame de Choiseul, passionately fond of her husband, was the martyr of this union, but at last submitted with a good grace; has gained a little credit with him, and is still believed to idolize him—But I doubt it—she takes too much pains to profess it.

I cannot finish my list without adding a much more common character—but more complete in its kind than any of the foregoing, the Maréchale de Luxembourg.[40] She has been very handsome, very abandoned, and very mischievous. Her beauty is gone, her lovers are gone, and she thinks the Devil is coming. This dejection has softened her into being rather agreeable, for she has wit and good breeding; but you would swear, by the restlessness of her person and the horrors she cannot conceal, that she had signed the compact, and expected to be called upon in a week for the performance.

I could add many pictures, but none so remarkable. In those I send you, there is not a feature bestowed gratis or exaggerated. For the

38. The Bishop of Rodez (François Colbert de Seignelay) observed to Miss Berry (quoted in her edition of the *Letters of the Marquise du Deffand to the Hon. Horace Walpole*, 1810, i. 13–14): 'La Duchesse de Choiseul était telle que l'a peinte Mr Walpole [in his letter to Gray], et mérite tout le bien qu'il en dit: son mari sans avoir pour elle un amour égal à celui qu'elle avait pour lui, avait néanmoins envers elle les plus justes égards et la plus grande considération; il n'a jamais cessé de les lui marquer. Par la dernière disposition de son testament, il veut que son corps et celui de Mme la Duchesse de Choiseul soient enfermés dans la même tombe. . . .'

39. Béatrix de Choiseul-Stainville (1730–94), m. (1759) Antoine-Antonin, Duc de Gramont (DU DEFFAND). 'L'extérieur de Mme la Duchesse de Grammont semblerait justifier ce qu'en dit Mr Walpole. Sa personne était grasse et forte, son teint éclatant, ses yeux vifs et petits, sa voix rauque, son abord et maintien pouvaient au premier coup d'œil paraître répoussant. Mais les qualités intérieures étaient bien différentes de ce qu'en pensaient ceux dont parle Mr Walpole. Son âme était élevée, généreuse et vraie, douce, franche, et pleine de charmes pour ses amis, et sa société en général; son caractère fort et décidé, son affection vive, ferme et attentive à tout ce qui pouvait être utile ou agréable à ceux qui la possédaient; on ne perdait son amitié que par des actions basses, ou par une conduite perfide. . . . Mme la Duchesse de Grammont fut saisie par ordre de Robespierre, enfermée au petit Châtelet, et se conduisit devant le tribunal révolutionnaire avec une dignité et une noblesse qui étonna ses sanguinaires juges. Elle ne dit pas un mot pour sa propre défense, et ne manifesta son énergie que pour sauver son amie la Duchesse du Châtelet traduite comme elle devant le même tribunal, lequel condamna l'une et l'autre à périr sur le même échafaud' (Bishop of Rodez, loc. cit.).

40. Madeleine-Angélique de Neufville (1707–87), m. (1) (1721) Joseph-Marie, Duc de Boufflers; m. (2) (1750) Charles-François-Frédéric de Montmorency-Luxembourg, Duc de Luxembourg, Maréchal de France (DU DEFFAND).

beauties, of which there are a few considerable, as Mesdames de Brionne,[41] de Monaco,[42] et d'Egmont,[43] they have not yet lost their characters, nor got any.

You must not attribute my intimacy with Paris to curiosity alone. An accident unlocked the doors for me. That *passe-partout*, called the fashion, has made them fly open—and what do you think was that fashion?—I myself—Yes, like Queen Elinor[44] in the ballad,[45] I sunk at Charing Cross, and have risen in the Faubourg St Germain. A *plaisanterie* on Rousseau,[46] whose arrival here[47] in his way to you[48] brought me acquainted with many anecdotes conformable to the idea I had conceived of him, got about, was liked much more than it deserved, spread like wild-fire, and made me the subject of conversation. Rousseau's devotees were offended. Madame de Boufflers, with a tone of sentiment, and the accents of lamenting humanity, abused me heartily,[49] and then complained to myself with the utmost softness. I acted contrition, but had like to have spoiled all, by growing dreadfully tired of a second lecture from the Prince of Conti, who took up the ball, and made himself the hero of a history wherein he had nothing to do. I listened, did not understand half he said (nor he neither), forgot the rest, said 'yes' when I should have said 'no,' yawned when I should have smiled, and was very penitent when I should have rejoiced at my pardon. Madame de Boufflers was more distressed, for he owned twenty times more than I had said: she frowned, and made him signs; but she had wound up his clack, and there was no stopping it. The moment she grew angry, the [lord of the house][50] grew

41. Louise-Julie-Constance de Rohan-Montauban (1734–1815), m (1748) Charles-Louis de Lorraine, Comte de Brionne (DU DEFFAND).

42. Marie-Catherine de Brignole (1739–1813), m. (1) (1757) Honoré-Camille-Léonor Goyon-de-Matignon de Grimaldi, P. of Monaco; m. (2) (1808) Louis-Joseph de Bourbon, Prince de Condé (DU DEFFAND).

43. Jeanne-Sophie-Élisabeth-Louise-Armande-Septimanie Vignerot du Plessis-Richelieu (1740–73), m. (1756) Casimir Pignatelli d'Egmont, Comte d'Egmont (DU DEFFAND).

44. Eleanor of Castile (d. 1290), m. (1254) Edward I of England.

45. In a broadside ca 1650 (BM Cat.) the ballad is entitled 'The Lamentable fall of Queene Elnor, who for her pride and wickednesse by Gods iudgement, sunke into the ground at Charing-crosse, and rose up at Queene Hive.' It is reprinted in *Roxburghe Ballads*, ed. Charles Hindley, 1873–4, ii. 362–9 (see especially stanza 18, quoted in MONTAGU i. 256, n. 17).

46. HW's letter 'Le Roi de Prusse à Monsieur Rousseau.' See *ante* i. 41.

47. 16 Dec. 1765 from Strassburg (J.-J. Rousseau, *Correspondance générale*, ed. Dufour, 1924–34, xiv. 318, 324).

48. Rousseau left Paris 4 Jan. and arrived in London 13 Jan. (Courtois, op. cit. 181–2).

49. 14 Jan. at Mme de Luxembourg's (DU DEFFAND v. 295).

50. 'House of the lord' in Miss Berry's text, emended by T-W.

charmed, and it has been my fault if I am not at the head of a numerous sect:—but when I left a triumphant party in England, I did not come hither to be at the head of a fashion.[51] However, I have been sent for about like an African prince or a learned canary-bird, and was, in particular, carried by force[52] to the Princess of Talmond,[53] the Queen's cousin, who lives in a charitable apartment in the Luxembourg, and was sitting on a small bed hung with saints and Sobieskis, in a corner of one of those vast chambers, by two blinking tapers. I stumbled over a cat, a foot-stool, and a chamber-pot in my journey to her presence. She could not find a syllable to say to me, and the visit ended with her begging a lap-dog. Thank the Lord! though this is the first month, it is the last week, of my reign; and I shall resign my crown with great satisfaction to a *bouillie* of chestnuts, which is just invented, and whose annals will be illustrated by so many indigestions, that Paris will not want anything else these three weeks. I will enclose the fatal letter[54] after I have finished this enormous one; to which I will only add, that nothing has interrupted my Sévigné researches but the frost. The Abbé de Malesherbes[55] has given me full power to ransack Livry.[56] I did not tell you, that by great accident, when I thought on nothing less, I stumbled on an original picture of the Comte de Grammont.[57] Adieu! You are generally in London in March:[58] I shall be there by the end of it.[59]

Yours ever,

Hor. Walpole

51. *Sic,* though the sense seems to demand 'faction.'

52. By the Duchesse d'Aiguillon on 15 Jan. (du Deffand v. 295, vi. 58).

53. Marie-Louise Jablonowska (1701–73), m. (1730) Antoine-Charles-Frédéric de la Trémoïlle, Prince de Talmond (du Deffand).

54. To Rousseau. The enclosure is missing.

55. Jean-Baptiste-Antoine de Malherbe (1712–71), O.S.B., *abbé commendataire* (titular abbot) of Grestain, 1735; of Thiron, 1743; of Livry, 1759; canon of Notre-Dame de Paris (La Chenaye-Desbois xiii. 45–6; *Répertoire . . . de la Gazette de France* iii. 499).

56. 12 miles east of Paris, where the orphaned Mme de Sévigné spent her youth under the care of her uncle, the Abbé Christophe de Coulanges (d. 1687), prior

of Notre-Dame des Anges at Livry (Edward Fitzgerald, *Dictionary of Madame de Sévigné,* 1914, ii. 5–6).

57. Philibert (1621–1707), Comte de Gramont. HW was contemplating a new edition of Anthony Hamilton's *Mémoires du Comte de Grammont,* 'with notes and cuts of the principal beauties and heroes' as early as 1751 (Montagu i. 118). The search for portraits, however, delayed publication until 1772 (*post* 21 July 1772; Cole i. 293; Hazen, *SH Bibliography* 96–8). HW found this picture (used as a frontispiece to HW's edition of the memoirs) 28 Nov. 1765, at the convent of the Grands Augustins. See du Deffand v. 276; HW to Conway 29 Nov. 1765.

58. Gray went to London 16 April ('Chronological Table,' *Gray's Corr.*)

59. HW arrived in London 22 April (du Deffand v. 314).

From GRAY, Wednesday 24 September 1766

Printed from MS in Waller Collection.
Address: To the Honourable Horace Walpole in Arlington Street, London.

Sept. 24, 1766, Pembroke Hall.

Dear Sir,

I HAPPENED to be in Norfolk[1] on the way to Houghton when I read an article in the newspaper,[2] relating to you, that shocked me. I wrote to Dr Gisburne[3] (who lives very near you)[4] to beg he would inform himself of your health, but I fear he is out of town, for I have received no answer. Today by accident I received a letter from Cole,[5] from whence I learn, thank God! that the worst part of that news was false, but that you have suffered much from a return of the gout, and are prevented only by weakness from going to Bath.[6] It would be a singular satisfaction to me if I might see three lines in your own hand, but it is impossible for me to judge whether this is a reasonable request. I flatter myself, if you can, you will indulge me in it, especially when you know that of those who are most about you, there is no one I can well write to. In a fortnight or less I hope to be in town.[7] Heaven preserve you, and restore you to health and ease. I hope this severe lesson will warn you against that careless regimen, to which you were so unreasonably attached. I am ever

Yours,

T. GRAY

1. Gray was absent from Cambridge 11–22 Sept. ('Chronological Table,' *Gray's Corr.*). He had recently been in Suffolk also (Gray to Nicholls, 23 Sept. 1766, *Gray's Corr.* iii. 935).

2. Perhaps in the *Daily Adv.* 13 Sept. 1766: 'On Thursday [11 Sept.] the Hon. Horace Walpole, Esq., was seized with a paralytic disorder at his house in Arlington Street, and continues very ill.' See also *Whitehall Evening Post* 11–13 Sept. 1766; COLE i. 118–21.

3. Thomas Gisborne (ca 1726–1806), M.D., Fellow of St John's College, Cambridge 1753–1806; physician to St George's Hospital 1757–81; appointed physician to the Royal Household 1759, and personal physician to George III, 1794 (Venn, *Alumni Cantab.;* information from Sir Owen Morshead).

4. In Cleveland Row, St James's (*Court and City Calendar*, 1766, p. 225).

5. Missing. Cole, writing from Bletchley (where he was rector 1753–68), probably repeated what HW had written him 18 Sept. 1766 (COLE i. 118–19).

6. HW set out for Park Place, Conway's country seat, 27 Sept., and proceeded to Bath 1 Oct., where he stayed until ca 21 Oct. (ibid. i. 119, n. 2; MONTAGU ii. 232).

7. Gray went to London 6 Oct. (Gray to Mason 5 Oct. 1766, *Gray's Corr.* iii. 939).

To Gray, ca Friday 26 September 1766

Fragment of HW's reply to *ante* 24 Sept. 1766. Quoted by Gray in his letter to Mason 5 Oct. 1766. Reprinted from *Gray's Corr.* iii. 938–9.

[Arlington Street, ca Sept. 26, 1766.]

. . . He (Pringle)[1] had another patient at the same time, who has ended very unhappily, that poor Dr B[rown].[2] The unfortunate man apprehended himself going mad, and two nights after cut his throat in bed. . . .

From Gray, Thursday 24 December 1767

Printed from MS in Waller Collection.

While Gray was in London (3 Nov.–14 Dec.), HW sent him some queries concerning *Historic Doubts:* see Cole i. 124. Our dating of Gray's movements after 1767 is partly based on his *Naturalist's Journal,* made available to us by Mr Carl H. Pforzheimer. It is a diary printed with eleven ruled columns for observations on natural phenomena, in which Gray, in addition to remarks on weather, plants, birds, etc., has written many notes which have biographical interest.

Address: To the Honourable Horace Walpole in Arlington Street, London.
Postmark: SAFFRON WALDEN 25 DE. FREE.

[Cambridge,] 24 Dec. 1767.

SURELY as the letter[1] is addressed to a *lady* and subscribed, 'Your most humble *Son,*' it can be to nobody but his mother.[2] I do not remember that there is any superscription[3] to it, for the *original* is not the

---

1. Sir John Pringle (1707–82), Bt, 1766; F.R.C.P., 1763. He attended HW during his illness (*ante* 24 Sept. 1766; *Gray's Corr.* iii. 938).

2. Dr John Brown. In his letter to Mason 5 Oct. 1766, Gray quotes Stonhewer's account of Dr Brown's suicide: 'This morning [23 Sept.] Dr B. dispatched himself: he had been for several days past very low-spirited, and within the last two or three talked of the necessity of dying in such a manner as to alarm the people about him. . . . He had contrived to get at a razor unknown to them. . . . I have tried to find out whether there was any appearance or cause of discontent in B., but can hear of none. A bodily complaint of the gouty kind . . . is all that I can get any information of; and I am told besides that he was some years ago in the same dejected way, and under the care of *proper attendants'* (*Gray's Corr.* iii. 938). The suicide occurred at Dr Brown's lodg-

ings in Pall Mall (*Lloyd's Evening Post* 24–26 Sept. 1766, quoted in *Gray's Corr.* loc. cit.). 'On Tuesday the coroner's inquest sat on the body of a gentleman of distinguished literary merit, who had cut a jugular vein with a razor at his lodgings in Pall Mall; and brought in their verdict lunacy' (*Daily Adv.* 25 Sept. 1766).

---

1. 'Letter of King Richard III to his mother, desiring her to give the Lord . . . his Chamberlain, the same office in Wiltshire as Colingbourne had. Written at Pountfret, the 3d day of Juyn (A.D. 1484?)' (*Catalogue of the Harleian Collection of Manuscripts . . . in the British Museum,* 1759, vol. i. *sub* MS 433, art. 6, f. 2b). It is printed by HW in *Historic Doubts* 39.

2. Lady Cecily Nevill (1415–95), m. (1424) Richard (Plantagenet), 3d D. of York; Edward IV's and Richard III's mother.

3. The salutation is 'Madam' (ibid.).

letter itself, but a transcript of it set down in a great register-book[4] belonging to the Privy Seal Office, in which this stands very near to the beginning. I have marked the number of the MS, and of the article, if you choose to consult the Museum about it. I told you false when I said the letter was dated,[5] but the reason I concluded so was that the articles,[6] as I remember, go on regularly in the book in order of time, and many come after it that belong to the first year of his reign.

In the page that contains his letter[7] about Jane Shore,[8] at a little distance below it are some abbreviated words in a cramp hand thus[9]

which seem to say something about the ninth year of Henry VII, but I think they relate not to this letter (which is directed to the *Bishop of Lincoln, his Chauncellor;* now Russel[10] Bishop of Lincoln was his Chancellor,[11] and not so to Henry VII) and the few succeeding articles are really of Henry VII and Henry VIII's time,[12] so I suppose the words to relate to them only.

4. Harl. MS 433: 'A book in folio, . . . being a register of the grants, etc., passing the Privy Seal, royal signet, or sign manual during the reigns of King Edward V and King Richard III, with some other entries . . .' (*Catalogue of the Harleian Collection* . . . , 1759, vol. i, introductory note under No. 433).

5. The letter 'can be of no other year than the year 1484' (James Gairdner, *History of the Life and Reign of Richard III,* Cambridge, 1898, p. 189).

6. The book, 340 folio pages, contains articles numbered 1–2378.

7. 'Letter of King Richard III . . . commanding him to dehort Thomas Lynom, his (the King's) solicitor from marrying with Jane Shore, late the wife of William Shore, now being in Ludgate' (*Catalogue of the Harleian Collection* . . . , 1759, vol. i, MS 433, art. 2378, f. 340b). The letter is printed in *Historic Doubts* 118–19.

8. (d. ?1527), m. (before 1483) William Shore, London goldsmith; mistress of Edward IV and of Thomas Grey, 1st M. of Dorset.

9. Gray's transcript, here reproduced, is a fairly accurate copy of the original, but 'by' in the first line is a mistaken transliteration of 'vj.' Mr A. J. Watson, with the help of Dr C. E. Wright and others in the Department of MSS in the BM, has kindly transcribed the original MS for us as follows:

> ffin vj s Copie
> Thom Drury dat
> Aᵒ ixᵒ Henr sept
> vt p copiã pred scrutatʳ

Dr Wright thinks it unwise to risk expansion of all the abbreviations, but, taking 'ffin[is]' in the sense of 'fee,' it is clearly a clerk's statement that he was paid six shillings for his work as a copyist.

10. John Russell (d. 1494), Bp of Lincoln, 1480.

11. From 1483 to 1485.

12. Gray, who had made his transcripts in 1759 (see *Gray's Corr.* ii. 642) and had probably not consulted the MS since, is mistaken here. Article 2378 is the last catalogued item in the MS; nothing follows it except two brief Latin entries on the same leaf, one of them an indecent joke about a

Mr Anstey's satire[13] seems to aim chiefly at this University, the patrons that protect it, the clients that make their court to them, their dedications, and clumsy flattery, their method of education, and style of politics, etc.; he has not indeed refused anything else ridiculous that came across him. I like it but little; the only things that made me laugh were:

> Sent venison, which was kindly taken
> And woodcocks, which they boil'd with bacon[14]

and the High Sheriff's frizzled lady, when she meets her husband, after he is knighted, at a ball.[15]

I have been confined to my room, ever since I came hither,[16] but not very ill. Adieu, I am

Ever yours,
T. G.

From GRAY, Sunday 14 February 1768

Reprinted from *Works* v. 368–70.

Feb. 14, 1768, Pembroke College.

I RECEIVED the book[1] you were so good to send me, and have read it again (indeed I could hardly be said to have read it before) with attention and with pleasure. Your second edition[2] is so rapid in its progress that it will now hardly answer any purpose to tell you either my own objections, or those of other people. Certain it is, that you are universally read here; but what we think is not so easy to come at. We

rooster, the other a copy of part of a legal document with a regnal date referring to the 15th year of either Edward II or Edward III. (In writing this note the editors received assistance from Messrs Hartley Simpson and Edmund Silk.)

13. *The Patriot, a Pindaric Address to Lord Buckhorse*, Cambridge, 1767, by Christopher Anstey (1724–1805), Fellow of King's College 1745–54; it was published anonymously 12 Dec. (*Daily Adv.* 12 Dec. 1767).

14. *The Patriot*, edn 1767, p. 10.

15.   ' . . . in velvet coat array'd, he
Meets at the ball his frizzled lady,
Who looks half pleas'd, and half affrighted,
E'er since her husband has been knighted.'
(Ibid. 43.)

16. Under 14 Dec. in Gray's *Naturalist's Journal:* 'Came to Cambridge.' On 28 Dec.

Gray wrote to Wharton: 'The gout came regularly while I was in town, first in one, then in the other foot, but so tame you might have stroked it. Since I got hither, *another* of my troublesome companions for life has confined me to my room, but abstinence has (I believe) got the better of that too, and tomorrow I go abroad again' (*Gray's Corr.* iii. 986).

---

1. *Historic Doubts on the Life and Reign of King Richard the Third. By Mr Horace Walpole* . . . Printed for J. Dodsley, published 1 Feb. 'in quarto, price 5s. sewed, with two prints of King Richard and his Queen' (*Daily Adv.* 1 Feb. 1768). 1200 copies were printed (*ante* i. 43).

2. It had been published on the 12th (*Daily Adv.* 8, 12 Feb.).

stay as usual to see the success, to learn the judgment of the town, to be directed in our opinions by those of more competent judges. If they like you, we shall; if any one of name write against you, we give you up, for we are modest and diffident of ourselves, and not without reason. History in particular is not our *forte;* for (the truth is) we read only modern books and the pamphlets of the day. I have heard it objected that you raise doubts and difficulties, and do not satisfy them by telling us what was *really* the case. I have heard you charged with disrespect to the King of Prussia,[3] and above all to King William[4] and the Revolution. These are seriously the most sensible things I have heard said, and all that I can recollect. If you please to justify yourself, you may.

My own objections are little more essential: they relate chiefly to inaccuracies of style, which either debase the expression or obscure the meaning. I could point out several small particulars of this kind, and will do so, if you think it can serve any purpose after publication. When I hear you read, they often escape me, partly because I am attending to the subject, and partly because from habit I understand you where a stranger might often be at a loss.

As to your arguments, most of the principal points are made out with a clearness and evidence[4a] that no one would expect where materials are so scarce. Yet I still suspect Richard of the murder of Henry VI. The chronicler of Croyland[5] charges it full on him, though without a name or any mention of circumstances.[6] The interests of Edward

3. Frederick the Great (1712–86). 'To judge impartially . . . we ought to recall the temper and manners of the times we read of. It is shocking to eat our enemies; but it is not so shocking in an Iroquois, as it would be in the King of Prussia' (*Historic Doubts* 31).
4. William III. 'The three estates of nobility, clergy, and people, which called Richard to the crown, and whose act was confirmed by the subsequent parliament, trod the same steps as the convention did which elected the Prince of Orange; both setting aside an illegal pretender, the legitimacy of whose birth was called in question. And though the partisans of the Stuarts may exult at my comparing King William to Richard III, it will be no matter of triumph, since it appears that Richard's cause was as good as King William's, and that in both instances it was a free election' (ibid. 45).
4a. I.e., distinctness.

5. The author of the third continuation of the history of the Abbey of Croyland (Crowland, Lincs), begun by Ingulph (d. 1109). The anonymous third continuation ('Alia Hist. Croylandensis continuatio') covers the years 1459–86. Gray probably used William Fulman's edition (*Rerum Anglicarum scriptorum veterum*, vol. i, Oxford, 1684, pp. 549–78). An argument for identifying the author as John Russell (*ante* 24 Dec. 1767) has been advanced by George L. Lam in an article entitled 'The Authorship of the Third Continuation of the Croyland Chronicle,' soon to be published.
6. Fulman, op. cit. 556. The Latin passage is also quoted by HW in *Historic Doubts* 8. In Gairdner's translation: 'I pass over in silence how at this period [1471] the body of King Henry was found in the Tower of London lifeless. May God spare and grant time for the repentance to him

were the interests of Richard too, though the throne were not then in view; and that Henry still stood in their way, they might well imagine, because, though deposed[7] and imprisoned[8] once before, he had regained his liberty and his crown, and was still adored by the people. I should think from the word *tyranni*, the passage was written after Richard had assumed the crown;[9] but, if it was earlier, does not the bare imputation imply very early suspicions[10] at least of Richard's bloody nature, especially in the mouth of a person that was no enemy to the house of York,[11] nor friend to that of Beaufort?[12]

That the Duchess of Burgundy,[13] to try the temper of the nation, should set up a false pretender[14] to the throne (when she had the true Duke of York[15] in her hands), and that the Queen-mother[16] (knowing

whoever [*et spatium pœnitentiæ ei donet, quicunque* etc.] thus dared to lay such sacrilegious hands on the Lord's Anointed; whereof the doer deserves the title of a tyrant, and the sufferer that of a glorious martyr' (James Gairdner, *History of the Life and Reign of Richard III*, Cambridge, 1898, p. 18). It is probable that, as Gray says, the author is accusing Richard; yet it is odd that, though this passage was written after Richard's death (see below, n. 9), the author should refer to him as though he were still alive. But the ambiguity may have been intentional, since he forbears to make a direct accusation.

7. By bill of attainder 1 Edward IV (Nov. 1461) (*Rotuli Parliamentorum* v. 476–83).

8. Henry VI was captured 13 July 1465 near Bungerly Hippingstones, Lancs, and conducted to the Tower 24 July. He was released ca 3 Oct. 1470, and re-assumed the crown 13 Oct. (C. L. Scofield, *Life and Reign of Edward IV*, 1923, i. 381–2, 541–2; Fulman, op. cit. 554; John Warkworth, 'Chronicle,' ed. J. O. Halliwell, 1839, p. 11 in *Camden Society* vol. x).

9. According to the author, it was written in 1486 (after Richard's death), in the space of ten days (21–30 April) (Fulman, op. cit. 578).

10. HW in *Historic Doubts* (p. 8) argues that the passage 'was written immediately after the murder was committed.' Both Gray's and HW's arguments suffer from their overlooking the date of composition of the continuation of the chronicle.

11. Russell, the possible author (see n. 5

above), held several offices under Edward IV and Richard III. In Henry VII's reign, the bishopric of Lincoln seems to have been his only office (DNB; but see also John Lord Campbell, *Lives of the Lord Chancellors*, 1846–69, i. 404–14; *Calendar of the Patent Rolls 1467–1477*, pp. 151, 451).

12. I.e., the Lancastrians. Henry VII's mother was Margaret Beaufort, descended from John of Gaunt, who was progenitor of the Lancastrian line.

13. Margaret of York (1446–1503), dau. of Richard, 3d D. of York, and sister of Edward IV and Richard III. She m. (1468) Charles the Bold, D. of Burgundy.

14. Lambert Simnel (b. ca 1477, living 1525). 'This youth first personated Richard, Duke of York, then Edward, Earl of Warwick; and was undoubtedly an impostor' (*Historic Doubts* 77). In the bill of attainder of John de la Pole, E. of Lincoln, 3 Henry VII (1487) 'oone Lambert Symnell' is called 'a child of x yere of age, sonne to Thomas Symnell, late of Oxforde Joynoure' (*Rotuli Parliamentorum* vi. 397). Simnel was proclaimed king by Lincoln 24 May 1487 at Dublin (ibid.).

15. Perkin Warbeck (ca 1474–99), another pretender, though HW considered him to be the true Duke, son of Edward IV (*Historic Doubts* 82–93). He proclaimed himself Richard IV at Whitesand Bay 7 Sept. 1497 (Gairdner, op. cit. 326). Margaret, Duchess of Burgundy, acknowledged him as her nephew in 1492 (ibid. 274–5).

16. Elizabeth Woodville.

her son was alive) should countenance that design, is a piece of policy utterly incomprehensible;[17] being the most likely means to ruin their own scheme, and throw a just suspicion of fraud and falsehood on the cause of truth, which Henry could not fail to seize, and turn to his own advantage.

Mr Hume's first query,[18] as far as relates to the Queen-mother, will still have some weight. Is it probable she should give her eldest daughter[19] to Henry, and invite him to claim the crown, unless she had been sure that her sons were then dead? As to her seeming consent to the match[20] between Elizabeth and Richard, she and her daughters were in his power,[21] which appeared now well fixed, his enemies' designs within the kingdom being everywhere defeated, and Henry unable to raise any considerable force abroad. She was timorous and hopeless; or she might dissemble, in order to cover her secret dealings with Richmond, and, if this were the case, she hazarded little, supposing Richard to dissemble too, and never to have thought seriously of marrying his niece.

Another unaccountable thing is that Richard, a prince of the house of York, undoubtedly brave, clear-sighted, artful, attentive to business; of boundless generosity, as appears from his grants; just and merciful, as his laws and his pardons seem to testify; having subdued the Queen and her hated faction, and been called first to the Protectorship and then to the Crown by the body of the nobility and by the

17. Gray is refuting HW's argument (*Historic Doubts* 76): 'The rigour exercised on her [Elizabeth] by Henry VII on her countenancing Lambert Simnel, evidently set up to try the temper of the nation in favour of some prince of the House of York, is a violent presumption that the Queen dowager believed her second son living. . . .'

18. 'Had not the Queen-mother and the other heads of the York party been fully assured of the death of both the young princes, would they have agreed to call over the Earl of Richmond, the head of the Lancastrian party, and marry him to the Princess Elizabeth?' (*Historic Doubts* 96.) Hume, following Sir Thomas More, believed Richard III to be the murderer of the princes (*History of England*, vol. ii, 1762, pp. 428–9). This query is one of

seven HW answered in *Historic Doubts* 96–102. No correspondence between HW and Hume survives on the subject of *Historic Doubts,* but HW evidently consulted him. See Hume to Mme de Boufflers, London, 17 Nov. 1767, *Letters,* ed. J. Y. T. Greig, Oxford, 1932, ii. 173; see also *Historic Doubts* 93n. For Hume's notes on the book see *post* 26 Feb. 1768.

19. Elizabeth of York.

20. Early in 1485 while Queen Anne was still living (Fulman, op. cit. 572).

21. Richard III offered to the Queen-mother and her daughters 'surety of their lives' if they would come 'out of the sanctuary of Westminster, and be guided, ruled, and demeaned' by him. The letter to Elizabeth is dated 1 March 1484 (quoted by Gairdner, op. cit. 165–6).

Parliament; with the common people to friend (as Carte[22] often asserts), and having nothing against him but the illegitimate family of his brother Edward,[23] and the attainted house of Clarence[24] (both of them within his power)—that such a man should see within a few months Buckingham,[25] his best friend, and almost all the southern and western counties on one day[26] in arms against him; that, having seen all these insurrections come to nothing, he should march with a gallant army against a handful of needy adventurers, led by a fugitive,[27] who had not the shadow of a title, nor any virtues to recommend him, nor any foreign strength to depend on; that he should be betrayed by almost all his troops, and fall a sacrifice[28]—all this is to me utterly improbable, and I do not ever expect to see it accounted for.

I take this opportunity to tell you that Algarotti[29] (as I see in the new edition of his works printed at Leghorn),[30] being employed to buy pictures for the King of Poland,[31] purchased among others the famous Holbein that was at Venice.[32] It don't appear that he knew anything of

22. Thomas Carte (1686–1754). For his character sketch of Richard see *A General History of England*, 1747–55, ii. 818–19.

23. Ibid. ii. 820; 'Richard had done enough for his purpose by bastardizing Edward IV's children. This secured him equally against the male and female issue.' The Act of Illegitimation is contained in the 'Act for the Settlement of the Crown upon the King and his Issue . . .' 23 Jan. 1 Richard III (1484) (*Rotuli Parliamentorum* vi. 240–2). This was copied for HW by Henry Rooke 'as near as could be from the original record in the Chapel of the Rolls.' Rooke's copy is with Lord Derby's collection of papers relating to the *Historic Doubts*.

24. George (1449–78), D. of Clarence, attainted of high treason 7 Feb. 17 Edward IV (1478) (*Rotuli Parliamentorum* vi. 193–5), and executed in the Tower 18 Feb. (C. L. Scofield, *Life and Reign of Edward IV*, 1923, ii. 209; see also COLE ii. 2).

25. Henry Stafford (1455–83), 2d D. of Buckingham.

26. 18 Oct. 1483 (*Rotuli Parliamentorum* vi. 245).

27. The Earl of Richmond (Henry VII).

28. In the battle of Bosworth, 22 Aug. 1485.

29. Francesco Algarotti (1712–64), cr. (1740) Count by Frederick the Great (*Neues*

Preussisches Adels-Lexikon, Leipzig, 1842, i. 96; NBG); man of letters; Gray's correspondent. In HW, Waldegrave MSS i. 41, HW quotes Frederick the Great's letter to Algarotti inviting him to Berlin, and then proceeds: 'This Algarotti was a noble Venetian, and author of *Il Newton[ian]ismo per le dame* [1737]. He was in England, and much acquainted with Lord Hervey and Lady Mary Wortley, who have both wrote commendatory verses to his works.'

30. *Opere del Conte Algarotti*, Leghorn, 8 vols, 1764–5.

31. Frederick Augustus II (1696–1763), Elector of Saxony and King of Poland.

32. 'In the palace of the Delfino family at Venice, where it was long on sale, the price first set £1500. When I saw it there in 1741, they had sunk it to £400 soon after which the present King of Poland bought it' (*Anecdotes, Works* iii. 77–8). Algarotti bought it for the King 4 Sept. 1743. The picture ('Madonna and Child with the Family of Jakob Meyer'), which in 1913 was in the Dresden Gallery, is generally agreed to be a seventeenth-century copy of the original (in 1913 in the Grand-ducal palace at Darmstadt) (Arthur B. Chamberlain, *Hans Holbein the Younger*, 1913, i. 232–45). The copy is said to have belonged to Maria de' Medici (ibid. 240–1).

your book,[33] yet he calls it the *Consul Meyer*[34] *and his family*,[35] as if it were then known to be so in that city.

A young man here, who is a diligent reader of your books, an antiquary, and a painter,[36] informs me that at the Red Lion Inn at Newmarket is a piece of tapestry containing the very design of your marriage of Henry the Sixth,[37] only with several more figures in it,[38] both men and women; that he would have bought it of the people, but they refused to part with it.

Mr Mason, who is here, desires to present his respects to you. He says that to efface from our annals the history of any tyrant is to do an essential injury to mankind, but he forgives it because you have shown Henry the Seventh to be a greater devil than Richard.

Pray do not be out of humour. When you first commenced an author, you exposed yourself to pit, box and gallery. Any coxcomb in the world may come in and hiss, if he pleases; ay, and (what is almost as bad) clap too, and you cannot hinder him. I saw a little squib fired at you in a newspaper[39] by some of the *house of York*,[40] for speaking lightly of chancellors. Adieu! I am ever

Yours,

T. GRAY

To GRAY, Thursday 18 February 1768

Reprinted from *Works* v. 371–4.

Arlington Street, February 18, 1768.

YOU have sent me a long and very obliging letter, and yet I am extremely out of humour with you. I saw *Poems by Mr Gray* advertised:[1] I called directly at Dodsley's[1a] to know if this was to be more

33. *Anecdotes of Painting.*

34. Jakob Meyer (living 1529), Mayor of Basel 1516, 1518, 1520. He was a staunch Catholic, and as a confession of faith he ordered in 1526 a votive picture from Holbein. It is described in Chamberlain, op. cit. i. 233–6.

35. See Algarotti, *Opere*, vi. 22–3.

36. Michael Tyson (1740–80), Fellow of Corpus Christi, Cambridge, 1767 (COLE i. 142).

37. *Ante* 15 Feb. 1754.

38. See COLE i. 169–70.

39. The *St James's Chronicle* 2–4 Feb. 1768 quotes (though without comment)

HW's unflattering remarks on three chancellors (*Historic Doubts* 63): Bacon, More, and Clarendon. HW also speaks of the 'suspicious testimony' of John Morton, Abp of Canterbury, Chancellor 1487–1500 (ibid. 18); and calls Thomas Rotherham, Abp of York, Chancellor 1474–83, a 'silly prelate' (ibid. 28).

40. I.e., some member of the Yorke family: Philip Yorke, Lord Hardwicke (d. 1764), had been Lord Chancellor, and his son Charles Yorke had been offered the chancellorship in 1765.

———

1. 'Speedily will be published, elegantly

than a new edition? He was not at home himself, but his foreman told me he thought there were some new pieces, and notes[2] to the whole. It was very unkind, not only to go out of town without mentioning them to me, without showing them to me, but not to say a word of them in this letter. Do you think I am indifferent, or not curious, about what you write? I have ceased to ask you, because you have so long refused to show me anything. You could not suppose I thought that you never write. No; but I concluded you did not intend, at least yet, to publish what you had written. As you did intend it, I might have expected a month's preference. You will do me the justice to own that I had always rather have seen your writings than have shown you mine; which you know are the most hasty trifles in the world, and which, though I may be fond of the subject when fresh, I constantly forget in a very short time after they are published. This would sound like affectation to others, but will not to you. It would be affected, even to you, to say I am indifferent to fame—I certainly am not, but I am indifferent to almost anything I have done to acquire it. The greater part are mere compilations; and no wonder they are, as you say, incorrect, when they are commonly written with people in the room, as *Richard* and the *Noble Authors* were. But I doubt there is a more intrinsic fault in them; which is, that I cannot correct them. If I write tolerably, it must be at once; I can neither mend nor add. The articles of Lord Capel[3] and Lord Peterborough,[4] in the second edition of the *Noble Authors*, cost me more trouble than all the rest together: and you may perceive that the worst part of *Richard*, in point of ease and style, is what relates to the papers you gave me on Jane Shore,[5] because it was tacked

printed, in one small volume, Poems, by Mr Gray. Printed for J. Dodsley, in Pall Mall' (*Daily Adv.* 13 Feb. 1768). It was advertised, as published 'this day,' in *Daily Adv.* 9 March 1768; *Whitehall Evening Post* 5–8 March 1768. Gray 'sent the packet' containing his poems 'to Dodsley (by Mr Baker)' on 8 Feb. (Gray's *Naturalist's Journal*).

1a. James Dodsley (1724–97), bookseller, Robert Dodsley's brother, partner, and successor.

2. See *post* 25 Feb. 1768.

3. Arthur Capell (1604–49), cr. (1641) Bn Capell of Hadham. HW inserted an article on Capell in the second edition of *Royal and Noble Authors* (1758) i. 212, mentioning the first edition of Capell's *Daily Ob-*

servations or Meditations, Divine, Morall, 1654 (sold SH i. 25). The second edition, entitled *Excellent Contemplations*, 1683, is not mentioned in *Royal and Noble Authors* until the 1787 edition, where HW incorrectly assigns it to 1685 (see *Works* i. 360). Presumably HW had not acquired it when he published the second edition of *Royal and Noble Authors*, but he had done so by 1763, for his copy (now WSL) is listed in the first section of the MS Cat. of HW's library, compiled in that year.

4. Charles Mordaunt (ca 1658–1735), 3d E. of Peterborough 1697, cr. (1689) E. of Monmouth. His life had been inserted in the second edition of *Royal and Noble Authors* ii. 125–7.

5. See *ante* 24 Dec. 1767.

on so long afterwards, and when my impetus was chilled. If some time or other you will take the trouble of pointing out the inaccuracies of it, I shall be much obliged to you: at present I shall meddle no more with it. It has taken its fate; nor did I mean to complain. I found it was condemned indeed beforehand,[6] which was what I alluded to. Since publication (as has happened to me before) the success has gone beyond my expectation.[7]

Not only at Cambridge, but here, there have been people wise enough to think me too free with the King of Prussia![8] A newspaper has talked of my known inveteracy to him.—Truly, I love him as well as I do most kings. The greater offence is my reflection on Lord Clarendon.[9] It is forgotten that I had overpraised him[10] before. Pray turn to the new State Papers[11] from which, *it is said,* he composed his history. You will find they are the papers from which he did *not* compose his history. And yet I admire my Lord Clarendon more than these pretended admirers do. But I do not intend to justify myself. I can as little satisfy those who complain that I do not let them know what *really did* happen. If this inquiry can ferret out any truth, I shall be glad. I have picked up a few more circumstances. I now want to know what Perkin Warbeck's proclamation[12] was, which Speed in his *History* says is preserved by Bishop Leslie.[13] If you look in Speed, perhaps you will be able to assist me.

6. Perhaps by Hume.

7. Dodsley printed 1200 copies (see *ante* i. 43 and 14 Feb. 1768, notes 1–2).

8. *Ante* 14 Feb. 1768, n. 3.

9. Edward Hyde (1609–74), cr. (1660) Bn Hyde; cr. (1661) E. of Clarendon. See *ante* 14 Feb. 1768, n. 39.

10. In *Royal and Noble Authors* (*Works* i. 385–90).

11. *State Papers collected by Edward Earl of Clarendon, commencing from the Year 1621. Containing the Materials from which his History of the Great Rebellion was composed, and the Authorities on which the Truth of his Relation is founded,* Oxford, 1767–86, 3 vols fol. The first volume was advertised as published 19 Jan. 1768 (*Whitehall Evening Post* 16–19 Jan. 1768). HW's copy was sold SH i. 66.

12. Perkin Warbeck's Proclamation (1497) was made in the name of Richard IV, 'by the grace of God King of England,' etc. The proclamation enumerates the crimes of Henry VII, 'our extreme and mortal enemy,' and concludes with a promise to 'peruse and call to remembrance the good laws and customs heretofore made by our noble progenitors, kings of England, and see them put in due and lawful execution.' It is dated July 1497 by A. F. Pollard, who has reprinted the text of the proclamation from BM, Birch MS 4160, No. 5 (a copy, dated 1616, of the original among the Cottonian MSS), in *The Reign of Henry VII from Contemporary Sources,* 1913–14, i. 150–5. The original MS was apparently lost in the fire of 1731 (see *post* 25 Feb. 1768). The proclamation survives in two other MS copies (see Pollard, op. cit. 150).

13. John Leslie (1527–96), Bp of Ross, 1566. HW alludes to the marginal note 'Leslæ. Epis. Ross.' in John Speed's *History of Great Britaine,* 1611, p. 741, where extracts are given from Perkin Warbeck's speech to James IV of Scotland and from the proclamation (see *post* 25 Feb. and 6

The Duke of Richmond[14] and Lord Lyttelton agree with you, that I have not disculpated Richard of the murder of Henry VI. I own to you, it is the crime of which in my own mind I believe him most guilt-less. Had I thought he committed it, I should never have taken the trouble to apologize for the rest. I am not at all positive or obstinate on your other objections, nor know exactly what I believe on many points of this story. And I am so sincere, that, except a few notes hereafter, I shall leave the matter to be settled or discussed by others. As you have written much too little, I have written a great deal too much, and think only of finishing the two or three other things I have begun[15]—and of those, nothing but the last volume of painters is designed for the present public. What has one to do when turned fifty, but really think of *finishing?*

I am much obliged and flattered by Mr Mason's approbation, and particularly by having had almost the same thought with him. I said, 'People need not be angry at my excusing Richard; I have not diminished their fund of hatred, I have only transferred it from Richard to Henry.'—Well, but I have found you close with Mason—No doubt, cry prating I, something will come out.[15a]—Oh! no—leave us, both of you, to Annabellas[16] and epistles to Ferney,[17] that give Voltaire an account of his own tragedies, to *Macarony Fables*[18] that are more unintelligible than Pilpay's[19] are in the original, to Mr Thornton's hurdy-gurdy

March 1768). Speed says nothing about Leslie's preserving the proclamation; he merely cites Leslie as one of several authorities for Perkin's history.

14. Charles Lennox (1735–1806), 3d D. of Richmond.

15. *Memoirs of the Reign of George III*, begun 18 Aug. 1766, *The Mysterious Mother*, begun 25 Dec. 1766 and finished 15 March 1768 (see *ante* i. 43), and the fourth volume of *Anecdotes of Painting* (Hazen, *SH Bibliography* 63).

15a. See Pope, *Epistle to Dr Arbuthnot*, ll. 275–6.

16. HW probably wrote 'Amabellas,' alluding to *Amabella: A Poem*, by Edward Jerningham (1737–1812), published 15 Feb. (*Public Advertiser* 13, 15 Feb. 1768).

17. *Ferney: An Epistle to M. de Voltaire*, by George Keate (1729–97), published 29 Jan. (*Daily Adv.* 29 Jan. 1768).

18. *Makarony Fables; with the New*

Fable of the Bees, published pseudonymously 22 Jan. (*Public Advertiser* 22 Jan. 1768). The author was John Hall-Stevenson (1718–85), of Skelton Castle ('Crazy Castle'), Cleveland, Yorks, friend of Sterne and author of *Crazy Tales*. For an account of the Demoniacs, a convivial club which he founded, see Louis C. Jones, *The Clubs of the Georgian Rakes*, New York, 1942, pp. 155–63.

19. Bīdpaī or Pilpay, the name given in the Middle Ages (from Sanskrit *Vidyapati*, chief scholar) to a famous collection of Hindu stories. They were first translated into English in 1570 by Sir Thomas North, from the Italian of Antonio Francesco Doni, under the title of *The Morall Philosophie of Doni;* and again in 1699 by Joseph Harris, from a French version, as *The Fables of Pilpay . . . containing many rules for the Conduct of Humane Life.*

poetry,[20] and to Mr ——,[21] who has imitated himself worse than any fop in a magazine would have done. In truth, if you should abandon us, I could not wonder—when Garrick's prologues and epilogues, his own Cymons[22] and farces, and the comedies of the fools that pay court to him, are the delight of the age, it does not deserve anything better.

Pray read the new *Account of Corsica*.[23] What relates to Paoli[24] will amuse you much. There is a deal about the island and its divisions that one does not care a straw for. The author, Boswell, is a strange being, and, like ——,[25] has a rage of knowing anybody that ever was talked of. He forced himself upon me at Paris[26] in spite of my teeth and my doors, and I see has given a foolish account of all he could pick up from me about King Theodore.[27] He then took an antipathy to me on Rousseau's account, abused me in the newspapers, and exhorted Rousseau to do so too:[28] but as he came to see me no more, I forgave all the rest. I

20. Bonnell Thornton (1724–68), published 13 Feb. *The Battle of the Wigs* (*Public Advertiser* 23 Jan., 13 Feb. 1768). Thornton was the author of *An Ode on Saint Cæcilia's Day, adapted to the Antient British Musick: viz the Salt-Box, . . . the Hum-Strum or Hurdy-Gurdy,* etc., 1763.

21. Not identified.

22. 'By His Majesty's Company at the Theatre Royal, Drury Lane . . . Cymon. A Dramatic Romance' (*Public Advertiser* 13, 14 Feb. 1768). HW's copy is now WSL.

23. James Boswell, *An Account of Corsica, the Journal of a Tour to that Island; and Memoirs of Pascal Paoli,* Glasgow, 1768. Boswell sent HW a presentation copy from Edinburgh 28 Feb., accompanied by a letter. HW's copy of the *Account of Corsica* is now in the possession of Mr Arthur A. Houghton.

24. Pascal Paoli (1725–1807), Corsican patriot who became the head of the independent Corsican state in 1755. When he was defeated by the French in 1769, he found asylum in England.

25. Mrs Toynbee (*Letters* vii. 164) inserted 'Cambridge' here. Richard Owen Cambridge was HW's Twickenham neighbour (*ante* 26 Sept. 1736; and see BERRY).

26. HW's Paris Journal says that on 21 Jan. 1766, 'Mr Boswell came' (DU DEFFAND v. 296). The entry in Boswell's journal-notes is dated 22 Jan., covering the events of the preceding day. As usual in his early

notes, he addresses himself in the second person: 'Went and found Horace Walpole . . . a lean genteel man. Talked to him of Corsica [and the Corsicans]. He said you should give something about them, as there are no authentic accounts. You said you intended to do so. He had seen Theodore, but whether from pride or stupidity he hardly spoke any. Horace has the original writing for getting him out of prison, and the great seal of the kingdom' (*Private Papers of James Boswell*, ed. Geoffrey Scott and Frederick A. Pottle, 1928–34, vii. 60–1). HW had replied briefly, ca 20 Jan., to a note from Boswell.

27. Theodore (1690–1756), Baron de Neuhoff, proclaimed King of Corsica April–Sept. 1736, died a prisoner in the Fleet. HW wrote about him in *The World* 22 Feb. 1753, and erected a tablet to him at the west door of St Anne's, Soho (*Works* i. 151–5). See also DU DEFFAND i. 183, and *ante* i. 28.

28. HW is referring to a letter in the *St James's Chronicle* 16–18 Dec. 1766, signed 'A Friend to Rousseau,' which reads in part as follows: 'I blush prodigiously for my countryman, Mr H.W., who rather than lose an unhappy piece of pleasantry, purchases the smiles of Mr Hume at the expense of the peace of the distressed Rousseau. . . . The only harm I wish the Prince of Cockle Shells is that he may feel in return the gall of an injured philosopher's pen. Jacques, stab him deep; believe me he

see he now is a little sick of Rousseau himself,[29] but I hope it will not cure him of his anger to me. However, his book will I am sure entertain you.

I will add but a word or two more. I am criticized for the expression *tinker up*[30] in the Preface. Is this one of those that you object to? I own I think such a low expression, placed to ridicule an absurd instance of wise folly, very forcible. Replace it with an elevated word or phrase, and to my conception it becomes as flat as possible.

George Selwyn says I may, if I please, write historic doubts on the present Duke of G[loucester][31] too. Indeed they would be doubts, for I know nothing certainly.[32]

Will you be so kind as to look into Leslie *De rebus Scotorum*,[33] and see if Perkin's proclamation is there,[34] and if there, how authenticated. You will find in Speed my reason for asking this.

I have written in such a hurry, I believe you will scarce be able to read my letter—and as I have just been writing French,[35] perhaps the sense may not be clearer than the writing. Adieu!

Yours ever,

HOR. WALPOLE

From GRAY, Thursday 25 February 1768

Reprinted from *Works* v. 374–6.

is mortal, and if unfeeling, make him susceptible! If I have any prophecy, the printing presses will be soon discharged from St - - - berry Hill, and English Horace ignobly buried with the *Noble Authors*. . . .' The only external evidence for attributing this piece to Boswell is HW's statement that it was his; the style however is Boswellian. See F. A. Pottle, 'The Part Played by Horace Walpole and James Boswell in the Quarrel between Rousseau and Hume,' in *Philological Quarterly*, 1925, iv. 351–63, where the complete text of the letter is reprinted. See also G. J. Williams to Selwyn 26 Dec. 1766 in John H. Jesse, *George Selwyn*, 1882, ii. 120–1.

29. 'While he was at a distance, his singular eloquence filled our minds with high ideas of the wild philosopher. When he

came into the walks of men, we know alas! how much these ideas suffered' (Boswell's *Account of Corsica*, 1768, p. 262; see also pp. 363–4).

30. 'Chronology and astronomy are forced to tinker up and reconcile, as well as they can, those uncertainties' (*Historic Doubts*, p. vi).

31. An allusion to the affair between the Duke and Lady Waldegrave, who had been secretly married in 1766. See *ante* i. 48.

32. HW seems to admit the marriage in his letter to Montagu 29 June 1770 (MONTAGU ii. 310).

33. *De origine, moribus, et rebus gestis Scotorum* . . . , Rome, 1578.

34. See *post* 25 Feb. 1768.

35. To Mme du Deffand (DU DEFFAND ii. 26–7).

Pembroke College, Feb. 25, 1768.

TO your friendly accusation, I am glad I can plead not guilty with a safe conscience. Dodsley told me in the spring that the plates from Mr Bentley's designs were worn out,[1] and he wanted to have them copied and reduced to a smaller scale for a new edition. I dissuaded him from so silly an expense, and desired he would put in no ornaments at all. The *Long Story* was to be totally omitted, as its only use (that of explaining the prints) was gone, but to supply the place of it in bulk, lest *my works* should be mistaken for the works of a flea or a pismire, I promised to send him an equal weight of poetry or prose; so, since my return hither, I put up about two ounces of stuff: viz. the *Fatal Sisters*, the *Descent of Odin* (of both which you have copies),[2] a bit of something from the Welsh,[3] and certain little notes, partly from justice (to acknowledge the debt, where I had borrowed anything), partly from ill temper, just to tell the gentle reader, that Edward I was not Oliver Cromwell, nor Queen Elizabeth the witch of Endor. This is literally all,[4] and with all this I shall be but a shrimp of an author. I gave leave also to print the same thing at Glasgow;[5] but I doubt my packet has miscarried,[6] for I hear nothing of its arrival as yet. To what you say to me so civilly, that I ought to write more, I reply in your own words (like the pamphleteer[7] who is going to confute you out of your own mouth): What has one to do, when *turned of fifty*, but really to

1. The *Designs* (*ante* 13 Feb. 1753) had been a great success, despite the fears of Dodsley and Gray. There were three editions dated 1753, and it was reprinted in 1765 and 1766; the same plates were used again in 1775 and 1789 (information from Mr A. T. Hazen).

2. See HW to Montagu 5 May 1761 (MONTAGU i. 364).

3. 'The Triumphs of Owen.'

4. See Gray to James Dodsley ca 1 Feb. 1768, *Gray's Corr.* iii. 999–1000.

5. 'Mr Beattie, Professor of Philosophy in the University of Aberdeen, first proposed this undertaking. When he found that it was most agreeable to the printers [Robert and Andrew Foulis], he procured Mr Gray's consent, and transcribed the whole with accuracy' (from the 'Advertisement' to *Poems by Mr Gray*, Glasgow, 1768). The Glasgow edition (64 pp.) is a large quarto, the London edition (122 pp.) a small octavo.

6. Gray sent the poems with footnotes and printers' instructions with his letter to Beattie of 1 Feb. 1768. Beattie received the packet 9 Feb., and acknowledged it 16 Feb., from Aberdeen. See *Gray's Corr.* iii. 1001–3, 1010–12.

7. The Rev. Frederick William Guydickens (Guidickins) (d. 1779), of the Middle Temple (GM 1779, xlix. 519; MONTAGU ii. 254). He published 10 March *An Answer to Mr Horace Walpole's late Work, entitled, Historic Doubts on the Reign and Life of King Richard the Third; or, An Attempt to confute him from his own Arguments. By F.W.G. of the Middle Temple.* See *Daily Adv.* 10, 11 March; *Public Advertiser* 12 March 1768. It was announced as 'In the press, and speedily will be published' in the *Daily Advertiser* 17 Feb. 1768.

think of finishing? However, I will be candid (for you seem to be so with me), and avow to you that till fourscore and ten, whenever the humour takes me, I will write, because I like it, and because I like myself better when I do so. If I do not write much, it is because I cannot. As you have not this last plea, I see no reason why you should not continue as long as it is agreeable to yourself, and to all such as have any curiosity or judgment in the subjects you choose to treat. By the way let me tell you (while it is fresh) that Lord Sandwich, who was lately dining at Cambridge, speaking (as I am told) handsomely of your book, said it was pity you did not know that his cousin Manchester[8] had a genealogy of the kings,[9] which came down no lower than to Richard III, and at the end of it were two portraits of Richard and his son,[10] in which that King appeared to be a handsome man. I tell you it as I heard it; perhaps you may think it worth inquiring into.

I have looked into Speed and Leslie. It appears very odd that Speed in the speech he makes for P. Warbeck,[11] addressed to James IV[12] of Scotland, should three times cite the *manuscript proclamation* of Perkin, then in the hands of Sir Robert Cotton;[13] and yet when he gives us the proclamation afterwards (on occasion of the insurrection in Cornwall) he does not cite any such manuscript. In Casley's *Catalogue of the Cotton Library*[14] you may see whether this manuscript proclamation still exists or not;[15] if it does, it may be found at the Museum.[16] Leslie will give you no satisfaction at all: though no subject of England, he could not write freely on this matter, as the title of Mary,[17] his

8. George Montagu (1737–88), 4th D. of Manchester. Lord Sandwich and he were fifth cousins (MONTAGU ii. 351).

9. See *post* 26 Feb. 1768.

10. Edward (1473–84), Prince of Wales (GEC, *sub* Cornwall).

11. *History of Great Britaine*, 1611, p. 741, dealing with Perkin Warbeck's claims to the throne. It is based on Polydore Vergil (pp. 596–7 in the Basel, 1570, edition of *Urbinatis Anglicæ historiæ*), Leslie (*De origine, moribus, et rebus gestis Scotorum*, Rome, 1578, pp. 333–4), and Perkin's MS proclamation (n. 13 below).

12. 1473–1513.

13. Sir Robert Bruce Cotton (1571–1631), Bt 1611, antiquary. He furnished Speed with materials for the *History of Great Britaine*, the proof-sheets of which he revised in 1609 (DNB). Cotton's owner-

ship of the original MS of the proclamation is stated in Speed's marginal note on p. 741 of his *History:* 'MS Perkini proclam. penes D.R.C. Baronet.'

14. For the full title see *ante* 2 Sept. 1760, n. 64.

15. Gray is alluding to the 'Appendix to the Catalogue of the Cottonian Library: showing what books were burnt or damaged by the fire that happened therein 23 Oct. 1731, and what were saved' (Casley, op. cit. 313). The MS is not mentioned by Casley, however; nor is it listed in Thomas Smith's *Catalogus librorum manuscriptorum Bibliothecæ Cottonianæ*, Oxford, 1696.

16. See *ante* i. 24 n. 155.

17. Mary Stuart (1542–87), Queen of Scots.

mistress, to the crown of England was derived from that of Henry VII.[18] Accordingly, he everywhere treats Perkin as an impostor,[19] yet drops several little expressions inconsistent with that supposition. He has preserved no proclamation; he only puts a short speech into Perkin's mouth,[20] the substance of which is taken by Speed, and translated in the end of his, which is a good deal longer; the whole matter is treated by Leslie very concisely and superficially. I can easily transcribe it, if you please; but I do not see that it could answer any purpose.

Mr Boswell's book I was going to recommend to you, when I received your letter; it has pleased and moved me strangely, all (I mean) that relates to Paoli. He is a man born two thousand years after his time! The pamphlet proves what I have always maintained, that any fool may write a most valuable book by chance, if he will only tell us what he heard and saw with veracity. Of Mr Boswell's truth I have not the least suspicion, because I am sure he could invent nothing of this kind. The true title of this part of his work is, 'A Dialogue between a Green-goose and a Hero.'

I had been told of a manuscript in Benet Library: the inscription of it is *Itinerarium Fratris Simonis Simeonis et Hugonis Illuminatoris, 1322*.[21] Would not one think this should promise something? They were two Franciscan friars that came from Ireland,[22] and passed through Wales to London, to Canterbury, to Dover, and so to France in their way to Jerusalem. All that relates to our own country has been

18. Leslie, Mary's apologist, wrote (among other tracts treating of the succession of women) *De titulo et jure Serenissimæ Principis Mariæ Scotorum Reginæ, quo regni Angliæ successionem sibi iuste vendicat libellus*, Rheims, 1580 (reprinted by S. Jebb in *De vita et rebus gestis Serenissimæ Principis Mariæ Scotorum Reginæ*, 1725, i. 37–116).

19. Under 1498 Leslie says that James IV, in order to keep faith with England, summoned 'Richard' (the name Perkin assumed) to him and charged that he, 'Ducem Eboracensem ementito titulo appellans, belli inter illum et Anglum auctor fuerat. Ponit quoque illi ante oculos amicitiam qua eum comprehendit; beneficia quibus ornavit; honorem quo prosecutus est' (*De origine*, p. 336).

20. See ibid. 334.

21. MS Corpus Christi Coll. Camb. 407, ff. 1–33. James Nasmith, who edited the MS in 1778, describes it in his *Catalogus librorum manuscriptorum quos Collegio Corporis Christi . . . in Academia Cantabrigiensi legavit . . . Matthæus Parker*, Cambridge, 1777, pp. 384–5.

22. Nothing is known of Symon Semeonis and Hugo Illuminator beyond what the *Itinerarium* contains. They were Franciscans of the monastery of Clane, co. Kildare (Mario Esposito, 'The Pilgrimage of an Irish Franciscan,' *Hermathena*, 1911, xvi. 266) or of the monastery of Clonmel, co. Tipperary ('Itinerarium Symonis Semeonis et Hugonis illuminatoris,' ed. P. Girolamo Golubovich, *Biblioteca bio-bibliografica della Terra Santa e dell' Oriente Francescano*, vol. iii, Florence, 1919, p. 246, n. 2).

transcribed for me, and (sorry am I to say) signifies not a halfpenny: only this little bit might be inserted in your next edition of the Painters:[23] 'Ad aliud caput civitatis (Londoniæ) est monasterium nigrorum monachorum nomine Westmonasterium, in quo constanter et communiter omnes reges Angliæ sepeliuntur—et eidem monasterio quasi immediate conjungitur illud famosissimum palatium regis, in quo est illa vulgata camera, in cujus parietibus sunt omnes historiæ bellicæ totius Bibliæ ineffabiliter depictæ, atque in Gallico completissime et perfectissime conscriptæ, in non modica intuentium admiratione et maxima regali magnificentia.'[24]

I have had certain observations on your *Royal and Noble Authors* given me to send you perhaps about three years ago; last week I found them in a drawer, and (my conscience being troubled) now enclose them to you.[25] I have even forgot whose they are.

I have been also told of a passage in Philip de Comines,[26] which (if you know) ought not to have been passed over. The book is not at hand at present, and I must conclude my letter. I am ever

Yours,

T. GRAY

To GRAY, Friday 26 February 1768

Reprinted from *Works* v. 376–8.
The date of the year is determined by the references to *ante* 25 Feb. 1768 and HW to Dalrymple 2 Feb. 1768.

Arlington Street, Friday night, February 26 [1768].

I PLAGUE you to death, but I must reply a few more words. I shall be very glad to see in print, and to have those that are worthy see your ancient odes; but I was in hopes there were some pieces too that I had not seen. I am sorry there are not.

I troubled you about Perkin's proclamation, because Mr Hume lays great stress upon it, and insists, that if Perkin affirmed his brother was

---

23. Which was published in 1782 (COLE ii. 319). The passage was not inserted.

24. The passage is taken from the second paragraph of the *Itinerarium*. Gray's 'Londoniæ' is his own gloss, and there is an omission of about four lines after 'sepeliuntur' (see Golubovich, op. cit. 247–8).

25. The enclosure has not been preserved.

26. (1445–1509). The passage relates to Richard III (see *post* 6 March 1768).

killed,[1] it must have been true, if he was true Duke of York. Mr Hume would have persuaded me that the proclamation is in Stowe,[2] but I can find no such thing there; nor, what is more, in Casley's *Catalogue,* which I have twice looked over carefully. I wrote to Sir David Dalrymple[3] in Scotland, to inquire after it, because I would produce it if I could, though it should make against me: but he, I believe, thinking I inquired with the contrary view, replied very drily, that it was published at York, and was not to be found in Scotland. Whether he is displeased that I have plucked a hair from the tresses of their great historian; or whether, as I suspect, he is offended for King William;[4] this reply was all the notice he took of my letter and book. I only smiled, as I must do when I find one party is angry with me on King William's, and the other on Lord Clarendon's account.[5]

The answer advertised is Guthrie's,[6] who is furious that I have taken no notice of *his History*.[7] I shall take as little of his pamphlet; but his end will be answered, if he sells that and one or two copies of his *History*. Mr Hume, I am told, has drawn up an answer too, which I shall see,[8] and, if I can, will get him to publish;[9] for, if I should ever choose to say anything more on this subject, I had rather reply to him[10] than to hackney-writers:—to the latter, indeed, I never will reply. A few notes I have to add that will be very material; and I wish to get some account of a book that was once sold at Osborn's,[11] that exists perhaps at Cambridge, and of which I found a memorandum t'other day in my note-book. It is called *A Paradox, or Apology for Richard III* by Sir

1. Not in the proclamation, but in his speech to James IV of Scotland (*ante* 25 Feb. 1768). For Perkin on Edward's murder see Polydore Vergil, *Urbinatis Anglicæ historiæ*, Basel, 1570, p. 596; Francis Bacon, *Historie of the Raigne of King Henry the Seventh*, 1622, p. 149.

2. Stow in his *Annales of England*, 1592, discusses Perkin pp. 793–802. Of the proclamation he merely says (under 1497) that after the invasion of Cornwall and landing at Whitesand Bay 7 Sept. 1497 'Perken made Proclamations in name of king Richarde the fourth, as sonne to king Edwarde the fourth' (p. 800).

3. See HW to Dalrymple 2 Feb. and Dalrymple to HW 9 Feb. 1768.

4. *Ante* 14 Feb. 1768, n. 4.

5. Ibid. n. 39.

6. Not Guthrie's but Guydickens's (see *ante* 25 Feb. 1768, n. 7).

7. *A General History of England*, 3 vols fol., 1744–51. See George L. Lam, 'Note on Guthrie's "History of England," ' N&Q 1942, clxxxiii. 71–2.

8. See *post* 8 March 1768, and *ante* i. 44–5. The notes are also discussed in HW to Cole 16 April 1768 (COLE i. 133–4).

9. Hume sent his notes in 1769 to Gibbon (then living at Buriton, Hants), who incorporated them in his review of *Historic Doubts*, published in 1769 in *Mémoires littéraires de la Grande Bretagne pour l'an 1768*, pp. 1–35. See *ante* i. 44.

10. HW did so in *Supplement to the Historic Doubts*. See *ante* i. 45.

11. Thomas Osborne (d. 1767), bookseller in Gray's Inn.

William Cornwallis.[12] If you could discover it, I should be much obliged to you.

Lord Sandwich, with whom I have not exchanged a syllable since the general warrants,[13] very obligingly sent me an account of the roll at Kimbolton;[14] and has since, at my desire, borrowed it for me and sent it to town. It is as long as my Lord Lyttelton's *History;*[15] but by what I can read of it (for it is both ill written and much decayed), it is not a roll of kings, but of all that have been possessed of, or been earls of Warwick:[16] or have not—for one of the first earls is Æneas.[17] How, or wherefore, I do not know, but amongst the first is Richard III in whose reign it was finished, and with whom it concludes. He is there again with his wife[18] and son,[19] and Edward IV and Clarence and his wife,[20] and Edward their son[21] (who unluckily is a little old man), and Margaret Countess of Salisbury, their daughter[22]—But why do I say with these? There is everybody else too—and what is most meritorious, the habits of all the times are admirably well observed from the most savage ages. Each figure is tricked with a pen, well drawn, but neither coloured nor shaded. Richard is straight, but thinner than my print;[23] his hair short, and exactly curled in the same manner; not so handsome

12. See *post* 6 March 1768. The author was Sir William Cornwallis (ca 1579–1614), Kt, 1599; M. P. Orford, 1604, 1614; essayist. He is confused by the DNB with his uncle, Sir William Cornwallis. See P. B. Whitt, 'New Light on Sir William Cornwallis, the Essayist,' *Review of English Studies*, 1932, viii. 155–69.

13. See *ante* ?18 March 1764, n. 10, and 25 Jan. 1766, n. 1.

14. Kimbolton Castle, Hunts, seat of the Duke of Manchester.

15. The title-page is commensurate with the bulk of the volumes. Lord Lyttelton published 7 July 1767 vols i–ii (553 and 578 pp. respectively, in quarto) of *The History of the Life of King Henry the Second, and of the Age in which he lived, in Five Books: To which is prefixed a History of the Revolutions of England from the Death of Edward the Confessor to the Birth of Henry the Second*. The concluding volume of the *History* (books iv–v) was published in 1771. See *Daily Adv.* 7, 10 July 1767.

16. The second Earl of Manchester had married the daughter of Robert Rich, 2d E. of Warwick.

17. 'The roll is on parchment, and is seven yards and a half long; perfectly preserved within, but by handling damaged on the outside, on which have been painted many coats of arms. The list begins with Guthalmus, and contains the effigies of several imaginary saints and heroes, many kings of England, and the portrait of Richard III, with whom it concludes, twice' ('Supplement to the *Historic Doubts,*' *Works* ii. 216).

18. Anne (1456–85), dau. of Richard Nevill, E. of Warwick; m. (1) (1470) Edward, P. of Wales (son of Henry VI); m. (2) (1472) Richard, D. of Gloucester (Richard III).

19. Edward, Prince of Wales.

20. Lady Isabel Nevill (1451–76), sister of Queen Anne (n. 18 above), m. (1469) George, D. of Clarence.

21. (1475–99), 18th E. of Warwick.

22. Lady Margaret (Plantagenet) (1473–1541), m. (ca 1491) Sir Richard Pole; she was cr. (1513) Cts of Salisbury.

23. In *Historic Doubts*, facing p. 103.

as mine, but what one might really believe intended for the same countenance, as drawn by a different painter, especially when so small; for
the figures in general are not so long as one's finger. His Queen is ugly,
and with just such a square forehead as in my print, but I cannot say
like it. Nor, indeed, where forty-five figures out of fifty (I have not
counted the number) must have been imaginary, can one lay great
stress on the five. I shall, however, have these figures copied, especially
as I know of no other image of the son. Mr Astle[24] is to come to me tomorrow morning to explain the writing.

I wish you had told me in what age your Franciscan friars lived;[25]
and what the passage in Comines[26] is. I am very ready to make *amende
honorable*.

Thank you for the notes on the *Noble Authors*. They shall be inserted when I make a new edition, for the sake of the trouble the person has taken, though they are of little consequence. Dodsley has asked
me for a new edition;[27] but I have little heart to undertake such work,
no more than to mend my old linen. It is pity one cannot be born an
ancient, and have commentators to do such jobs for one! Adieu!

Yours ever,

Hor. Walpole

Saturday morning.

On reading over your letter again this morning, I do find the age in
which the friars lived—I read and write in such a hurry, that I think I
neither know what I read or say.

From Gray, Sunday 6 March 1768

Reprinted from *Works* v. 379–80.

Pembroke Hall, March 6, 1768.

HERE is Sir William Cornwallis, entitled *Essayes of Certaine
Paradoxes*. Second edition, 1617, London.

24. Thomas Astle (1735–1803), antiquary
and paleographer (see Cole).
25. See postscript below.
26. See *post* 6 March 1768.
27. HW finally published it in 1787 'Enlarged with many new articles, with several
passages restored from the original MS,
and with many other additions,' printed at
SH by Thomas Kirgate. Its pagination, pp.
[245]–564, is that of *Works*, where it was
printed with a new title-page. See Hazen,
SH Bibliography 36, 91. The notes mentioned by HW have not been identified.

King Richard III
The French pockes
Nothing   } praised.[1]
Good to be in debt
Sadnesse
Julian the Apostate's vertues

The title-page will probably suffice you; but if you would know any more of him, he has read nothing but the common chronicles, and those without attention: for example, speaking of Anne the Queen, he says she was *barren,*[2] of which Richard had often complained to Rotheram.[3] He extenuates the murder of Henry VI and his son:[4] the first, he says, might be a malicious accusation, for that many did suppose he died of mere melancholy and grief; the latter cannot be proved to be the action of Richard (though executed in his presence); and if it were, he did it out of love to his brother Edward. He justifies the death of the lords[5] at Pomfret, from reasons of state, for his own preservation, the safety of the commonwealth, and the ancient nobility. The execution of Hastings[6] he excuses from necessity, from the dishonesty and sensuality of the man; what was his crime with respect to Richard, he does not say. Dr Shaw's[7] sermon was not by the King's command, but to be imputed to the preacher's own ambition; but if it was by order, *to charge his mother with adultery was a matter of no such great moment, since it is no wonder in that sex.*[8] Of the murder in the Tower he doubts, but, if it were by his order, the offence was to God, not to his people; and *how could he demonstrate his love more amply, than to venture his soul for their quiet?*[9] Have you enough,

1. The six essays (in the 1st edn, 1616: printed in small quarto, in two parts, without pagination) are entitled: 1. The Praise of King Richard the Third. 2. The Praise of the French Pockes. 3. The Praise of Nothing. 4. That it is good to be in Debt. 5. The Praise of Sadnesse. 6. The Praise of the Emperour Julian the Apostata: His Princely vertues, and finall Apostacie.

2. 'The Praise of King Richard the Third,' Cornwallis, op. cit. C_2 verso.

3. Thomas Rotherham (1423–1500), Abp of York 1480–1500.

4. Cornwallis, op. cit. A_3 verso.

5. Anthony Wydville or Woodville (born 1442), 2d E. Rivers, and Sir Richard Grey, K.B., 1475, Elizabeth Woodville's son by her first marriage, were beheaded at Pomfret 25 June 1483. See ibid. A_4.

6. Sir William Hastings (?1431–83), Kt 1461, cr. (1462) Bn Hastings; beheaded 13 June 1483. See ibid. B_1 recto and verso.

7. Ralph Shaw (d. 1484), S.T.B., who preached a sermon 22 June 1483 at St Paul's Cross impugning the validity of Edward IV's marriage to Elizabeth Woodville (James Gairdner, *History of the Life and Reign of Richard III,* Cambridge, 1898, pp. 79–82).

8. Ibid. B_2.

9. Ibid. B_4 recto and verso.

pray? You see it is an idle declamation, the exercise of a schoolboy that
is to be bred a statesman.

I have looked in Stowe: to be sure there is no proclamation there.[10]
Mr Hume, I suppose, means *Speed,* where it is given,[11] how truly I
know not; but that he had seen the original is sure,[12] and seems to
quote the very words of it in the beginning of that speech[13] which Perkin makes to James IV and also just afterwards, where he treats of the
Cornish rebellion.[14]

Guthrie, you see, has vented himself in the *Critical Review.*[15] His
History I never saw, nor is it here, nor do I know any one that ever saw
it. He is a rascal,[16] but rascals may chance to meet with curious records,
and that commission to Sir J. Tyrrell[17] (if it be not a lie) is such; so is
the order for Henry VI's funeral.[18] I would by no means take notice of
him, write what he would. I am glad you have seen the Manchester
Roll.

It is not I that talk of Philip de Comines; it was mentioned to me as

10. See *ante* 26 Feb. 1768, n. 2.

11. Speed in his *History,* 1611, pp. 741–2,
gives only an extract from the middle of
the proclamation. See *ante* 18 Feb. 1768,
notes 12–13.

12. See *ante* 25 Feb. 1768, n. 13.

13. See ibid. n. 11.

14. 7 Sept. 1497 (*ante* 26 Feb. 1768, n. 2;
Speed, op. cit. 741). Gray refers to Speed's
extract from the proclamation (n. 11
above).

15. For Feb. 1768, xxv. 116–26.

16. HW had been at odds with him since
the controversy about Conway's dismissal
(*ante* 17 Aug. 1764).

17. Sir James Tyrell (d. 1502), Kt, 1471,
whom HW considered too eminent to have
been commissioned to murder the Princes.
Guthrie (alluding to *Historic Doubts* 55–8)
says, 'Had Mr Walpole condescended to
consult records, he might have spoken of
Tyrrel with much more precision, and in
a manner which we think renders it highly
probable that he was the murderer of the
young king. Tyrrel was little better than a
common executioner, under the denomination of one of the commissioners for exercising the office of High Constable of England. His commission for this infernal
office is dated November 4, 1482; and his
business is described in that commission.

. . .' Guthrie goes on to summarize the
letters patent 14 Nov. 22 Edward IV (1482),
found in Rymer, *Fœdera* xii. 169, appointing Tyrell, etc. 'Commissarios nostros Gen-
erales in Officio Constabulariatus nostri
Angliæ.' This commission gives them 'auc-
toritatem et potestatem ad cognoscendum,
procedendum, et statuendum de et super
causis, querelis, negotiis, excessibus, crimi-
nibus,' etc. See also *Calendar of Patent
Rolls 1476–1485,* p. 317. For HW's criticism
of Guthrie on this point see 'Supplement to
the *Historic Doubts*' (*Works* ii. 187–91).

18. 'He has likewise forgot that by the
accounts, still extant in the Tower, of dis-
bursements for Henry's maintenance while
a prisoner, Sayer, his keeper, was paid for
his board down to the 12th of June; and
that the bill for his funeral expenses is
dated the 24th of the same month, on
which day he probably died' (Guthrie in
Critical Review xxv. 118). For the payments
to William Sayer and Robert Radclyf for
their own and their charge's expenses see
Rymer, *Fœdera* xi. 712, under 12 June 11
Edward IV (1471). See ibid. xi. 712–13 for
the bill of Henry VI's funeral expenses,
dated 24 June 11 Edward IV. This document from Rymer is quoted by Guthrie in
a footnote in the *Critical Review* xxv.
118–19.

a thing that looked like a voluntary omission; but I see you have taken notice of it in the note to page 71,[19] though rather too slightly. You have not observed that the same writer says, c. 55,[20] *Richard tua de sa main, ou fit tuer en sa presence, quelque lieu apart, ce bon homme le Roi Henry.*[21] Another oversight I think there is at p. 43, where you speak of the *roll of parliament*[22] and the contract with Lady Eleanor Boteler,[23] as things newly come to light; whereas Speed has given at large the same roll in his *History.*[24] Adieu! I am ever

Yours,

T. GRAY

To GRAY, Tuesday 8 March 1768

Printed from MS in the Pierpont Morgan Library, formerly in the Waller Collection. Sold at Sotheby's Dec. 1921 (lot 24) to Maggs; Maggs Cat. No. 421, April 1922 (lot 838).

Arlington Street, March 8, 1768.

I DON'T mean to trouble you with any farther searches; but I must thank you for your readiness to oblige me. I will try to return it by keeping the roll as long as I can, that you may see it, if you look Londonwards;[1] it is really a great curiosity, and will furnish one with remarks. Not that I am going to answer such trumpery as Guthrie's, who does not seem to disagree with me (though I scarce can discover the scope of his jumbled arguments) but is angry I did not declare I agreed with him, though I vow I never saw his book. It shall rest in peace for

19. Of *Historic Doubts.* 'I must however, impartially observe that Philip de Comines says, Richard having murdered his nephews, degraded their two sisters in full parliament. . . . For my own part I know not how to believe that Richard would have passed that act, if he had murdered the two princes.' HW's copy of *The Memoirs of Philip de Comines,* translated by Thomas Uvedale, 1712, was sold SH iii. 95.

20. This numbering of chapters is characteristic of the early sixteenth-century editions of Philippe de Comines' *Cronique et hystoire* (1st edn, 1524); the division into books and chapters began with the first edition of the *Mémoires,* Paris, 1552. Twelve French editions of the *Cronique* were published between 1524 and 1551 (*Bibliotheca*

Belgica, 1880–90, ser. I, vol. v, *sub* Comines).

21. In the Paris, 1546, edition, the passage is on f. 68 recto, in 'Chapitre LV.'

22. Cited *ante* 14 Feb. 1768, n. 23.

23. Lady Eleanor Talbot (d. ca 1468), dau. of John Talbot, 1st E. of Shrewsbury; m. Sir Thomas Boteler, son of Sir Ralph Boteler (*ante* 3 March 1754, notes 43, 81). See also COLE i. 304.

24. 1611 edn, pp. 711–13.

1. Gray 'came to London' 7 April where he stayed until 30 May (Gray's *Naturalist's Journal; Gray's Corr.* iii. 1033). He was 'at Twickenham' 16–17 April (Gray's *Naturalist's Journal*), and with Mason visited HW at SH on the 17th (COLE i. 134).

me, as all such writers ever shall. The few criticisms I have suffered have done more than my own arguments could: they have strengthened my opinion, seeing how little can be advanced to overturn it. Mr Hume has shown me an answer he has drawn up. It is nothing but his former arguments enlarged: no one new fact or new light. I am trying to persuade him to publish it, that I may have occasion to add a short appendix,[2] with some striking particulars; not, to dispute more with him. I propose too to give eight or nine figures[3] from Rous's roll.[4] In the Coronation roll,[5] is this entry, which you and I overlooked: *Things ordered in haste by my Lord Duke of Buckingham.* Then immediately follow the robes for Edward V[6]—proof I think of the design that he should walk.

I shall correct a mistake I find (by Guthrie) I made, about the Duke of Albany.[7] For the confession of the Lady Butler, I take it to be an absolute lie.[8] The commission of Sir James Tirrel I have not had time to search for in Rymer,[9] where I suppose it is, if anywhere. But you did not observe that it is dated in November 1482. Consequently under Edward *IV* and if true, contradicts Sir T. More, who says Tirrel was kept down.[10] If the date should be 83; it was subsequent by two or three

2. See *ante* 26 Feb. 1768, n. 10.

3. See the two folding plates, each with five figures, in 'Historic Doubts,' *Works* ii, between pp. 166 and 167.

4. John Rous (ca 1411–91), antiquary. In the 'Supplement to the *Historic Doubts'* where a description of the roll is given, HW quotes the inscription on the reverse, 'This roll was labur'd and finish'd by master John Rows of Warwick' (*Works* ii. 216).

5. Of Richard III: see *Historic Doubts* 65–7. 'This precious monument . . . exists in the Great Wardrobe. . . . It is the account of Peter Courteys, Keeper of the Great Wardrobe, and dates from the day of King Edward IV his death, to the Feast of the Purification in the February of the following year. Peter Courteys specifies what stuff he found in the Wardrobe, what contracts he made for the ensuing coronation, and the deliveries in consequence.' When challenged by Dr. Milles (see *post* 12 Sept. 1770), HW later agreed that the document in question was not the coronation roll but a Wardrobe account. See *Works* ii. 231*–2*.

6. See *Historic Doubts* 65–6. See also the coronation roll (Bodl. Ashm. MS 863, pp. 437–42), printed in L. G. W. Legg, *English*

Coronation Records, 1901, pp. 193–7, where the names of those who marched in the procession of 5 July 1483 are given. Contrary to HW's belief, it was Richard's son Edward who marched, not Edward V.

7 Alexander (ca 1454–ca 1485), cr. (?1456) D. of Albany; son of James II of Scotland. Guthrie *(Critical Review,* 1768, xxv. 126), alluding to *Historic Doubts* 109n, expresses surprise that HW should 'mention the Scotch Duke of Albany being with Richard at York, as a proof of Richard being on good terms with the Court of Scotland; when nothing is more certain than that the Duke of Albany lived then an exile, proscribed from his country, and that Richard had assisted him in his attempt to dethrone his elder brother James III.' For HW's correction of his mistake see 'Supplement to the *Historic Doubts'* (*Works* ii. 191).

8. 'Lady Eleanor Butler . . . acquitted the King of any promise, but not herself of frailty, in open court' (Guthrie, op. cit. 124).

9. See *ante* 6 March 1768, n. 17.

10. 'The man [Tyrell] had an high heart, and sore longed upwarde, not rising yet so

months to the time assigned for the murder. But enough of all this till I see you.

Have you read the two new volumes of Swift?[11] The second is the dullest heap of trumpery, flattery, and folly. The first is curious indeed! what a man! what childish, vulgar stuff! what gross language to his goddess![12] what a curious scene when the ministry thought themselves ruined![13] what cowardice in such a bully![14]—then his libels, and his exciting the ministers to punish libels in the same breath![15]—the next moment generous and benevolent. But his great offence with me, is preventing a poor fellow from being pardoned, who was accused of ravishing his own strumpet.[16]

I think you will like Sterne's sentimental travels,[17] which though often tiresome, are exceedingly good-natured and picturesque. Good night!

Yours ever

H. W.

PS. I this moment hear that the robbery and setting fire to Mr Con-

fast as he had hoped, being hindered and kept under by the meanes of Sir Richarde Ratclife and Sir William Catesby . . .' ('The History of King Richard the Thirde,' Workes of Sir Thomas More, 1557, p. 68).

11. Letters written by the late Jonathan Swift . . . , ed. Deane Swift of Goodrich, 1768, 2 vols, 4°, published 1 March (London Chronicle 25–27 Feb., 27 Feb.–1 March 1768, xxiii. 197, 207). This second series of Swift's letters was added to the quarto edition of the Works (1755–79) started by Hawkesworth (see H. Teerink, Bibliography of . . . Swift, The Hague, 1937, pp. 84 et seq.). HW's set was sold SH v. 22 and is now WSL.

12. 'Stella' or 'Mrs Johnson'; she was Esther Johnson (1681–1728), whom Swift supposedly married secretly in 1716 (for a summary of this controversial issue see Maxwell B. Gold, Swift's Marriage to Stella, Cambridge, 1937).

13. Letter XXXVI (to Stella), 1–15 Dec. 1711 (Swift's Letters, quarto edn, vol. iii, 1768, pp. 258–65).

14. 'I have desired him [Erasmus Lewis] to engage Lord Treasurer, that as soon as he finds the change is resolved on, he will send me abroad as Queen's secretary some-

where or other, where I may remain till the new ministers recall me; and then I will be sick for five or six months till the storm has spent itself. . . . I should hardly trust myself to the mercy of my enemies while their anger is fresh' (9 Dec. 1711: ibid. 263).

15. 'The pamphleteers begin to be very busy against the ministry: I have begged Mr Secretary [Henry St John] to make examples of one or two of them; and he assures me he will. They are very bold and abusive' (21 Sept. 1711: ibid. 215).

16. 'I was this forenoon with Mr Secretary at his office, and helped to hinder a man of his pardon, who is condemned for a rape. The under-secretary was willing to save him, upon an old notion that a woman cannot be ravished: but I told the secretary, he could not pardon him without a favourable report from the judge; besides, he was a fiddler, and consequently a rogue, and deserved hanging for something else; and so he shall swing. . . . 'Tis true, the fellow had lain with her a hundred times before; but what care I for that?' (25 July 1711: ibid. 187).

17. Laurence Sterne's Sentimental Journey was published 27 Feb. (Public Advertiser 12 Feb., 27 Feb. 1768).

way's house[18] was committed by a servant[19] belonging to the Duke of
Richmond. I know no more yet. They had a great escape of their lives,
though the loss and damage is considerable; and they have been most
unhappy, as they have none but old and faithful servants, and could
not be persuaded any of them were guilty.

From Gray, ca April 1769

Printed from MS in Waller Collection.

Dated by the allusion to Palgrave, who, as it appears from Gray to Brown 17
April 1769,[1] was in London at this time. Gray 'went to London' 6 April, and returned 'to Cambridge by Hadham' 14 May (Gray's *Naturalist's Journal*).

Address: To the Honourable Horace Walpole.

Friday [ca April 1769], Jermyn Street.[2]

M R GRAY (upon the information of Mr Palgrave)[3] lets Mr Walpole know, that there is at *Luton*[4] a chapel built in Henry VII's
time, by a Lord Hoo and Hastings,[5] and lined throughout with most
beautiful Gothic woodwork;[6] this is going to be demolished,[7] and, he
imagines, Mr Walpole may have its inside for a song.

18. 'Yesterday morning [Wednesday, 2 March] between five and six o'clock a fire was discovered in the library of the Right Hon. Henry Seymour Conway, at his house in Warwick Street, near Charing Cross, which consumed a great number of books and writings, and greatly damaged the apartment. It is supposed to have been burning some hours before found out' (*Daily Adv.* 3 March 1768).

19. James Sampson, who was executed 11 May 1768 (DU DEFFAND ii. 40, n. 1). The *London Chronicle* 8–10 March 1768 (*sub* 10 March, xxiii. 238) says that he 'was recommended to the General' by the Duke of Richmond, 'and had a place given him in the Tower of £100 a year. It seems he had married a servant of Lady Aylesbury's, the General's lady, and therefore was frequently at the house; but the night of the robbery he concealed himself in the house, and so made his way out, that it was not known of his having been there.'

1. Conjecturally dated 'c. April 20, 1769' in *Gray's Corr.* iii. 1058. Shortly before his death Mr Whibley found the original MS of the letter to Brown with the postmark 17 AP.

2. Except for occasional sojourns in Southampton Row (*ante* ca 28 Oct. 1760), Gray's London address from 1753 to 1770 was 'Mr [William] Roberts, hosier and hatter, at the Three Squirrels in Jermyn Street' (*Gray's Corr.* i. 375–6, iii. 1093, 1186, n. 1). Roberts in 1783 was at the same address (information from Sir Ambrose Heal).

3. William Palgrave (ca 1735–99), Fellow of Pembroke College, Cambridge, 1764–99; Gray's friend and correspondent (*Gray's Corr.* ii. 576, n. 1).

4. Luton Hoo, Beds, seat of the Earl of Bute, who bought it in 1763 with the manor of Luton (*Vict. Co. Hist., Beds* ii. 353–5).

5. Sir Thomas Hoo (d. 1455), K.G., 1445, cr. (1448) Bn Hoo and Hastings. He lived in the time of Henry VI, not Henry VII.

6. For description and engravings, see Henry Shaw, *History and Antiquities of the Chapel at Luton Park*, 1830. According to Shaw, the embellishments of the chapel, which were installed in the late seventeenth century by Sir Robert Napier of Luton, were probably taken 'from some part of Luton church.' He dates them 1475–1546 (pp. 13–14).

7. 'I hear it [the chapel of Luton] is to

From Gray, Friday 26 May 1769

Printed from MS in Waller Collection.
Address: To the Honourable Horace Walpole in Arlington Street, London.
Postmark: 27 MA.

Pembroke Hall, 26 May 1769.

OLD Cole lives at *Water-Beach*[1] near the road from Cambridge to Ely; but I believe you had best send the book[2] to me, and I will take care it shall be delivered to him.[3] I have not seen it yet, but propose to buy it[4] on your recommendation; if it has a hundredth part of Linnæus's[5] merit, it must be divine! What the title means, I do not conceive.

To Gray, ca August 1770

Missing. Implied in *post* 12 Sept. 1770.

From Gray, Wednesday 12 September 1770

Printed from MS in Waller Collection.
Address: To the Honourable Horace Walpole in Arlington Street, London.
Postmark: ROYSTON 13 SE.

be preserved; and am glad of it, though I might have been the better for its ruins' (HW to Lord Strafford 3 July 1769). Shortly before 1830 a new chapel was erected at Luton Park by the Marquess of Bute, and the original embellishments transferred to it (Shaw, op. cit. 1).

----

1. Five miles NE of Cambridge. Cole lived there from 1767 to 1770.
2. *A Biographical History of England, from Egbert the Great to the Revolution: consisting of Characters disposed in different Classes, and adapted to a Methodical Catalogue of Engraved British Heads,* by James Granger (1723–76), vicar of Shiplake, Oxon, 4 vols quarto, published 26 May (*Daily Adv.* 26 May 1769). It was dedicated to HW.
3. In his diary for 5 June 1769 Cole wrote, 'Mr Gray of Pembroke and Mr Tyson of Benet came by eleven o'clock and stayed till past seven. Mr Gray brought me

the two sets of Mr Granger's books: one which I had bought and lent him, the other with blank leaves which Mr Walpole made me a present of' (Add. MS 5835, f. 207 verso). See also COLE i. 157–9.
4. It is not in the MS catalogue of Gray's library.
5. Carl von Linné (1707–78). Gray in 1759 bought the 10th edition of *Caroli Linnæi . . . Systema naturæ,* 2 vols 8vo, Stockholm, 1758–9 (Gray first quotes it in his letter of 18 Sept. 1759 to Wharton). He had his copy (now at Harvard) interleaved, and his profuse annotations and drawings tend to confirm Mason's assertion that 'the favourite study of Mr Gray, for the last ten years of his life, was natural history' (Mason, *Mem. Gray* 341). See also chapter vii ('The Disciple of Linnæus') in W. Powell Jones, *Thomas Gray, Scholar,* Cambridge, Mass., 1937, pp. 125–41; C. E. Norton, *The Poet Gray as a Naturalist,* Boston, 1903.

Pembroke Hall, 12 Sept. 1770.

I AM ashamed to excuse myself to you, though it was not negligence, but forgetfulness. The other day going into the Public Library[1] I first recollected your commission,[2] and consulted the chronicle of Croyland. The only edition I find of it[3] has certainly these words—sed quo genere *violenti* interitus, ignoratur.[4] Either you have made use of some edition where that essential word is omitted, or cited after *Buck*[5] without suspecting his fidelity. I am ever

Yours,

THO. GRAY

To GRAY, September 1770

Missing. Probably written at SH. Mentioned *post* 17 Sept. 1770.

From GRAY, Monday 17 September 1770

Printed from MS in Waller Collection.
Address: To the Honourable Horace Walpole in Arlington Street, London.
Postmark: ROYSTON 18 SE.

Sept. 17, 1770, Pembroke College.

I WRITE, having nothing essential to say, merely because you are ill,[1] and have but too much time to read me. I plead no merit in my sympathy, because I have the same enemy, and am daily expecting

1. The University Library at Cambridge.
2. To verify a passage (*Works* ii. 228*) in the 'Reply to the Observations of the Rev. Dr Milles' (*Works* ii. 221*–44*). See *ante* i. 46. Milles accused HW of misquoting the 'Croyland Chronicle' in *Historic Doubts* 69–70n. See n. 5 below.
3. William Fulman's (*ante* 14 Feb. 1768, n. 5) was the only available edition at this time. See preface to H. T. Riley's translation of *Ingulph's Chronicle of the Abbey of Croyland*, 1893.
4. Fulman, op. cit. 568: 'Vulgatum est, dictos Regis Edwardi pueros, quo genere violenti interitus ignoratur, decessisse in fata.'
5. Sir George Buck (Buc) (d. 1623). Gray guessed correctly; HW cited Buck's *History of the Life and Reigne of Richard the*

Third, 1647, p. 84, for this passage (HW's copy was sold SH i. 150). Buck's paraphrase omits 'violenti,' and his marginal 'Prior Croyland' gave HW the impression that Buck was citing not the author of the third continuation of the 'Croyland Chronicle' but the Prior of Croyland, another authority (see *Historic Doubts* 69–70n. In his 'Reply' (*Works* ii. 228*) HW said: 'Whether Mr Buck omitted the word "violent" by design or not, it is impossible for me to ascertain. For myself, I probably copied him, and was not so careful as I ought to have been in collating the passage with the original. I will, however, take any shame to myself for the omission.'

1. HW complained to Mann 20 Sept. 1770: 'I am laid at length upon my couch

her attacks,[2] the more violent perhaps for having been now for some years suspended. Talk not of round windows, nor of dying in them; our distemper (remember) is the means of health and *long life;* now this latter is only the name of another distemper, of which I know enough already to say, when the gout pinches me, *'tis well it is nothing worse.* I do not understand why (with your temperance) you are treated so severely; but suspect it is owing to a little indolence and want of motion between the fits, as I have lately heard you complain of a tenderness in your feet that would not let you walk as usual. Man is a creature made to be jumbled, and no matter whether he goes on his head or heels, move or be moved he must. I am convinced I owe my late and present ease to the little expeditions I always make in summer. The smartness of the pain you undergo is an undoubted sign of strength and *youth,* and the sooner it will be over. I know this is poor comfort, but I flatter myself that in some few days you will be at ease, and will have the good nature to tell me so.

I have neither seen Tyson nor Cole of late, but will take care they shall know what you say. The latter lives at Milton[3] near the Ely road. For myself I shall hardly be in town before the end of November.[4] Adieu! I am

Yours ever,

T. G.

From Gray, Sunday 17 March 1771

Fragment. Printed by Mason as a footnote to Gray to Beattie 2 July 1770. Reprinted from Mason, *Mem. Gray* 385.

[Cambridge,] March 17, 1771.

HE must have a very good stomach that can digest the *Crambe recocta*[1] of Voltaire.[2] Atheism is a vile dish, though all the cooks

. . . having had the gout above these three weeks in my hand, knee, and both feet, and am still lifted in and out of bed by two servants.' HW was put to bed 8 Sept. and had not been 'out of it since but three times to have it made' (HW to Lady Ossory 15 Sept. 1770; see also DU DEFFAND ii. 460).

2. Under 3 Oct. Gray entered in his *Naturalist's Journal,* 'From about this time to 19 Oct. I was confined by a fit of the gout.' See also Gray to Mason 24 Oct. 1770, *Gray's Corr.* iii. 1149.

3. Cole moved to Milton early in 1770 (COLE i. 142, n. 42).

4. Gray 'went to London' 30 Dec., and 'stayed a fortnight' (Gray's *Naturalist's Journal* under 30 Dec. 1770, 12 Jan. 1771). He 'returned to Cambridge' 14 Jan. (ibid. under 14 Jan.).

1. Warmed-over cabbage; adapted from *Juvenal* vii. 154.

2. Gray had apparently read the first few volumes of Voltaire's *Questions sur l'En-*

of France combine to make new sauces to it. As to the soul,[3] perhaps they may have none on the Continent, but I do think we have such things in England. Shakespear, for example, I believe had several to his own share. As to the Jews (though they do not eat pork) I like them because they are better Christians than Voltaire.[4]

From GRAY, ca Saturday 23 March 1771

Missing. Written at Cambridge. Mentioned in the postscript to *post* 25 March 1771.

To GRAY, Monday 25 March 1771

Printed from MS now WSL. In 1828 it was bequeathed by Mrs Damer to Sir Wathen Waller, 1st Bt; sold at Sotheby's 5 Dec. 1921, lot 25, to Maggs; offered by Maggs, Cat. No. 425 (Summer, 1922), lot 1838; No. 449 (1924), lot 443. Purchased by B. J. Beyer; Beyer to H. V. Poor; Mrs Poor to WSL, 29 Oct. 1935.
Address: To Mr Gray at Pembroke College, Cambridge.

Arlington Street, March 25, 1771.

I AM very much pleased with the head of Richardson,[1] and very angry with Bannerman,[2] who shall do nothing for me, since he will not do anything for me. I only suspend the bull of excommunication, till I am sure I shall not want him. If the young man copies mezzotinto, as well as he does etching, which is not probable, I shall beg you to seize the prints in Bannerman's hands, if it is not inconsistent with the charters of the City of Cambridge, and deliver them to Mr Tyson's en-

---

cyclopédie par des amateurs, 9 vols 8vo, [Geneva], 1770–2 (another nine-volume set with a London imprint appeared 1771–2). Voltaire's new publication reprinted a number of articles not only from the *Dictionnaire philosophique* and *La Raison par alphabet,* but also from his miscellaneous writings.

3. See the article 'Âme' in seven sections (*Questions* i. 171–203).

4. Gray alludes to the 'Critical Remarks on some Passages of Voltaire,' appearing in the GM, between Sept. 1770 and Nov. 1773, which systematically examined the treat-

ment of the Jews and the Old Testament in the *Dictionnaire philosophique.*

---

1. An engraving of Jonathan Richardson (1665–1745) by Charles Bretherton (d. 1783) (COLE i. 313, n. 17) faces p. 15 in vol. iv of the *Anecdotes of Painting.* The fourth volume of the *Anecdotes,* although already in the press at SH, was not published until 1780 (Hazen, *SH Bibliography* 63).

2. Alexander Bannerman (fl. 1762–72), engraver, who had engraved 32 plates in vols i–iii of the *Anecdotes,* was re-engaged by HW 'for some of the heads' in vol. iv (COLE i. 198).

graver.³ But as you talked of being in town in March, I hope to settle this with you by a verbal negotiation.

I have had my house in town broken open,⁴ and everything broken open in my house, and I have not lost to the value of sixpence. The story is so long, that if I began to tell it you, you would be here before it was finished, though you should not arrive till Christmas. It is talked of more than my Lord Mayor,⁵ and my Lord Mayor knows as much what to make of it, as anybody does. If you know any saint that dragged a beautiful young woman into a wood to ravish her, and after throwing her on her back and spreading open her legs, walked quietly away without touching her, to show his continence, you have a faint idea of my house-breakers. Some people have confounded me with my cousin⁶ just arrived from France, and imagine they sought for French papers;⁷ others say I am Junius⁸—but Lord help me! I am no such great man, nor keep treason in my glass-case of china.⁹ My miniatures, thank you, are very safe, and so is Queen Elizabeth's old face,¹⁰ and all my coins and medals,¹¹ though the doors of the cabinets were broken to pieces. You never saw such a scene of havoc as my first floor was, and yet five pounds will repair all the damage. I have a suspicion about the

3. Probably Bretherton's father, James Bretherton (d. 1806), who engraved four plates for *Anecdotes*, vol. iv (facing pp. 27, 48, 91, 107). See COLE i. 313, n. 17.

4. The night of Sunday 17 March (see HW to Mann 22 March 1771).

5. Brass Crosby (ca 1725–93), Lord Mayor of London 1770–1, was summoned on 19 March before the House of Commons for refusing to honour a proclamation apprehending John Wheble and Richard Thompson, the printers of the *Middlesex Journal* and the *Gazetteer*, for printing illegally the current debates of the House. The conflict (issuing from the controversy over the legality of general warrants: see *ante* 25 Jan. 1766, n. 1) ended 27 March with Crosby's imprisonment in the Tower. See HW to Mann 22, 30 March 1771; *Mem. Geo. III* iv. 188–96, 198–203; GM 1771, xli. 139–41; *London Chronicle* 12 through 28 March 1771, xxix. 250–302.

6. Hon. Robert Walpole (1736–1810), secretary to the English embassy at Paris (DU DEFFAND ii. 133, n. 5).

7. See Mme du Deffand to HW ca 2 April 1771 (DU DEFFAND iii. 55).

8. For the Junius controversy see *The Letters of Junius*, ed. Charles W. Everett, 1927; William J. Smith in *Grenville Papers*, 1852–3, iii. pp. xiii–ccxxviii; DNB *sub* Sir Philip Francis; *Cambridge Bibliography of English Literature*, ed. F. W. Bateson, New York, 1941, ii. 630–2. For an attempt to identify Junius with HW see a letter from Charles E. Grey to John Wright in *Letters of Horace Walpole*, ed. Wright, 1840, vi. pp. xxi–xxviii.

9. In Paris it was thought that Choiseul's enemies were looking for a secret correspondence between him and HW (DU DEFFAND iii. 52, n. 1; 55).

10. Probably a unique 'fragment of a gold coin of Elizabeth's, very extraordinary portrait' (SH x. 8), which HW bought at Lord Oxford's sale in 1742 ('Des. of SH,' *Works* ii. 450; HW to Mann 22 March 1742 O.S.).

11. The 'cabinet of modern medals,' containing 'a series of English coins, with downright John Trot guineas, half-guineas, shillings, sixpences, and every kind of current money' (HW to Mann 22 March 1771).

person,[12] whom we are watching, but not the least guess at his self-denial. He burst a great hole in the door of the area; and must have had an iron crow to force open the chest, for the brass flapper is bent and shivered into seven pieces, but contented himself with tumbling the prints and tapestry chairs. Silver candlesticks, linen, spoons, nothing struck his fancy; yet he was in no hurry, for he ransacked the offices, and every room of the first floor, and nobody knows when he came in or went out, though he seems to have taken no precaution not to be heard. There were only the two maids in town, who were waked by a passenger that found the street door open between five and six in the morning. In short, this is the first virtuoso that ever visited a collection by main force in the middle of the night. Adieu!

Yours ever

H. Walpole

Monday night.

PS. I had sealed my letter, but am forced to open it again and put it in a cover,[12a] for I have this minute received yours and Thornhill.[13] The likeness is well preserved and I shall not quarrel with the price, but it is too black, and the wig very hard—however as Worlidge's[14] style is fashionable, two or three more by the same hand may not displease, therefore pray trouble yourself to give the young man two more,[15] but none to Bannerman. Tell me how I shall send the money[16] I owe you, besides a thousand thanks.[17]

12. Not identified.

12a. The cover is missing, but the seal is still on the outside of the one sheet which contains both letter and postscript.

13. Sir James Thornhill (1675–1734), Kt, 1720, painter. His portrait, engraved by Charles Bretherton, faces p. 20 in vol. iv of the *Anecdotes of Painting*.

14. Thomas Worlidge (1700–66), painter and etcher. For his self-portrait, engraved by Chambars, and his biography by HW, see *Anecdotes* iv. 66–7.

15. In addition to the engravings of Richardson and Thornhill, Charles Bretherton did also a half length of James Anthony Arlaud (*Anecdotes*, vol. iv, plate facing p. 38).

16. HW later made a note that he owed, or had paid, Gray three guineas 'for heads' (du Deffand iii. 75).

17. Shortly before setting out for Paris on 7 July 1771 (du Deffand v. 333) HW saw Gray for the last time (Cole i. 228). Gray died 30 July at Pembroke of 'gout in his stomach,' as his contemporaries believed. 'Sir Humphry Rolleston, after considering the evidence afforded by the letters as to Gray's illness, concludes that he suffered from chronic kidney disease, which terminated in uræmia' (*Gray's Corr.* iii. 1272, n. 2). HW did not hear of his death until 11 Aug. (du Deffand v. 338, Cole loc. cit.). For HW's shocked reception of the news see his letters to Conway 11 Aug., to Cole 12 Aug., and to Chute 13 Aug. (postscript to his letter of 5 Aug. 1771).

APPENDICES

APPENDICES

APPENDIX 1: THE NICOLL AFFAIR

WALPOLE'S NARRATIVE

Printed from MS now WSL, who also owns a draft dated 7 August 1751, both in HW's hand. There is another copy, in a clerk's hand, in the possession of C. L. Chute, Esq., of the Vyne, Hants.

A Narrative
of the Proceedings on the intended Marriage between Lord Orford and Miss Nicholl:[1] in a Letter addressed to Mrs Harris, my Lord's Grandmother.

Madam,

AS I informed you upon talking over the situation of Lord Orford's affairs, that if you approved it, I believed it would be in my power to bring about a great and very advantageous match for him, which, with great tenderness for him, you seemed extremely to approve: As I had very nearly accomplished so desirable a business; and as it has failed by the means of persons almost as much concerned as myself to promote it; I think it absolutely incumbent upon me to explain to you, Madam, the whole detail of this affair, and to prove to you, that though I have been maliciously, and to serve other purposes, accused of not wishing well to this marriage, the very accusers of me have been the persons who for their own views have defeated this design. Their accusation of me I despise and forgive; the injury they have done Lord Orford is unpardonable.

You will excuse me, Madam, if in unravelling this mystery of double-dealing, I am forced to run into a long detail of many circumstances, which no ways concern you, but are essential to the opening and explaining the whole scheme and management of the illustrious personages concerned in this notable drama.

1. Margaret Nicoll (ca 1735–1768), dau. and heiress of John Nicoll (d. 1747) of Colney Hatch and of Minchenden House, Southgate, Middlesex; m. (1753) James Brydges (1731–89), styled M. of Carnarvon 1731–71, 3d D. of Chandos 1771 (GEC; G. F. Beltz, *Review of the Chandos Peerage Case,* 1834, pedigree I; GM 1747, xvii. 592).

On the late Mr Whithed's death,[2] who was in treaty of marriage with Miss Nicholl, an immense fortune, Mr John Chute, as near a relation to the young lady as any she has,[3] told me, that from the regard he had for me and my family, and from the good opinion he had of my nephew Lord Orford, he should be most happy, if now he had lost his own near relation and friend Mr Whithed, he could bring about a marriage between Lord Orford and Miss Nicholl, who was continually sending him complaints of the inhuman treatment she underwent from Mr and Mrs Okeover,[4] her guardians and uncle and aunt, the latter of whom was her next heir, and who though allowed by Chancery a thousand pounds a year for her maintenance (pray, Madam, observe this article, as you will hereafter perceive how many iniquities this bait has incited) yet in three years and an half had given her but fourteen guineas and many blows, and had dealt out several of the latter on her not being able to recollect how she, a fortune of £150,-000,[5] had disposed of fourpence, a fraction of one of the aforesaid fourteen guineas. It was impossible for me not to feel all the friendship and advantage of this offer. I acquainted you, Madam, with it, I told Lord Orford of it, and from the fullness of my heart (a weakness which old age is incapable of, and incapable of resisting making advantage of) mentioned it to my Uncle Horace—an unlucky circumstance, as it gave time to muster and instruct a crew of dirty agents, attorneys and solicitors, and such like vermin,[6] who have incomparably executed the offices for which they were so ably and aptly chosen.

It is unnecessary to repeat with what difficulty, by means of a correspondence settled between Mr Chute's servant[7] and Miss Nicholl's woman,[8] a person whom my uncle's agents have amply rewarded for the share she had in serving Lord Orford's interest,[9] Miss Nicholl's es-

2. 30 March 1751 (*London Magazine* 1751, xx. 189; see also *ante* 8 Feb. 1747, n. 31).

3. An exaggeration. Mary Okeover (see below) was her aunt. Chute's mother's sister, Winifred Keck, married John Nicholl of Colney Hatch, Miss Nicholl's grandfather; thus Chute was her first cousin once removed (*Le Neve's Pedigrees of the Knights*, ed. G. W. Marshall, 1873, pp. 418–19; Daniel Lysons, *Environs of London*, 1795–6, ii. 23).

4. Leake Okeover (1701–63) of Okeover, Staffs, and his wife Mary (d. 1765), dau. of

John Nicoll, Miss Nicoll's grandfather (George Wrottesley, 'Account of the Family of Okeover of Okeover,' *Collections for a History of Staffordshire*, n.s. vii, 1904, pp. 111–14; Venn, *Alumni Cantab.*).

5. 'Above £150,000' (see *ante* i. 23–4); '£152,000' (HW to Mann 14 May 1777).

6. HW is referring especially to Francis Capper (*post* n. 18) and Thomas Nuthall (*post* n. 17).

7. Presumably 'Myrtila,' the Italian valet or footman mentioned *post* ii. 219 and 224.

8. Later identified as Mrs Gardiner.

9. Here the sarcasm, which HW uses

cape from her guardians was at last effected,[10] and she lodged a few miles out of town with Mrs Chute,[11] sister-in-law of Mr Chute, and widow of Mr Francis Chute,[12] a gentleman who suffered the greatest hardships and expenses from attachment to my father,[13] which have been acknowledged by my father's brother in the grateful manner you will hear hereafter. Mr J. Chute immediately went to my Lord Chancellor,[14] and acquainted him with Miss Nicholl's escape, and the reasons of it—a proceeding at least as honourable as any that will appear in the course of this narration, even of persons whose age, characters, professions or connections made it incumbent upon them to preserve an outside of dignity and integrity. My Lord Chancellor disapproved the concealment of the young lady, and advised her being restored to her guardians, till her cause could be heard. Mr Chute had no unworthy purposes to serve: He immediately went to Miss Nicholl, and notwithstanding the most violent exclamations and terrors on her part, persuaded her to return to, and actually conducted her back to Mr Okeover's.[15] I should tell you, Madam, that one great inducement to Mr Chute's attempting Miss Nicholl's delivery, was the solicitation of one Harrison,[16] a clergyman and her trustee, who had a living from Mr Chute's brother, and lived then in Mr Okeover's house. I should not introduce this worthy personage upon the stage, though such a harlequin in his character as to be fit for any theatre, if he had not been adopted by my uncle's lawyers, for no reason that I can conceive, but

throughout the narrative, is obvious; occasionally it is less so, even to the point of ambiguity.

10. On 4 May 1751 (post ii. 230).

11. Ann (living 1754: see HW to Chute 21 May 1754), widow of Francis Chute. She is described post ii. 229 as 'of Somerset House.'

12. Francis Chute (d. 1745), F.R.S., John Chute's elder brother; a barrister and King's Counsel (Record of the Royal Society, 1912, p. 341; C. W. Chute, History of the Vyne, 1888, pp. 96–7; London Magazine 1745, xiv. 205). He was presumably the 'Mr Chute,' a Middle Temple barrister, who wrote Beauty and Virtue. A Poem sacred to the Memory of Anne late Countess of Sunderland, 1716 (Giles Jacob, The Poetical Register, 1723, ii. 290; BM Cat.); it is probable too that he was the Francis Chute who wrote The Petticoat, 1716, published

by Curll as being by 'J. Gay' (Ralph Straus, The Unspeakable Curll, 1927, pp. 78, 133, 241–2).

13. In May 1741 Francis Chute was elected M.P. for Hedon, Yorks; but in March 1742 he was unseated on petition, a fate suffered as the result of his attachment to Sir Robert Walpole, whose downfall had occurred at the end of January (Journal of the House of Commons xxiv. 15, 110–11; Return of Members of Parliament, 1878, ii. 94; HW to Mann 5 Dec. 1746, O.S.).

14. Lord Hardwicke.

15. Presumably in London; the Okeovers did not live on the family estate in Staffordshire (Wrottesley, op. cit. 111).

16. The Rev. Mr Harrison, whom HW pillories in this narrative, was living in 1754, but has not been further identified (see HW to Chute 21 May 1754).

his having done all he could to defeat Lord Orford's marriage. This reverend match-broker, for so I must call him, from his having formerly proposed to have the young lady bought of Mr Okeover, had been engaged in the design of her marriage with Mr Whithed; though with so much holy subtlety, and chicane, that Mr Whithed had often been on the point of discarding him, but was restrained by the elder Mr Chute, who advised gentle management of the priest, and constantly when he spoke of him, said, 'One must sometimes hold a candle to the devil.' On Mr Whithed's death, the humane parson pressed Mr J. Chute to endeavour Miss Nicholl's rescue, telling him, he did not know what the Okeovers might not be capable of; and that he even thought her life in danger in their hands. An apprehension, which he conquered with the greatest firmness soon after; for on Mr Chute's acquainting him that Nuthall[17] the solicitor had brought him Capper[18] the conveyancer's opinion, that it would not be safe (as to the young lady's life) to petition my Lord Chancellor for her change of guardians, while she was in their hands, but that she must run away first; and that it would even be prudent not to communicate her intended flight to her trustees, that they might declare their ignorance of it, Harrison approved of the measure, provided she ran away to Mr Antony Chute of the Vine; but soon grew so cold upon it, that Miss Nicholl, sending new complaints of her ill usage, though under affliction for Mr Whithed, advertised Mr J. Chute, that the Doctor, who had trembled for her life, had now tried to persuade her to venture it for three months longer, by which time he told her he hoped to find her a proper husband; an office he was so good as to take upon himself, not to be sure with any lucrative view, but I suppose not thinking Lord Orford's rank or fortune proportionate to Miss Nicholl, with the design of which Mr J. Chute had trusted him, and was betrayed by him, as he has since been by two or three persons to whom the same confidence was

17. Thomas Nuthall (living 1775), solicitor to the East India Company, and solicitor to the Treasury 1765–75; appointed secretary of bankrupts, 1766 (GM 1765, xxxv. 348; 1766, xxxvi. 391; *Royal Kalendar,* 1775, p. 93).

18. Though Capper's grammar may have retained traces of rusticity (see *post* ii. 230), HW's picture of him as a low ignoramus is not borne out by the available facts. Francis Capper (1698–1764) of Bushey, Herts, was educated at Corpus Christi College and Trinity Hall, Cambridge; called to the bar at the Inner Temple, 1721; admitted to Lincoln's Inn, 1722, and called to the bench there, 1743; held various offices at Lincoln's Inn, becoming treasurer in 1753; Commissioner of Hackney Coaches 1722–58 (*Miscellanea Genealogica et Heraldica,* 4th ser., ii. 76; Venn, *Alumni Cantab.; Records of Lincoln's Inn: Admissions,* 1896, i. 389; ibid.: *Black Books,* 1897–1902, iii. 329, 353; Burke, *Landed Gentry,* 1879, i. 266).

made—not clergymen indeed! Mr Harrison even at the critical time went into the country, as he pretended to assist at Mr Thistlethwaite's election,[19] though he knew it was given up by Mr Stanley,[20] the other competitor by a public advertisement, and being urged with that knowledge, he replied with that doubt which so well becomes a searcher after truth, that all might not be true that was in the newspapers. Mr J. Chute who could not, like the parson, one day believe her life in danger, and the next not, facilitated Miss Nicholl's escape, as I have mentioned before.

On her return to her guardians, my Lord Chancellor appointed a hearing of the affair in a few days. It was necessary to have lawyers: Mr Chute and I were so happy as not to have great acquaintance in that profession. It was suggested too, that in case Miss Nicholl and her trustees could not presently agree upon a guardian, it would be necessary to find an intermediate person, with whom she might be placed, on her leaving Mrs Okeover. I had recourse to my uncle under these difficulties, depending upon the zeal he had expressed for Lord Orford's welfare, and thinking I should do him the greatest pleasure to give him an opportunity of finishing a life worn out in the service of his country, and so broken with age and infirmities that there was little prospect of his getting over another year,[21] in contributing to the re-establishment of his brother's family by so considerable an alliance. My uncle with very becoming earnestness, not only recommended but pressed upon me his own conveyancer and solicitor, whose abilities and integrity he magnified exceedingly. As they managed his money-matters, I thought I had grounds to believe them honest. As our affair lay in very little compass, and had nothing ill to be palliated or concealed, I did not think it much signified what genius they had. Their honesty will appear in the course of this narrative—for their abilities, the solicitor I believe has just such as are fit for such dirty business: for the conveyancer, I found him a fat-headed fellow,[22] exceedingly mean

19. Alexander Thistlethwayte (see *ante* 16 April 1751, n. 3) was elected M.P. for Southampton, *vice* Whithed, 8 May 1751 (Return of Members of Parliament, 1878, ii. 103).

20. Doubtless Hans Stanley (ca 1720–1780: see DU DEFFAND and MONTAGU), who was elected M.P. for Southampton borough in 1754.

21. Whether this is sarcasm or a disin-genuous attempt to make Horace Walpole, Sr, appear to be in his dotage, is not certain. It is contradicted by HW to Mann 22 April 1751, O.S., where HW describes his uncle as 'not merely well for his age, but plump, ruddy, and without a wrinkle or complaint' (see also William Coxe, *Memoirs of Horatio, Lord Walpole*, 1820, ii. 449–50). He lived until 1757.

22. Draft reads 'fat-headed dull fellow.'

and cringing in his appearance, and dull in his intellects, and as I have
since learnt of no esteem in his profession—in short such a man as I
should scarce have thought a proper instrument for a plot—but it
seems the bluntest tools may be used to do mischief with! My uncle
even told me that he did not doubt but such was Capper's attachment
to him that he could prevail on him to take Miss Nicholl under his care
for a week or even a fortnight—*but Lord! It would be purely to oblige
him, for Mr Capper was not a sort of man to disturb the repose of his
family for any lucrative views; nor one that for the world would take
such a charge upon himself for a longer season!* How Mr Capper came
to change his way of thinking so much as he has since done on this
head, or how my uncle came to know so little of his friend's disposition, or whether it was still to *oblige my uncle* that he submitted and
was willing to submit to this burthen much longer, I do not pretend to
determine.

Mr J. Chute then proposed his sister-in-law Mrs Chute for guardian.
My uncle, who had already removed the cause into his own court,[23]
would not hear of it. To humour an old man's frowardness, several
other persons were proposed; but not coming within the description
that he had laid down in his own mind, he rejected all but Mrs Fowle,[24]
his own niece, a very worthy lady and married to a man of great honour, as sufficiently appeared afterwards, by their refusing to accept the
trust the moment they knew it was not to serve Lord Orford.[25]

When the hearing came on before my Lord Chancellor, the Okeovers objected to Mrs Chute. How their objections came to be admitted, must be decided by the lawyers, after they had given up the
young lady without any terms but those of not hearing her complaints
read, which they could not stand. If any farther justification were
wanting to Mr Chute, it was Mr Okeover's running away for debt,[26]
the moment he could no longer apply Miss Nicholl's allowance to

23. Draft reads 'erected himself into di-
rector of the whole cause.'
24. Elizabeth Turner (d. 1763), dau. of
Sir Charles Turner and Mary Walpole
(HW's aunt), m. John Fowle (d. 1772) of
Broome, Norfolk, bencher of Gray's Inn
and auditor of excise 1750–72 (Thomas
Wotton, *English Baronetage*, 1741, iv. 217–
18; GM 1763, xxxiii. 97; Venn, *Alumni Can-
tab.*; Francis Blomefield and Charles
Parkin, *Topographical History of . . .
Norfolk*, 1805–10, x. 110.

25. Horace Walpole, Sr, and Capper say
that Fowle refused the guardianship because of Chute's conduct. See *post* ii. 223–4,
231.
26. See also HW to Mann 30 May 1751,
O.S., where HW says that Okeover had
'gone into the Fleet.' HW's charge is supported by Wrottesley's statement that Okeover 'greatly diminished the patrimony of
the family by his extravagance,' sold several of his estates, and shut up the house at
Okeover (Wrottesley, op. cit. 111).

satisfy his own creditors. At this juncture little Capper presented himself at my Lord Chancellor's footstool with as much abject servility as if he were the criminal, and offered to take care of the young lady till her relations could agree upon a guardian, which they were to name to my Lord Chancellor in a week or ten days after. But before the audience was dismissed, a new character stepped forth, whom it will be necessary to make known, though with not quite so many triumphal arches as he erected to his own nameless name on carrying a contested election.[27] His industry sunk beneath the conveyancer's sleight of hand: in an equal contention for a thousand pound a year, and with equal want of capacity, it was easy to foresee which would be victor, the lawyer or the senator. This hero was Mr Tracy,[28] Member of Parliament for Worcester, nephew to the Mr Chutes, and brother-in-law to the fair Mrs Tracy-Atkins.[29] He told Mr J. Chute that in case Mrs Chute were not accepted, he hoped his wife[30] might be the guardian. Indeed in that case Miss Nicholl had some chance of being well looked after, as Mrs Tracy herself was often out of her senses and forced to have a keeper. Mr Chute waived it in civil terms, having before agreed to Mrs Fowle, and told Mr Tracy that it did not depend upon him. Mr J. Chute then wrote to his brother to beg his recommendation for Mr Fowle. In the mean time Mr Tracy had wrote to beg it for himself, telling Mr Antony Chute a most exact truth (as appears from Mr J. Chute's answer) that his brother John approved of him—and obtained it. How assured Mr Tracy was of Mr J. Chute's approbation will appear farther, from his letting Mr J. Chute make him the confidence of the intended marriage after this, and never mentioning one word of his negotiations at the Vine. Mr J. Chute at the same time told Mr Tracy that my uncle had engaged to make him easy, which it seems he thought he had pretensions to do, from Mr Tracy's being a constant hanger-on of his, and a perpetual solicitor for his interest with the ministry. This confidence made upon honour, Mr Tracy, by a dispensation which he gave himself, inserted afterwards in an affidavit. Mr Antony Chute wished Mr Tracy could be prevailed upon to give up

27. See next note.
28. Robert Tracy (1706–67) of Stanway, Glos, son of Chute's half-brother John Tracy; M.P. Tewkesbury 1734–41, Worcester, 1747 (return amended Feb. 1748)–1754 (Return of Members of Parliament, 1878, ii. 75, 88, 105, 119; see also *ante* 12 Sept. 1756, n. 1).

29. Katherine Lindsey (d. 1788) m. (1735) John Tracy Atkyns (GM 1735, v. 619; 1788, lviii pt i. 368; DNB).

30. Anna Maria, dau. of Sir Roger Hudson (*Bristol and Glos Archæological Society*, 1905, xxviii. 298).

his recommendation, not knowing I suppose that a thousand pound a year might be the consequence of his adhering to it.

Mr J. Chute then sent his brother a letter from Miss Nicholl to beg his recommendation of Mr Fowle, which he not only granted, but sent a revocation of that for Mr Tracy, and commissioned his brother to claim this retractation, in case Mr Tracy should *sink* it.

During these transactions, I acquainted Lord Orford with the progress we had made in the affair, but was so unhappy as to find him very cold in it. Whether he was not tempted by the little-favourable picture of Miss Nicholl's person,[31] or whether he had heard the disagreeable reports of her temper, I know not. The former, I own, I flattered myself might improve; and for the latter, I though her too much a child to judge of it; and even suspected that it might have been propagated by her aunt's resentment. Whatever were the motives, Lord Orford was then so little earnest upon the match, that Mr Fowle declined accepting the trust; not carrying his views so far, as I have grounds to suspect my uncle did his; especially when he began to perceive that the young fortune might come by a rebound into his own family.

On Mr Fowle's refusal, Mr J. Chute sent his brother another letter from Miss Nicholl, to beg his recommendation of Mrs Chute. To this he returned an indefinite answer. Mr J. Chute wrote again himself: Mr A. Chute complied; but before the messenger could return, recalled his approbation, and only sent another vague answer. On these disappointments another guardian was looked out for. Nuthall proposed to Miss Nicholl one Mr Heckstetter,[32] an intimate of his own— so is Mrs Heckstetter,[33] if one could believe the scandalous chronicle of Capper's family; but as it is the last place I should resort to for anybody's character, I declare I am persuaded that Mrs Heckstetter is a lady of a very unblamable reputation. Mr Nuthall had so much influence with Miss Nicholl in this recommendation that he even drew her afterwards into swearing that Mr Heckstetter had been her own thought. Mr J. Chute to show his impartiality and compliance with whatever my uncle's creatures proposed, wrote then to his brother in favour of Mr Heckstetter, to which he not only received a peremptory refusal, but even a most severe answer, reproaching Mr J. Chute with

31. See *post* ii. 224.
32. David Heckstetter (d. 1757) of Southgate, a justice of the peace; presumably the son of Sir David Heckstetter (d. 1721), a Hamburg merchant (GM 1757, xxvii. 290; *London Magazine*, 1757, xxvi. 308; Sir William Musgrave, *Obituary*, 1899–1901).
33. Not further identified.

all the trouble he had given him in behalf of Miss Nicholl; and com-
mending Mr Tracy, Mr Atkins,[34] and the Proteus-Doctor, of whose
usage Mr J. Chute had very justly complained. It should be mentioned
that Mr Atkins had promised Mr J. Chute to justify all his proceedings, to his brother to whom he was going to make a visit, and that he
would acquaint Mr A. Chute with all Harrison's impertinence and
double-dealing. A promise which Mr Atkins fulfilled in the most honourable manner, by inflaming the breach between the two brothers to
the greatest height,[35] and by vindicating the parson, who I do not
doubt returned the favour by a plenary absolution. Lucky indeed was
this turn for the peace of the family; for in the warmth of Mr Atkins's
friendship for Mr J. Chute, he had assured him that he would prevail
on Mr A. Chute to take from Harrison a small living to which he had
preferred him, and might, it being a donative, resume: and so far did
this idea transport the house of Tracy, that looking on every emolu-
ment as lawful prey, Mr and Mrs Atkins were on the point of quar-
relling whether the donative, not yet vacant nor in their disposal,
should be given by Mr A. Chute to my Lord Tracy's[36] or to Mrs Travel's, Mr Tracy's sister's son.[37]

The affair being in this unsettled situation, my Lord Chancellor referred it to a Master in Chancery;[38] when Mr Tracy persisting in endeavouring to force Miss Nicholl into his power, absolutely against
her consent, her friends found it necessary to represent the impro-
priety of placing her with a gentleman who had so far damaged his

34. John Tracy Atkyns (d. 1773), brother
of Robert Tracy; barrister and Chancery
Court reporter (DNB).

35. HW's excessive concern to justify his
conduct in this affair proceeded at least in
part from a worthy motive: his friendship
for Chute. He felt that Chute's efforts to
promote the Orford-Nicoll match had resulted chiefly from Chute's attachment to
the Walpoles, and that therefore he was
himself indirectly responsible for a quarrel
which might have caused Chute to be dis-
inherited. How deeply HW's feelings were
involved is shown by his joy upon learning
that Anthony Chute had died intestate,
thus leaving Chute in possession of the
Vyne (HW to Chute 21 May 1754; see also
HW to Mann 30 May 1751, O.S.).

36. John Tracy (1722–93), son of Thomas
Charles Tracy (1690–1756), 5th Vct Tracy;

B.D. 1757; D.D. 1761; warden of All Souls,
Oxford 1766–93; succeeded his brother as
7th Vct, 1792; Robert Tracy's second cousin
(GEC; John Lodge, Peerage of Ireland, 1789,
v. 11–12).

37. Probably Francis Travell (ca 1728–
1801) of Swerford, Oxon, son of John Travell; Exeter Coll., Oxford, B.A. 1751. His
mother, who d. 1763, has not been further
identified; but the Tracy connection is established by a brother, Ferdinando Tracy
Travell (d. 1808), evidently named for Robert Tracy's grandfather (Foster, Alumni
Oxon.; C. W. Boase, Registrum Collegii
Exoniensis, Oxford, 1894, p. 145; Lodge,
loc. cit.; GM 1801, lxxi pt ii. 674).

38. Thomas Bennet (d. 1764) (post ii.
231; Court and City Register, 1751, p. 112;
London Magazine 1764, xxxiii. 382).

fortune as to be reduced to keep his parliamentary residence at a milliner's; and with his wife whose intellects were in as crazy a situation
as her husband's fortune. Affidavits were made of her frenzy: two in
particular from the report of her sister-in-law Mrs Atkins. The known
story of Mrs Tracy's inviting Mr Binks the Quaker[39] to bed to her and
her husband when he had risen one night in his shirt to assist at a fit
of Mr Tracy, was ready to be sworn, but was dropped, as it would have
been too decisive to determine from what particular furor this charity
proceeded. A physician swore Mrs Tracy had been ill, but not mad—
indeed he dated his affidavit before the time alleged. Mrs Atkins could
recollect nothing but that she might have talked of her sister's disorder. But as it was well observed by Miss Nicholl's counsel, Mr Tracy
himself was too conscientious to say one word against his wife's madness, which he would probably have done if he could have denied the
deposition of her having consulted a clergyman whether her husband
might not put her to death with her own consent. It seems the Master
had more regard to his silence than to his vapouring at the hearing, for
his report was not favourable to Mr Tracy; who was as unlucky at can-
vassing for recommendations, for as if a great fortune were a borough,
and to be carried by vote, he had solicited several people of quality for
their interest. One noble person to whom he had sent a panegyric on
himself, drawn as he said by a partial friend, and begging to have it
signed if the least resemblance could be discovered, returned it with
his name, but after having scratched out the words, *persons of good
understanding;* which indeed, putting Mrs Tracy's madness out of the
question, would have been very difficult for anybody to have vouched,
who had the honour of knowing Mr Tracy.—But I have done with this
cabal; and shall only observe that I don't doubt but the Master would
have thought it as proper to have placed the young lady with any man
who made a livelihood of letting out his wife to other men's pleasures.

  While Mr Tracy was thus open-mouthed in his pursuit, I could not
help observing that another set of people were as intent (darkly and
silently) upon securing the young lady for views of their own.[40] No attempts were made, but by me, towards an interview between her and
Lord Orford. On the contrary, she was continually carried out of town
and kept at Capper's in the country, where such instructions were
given her and such erudition put into her hands by that young but ex-

39. Not further identified.

40. Much of what follows was denied by

Horace Walpole, Sr, Miss Nicoll, Capper,
and Nuthall. See *post* ii. 218-31 *passim.*

perienced dame Miss Capper,[41] as made her and Lord Orford's friends apprehend that no matrimony would come up to the ideas that she had collected in her noviciate. As often as I proposed to my uncle to let Lord Orford see her, he put me off with the foolishest excuses—and yet I found this proceeded from no inattention or application to other business, for he began now to inform me that good Mr Capper was inclined to undergo the fatigue of the guardianship a little longer. I replied little to this benign offer—My uncle repeated it, and even pressed me to mention it to Mr Chute; and forgetting entirely or over-looking indecently all he had said to me of the difficulties Capper would make if desired to keep her, he continued soliciting me in the most troublesome manner day by day, by word of mouth and by letter to agree to her staying with Capper. I saw no reason for it: I even saw that she was kept out of Lord Orford's way. I had reason to apprehend a design to marry her to my uncle's son,[42] and I knew others had sur-mised and said the same. Instead of endeavouring to persuade Mr Chute to come into this foolish (or as I suspected treacherous) scheme, I warned him against it, acquainted him with my suspicions, and begged him to let Miss Nicholl know how very improper a match I feared was preparing for her. In the mean time knowing my uncle was to go out of town in a week, I pressed him to make a meeting for Lord Orford with Miss Nicholl at his house. He shuffled it off—I grew so warm, that at last he yielded—I begged Lord Orford might not know of the intended interview nor the young lady—Miss Capper, all whose precepts and discoveries are delivered under the nonsensical veil of fortune-telling, cast coffee grounds to let Miss Nicholl know whom she was to meet. They met.[43] At night I received a letter[44] from my uncle to tell me Lord Orford thought Miss Nicholl well enough in her per-son,[45] and referred to me whether it would not be advisable to let her stay where she was. I did not see how one was a consequence of the other; and refused my concurrence. My uncle wrote again[46] to me on the same subject with as little effect. This eagerness was suspicious:

41. Mary Capper (1738–86) m. (1761) the Rev. George Smallridge, rector of Bothal and Shipwash, Northumberland (*Miscellanea Genealogica et Heraldica*, 4th ser., ii. 79).

42. Richard Walpole (see *ante* 31 Dec. 1751, n. 5).

43. On June 20 at the Cockpit, old Horace's London house. HW was also there,

but apparently was not introduced to Miss Nicoll. See *post* ii. 210 and 223.

44. *Post* ii. 214–15.

45. Draft reads 'not so disagreeable as he expected.'

46. Presumably the letter of June 21, *post* ii. 216. Old Horace did not, however, renew his suggestion that Capper should be named guardian, as HW seems to imply.

might not he want to carry his point before he went out of town? I knew there was no probability of her being in any hands where Lord Orford might not see her with at least as much facility as he had hitherto done, especially while she had such a confidence in Mr Chute, that she had told him that the night of her escape she would have married whomever he had brought to her. This or any other declaration had no weight with him who wished to place her with nobody but a man of so many good qualities and such honour as Lord Orford. This connection did not suit the views of the cabal. As Mr Chute would not be the bubble to play her into their hands, they were determined to break off the intimacy by making a bubble of the young lady—and accordingly having patched up a treaty with Harrison, as if the conveyancer's disposition to mischief wanted the parson to say grace to his treachery, the lawyer and the doctor instilled such prejudices into Miss Nicholl, that when Mr Chute went to visit her the day after she had seen Lord Orford, he was extremely surprised not only to find the greatest coldness in her, but so total a silence that he could not extract the least answer from her, though he even went so far as to assure her that if it was her desire, he would do his utmost to promote her remaining with Capper. After an hour and half soliciting for an answer, she referred him for one to Capper. At last, after many offers of friendship on his part, which she only returned with some ambiguous tears, and straining for a few more, insomuch that Mrs Gardiner her woman, who was present all the time, said, *Madam, it looks as if you had a mind to make your eyes red that the family may ask if you have been crying,* Mr Chute left her.[47]

The next morning I received a note from my uncle to desire to see me. I went and found him with his eldest son.[48] He put on much passion—whether real or affected, I know not; either was indifferent to me, and equally ridiculous. He complained vehemently that Mr Chute had abused him to Miss Nicholl and terrified her: that Capper had wrote him word of it, and was determined immediately to get rid of her, that his family might be at peace—(This was the old foolish pretence![49])—that three or four of Capper's family had overheard Mr Chute's extravagant behaviour—(That they had listened I dare say was true[50]) Mrs Gardiner can tell how terrifying Mr Chute was!—that

47. For Miss Nicoll's account of this interview see *post* ii. 218–20.
48. Horatio, later 2d Bn Walpole.
49. Draft reads 'lie.'
50. Draft reads 'no lie.'

Mr Chute had even told her that my uncle would give Capper ten thousand pound for her—if Mr Chute said that he even suspected my uncle would be willing to give so much, I can't help thinking he was much mistaken: I don't know that my uncle ever took seven per cent for money—but I am very sure he never gave it.—He concluded this rhapsody with desiring I would send him his letters to have them copied, which he would return, and I might have copies of mine. I immediately pulled out all his letters that I had about me, which were all but one, and not enough respecting the awful tribunal I was before, threw them down in a passion, and said I scorned to make any use of his letters, and would never touch one of them again; and used some expressions of Capper, which I will not repeat, not from thinking on the coolest reflection that he did not deserve them, but choosing if he has a mind for a prosecution, that he should have them from the evidence of those who heard me, not under my hand. My uncle said it was very ill usage of his *friend*—whatever names I called Capper, I should not have used my uncle so ill as to call him *his friend*—and then told me he believed that *I had no mind myself to bring about the marriage.* This was such unjust and injurious provocation, that I started up and told him with great warmth that I would quit his house that instant, and never have anything to say to him more—and went out— He and his son followed me into the hall, and my cousin entreated me to return. I did, but on my uncle's sputtering out the same provocation (I wonder it made me angry instead of making me laugh) I left the house without making him any answer. He sent a note after me for his last letter—I sent it with the following lines:

Copy of a letter to my uncle Horace Walpole.[51]

Arlington Street, June 22, 1751.

Sir,

You need not give yourself the trouble to have the letters copied, or to send them back, for to me they are mere waste paper. Whether I am desirous Lord Orford should marry Miss Nicholl or not (though I pressed their meeting at your house which you would have declined, and you know you said it would be better to stay till she was settled somewhere) I do not think fit to justify to you; I shall to the world in

51. There is also a draft (now WSL) in HW's hand, and a copy (in the possession of F. L. Holland, Esq.) in the hand of Horace Walpole, Sr.

the most public manner. You told me we had quarrelled formerly and you believed it would come to that again—you know whether I ever sought a reconciliation, or whether it was possible for any man ever to show more indifference to another's friendship than I have always done for yours: after taxing me with not promoting Lord Orford's welfare by any means in my power, there are no terms on which I should not disdain your friendship.

I am Sir, for the last time of my life, your humble servant

HOR. WALPOLE

In a day or two after I sent the following letter to Capper:[52]

Arlington Street, June 24, 1751.

Sir,

As I have been taxed with not wishing any longer to promote the match between Lord Orford and Miss Nicholl, it becomes necessary for me to justify myself from that charge by removing every obstacle that has been thrown in the way. I have no way of bringing about this marriage but by Mr Chute, who has shown so much friendship to Lord Orford and me in this business, and on whose interest with the young lady I alone depended. She was at my desire placed with you, as a friend to my family: since she has been with you she has been prejudiced in the most unworthy manner against Mr Chute, without the least provocation from him, and you have even taken upon you to forbid his being admitted to her, though her nearest relation and greatest friend, while your scruples were so great that you could not refuse her seeing the parson, whom I should call by a very harsh term, if his profession, as well as that of the law, did not exempt him from any suspicion of dishonesty. A meeting was even negotiated for him with her this week on the very day she was to have breakfasted with Mr Chute, who though my friend was put off by a preference to the parson, who I am afraid you knew had done all he could to prevent her marrying Lord Orford; and whom you, Sir, with less reverence for the church than I have, had called by the most injurious appellations. I cannot doubt but on this representation you will immediately endeavour at renewing the friendship between Miss Nicholl and Mr Chute, lest you, instead

52. There is also a draft (now WSL) in HW's hand, and a copy (in the possession of Mr Holland) in a hand identified (*post* ii. 221 and n. 2) as Mrs Capper's.

of me, should stand in the predicament of hindering Lord Orford's marriage. At the same time I am persuaded you will acquaint him when the affair of her guardianship is to be determined, a transaction in which of late he has been kept wholly in the dark, not with any design to be sure on your part, but from a forgetfulness occasioned by the multiplicity of your business! I shall at the same time have the pleasure of congratulating you on being eased of so weighty a charge, and which you have been so wrongfully accused of wishing still to undergo, in order to promote a marriage with another relation of mine, more worthy I must confess than Lord Orford, but not just the one with whom I had wished to see her established. My uncle, by accusing me of not desiring the match with the latter, gives me full authority, if I had as little charity, to believe what has been suspected of his intention in favour of his own son.—But I do not entertain surmises so rashly. I am convinced that Mrs Walpole's[53] visit to Miss Nicholl immediately after her arrival at your house, was calculated purely to serve Lord Orford's interest, though they happened to forget ever to propose his being of the party. I am convinced that my uncle's declining to *negotiate* a meeting at his house between them, as often as I proposed it, and not consenting to it at last till I pushed it with too much peevishness, was entirely the result of his good wishes to Lord Orford. I am convinced that my uncle's desiring Lord Orford (as the latter has twice told me) to pretend to give in to the match, though he should not design it, in order to her being placed with Mr Fowle, was grounded on the same good intention, especially as my uncle said he might have opportunities of seeing her at Mr Fowle's in Norfolk—How likely he was to do that, or whether he or Mr Richard Walpole were most likely to see her there,[54] I leave to less partial judges than myself to determine. I am convinced, that my uncle who originally objected to Miss Nicholl's being with a Mrs Steele,[55] because she has a son of fifteen at school, forgot your son[56] by some years older, merely from zeal to serve Lord

53. Mary Magdalen (d. 1783), dau. of Peter Lombard of Burnham Thorpe; m. (1720) Horatio Walpole (GEC; William Coxe, *Memoirs of Horatio, Lord Walpole*, 1820, ii. 465). See HW to Mann 20 Sept. 1772.

54. Wolterton and Houghton, respectively the Norfolk seats of Horace Walpole, Sr, and Lord Orford, both lay at a considerable distance from Broome, John Fowle's seat in south Norfolk. Houghton, however, was probably closed, or at least was not often visited by Lord Orford (see HW to Mann 29 April 1745, O.S., and 16 July 1751, O.S.).

55. Not further identified

56. Richard Capper (1730–1800); educated at Eton; later of Lincoln's Inn (*Miscellanea Genealogica et Heraldica*, 4th ser., ii. 80).

Orford. Lastly, I am convinced that the agreeable picture which your daughter Sir, drew to Miss Nicholl of Mr Richard Walpole, particularly of how much taller he was than the rest of his brothers, was solely intended to give her a favourable idea of Lord Orford.—Indeed I don't know whether it would not be carrying my partiality too far, if I were to believe that the mysteries of divination into which Miss Nicholl has been initiated at your house, were all opened to her with a view to Lord Orford. Would not it look like too great prepossession in favour of Miss Capper, if I were to say, that when she and Miss Nicholl were crawling blindfold about the garret after ashes and water and a bough and goose giblets, the types of their future husbands,[57] that I think one of these emblems being christened by the name of a French periwig-maker, was an intended recommendation of my nephew? You and I, Sir, who know the world, can smile at these girlish devices, and at the bawdy books of fortune-telling with which Miss Nicholl has been furnished under the same matronlike government; but I much question whether my Lord Chancellor may not have narrower notions, and not hold this to have been the sort of education he intended for the young lady when he delivered her into your hands. Nor would his lordship I presume be better pleased if he should be made believe by false reports that there is a scheme for continuing her under your care in order to facilitate a very unsuitable match for her.

You see, Sir, that I at least have no suspicions of a plot for marrying her to my cousin rather than to my nephew: if Mr Chute had, perhaps ill-judging people might think that he, as a relation and one who by delivering her from the former tyranny, had some obligations to look after her being well and properly disposed of, ought to warn her against such designs—You, Sir, it seems thought otherwise, and placed two or three spies to overhear what cautions he might think it incumbent upon him to give her. My uncle says you have several witnesses who did overhear him expressing himself so warmly as to frighten the young lady. Who the witnesses were, or what part of your family, I know not; the world perhaps will think that *those who listen, will lie*. At this end of the town, we are more apt to be attentive to the point of honour, than to the prudence of getting evidence; and scorn to hearken at a door, though it might produce the strongest affidavits. Don't, Sir, think that by this I mean any reflections; I allow for the dif-

57. See *post* ii. 224.

ference of customs, and can conceive that this practice may be very reputable among the sober families about Chancery Lane. Whatever it was Mr Chute said, it seems my uncle highly resents it;—I am sorry for it! Mankind will think that less anger would look like less disappointment; and I would have everybody be just as clear as I am that he had no thoughts of the marriage for his son.

I have heard from an eminent lawyer, that a near relation of Lord Orford's,[58] whom I will not name, lest I be thought to insinuate more than I mean, has declared that Lord Orford has so great an aversion to Miss Nicholl, that if he were married to her and even in bed with her, he would not be able to ——[59] I will not say what, lest I shock the modesty of your fortune-telling family; who I suppose scarce proceeded to instruct her in the duties of a husband, with the same care that they prepared her for one.

As there are no farther thoughts of troubling you with the guardianship, I shall say no more on that head. That I could never have come into it,[60] after the town had got a notion of a project for my cousin, is certain; though my uncle was so good as to assure me, that I might very consistently with my honour—but such casuistry is too nice for my homely understanding.

I beg your pardon for giving you so long a trouble: I shall hear with pleasure that you have renewed the friendship between Mr Chute and Miss Nicholl, lest the world should think there were any sinister views in interrupting it; and that you are delivered from the fatigue of the guardianship. If you should not think proper to undeceive the young lady in her present wrong opinion of Mr Chute, it will be necessary for me to do, as he has been wounded by instruments of my family; and I choose to give you this notice that you may have proper persons to overhear what shall be said to her.

I am Sir with as much truth as
esteem your obliged and obedient servant

Hor. Walpole[61]

58. Presumably Horace, Sr; see next note. The 'eminent lawyer' must be Capper himself.

59. 'A hard suspicion upon his vigour! Has not it been found possible to consummate even with Mrs Walpole?' (HW).

60. I.e., could never have approved of Capper as guardian. See *post* ii. 215.

61. See old Horace's observations on this letter, *post* ii. 221–4.

To this I received no answer. I then sent the following letter to Miss Nicholl.[62]

June 28, 1751.

Madam,

It will undoubtedly at first sight appear impertinent in me who am an entire stranger to you, to take the liberty of sending you a letter; but when you have heard my reasons for it, I am persuaded you will not only excuse me, but be convinced I mean nothing but your service and credit; and that I do mean both, I appeal to any persons to whom you shall at any time give yourself the trouble of showing this letter: there is no secret in it, nothing that will not bear the light.

When Mr Chute, Madam, had effected your delivery from Mrs Oke-over (a service you have since much acknowledged, and which I am persuaded you have too much honour and gratitude ever to forget) and there was a difficulty to know where to place you till a guardian should be appointed, I recommended to Mr Chute one Capper a con-veyancer, a man whom indeed I did not know so well as I do since, but of whom I had heard an extraordinary good character from a relation of my own, whom I flattered myself I might depend upon—I beg your pardon, Madam, for trusting so lightly to others; and in this point must acknowledge Mr Chute and I were both very blamable. Since you have been at that man's house, the greatest mysteriousness has been practised in protracting and concealing the days on which there were to be any hearings of your cause; and after you had chosen Mr Heck-stetter, a gentleman found out for you by this cabal, direct and indirect applications were made to me to induce Mr Chute to approve your re-maining with Mr Capper, which looked but too much like their ap-prehending that Mr Heckstetter was a gentleman of too much honour to concur in any practices that were not for your service. As I had be-fore great suspicions, and so had several other persons, that there was a project for marrying you to a young man whose fortune is by no means suitable to yours, I could not in honour connive at what would have been so injurious to you: I acquainted Mr Chute with what others thought, and with my own suspicions; and it was at my desire, as a man of honour that he acquainted you with them. Indeed it was incumbent upon him to warn you against such practices, whether they were designed or not, if he had the least intimation of any such scheme.

62. There is also a draft (now wsl) in HW's hand, and a copy (in the possession of Mr Holland) in the hand identified as Mrs Capper's.

He did give you such warning, Madam—but what did his friendship do more? after having discharged his duty to you, he told you, as you know, that if you were inclined to stay with Mr Capper, he would do all in his power to promote it. How did Mr Capper return this? by representing Mr Chute to my uncle, as having grossly abused him, and terrified you; and by setting you against Mr Chute, and doing all in his power to break off the friendship between you and Mr Chute, and by ordering him not to be admitted to you; and by introducing the parson to you, who you know, Madam, did all he could to prevent your leaving Mrs Okeover, who has done all he could to deliver you into the hands of a madwoman and her husband of whom you have expressed your abhorrence, and who has underhand joined in the most scandalous manner with the vilest and most mischievous wretches, to prejudice Mr Chute's brother against him, whose friendship he has lost, Madam, as you know and have owned, merely in trying to serve you.

Upon this foot I last Monday wrote Capper a long letter with my opinion of his conduct. He has not been able to justify himself in any one point. Judge you, Madam, if a man and his family who deal in whispers and mischief, and cannot defend their conduct, are worthy your countenance. They are indeed, Madam, many ways unworthy of it. They are below you in birth, education, understanding, and conversation. You are born to live in another world, than with scriveners' wives[63] and daughters. You can learn nothing from them fit for you to know; you may receive much prejudice from them.

I am very far, Madam, from attributing to you any part of the injustice done to Mr Chute. Your youth and inexperience have been imposed upon, which I am ready to convince you of, whenever you will give me an opportunity. Be so good to compare our conduct with that of the family you live in: they backbiting and instilling falsehoods into you, and shunning explanation, which we desire and *will* come to, in the most public manner. I am so far from imitating them in doing anything underhand, that I beg Madam, you will communicate this letter to Capper; at the same time entreating you to do me the honour to preserve a copy of it, as you will at least, when you have more experience, discover how honourable our proceedings have been towards you.

In short, Madam, not to trouble you any longer, the drift of this

63. Mrs Capper was Mary (ca 1703–1763), dau. of Thomas Bennet, bookseller; m. Francis Capper in 1725 (*Miscellanea Genealogica et Heraldica*, 4th ser., ii. 75–6).

letter is to beg you would be so good as to hear me for a quarter of an hour with Mr Chute in his defence; and as we shall say nothing we cannot and will not stand by, we desire it may be in the presence of Mr Capper and his family, which will not only show you how fair our dealings are, but will save him the trouble and meanness of placing spies to overhear what is said to you. As I am determined for the justification of Mr Chute and myself that this whole affair shall be made as public as possible, we are desirous your name should appear in it with as much honour as possible: we have no doubt but it will be impossible for those people to prevail on you to say or deny anything but what is strictly fact, and we desire nothing of you but to say what is so.

> I am Madam
> your most obedient humble servant
>
> HOR. WALPOLE

PS. If Mr Capper should prevail on you to make no more answer to this letter than he was able to do to that I wrote to him, it will avail him very little, for both will be made very public.[63a]

To this neither did I receive any answer. Instead of being able or trying to vindicate his conduct, the muddy-headed conveyancer had recourse to those tricks, with which Alma Mater the law so plentifully furnishes her industrious votaries. Nor was the solicitor wanting to assist his worthy associate in carrying on the juggle. As Mr Chute was kept wholly in the dark as to all the proceedings on the cause, he every now and then sent to Nuthall to know when there would be any hearing. Twice, I am not sure if not thrice, he received letters from Nuthall acquainting him there would be a hearing such a day; these letters came on the very day of the hearing, but always antedated by three days; and the last time, so impudent or so bungling was this imp of the law, the wafer was wet.

In short, Madam, to wind up this iniquitous affair, after Miss Nicholl had been three months in Capper's hands, the cause was carried back to my Lord Chancellor, where without Mr Chute's knowing anything when it was to be heard and decided, it was determined that Miss Nicholl should be placed with Mr Heckstetter,[64] with a permission (a

---

63a. HW had intended to publish his narrative (HW to Mann 31 Aug. 1751).

64. The following clipping from the *London Gazetteer*, No. 800, ca 31 July 1751,

very unaccountable one) that she might go to Mr Capper's in the country whenever she pleased; and with as unaccountable (though very unnecessary) a prohibition of Mr Chute's seeing her but in presence of Mr Heckstetter or his wife. The codicil to this sentence was a dismission of Miss Nicholl's woman.

I do not doubt but my Lord Chancellor had had ample lies and grievances laid before him to occasion this resolution—but the more he was imposed upon (and imposed upon he certainly was, Mr Chute having nobody to speak for him, and the very lawyers employed by him, being the persons who betrayed him) the more incumbent is it upon these underlings to set forth, if they can, any justification or palliative of the lies they must necessarily have told to extort this sentence. How ready they are to asperse, will appear to you, Madam, when I tell you and am ready to prove, that these tools, selected by my uncle to carry on Lord Orford's interest, have done nothing but represent him to Miss Nicholl as a beggar and every way an unsuitable husband for her.

I beg your pardon, Madam, for the long trouble I have given you; it was necessary to show you how Lord Orford's service was defeated, and how I have been betrayed and falsely accused—an accusation[65] so absurd, that I wonder I have given myself so much trouble to expose and refute it. What indeed could be more ridiculous than to accuse me of not wishing well to the match for Lord Orford, only because I *did* promote it preferably to that with my cousin? or why, when only Mr Chute and I had projected and undertaken this affair, was the intervention of that

---

is preserved with HW's copy of his narrative:

'On Saturday last [27 July] was decided before the Lord High Chancellor a very remarkable contest, for the appointment of a new guardian to a young lady of the first fortune in this kingdom, in the room of her aunt, the testamentary guardian, and next taker in case of her death, under her father's will, from whom the young lady had some time ago been obliged to withdraw herself, on account of the very great severity and rigour she had been treated with. This affair has been three months in litigation in the Court of Chancery, owing to the obstinacy of this former guardian; who in conjunction with some of the young lady's relations, seemed bent on forcing her into hands equally improper in themselves,

and obnoxious to her; but the Court of Chancery, upon hearing the merits on both sides, and the arguments of the most eminent counsel of this kingdom, was pleased to confirm the young lady's own prudent choice of a new guardian, to the great comfort and joy of her mind, and the satisfaction of all who wish her future happiness and welfare.'

65. The original conclusion of the draft was as follows: '—— an aspersion I shall take due care to repel by making this narrative sufficiently public——I wish I may ever have it as much in my power to serve Lord Orford.

I am Madam etc.
HOR. WALPOLE
Aug. 7, 1751.'

booby Capper the one thing necessary to its accomplishment?—But I have done—Provocation I had had much and had given none; if I have now given any, as I hope I have, in the course of a justification that I owed to myself, they who chose to lay their own ill disposition to my charge, may thank themselves for it—I shall have no longer any concern but in having miscarried in my good intentions to Lord Orford.

I am Madam

your most obedient
humble servant

HOR. WALPOLE

SUPPLEMENTARY DOCUMENTS

The following documents, supplementing HW's narrative, are printed from photostats of copies in the possession of F. L. Holland, Esq.

HORACE WALPOLE, SR, TO HW

Copy in the hand of Horace Walpole, Sr.

June the 20, 1751.

Dear Sir,

MY Lord Orford told me after you left us, with respect to the young lady, that he thought her much better than he expected by the account he had had of her, that he did not by any means dislike her, but that in a matter of this nature and importance it was not proper without a more particular acquaintance to come to a final determination. He then asked under whose care she was to be placed. I told him I did not know, there was a great contest among the relations about that matter. His Lordship then said, why should she not continue with Capper. I replied I did not know whether it would be agreeable to the young lady or your friend Mr Chute, who had the greatest credit with her.

I thought proper to acquaint you with this discourse while it was fresh in my mind, for Mr Chute's and your consideration. For my own part I am of opinion that by time and management this so much to be desired alliance for many reasons may be brought about. Under whose care it may be proper to place the young lady I shall say nothing, because I never pleased your friend in that respect. But as he is zealously concerned for her welfare and for the match with Lord Orford, and has the greatest influence with Miss Nicoll, if she is placed where opportunities may offer for their being acquainted next winter, what we want and what we wish may be happily accomplished to the satisfaction of both parties, for I cannot forbear adding that Lord Orford let fall in the course of our conversation several observations to her advantage. I am with the greatest regard and affection,

> Dear Sir etc.
>
> H. WALPOLE

HW TO HORACE WALPOLE, SR

Copy in the hand of Horace Walpole, Sr.

[June 21, 1751.]

Dear Sir,

AFTER all I have done to promote it, there can be no doubt of my zeal for Lord Orford's marrying Miss Nicoll, but as Mr Tracy has been so impertinent as to accuse our whole family of a design to marry her to some one of the family, who is not a proper match for her, since we cannot persuade Lord Orford to take her, and said that was the inducement for keeping her at Mr Capper's, I can never give my consent to her staying there, nor can venture to propose it to Mr Chute, though I am persuaded his friendship for me would incline him to concur in it, if I asked it. But I must a little consider what the world will think of me, and as Lord Orford may still if he chooses it, have opportunities of seeing Miss Nicoll, when she is at Hecks[t]etter's, I must desire you would drop the scheme of her remaining at Mr Capper's, as I think it absolutely inconsistent with my honour to consent to it, and do insist upon its not being proposed.

> I am
>
> Dear Sir etc.
>
> HOR. WALPOLE

HORACE WALPOLE, SR, TO HW

Copy in the hand of Horace Walpole, Sr.

Cockpitt,[1] June 21, 1751.

Dear Sir,

I AM so far from having any scheme for Miss Nicol's continuing at Mr Capper's, that as he was with me this morning, I told him that having reason to think that those who had the greatest concern for the young lady and have the greatest credit with her had no inclination to it, I would not desire him to take that great charge upon himself, at which he was extremely pleased saying that nothing but a regard for our family would have induced him to be at all concerned at first, although he and his family are very well satisfied with the young lady's behaviour, yet it is a matter of too great a nicety and consequence for him to be trusted with, and therefore, dear Horace, your honour in this respect will be very safe, and thank God I shall have nothing more to say to it directly or indirectly. There seems something mysterious in this affair that I do not comprehend, nor am I at all curious to unriddle, it being no business of mine any otherwise than still to repeat that if you and Mr Chute continue to be of the same opinion and as zealous for Lord Orford's marrying Miss Nicol as you appeared at first, I think it may be happily effected, and I earnestly entreat you to put it [out] of your own and your friend's head as if I have ever had any scheme or view to have Mr Capper guardian to the young lady, and what has fallen from me was only as a common friend to promote that honourable design in which I thought we were all agreed and to which I still wish well. I am

Most affectionately yours

H. WALPOLE

FRANCIS CAPPER TO HORACE WALPOLE, SR

Copy in the hand of Horace Walpole, Sr.

Friday, 21 June 1751.

UPON my return to my chambers this day about two, I received an earnest message from my wife to desire to see me. Upon my coming home, she told me that Mr John Chute had been at my house

1. A portion of Lord Clarendon's premises, in Whitehall. Old Horace had obtained a 50-year lease of the house in 1727 (*Survey of London*, vol. xiv, 1931, p. 90).

this morning to see Miss Nichols, that he went upstairs to her, told her in a violent rage that I was to get her for your third son, that I had been carrying on a scheme for that purpose and that you would give him £10,000 to gain his consent. She, terrified, told him she had never heard it or could suspect it, but he said it was no wonder I did not speak, it would disappoint the scheme if I did, and declared he would be revenged, and uttered other falsehoods and absurdities. If he is not besides [sic] himself, his behaviour is of the blackest sort and prone for any mischief, for what could prompt him to utter such untruths, to abuse me so undeservedly? I am determined he shall not enter my house while Miss Nichols is in it, whom he has left in the utmost distress, and beg if you see Mr Nuthall, you would press him to expedite the appointment of the guardianship that I may live at ease in my own house. I am Sir with the greatest respect, etc.,

FRANCIS CAPPER

HORACE WALPOLE, SR, TO LORD ORFORD

Copy in the hand of Horace Walpole, Sr.

June 22, 1751.

My dear Lord,

NOT having time to pay my respects to your Lordship before I go into the country, which will be early tomorrow morning, I think myself obliged to trouble your Lordship with an account of a disagreeable affair that has happened between your Uncle Horace and myself occasioned by a most unaccountable behaviour of his friend Mr Chute.

After you left me last Thursday I wrote a letter to your uncle, of which the enclosed No. 1[1] is a copy, and I received from him the next morning an answer, of which the enclosed No. 2[2] is a copy, which I must own surprised me by supposing that I had a scheme for putting Miss Nicol under the care of Mr Capper, and insisting (as what would be derogatory to his honour) that such a proposal should not be made. Your Lordship will judge by my said letter No. 1 whether I gave any occasion for so much warmth and concern on that account.

No. 3[3] is a copy of my letter to your uncle in answer to his of No. 2.

1. Old Horace to HW 20 June 1751 (*ante* ii. 214–15).

2. HW to old Horace 21 June (*ante* ii. 215).

3. Old Horace to HW 21 June (*ante* ii. 216).

Yesterday in the evening I received a letter from Mr Capper of which No. 4[4] is a copy, which I own surprised and affected me extremely. I shall make no observations upon it, but such unprovoked, malicious, and groundless accusations of Mr Chute's with regard to my design with respect to Miss Nicoll made me desire a conference with your uncle Horace. We had very warm altercations about the behaviour of his friend Mr Chute as set forth in the contents of Mr Capper's letter to me, in which I having in the heat of discourse let fall, perhaps too hastily,[5] that I questioned your uncle's inclination at present for your marriage with Miss Nicoll, he called it an injurious reproach and in a passion left my house.

As I had kept no copies of the letters I had wrote to him and therefore desired to see the originals that I might take copies of them for fear of future mistakes or misrepresentations about them, he having one of the originals with him, he left it with me for that purpose. In sending me the other I received a very remarkable letter[6] from him of which the enclosed No. 5 is a copy, upon which I shall say nothing more than if the result of this dispute should end in our contesting who should endeavour to promote your Lordship's welfare most I should look upon it as not being a very unfortunate issue, and shall make myself as easy as I can under your uncle's displeasure.

MARGARET NICOLL'S STATEMENT

Written ca 23 June 1751. Copy in unidentified clerk's hand.

THE behaviour of Mr John Chute towards Mr Capper and his family has been so dishonourable that I think it but justice in me to set down the particulars of his behaviour that the world may judge of the disinterestedness of Mr Capper and his family and how unjustly they have been aspersed by Mr John Chute, and from the time I came into their house I can safely take my oath that I never saw Mr Richard Walpole nor so much as heard him mentioned either in public or private as a man of particular merit, and I can further with the greatest truth say, that I believe them to be people of the strictest honour, whatever Mr John Chute may have insinuated to the contrary, for his com-

4. Capper to old Horace 21 June.
5. Coxe, whose account of Lord Walpole's character is generally favourable, acknowledges that 'he was by nature chol-

eric and impetuous' (*Memoirs* ii. 453).
6. HW to old Horace 22 June (*ante* ii. 205–6).

mon topic of conversation lately to me, has been to abuse and lessen
Mr Capper and his family; but more particularly on Friday the 21st
June 1751, he sent his valet Myrtila in the morning to reprove me for
seeing Mr Harrison my trustee, which I took with some disdain and
walked out of the room, and the valet went away some time after and
returned in about an hour and said that Mr John Chute would wait on
me presently with good news, which was as follows. He told me that he
had been let into a scheme of Mr Capper's being proposed to him for
my guardian and that Mr Hechstetter was to resign and told me that
was the time for me to propose Mrs Chute. I said that I did not believe
there was any such design, and I believed that Mrs Chute would not be
consented to for my guardian. He said, 'What! Would not I have Mrs
Chute if I could,' and I making him no reply, he said, 'Do not be afraid,
you shall not want for money,' and I still continuing silent, he flew into
a violent passion and said this was not my own inclination, but that
my silence was owing to my being deceived by that devil Miss Capper,
but he would be revenged on her, an insinuating toad, and said that it
was she that had persuaded me against Mrs Chute. I assured him upon
my honour and life that Miss Capper had never set me against Mrs
Chute. He then asked me if I would not have Mrs Chute if I could. He
repeated this over and over, and at last fell down on his knees before
me, and starting up with vehemence, flew around the room, and sitting
down in the window he said, 'Your servant, Miss Nicoll, if these are
your tricks I have done with you. Is this all the thanks you give me, you
base wretch and ungrateful creature? You will not say that you would
have Mrs Chute if you could,' and then spoke low, 'O! Miss Nicoll,
you have broke my heart. I will go where you shall never see me more.
I'll hang myself. I only wish to live to serve you.' He then went to the
door as if he was going, and I said, 'Sir, what do you mean by this
usage? I have not had it in my power as yet to return the obligations I
have to you, and as soon as I have, you shall have no cause to upbraid
me with ingratitude.' Then he flew into a most violent rage and with
the utmost anger asked me over and over if I thought he was to be paid
with money, and said it was not my money he wanted, it was that bitch
Miss Capper that had put that in my head. He sat silent some time and
then with a soft tone said, 'I thought to have told you something of importance but you will not hear me.' I burst into tears and told him indeed I would. He then asked me why I cried. I told him I could not help

it, and I can safely affirm I was never more terrified in my life (though I did not tell him so). He then said if I went on crying he would not tell me what it was, and he knew that I would not hear him. I desired him to speak, and I would hear him. Then he said it was a plot laid against me. I said by whom. He replied, by Capper and his daughter who were going to sell me. I said, 'What do you mean Sir?' and he said, 'I should have been with you by nine o'clock this morning but was prevented by a message from old Horace Walpole to desire me to consent for Capper to be your guardian.' I said I could not believe it. He protested it was true, and that there was a consultation held at Capper's chambers every morning between old Horace Walpole and his creature Capper to get Hechstetter to resign, 'and then Capper will have you all to himself and will sell you to a younger son of that old fox Horace Walpole and then you will know how much I have been your friend,' and that that devil Miss Capper was fixed upon by them as a proper person to recommend Dick Walpole to me. And I said, 'Sir indeed she never did, and I can safely take my oath of it,' and he replied, 'I do not know that they have, but I leave that to your own sense to determine if they had named it to you, if their scheme could have gone forward, but old Horace Walpole would give me ten thousand pounds to sell you to his son Richard Walpole.' I said I was sure there was no such scheme and could never believe it, and he said, 'Then you will not believe that Capper is a villain, though I came on purpose to let you know it, and I may have ruined myself forever if I have been overheard, and yet you will not say that you believe me, or that you would have Mrs Chute if you could,' and then pressed me over and over to say Mr Capper was a villain, which I said I could not believe and therefore would not say it, at which he flew into another rage with me. 'And will you have Capper for your guardian?' He asked me this over and over again. 'Do but say who you will have; if it is Tom Long the carrier I will be for him too,' and I replied, 'Sir you know Mr Hechstetter is to be the person.' And he said a great deal more which I can't now recollect, and he was with me three hours all but ten minutes and left me in the greatest fright and disorder, but all this I can safely take my oath of.

MARGARET NICOLL

FRANCIS CAPPER TO HORACE WALPOLE, SR

Copy in the hand of Horace Walpole, Sr.

25 June 1751.

UPON my return from the country yesterday I received the enclosed letter:[1] the original I'll keep by me as a memorial to what
pitch passion and views of interest can carry men. I know my own innocence too well to be much affected with it, and intend no answer nor
ever to speak to the author, if I can avoid it, whom till of late I thought
a wiser and a better man than to submit to such low arts of scurrility. It
is with great concern I see the young lady beset with such sort of
friends, and if she was known, the world I am sure would be of her
side, as her case is truly injured innocence; and as she has a good
temper and person, and wants only the advantage of quiet and a good
education, I am in great hopes that Lord Chancellor will appoint her
a proper guardian within a week. I hope you bore your journey well.
I almost write with tears to see how injuriously you are treated by the
enclosed. However whatever schemes Mr John Chute and others may
think to execute, it shall not be in their power to do anything in my
house, and as I have found him out, will not let him see her, which
seems to me the best method to prevent his mischief. I think what you
foresaw must be the case, and that they never thought of Lord Orford
but under false pretences, and yet I hope his Lordship may proceed if
he makes the proper application to the court and approves of it.

I am, Sir, etc.

FRANCIS CAPPER

I got my wife to copy the letter,[2] as not thinking it proper to let my
clerk see the original.

NOTES BY HORACE WALPOLE, SR

Copy in the same hand as that in the copy mentioned in n. 2 on the preceding
letter: presumably Mrs Capper's.

WITHOUT entering into a particular discussion of the scurrilous, sneering, and ironical abuse and ribaldry of this ingenious
performance[1] which is below the dignity of a gentleman, or an honest

1. HW to Capper 24 June (*ante* ii. 206–9).   1. HW to Capper 24 June.
2. Presumably the copy in the possession
of Mr Holland.

man, it may be proper to take notice of some pretended facts that are entirely false or falsely represented in it.

1. As to the reflection with respect to Mrs Walpole's visiting Miss Nicoll, in not having proposed to make Lord Orford one of the party:

Lord Orford had declared his indisposition to hearken to any proposition relating to marriage for the present, and impressions had been made upon him to the disadvantage of Miss Nicol; and therefore although Mrs Walpole returned Mrs Capper a visit she owed her with a view of seeing Miss Nicoll at the same time, would it not have been ridiculous and absurd to have proposed that Lord Orford should be one of the party to accompany Mrs Walpole in a visit to a lady's where his Lordship had not the least acquaintance with any of the family?

2. As to the reflection of Mr Walpole the uncle having declined upon the application of his nephew to negotiate a meeting at his house at the Cockpit between Lord Orford and Miss Nicol, and not consenting to it at last until the nephew had pushed it with too much peevishness:

The fact is this: about the middle of June whilst the contest about the guardianship of Miss Nicoll was still depending among the relations, and Lord Orford still continued to show a disinclination to matrimony, Mr Walpole the nephew in a visit he made his uncle at the Cockpit desired him to appoint a day for Lord Orford and his dining with him and to manage it so that Mrs Capper and her daughter, bringing Miss Nicoll with them, though without Lord Orford's knowledge, might make Mrs Walpole a visit in that afternoon. The uncle said, 'Surely, nephew, it would be better to stay till Miss Nicoll is settled, and not press this matter whilst his Lordship continues not to have the least inclination to it, but let us give him time to reflect upon what has been represented to him on this head, it being as his governor says his Lordship's temper not to agree to any proposal at first until upon consideration he shall have made it his own and renewed the discourse of it on his own motion.' Mr Walpole the nephew with some warmth replied that his Lordship must come to some final determination immediately, for Mr Chute was resolved that his cousin should be disposed of to somebody or other. The uncle coolly said he saw no occasion for so much haste as the young lady was but sixteen years of age, and the delay of half a year after she should be settled, that she might be fashioned by a better education, and Lord Orford might have opportunities of seeing her and being acquainted with her next winter, could not be liable to any great inconvenience. However upon the nephew's earnestness the uncle agreed to his request, and a day was then fixed, and his Lordship and Mr Walpole of Arlington Street accordingly dined with Mr Walpole at the Cockpit the 20th of June last, and the ladies from Mr Capper's with Miss Nicoll made a visit to Mrs Walpole as was concerted in the afternoon and stayed above an hour. Lord Orford was present all the while. As soon as the ladies took their leave, Mr Walpole of Arlington Street went away too, leaving his Lordship and Mr Walpole the uncle alone; and in consequence of a conversation which they had together relating to Miss Nicoll, Mr Walpole with some pleasure wrote his nephew an account of it the same evening, as conceiving some hopes that his Lordship in time and by prudent management might be disposed to the match. But this letter instead of giving him of Arlington Street any satisfaction, he was extremely ruffled with it, as appears by his answer of June the 21st pretending to be alarmed with a design for putting Miss Nicoll under the guardianship of Mr Capper in order to marry her to Mr Richard Walpole, although there could not be the least pretence for such an alarm or the least shadow of reason for apprehending such a design in the whole course of this transaction.

3. As to Mr Walpole of the Cockpit having desired Lord Orford to pretend to give in to the match although his Lordship should not design it, Mr Walpole of the Cockpit does not deny that he advised Lord Orford not to declare openly his disinclination to the marriage until he should have considered it more seriously.

But as to his having said so in order to have Miss Nicoll placed with Mr Fowle, with an intention (as the letter to Mr Capper says) that Lord Orford might have opportunities of seeing her at Mr Fowle's in Norfolk, implying at the same time by a malicious and ironical sneer that Mr Richard Walpole was more likely to see [her] there than his Lordship:

It is to be observed that Mr Walpole of Arlington Street was the person that first proposed to have Mr Fowle appointed guardian to the young lady, and for that purpose Mr Walpole the uncle sent for him from the Bath, it being generally allowed that she could not be placed in a better house, and Mr Fowle was once named in Chancery; but upon his arrival in town Mr Fowle, perceiving the wild and extravagant way of talking and acting of Mr J. Chute, earnestly entreated that he might be excused and would by no means be concerned in the affair.

And the notion of any design being carried on by Mr Walpole of the Cockpit with Mr Capper to marry his third son Mr R. Walpole to Miss Nicol, had by the confession of Mr Walpole of Arlington Street his friend no other ground than that Mr Tracy (who contested with them the guardianship of the young lady) had said so.[2]

And therefore the making that the foundation of all the scurrilous, abusive, injurious, unjust, pitiful, and unprovoked behaviour of those two gentlemen, to ruin the character of Mr Capper, a counsellor-at-law of great practice and of known abilities and integrity, and to defame the unblemished reputation of his family is so black a scene of iniquity that no words can aggravate or describe, but must have been contrived to cover some bad intentions of their own.

N.B. Mr Walpole of Arlington Street was the person that gave Lord Orford the most disadvantageous description of Miss Nicoll's person.

THOMAS NUTHALL TO HORACE WALPOLE, SR

Copy in the hand of Horace Walpole, Sr.

London, June 26, 1751.

Sir,

I HOPE this will find you and your family safe at Woolterton, which it will give me great pleasure to hear.

If any of your nephew's exploits and performances can appear wonderful to you, I think his letter to Mr Capper which is sent you this post must be of this kind. I intend only to explain a passage or two in it which without my assistance must appear very mysterious; I mean first about the goose giblets, ashes, and water, etc.[1] This tale took its rise from an innocent trick proposed by Miss Nicoll to Miss Capper, by which she said she should discover whether she should marry a widower, bachelor, or live unmarried. It was never put in practice but the proposal for trying the trick was overheard by Mr Chute's Italian footman who carried it to his master, and you see it is improved into this formidable accusation against Miss Capper, who never mentioned

2. See HW to old Horace 21 June (*ante*   1. See *ante* ii. 208.
ii. 215).

or thought of it. Then as to the bawdy books and explanation of dreams, that is likewise a notable circumstance and arose from this. At Garston Mr C., Miss N., and Miss Capper took a walk, and looking into a cottage where a poor woman lived, Miss N. took up a sort of riddle-book called Mother Bunch's Tales,[2] and carried it away with her, giving the old woman half a crown for it. Miss Capper had no more to do with this than with the goose giblets, but you see how little quarter innocence is to expect from these heroes. I had a mind to explain these two dark passages in your nephew's letter, a wickeder fellow than whom I think does not exist, for though his friend may come pretty near him, I think he can't exceed him in infamy. They have not yet been at Mr Capper's, and I doubt not but all these bullyings will vanish in smoke. I am

Sir, etc.,

THOMAS NUTHALL

The affair comes on by consent on Friday.

JOHN CHUTE TO MARGARET NICOLL

Copy in the hand of Horace Walpole, Sr.

Bond Street, Saturday morning [June 29, 1751].

My dear cousin,

THE insolence of those you are hitherto in the hands of, in presuming to refuse admittance to you, does not at all surprise me; they are low dirty people, and it is no wonder that after they had acted the part of such in listening and overhearing what passed the other day between you and me, their resentment should make them capable of any impertinence; but I cannot account for my dear cousin Nicol's submitting her own good sense and good nature to serve the purposes of people so very unworthy to have the direction of it. I cannot comprehend it possible I should any way have offended you, nor had I ever the least reason to imagine you are displeased with any part of my conduct, till since I had last the pleasure of waiting upon you, when I only laid those considerations before you which I had often done at other

---

2. *Mother Bunch's Closet Newly Broke Open*, 1685; many later editions (see edition by G. L. Gomme and H. B. Wheatley, 1885). It is not a 'riddle-book,' but, as HW said, a 'bawdy book of fortune-telling.'

times without offending you. Now supposing my suspicions to be ill-grounded, there is yet nothing you could take amiss, admitting there was no design of leading you into steps which might end in a disadvantageous establishment. Is it a fault in a sincere friend to warn you against all possible dangers you are liable to be exposed to? I beg the favour of you to read the letter[1] which accompanies this with calm attention. You will find I did not assert a falsehood when I told you of the scheme for the guardianship; you will find there was reason to be alarmed; in that you will find my full justification, provided you are so good as not to forget what was all along the principle of my conduct, an inviolable attachment to your interest which I had long since shown myself capable of neglecting all risks to promote.

I was at the Master's last night, but could not stay the end. I hope the affair is decided to your wish. I should be glad of the favour of a line to let me know when I may hope for that of your permission to wait upon you. I have the honour to be with the sincerest affection

My dear cousin Nicoll's etc.

JOHN CHUTE

THOMAS NUTHALL TO HORACE WALPOLE, SR

Copy in the hand of Horace Walpole, Sr.

London, June 29, 1751.

Sir,

M R C[HUTE] and your gracious nephew have left Mr Capper's family quiet all this week, or more properly since the letter of which you had a copy, till this day when a letter from each of the gentlemen was delivered to Miss N.[1] by her maidservant, who received them under a cover from Mr C. by a porter. You may imagine they have given great disquiet to that family, as they are as extraordinarily villainous and wicked as the other performance you had before a copy of. No answer will be given to any of these libels, and I am in hopes that the disappointment may have a good effect, or at least prevent a farther literary correspondence on their part.

I was sent to by C[hute] yesterday morning to know when the hear-

1. HW to Miss Nicoll 28 June (*ante* ii. 210–12).

1. HW's and Chute's letters of 28 and 29 June (*ante* ii. 210–12 and 225–6).

ing came on, and last night at six just as we were beginning, the two squires came in, and after having seated themselves behaved with more impudence during the attendance than I am capable of informing you. Indeed they did not stay it out, but they were making faces and affronting Tracy, Harrison, and the rest all the time. They are inveterate against Tracy, and only wish for Mr H[eckstetter]² in hopes of getting admittance once more. We shall finish before the Master on Tuesday, and we are satisfied he is entirely on our side. This consideration in some measure supports my client's spirits, who is indeed to be pitied, and behaves as properly and as steadily as any one of twice her years and experience could possibly do.

The enclosed³ will take up so much of your time that I will give you no further trouble than to assure you that I am etc.,

THOMAS NUTHALL

I had good quarter from the two heroes last night, and was often whispered to by your nephew. They have not quarrelled with me yet, but I expect it and am prepared and wish they had begun and ended there.

THOMAS NUTHALL TO HORACE WALPOLE, SR

Extract in the hand of Horace Walpole, Sr.

Crosby Square, London, July 9, 1751.

Sir,

THE two heroes, who have been for some time quiet, have at length produced their prodigy. Yesterday morning four of the enclosed ballads¹ were sent under covers directed to Miss Capper, Mrs Capper, Miss Nicol's footman, and Mr Capper's footman by name. This has given the two young ladies particularly great uneasiness, and Miss N. yesterday sent her relation back all his presents by her footman, with a

2. It is to be observed that, as between Robert Tracy and David Heckstetter, the remaining candidates for the guardianship, HW and Chute sided with Horace Walpole, Sr, in preferring Heckstetter. HW's and Chute's continued interest in the hearings must have arisen only from their apparently unjustified fear that Capper would be appointed guardian.

3. Presumably Chute's and HW's letters to Miss Nicoll.

———

1. The enclosure unfortunately has not been preserved, and no copy of the lampoon is known to the editors. There is no evidence, aside from Nuthall's and Capper's assertions, that it was written by Chute or HW.

message that she desired she might never see or hear from him again. How this will be taken I don't know, but I suppose it will fall to her turn to be abused now. When she is safe at Southgate, I dare say these disturbances will be all at an end. I am etc.,

THOMAS NUTHALL

FRANCIS CAPPER TO HORACE WALPOLE, SR

Extract in the hand of Horace Walpole, Sr.

13 July 1751.

MR NUTHALL tells me he has acquainted you with the treatment which I and my family have met with from Mr John Chute and his companion. It has been so infamous that those who have been guilty of it in such a gross and absurd manner in sending that scurrilous and abusive letter to me filled with falsities, and two other letters to Miss Nichols, must have worn out of their minds any regard to truth or good manners. And at last came (as I suppose) from the same hand a copy of verses in print filled with bawdry and nonsense directed to my wife and daughter. I know not these arts; I did not think that one of the parties was capable of the practice till experience convinced me of the contrary. Miss Nichols is very sensible of the insults and abuse, but cannot resent it in any other manner than by avoiding any occasion of seeing them, and she sent back by her servant to Mr John Chute some petty presents which he had made her, and with a message to him that she desired never to see him or hear from him again, and by what I can observe in her his behaviour has made the deepest impressions of resentment in her mind. I much pity her that her great fortune should expose her to this treatment, and as much as I can see, she is a very deserving young lady, and as she says, would be very happy if others would let her choose for herself and go to Mr Hecks[t]etter for her residence and education, etc.

FRANCIS CAPPER

FRANCIS CAPPER TO HORACE WALPOLE, SR

Extract in the hand of Horace Walpole, Sr.

27 July 1751.

THE counsel for Mr Tracy was heard through, and the case appeared to Lord Chancellor so clear that he determined the matter in Miss Nicol's favour without hearing any one of her counsel.[1] It was highly agreeable to her, and I hope it must tend to the advancement of her quiet and views, she having conceived an aversion to reside in the family of Mr Tracy. Lord Chancellor has inserted in his order that neither Mr John Chute nor Mrs Ann Chute of Somersett House should have liberty to see her but in the presence of Mr [Heckstetter][2] and his lady. But Miss Nicoll will refuse to see either of them on any terms. I have been a witness of her temper and behaviour for eleven weeks past, and I do declare that those who blame her do it from other motives than any occasion given by her, and when she has had the advantages of proper masters, she will appear to become her fortune. She went home from me this day, so that I begin to enjoy the quiet I have always coveted.

I am etc.,

FRANCIS CAPPER

CHUTE'S BILL

Copy in same clerk's hand as in Miss Nicoll's statement. Undated, but probably presented after the final hearing on July 27.

Money laid out for Miss Nicoll by John Chute, Esq.

To chairmen by her direction May 4th	22	1	—[1]
To Mrs Chute, a bill which was for sundry expenses of coach-hire, chair-hire, messengers, porters, etc., on Miss Nicoll's account	8	—	6
To journeys and couriers to the Vine on Miss Nicoll's account	17	8	1
	1	—	2

1. See *ante* ii. 212–13, n. 64.
2. MS reads 'Enchetter.'

———

1. For the trip from the Okeovers' to Mrs Chute's, 'a few miles out of town' (*ante* ii. 195). The first digit has been altered to a pound-sign, so that it appears to read £2; yet in estimating the total the figure has been counted as £22. Other items in the bill are likewise suspiciously high.

To journeys in postchaises to attend Miss Nicoll's affairs by her express desire when she was at Garston in Herts	4	16	—
To a postchaise and a coach and four to Sh. Bush[2] .	1	—	—
To a snuff-box which was bought by Miss Nicoll's order, though by her mistaken for a present . .	3	3	—
To coach and chair-hire during my frequent attendance upon Miss Nicoll in town, which was always in compliance with her immediate desire; to sundry other small expenses	15	15	—
To a person who cleaned Miss Nicoll's teeth . . .	1	11	6
	£74	15	3

FRANCIS CAPPER'S STATEMENT

Draft, undated, but later than August 7, the date of HW's narrative. The substance of the statement makes it certain that it originated with Capper, and the fact that it contains many corrections suggests that it is in his own hand.

THE 4 May Miss Nicolls left Mrs Okever, was carried away in a chair procured by John Chute to Mrs Ann Chute's habitation. On the 6th May being Monday she was brought back by Mr Chute to Mrs Okever her former guardian, and by advice a petition was preferred to the Lord Chancellor to remove Miss Nicolls from Mrs Okever's care and to place her in some other family where she might live with more satisfaction.

That petition was presented to the Lord Chancellor, who ordered an attendance for hearing thereof on the 11th of the same month, when all parties attended at the house of the Lord Chancellor. And the counsel on both sides thinking it was better not to go into the particulars of the matter of the petition as the young lady was coming so early into the world and had so large a fortune, and neither side having thought of a fit person with whom to place her, Mr Nuthall and Mr Heaton[1] the solicitors on both sides applied to Mr Capper one of the counsel for Miss Nicolls that she might go into his family till a fit person should be thought of with whom and by her consent she might be educated; that Mr Capper was unwilling to it and would consent no otherwise than for nine or ten days, until a fit person could be

2. Shepherd's Bush, west of London.   1. Not further identified.

named to the Lord Chancellor for his approbation for the purpose aforesaid. And accordingly with the consent of Mrs Okever, then present in court, Miss Nicolls was placed with Mr Capper to remain about a fortnight as it was then understood and a liberty was given to the parties by that time to name some other person.

That John Fowle Esq. was the person thought of, and both Miss Nicolls and Mrs Okever would have consented to it, but some of her relations not seeming satisfied, Mr Fowle would not undertake the office and refused to be the young lady's guardian. And the Chancellor thereupon referred it to Master Bennett to see who was a proper person with whom to place Miss Nicolls to have the care of her education. That the forms of proceedings before the Master and the struggle given by some of the relations to be her guardian, to whom she was averse, protracted the appointment of the guardianship to about the beginning of August last.

That in this interval the young lady continued with Mr Capper, where any of her friends or relations or acquaintance had resort to her, and Mr John Chute while she continued in town scarce forbore any day visiting her, and he often would sit in her room with her and her maidservant, and when she was in the country would come to her then to acquaint her concerning her affairs, and it had been observed by some of Mr Capper's family that the young lady seemed uneasy several times after his leaving her.

That Mr Capper often begged of Mr Nuthall her solicitor to get the Master's report for appointment of a guardian as the care of the young lady while in his family was so great a charge, and besides the numerous visits that were made at his house on her account gave him some uneasiness. That on the 21st of June last Mr Chute, while Mr Capper was at Westminster Hall, came upon a visit to the young lady at his house in the morning, went as usual into her room where her maidservant was, and there endeavoured to engage her to elect Mrs Ann Chute for her guardian and behaved like a madman, not caring what he said or did, and was so loud that Mrs Capper heard him while she was sitting in the dining-room up one pair of stairs, and the servants who were at work in the room next to that where Miss Nicolls was, the particulars of which discourse and behaviour between her and Mr Chute the young lady has wrote down.

That Mrs Capper sent to her husband to Lincoln's Inn at his return from Westminster on that day to dine at home, as he intended to be in

Commons that day in the Hall at Lincoln's Inn, and sent word she had earnest business to communicate to him; that Mr Capper immediately went home and found all his family in disorder by what had happened and the young lady in tears, who begged of him that he would deliver her from Mr John Chute and that she would never see him again and at the same time acquainted Mr Capper with most of the particulars, which two or three days afterwards she put into the said writing, and that most of his discourse at former visits had tended to desire her to think of Mrs Chute only as her guardian and to disparage Mr Capper and his family to her, which was of the occasion of her crying as she had been kindly entertained by them. And two persons dining with him in his family that day saw the great disorder of the lady, in so much that she was obliged to go from table and retire into her own chamber without eating her dinner. That Mr Capper being acquainted of John Chute's behaviour and of his scandalous falsehoods, ordered all the servants in his family to deny Mr John Chute entrance and to forbid him to come any more to Miss Nicolls, and as some of the said falsehoods concerned the character and credit of Mr Horace Walpole the elder, Mr Capper sent him a letter the same day to acquaint him with what John Chute had thus said to Miss Nicolls in private concerning the story of her marriage, and that John Chute had told her that Mr Walpole would give him £10,000 for his favour therein or to that effect. Mr Chute never came after to the house of Mr Capper as he knows of. On Monday following Mr Capper received from Mr Horace Walpole the younger a very rude and opprobrious letter, whom he had never angered or had any concern with, and in a short time after a ballad filled with bawdry and nonsense was sent to Mr Capper's wife and daughter and sent and dispersed to several of his acquaintance and on covers without any name. That in a very short time afterwards two letters[2] came to Miss Nicolls, the one from Mr Horace Walpole the younger, the other from Mr Chute, to disparage Mr Capper to her in regard to his station in life and other opprobrious language, and which two letters after Miss Nicolls had read over she gave to Mr Capper to keep; and Mr Chute having at some of the times before when he had visited the lady made her two or three small presents of marble figures, she with resentment called up her servant and sent them back under a cover to John Chute to tell him to take them back and not to

2. The chronology here is inaccurate: the letters preceded the ballad.

visit her or trouble her with any letters again, and expressed great resentment that Mr Horace Walpole the younger should interfere concerning her, whom she was never acquainted with.

The treatment Mr Walpole the elder and Mr Capper has since met with from Mr Walpole the younger and John Chute has been so infamous that it would scarce be credited but from the narrative sent about by the said Walpole.

APPENDIX 2

WALPOLE'S MEMOIR OF ASHTON

Printed from HW, Waldegrave MSS 1. 57–8, 87. Undated: begun ca 1749.

Nobilis impietas Herodis, splendida culpa!
Qua vitam donat millibus ante diem.

THESE two lines for what they call Bibling verses, or an epigram
taken out of a chapter of the New Testament read to the Fellows
of King's College Cambridge while they dine, were wrote by Thomas
Ashton, since a celebrated preacher. He was eldest son of a schoolmaster at Lancaster, and born about the year 1715: educated on the
Foundation at Eton College, and afterwards Fellow of King's. From
thence he was tutor to the Earl of Plymouth; during which time was
addressed to him by H.W. from Florence an epistle in verse, since
printed in the second volume of Dodsley's miscellanies 1748. He went
into Orders in 1742 having left Lord Plymouth, and was by the Crown
presented to the living of Aldingham, about 7 miles from Lancaster,
and made chaplain to Sir R[obert] W[alpole] Earl of Orford in 1745.[1]
He was preacher in Queen's Street Chapel, where he soon became so
famous, that he had his salary raised from 40 to 100 pounds per annum
and might have had what terms he pleased to continue there, which yet
he would not do but two years, during which time he was elected Fellow of Eton College. He printed a sermon[1a] on the Rebellion preached
at Queen's Street Chapel, and another[2] on its suppression preached at
Eton; besides which there have been published of his writing, an epitaph in verse on the death of Rich[ar]d West,[3] (son to the Chancellor
of Ireland, and grandson to Dr Burnet, a very ingenious young man
who died about five or six and twenty, and who wrote an admirable
monody on the death of Queen Caroline, printed in Dodsley's miscellanies, and several other pretty poems MSS [sic]) and an essay on the
death of Lord Orford 1745.[4] At Eton School Mr Ashton paraphrased

1. But see ante 4 May 1742, n. 12.
1a. A Sermon preached at the Chapel in
Great Queen Street . . . on occasion of the
present Rebellion, 1745 (BM Cat.).
2. A Sermon preached in the Collegiate
Chapel at Eton, on . . . the Suppression of
the late unnatural Rebellion, 1746 (BM

Cat.). This and the other sermons mentioned below were reprinted by Ashton in
Sermons on Several Occasions, 1770.
3. See HW to Mann June 1742. The
verses were printed in the London Magazine 1742, xi. 305, and elsewhere.
4. A Character of the Life and Adminis-

THOMAS ASHTON, BY REYNOLDS, 1763

in English verse the —— Psalm, and in 1748[5] the —— Psalm, on a most
extraordinary escape which happened to him alone in March that year
between Lancaster and Aldingham, when two other persons with him
were drowned.[6] At Cambridge he wrote a little poem on the death of
Mr Sunderland[7] of Clare Hall, and a few occasional little pieces since,
and thus translated Pope's *Epitaph on Sir Isaac Newton:*[7a]

> Nature and nature's works[8] lay hid in night;
> God said let Newton be and all was light.

> Naturæ facies caligine mersa jacebat,
> Tandem Newtonus se ostendit et omnia secum.

The last line is imitated from this beautiful line of Ovid,

> Cum vero Titan se ostendit et omnia secum.[9]

Mr West, who is mentioned above made as happy an answer to the
known epigram on Tom Hearne;

> 'Pox on't,' quoth Time to Thomas Hearne,
> 'Whatever I forget you learn.'

> Answer.
> 'Damn it,' quoth Hearne in furious fret,
> 'Whate'er I learn you soon forget.'[9a]

And he thus travestied the lines of Pope on the grotto at Twickenham:

> Thou who shalt stop where the lean bard's backside
> Shines a broad circle o'er the shadowy tide. . . .[10]

Mr West is buried at Hatfield. Here are two epitaphs which Mr A.
made for him and for himself.[10a]

*   *   *   *   *

tration of the late . . . Earl of Orford,
1745. The essay was published anonymously; HW's copy, in which he identifies
the essay as Ashton's, is now WSL.

5. An error for 1746: see next note.

6. A copy of these 'Thanksgiving verses,'
dated from Aldingham, 6 March 1746,
'after his wonderful escape from being
swallowed up on Lancaster Sands,' is preserved in the British Museum (Add. MS
32,096, f. 164).

7. Probably John Sunderland, admitted

a sizar at Clare, 1735 (Venn, *Alumni Cantab.*). The verses have not been found.

7a. Pope, *Works,* ed. Elwin and Court-
hope, iv. 390.

8. Properly 'laws.'

9. 'At cum se Titan ostendit et omnia
secum' (*Heroides* xv. 135).

9a. In *Works* i. 204.

10. And so on through sixteen lines.

10a. Only the latter appears. HW left a
space for the other, but did not fill it in.

Hic jacet
Quod reliquum est Thomæ Ashton,
Qui siquid laudandum præ se ferret, Deo tribuit,
    Siquid non item, sibi.
Qui vera semper, quamvis ridens, dicere,
Honesta, quamvis liber, agere conabatur.
Qui in ætate, decentius lasciva, desipere desiit;
Recteque facere, quam scite loqui, satius duxit.
Qui hac dum fruebatur vita, meliorem sperabat;
    Deoque tandem optimo maximo
Credentem sese, non credulum, dedidit.

In May 1750 Mr Ashton published a dissertation in the controversy between the Bishop of London and Dr Middleton on 2 Peter 1. 19.[11]

In March 1752 he published a defence of his dissertation, entitled *Observations on a Book entitled an Essay etc. by a late Fellow of King's College Cambridge*. In February 1756 a Sermon on the General Fast, preached at St Botolph's, Bishopsgate, and soon after a defence[12] of his sermon against one of the Monthly Reviews which had censured it.

He took his doctor's degree at Cambridge July 1759.

At the end of 1760 he married Miss Amyand,[13] sister of Mr Claudius Amyand, and daughter of the late serjeant surgeon of that name.

January 30th 1761 he preached before the House of Commons; the sermon[14] was published.

April 8th in the same year he was chosen preacher to the Society of Lincoln's Inn, in the room of Dr Warburton, promoted to the see of Gloucester.

In the winter of 1763 he had a stroke of apoplexy as he was preaching in the chapel at Eton College.

11. See *ante* 12 June 1750.
12. Neither Ashton's defence nor the attack which provoked it has been found.
13. Judith, 6th dau. of Claudius Amyand (*Eton Coll. Reg.*).
14. *A Sermon preached before the Honourable House of Commons . . . on Friday, January 30, 1761*, etc., 1761 (BM Cat.).

APPENDIX 3

West's Imitation of Propertius

Reprinted from *Gray-HW-West-Ashton Corr.* i. 229–31. See *ante* 21 June 1739, O.S.

Imitated from Propertius *El.* 15 [i.e., 17], *Lib.* 3: *Nunc, oh Bacche tuis,* etc.

NOW prostrate, Bacchus, at thy shrine I bend:
This once be gracious, father, and attend!
Thine, great Lyæus, is the power confess'd
To chase our sorrows, and restore our rest:
'Tis thine, each joy attendant on the bowl,
Thine each gay lenitive that glads the soul.
God of the rosy cheek and laughing eye,
To thee from Cynthia and from love I fly;
If ever Ariadne was thy care,
Now show thy pity, and accept my prayer.
  Then, Bacchus, if by thee renew'd I find,
As once, my old serenity of mind,
My Umbrian hill shall flourish with the vine,
Thine, Bacchus, all my labours shall be thine.
With my own hands the generous growth I'll rear,
Rank the young shoots, and watch the rising year,
Till all my boughs with the red autumn bend,
And the large vintage in my vats descend.
  Hail, mighty Bacchus, to my latest hour
In grateful strains I'll celebrate thy power;
And as I strike the dithyrambic string,
Thy name, thy glory, and thy power I'll sing:
Thy birth I'll sing, thy mother's fatal fires,
Thy Indian trophies, and Nysæan choirs:
I'll sing Lycurgus by his pride undone:
The dire disaster of Agave's son:
And the false Tuscans hurled into the main.
I'll sing the wonders of the Naxian plain,
Thy lakes of honey and thy floods of wine;
Such blessings, father, are reserved for thine!
Now, io Bacchus! to the general song,

Bacchus, to thee I'll lead the pomp along:
O'er thy white neck the vivid ivy spread,
The Lycian mitre nodding on thy head:
Divine with oil thy honest face shall glow,
And to thy feet the dancing robe shall flow.
Meantime thy orgies in procession come:
Dircæan Thebes shall beat the hollow drum,
Th' Arcadian reed shall give a softer sound,
And Phrygian cymbals rattle hoarse around:
High at thy shrine the flamen priest shall stand
White-robed, with ivy crowned, and in his hand
The golden vase: th' inferior throng shall sing:
Io! again shall through the temple ring.
    And I thy bard these wonders will rehearse,
And sound thy glories in no common verse:
Of thee this only recompense I ask,
A slight reward for such a toilsome task,
'Tis but to ease my bosom of its pain,
And never may I feel the pangs of love again.

APPENDIX 4

Walpole in Rome

Printed from HW, Waldegrave MSS 2. 40–2.

This *jeu d'esprit* (resembling the parody printed *ante* ca 15 Oct. 1735) is undated, but probably belongs to 1740.

Some Fragments of a Journey to Italy.

* * * * Having heard that the best view of the city was from the top of St Peter's, which, as everyone knows, is not only the highest church in Rome, but in the world; for the tower of Babel, which as Sigonius supposes was a temple, is no longer standing; and the tower of Pequin, being an idolatrous place of worship, cannot properly be called a Christian church; I having a great desire to see at one prospect this mistress of the world—did not go up. From hence you command not only the city, but the whole *campania* of Rome, with those beautiful hills of Tivoli (the Tibur of the ancients) Frescati, Albano and Palestrina. I made an excursion to these four places, at the latter of which are great ruins of the famous Temple of Fortune; they lay about half a mile from the town, but it being a very rainy day, I did not go to see them.

In the environs of Rome, there is nothing which strangers are more carried to see, than the fountain of Egeria; there are now small remains, for which reason, I did not go thither. Within ten miles of Rome was fought the famous battle between the Romans and the Æqui, which, says Livy, was to decide the future fate of the empire of the world. The field of battle was extant in his time, as some antiquarians suppose it still to be; but their entire ignorance of the spot prevented my visiting it.

Among the many ancient gems, which are to be seen at Rome in greater quantities than in the rest of the world put together, if you except the collections of the King of France, and the Great Duke of Tuscany, with some other private collections which are in every city of Italy; the most famous is that of the Strozzi family. The chief jewel of this noble cabinet, and which indeed has not its fellow in the world, is the Medusa, of which there are so many copies in England. The countenance is the most beautiful that can be imagined, that Grecian beauty so often described by the poets. Her snakes add a lovely horror to her face, and set off the sweetness of her natural look, as I have heard, for I never saw it. Among the magnificent ruins of Rome, nothing has been more talked of, than the Septizonium Severi. Antiquaries disagree about the use of this structure; some supposing it was a sepulchral monument erected by that Emperor for himself. Others think it was an aviary for Egyptian birds, in which Severus much delighted. The learned Gruter is of opinion that it was the repository for the Empress's girdles etc. I will not pretend to decide which of these conjectures may be the true, but leave my reader to consult Montfaucon, who has compared the several arguments and added one of his own to prove it a Gothic structure, and to show that the Septizonium stood above three yards distant from the edifice in question. This noble remnant of antiquity I had the misfortune not to see, it having been pulled down about twenty years before my coming to Rome.

* * * * I shall finish this article of churches with those two celebrated chapels in the Vatican of Sixtus Quintus, and Paul the Third. In this latter among numberless beauties, is that most magnificent work of Michael Angelo, the Last Judgment. It is needless to enter into a particular description of this picture, of which so many volumes have been wrote, and to which I am the less capable of adding anything, as I never saw either this or the above-mentioned chapel, each of them being enclosed in the Conclave, which was sitting to choose a successor to Clement the Twelfth, who dying about two months before my arrival, prevented my being presented to him. I should have been introduced to the new Pope by Cardinal Alexander Albani, to whom I take this opportunity of returning my thanks for numberless civilities which he would have shown me if he had been at liberty, but I left Rome before the election.

Few foreigners come to Rome without taking a journey to Ostia, but I had heard so little in its praise from those who had been there, that I did not take the trouble to go myself.

* * * * on the road to Naples, I passed within two miles of Old Capua, that luxurious retreat, which conquered Hannibal more than all the Roman legions could do. The softness * * *

* * * for above a mile in a channel of cinders and sulphur, whose noisome stench and pestiferous * * * to the foot of the mountain: here you ascend half way on mules, which you are obliged to quit and clamber up as you can for a mile and half to the first mouth, but these

accounts discouraged me so much, that I was contented with taking a view of the whole mountain at a distance.

About four miles from the city at the mouth of the bay lies the little isle of Caprea, so famous for the retirement and brutal pleasures of Tiberius. I did not take a boat to go there, and in about four hours did not make shore. Here I did not see anything very remarkable, the senate on that Emperor's death having sent a body of pioneers to destroy all his works, of which there are now scarce any remains.

* * * * by the marble bridge at Narni, which, I have been told by those that have seen it, was built by Augustus. The next place of note is Terni; here is that noble cascade, which is allowed to fall from a much greater height, than that at Tivoli, but of this I could form no ocular judgment, having only seen the latter.

* * * * I will not say anything of the wealth of the Holy House of Loreto; of the grandeur of Milan, the commodiousness of the port of Leghorn, the bending tower of Pisa, the * * of Lucca etc. etc., having never seen any of them; though I know * * * *

APPENDIX 5

ANECDOTES OF LADY MARY WORTLEY MONTAGU AND LADY POMFRET

Printed from HW, Waldegrave MSS i. 5–7, 28–9, 2. 38. Written ca 1740.

i.[1]

Unseen, unheard the throng around me move,
Not wishing praise, insensible of love;
No whispers soften, and no beauties fire;
Coldly I see the dance and careless hear the lyre.

THESE lines from Lady Mary Wortley's Epistle to Lord Bathurst.[2] The world will probably not only see her poems, but her memoirs,[3] which she has wrote herself. Partially no doubt, for even no man, unless his impudence were equal to hers, could venture to describe them all. Mr Pope under the characters of Sapho[4] and Avidien's wife[5] has struck some of the particulars. He was once her friend, as may even appear from some of her first compositions: particularly from her *Town Eclogues,* which she owns were first thought of in company with Pope and Gay,[6] the latter of whom pursued the same scheme, though

1. HW's hints at scandal concerning Lady Mary, and the generally unflattering picture of her in his letters and in Pinkerton's *Walpoliana,* have led her nineteenth-century apologists—her descendants Lady Louisa Stuart and Lord Wharncliffe, her editor W. Moy Thomas, and others—to accuse HW of an inherited prejudice resulting from Lady Walpole's dislike of Lady Mary as patroness of Maria Skerrett, and from Sir Robert's political enmity towards Lady Mary's husband, Edward Wortley Montagu. The truth or falsity of much of the gossip HW relates, now supplemented by the anecdotes here printed for the first time, cannot be tested; but his letters contain evidence that he felt no special animus towards her. He admired her poems highly, and was responsible for the 1747 edition of her *Town Eclogues* (HW to Mann 24 Nov. 1747, O.S.; see also *ante* ca Jan. 1748, n. 40). He also, in the main, spoke well of her letters (HW to Mann 14 Oct. 1751, O.S.,

and 10 May 1763), except when Pinkerton was rash enough to say he preferred them to Madame de Sévigné's (HW to Pinkerton 22 June 1785). In January 1761 HW sent her a set of *Royal and Noble Authors,* which she had 'scolded' him for not having given her before (HW to Mann 5 Dec. 1760, 27 Jan. 1761); and after her return to England, in January 1762, he went to see her (ibid. 29 Jan. 1762).

2. So first printed; but later, as addressed to Lord Burlington. See Lady Mary's *Letters and Works,* ed. Lord Wharncliffe and W. Moy Thomas, 1887, ii. 477, n. 1.

3. HW is probably referring to Lady Mary's journal, which her daughter, Lady Bute, guarded carefully and eventually burned (*Letters and Works,* 1887, i. p. lxxxiv; see also HW to Mann 3 Oct. 1762).

4. *Satires* i. 83, *Moral Essays* iii. 121, etc.

5. *Satires* ii. 49.

6. 'The famous Ballad of Black-eyed Susan ['Sweet William's Farewell to Black-

with far inferior success. The first grounds of the coolness between her and Pope,[7] as she says, was a song, which he had made on her, and which some years afterwards he handed about as designed for Mrs Howard, after Countess of Suffolk and mistress to King George II. That song ends with this line—*Who would think Mrs Howard ne'er dreamt it was she?*[8] On seeing this, Lady Mary sent him the original copy in his own handwriting. Great quantities of Lady Mary's amours and infamies are known: her first setting out was with an amour with Lord Stairs, who is mentioned in her Eclogues by the name of *Sharper*.[9] Soon after this affair she was courted by Lord Lonsdale, elder brother of the present Lord, and by Mr Wortley: to both she was cruel; this was before her marriage, for she has never been known to refuse any favour but that of her perpetual possession. At the same time her father fell in love with Lady Anne Bentinck who forsook for him Sir Conyers Darcy, who had long been her lover, and on whose despair, Rowe made the ballad of *Colin's Complaint*. However she would not have the Duke of Kingston,[10] unless he would marry off his two daughters, Lady

eyed Susan'] was wrote by Gay on the amour between Earl Berkley and Mrs Coke, wife to the vice-chamberlain. One of Lady Mary Wortley's *Town Eclogues,* "Lydia" or "The Toilette" is on the same subject' (HW, Waldegrave MSS 1.8. Though Lady Mary seems to have laid claim to 'The Toilette,' it was also by Gay: see Lady Mary's *Letters and Works,* 1887, ii. 458, n. 2).

7. 'On the first breaking out of the quarrel between Pope and Lady Mary Wortley, he sent her word, he would set her down in black and white; to which she replied, if he did, she would have him set down in black and blue. This she could easily do, as she was always known to keep one or two strong footmen' (HW, Waldegrave MSS 1.9). For a poetic version of Lady Mary's threat, though not attributed to her, see Hervey, *Memoirs* i. p. xliii. The various theories concerning Lady Mary's quarrel with Pope are summarized by Leslie Stephen in DNB.

8. The song begins, 'I said to my heart, between sleeping and waking,' and was included by Pope and Swift, as being 'by a person of quality,' in their *Miscellanies. The Last Volume* [iii], 1727, pp. 166–7. But although HW attributes this anecdote to

Lady Mary herself, it cannot be reconciled with the known facts about the verses. The author was probably Lord Peterborough, to whom the lines were later assigned by HW himself in his *Royal and Noble Authors* (*Works* i. 439); and this attribution, which has been generally accepted, is also to be found in a MS draft of the lines, dated 1723 and probably in Pope's hand, among the Pope MSS in the Pierpont Morgan Library. Additional cause for rejecting the accuracy of the anecdote is the fact that in the third stanza a compliment is paid to Lady Mary under the name of 'Sappho.' (In writing this note the editors have been assisted by Messrs Norman Ault, Robert Halsband, and Maynard Mack.)

9. 'Sharper' is mentioned in 'Thursday. —The Basset-table,' the authorship of which is discussed *ante* ca Jan. 1748, n. 40. For another allusion to the affair with Lord Stair, for which HW is named as authority, see Sir James Prior, *Life of Edmond Malone,* 1860, pp. 150, 151.

10. Lady Mary's father, the Marquess of Dorchester (he did not become Duke of Kingston until 1715, three years after her marriage). In 1714 he married Lady Isabella (not Anne) Bentinck, who, according to Lady Louisa Stuart, 'had long been the

Mary and the since unfortunate Lady Marr. The Duke immediately ordered Lady Mary to choose a husband or retire into the country. In this dilemma, she sent to Lord Lonsdale, who was newly fallen in love with the fine Lady Sunderland, and desired to be excused. Reduced to Mr Wortley, she married Mr Wortley. Her usage of her children, I mean of those two which she owned by her husband, was monstrous. To her son[11] her cruelty is known; that to her daughter, the amiable Lady Bute, is less public. After having drawn Lord Bute into an amour with her, just when they were going to be married, she pretended to disapprove it, and thereby saved giving her a fortune; nay a wedding dinner; for the next day when the new pair went to wait on Mr Wortley and Lady Mary at Twickenham, they let them stay there till five o'clock, and then sent them away without asking 'em to dine.[12] Her sister she used more inhumanly;[13] this lady lost her senses, upon fear of her husband's displeasure, for during his exile upon the Preston rebellion she had kept up a correspondence with the ministry to obtain his pardon, which my Lord found out, before it was concluded. On his death, Lady Mary got the charge of her sister, and kept her in a madhouse long after she had recovered her senses, merely to keep the pension which she was allowed for her maintenance, which was so mean and so ill taken care of, that the woman who guarded her, used to make her eat her whole portion in the morning, that she might not have the trouble of waiting on her the rest of the day. Lady Mary at the same time had the charge of Lady Marr's daughter, Lady Margret[14] Erskine, who behaved with great deference to Lady Mary, at the same

object of his Grace's pursuit' (Letters and Works, 1887, i. p. xcvii). Lady Mary's correspondence with her future husband, though largely given over to wrangling, demonstrates considerable affection, and does not support HW's assertion that her marriage to Montagu was a mere pis aller. The marriage, which followed an elopement, was carried out against the wishes of Lord Dorchester, who had arranged another match for her, probably with the Hon. Clotworthy Skeffington, later 4th Vct Massereene (C. H. Collins Baker in TLS 4 Sept. 1937; 'George Paston' [Emily Morse Symonds], Lady Mary Wortley Montagu and her Times, 1907, pp. 30–154).

11. Edward Wortley Montagu, Jr (1713–76), who was highly talented but very dissolute and perhaps mentally unbalanced.

12. We have found no corroboration of this story, but Lady Mary was estranged from Lady Bute for some time after her marriage.

13. Moy Thomas (Letters and Works, 1887, i. pp. lviii–lxii) defends Lady Mary against the charge of having maltreated her sister, an accusation which seems to have originated with Lady Mar's brother-in-law Lord Grange, who contested with Lady Mary the guardianship of Lady Mar and who was notorious for having confined his own wife on St Kilda. Pope's allusion to a peeress who 'starved a sister' (Epilogue to the Satires i. 112, ii. 20) gave currency to the tale. Lady Mary's published letters to her sister are very affectionate.

14. Properly Frances. See also HW to Mann 14 Oct. 1751, O.S.

time denying herself almost necessaries to save money for her mother, till the day she was of age, when she instantly left Lady Mary, and went and delivered her mother from her confinement.

One of her many amours was with Mr Chandler, eldest son to the Bishop of Durham, to whom she wrote that admirable Description of a Lover, which begins thus,

> At length by so much importunity press'd,
> Take (Chandler) at once the inside of my breast, etc.

though in the copies which she gives now she writes (Molly)[15] meaning Miss Skerret, her relation[16] and élève. She afterwards wrote an answer to this, as from Chandler, a description of what a mistress should be: but this I believe she has suppressed. After friendships and the same number of enmities with half the town, after being reduced to a page or half-pay officer, her avarice still combating her lust, abused by the men and shunned by the women, in the year 1739 she left England with only one man and maid and most of her jewels, and passed into France, saying England was grown so dull she could not stay there.[17] From Dijon and Lyons, she went to Turin, where she was stopped by a custom-house officer who went to strip her in search of a pound of snuff; from thence to Venice, which she was forced to leave in less than a year, having equalled the character which she left in England, by persecuting with her fulsome love a noble Venetian,[18] besides a thousand other extravagancies, as dancing all night at a public ball made for the Prince of Saxony,[19] etc., etc., and having been able to maintain no acquaintance but with two or three abbés who translated

---

15. This is confirmed by Moy Thomas, who says that he found *The Lover: a Ballad* 'in a commonplace-book of Lady Mary's, headed in her handwriting, "To Molly"' (*Letters and Works*, 1887, ii. 498, n. 1; see also Paston, op. cit. 545). In the early editions the poem was printed as addressed 'To Mr C——,' which was expanded to 'Congreve' in the collected edition of 1803 and in subsequent editions; but HW's identification of Chandler is presumably correct, since Lady Mary herself identified for HW the persons mentioned in her poems (see *ante* ca Jan. 1748, n. 40), and it is further supported by the 1782 edn of Dodsley's *Collection*, where the poem is given as addressed to Chandler. For Rich-

ard Chandler (later Cavendish) (d. 1769) see GM 1793, lxiii pt ii. 974.

16. No evidence of any relationship has been discovered.

17. Upon being questioned by Lady Shadwell, Lady Mary gave this as the reason for her leaving England (Emily J. Climenson, *Elizabeth Montagu*, 1906, i. 50–1).

18. Probably Pietro Grimani, Procurator of St Mark's, Venice (see Paston, op. cit. 369, 375, 378). Elizabeth Montagu, upon learning that Lady Mary was in Venice, jokingly predicted that she would 'limit her ambition to an intrigue with the Pope or the Doge of Venice' (Climenson, op. cit. i. 51). Grimani became Doge the following year.

19. See Paston, op. cit. 378.

her verses into Italian.[20] From thence she went to Florence, where she was received into the house of Lady Pomfret, with whom she had contracted an acquaintance, a short time before her leaving England, having long sought it during the life of the Queen. But here she broke through all bounds; made open love to my Lord, and to every man that came to the house; flew out into all extent of bawdy conversation before my Lady and her daughters and told double lies of the family and every one that came into it. In short Lady Pomfret was forced to dismiss her into whatever part of Italy or the world she could find to settle in.[21]

General Charles Churchill, on hearing some of her adventures related, which happened when she was a maid, swore, 'Zounds! Then it was before she could speak.' Lady Mary hated him as much as he her; the verses which she wrote behind his picture at Vanloo's are a proof.[22]

*　*　*　*　*

To

the Postchaise

that carries Lady Mary Wortley Montagu

(Wrote at Toulon 1741.)

Sic te diva potens Cypri,
　Sic fratres Helenæ, lucida sidera,
Ventorumque regat pater,
　Obstrictis aliis præter Iapyga,
Navis, quæ tibi creditum
　Debes Virgilium, finibus Atticis

20. HW is referring especially to Antonio Conti, with whom Lady Mary had been previously acquainted and whom she met again in Venice (*Letters and Works*, 1887, ii. 53). He translated *The Lover*, the *Epistle to the Earl of Burlington*, and some shorter poems, and made a verse paraphrase of her essay on a maxim of La Rochefoucauld (Antonio Conti, *Prose e poesie*, Venice, 1739–56, ii. pp. i–xxii).

21. Neither Lady Mary's nor Lady Pomfret's published letters support HW's assertion that Lady Mary was 'dismissed.' She arrived in Florence 22 Aug. 1740 for what Lady Pomfret expected to be only a brief visit, and departed 16 Oct. for Rome,

from whence she wrote to Lady Pomfret and received a reply (*Letters and Works*, 1887, ii. 82, 83; *Hertford Corr.* ii. 82, 116, 134).

22. HW transcribed the lines, as being by Lady Mary, in HW, Waldegrave MSS 2. 39; but he later added this note: 'I have since learnt that these lines were Mallet's, and Lady Mary, as she was a little apt to do, seized them for her own.' Lord Wharncliffe included the lines in his original edition of Lady Mary's works (1837), but Moy Thomas, finding them published among Mallet's poems, omitted them. See *Letters and Works*, 1887, ii. 516.

Reddas incolumem precor,
At serves animæ dimidium meæ.
[Horace, *Odes* I. iii.]

The Queen of Lust from dangers ward thee,
And hotter Helen's brothers guard thee!
And may the King of Winds restrain
Each storm that blows across the plain,
Chaining up all, except one gale
To scatter whiffs and cool her tail!
O chaise, who art condemn'd to carry
The rotten hide of Lady Mary,
To Italy's last corner drive;
And prithee set her down alive;
Nor jumble off with jolts and blows,
The half she yet retains of nose!

ii. (Lady Pomfret.)

Haec eadem ut sciret, quid non faciebat Amyntas?[23]

To gain such art what pains Sabina[24] took,
With lip of blackamoor and fist of cook;
Each force of finger and of breath she spent,
Beneath such force the tender organ bent;
Yet still she beat, and puff'd and sweat and star'd,
No minstrel in a bacchanal more hard ——
(Fragment of a Town Eclogue.[25])

SABINA was half witted, half learned, half ill-natured, half proud, half vulgar. Having ruined her husband's estate by buying pennyworths, she went abroad to save money; continued to buy all the trumpery she met with, as often as she thought it cheap, which was as often as she met with it. She read much, chiefly history, which she began at Charlemagne; before his time, she looked on all as fabulous and uncertain; and one day in a dispute about commonwealths, when some of the Grecian ones were mentioned to her, she said, 'Ay, but no-

23. Virgil, *Eclogues* ii. 35.
24. 'Lady Pomfret' (HW).
25. Presumably by HW himself. While in Florence HW composed a 'Town Eclogue,' called 'Sunday, or the Presence Chamber' (HW, Waldegrave MSS 2. 34–8), as a sequel to Lady Mary's eclogues.

body knows anything about them.' However for the ornaments of her discourse, she would sometimes deviate into the earlier ages, particularly one day, as she was getting into a coach, the step was too high, she said, ' 'Tis as difficult to get up here, as 'twas for Cæsar to take Utica.' She kept a correspondence with Lady Hertford[26] and Lady Bell Finch, and continually employed her second daughter, to copy out the letters from and to herself, and made all the proper names be wrote in red ink. In the Queen's time, she wrote out *Henry and Emma*[27] in gold letters on vellum, and painted the capitals, for one of the Princesses. After she was forty years old, she took it into her head to learn on the flageolet, and at concerts, when she heard the flute, would set tooting, and staring; and whistling with her lips, playing with one hand on her swelled belly, and t'other in her breeches. She pretended great criticism in English; one day a person happened to say *peasants;* Lady Walpole, her great friend and fellow-pedant, said, 'Say *country fellows*'; the person appealed to Lady P. who answered, '*Peasants* is more poetical, but *country fellows* is better grammar.' This happened at Florence, where she applied extremely to Italian, but never spoke beyond the consistency of a parrot's Portuguese: yet in the many disputes that she used to have with her husband she would always speak Italian, because she said she would not have the servants think she was in the wrong.

26. Lady Pomfret's correspondence with Lady Hertford, covering the years 1738 to 1741, was published in 1805.

27. By Matthew Prior.

APPENDIX 6

West's *Pausanias*

See *ante* 29 March 1741, O.S. Printed from MS now wsl. The abrupt beginning of the fragment suggests that part of the letter may have been lost. West's historical source was Thucydides i. 128–34.

You do not fail me—

ARGILIUS.
Ah! how can you imagine—

CLEODORA.
Nay but no more: Pausanias may be coming:
I fain would learn of you before you go,
Whither your journey lies: I only wish
It may not be [to] Asia. Adieu! Argilius.

ARGILIUS.
Then till we meet once more—Adieu!
My Cleodora.

ARGILIUS alone.
'I only wish it may not be to Asia!'—
What means she by those words? She even repeated them
With anxious earnestness. Is it her fears?
And can she be alarm'd about my safety?
And is my voyage of such moment to her?
O heavens! and does she love me?—ah! no, I dream.
Wretched Argilius! Thou art lost: she deems thee
A traitor to thy country, and I know
Her generous spirit so abhors a falsehood,
Though 'twere to serve her, that she ne'er could love thee.
Am I a traitor then? O Spartans! Spartans!
If ever treason lodg'd within this bosom,
Let vultures gnaw my heart, and may my name
Be branded with immortal curses!
Pausanias! Pausanias!
Now sure I give you the severest proof
Of my fidelity—though general Greece

Suspect you false, though you yourself mistrust me,
Though I lose Cleodora by it, yet
I'm your friend.
Pausanias false? It cannot, cannot be.
Gods! have the Greeks so soon forgot Platæa?
Have they forgot him, when,
Terrible as Mars, upon the edge of battle
He stood, and waving through the frighted air
His dreadful falchion, cried, now, Spartans, now
Revenge Leonidas! Liberty or death!
Then, rushing like a whirlwind o'er the plain,
He led his fierce battalions; down before him
Whole nations fell, and Asia trembling fled.
—Go! now impeach him, go, ungrateful Spartans,
Go, emulate th' Athenians: Thus they served
The brave Miltiades. But 'tis the fate of patriots,
Never rewarded, seldom understood.
Pausanias false! heavens! I can't bear th' idea.
Yet, had I cause but to suspect him such;
For without cause suspicion is unjust,
Nay 'tis ungenerous, 'tis base in friendship;
Yet, had I cause—by heavens! this hand, this hand
Should be the first to plunge the dagger in,
And sacrifice my friend, to save my country.
Hah! here he comes—

ARGILIUS. PAUSANIAS.
ARGILIUS.
—My Lord Pausanias, welcome.

PAUSANIAS.
Argilius! I am sick of the ephori:
They worry me to death. Pray be sincere:
D'you take me for a villain?

ARGILIUS.
What, my Lord!
Can any Spartan take you for a villain?

PAUSANIAS.

Why yes; our ephori. (Now will I tell
Nothing but truth, and yet I'll make this boy
Believe me honest—) They have brought against me
Impeachment on impeachment, run o'er my life,
Tax'd all my actions—

ARGILIUS.
And Platæa's too,
I hope.

PAUSANIAS.
No, Diotimus was so good
To mention it with praises: Then they question'd me
For sending embassies to Artabazus;
The story of Byzantium too; in brief
They dealt with me, as though I were a traitor.

ARGILIUS.
'Twas thus
Th' Athenians dealt with brave Miltiades.

PAUSANIAS.

Yes, but I will not rot in chains, as he did.
What, shall I tamely fall a sacrifice
To crooked jealousies and false surmises?
Not so, Argilius. 'Tis a bad world we live in;
And virtue, to defend herself, must stoop
To means, which virtue of herself would scorn:
Bare innocence is nowadays no safeguard.
I therefore found it vain to plead my cause
In words, but treated them as they deserv'd:
So I e'en threw my Persian gold among them,
And set the rogues a-scrambling, till they loos'd
Their hold upon me.

ARGILIUS.
O Lycurgus! couldst thou
But now return on earth, and view thy city!

PAUSANIAS.

Young man! thou talk'st a Spartan. But thank heaven!
We are not so far gone: Poverty still
And virtue are acquainted with each other:
Sparta as yet has many sons to boast of:
Our children may improve upon us—O Argilius!
Think how it stabb'd me to descend so low,
As to be forc'd to purchase my acquittance,
Meanly to purchase it, by such unmanly,
Such ignominious means, as, while they saved me,
Yet left the blemish on my injured honour.
But I was forc'd to't: I must else have perish'd
The sacrifice of popular brutality.
But bribery!—
Oh 'tis a vile dishonourable screen!
'Tis a blind judge, that settles no distinction
'Twixt guilt and innocence. Why, had I been the traitor,
Which they would make me, I had thus escaped
With as much credit to the full, as now!
(So! I have told my story: let the fool
Work on it, as he may.)

ARGILIUS.
But Diotimus,

He never could—

PAUSANIAS.
No: for I knew the man,
Him and some others of a nobler stamp
I knew too well, to think such sordid trash
Could ever tempt them. But 'tis hard, in truth
'Tis hard, when even honest men suspect us:
The rest I heed not; but I wouldn't methinks,
Have Diotimus, and such men my foes.
I know but one thing that can bear me out:
And that's my conscience. Prithee, Argilius,
Do I look like a traitor?

ARGILIUS.
                              Nay, my Lord,
No more of that—but what! did Diotimus
Drop the impeachment then?

PAUSANIAS.
                              I'll tell you.
Soon as he saw which way the torrent ran,
He let it go no farther: he only laid
A fine upon me: At the close of all
He made a speech, in which he much enlarg'd
Upon Platæa, and said 'twas worthier Spartans
To scare the coward Persian with their sword,
Than treat with them in vile ambassadry.
I answer'd nothing.
But treated his suspicions with contempt:
And yet, I own, my very heart within me
Bled to be so suspected by that man!
—But enough of this.
The day declines already on our hands:
Now to the scope and purpose of our meeting;
You must forthwith to Asia; instant business
Demands you hence. Argilius, I am loath
To part with you: but who have I beside
I can rely on? Oh! I am beleaguer'd
With dark informers and malicious spies:
You are my only friend—Now Diotimus
Would call this vile ambassadry.

ARGILIUS.
                              My Lord!
No further, I conjure you—

PAUSANIAS.
                              Well! I will not.
Here are the letters: This for Artabazus:
For Intaphernes and Pharnaspes these.
I'd tell you their full import, but I'm bound
In honour to conceal them: In good time
You shall know all; at present be assured,

The general weal of Greece is lodg'd in them,
And therefore with the rest, your own in common.
But you must hence without delay for Argos;
A vessel there lies ready to convey you
To Ephesus. Argilius! need I add?
You must be cautious. Sparta is all eyes,
And should they once suspect—

ARGILIUS.
        Fear not, my Lord,
You did me justice, when you said just now,
You might rely on me: And for the rest,
Heaven still protects the virtuous enterprise.

PAUSANIAS.
I fear nor heaven, nor you—with caution added.
Argilius, adieu! I must now meet
The helot Clytus: He is brave and honest,
Though born a slave. You see, what I'm reduced to:
I'm so beset with foes, I'm even forc'd
To fly to slaves for succour. This it is
To serve a thankless country! Be it so!
Since 'tis the will of heaven, I'm satisfied.
But fie! we lose the time in talk. Argilius!
With this embrace, once more adieu! my friend.

ARGILIUS.
Adieu! my Lord! and may your virtue soon
Shine forth without a cloud to hide its lustre!

PAUSANIAS alone.
Adieu young Spartan! and I think, for ever!
Those letters bear the mandate of thy fate:
Alas! thou'lt never live to bring their answer.
In truth thou dost deserve a nobler doom,
And, were it safe to spare thee, I would spare thee:
But 'tmust not be—and yet—no more—
—So farewell for ever!—
—Why! What an easy thing it is to impose
On the dull brain of tame credulity!

The world's made up of fools; and he's a fool
That does not use them so. Now honest ones
Are of all fools the fittest for our purpose:
Poor useful instruments—
They're made to be employ'd, and then dispatch'd:
So we but manage them, and never trust them,
They add a credit to our undertakings:
For none suspects, where honesty's concern'd.
Hah! honesty! what is it?
That boasted basis of our reputation,
That band of justice between man and man,
That law of life, and cement of society,
What is it? Words. 'Tis all self-love at bottom.
Or fear of punishment, or dread of shame,
Or force of custom, or mere constitution
Make all men what they are—For me,
I was not framed for this vile Spartan coop,
This wretched policy of sage Lycurgus!
No, my ambition asks a larger field—
   As for the herd, why let 'em creep—
   It is their calling, and they *must* obey:
My soul was nobler born and destin'd unto sway.

APPENDIX 7

WALPOLE'S DUTIES AS USHER OF THE EXCHEQUER

Extract from *The Sixth Report of the Commissioners appointed to Examine, Take, and State, the Public Accounts of the Kingdom,* 1782, Appendix No. 61, pp. 159–60. See *ante* i. 7 and n. 35.

THE examination of Charles Bedford, Esq., deputy to the Honourable Horace Walpole, Usher of the Exchequer; taken upon oath the 3d, 5th, and 6th December 1781.

This examinant saith, that he is Deputy Usher of the Receipt of the Exchequer to the Honourable Horace Walpole, the Usher; he was appointed by deed, under the hand and seal of the Usher, and has been deputy seven years. The Usher is appointed by letters patent for life, to exercise his office by himself, or his deputy or deputies. He believes it has always been usual for the Usher to execute his office by deputy; the present Usher transacts no part of the business himself; it is all done by the deputy.

The office consists of the Usher, his deputy, and a clerk,[1] who is now also yeoman usher; the Usher appoints them all.

It is the business of this office to supply the Treasury and Exchequer with all kinds of stationery ware, tables, desks, and turnery ware,[2] and the Exchequer with coals; to keep the keys of the doors of the Exchequer, and to employ the persons who do repairs to the Exchequer, and the inside of the Treasury. The advantages to the Usher arise either from certain small half-yearly payments, or from the profits he makes by his supplying the Treasury and Exchequer with these articles, at a rate according to an ancient table of allowed prices, kept in the offices of the Usher and Auditor. He has a profit of forty per cent upon extraordinary articles not included in the table, and three shillings and sixpence in the pound on bills for repairs. He delivers nothing to any office without a note, specifying the article wanted; and every half year he makes out an account for each office of every article he has served to that office, which accounts are both compared with the notes, and signed by the deputies or first clerks in each office, and are

---

1. William Harris, who had been clerk in the office since 1771 (HW to Grosvenor Bedford 27 Feb. 1771 to Charles Bedford 18 Oct. 1780; *Court and City Register* 1781, p. 96).

2. Furniture turned on a lathe.

the Usher's vouchers. Two liberates[3] are then made out, one for the old, the other for the new offices; these liberates contain all the articles in those vouchers, with the prices; they are carried with the vouchers to the Auditor; they are there examined and signed by him, then signed by the Chancellor of the Exchequer, after which they are paid, by orders under the general letters patent dormant. All these fees and profits that accrued to the Usher during the year ending at Michaelmas 1780, amounted to five thousand two hundred and ninety-three pounds six shillings and one farthing; out of which he paid, for taxes, four hundred and seventy-six pounds and fivepence farthing; for fees at the Treasury and the Exchequer, forty-six pounds eighteen shillings; for incidental expenses, one hundred and five pounds fourteen shillings and tenpence; to his deputy, a salary of one hundred and forty-four pounds, and one third of the poundage on the bills for repairs, two hundred and thirty-four pounds four shillings and sixpence; to the clerk, a salary of fifty pounds, and as yeoman usher, thirty-six pounds, eight shillings and threepence, amounting together to one thousand and ninety-three pounds six shillings and one farthing; which reduced his clear receipt for that year, to four thousand two hundred pounds, which sum he paid to Mr Walpole; the sums contained in the four liberates for that year amounted to fourteen thousand four hundred and forty pounds three shillings and sixpence.

3. Writs issued out of Chancery for the payment of any royal allowance.

APPENDIX 8

THE AUTHORSHIP OF *Remarks on Mr Walpole's Catalogue*, 1759

See *ante* i. 31 and n. 215.

THOUGH HW calls the author of the *Remarks* 'one Carter,' the person he seems to have had in mind was William Cartwright (ca 1730–1799), said to have been born at Leek, Staffordshire, the son of William Cartwright, an exciseman. He was bound apprentice to John Dod, a Shrewsbury apothecary, but became associated with the non-jurors, and in 1758 was invested with deacon's and priest's orders by the non-juring Bishop Kenrick Price. He was in London in 1759, as HW says, acting as 'journeyman' to an apothecary; and he remained there until 1769, when he returned to Shrewsbury and resumed the apothecary's trade, at the same time collecting about him a non-juring congregation which met in his house. In 1781 he was consecrated bishop by Price. After Price's death in 1790 Cartwright succeeded him as bishop of the Manchester remnant; but he died a communicant of the Established Church, and is described on his tombstone at St Giles's, Shrewsbury, merely as an 'apothecary.'[1] On what authority HW attributed the pamphlet to Cartwright is unknown. No other published writings have been found ascribed to him.

An entirely different and more probable identification of the author of the *Remarks* is given by Richard Bull in a note in his copy (now WSL), as follows: 'The author of this book was one Osborne in Marsham Street, Westminster, who was a Tory and a rank Jacobite. He was also the author of *The True Briton*, in three volumes 8vo. 500 copies of these *Remarks* were printed; but Gibson and Russell, the booksellers who sold them, had only a few delivered to them at a time, and which were always brought by Osborne himself. Not many of them were sold, nor is it known what became of the rest, but by the book becoming so very scarce, it is supposed they were bought up by somebody. I received the above information from Gibson, one

---

1. See Henry Broxap, *The Later Non-Jurors*, Cambridge, 1924, pp. 257, 277, 278, 287–8; *idem, A Biography of Thomas Deacon*, Manchester, 1911, pp. 155–6; *Salopian Shreds and Patches* 27 Aug. 1879, iii. 207–8; *Shropshire Notes and Queries* 9 June 1911, ser. III, vol. i, p. 24.

of the booksellers above mentioned. He now lives near the Seven Dials and is in another way of business.'

The 'Osborne' who wrote *The True Briton* (1751–3) was certainly —as is clear from reciprocal puffs in the two journals—the George Osborn who wrote an earlier Jacobite paper, *The Mitre and Crown*, 1748–51.[2] The ranting style of the *Remarks* is very similar to that of these two papers. But Osborn is even more obscure than Cartwright; nothing has been learned about him beyond a few facts gleaned from his own writings. On the title-page of *The Mitre and Crown* he describes himself as 'a gentleman late of the Temple'; and in the last issue, for Feb. 1751 (iii. 190–1), he writes, '. . . As to *Primitive Christianity*, I hope to digest my thoughts on that head into a short and clear treatise in a very little time.' This treatise, if ever published, has not been traced. In *The True Briton* for 1751 (i. 15) Osborn complains of the public's indifference to the poems he wrote on two Lord Mayors, John Blachford and Francis Cokayne (who held office successively in 1750 and 1751),[3] which were printed by J. Fuller and sold for a penny. These also have not been traced. There was a George Osborne, son of Thomas Osborne of St Anne's, London, who was at Eton 1717–22 and Corpus Christi College, Oxford, 1723–6.[4]

2. See Samuel Halkett and John Laing, *Dictionary of Anonymous and Pseudonymous English Literature*, 1926–34, iv. 96.

3. A. B. Beaven, *Aldermen of London*, 1908–13, ii. 129.

4. *Eton Coll. Reg.;* Foster, *Alumni Oxon.;* Thomas Fowler, *The History of Corpus Christi College*, Oxford, 1893, p. 430.

INDEX

References in bold-face type indicate further biographical information in the footnotes. Women are indexed under their maiden names, titled persons under their family names.

—— is ashamed of his contributions to, ii. 35

HW's poems published in, i. 21–2, ii. 234

West's 'Monody' printed in, ii. 234

Collège des Quatre Nations:
Mazarin's tomb at, i. 165

Colman, George (1732–94), dramatist; manager of Covent Garden Theatre:
HW's 'Nature will Prevail' pleases, i. 48

Colonna, Filippo (1663–1714):
Clement XI will not permit, to sell antique fragments, i. 213

Comédie-Française:
Comédie-Italienne better than, ii. 145
excellent, but unpopular except on fashionable nights, i. 162

Comédie-Italienne:
better than Comédie-Française, ii. 145

Comfits:
at Florentine wedding, i. 230

Comines, Philippe de (1445–1509), chronicler:
Gray mentions passage in, ii. 175, 180–1
HW inquires about, ii. 178

Committee of Secrecy:
Prior examined by, i. 186
to investigate Sir Robert Walpole's administration, i. 248

Common Sense, or The Englishman's Journal:
Glover extravagantly praised in, i. 133

Compiègne:
HW alludes to, i. 178

Complete Collection of Genteel and Ingenious Conversation. See under Swift, Jonathan

Complaisant, Le. See under Ferriol, Antoine

Comus. See under Milton, John

Conclave:
Albani and Corsini factions in, irreconcilable, i. 220
continues, with increasing divisions, i. 226–7
factions and feuds in, i. 212–3, 215–7
HW and Gray visit Rome during, i. 9, 203
HW expects, to be drawn out to great length, i. 220
HW mentions, ii. 240
zelanti at, oppose factions, i. 220

Congreve, William (1670–1729), dramatist:
Double Dealer, Gray quotes, i. 56–7
translation of Horace by, too free, i. 101
Way of the World: Gray alludes to, i. 77; Gray sees, i. 113; HW alludes to, i. 206; West mentions, i. 131

Conserves:
monks serve, i. 182

Conti, Prince de. See Bourbon, Louis-François de (1717–76)

Conti, Gioacchino (1714–61), called Gizziello; singer:
Gray admires, except for mouth, i. 102

Convents:
HW's lines on, praised by Gray, ii. 36

Conversazione:
HW and Gray attend, at Turin, i. 191

Conway, Anne, m. ante 1733 Musgrave Heighington:
Gray alludes to, i. 84

Conway, Anne Seymour (d. 1774), m. (1755) John Harris; HW's cousin:
(?) Conway writes to, i. 146
receives share of uncle's fortune, i. 25
(?) West supposes HW wants to see, i. 235

Conway, Francis Seymour (1718–94), 2d Bn Conway; cr. (1750) E. and (1793) M. of Hertford; HW's cousin and correspondent:
Paris visited by, i. 166
receives share of uncle's fortune, i. 25
'reckoned one of the prettiest persons about town,' i. 176

Conway, Francis Seymour (1743–1822). See Seymour-Conway, Francis

Conway, Henry Seymour (1719–95), field marshal; HW's cousin and correspondent:
dismissal of, alluded to, i. 40
Gray mentions, ii. 10, 83
HW answers pamphlet against, i. 40
HW mentions, ii. 52
HW's Fugitive Pieces dedicated to, i. 29
HW travels abroad with, i. 8–9
house of, robbed and set on fire by servant, ii. 183–4
letter of, to sister, i. 146
More, Mr, is prompted by, i. 180
plays chess with abbé, i. 181
receives share of uncle's fortune, i. 25
Rheims to be visited by, i. 166
to stay at Geneva, i. 183

Conway, Jane Seymour (1716–49), Henry Seymour Conway's half-sister:
(?) Conway writes to, i. 146
(?) West supposes HW wants to see, i. 235

Cooper, Anthony Ashley (1671–1713), 3d E. of Shaftesbury:
Characteristics: West recommends 'Inquiry concerning Virtue' in, i. 133; West refers to, i. 124

Cope, Sir John (d. 1760), K.B.; M.P.:
afflicted with gout, erysipelas, and love, ii. 87
Bath's verses about, ii. 87

Copernican system:
Gray alludes to, ii. 139

Copies of Seven Original Letters from King Edward VI to Barnaby Fitz-Patrick:
HW writes advertisement to, i. 46

Coquebert, Henri (fl. 1757–76), of Rheims:
(?) HW mentions, i. 178

Cordeliers:
church of, at Angers, ii. 69

Cordus, Valerius (1515–44), physician:
Dispensatorium, Gray's note for HW, ii. 126

Corneille, Pierre (1606–84), dramatist:
Cid, Le, HW and Gray to see, i. 167
Cinna, HW parodies, i. 14

Cornhill:
Gray visits in, i. 113

Traité du poème épique, West alludes to, i. 117

Le Brun, Charles (1619–90), painter:
Le Sueur's pictures supposedly defaced by, i. 170

Lee, Nathaniel (ca 1653–92), dramatist:
Œdipus by Dryden and, West alludes to, i. 92
Rival Queens: Gray alludes to, i. 67, 113; HW alludes to, i. 201

Leghorn:
Algarotti's works printed at, ii. 165
HW fancies West's landing at, i. 229
HW has not seen, i. 230

Legris de Latude, Claire-Joseph-Hippolyte (1723–1803), called Mlle Clairon; actress:
Dumesnil is preferred to, ii. **145**

Leicester, E. of. *See* Coke, Thomas (1697–1759)

Leicester Fields:
West mentions, i. 173

Leleu, Mme de. *See* Maugras, Marguerite-Antoinette

Lelu. *See* Leleu

Lennard, Lady Anne (1684–1755), m. (1) (1716) Richard Barrett; m. (2) (1718) Henry Roper, 8th Bn Teynham; m. (3) Robert Moore; Bns Dacre s.j.:
third husband of, mentioned, i. **179**

Lennox, Charles (1735–1806), 3d D. of Richmond:
disagrees with HW about Richard III, ii. 169
servant of, robs Conway, ii. 184

Lennox, Lord George Henry (1737–1805), colonel:
appointed aide-de-camp, ii. **121**

Lennox, Lady Sarah (1745–1826), m. (1) (1762) Sir Thomas Charles Bunbury; m. (2) (1781) Hon. George Napier:
HW mentions, ii. **120**

Lenox. *See* Lennox

Lens, Bernard (1682–1740), miniature-painter:
HW learns drawing from, i. **7**

Leonidas. See under Glover, Richard

Lepell, Mary (1700–68), m. (1720) John Hervey, Bn Hervey of Ickworth 1733:
HW mentions, ii. 120
HW writes elegy for monument of, i. **43**

L'Epine, Francesca Margherita de (d. 1746), m. (1718) John Christopher Pepusch; singer:
praised by inebriate, i. 64

Leslie, John (1527–96), Bp of Ross:
De Origine, Moribus, et Rebus Gestis . . . Scotorum, HW asks Gray to look into, ii. 171, 173–4
Speed cites, ii. 168

Le Sœur. *See* Le Sueur

'Lesson for the Day, The,' by HW:
HW sends, to Mann, i. 13
imitations of, i. 13
printed with spurious additions, i. 13

Le Sueur, Eustache (1616–55), painter:
'La Vie de Saint-Bruno' by, HW admires, i. 169–70, ii. 145

Leszczyńska, Marie. *See* Marie-Catherine-Sophie-Félicité

Letter from Xo Ho, A, by HW:
five editions of, i. 27

Letter to the Tories, A:
attributed to Lyttelton, i. 18–9

Letters to the Whigs, by HW:
editions of, i. 19–20
Letter to the Tories answered in, i. 19–20

Letters Writ by a Turkish Spy:
Gray imitates, i. 70–2

Lettres écrites de la montagne. See under Rousseau, Jean-Jacques

Leucadian promontory:
Gray alludes to, i. 114

Leveson-Gower, Baptist (ca 1704–82), M.P.:
anecdote of Wynne remembered by, i. **33**

Lévesque de Burigny, Jean (1692–1785), writer:
Vie de Grotius, Gray refers HW to, ii. 128

Lewen, Lætitia van (1712–50), m. (1729) Rev. Matthew Pilkington:
verses by, in Cibber's book, ii. **13**, 21

Lewis, —— (fl. 1715–37), m. (*ante* 1715) John Thurmond; actress:
inebriate praises, i. 64

Lewis, Mrs Thomas. *See* Turnour, Elizabeth

Lewis. *See also* Louis

Liddell, Anne (ca 1738–1804), m. (1) (1756) Augustus Henry Fitzroy, 3d D. of Grafton; m. (2) (1769) John Fitzpatrick, 2d E. of Upper Ossory:
HW writes epigram on, i. **36**

Life of Mahomet. See under Boulainvilliers, Henri de

'Life of Sir Thomas Wyat the Elder,' by HW:
in *Miscellaneous Antiquities,* i. 47

Ligniville, Anne-Marguerite de (ca 1687–1772), m. (1704) Marc de Beauvau, Prince de Craon:
pharaoh at house of, i. **234**

Linacre, Thomas (?1460–1524), physician and classical scholar:
mentioned in Latin verses, ii. 110

Lincoln, Bp of. *See* Russell, John (d. 1494)

Lincoln, Dean of. *See* Green, John (ca 1707–79)

Lincoln, E. of. *See* Fiennes-Clinton, Henry (1720–94)

Lincoln Cathedral:
HW mentions MSS at, ii. 104

Lincoln's Inn:
Ashton chosen preacher to, ii. 236
Capper at, ii. 231–2
HW is entered at, i. 5

Lindsey, Katherine (d. 1788), m. (1735) John Tracy Atkyns:
affidavits by, of sister-in-law's lunacy, ii. 202
Tracy, Robert, brother-in-law of, ii. 199

Linnæus (Carl von Linné) (1707–78), naturalist:
Gray alludes to, ii. **185**

Linton, Kent:
HW erects tomb for Galfridus Mann at, i. 29

Liqueur:
French, Gray recommends, ii. 147

'Oronoko. *See under* Southerne, Thomas
Orosmades (Orozmades). *See* Gray, Thomas
Osborn, George, Jacobite:
 (?) author of pamphlet attacking HW, i. 31–2, ii. 258–9
Osborn. *See also* Osborne
'Osborne, Francis.' *See* Pitt, James
Osborne, Thomas (d. 1767), bookseller:
 HW mentions, ii. 176
Ossory, Cts of Upper. *See* Liddell, Anne (ca 1738–1804)
Ostentation:
 French love of, HW comments on meanness in, i. 164
Othello. See under Shakespeare, William
Otterbourne, Thomas (fl. 1393–1420), chronicler:
 Chronica Regum Angliæ, Gray quotes, ii. 78
Ottoboni, Pietro (1667–1740), cardinal:
 collection of, being sold, i. 214
 dies in Conclave, i. 214
 HW buys bust at sale of, i. 232–3
 ostentation of, shown by gift of cameos to E. of Carlisle, i. 214
Ovid (Publius Ovidius Naso) (43 B.C.–A.D. ca 18):
 HW might have compared *Georgics* to, i. 198
 Heroides, Ashton imitates line of, ii. 235
 Metamorphoses: Gray quotes, i. 145; West alludes to, i. 100; West quotes, i. 124
 West refers to, i. 134
Owen, William (d. 1793), at Homer's Head; bookseller:
 (?) HW's pamphlet seized at shop of, i. 23
 Magazine of Magazines published by, ii. 44
Oxford, Cts of. *See* Holles, Henrietta Cavendish (ca 1693–1755)
Oxford, E. of. *See* Harley, Edward (1689–1741)
Oxford University:
 Botanic Garden at, i. 123
 Fox, Henry, attends, i. 33
 HW asks West for account of Etonians at, i. 94
 HW asserts liberties of, in pamphlet, i. 22–3
 Ministry proposes that the Crown should nominate Chancellor of, i. 22–3
 Sheldonian Theatre at, i. 100
 West's attendance at, mentioned, i. 233
 —— to return to, i. 157
 See also Christ Church; Magdalen College; Queen's College

Padua, John of. *See* John of Padua
Painting, encaustic:
 HW's account of, discontinued, i. 34
Palgrave, William (ca 1735–99), Fellow of Pembroke College, Cambridge:
 Gray sends HW information from, ii. 184
Palombo, secretary to Sir Horace Mann:
 HW mentions, i. 202
Panciatichi, Giovanni Gualberto (1721–50), of Florence:
 Cambridge visited by, ii. 31

Pandolfini, Roberto (d. *post* 1750), of Florence:
 Cambridge visited by, ii. 31
Paoli, Pascal (1725–1807), Corsican patriot:
 Boswell's account of, ii. 170, 174
Paradise Lost. See under Milton, John
Parallel in the Manner of Plutarch, etc. *See under* Spence, Joseph
Paris, Abp of. *See* Beaumont du Repaire, Christophe de (1703–81)
Paris:
 (*Paris streets and buildings will be found under their own names*)
 conversation in, petty and disgusting, ii. 143–4
 HW and Gray visit, i. 8
 HW describes pleasures of, i. 162
 HW visits, i. 11, 41, 42, 46, 49–50, ii. 140, 142
 Italian playhouse in, unpopular, i. 162
 men of, take up gravity, ii. 149–50
 people of, HW dissatisfied with, ii. 143–4
 Turner expects to visit, annually, i. 137
 ugly and beastly, ii. 143
 women of, often well informed and witty, ii. 150
'Parish Register of Twickenham, The,' by HW:
 remarkable persons listed in, i. 33
Park Place, Berks, Henry Seymour Conway's seat:
 Gray mentions, ii. 83
Parliament:
 Acts of: burnt in explosion, i. 104; mentioned, i. 17, 19
 HW asks West for news of, i. 238
 HW retires from, i. 42, 44
 House of Commons: Ashton preaches before, ii. 236; contested election in, i. 26; HW's first speech in, falsely reported in magazines, i. 12
 House of Lords: assizes bill amended by, i. 20; possible divorce trial in, i. 219
 new, ends Sir Robert Walpole's administration, i. 11
Parma, Ps of. *See* Elizabeth (Farnese) (1692–1766)
Parma:
 HW and Gray visit, i. 9
 Modena, D. of, might have had, i. 242
Parsons, Sir Humphrey (ca 1676–1741), Lord Mayor of London:
 West mentions, i. 236
Partridge, John (ca 1719–1809), clerk of Stationers' Company:
 (?) HW mentions, ii. 120
Pasarella, Jacopo (d. 1495), Bp of Imola and of Rimini:
 dispensation granted by, for Henry VII's marriage, ii. 79
'Patapan, or The Little White Dog,' by HW:
 never printed, i. 14
Patriot, The. See under Anstey, Christopher
Patriotism. See under Bentley, Richard (1708–82)